DRAINING
DEVELOPMENT?

DRAINING
DEVELOPMENT?

Controlling Flows of Illicit Funds
from Developing Countries

Edited by

PETER REUTER

THE WORLD BANK

1818 H Street NW
Washington DC 20433
Telephone: 202-473-1000
Internet: www.worldbank.org

1 2 3 4 15 14 13 12

Rights and Permissions

ISBN (paper): 978-0-8213-8869-3
ISBN (electronic): 978-0-8213-8932-4
DOI: 10.1596/978-0-8213-8869-3

Library of Congress Cataloging-in-Publication Data
Draining development? : controlling flows of illicit funds from developing countries / edited by Peter Reuter.
    p. cm.
    Includes bibliographical references and index.
    ISBN 978-0-8213-8869-3 — ISBN 978-0-8213-8932-4 (electronic)
1. Tax administration and procedure—Developing countries.   2. Money laundering—Developing countries.   3. Tax evasion—Developing countries.   4. Transfer pricing—Taxation—Law and legislation—Developing countries.   I. Reuter, Peter, 1944–
    HJ2351.7.D73 2011
    364.1'33—dc23
                                                                                        2011039746

Cover design by Drew Fasick of the Fasick Design Group.

Contents

Tables

Foreword

The subject of *Draining Development?* is one that we feel very strongly about.

Estimates on the magnitude of illicit financial flows from developing countries vary enormously, but even the most conservative suggest that the total outflow exceeds significantly the amount of official development assistance from the Organisation of Economic Co-operation and Development countries. When we look at the financing needs of the developing world—what it will take to achieve the Millennium Development Goals—it is clear that development aid alone is insufficient. To have any hope of reaching the Millennium Development Goals, poor countries must attack the illicit outflow of monies and recover what is now illegally held abroad.

Nigeria's experience illustrates the challenges. In the early 2000s, the Nigerian government made a concerted push to recover the funds that illegally fled their country. They encountered problems both in Nigeria and abroad: outdated rules and poorly trained staff at home, and overseas there was bank secrecy, opaque corporate and trust vehicles, and time consuming procedures precluding cooperation. The playing field was tilted against Nigeria's national interests.

No developing country should have to repeat what Nigeria had to go through to recover funds that rightly belong to its citizens. The effort required thousands of hours of investigative work to locate where the money was hidden, and then the government had to pay millions of dollars in legal fees to recover just a portion of it.

Although recovery is becoming easier, too many obstacles remain. Laws governing trusts and corporations in many countries still provide anonymity to asset holders. Even where the laws are up to date, enforcement often continues to lag. A recent Global Witness report on banks and money laundering provided a damning indictment of the enforcement efforts of many nations.

No matter how successful we are in reducing barriers to asset recovery, it will continue to be a time-consuming and expensive proposition. Differences in legal systems, the demands of due process, the need to respect property rights—all of these factors ensure that recovery will never be a straightforward affair.

That is why *Draining Development?* and the information and analysis it provides on illicit financial flows are so important. Far better than reducing barriers to asset recovery is to not have to recover the assets in the first place. If we can find ways to stop the illegal outflow of money, developing countries can refocus their energies on development.

But as the chapters in this volume show, money flows out illicitly for many reasons, including tax evasion, the smuggling of illegal goods, the trafficking of human beings and other organized crimes, the manipulation of transfer prices and trade mispricing, customs fraud, the failure of money laundering controls, terrorist financing, and bribery. In addition to depleting already meager public coffers and hiding the profits of crime, illicit financial flows pose a risk to the stability of global financial markets; contribute to suboptimal investment decisions; undermine tax morale and accountability between citizen and state; and add to growing income inequality both within and between countries. The consequences are incalculable.

It is our contention that the illicit outflow of money from developing countries, in particular, has not received the attention it deserves—either from the development community or from policy makers in developed or developing countries. This book represents an important step toward garnering the attention the issue deserves. Norway is proud to have assisted the World Bank in this endeavour, and together we would like to thank the authors and the editor for the fine work they have produced.

Erik Solheim, Minister of the Environment and International Development, Norway
Otaviano Canuto, Vice President, World Bank

Acknowledgments

This project was initiated by Norway's Ministry of Foreign Affairs, which provided funding to the World Bank. Harald Tollan was the Ministry staff member who oversaw the grant; he gave helpful guidance on the project at several critical points.

At the World Bank, Rick Messick served as more than a project monitor. He was an active participant from beginning to end, helping identify authors, commenting on my ideas for topics and providing comments on my own chapters. He also navigated the complexities of the World Bank procurement system to enable (all but one) conference participants to actually reach Washington on time, no mean achievement.

Amir Farmanes, then a doctoral student at the School of Public Policy at the University of Maryland served as project assistant and played a major role in organizing the September 2009 conference at which the first versions of the papers were delivered.

The discussants at the conference included: Odd-Helge Fjeldstad (Christian Michelsen Institute, Bergen, Norway); Phil Keefer (World Bank); Grace Pérez-Navarro (OECD, Paris); Mick Keen (IMF); Richard Danziger (International Organization for Migration, Geneva, Switzerland); Marijn Verhoeven (World Bank); Ted Moran (Georgetown University); Rob Weiner (Georgetown University); Dilip Ratha (World Bank); Robert Kudrle (U. Minnesota, Minneapolis); Sony Kapoor (Re-Define); Nicos Passas (Northeastern University); Victoria Greenfield (US Naval Academy); Gabriel DeMombynes (World Bank); Simon Pak (Pennsylvania State University, Great Valley); Alan Carter (HM Revenue and Custom, London); Jack Blum (Baker, Hostettler, Washington); Maxwell Nkole (former chief of Zambian Anti-Corruption agency). Their comments materially helped strengthen the book. I am also grateful to the other speakers at the conference: Nuhu Ribadu (then at the Center for Global Development), Raymond Baker (Global Financial Integrity) and Stephen Shay, (U.S. Treasury Department).

Stephanie Blankenburg and Mushtaq Khan served as gracious hosts for a preliminary working conference to discuss early drafts of the papers at the School of Oriental and African Studies in London. Max Everest-Phillips in addition to writing one of the book chapters, was invaluable in identifying a number of the other authors for important topics.

Finally, I would like to thank Robert Zimmerman for editing the manuscript, and Susan Graham, Stephen McGroarty, and Andres Meneses of the World Bank's Office of the Publisher for managing the production of the book.

Contributors

Marcela Anzola is a legal scholar at the University of Texas, Austin.

Stephanie Blankenburg is at the Department of Economics, School of Oriental and African Studies, University of London.

Alex Cobham is Chief Policy Adviser, Christian Aid, London.

Tim Daniel is a London-based partner in the U.S. law firm Edwards Wildman Palmer LLP.

Lorraine Eden is Professor of Management, Mays Business School, Texas A&M University, College Station, Texas.

Max Everest-Phillips is Director of the Governance and Institutional Development Division, Commonwealth Secretariat, London.

Clemens Fuest is at the Oxford University Centre for Business Taxation, Oxford.

Mushtaq Khan is at the Department of Economics, School of Oriental and African Studies, University of London.

Pierre Kopp is Professor of Economics, Department of Economics, Panthéon-Sorbonne University, University of Paris 1.

Carlos A. Leite is a former economist at the International Monetary Fund and was a tax specialist with Deloitte Touche Tohmatsu Limited, Toronto, at the time of writing.

Michael Levi is Professor of Criminology, School of Social Sciences, Cardiff University, Cardiff, United Kingdom.

James Maton is a London-based partner in the U.S. law firm Edwards Wildman Palmer LLP.

Mick Moore is at the Institute for Development Studies, University of Sussex, Brighton, United Kingdom.

Richard Murphy is Research Director of the Mapping the Faultlines Project at the Tax Justice Network, London.

Volker Nitsch is Professor of Economics, Department of Law and Economics, Technische Universität Darmstadt, Darmstadt, Germany.

Peter Reuter is Professor at the School of Public Policy and Department of Criminology, University of Maryland, College Park.

Nadine Riedel is at the Oxford University Centre for Business Taxation, Oxford.

Francisco E. Thoumi is Tinker Visiting Professor of Latin American Studies, University of Texas, Austin.

Abbreviations

AFDI	Annual Inquiry into Foreign Direct Investment (U.K. Office for National Statistics)
ALP	arm's-length principle
AML	anti–money laundering
ATM	automated teller machine
BLS	U.S. Bureau of Labor Statistics
BNP	BNP Paribas (Suisse) SA
CBN	Central Bank of Nigeria
c.i.f.	cost, insurance, and freight
CIT	corporate income tax
DNE	National Narcotics Directorate (Colombia)
DTA	double tax agreement
EU	European Union
FATF	Financial Action Task Force
FDI	foreign direct investment
FDN	Nicaraguan Democratic Foundation
Fiscalía	Attorney General's Office (Colombia)
FIU	financial intelligence unit
f.o.b.	free on board
FSI	financial secrecy index
GDP	gross domestic product
HS	harmonized system (product classification)
IAS	International Accounting Standard (International Accounting Standards Board)
IFF	illicit financial flow
IFRS	International Financial Reporting Standard

ILO	International Labour Organization
IMF	International Monetary Fund
IOM	International Organization for Migration
IRS	Internal Revenue Service (United States)
KACC	Kenya Anti-Corruption Commission
MNC	multinational corporation
MNE	multinational enterprise
MOF	Ministry of Finance (Zambia)
NGO	nongovernmental organization
OECD	Organisation for Economic Co-operation and Development
OFC	offshore financial center
OFDI	outward foreign direct investment
PEP	politically exposed person
SAR	special administrative region (China)
SAR	suspicious activity report
SITC	Standard International Trade Classification
TJN	Tax Justice Network
TPM	transfer price manipulation
UNCAC	United Nations Convention against Corruption
UNCTAD	United Nations Conference on Trade and Development
VAT	value added tax

Note: All dollar amounts are U.S. dollars (US$) unless otherwise indicated.

Introduction and Overview: The Dynamics of Illicit Flows

Peter Reuter

Abstract

A remarkable consensus emerged during the first decade of the 21st century on the need for the wealthy countries of the world to increase their aid sharply to developed states. At Monterrey, Mexico, in 2002, the world's leaders committed to a "substantial increase in official development assistance [to help] developing countries achieve internationally agreed development goals and objectives" (United Nations 2003, 14). Three years later, at Gleneagles, United Kingdom, the heads of the G-8 nations reaffirmed this commitment, and in Doha, Qatar, in 2008, the nations of the world again recognized the need to increase development aid and pledged to do so. However, although development assistance steadily increased over the decade, rising from US$58 billion in 2000 to a projected US$125 billion in 2010, it still falls far short of what the developed world promised, and what many believe poor countries need if their citizens are to escape poverty.

As it became clear over the decade that the wealthy world's commitments would not match the rhetoric, the development community began searching for other sources of funding to fill the development finance gap. At the same time, reports of massive, illegal outflows from developing countries began appearing. In 2004, Transparency International estimated that 10 of the most notoriously corrupt heads of state in developing countries may have, together, spirited as much as US$60 billion out of their countries during their respective tenures in office (Transparency International 2004). In 2005, Raymond Baker estimated that more than US$540 billion flowed out of developing countries each year thanks to a combination of tax evasion, fraud in international trade, drug trafficking, and corruption (Baker 2005). In 2007, Christian Aid and the Tax Justice Network produced studies reporting similar figures (Kapoor 2007; TJN 2007).

These reports and their implications were not lost on those looking for ways to fill the development finance gap. If, in fact, the amount of money illicitly flowing out of developing countries was anywhere near the amounts estimated in these reports, even partially staunching the flow held significant promise for filling the gap. Two questions thus immediately arose. Are the outflows large enough to justify efforts to staunch them? And, if so, what can be done?

In 2008, the Norwegian government asked the World Bank to undertake a research project that would address these questions. The Bank, in turn, commissioned the editor of this book to organize a conference with authors of original papers and to edit the proceedings. The purpose of this book is to assess what is known about the composition of illicit flows, the processes that generate these flows, the role of tax havens in facilitating them, and the effectiveness of programs aimed at either preventing the flows or locating and recouping them once they have left.

The book provides the first collection of analytic contributions, as opposed to advocacy essays and black box estimates, on illicit financial flows (IFFs). Some of the chapters present new empirical findings; others, new conceptual insights. All of them enrich the understanding of the dynamics of the illicit flows phenomenon. The book does not offer a new estimate of the global total of these flows because the phenomenon is too poorly understood.

The chapters are based on papers first presented at a September 2009 conference at the World Bank. Each paper had one or two assigned discussants, and the revisions reflect the often searching critiques of the discussants, as well as additional comments from the editor and from two external peer reviewers. The chapters have been written to be accessible to nonexperts.

Following this introduction, the book has five parts: I. The Political Economy of Illicit Flows; II. Illegal Markets; III. To What Extent Do Corporations Facilitate Illicit Flows?; IV. Policy Interventions; and V. Conclusions and the Path Forward.

The Short History of Illicit Financial Flow Estimates

Raymond Baker's *Capitalism's Achilles Heel: Dirty Money and How to Renew the Free-Market System*, published in 2005, gave shape to the topic. Baker reported on the results of 550 interviews he had conducted with senior business executives around the world in the early 1990s to estimate the extent of illicit flows involving corporate mechanisms, mostly in transactions between unrelated parties. He examined government and academic reports on other sources of the flows, such as illegal markets, and, accompanied by explicit statements on the reasons for his judgments, offered assessments of the amounts that might be flowing internationally out of developing countries as a consequence. A summary of his quantitative findings is provided in table 1.1.

Baker estimates that over 60 percent of total illicit flows arise from legal commercial activities, and most of the remainder from criminal activity. The former leave the developing world through three channels: the mispricing of goods traded between independent parties, the distortion of transfer prices charged on goods traded within a multinational firm, and fraudulent transactions.

Baker provides minimal detail about the derivation of these figures. Thus, there is no information on the methods used to convert the

Table 1.1. Crossborder Flows of Global Dirty Money

US$, billions

	Global		From developing or transitional countries	
Type	High	Low	High	Low
Criminal	549	331	238	169
Corrupt	50	30	40	20
Commercial	1,000	700	500	350
Total	1,599	1,061	778	539

Source: Baker 2005.

interviews with 550 senior corporate executives in 11 nations into estimates of trade mispricing in the global economy. This is not a simple task. For instance, the nature of the sample is critical to such an exercise (in terms of dimensions such as the commodities and services involved or the countries with which these are traded). Similarly, between the early 1990s, when Baker did his interviews, and 2005, when the estimate was published, there were many changes that could have either raised or lowered the share of mispriced transactions.

For the criminal revenues, Baker uses figures that are often cited in the semiprofessional literature. Consider drug markets, for example: this represents the most well studied illegal industry. Baker uses figures from the United Nations Office on Drugs and Crime that cite a total of US$400 billion in retail sales and US$120 billion in wholesale revenues. There is, however, a critical literature suggesting that these are substantial overestimates, perhaps twice the true value.[1]

As Baker and his colleagues have acknowledged, given the scarcity of available data, the numbers Baker presents are not precise estimates, but, rather, are indications of orders of magnitude that are meant to prompt academic researchers, the International Money Fund (IMF), and the World Bank to collect more accurate and complete data and devise more rigorous estimating techniques. Nonetheless, as is the norm with such work, popular accounts of Baker's conclusions have focused on the money amounts, which are in the hundreds of billions of dollars, and ignored the caveats that accompany them.

Moisés Naím's *Illicit: How Smugglers, Traffickers, and Copycats Are Hijacking the Global Economy*, also published in 2005, has added to the prominence of the topic. Naím's emphasis is on the expansion of the variety of illicit international trade involving banned goods, such as drugs, or the counterfeit and theft of intellectual property. He offers no original estimates, but includes alarmingly high numbers, such as an international trade volume in illegal drugs amounting to US$900 billion. Though Naím's book does not use the term "illicit financial flow," it reinforces the sense that there are large flows of dirty money from the developing world to the developed nations.

Global Financial Integrity, an organization founded by Raymond Baker in 2006, has turned out a number of reports on illicit flows.[2] These have attracted a great deal of media attention. Beyond one that is much discussed in this volume (Kar and Cartwright-Smith 2008), it has also published studies showing the importance of these flows to specific countries and regions (on Africa, for example, see Kar and Cartwright-Smith 2010). However, as with the estimates in Baker's book, popular accounts generally ignore the caveats attached to the estimates in favor of the raw numbers. Though several contributors to this volume have raised questions about the validity of the current estimates, there is no doubt that these numbers have helped galvanize attention on illicit flows and ways to deal with them.

In addition to the work mentioned above, there has been a steady flow of reports from organizations such as the Tax Justice Network (for example, TJN 2007) and Christian Aid that focus, in particular, on the role of contracts involving multinational corporations. These contracts have apparently allowed the exploitation of natural resources by the corporations through failure to specify properly the price at which the gold, timber, and so on is to be exported from developing countries. The transfer may be legal, but, it is often alleged, the underlying contract is the result of corrupt dealings between officials and the multinational corporations; the flows are thus appropriately classified as illicit.

One disappointing note is that, since the appearance of Baker's volume in 2005 to broad acclaim, our volume is the first substantial attempt to address the issue from a scholarly perspective. Of the over 100 Google Scholar citations to *Capitalism's Achilles Heel*, none is from a major academic journal.[3]

When this volume was in final preparation, an odd affirmation of the reality of IFFs appeared fleetingly on the Internet site of the Bank of China.[4] The headline-catching sentence was as follows:

> According to a research report published by the Chinese Academy of Social Sciences, since the middle of the 1990s, the overall number of the escaped Party and Government cadres, officials in the judicial and public security branches, senior-level administrators in the state-owned enterprises, as well as staff in the Chinese institutions stationed abroad, added up to 16,000–18,000, and these corruptors have taken with them around RMB 800 billion (circa US$100 billion).

The report then detailed many major cases, identifying not only the offenders, but also the methods that they had used to move the money out of the country. The RMB 800 billion was not intended to be an esti-mate of the gross flows. It was an estimate of how much had been detected in roughly a 10-year period, surely a modest fraction of all IFFs, particularly because it included only official corruption and not other sources such as tax evasion and criminal earnings.

The Policy Response to Illicit Financial Flows

Norway has led government efforts to focus attention on the issue. In 2008, the Norwegian government created a commission to prepare a report on illicit flows.[5] It has also funded, with other nations, the Task Force on Financial Integrity and Economic Development, for which Global Financial Integrity serves as the secretariat, and funded the confer-ence that led to this volume.[6] The governments of Germany and the Neth-erlands have also paid attention to the topic. This is reflected, for example, by Germany's sponsorship of a side event on tax flight at the fall 2008 meetings of the World Bank and IMF and the funding by the Netherlands of an ongoing World Bank study on illicit flows in East Africa in 2010.

Despite (or because of?) the absence of serious scholarly attention, illicit flows have become a topic of high-level policy discussion. For example, the G-20 Pittsburgh summit in September 2009, near the height of the global fiscal crisis, addressed the issue in its communiqué.[7] It was also discussed at the October 2009 annual meetings of the World Bank and IMF Boards (Development Committee 2010).

IFFs have often been identified as a contributing factor in the current global financial crisis and a source of instability in the world financial system because of the illicitness.[8] Tax havens, more appropriately called secrecy jurisdictions, have been inculpated in many major scandals over the last decade; they have been under attack because they can undermine effective financial regulation in other nations, both developed and devel-oping.[9] Once the spotlight is turned on them, it is hard not to notice that they also serve as the destination for the bribes received by many dic-tators; for example, James Maton and Tim Daniel, in chapter 13 in this volume, describe how Sani Abacha, the dictator of Nigeria in the late 1990s, kept substantial liquid funds on the Isle of Jersey.

More importantly, IFFs have been identified as a major impediment to growth and to the development of sound financial systems and governance in developing countries, an issue dealt with by Mick Moore in chapter 14 in this volume. Attention to the issue has also grown as the demand for greater resources to finance development has collided with the shrinking volume of funds arriving from developed countries following the financial crisis and, more generally, with the lack of support by taxpayers. The greater attention has highlighted that illicit flows may be engendered by official development assistance given that aid represents, in some countries, a substantial share of the money available to central governments. It also highlights that misuse of the funds helps undermine support for foreign aid. Still, if there are large flows of illicit funds out and if they can be curbed, the development finance gap can be met painlessly.

Definition is an important source of controversy in the study of this phenomenon.[10] "Illicit financial flows" is an ill-defined term, and the boundaries are disputed. "Illicit" is not the same as "illegal." No one will deny that the deposit of Mobutu Sese Seko's corrupt earnings in Swiss banks is an illicit flow. However, there will be less agreement, for example, about flows that represent efforts to evade the arbitrarily administered taxes and regulations of corrupt governments; efforts to evade the oppressive economic legislation of President Ferdinand Marcos might have been illegal, but they were not necessarily illicit. Perhaps the defining characteristic of illicit is that (1) the acts involved are themselves illegal (corruption or tax evasion) in a regime that has some democratic legitimacy, or (2) the funds are the indirect fruits of illegal acts (for example, benefits given to those who have provided illegal funding for a presidential election). Thus, illicit funds are not merely the consequence of bad public policy and do not include all international illegal financial flows from illegitimate regimes. The questions about definition are taken up in a number of chapters, notably, those of Stephanie Blankenburg and Mushtaq Khan (chapter 2) and Max Everest-Phillips (chapter 3).

The remainder of this chapter gives brief summaries of the individual chapters.

The Political Economy of Illicit Flows

In chapter 2, Stephanie Blankenburg and Mushtaq Khan, economists at the School of Oriental and African Studies, in London, develop an analytical framework that identifies core determinants and drivers of illicit capital flight from developing countries. They begin with an extensive history of the use of the term capital flight and the variety of concepts and measures that have been attached to this label. This is an essential starting point because the central estimates of the scale of illicit flows are based on methods developed to estimate the volume of capital flight. Moreover, the concept of capital flight has morphed a number of times since it was first formulated by Kindleberger (1937); even now, there is considerable ambiguity as to whether capital flight refers to short- or long-term capital movements.

Blankenburg and Khan then relate systematically the concepts of dirty money, illegal capital flows, and capital flight, which are often used almost synonymously, but which represent different behaviors and challenges. Some definitions are legalistic and rule oriented; others are broad and oriented toward defining the phenomenon in terms of motivations or effects.

A significant component of the illicit funds leaving developing countries results from the structural features of the societies of these countries, such as laws that advance the interests of a ruling elite; paradoxically, these features cause domestic capital to seek profitable investment opportunities in more advanced economies. Policy measures to control and reduce illicit capital flight from developing economies will be effective only to the extent that they take account of these structural investment constraints. Market-improving good governance reforms are insufficient and can sometimes even be counterproductive in this respect.

The heart of Blankenburg and Khan's argument is that, in many developing countries, governments lack legitimacy; government policies do not represent the result of the working out of a bargain among various interest groups, but, rather, the imposition of the power of a small set of economic actors. Illegal financial flows may not be illicit flows because of the state's lack of legitimacy.

Max Everest-Phillips, a governance adviser at the U.K. Department for International Development at the time of writing, also examines, in chapter 3, the determinants of IFFs through a political economy analysis. His focus, though, is tax evasion. Reviewing the experiences of a large array of countries and tax systems, he argues that the root cause of all illicit capital outflows is ultimately not poor policy or capacity constraints in administration, but the failure of political will. Controlling tax evasion (and the other dimensions of illicit flows: criminality and corruption) requires political incentives to build an effective state. An effective state includes effective tax systems, which derive from formal and informal institutional arrangements (political settlements) that establish the ambition to promote prosperity and raise public revenue. Such a commitment arises if political leaders and taxpayers perceive the need for effective tax systems so as to provide the state with the resources required to enforce property rights, deliver political stability, and promote economic growth. The extent and the form of tax evasion derive from the political consensus to tax effectively and to develop the administrative capacity to do so. In turn, this shapes and reflects the intrinsic willingness to pay taxes (tax morale) of taxpayers. The political economy of controlling illicit capital flows, including tackling tax evasion, demonstrates the necessity of addressing ineffective governance and the weak state legitimacy of many developing countries. If regime leaders and elites are not prepared to tax themselves and prevent free-riding, genuine political ownership of efforts to curb illicit capital flows will be problematic.

In chapter 4, Clemens Fuest and Nadine Riedel, economists at Oxford University, assess tax evasion and avoidance in developing countries and the role of international profit shifting, which may serve as a channel for illicit financial flows. They begin, as does Volker Nitsch in chapter 10, by expressing skepticism about the existing estimates of the extent of tax losses to developing countries that occur as a result of the movement of capital from developing countries to tax havens. The available data are limited, and estimates reflect broad assumptions, often selected in a way that generates high estimates. For example, it is often assumed that the capital would, if kept at home, pay the full tax rate, even though there are numerous loopholes that allow corporations to incur much lower tax obligations.

Empirical evidence on the magnitude of the problem and on the factors driving income shifting is scarce and confined to studies of developed nations. Fuest and Riedel discuss methods and available data sets that can be used to gain new insights into the problem of corporate income shifting. The authors argue that the results of many existing studies on tax evasion and avoidance in developing countries are difficult to interpret, mainly because the measurement concepts used have a number of drawbacks. They discuss alternative methods and data sets and present descriptive evidence that supports the view that profit shifting takes place from many developing countries into tax havens.

Illegal Markets

The international flows of funds in illegal markets, apart from the markets for drugs, have not been the subject of systematic empirical study. Nonetheless, it is routinely asserted that they also generate large flows from developing countries, where cocaine and heroin are produced and from which many humans are trafficked. For example, as noted above, Raymond Baker (2005) estimates that illegal markets account for US$168 billion–US$231 billion of the illicit flows from developing nations.

In "Illicit Capital Flows and Money Laundering in Colombia" (chapter 5), Francisco Thoumi, a Colombian economist, and Marcela Anzola, a Colombian legal scholar, assess illicit flows in Colombia primarily generated by the trade in illegal drugs. They show that Colombia's principal problem is the inflow rather than outflow of drug moneys and that this has had important economic and political consequences for the nation. For example, these flows have exacerbated the concentration of land ownership in rural areas and, by providing access to foreign funds, also exacerbated the long-running insurgency. Though Colombia has enacted model asset-recovery and anti–money laundering (AML) control laws, a detailed examination of the record of the last decade indicates that it has failed to provide a serious threat to the financial well-being of traffickers. In turn, this reflects the failure of the Colombian state to establish norms of compliance with financial laws.

Thoumi and Anzola argue that the key to these failures of well-written laws, as well as an important factor in Colombia's prominence in the international cocaine trade, is the broad lack of compliance with legal norms and the general weakness of the state.

In "Human Smuggling and International Financial Flows" (chapter 6), Pierre Kopp, an economist at the University of Paris (Sorbonne), examines the markets for human smuggling in the first such essay by an economist. These markets are varied, ranging from successfully assisting workers to cross illegally into the United States to coercively employing sex workers from Thailand in Belgium. Drawing on basic economic concepts, Kopp shows that the financial flows vary by type of trafficking. In some of these markets, there will be flows back to the country of human origin, but, in others, the value added will occur and remain in the destination country. Kopp concludes that there are no authoritative estimates of the scale of these markets and little prospect that such estimates will be generated either globally or at the national level; prices for services vary substantially, and there is no systematic basis for estimating the scale of the human trafficking itself.

To What Extent Do Corporations Facilitate Illicit Flows?

The chapters in part III mostly deal with inherently technical questions that cannot be avoided in seeking to understand the flow between the developing and developed worlds. In particular, transfer pricing, the methods by which multinational firms price transactions between affiliates in different countries with varying tax rates, may permit large transfers of taxable revenue that are properly viewed as illicit, even if not formally illegal. Trade mispricing, in which export or import documents carry false prices, also may be important both as a source of tax evasion and as a channel for movement of illicit funds.

In "Transfer Price Manipulation" (chapter 7), Lorraine Eden of the Mays Business School at Texas A&M University provides an overview of the methods by which firms set prices in these internal, but international, transactions. There is a well-established set of theoretical principles and, in some nations, generally in the Organisation for Economic Co-operation and Development (OECD), a detailed set of rules to implement these principles. However, in the real world, there are many potential sources of deviation that allow for considerable discretion and potential abuse. Moreover, some countries, mostly in the developing world, have not created rules specific to the setting of these prices.

Eden reviews the thin empirical literature on the extent of income transfer by transfer price manipulation (TPM). Whether through analysis of individual transactions or more aggregate methods, most studies find evidence that TPM occurs in response to changing corporate tax rate differentials. However, the research task is complicated by the large variety of factors that influence a corporation's incentives for TPM; ad valorem taxes, restrictions on the repatriation of profits, and political instability all play a role. The literature is also dominated by studies focused on where the data are available, particularly the United States. Eden concludes that TPM occurs, but she is not able to estimate how important it is anywhere, let alone in individual developing countries.

More detail that is specific to the case of developing countries is provided in "The Role of Transfer Pricing in Illicit Financial Flows" (chapter 8) by Carlos Leite, a former IMF economist and Deloitte Touche Tohmatsu analyst in Toronto. Leite illustrates the inherent uncertainties in many dimensions of transactions. For example, what is a reasonable method of allocating risk among different affiliates in a multinational corporation? He uses the example of an oil company in a developing country. The company entered into a complex contract that generated unexpectedly high profits in the country, which lacked any specific regulations for transfer pricing. The company was thus able to shift the profits to the country in which its oil trading subsidiary resided and in which it may have paid only a 1 percent tax. Should this be treated as tax avoidance, particularly given the firm's legitimate fear of expropriation by the new regime in the developing country, or tax evasion, given that any reasonable set of transfer pricing rules would have required declaration of the income in the developing country? Leite's chapter emphasizes the extent to which many transfer pricing decisions that affect developing countries lie outside the realm of the OECD principles.

Richard Murphy, an accountant and a principal analyst in the Tax Justice Network effort to bring attention to the corporate and tax haven roles in illicit flows, tackles the scale of the corporate flows in "Accounting for the Missing Billions" (chapter 9). Basing his analysis on the approach of an auditor, Murphy first tests the hypothesis that substantial transfer mispricing by major corporations might contribute to a loss of at least US$160 billion a year to developing countries in the context of the total likely corporate profits tax paid or not paid worldwide in a year. Second, he explores the hypothesis that activities in developing countries and in the extractive industries in particular might be especially prone to this abuse. This reflects both the lack of any effective monitoring capability in many developing countries and the fact that transfer prices can greatly affect not only taxes on corporate profits, the usual focus of transfer mispricing, but royalties and other price-sensitive taxes. Third, Murphy considers whether this sum could be hidden from view within the accounts or financial statements of the multinational corporations that might be perpetrating the mispricing. Finally, he explores the possibility that the corporations might use secrecy jurisdictions (usually called tax havens) to assist in hiding these transactions from view. In each case, Murphy finds that the hypothesis is plausible and that, as a consequence, losses of the estimated amount are also plausible, although not proven to exist as a result of this work. In addition, the chapter identifies the potentially important role of the Big Four firms of accountants with regard to this issue based on their significant presence in secrecy jurisdictions, their role as auditors of most of the world's multinational corporations, and their important role in setting International Financial Reporting Standards.

Volker Nitsch, an economist at Technische Universität Darmstadt, Germany, addresses a related issue in "Trade Mispricing and Illicit Flows" (chapter 10). A potential vehicle for the unrecorded movement of capital out of a country is the falsification of invoices in international trade transactions. In contrast to transfer pricing, this involves transactions between formally unrelated parties. Exporters may understate the export revenue on their invoices (whether by giving low figures for the price or quantity), and importers may overstate import costs, while their trading partners are instructed to deposit the balance for their benefit in a foreign account. The chapter critically reviews empirical approaches to quantify the extent of trade mispricing. Various reasons for discrepancies in bilateral trade statistics are discussed, and incentives for faking trade invoices other than capital flight are highlighted. Overall, the accuracy and reliability of estimates of IFFs based on trade mispricing are questioned.

Policy Interventions

Alex Cobham, an economist with Christian Aid, examines the role of tax havens in "Tax Havens and Illicit Flows" (chapter 11). This chapter makes three contributions. First, it provides a brief, critical survey of the state of knowledge on the impact of havens on development. Second, it uses existing data to extend that knowledge by examining the detail on bilateral trade and financial flows between havens and developing countries and identifying the exposure of developing countries of different types. Third, the chapter sets out a research agenda that would allow greater certainty about the scale of the impact of tax havens on development.

Two results emerge. First, the exposure of developing countries to tax havens is on a par with, if not more severe than, that of high-income OECD countries. Thus, efforts to ensure that developing countries benefit from moves to require greater transparency in terms of international tax cooperation in particular may be of great value. Second, the differences in developing-country exposure across different income groups and regions are substantial, and recognition of this must lead to more detailed and careful study and, over time, policy responses.

OECD member countries and others, through the intergovernmental Financial Action Task Force, have invested considerable effort in the implementation of a comprehensive set of laws and regulations against money laundering in all nations; this is seen as a major tool to prevent illicit outflows.[11] Michael Levi, a criminologist at Cardiff University, in "How Well Do Anti–Money Laundering Controls Work in Developing Countries?" (chapter 12), examines how well the AML system in developing countries has worked for those countries. Levi finds evidence that, for many countries, perhaps particularly those most in need of effective AML controls, the regime has minimal capacity to detect or punish violations. Indeed, there are few instances in which domestic AML controls have generated cases against kleptocrats or their families. Levi examines five cases of grand corruption to show the extent to which the flows of funds could plausibly have been detected by a domestic system of rules and finds the results quite mixed. He concludes by noting the many difficulties of creating an effective AML regime if the government is thoroughly corrupted, reinforcing a message in the Daniel and Maton chapter.

Though illicit flows are a relatively recent issue, components of the response to the flows have been prominent for some time. In particular, there has been growing emphasis since the 1990s on the recovery of stolen assets and the spread of AML controls around the globe.

Tim Daniel and James Maton, London-based lawyers at Edwards Wildman UK who have represented governments in successful suits against corrupt officials in a number of developing countries, describe and analyze experiences in attempting to recover stolen assets in "The Kleptocrat's Portfolio Decision" (chapter 13). Though success is rarely complete in that not all the assets are recovered, Daniel and Maton find growing willingness on the part of British and Swiss courts to render judgments that facilitate the collection of such assets. They provide a particularly detailed and compelling account of the recovery of assets from the estate and family of Sani Abache, the military ruler of Nigeria in the 1990s. The experience in recent cases suggests that the use of secrecy jurisdictions to hide beneficial ownership is often only a modest obstacle to recovery. More often, the problem lies in the home country, where the successor government may be unwilling to provide the legal and evidentiary support for effective recovery or where the local courts thwart overseas suits; the case against Tommy Suharto in Indonesia, whereby a Guernsey court froze assets while waiting for action by the Indonesian government, which is still not forthcoming years later, provides one illustration of the problem.

Conclusions

Mick Moore, a tax economist at the Institute of Development Studies at the University of Sussex, assesses some of the consequences of IFFs in "The Practical Political Economy of Illicit Flows" (chapter 14). The increasing scope to expatriate capital illicitly exacerbates problems of corruption, low investment, the unequal sharing of tax burdens across different parts of the private sector, the low legitimacy of private enterprise, and relatively authoritarian and exclusionary governance. The international community is already developing a range of interlocking tools to deal with the nexus of problems around illicit capital flows, capital flight, corruption, money laundering, tax avoidance, tax havens, and transfer mispricing. Improvements in the design of these tools and greater vigor in implementation should have especially beneficial effects within many of the poorest countries, notably, in increasing private investment and economic growth, reducing the popular mistrust of private enterprise, and providing more space for more democratic governance. More effective international action against illicit capital flows would be complementary rather than competitive with attempts to improve from within the quality of public institutions in the poorest countries.

The final chapter (15) presents the editor's overview of the topic and how the issues should be dealt with in terms of future research. The chapter argues that illegal markets, though significant in absolute terms, are unlikely to be the source of substantial illicit flows out of developing countries because most of the value added is in rich countries, and much of it that is earned by developing county nationals is repatriated home. It also argues that, whatever the problems with existing IFF estimates, the phenomenon is large enough to command serious attention. Illicit flows is a coherent concept in policy terms; what links the international outflows from tax evasion, corruption, and drug markets is the fact that they can all, in principle, be stopped by the same set of policies and laws. A central question is whether there is a set of measures that has the prospect of making a substantial difference to these flows. The alternative view is that these outflows are much less of a problem than the underlying phenomena that generate them and that the debate on outflows may actually divert attention from these phenomena. The chapter suggests a research path for clarifying this issue. Illicit financial flows have complex origins and varied consequences and present difficult policy options. The research program appropriate to study them will also be complex, varied, and difficult.

Notes

1. For an early critique, see Reuter (1996). For a much more detailed analysis published after 2005, see Kilmer and Pacula (2009).
2. See http://www.gfip.org/.
3. A 2010 paper written for the United Nations Department of Economic and Social Affairs by a well-known development economist does make extensive use of Baker (see FitzGerald 2010).
4. The odd feature was that the item was withdrawn within a few hours of appearing on the website. Even in that brief period, it captured public attention. See, for example, Chen and Pansey (2011). Apparently, the report, "Investigation on the Asset Transfer Routes Used by Corrupt Officials and the Corresponding Surveillance Methods," was given a Bank of China award for the quality of the research but was never intended to be made public. The translated report can be found on the website of this volume, http://go.worldbank.org/N2HMRB4G20.
5. See Norway, Minister of the Environment and International Development, 2009, *Tax Havens and Development: Status, Analyses and Measures*, Oslo: Government Commission on Capital Flight from Poor Countries, http://www.regjeringen.no/upload/UD/Vedlegg/Utvikling/tax_report.pdf.
6. See Task Force on Financial Integrity and Economic Development, Washington, DC, http://www.financialtaskforce.org/.

7. Leaders' Statement, G-20 Pittsburgh Summit, September 24–25, 2009, paragraphs 22 and 42, http://www.g20.org/Documents/pittsburgh_summit _leaders_statement_250909.pdf.

8. See "Final Report from the Task Force on the Development Impact of Illicit Financial Flows" at http://www.leadinggroup.org/IMG/pdf_Final_report_Task _Force_EN.pdf.

9. *Wall Street Journal*, 2009, "Tax Havens Pledge to Ease Secrecy Laws," March 13, http://online.wsj.com/article/SB123685028900906181.html.

10. A typical definition of illicit, presented at dictionary.com, shows two meanings. "1. not legally permitted or authorized; unlicensed; unlawful," and "2. disapproved of or not permitted for moral or ethical reasons." See http://dictionary .reference.com/browse/illicit.

11. See Financial Action Task Force, Paris, http://www.fatf-gafi.org/.

References

Baker, R. W. 2005. *Capitalism's Achilles Heel: Dirty Money and How to Renew the Free-Market System*. Hoboken, NJ: John Wiley & Sons.

Chen, L., and G. Pansey. 2011. "Capital Flight Accompanies Corruption in China, Bank Warns." *EpochTimes*, June 25. http://www.theepochtimes.com/n2/china /capital-flight-accompanies-corruption-in-china-bank-warns-57712.html.

Development Committee (Joint Ministerial Committee of the Boards of Governors of the Bank and the Fund on the Transfer of Real Resources to Developing Countries). 2010. "Strengthening Governance and Accountability Review, Results, and Roadmap." Report DC2010–0007, April 21. http://siteresources .worldbank.org/DEVCOMMINT/Documentation/22553919/DC2010-0007% 28E%29Governance.pdf.

FitzGerald, V. 2010. "International Tax Cooperation and International Development Finance." Paper prepared for the 2010 World Economic and Social Survey, United Nations Department of Economic and Social Affairs, New York. http:// www.un.org/esa/analysis/wess/wess2010workshop/wess2010_fitzgerald.pdf.

Kapoor, S. 2007. "Haemorrhaging Money: A Christian Aid Briefing on the Problem of Illicit Capital Flight." Christian Aid, London.

Kar, D., and D. Cartwright-Smith. 2008. "Illicit Financial Flows from Developing Countries, 2002–2006." Global Financial Integrity, Washington, DC. http://www . gfip.org/storage/gfip/economist%20-%20final%20version%201-2-09.pdf.

————. 2010. "Illicit Financial Flows from Africa: Hidden Resource for Development." Global Financial Integrity, Washington, DC. http://www.gfip.org /storage/gfip/documents/reports/gfi_africareport_web.pdf.

Kilmer, B., and R. Pacula. 2009. "Estimating the Size of the Global Drug Market: A Demand-Side Approach." In *A Report on Global Illicit Drug Markets, 1998–2007*, ed. P. Reuter and F. Trautmann, 99–156. Brussels: European Commission.

Kindleberger, C. P. 1937. *International Short-Term Capital Movements*. New York: Augustus Kelley.

Naím, M. 2005. *Illicit: How Smugglers, Traffickers, and Copycats Are Hijacking the Global Economy*. New York: Anchor Books.

Reuter, P. 1996. "The Mismeasurement of Illegal Drug Markets: The Implications of Its Irrelevance." In *Exploring the Underground Economy: Studies of Illegal and Unreported Activity*, ed. S. Pozo, 63–80. Kalamazoo, MI: W. E. Upjohn Institute for Employment Research.

TJN (Tax Justice Network). 2007. *Closing the Floodgates: Collecting Tax to Pay for Development*. London: TJN. http://www.innovativefinance-oslo.no/pop.cfm?FuseAction=Doc&pAction=View&pDocumentId=11607.

Transparency International. 2004. *Global Corruption Report 2004*. London: Pluto Press. http://www.transparency.org/publications/gcr/gcr_2004.

United Nations. 2003. "Monterrey Consensus of the International Conference on Financing for Development: The Final Text of Agreements and Commitments Adopted at the International Conference on Financing for Development, Monterrey, Mexico, 18–22 March 2002." Department of Public Information, United Nations, New York. http://www.un.org/esa/ffd/monterrey/Monterrey Consensus.pdf.

Part I

The Political Economy
of Illicit Flows

2

Governance and Illicit Flows

Stephanie Blankenburg and Mushtaq Khan

Abstract

The concern about illicit capital flows from developing countries reflects a variety of relevant policy issues, but is often motivated by weakly formulated underlying analytical frameworks. We review the literature on illicit capital flows and suggest that the common underlying concern that motivates the different approaches is the identification of flows that potentially damage economic development. Implicitly, if these flows could be blocked, the result would be an improvement in social outcomes. Illicit flows can be illegal, but they need not be if the legal framework does not reflect social interests or does not cover the relevant flows. A minimal definition of an illicit capital flow has to consider both the direct and the indirect effects of the flow and has to assess these effects in the context of the specific political settlement of the country in question. To demonstrate the implications in simplified form, we distinguish among advanced countries, intermediate developers, and fragile developing countries. The types of flows that would be considered illicit are shown to be significantly different in each of these cases. The analysis provides a rigorous way of identifying policy-relevant illicit flows in developing countries. Given the potential importance of these flows, it is vital to have a rigorous framework that at least ensures that we minimize the chances of causing inadvertent damage through well-intentioned policies. Indeed, the analysis shows that many loose definitions of illicit capital flows are problematic in this sense.

Introduction

The concept of illicit capital flows has come to prominence relatively recently, reflecting growing concerns about the ramifications of an insufficiently regulated and apparently increasingly predatory international financial system. In advanced economies, the 2008 global financial crisis brought into sharp relief the growing gap between the effectiveness of national regulatory tools and the global operations of private financial agencies. As illustrated, for example, by the standoff between the U.S. Securities and Exchange Commission and Goldman Sachs employees over the collateralized debt obligation deal, Abacus 2007–AC 1, the debate in advanced countries has highlighted important ambiguities about what constitutes legitimate financial market behavior.

In the case of developing countries, the international concern about illicit capital flows is motivated primarily by concerns that vital developmental resources are being lost to these economies because of the ease with which capital flight can flourish in the context of a burgeoning, yet opaque international financial system (for example, see Eurodad 2008a; Global Witness 2009; Kar and Cartwright-Smith 2008; Baker 2005). Closely related to this is the idea that illicit capital flows from developing economies are indicative of deeper structural problems of political governance in these countries. Finally, there also are worries about how illicit capital flows from developing countries may affect advanced countries through diverse mechanisms, such as directly or indirectly financing crime or terror. In this chapter, we are concerned mainly with the impact of illicit capital flows on developing countries and the effectiveness of policy to control such outflows.

The next section situates the literature on illicit capital flows within the wider context of economic analyses of capital flight from developing economies and provides our definitions. The following section elaborates our definition of illicit capital flows. We simplify the range of variation across countries using a three-tier typology of different economic and political contexts: advanced economies; an intermediate group of normal developing countries in which a stable political settlement exists even though institutions still have a large element of informality; and a final tier of fragile and vulnerable developing countries in which the political settlement is collapsing, and economic processes, including illicit capital flight, are driven by the collapsing polity. A definition of illicit capital flight has to be consistently applicable across these substantially different institutional and political contexts. Keeping this in mind, we define illicit capital flows as flows that imply economic damage for a society given its existing economic and political structure. The penultimate section develops some basic policy tools to operationalize this analytical framework. The final section concludes.

Illicit Capital Flows and Capital Flight: Concepts and Definitions

The term *illicit* has strong moral undertones, but a closer look at the actual use of the term almost always reveals an underlying concern with the developmental damage that particular capital flows can inflict. We believe that, from a policy perspective, this has to be made explicit, as well as the precise methodology that is being applied to determine the damage. We start by defining an illicit capital flow as a flow that has a negative impact on an economy if all *direct* and *indirect* effects in the context of the *specific political economy* of the society are taken into account. Direct effects refer to the immediate impact of a particular illicit capital flow on a country's economic growth performance, for example, through reduced private domestic investment or adverse effects on tax revenue and public investment. Indirect effects are feedback effects on economic growth that arise from the role played by illicit capital flows in the sustainability of the social and political structure and dynamics of a country. For clarity of exposition, we specify the political economy of a society in terms of the political settlement. A *political settlement* is a reproducible structure of formal and informal institutions with an associated distribution of benefits that reflects a sustainable distribution of power. Sustainability requires that the formal and informal institutional arrangements that govern societal interaction in a country and the distribution of benefits to which they give rise achieve a sufficient degree of compatibility between economic productivity and political stability to allow the society to reproduce itself without an escalation of conflict (Khan 2010).

There are two important elements in this definition. First, the judgment of impact has to consider both direct and indirect effects because we are interested in the overall net effect of particular financial flows on the developmental prospects of a country. Second, the specific political settlement of the country is important because the indirect effects, in particular, depend on the interplay between the economic and political structure of the country, and this can vary greatly across contexts. To simplify, we focus on three broad variants of political settlements, but finer distinctions can be made. The assessment of both direct and indirect effects is necessarily based on a counterfactual assessment of what would happen if the illicit capital flow in question could hypothetically be blocked. The assessment is counterfactual because, in many cases, the flows cannot actually be blocked or only partially so. The assessment is therefore subject to the analytical perspective of the observer, but we believe that this needs to be done in an explicit way to facilitate public debate. Our definition allows us to make sense of the perception that not all illegal flows are necessarily illicit, while some legal flows may be illicit. The task of policy is to identify both the particular capital flows that can be classified as illicit, but also the subset of illicit flows that can be feasibly targeted.

What constitutes damage in the sense of a negative developmental impact depends on how we define development. When illicit capital flows are equated with illegal outflows (as in Kar and Cartwright-Smith 2008; Baker and Nordin 2007), the implicit suggestion is that adherence to prevailing legal rules is sufficient for promoting the social good.[1] Yet, the use of the notion of illicitness also suggests that damaging developmental outcomes may not always correspond to violations of the law and that, therefore, social, economic, and political damage needs to be more precisely defined. Moreover, if we are not to suffer the criticism of paternalism, our criteria have to be widely accepted as legitimate in that society. In practice, it is difficult to establish the criteria that measure development and therefore can be used to identify damage in any society, but particularly in developing ones. A social consensus may not exist if there are deep divisions about social goals. However, as a first step, we can insist that analysts and observers making judgments about illicit flows at least make their own criteria explicit. This will allow us to see if these criteria are so far away from what are likely to be the minimal shared assumptions in a society as to make the analysis problematic. In addition, because the effect of capital flows (and economic policies in general) is often heavily disputed, we also require an explicit reference to analytical models that identify how particular capital flows affect particular developmental goals. Making all this explicit is important because observers may disagree in their choices on these issues.

Our definition suggests that capital flows that are strictly within the law may be illicit if they damage society and that, conversely, flows that evade or avoid the law may sometimes be benign, and blocking some of these flows may have adverse consequences. However, all illegal capital flows may be judged illicit from a broader perspective if the violation of laws is judged to be damaging for development regardless of the specific outcomes associated with lawbreaking. We argue that this position is easier to sustain in advanced countries where the formal structure of rules is more or less effectively enforced by rule-based states and where political processes ensure that legal frameworks are relatively closely integrated with the evolution of socially acceptable compromises to sustain political stability and economic growth. The ongoing global financial and economic crisis has demonstrated that this picture does not always hold true even in advanced countries. Meanwhile, developing countries are typically characterized by significant informality in social organization; laws, if they exist, are, in general, weakly enforced and do not typically reflect worked-out social compromises and economic programs, and significant aspects of the economy and polity therefore operate through informal arrangements and informality in the enforcement of formal rules (Khan 2005, 2010). Violations of formal rules are widespread in these contexts and do not necessarily provide even a first approximation of social damage.

To keep the analysis broad enough to include different types of societies, what then should we be looking for to judge damage to society? Is damage to be judged by the effects of particular flows on economic growth, or income distribution, or different measures of poverty, or some combination of the above? We suggest that we should use the least demanding way of judging damage because the more minimal our requirement, the more likely we are to find broad support across observers who may disagree at the level of more detailed specifications.

An illicit financial flow (IFF), according to our minimal definition, is one that has an overall negative effect on economic growth, taking into account both direct and indirect effects *in the context of the specific political settlement of a country.* A flow that has not directly affected economic growth, but has undermined the viability of a given political settlement without preparing the ground for an alternative sustainable political settlement may be seen to have, indirectly, a negative effect after we account for adjustments that are likely as a result of a decline in political stability. It is now increasingly recognized that the different ways in which the political and social order is constructed in developing countries have important implications for how institutions and the economy function (North et al. 2007). Because the construction of political settlements (and, in North's terminology, of social orders) differs significantly across societies, the economic and political effects of particular financial flows are also likely to be different.

Our definition has some overlaps with, but also important points of departure from, the way in which damaging capital flight has been analyzed in the economics literature. The loss of developmental resources through capital flows from poor to rich economies has been an important topic of development economics since its inception. In particular, the literature on capital flight had made the problem of abnormal capital outflows from developing countries its main interest long before the policy focus on illicit capital outflows from such economies emerged. A brief review of this literature allows us to identify systematically different core drivers of capital flight highlighted by different strands of the literature. Our review also establishes the problems associated with ignoring the structural differences in the types of political settlements across countries, problems that our definition of illicit capital flight specifically addresses.

From capital flight as abnormal capital outflows to single-driver models of capital flight

In 1937, Charles Kindleberger famously defined capital flight as "abnormal" capital outflows "propelled from a country . . . by . . . any one or more of a complex list of fears and suspicions" (Kindleberger 1937, 158).

A specialist of European financial history, Kindleberger had in mind well-known episodes of European capital flight going back to the 16th century, as well as the troubles of crisis-ridden Europe in the 1920s and 1930s. In most of these historical cases, this "complex list of fears and suspicions" can be attributed to specific events or to exceptionally disruptive periods of political, social, and economic change or confrontation. To differentiate ex post between abnormal capital outflows driven by profound uncertainty (fear and suspicion) about the future on the one hand and, on the other hand, normal capital outflows driven by usual business considerations was a rather straightforward exercise in those contexts.

For policy purposes, however, such ex post analyses are of limited relevance. What matters is sufficient ex ante knowledge of the factors that differentiate abnormal from normal situations. Such ex ante knowledge—to facilitate effective preventive policy options—will have to include consideration of the determinants of precisely those economic, political, and social factors that may trigger the disruption that we regard as obvious from an ex post perspective. There may not be any general or abstract solution in the sense that what qualifies as capital flight requiring a policy response may differ across countries. A half-century on from his original contribution, Kindleberger himself struck a considerably more cautious note in this respect, as follows:

> It is difficult—perhaps impossible—to make a rigorous definition of capital flight for the purpose of devising policies to cope with it. Do we restrict cases to domestic capital sent abroad, or should foreign capital precipitously pulled out of a country be included? What about the capital that emigrants take with them, especially when the people involved are being persecuted ... ? Does it make a difference whether the emigration is likely to be permanent or temporary, to the extent that anyone can tell ex ante? And what about the cases where there is no net export of capital, but capital is being returned to the country as foreign investment ... ? Is there a valid distinction to be made between capital that is expatriated on a long-term basis for fear of confiscatory taxation, and domestic speculation against the national currency through buying foreign exchange that is ostensibly interested in short-term profits? (Kindleberger 1990, 326–27)

As attention shifted to capital flight from contemporary developing economies, in particular in the wake of the Latin American debt crisis of the early 1980s, a growing consensus emerged about the difficulty of isolating specific determinants of abnormal capital outflows ex ante (Dooley 1986; Khan and Ul Haque 1985; Vos 1992). While there was some agreement on basic characteristics of abnormal outflows (that they tend to be permanent, not primarily aimed at asset diversification, and not generating recorded foreign exchange income), the original effort to identify the characteristics of abnormal capital outflows was replaced by definitions of capital flight in terms of a single-core driver, perceived differently by different approaches (Dooley 1986, 1988; Cuddington 1987).

Capital flight as portfolio choice

First, the portfolio approach adopts standard models of expected utility maximization by rational economic agents to explain capital flight as a portfolio diversification response to higher foreign returns relative to domestic returns on assets (Khan and Ul Haque 1985; Lessard and Williamson 1987; Dooley 1988; Collier, Hoeffler, and Pattillo 2001). More specifically, this involves a counterfactual comparison of after-tax domestic and foreign returns, adjusted for a range of variables, such as expected depreciation, volatility of returns, liquidity premiums, and various indicators of investment risk, including indexes of corruption. In this view, capital flight is caused by the existence of market distortions and asymmetric risks in developing countries (relative to advanced economies). The underlying market-theoretical model of economic development builds on four core premises: (1) economic behavior relevant to capital flight is correctly described by expected utility maximization, (2) markets exist universally (and thus can be distorted), (3) individual agents possess the ability to compute the probabilities of investment risk globally and on the basis of counterfactual investment models, and (4) computable probabilities can be attached to all events.

These are obviously fairly restrictive assumptions in any case. In the present context, however, the most important conceptual drawback is illustrated by the following remark of a Brazilian economist:

> Why is it that when an American puts money abroad it is called "foreign investment" and when an Argentinean does the same, it is called "capital flight"? Why is it that when an American company puts 30 percent of its equity abroad, it is called "strategic diversification" and when a Bolivian

businessman puts only 4 percent abroad, it is called "lack of confidence"? (Cumby and Levich 1987, quoted in Franko 2003, 89)

The obvious answer is that, relative to overall domestic resources, more domestic capital tends to flee for longer from Argentina and Bolivia than from the United States and that this is so because structural uncertainty about future investment opportunities is higher in the former economies. To prevent relatively scarce capital from voting with its feet in situations of great structural uncertainty, developing countries are more likely to impose regulatory barriers on free capital movement, thus turning what might simply appear to be good business sense into illegal capital flight.

By focusing on a single broad motive for capital flight, namely, utility maximization in the presence of differential policy regimes and investment risks, the portfolio approach conflates short-term utility (and profit) maximization with structural political and economic uncertainties. No systematic distinction is made between the drivers of asymmetric investment risks in developing economies, which may range from inflation and exchange rate depreciation to expectations of confiscatory taxation and outright politically motivated expropriation. Similarly, policy-induced market distortions can range from short-term fiscal and monetary policies, common to all economies, to policies promoting long-term structural and institutional changes with much more wide-ranging (and often more uncertain) implications for future investment opportunities. This failure to distinguish between different drivers of capital flight considerably weakens the effectiveness of the policy implications arising from this approach. This consists essentially in the recommendation of market-friendly reforms to eliminate such market distortions on the assumption that these will also minimize asymmetric investment risks. If, however, markets do not as yet exist or suffer from fundamental structural weaknesses, market-friendly reforms may be insufficient to minimize differential investment risk relative to, for example, advanced economies.

This problem is, in fact, at least partially recognized by advocates of this approach. Some authors use a narrow statistical measure of capital flight, the hot money measure, which limits capital flight to short-term speculative capital outflows of the private nonbank sector (taken to be the primary source of net errors and omissions in a country's balance of payments) (for example, see Cuddington 1986, 1987). In contrast, the most widely used statistical definition of capital flight, often referred to as the residual measure, includes recorded and nonrecorded acquisitions of medium- and short-term assets and uses broader estimates of capital inflows (World Bank 1985; Erbe 1985; Myrvin and Hughes Hallett 1992).[2] Cuddington thus reemphasizes the idea that abnormal capital outflows of money running away are a reaction to exceptional circumstances and events rather than ordinary business, although, in times of extensive deregulation of international financial markets, this conjecture may be less convincing. Other authors have taken a different route to distinguish portfolio capital flight from other forms of capital flight, in particular that induced by extreme political instability, such as civil war (Tornell and Velasco 1992; Collier 1999). In the latter case, capital flight can occur despite lower actual foreign returns relative to potential domestic returns (if peace could be achieved) and is part of a wider outflow of productive resources, including labor.

The social controls approach to capital flight

A second strand of the capital flight literature defines capital flight as "the movement of private capital from one jurisdiction to another in order to reduce the actual or potential level of social control over capital" (Boyce and Zarsky 1988, 192). To the extent that such capital flight is motivated primarily by the pursuit of private economic gain, this social control definition is not radically different from the portfolio approach. In both cases, capital flight occurs in response to policy intervention. However, the "social controls" approach rests

> upon an explicit premise absent in much conventional economic theory, namely that individual control over capital is rarely absolute or uncontested, but rather subject to social constraints, the character and extent of which vary through time. Unlike many authors, Boyce and Zarsky, therefore do not consider capital flight to be necessarily "abnormal." (Rishi and Boyce 1990, 1645)

As with the portfolio approach, there is no systematic distinction between fundamentally different drivers of capital flight. All capital flight occurs in response to government controls, whether these concern short-term macroeconomic stabilization through fiscal and monetary policy measures or more long-term structural interventions. However, in this case, the underlying model of the economy is not that of universal and competitive markets inhabited by maximizers of expected utility and profits, but rather that of a mixed economy in which markets are one set of several institutions ultimately governed by a (welfare or developmental) state or, more broadly, by social interventions from outside the market sphere. Different from the portfolio approach, the main policy implication is therefore not simply a focus to promote markets, but to minimize capital flight through the strengthening of existing social controls or the introduction of alternative, more effective administrative measures to control private capital movements.

The social controls approach remains ambiguous, however, about the origin and legitimacy of social (capital) controls. A weak version of the approach identifies governments as the core players in social control, and no explicit judgment is made about the legitimacy or effectiveness of specific government controls. This position comes closest to the portfolio approach. In this vein, Walter, for example, argues that capital flight

> appears to consist of a subset of international asset redeployments or portfolio adjustments—undertaken in response to significant perceived deterioration in risk/return profiles associated with assets located in a particular country—that occur in the presence of conflict between objectives of asset holders and the government. It may or may not violate the law. It is always considered by authorities to violate an implied social contract. (Walter 1987, 105)

By contrast, the strong version adopts the more heroic assumption that social (capital) controls reflect some kind of a social consensus about the ways in which economic development is best achieved. The implied social contract here is not one merely perceived by government authorities to exist, but one based on genuine social approval. A recent example is the observation of Epstein, as follows:

> When people hear the term "capital flight" they think of money running away from one country to a money "haven" abroad, *in the process doing harm to the home economy and society*. People probably have the idea that money runs away for any of a number of reasons: to avoid taxation; to avoid confiscation; in search of better treatment, or of higher returns

somewhere else. In any event, people have a sense that *capital flight is in some way illicit, in some way bad for the home country,* unless, of course, capital is fleeing unfair discrimination, as in the case of Nazi persecution. (Epstein 2006, 3; italics added)

For Epstein (2006, 3–4), capital flight is therefore an "inherently political phenomenon" and also mainly "the prerogative of those—usually the wealthy—with access to foreign exchange." This view entails a more explicitly normative position than either the portfolio approach or the weak version of the social controls approach in that capital flight is characterized not only as economically damaging for development, but also as illegitimate from the perspective of an existing consensus about the social (developmental) good.

Capital flight as dirty money

Both the portfolio approach and the social controls approach broadly interpret capital flight as a response by private capital to expectations of lower domestic returns relative to foreign returns on assets. Both are outcome oriented in that their primary concern is with the macroeconomic analysis of the perceived damage inflicted by capital flight on developing economies rather than with the origins of flight capital or the methods by which it is being transferred abroad. They differ with regard to their analytical benchmark models of a normal or ideal economy. Whereas the portfolio approach subscribes to variants of the standard model of a competitive free-market economy, the social controls approach adopts a mixed economy model in which the social control of private capital, for example by a welfare state, is normal. This translates into different single-driver models of capital flight. In the first case, the driver is simply profit (or utility) maximization (or the minimization of investment risk) at a global level, and the damage done arises not from capital flight per se, but from market distortions that lower relative returns on domestic private assets. In the second case, the driver is the avoidance of policy controls, and the damage arises from private capital breaking implicit or explicit social contracts. These models overlap only in so far as (1) market distortions arise from domestic policy interventions rather than other exogenous shocks and (2) social controls are judged, in any particular context, to be poorly designed so as to undermine rather than promote economic development and thus violate the implicit or explicit social contract.

The more recent literature on illicit capital flows adopts an explicitly normative perspective on capital flight that focuses primarily on adherence to the law or perceived good practice. Illicit capital flows are flows that break the implicit rules asserted as desirable by the observer. A cross-border movement of capital that, at any stage from its generation to its use, involves the deployment of illegal or abusive activities or practices is illicit. Probably the most well known example of this procedural or rule-based perspective on capital flight is Baker's notion of dirty money that distinguishes criminal, corrupt, and commercial forms of illicit capital flows (a term used interchangeably with dirty money) (Baker 2005; Baker and Nordin 2007). Criminal flows encompass "a boundless range of villainous activities including racketeering, trafficking in counterfeit and contraband goods, alien smuggling, slave trading, embezzlement, forgery, securities fraud, credit fraud, burglary, sexual exploitation, prostitution, and more" (Baker 2005, 23). Corrupt flows stem "from bribery and theft by (foreign) government officials" trying to hide the proceeds from such activities abroad, and the commercial component of dirty money stems from tax evasion and mispriced or falsified asset swaps, including trade misinvoicing and abusive transfer pricing (Baker 2005, 23). Of these components of dirty money, illicit commercial flows have been estimated to account for around two-thirds of all illicit outflows, and proceeds from corruption for the smallest part, around 5 percent of the total (Eurodad 2008b).

This rule-based dirty money approach leads to a conceptual definition of capital flight that is narrower than the definitions adopted by more conventional approaches. First, definitions of capital flight here are mostly limited to unrecorded capital flows. Thus, Kapoor (2007, 6–7), for example, defines capital flight as the "unrecorded and (mostly) untaxed illicit leakage of capital and resources out of a country," a definition taken up by Heggstad and Fjeldstad (2010, 7), who argue that its characteristics include

> that the resources are domestic wealth that is permanently put out of reach for domestic authorities. Much of the value is unrecorded, and attempts to hide the origin, destination and true ownership of the capital are parts of the concept.

This does not necessarily translate into the adoption of narrow statistical measures of capital flight, such as hot money estimates that take account only of unrecorded capital flows in the balance of payments. Rather, measures of illicit capital flows attempt to capture as many likely conduits for such flows as possible, in practice integrating different conventional measures of capital flight with estimates of trade misinvoicing (Kar and Cartwright-Smith 2008).

Second, consistent with the conceptual focus on dirty money, the core driver of capital flight is also more narrowly defined, as follows:

> The term flight capital is most commonly applied in reference to money that shifts out of developing countries, usually into western economies. Motivations for such shifts are usually regarded as portfolio diversification or fears of political or economic instability or fears of taxation or inflation or confiscation. All of these are valid explanations for the phenomenon, *yet the most common motivation appears to be, instead, a desire for the hidden accumulation of wealth.* (Kar and Cartwright-Smith 2008, 2; emphasis added)

However, capital flight in response to return differentials, asymmetric investment risks, or perceived macroeconomic mismanagement through social controls can also occur in the open, in particular in a highly deregulated financial environment. Thus, the main concern of conventional approaches to capital flight is with wealth accumulation abroad in general, rather than exclusively or even primarily with hidden wealth accumulation.

Finally, illicit capital flows are also often equated with illegal outflows, on the grounds that funds originating in (or intended for) illicit activities have to be hidden and will eventually disappear from any records in the transferring country (Kar and Cartwright-Smith 2008; Baker and Nordin 2007). This narrows conventional definitions of capital flight because the latter's focus on capital outflows that are, in some sense, damaging to the economy is not limited to illegal outflows. How extensive the overlap between illegal and damaging capital outflows is will depend on how closely and effectively legal frameworks encapsulate the social or economic good, defined in terms of the respective underlying benchmark models of an ideal or licit state of affairs.

In fact, the equation of illegal and illicit capital outflows is not systematically sustained, even in the dirty money approach. At least some of the activities included in the analysis of dirty money are not illegal, but refer to practices characterized as abusive, such as aspects of transfer pricing, specific uses made of tax havens, and corrupt activities that have not necessarily been outlawed. Rather, the procedural or rule-based focus on adherence to the law in this approach to capital flight is based on an implicit claim that adherence to the law will promote economic development or, more generally, the social good. If the principal motivation for capital flight is, in fact, "the external, often hidden, accumulation of wealth, and this far outweighs concerns about taxes" (Baker and Nordin 2007, 2), the policy response has to be directed primarily at eliminating the dirty money structure through the enforcement of national and global standards of financial transparency and democratic accountability. The core obstacle to economic development then becomes the lack of good governance, corruption, and the absence of or weaknesses in the rule of law (rather than specific legislation).

Thus, the dirty money approach to illicit capital flows from developing countries differs from more conventional definitions of capital flight mainly in that it appears to be rooted less in outcome-oriented models of economic growth and development, but in a specific rule-based liberal model of good governance and a good polity, perceived to be a necessary condition for achieving any more substantially defined social good.

From the above, we see that the literature identifies three core drivers of capital flight from developing economies, each implying a different underlying view of what constitutes damage to these economies and each adopting a monocausal perspective. Figure 2.1 summarizes features of these approaches, as follows:

1. In the portfolio approach, social damage is a result of interference with competitive markets that are presumed to otherwise exist. Capital flight is driven by economic incentives to escape such interference given profit-maximizing investment strategies. The best way to eliminate capital flight in this perspective is to remove the damaging government interventions in competitive markets. This largely ignores the fact that competitive markets require government regulation even in advanced economies and that extensive market failures imply that significant government intervention may be required to achieve developmental outcomes in developing economies.

2. The social controls approach is almost the mirror image of the port-folio approach. All social controls over private capital movements are presumed to reflect a legitimate social contract that is welfare enhancing. As a result, capital outflows that violate social controls imposed by a welfare-developmental state are damaging and illicit, presumably because the indirect effects of violating the social contract will be socially damaging. The best way to eliminate capital flight is to reinforce social controls. This largely ignores the fact that not all formal social controls and regulations in developing countries are legitimate, growth enhancing, or politically viable.

3. In the dirty money approach, social damage is the result of violating the rule of law. Capital flight is driven by the desire to accumulate wealth by hiding from the rule of law. No substantial view on what constitutes social, economic, or political damage is typically offered. This largely ignores the fact that, in developing countries in particular, existing legal frameworks may not adequately encapsulate the economic and political conditions necessary to achieve whichever substantial idea of the social good is adopted (economic development, social justice, the preservation of specific human rights, and so on).

Figure 2.1. Definitions of Capital Flight

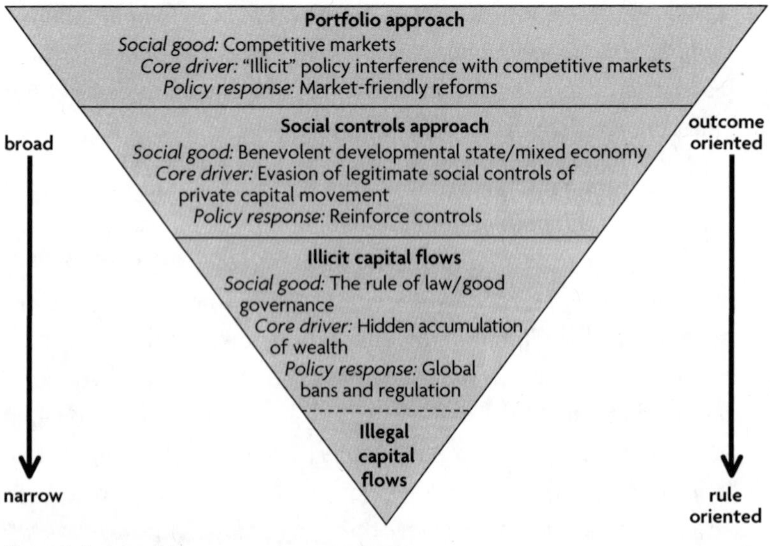

Portfolio approach
Social good: Competitive markets
Core driver: "Illicit" policy interference with competitive markets
Policy response: Market-friendly reforms

Social controls approach
Social good: Benevolent developmental state/mixed economy
Core driver: Evasion of legitimate social controls of private capital movement
Policy response: Reinforce controls

Illicit capital flows
Social good: The rule of law/good governance
Core driver: Hidden accumulation of wealth
Policy response: Global bans and regulation

Illegal capital flows

broad — narrow

outcome oriented — rule oriented

Source: Author compilation.

Illicit Capital Outflows: An Alternative Policy Framework

The discussion above suggests that the search for a conceptual definition of capital flight in general and of illicit capital outflows from developing countries in particular has been motivated by differing perceptions of what constitutes the social or developmental good. Implicit differences in the values and theoretical models of observers explain the significant differences in how illicit capital flows have been defined. These hidden differences are not conducive for developing effective policy responses on the basis of which some minimum agreement can be reached. We believe we can go to the core of the problem by defining illicit capital flows as *outflows that cause damage to the economic development of the country, taking into account all direct and indirect effects that are likely, given the specific political settlement.*

An implicit assumption in many conventional approaches is that all flight capital, however defined, will yield a higher rate of social return in developing economies if it can be retained domestically (Schneider 2003a; Cumby and Levich 1987; Walter 1987). From a policy perspective, locking in potential flight capital is supposed to reduce the loss of developmental resources directly and indirectly stabilize domestic financial markets and improve the domestic tax base (Cuddington 1986). In contrast, we argue that the problems faced by countries with capital flight can be different in nature. The widely shared premise of a general negative relationship between capital outflows and domestic capital accumulation simply is not valid (Gordon and Levine 1989). Dynamic links among capital flows, economic growth, technological change, and political constraints mean that, even in advanced economies, the regulation of capital outflows is an uphill and evolving task. In developing countries, too, some capital outflows may be desirable to sustain development. Moreover, the idea underlying some of the illicit capital flow literature that adherence to the law is sufficient for identifying the social or economic good clearly does not always apply.

On the basis of our minimalist definition of illicit capital flows, we proceed to develop a simple three-tier typology of economic and political constellations and governance structures and the ways in which these pose policy challenges in controlling illicit capital outflows. Specifically, we distinguish between advanced economies (in opposition to developing countries in general), and, within the latter group, we distinguish between normal or intermediate developing countries and fragile developing countries.

Advanced economies: The differences with respect to developing economies

Advanced economies are likely to be supported by rule-based states and political institutions such that the social compromises for political stability and the economic policies required for sustaining growth—the political settlement—are reflected and codified in an evolving set of laws. In these contexts, it is not unreasonable to expect that *as a first approximation, damaging capital flows are likely to be capital flows that violate existing laws.* Illegal capital flows are likely to be damaging and can justifiably be described as illicit in this context. However, some damaging flows may not be illegal if laws do not fully reflect these conditions or have not caught up with the changing economic and political conditions involved in sustaining growth. For instance, the proliferation of inadequately regulated financial instruments that resulted in the financial crisis of 2008 was driven by financial flows that were, in many cases, not illegal, but turned out, ex post, to be seriously damaging. A focus on identifying damaging financial flows independently of the existing legal framework may therefore be helpful even in advanced countries, though, most of the time, a focus on illegal financial flows may be adequate.

Advanced economies, by definition, have extensive productive sectors, which is why they have high levels of average income. As a result, formal taxation can play an important role not only in providing public goods, but also in sustaining significant levels of formal, tax-financed redistribution. Both help to achieve political stability and sustain existing political settlements. Taxation may be strongly contested by the rich, but an implicit social contract is likely to exist whereby social interdependence is recognized and feasible levels of redistributive taxation are negotiated. Significant fiscal resources also provide the resources to protect property rights and enforce a rule of law effectively.

Tax evasion and capital flight in this context are likely to represent individual greed and free-riding behavior rather than escape routes from unsustainable levels of taxation. Moreover, if economic policies and redistributive taxation represent the outcome of political negotiations between different groups, illegal capital flows would also be illicit in the sense of damaging the sustainability of the political settlement and thereby, possibly, having damaging indirect effects on economic growth. Transparency, accountability, and the enforcement of the rule of law can therefore be regarded as mechanisms for limiting tax-avoiding capital flight and other forms of illicit capital flows in advanced countries.

Nonetheless, even within advanced countries, if legal arrangements cease to reflect economic and redistributive arrangements acceptable to major social constituencies, the correspondence between illegal and illicit can break down. The more recent discussion of illicit capital flows in advanced countries has to be considered in a context in which the increase in the bargaining power of the rich to define economic laws in their own interest has exceeded the pace at which other social groups have accepted these changes. This allows us to make sense of the more recent preoccupation with IFFs in many countries of the Organisation for Economic Co-operation and Development (OECD) where the concern with dirty money has been closely associated with changes in the structure of many of these economies as a result of the decline in manufacturing and a growth in the service sectors, in particular, finance. The result has been not only a gradual change in the formal structure of taxation and redistribution in ways that reflect the regressive changes in power, but also a growing tendency of the super-rich to evade even existing legal redistributive arrangements through financial innovations or outright illegal capital flows. The avoidance and evasion of taxation have not been uncontested in advanced countries. Many social groups have criticized these developments and questioned the legitimacy of capital flows that seek to avoid and evade taxes. This constitutes an important part of the concern with illicit capital flows in advanced countries.

Palma (2005) points to the significant decline in manufacturing profits as a share of total profits in advanced countries over the last three decades and the concomitant search for global financial, technological, and resource rents (see also Smithin 1996). The decline in manufacturing can at least partly explain the significant change in income distribution in OECD countries, generally in favor of the highest income groups. For example, in the United States, the average real income of the bottom 120 million families remained roughly stagnant between 1973 and 2006, while that of the top 0.01 percent of income earners increased

8.5 times, meaning that the multiple between the two income groups rose from 115 to 970. During the four years of economic expansion under the George W. Bush Administration, 73 percent of total (pretax) income growth accrued to the top 1 percent of income earners compared with 45 percent during the seven years of economic expansion under the Clinton Administration (Palma 2009). The structural change in advanced countries is obviously complex and differs across countries, but there has been a significant structural change over the last few decades, and the redistributive arrangements that emerged out of the postwar political consensus have faced renegotiation as a result.

The contemporary concern with illicit capital flows in advanced countries is motivated by a growing dissatisfaction both with the enforcement of law and with the extent to which the law in critical areas still effectively supports the social good. Narrower debates about illegal capital flows have focused on capital movements that have flouted existing legal redistributive arrangements because of the growing power of the rich to evade taxes through complex financial instruments and the threat of relocation to other jurisdictions. But a more profound concern with illicit capital flows is based on a feeling of unease that the increase in the political power of these new sectors has enabled them to change laws without the acquiescence of groups in society that would once have had a say. This includes changes in laws that have weakened regulatory control over capital seeking to move much more freely in search of risky profits or tax havens. Even legal capital flows could be deemed to be illicit from this perspective if economic welfare or political stability were threatened by a unilateral redefinition of the implicit social contract.

The steady deregulation of financial flows in advanced countries in the 1980s and 1990s is a case in point. Changes in regulatory structures increased returns to the financial sector, arguably at the expense of greater systemic risk for the rest of society, and diminished the ability of states to tax these sectors (Eatwell and Taylor 2000). Some of the associated financial flows could therefore easily be judged to have been illicit according to our definition. Underlying this judgment is the implicit claim that the restructuring of law is based on an emergent distribution of power that is not legitimate because it eventually produces economic and political costs in which many social constituencies no longer acquiesce and that thereby threatens to become unsustainable (Crotty 2009; Wray 2009; Pollin 2003).

The concern here is that some of these financial flows were illicit either because they were directly damaging to the economy or because they damaged the political settlement in unsustainable ways and may eventually bring about economic costs in the form of social protests and declining political stability. These are obviously matters of judgment, but our definition provides a consistent way of structuring the policy debate without getting locked into a monocausal definition.

As long as the new sectors grew rapidly, the critique that some capital flows were illicit (even if legal) remained a fringe argument. However, the financial crisis of 2008, largely the result of excessive risk taking by an insufficiently regulated financial sector, showed, ex post, that some of these financial flows were not only questionable in terms of their legitimacy and their impact on social agreements, they were damaging in a straightforward sense of economic viability. If the political process in advanced countries responds to these pressures by enacting laws that combine socially acceptable redistributive arrangements with regulatory structures that make sense for sustained economic growth, the law could once again reflect a broadbased social compromise grounded on maintaining politically sustainable economic growth. Under these circumstances, illicit capital flows will once again become coterminous with illegal capital flows.

Even so, the basic features of advanced countries that we discuss above have often created an expectation that a rule of law can and should be enforced at a global level, making illicit capital flows relatively easy to identify and target. Unfortunately, while this analysis makes sense at the level of individual advanced countries, it falls apart as an analytical framework at a global level. It ignores the obvious fact that global laws guiding economic policy or capital flows would only be legitimate if there were a global social consensus based on the same principles of redistributive taxation and social provision on which cohesive societies are constructed at the level of individual countries. It also presumes that a global agency would have the fiscal resources to enforce laws at the global level in the same way that individual advanced countries can enforce national laws. None of these presumptions are reasonable given the current global gaps among countries in terms of economics and politics. By our definition, the absence of a sustainable global political settlement based on global redistributive and enforcement capabilities makes problematic any attempt to define IFFs at the global level.

To understand this more clearly, the differences between the political settlements in advanced and developing countries need to be spelled out. First, developing countries are structurally different because their internal political stability and economic development are not (and cannot normally be) organized through formal rules and laws to the extent observed in advanced countries. *In developing countries, the legal framework is not an adequate guide for identifying illicit capital flows even as a first approximation.* There are two essential limitations on a purely legal analysis of what is illicit in the typical developing country. First, in the realm of politics, the internal political stability of developing countries is not solely or even primarily based on social agreements consolidated through legal fiscal redistributions. For a variety of reasons, including limited fiscal space and more intense conflicts given the context of social transformations, redistributive fiscal arrangements are typically less transparent and less formal compared with those in advanced countries. The political problem involves delivering resources to powerful constituencies that would otherwise be the source of political instability in a context of fiscal scarcity.

If politically powerful constituencies have to be accommodated legitimately and transparently, acceptable redistributions to more deserving groups such as the severely poor have to be agreed upon simultaneously to achieve political legitimacy. The fiscal sums typically do not add up in developing countries for a redistributive package that would pass the test of public legitimacy, as well as provide the redistribution required by powerful groups. As a result, it is not surprising that the critical redistributions to powerful constituencies typically occur through patron-client politics and other mechanisms characterized by limited transparency. If successful, these arrangements achieve political stabilization by incorporating sufficient numbers of politically powerful factions within the ruling coalition. Even in developing countries where significant fiscal redistribution takes place, critical parts of the overall system of political redistribution are not based on transparently negotiated arrangements codified in fiscal laws and economic policies (Khan 2005).

Second, the economies of developing countries are also significantly different from the economies of advanced countries. Their formal or regulated modern sectors are normally a small part of the economy, and a much larger informal sector is unregulated or only partially regulated.

Much of the economy, including the formal sector, suffers from low productivity and does not generate a big enough taxable surplus to pay for across-the-board protection of property rights and adequate economic regulation. The achievement of competitiveness also often requires periods of government assistance and strong links between business and politics. This is because, even though wages may be low, the productivity of the modern sector is often even lower. Developing countries have poor infrastructure and poor skills in labor and management, and, in particular, they lack much of the tacit knowledge required to use modern technologies efficiently, even the most labor-intensive ones.

The strategies through which developing countries progress up the technology ladder while maintaining their internal political arrangements can differ substantially across countries (Khan and Blankenburg 2009). These strategies usually involve creating opportunities and conditions for profitable investment in at least a few sectors at a time. Because the creation of profitable conditions across the board is beyond the fiscal capacities of developing countries, these strategies inevitably create privileges for the modern sector and, often, for particular subsectors through government interventions in prices, exchange rates, interest rates, regulations, taxes, subsidies, and other policy instruments. The strategies for assisting learning in countries with industrial policies, such as the East Asian tigers, are well known. But the growth of modern sectors in all developing countries has required accidents or smaller-scale policy interventions that overcame the built-in disadvantages of operating profitably given the adverse initial conditions (Khan 2009). Some of this assistance may be formal and legal, but other aspects of assistance may be informal and even illegal. For instance, some firms may informally have privileged access to land, licenses, and other public resources. Some of these privileges may be important in offsetting initial low productivity or the higher costs created by poor infrastructure and the poor enforcement of property rights and the rule of law. Deliberately or otherwise, these arrangements can assist some firms in starting production in adverse conditions and engage in learning by doing, but they can also simply provide privileges to unproductive groups (Khan and Jomo 2000; Khan 2006).

Thus, in many cases, business-government links in developing countries are predatory from the perspective of the broader society. Resources captured by privileged firms in the modern sector are wasted, and, in these cases, the modern sector remains inefficient at significant social cost. However, in other cases, periods of hand-holding and bailouts do lead to the emergence of global competitiveness through formal and informal links between emerging enterprises and the state. The efficacy of developmental strategies depends on the nature of the relationships between business and politics, the compulsions on both sides to generate productivity growth over time, the time horizons, and so on, but not in any simple way on the degree to which formal laws are upheld (Khan and Blankenburg 2009; Khan 2009).

It is not surprising that all developing countries fail the test of adherence to a rule of law and political accountability. Yet, some developing countries perform much better than others in terms of politically sustainable growth that eventually results in poverty reduction, economic development, and movement toward the economic and political conditions of advanced countries. These observations suggest that what constitutes a damaging financial flow may be more difficult to identify in developing countries. Because of the significant differences in the economic and political conditions across developing countries, we find it useful to distinguish between normal developing countries, which we call intermediate developers, and fragile developers that suffer from more serious crises in their political settlements.

Normal developing countries: The intermediate developers

Our term *intermediate developers* refers to the typical or normal developing country in which internal political and economic arrangements sustain political stability. Their internal political settlements can be quite varied, but also differ from those in advanced countries in that their reproduction typically requires significant informal arrangements in both redistributive arrangements and the organization of production. Nonetheless, in most developing countries, there is a political settlement that has characteristics of reproducibility, and these societies can sustain economic and political viability. This does not mean that the governments are universally recognized as legitimate, nor are violence and conflict entirely absent, but the political arrangements are able to achieve development (at different rates) without descending into unsustainable levels of violence.[3] Countries in this category include, for example, China and most countries of South Asia, Southeast Asia, and Latin America. In contrast, fragile developers are countries, such as the Democratic Republic of Congo or Somalia, in which a minimally sustainable political settlement among the contending forces in society does not exist and in which the fundamental problem is to construct this in the first place.

Our analysis of illicit capital flows from intermediate developers can be simplified by distinguishing between political and economic actors according to their motivations for making decisions about financial flows. The former are likely to be concerned about threats to the processes through which they accumulate resources and about the political threats to these resources; the latter are likely to be primarily concerned with profit opportunities and expropriation risk. In reality, political and economic actors may sometimes be the same persons; in this case, we have to look at the motivations jointly. The simplification may nonetheless help one to think through the different analytical issues involved so that appropriate policies can be identified in particular cases.

Financial outflows driven by political actors. An obvious reason why political actors in developing countries may engage in capital flight is that their opponents may expropriate their assets if the opponents come to power. A significant amount of the resource accumulation is likely to have violated some aspect of the structure of formal laws. The legality can be questioned by the next ruling coalition for a number of reasons, including expeditious political reasons, for instance, to undermine the ability of previous ruling factions to return to power. Let us assume that this capital flight is immediately damaging because it represents a loss of resources. The issue from the perspective of an analysis of (illicit) capital flight involves assessing the consequences of hypothetically blocking specific financial outflows in these circumstances. The important point is that patron-client politics cannot be immediately replaced by fiscal politics because these countries are developing economies with a limited tax base. Therefore, the fundamental mechanisms through which political entrepreneurs gain access to economic resources are unlikely to disappear in the short run in most developing countries, with the exception of those that are close to constructing Weberian states.

Given the nature of political settlements in developing countries, attempting to block financial outflows driven by politicians is unlikely to lead to a liberal rule of law because any new ruling coalition will also require off-budget resources to maintain political stability and will keep resources available for elections (and for their own accumulation). If these resources can be expropriated by a new coalition after an election, this can significantly increase the stakes during elections. Expropriating the financial resources of former politicians may therefore have the paradoxical effect of increasing instability (the case of Thailand after 2006, for example). It can increase the intensity with which assets of the current ruling coalition are attacked by the opposition, and it can increase the intensity of opposition by excluded coalitions as they attempt to protect their assets from expropriation. Indeed, the evidence from stable intermediate developers such as Brazil or India suggests that the stability of the political settlement in the presence of competition between patron-client parties requires a degree of maturity whereby new coalitions understand that it is not in their interest to expropriate the previous coalition fully. An informal live-and-let-live rule of law guiding the behavior of political coalitions can reduce the costs of losing and allow elections to mature beyond winner-takes-all contests. However, this type of informal understanding is vulnerable.

If the competition between political factions has not achieved a level of maturity that informally sets limits on what can be clawed back from a previous ruling coalition, a premature attempt at restricting financial flows may have the unintended effect of significantly raising the stakes in political conflicts. If the ruling coalition cannot protect some of its assets in other jurisdictions, it may feel obliged to use violence or intimidation to stay in power, and this can increase the likelihood of eventual expropriation. Paradoxically, some amount of flexibility in politically driven financial flows at early stages of state building may help lower the stakes at moments of regime change. Thus, restrictions on political financial flows are only likely to improve social outcomes if live-and-let-live compromises between political coalitions have already been established. For instance, in more stable political settlements such as in Argentina, Brazil, or India, a gradual increase on restrictions on financial outflows could lead to better social outcomes as long as current politicians feel that the risk of domestic expropriation is low and the restrictions simply restrict excessive illegal expropriation by political players. If formal rules restrict political accumulation that is beyond what is normally required to sustain political operations in this political settlement, then financial flows that violate these rules can justifiably be considered illicit. In contrast, if the informal understanding between competing parties is still vulnerable and live-and-let-live arrangements have not become entrenched (as in Bangladesh, Bolivia, Thailand, and, to an extent, República Bolivariana de Venezuela), attempts to limit financial outflows driven by political players are likely to be evaded or, if forcefully enforced, can occasionally have damaging consequences in raising the stakes during elections. According to our definition, we should not consider all capital outflows by political actors to be illicit in these contexts, with critically important policy implications. Clearly, these judgments reflect an attempt to take into account direct and indirect effects and are open to a degree of disagreement. However, we believe that these judgments have to be made and that they are best made explicitly.

Financial outflows driven by economic actors. Financial outflows driven by economic actors can be motivated by concerns about expropriation or low profitability (in addition to tax evasion and tax avoidance). These factors help explain the frequent paradox that economic actors in developing countries often shift assets to advanced-country jurisdictions where tax rates are higher and the returns achieved, say, on bank deposits, are nominally lower (Tornell and Velasco 1992). Some of these flows are damaging, and blocking them (if that were possible) is likely to leave society more well off. Others are not damaging, or, even if they are damaging, attempts to block them would not be positive for society after all the direct and indirect effects are weighed.

Financial outflows with net negative effects. The simplest cases involve capital flight whereby both the direct and indirect effects are negative, such as those driven by tax evasion or tax avoidance. The direct effect of these outflows is likely to be negative if tax revenue and, with it, public investment is reduced, and, in addition, the indirect effect is also likely to be negative if the taxes are socially legitimate and their loss undermines political stability. The capital flight in these cases is clearly illicit. Another clearcut case is that of theft of public resources with the collusion of political actors. A particularly serious example is the two-way capital flow involved in the odious debt buildup resulting if external borrowing by governments is turned, more or less directly, into private asset accumulation abroad by domestic residents. Examples include the Philippines and several Sub-Saharan African economies (Boyce and Ndikumana 2001; Cerra, Rishi, and Saxena 2008; Hermes and Lensink 1992; Vos 1992). Odious debt has no redeeming features, and, if it can be blocked, the developing country is likely to be more well off in terms of direct investment effects. In normal cases where a political settlement involving powerful domestic constituencies exists, theft on this scale by a subset of the ruling coalition is likely to undermine the political settlement and have additional negative effects on growth. Blocking these financial outflows is therefore likely to have a positive effect on growth through both direct and indirect effects. The flows are thus rightly classified as illicit.

Many cases are more complex. Consider a plausible case wherein capital flight is driven by attempts to evade environmental restrictions, labor laws, or other socially desirable regulations that reduce profits. In principle, these could be welfare-enhancing regulations, and capital flight to evade them could be judged illicit. However, a more careful evaluation suggests that the issue may vary from case to case. Because developing countries are often competing on narrow margins with other developing countries, investors may threaten to leave and begin to transfer resources away from a country. What should the policy response be? If social policies in the developing country are significantly out of line with competitors, these policies may have made the country uncompetitive. Yet, removing all social protections is also not desirable. The real issue in this case is coordination in social policy that takes into account differences in initial conditions across countries, not an easy task. If such a coordinated policy structure is not possible across countries, the enforcement of restrictions on capital flight is unlikely to improve growth because domestic investors may become globally uncompetitive. These capital flows would therefore not be illicit according to our definition because blocking capital flight without deeper policy coordination may fail to improve economic outcomes in a particular country. This has important policy implications: all our effort should not be put into trying to block capital flight regardless of the underlying causes. Rather, the policy focus should be either to achieve the coordination of social policies across developing countries or, more realistic, to change policies such that regulations are aligned across similar countries.

An even more important example concerns policies to overcome major market failures such as those constraining technological capabilities. Growth in developing countries is typically constrained by low profitability because of the *absence* of formal and informal policies to address market failures and, in particular, the problem of low productivity because of missing tacit knowledge about modern production processes (Khan 2009). In the absence of policies that assist technological capability development, capital is likely to flow out of the developing country despite low wages. Countervailing policies, variously described as technology policies or industrial policies, involve the provision of incentives for investors to invest in particular sectors and to put in the effort to acquire the missing tacit knowledge. In the presence of such policies, some restrictions on capital movements may be potentially beneficial. The provision of incentives to invest in difficult processes of technology acquisition and learning may be wasted if domestic investors can claim the assistance without delivering domestic capability development. Unrestricted financial outflows may allow domestic investors to escape sanctions attached to poor performance. If the policy is well designed and the state has the capability to enforce it, restrictions on financial outflows may be socially beneficial. Some amount of capital flight may still take place, and liberal economists may want to argue that this is a justification for removing the policy and returning to a competitive market. However, if the market failures constraining investments are significant, this may be the wrong response, *if a credible technology policy exists*. The restrictions on capital flight in East Asian countries in the 1960s and 1970s worked dramatically because they combined significant incentives for domestic investment with credible restrictions on capital flight. In such cases, capital flight would be directly damaging in the sense of lost investment and not have any indirect positive effects either. It would therefore be illicit according to our definition.

The mirror image of this is capital flight driven by the *absence* of profitable domestic opportunities in a country without effective technology policies. Capital is likely to seek offshore investment opportunities. Even if this capital flight appears to be damaging in an immediate sense, it may not be. This is because attempting to block capital fleeing low profitability is unlikely on its own to solve the deeper problems of growth. Indeed, enforcing restrictions on capital outflows in a context of low profitability and absent policies to correct market failures could para-doxically make economic performance worse by reducing the incomes of nationals. Capital flight in these contexts is not necessarily damaging in terms of direct effects on growth, and the indirect effects may also not be negative unless we optimistically believe that blocking these flows will force the government into adopting the appropriate policies for tackling market failures. Because this is an unlikely scenario, it would be mislead-ing to classify these financial outflows as illicit. There is an important policy implication: developing countries need to design policies to address low productivity and to absorb new technologies. Attempting to block financial outflows without solving these problems will not neces-sarily improve social outcomes.

A different and even more obvious case is one in which capital flight is induced by the *presence* of bad policies such as the protection of domestic monopolies that disadvantage investors who are not politically connected or privileged with monopoly rights. In this situation, if capi-tal leaves the country, the direct effects may appear to be damaging in the sense of lost investment, but may not be if domestic investment oppor-tunities are poor. The problem is not the capital flight, but the growth-reducing arrangements that induce it. Blocking financial outflows could, in an extreme case, lead to the consumption of capital by some investors because profitable investment opportunities may be unavailable. The indirect effects of blocking financial outflows in this context may also not be positive, and the financial outflow is not usefully described as illicit. The appropriate response would be to remove some of the under-lying restrictions on investment.

Finally, a particularly interesting set of cases concerns financial out-flows associated with activities that are directly growth-sustaining, but have significant negative effects on a society's political settlement and, therefore, on long-run growth through indirect effects. A classic example is the business associated with narcotics and drugs. For many countries, including relatively developed countries like Mexico, the income from the production and marketing of drugs is a significant contributor to overall economic activity. By some measures, there could be a significant positive effect on growth as a direct effect. However, given the legal restrictions on the business in many countries, the activity inevitably involves criminality and massive hidden rents that disrupt the under-

lying political settlement of the producing country. The indirect negative effects are likely to far outweigh any positive direct effect. It would be
quite consistent with our definition to describe the financial flows associated with these sectors as illicit.

Financial outflows with positive or neutral effects. We discuss in passing
above a number of examples in which financial outflows do not have a
net negative effect if both direct and indirect effects are accounted for. In
some cases, this can involve making difficult judgments that are specific
to the context. For instance, in the presence of significant market failures
facing investors, it may sometimes be useful not to enforce restrictions
on capital flight too excessively. In textbook models, developing countries lack capital and, therefore, capital should flow in if policies are
undistorted. In reality, the productivity in developing countries is so low
that most investments are not profitable, and temporary incentives are
needed to attract investments (Khan 2009). It is possible that some of
these incentives have to be made available in other jurisdictions to be
credibly secure from expropriation. In these contexts, the strict enforcement of restrictions on financial flows may reduce the degree of freedom
states have in constructing credible incentives for investors taking risks
in technology absorption and learning.

For example, a significant part of the foreign direct investments in
India in the 1980s and 1990s came from jurisdictions such as Mauritius.
A plausible interpretation is that much of this was Indian domestic capital going through Mauritius to come back for reinvestment in India. One
side of this flow was clearly a hidden financial outflow, the other a transparent inflow in the form of foreign direct investment. As a result, the
developing country may not be a net capital loser, and, indeed, the incentives provided through this arrangement may make new productive
investment possible in areas where investment may not otherwise have
taken place. As in the case of odious debt, recycling is also only one side
of a two-way flow and is generally assumed to be driven by tax and regulatory arbitrage and to be harmful for society (for example, see Kant
1998, 2002; Schneider 2003b, 2003c). However, in the case of countries
with low productivity and missing tacit knowledge, the rents captured in
this way may, in some situations, serve to make investments more attractive and thereby increase net investments. The direct effect may be to

promote growth. Recycling through a foreign jurisdiction may also be a mechanism for hiding the source of funds in cases in which much of the initial capital base of emerging capitalists has involved questionable processes of accumulation that could be challenged by their competitors in terms of a formal interpretation of laws. Declaring these flows illicit for the purpose of blocking them may be a mistake. The direct effect is likely to be a reduction in investment because these types of accumulation may continue to remain hidden or be diverted into criminal activities. The expectation of positive indirect effects, for instance by creating disincentives for accumulating resources through questionable informal processes, may also be misguided given the structural informality in developing countries discussed elsewhere above. These are matters of judgment in particular cases.

Sometimes, capital outflows may appear to be illicit simply because they are disallowed by ill-considered laws that cannot be enforced. If the laws were enforced, society might become even less well off. For instance, in some developing countries, vital imports may be illegal for no obvious reason, forcing importers to engage in illegal financial transfers to get around the restrictions. In many developing countries, remitting foreign exchange out of the country may also be disallowed for many purposes, including vitally important ones. An example is the widespread practice of illegally remitting foreign exchange from Bangladesh to foreign employment agencies that want a commission for arranging overseas employment for Bangladeshi workers. If, as a result, domestic workers are able to find employment on better terms than in the domestic market, their higher incomes are likely to have a positive effect on welfare, and their remittances are likely to support domestic growth. If illegal financial outflows involve payments to people smugglers, and most domestic workers end up less well off, the direct effects alone would make us classify the financial flows as illicit. A careful analysis is required in each case, but, in many cases, the problem may be an inappropriate legal or regulatory structure.

Table 2.1 summarizes some of the examples we discuss. Only flows falling in the middle row of the table are properly illicit according to our definition. Defining as illicit the other capital flows listed may be a policy error even in the case of financial flows in which the direct effect appears to be damaging. Nor is the legal-illegal divide of much use in the typical

Table 2.1. Logical Framework for Identifying Illicit Flows from Developing Countries

Net effect on growth (including indirect effects)	Direct effect on growth	
	Direct effect negative (flow can be legal)	Direct effect positive or neutral (flow can be illegal)
Net effect negative (flow is illicit even if legal)	Examples: Capital outflows to evade/avoid legitimate taxes Evasion of restrictions that support an effective industrial policy Financial outflows of political actors in the presence of live-and-let-live agreements	Examples: Financial flows associated with the production of drugs and narcotics
Net effect positive or neutral (flow is not illicit even if illegal)	Examples: Financial outflows of political actors in the absence of informal agreements restricting expropriation	Examples: Unauthorized payments to overseas agencies to provide jobs that are better than domestic opportunities (Bangladesh) Recycling that bypasses critical market failures in developing economies and increases investment by domestic investors in their own country Outflows from countries in which profitability is low because of absent industrial policy or presence of damaging policies such as protection for domestic monopolies

Source: Author compilation.

developing-country case if the aim is to identify financial flows that need to be blocked to make the developing country more well off. In any particular country, many financial flows may be simultaneously driven by different underlying causes. The judgment that has to be made involves identifying the drivers of the most significant financial flows and assessing whether these are damaging in the context of the specific political settlement.

Developing countries in crisis: The fragile developers

Fragile developing countries are ones in which the internal political settlement is close to collapsing or has collapsed, and political factions are engaged in violent conflict. This group includes, for example, Afghanistan, the Democratic Republic of Congo, and Somalia. It also includes a number of other developing countries in North and Sub-Saharan Africa,

Latin America and the Caribbean, and Central Asia in which political settlements are highly vulnerable to collapse in the near future. IFFs may appear to be at the heart of their fragility and, indeed, may be fueling conflicts. However, we argue that it is difficult to define what is illicit in such a context of conflict. Fundamental disagreements about the distribution of benefits are unlikely to be resolved without recourse to systemic violence.

Violence is, nonetheless, not the distinctive feature of fragile countries; there may also be pockets of intense violence in intermediate developers such as Bolivia, Brazil, India, or Thailand. Rather, fragile countries are characterized by a significant breakdown of the political settlement and, in extreme cases, also of social order. While pockets of rudimentary social order may spontaneously emerge in such societies, this is largely limited to the organization of violence and subnational economies supporting the economy of violence. There is a grey area between intermediate developers facing growing internal conflicts and a developing country classified as fragile. Nonetheless, in intermediate developers, while a few political groups and factions may be engaging in significant violence, most significant political factions are engaged in the normal patron-client politics of rent seeking and redistribution using the formal and informal mechanisms through which political settlements are constructed in these countries. A political settlement is possible because there is a viable distribution of resources across the most powerful groups that reflects their relative power and that can be reproduced over time. This is a necessary condition describing a sustainable end to significant violence and the emergence of a political settlement.

The defining characteristic of fragility is that a sustainable balance of power and a corresponding distribution of benefits across powerful political actors have not emerged. Violence is the process through which contending groups are attempting to establish and test the distribution of power on which a future political settlement could emerge. But this may take a long time because the assessment by different groups of what they can achieve may be unrealistic, and some groups may believe that, by fighting long enough, they can militarily or even physically wipe out the opposition. In some cases, this belief may be realistic (Sri Lanka in 2010); in other cases, the attempt to wipe out the opposition can result in a bloody stalemate until negotiations about a different distribution of benefits can begin (perhaps Afghanistan in 2010). The analysis of what is socially damaging needs to be fundamentally reevaluated and redefined in these contexts, and this has implications for our assessment of illicit flows.

The historical examples tell us that apparently predatory resource extraction has been the precursor of the emergence of viable political settlements that have generated longer-term social order and viable states (Tilly 1985, 1990). Yet, in contemporary fragile societies, new circumstances make it less likely that conflicts will result in the evolution of relationships between organizers of violence and their constituents that resemble state building. First, natural resources can give organizers of violence in some societies access to previously unimaginable amounts of purchasing power, destroying incentives for internal coalition building with economic constituents in the sense described by Tilly. Second, the presence of advanced countries that manufacture sophisticated weapons and can pump in vast quantities of resources in the form of military assistance or aid also changes the incentives of domestic organizers of violence. Instead of having to recognize internal distributions of power and promote productive capabilities, these people recognize that the chances of winning now depend at least partly on international alliances and the ability to play along with donor discourses. Domestic organizers who try to fight wars by taxing their constituents in sustainable ways are likely to be annihilated by opponents who focus on acquiring foreign friends.

These considerations should give us serious cause for concern in talking about IFFs in these contexts in which the indirect effects of financial flows through the promotion or destruction of political stability are likely to far outweigh the direct effects on growth. By its nature the construction of politically stable settlement involves winners and losers: strategies of state or polity formation are not neutral in any sense.

The terminology of illicit flows in these contexts should preferably be avoided, or its use should be restricted to financial flows that are illicit explicitly from the perspective of the observer. For instance, the flow of narcotics incomes, grey or black market transactions in the global arms market, or sales of natural resources by warlords may go against the legitimate interests of outsiders, and they are entitled to declare the associated financial flows as illicit *from the perspective of their interests*. This is justifiable if these flows are causing damage to the interests of other countries.

We should not, however, pretend that blocking particular flows is in any way neutral or necessarily beneficial for the construction of viable political settlements, because there are likely to be many possible settlements that different groups are trying to impose. Moreover, competing groups of outsiders are also likely to be providing aid, guns, and, sometimes, their own troops to their clients within the country. There is no easy way to claim that some of these resource flows are legitimate and constructive and others are not without exposing significant political partiality toward particular groups.

The real problem is that we do not know the outcomes of these conflicts, and the internal distribution of power is both unstable and changing. Because the sustainability of the eventual sociopolitical order that may appear depends on the emergence of a sustainable distribution of power among the key groups engaged in conflict, we cannot properly identify ex ante the resource flows that are consistent with a sustainable political settlement. The resource flows are likely to help determine the political settlement as much as sustain it.

It follows that the analysis and identification of illicit capital flows must be different across intermediate developers and across fragile developers. Fragile societies typically do not have internationally competitive sectors in their economies, nor do their competing leaders have the capacity to encourage productive sectors effectively. The adverse conditions created by conflict mean that significant countervailing policies would have to be adopted to encourage productive investment in these contexts. Though this is not impossible, as the example of the Palestinian Authority in the five years immediately following the Oslo Accords shows (Khan 2004), the likely direct growth effect of particular financial flows is a moot question in most cases of fragility.

Globally competitive economic activities do take place in many conflicts, but these are of a different nature from the development of technological and entrepreneurial skills with which intermediate developers have to grapple. One example is natural resource extraction that is a special type of economic activity because it does not require much domestic technical and entrepreneurial capability. The returns may be large enough for some foreign investments or for extraction based on artisanal technologies even in war zones. A similar argument applies to the cultivation of plants associated with the manufacture of narcotics. The financial flows from these activities are likely to be directly controlled by political actors and may provide the funds for sustaining the conflict. The only type of capital flight that is likely to emanate directly from the decisions of economic actors is the obvious one of attempting to escape destruction or appropriation. But if individuals try to move their assets out of a war zone to avoid expropriation, it would be unhelpful to characterize these as illicit.

Of most concern in fragile societies are the flows organized by political actors, as these are bound to be connected with ongoing conflicts in some way. In the case of intermediate developers, our concern is that, under some conditions, restrictions on financial flows may inadvertently increase the stakes for holding on to power. A similar, but obviously more serious set of uncertainties affects the analysis of conflicts. In theory, if all parties to a conflict were blocked from accessing the outside world, this may have a positive effect in forcing them to recognize the existing distribution of power and reaching a compromise more quickly than otherwise. In the real world, a total sealing off is unlikely. Some parties to the conflict are likely to be recognized by outside powers as legitimate well before an internal political settlement has been arrived at and receive financial and military assistance.

Two entirely different outcomes may follow. The less likely is that the groups excluded by the international community recognize the hopelessness of their situation and either capitulate or agree to the settlement that is offered. A more likely outcome, as in Afghanistan, is that external assistance to help one side while attempting to block resource flows to the other by declaring these to be unauthorized or illicit can increase the local legitimacy of the opposition and help to intensify the conflict. In the end, every group is likely to find some external allies and ways to funnel resources to fight a conflict where the stakes are high. Paradoxically, finding new foreign allies becomes easier if the enhanced legitimacy of the excluded side makes it more likely that they will win. These considerations suggest that a neutral way of defining IFFs is particularly difficult, perhaps impossible, in the case of fragile developers.

Table 2.2 summarizes our analysis in this section.

Table 2.2. Illicit Financial Flows in Different Contexts

Country type	Defining features	Main policy concern	Main types of illicit capital flows	Policy focus in addressing illicit capital flows
Advanced economies	High average incomes and long-term political stability. Political process responds effectively to economic underperformance and distributive concerns.	Laws and fiscal programs should maintain social cohesion and economic growth.	Mainly flows that violate existing laws (for example, tax evasion). Occasionally refer to legal flows where laws no longer reflect social consensus or economic sustainability.	Strengthen enforcement and regulation. At moments of crisis, attempt to bring law back into line with broad social consensus on economic and political goals.
Intermediate or normal developers	Lower average incomes, and politics based on a combination of formal and informal (patron-client) redistributive arrangements. Achieves long-term stability without sustained violence.	Develop, maintain, and expand viable development strategies, in particular the development of broadbased productive sectors.	Flows that undermine developmental strategies. Capital flight in a context of a failure to raise domestic profitability is problematic, but is not necessarily illicit. Flows associated with internationally criminalized activities like drugs.	Economic policies to enhance profitability primarily by addressing critical market failures. Build governance capabilities to enforce restrictions on financial flows that make these policies less vulnerable to political contestation.
Fragile developing countries	Breakdown of existing political settlements resulting in the outbreak of sustained violence that undermines longer-term conditions for the maintenance of basic sociopolitical order.	State building and reconstruction of a viable political settlement to allow society to embark on a sustainable path of economic development.	Not possible to define illicit flows in a neutral way when elites are in conflict. The effects of financial flows have to be judged primarily in terms of their effects on the establishment of a particular political settlement.	A viable political settlement requires competing groups to accept a distribution of benefits consistent with their understanding of their relative power. Difficult for outsiders to contribute positively and easy to prolong conflicts inadvertently.

Source: Author compilation.

Policy Responses to Illicit Flows

Our discussion above suggests that capital outflows from developing countries qualify as illicit according to our definition if they have a negative economic impact on a particular country after we take both direct and indirect effects into account in the context of a specific political settlement. Both judgments about effects are counterfactual in the sense that we are asking what would directly happen to growth if a particular flow could be blocked, and then we are asking what would happen after the indirect effects arising from adjustments by critical stakeholders to the new situation have taken place. The latter assessment depends on our knowledge about the economy and polity of the society as summarized in the political settlement. This methodology allows us to derive some useful policy conclusions in the case of intermediate developers. By contrast, the use of the illicit flow terminology involves significant dangers in the case of fragile countries. Policy makers should at least be explicitly aware of this.

In this section, we discuss a sequential approach for the identification of feasible policy interventions to address illicit capital outflows that satisfy our definition and that occur in intermediate developers.

Assume that a particular capital outflow from an intermediate developer is illicit according to our definition. The core policy concern here is a microlevel assessment of how any particular set of measures to restrict the illicit capital outflow affects the macrodynamics of the economy and society in question. While our assessment about the nature of an illicit flow has taken into account the indirect effects of blocking the flow, the implementation of any policy almost always gives rise to unintended consequences, and all the indirect effects may not be understood. More often than not, policy failure is the failure to take such unintended consequences into account ex ante.

An illustration of such unintended consequences, in this case pertaining to the international regulation of financial flows, is provided by Gapper's analysis (2009) of the Basel Accords I (1998) and II (2004), which were designed to regulate global banks essentially by setting higher capital adequacy standards and improving the measurement of leverage. Ironically, these standards inadvertently accelerated rather than muted financial engineering by banks, in particular the securitization of risky mortgage debts. The accords raised the threshold of responsible banking, but simultaneously created incentives to find a way around the thresholds that would prove more disastrous to the global economy. As Gapper remarks (2009, 1), "it would be wrong to throw away the entire Basel framework . . . because global banks found ways to game the system." The obvious implication is that one must strengthen rather than throw away existing regulations.

More generally, in our view, *an effective policy response to illicit flows requires a step-by-step, sequential assessment of the macrolevel effects of blocking particular capital flows*. To illustrate what this entails in the case of an intermediate developer, consider the example provided by Gulati (1987) and Gordon Nembhard's analysis (1996) of industrialization policies in Brazil and the Republic of Korea from the 1960s to the 1980s. Both authors argue that trade misinvoicing in these countries during this period followed an unusual pattern in that imports tended to be under-invoiced. Both authors explain this in terms of domestic producers and traders, "rather than being preoccupied with evading controls to earn foreign exchange, may be more concerned about meeting export and production targets and maximizing government plans" (Gordon Nemb-hard 1996, 187). In these two countries (but not necessarily in others), there were potentially avoidable losses from trade misinvoicing, and these flows were therefore illicit. Nonetheless, the losses were significantly smaller than the gains from the incentives created for higher investments in sectors promoted by the industrial policy. To decide whether or not to block illicit trade misinvoicing in these circumstances (and, if so, how), the most important aspect of policy design is to prepare a microlevel analysis of the impact of different ways of blocking these flows on the overall economy. This analysis has to take account of economic and political circumstances and the likely impact of particular regulatory strategies. Figure 2.2 illustrates the iterative process required to arrive at policy decisions that avoid unintended negative consequences.

Figure 2.2. Choosing Attainable Benchmarks for Policy Design

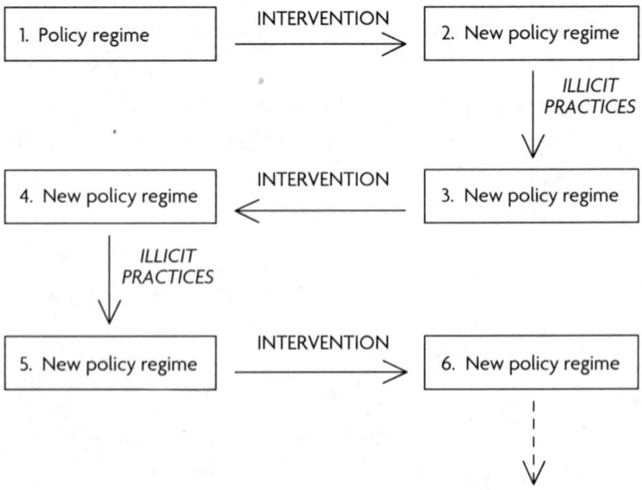

Source: Author compilation.

Assume that the policy intervention from stage 1 to stage 2 in figure 2.2 introduces an industrial policy regime to promote manufacturing exports. This, in turn, provides incentives for some illicit practices, giving rise to stage 3. Despite the presence of the illicit practices arising from the implementation of the industrial policy introduced in stage 2, the overall development outcome at stage 3 is reasonably good. There are several possible responses to the observation of illicit practices at stage 3. One option is to abandon the export-promoting industrial policies on the grounds that these create the incentive to underinvoice imports. This would be in line with the portfolio approach to capital flight that adopts competitive markets as the benchmark model. However, if critical market failures were significant to start with, developmental outcomes at position 1 may be worse than at position 3. Hence, an immediate response to the illicit flow problem at stage 3 that does not take account of developmental problems at stage 1 may be self-defeating. Indeed, in terms of our definitions, the financial flows at position 3 are not illicit with respect to position 1, though they are illicit with respect to position 2.

An obvious option would be to run a more efficient customs administration to raise the transaction costs of import underinvoicing, ideally to the point at which this becomes unprofitable. This is the preferable policy option: it could shift the policy framework from position 3 to position 4. The result would be a reduction in underinvoicing that then takes us to position 5, a combination of the new policy framework and a new (reduced) level of illicit flows. The developmental outcomes at stage 5 would be better than those at stage 3, and, so, this response to the illicit flow problem would be entirely justified. Yet, to get from position 3 to position 5 requires a careful microlevel analysis of the costs and benefits of different policies. If import underinvoicing and the illicit profits associated with it could be eliminated without jeopardizing the participation of private sector firms in the export promotion program, the policy of better enforcement would be effective and economically justified.

In contrast, consider the case (such as Brazil in the 1970s rather than Korea) in which tolerating some import underinvoicing is an informal incentive to ensure private sector participation in a growth-enhancing export promotion program. If the extra incomes from this source are important to ensuring private sector participation in the policy, an attempt to remove these rents could inadvertently result in more damaging rent seeking by the private sector or the sector's political refusal to participate in industrial policy programs. If either happened, the economy would be less well off and could revert to the less preferable position at stage 1. This assessment would depend on our understanding of the political settlement and the power of the private sector to resist the imposition of policies that the sector perceives to be against its interests. The attempt to control the illicit flows would then have failed in a developmental sense even if the illicit flows disappeared. The core policy task in this case would not be to block the illicit capital flows associated with stage 3 (import underinvoicing), but to support the creation of state capacities and an adjustment of the political settlement that would allow the effective implementation of efficient customs administration in the future without reliance on informal perks such as import underinvoicing. More generally, this suggests that a careful sequential microanalysis of the macro-outcomes of blocking particular illicit capital flows is required, locating particular strategies in the context of specific initial conditions.

Conclusion

Our core concern has been to show that what constitutes an illicit capital outflow can vary across countries, depending on the core political and economic features. The number of capital outflows that are *unequivocally* illicit in our minimal definition is likely to be more limited than the number that might be defined as such in single-driver approaches based on questionable underlying economic models. Quantitative estimates of illicit flows using our definition are therefore likely to be considerably less spectacular than, for example, recent estimates of dirty money (see Kar and Cartwright-Smith 2008). This is precisely our point. We argue that, *if* economic development is to be the main concern in this debate, then the promotion of economic growth in the context of a distribution of benefits that is politically viable has to be the condition that any policy intervention must meet. Wider criteria than this to define illicit capital outflows as a target for policy intervention by necessity rely on some broader notion of the social or economic good based on an abstract underlying model that may have little relevance in seeking development in the real world.

Our analysis also questions the validity of a core premise of the capital flight literature, namely, that all flight capital, if retained domestically, will yield a higher social rate of return (Schneider 2003a; Cumby and Levich 1987; Walter 1987). The purpose of our analytical typology is to show that, from the point of view of economic and political development, blocking all capital outflows from developing countries is not desirable. Moreover, as we outline in table 2.1, blocking some apparently *damaging* flows can also do more harm than good if these flows are driven by deeper problems (such as the absence of industrial policy, live-and-let-live rules between competing political factions, or the presence of domestic monopolies). In these cases, we argue, it is a mistake to describe the resultant flows as illicit. The policy implication is not that nothing should be done in such cases. It is rather that the solution is to look for policies that address the underlying structural problems. In the case of fragile developers, our analysis points out the dangers of too easily defining what is illicit. Finally, our sequential impact assessment suggests that there are dangers even in simplistically attacking capital flows that we do deem illicit. Even in these cases, it is possible that some policy responses are more effective than others, and policies that tackle illicit capital flows in isolation from the wider political settlements of which they are a part may leave society less well off.

Consider the following example on anti–money laundering (AML) policies. The cost-effectiveness of the AML regime promoted by the intergovernmental Financial Action Task Force is doubtful even for advanced economies (Reuter and Truman 2004; Schneider 2005).[4] Sharman (2008) extends this analysis to developing countries, with a special focus on Barbados, Mauritius, and Vanuatu, and finds that AML standards have had a significant net negative impact on these three developing countries. Essentially, the costs imposed on legitimate businesses and states having limited administrative and financial capacity far outweighed the extremely limited benefits in terms of convictions or the recovery of illicit assets. Yet, according to Sharman, rather than rethinking the policy model, its enforcement was strengthened mainly by blacklisting noncompliant countries and through competition between states for international recognition and imitation.

Sharman (2008, 651) highlights the case of Malawi, as follows:

Malawi is not and does not aspire to be an international financial center, nor has it been associated with money laundering or the financing of terrorism. Speaking at an international financial summit in September 2006, the Minister of Economics and Planning recounted how his country had come to adopt the standard package of AML regulations. The Minister was told that Malawi needed an AML policy. The Minister replied that Malawi did not have a problem with money laundering, but was informed that this did not matter. When the Minister asked if the package could be adapted for local conditions he was told no, because then Malawi would not meet international standards in this area. The Minister was further informed that a failure to meet international AML standards would make it harder for individuals and firms in Malawi to transact with the outside world relative to its neighbors, and thus less likely to attract foreign investment. The Minister concluded: "We did as we were told."

Notes

1. "The term, *illicit financial flows*, pertains to the crossborder movement of money that is illegally *earned, transferred*, or *utilized*." (Emphasis in original.) Global Financial Integrity summary fact sheet on illicit financial flows, http://www.gfip.org/storage/gfip/documents/illicit%20flows%20from%20developing%20countries%20overview%20w%20table.pdf.
2. The most commonly applied variant of this residual measure subtracts capital outflows or uses of foreign exchange (the current account deficit and increases in central bank reserves) from capital inflows (net external borrowing, plus net foreign direct investment). An excess of inflows over outflows is interpreted as indicative of capital flight. Nonbank variants of this measure include net acquisitions of foreign assets by the private banking system in capital outflows.
3. Our intermediate developers should not be confused with middle-income countries. Relatively poor and middle-income developing countries can both have sustainable political settlements, and both can suffer from internal political crises that result in fragility as a result of a collapse in the internal political settlements.
4. See Financial Action Task Force, Paris, http://www.fatf-gafi.org/.

References

Baker, R. W. 2005. *Capitalism's Achilles Heel: Dirty Money and How to Renew the Free-Market System.* Hoboken, NJ: John Wiley & Sons.

Baker, R. W., and J. Nordin. 2007. "Dirty Money: What the Underworld Understands That Economists Do Not." *Economist's Voice* 4 (1): 1–3.

Boyce, J. K., and L. Ndikumana. 2001. "Is Africa a Net Creditor? New Estimates of Capital Flight from Severely Indebted Sub-Saharan African Countries, 1970–96." *Journal of Development Studies* 38 (2): 27–56.

Boyce, J. K., and L. Zarsky. 1988. "Capital Flight from the Philippines, 1962–1986." *Philippine Journal of Development* 15 (2): 191–222.

Cerra, V., M. Rishi, and S. C. Saxena. 2008. "Robbing the Riches: Capital Flight, Institutions and Debt." *Journal of Development Studies* 40 (8): 1190–213.

Collier, P. 1999. "On the Economic Consequences of Civil War." *Oxford Economic Paper* 51 (1): 168–83.

Collier, P., A. Hoeffler, and C. A. Pattillo. 2001. "Flight Capital as a Portfolio Choice." *World Bank Economic Review* 15 (1): 55–80.

Crotty, J. 2009. "Structural Causes of the Global Financial Crisis: A Critical Assessment of the 'New Financial Architecture.'" *Cambridge Journal of Economics* 33 (4): 539–62.

Cuddington, J. T. 1986. *Capital Flight: Estimates, Issues, and Explanations.* Princeton Studies in International Finance 58 (December). Princeton, NJ: Princeton University.

———. 1987. "Capital Flight." *European Economic Review* 31 (1–2): 382–88.

Cumby, R. E., and R. M. Levich. 1987. "On the Definition and Magnitude of Recent Capital Flight." In *Capital Flight and Third World Debt,* ed. D. R. Lessard and J. Williamson, 26–67. Washington, DC: Peterson Institute for International Economics.

Dooley, M. P. 1986. "Country-Specific Risk Premiums, Capital Flight and Net Investment Income Payments in Selected Developing Countries." Departmental memorandum, March, Research Department, International Monetary Fund, Washington, DC.

———. 1988. "Capital Flight: A Response to Differences in Financial Risks." *IMF Staff Papers* 35 (3): 422–36.

Eatwell, J., and L. Taylor. 2000. *Global Finance at Risk.* New York: New York Press.

Epstein, G. A., ed. 2006. *Capital Flight and Capital Controls in Developing Countries.* Cheltenham, U.K.: Edward Elgar.

Erbe, S. 1985. "The Flight of Capital from Developing Countries." *Intereconomics* 20 (6): 268–75.

Eurodad (European Network on Debt and Development). 2008a. "Eurodad Fact Sheet: Capital Flight Diverts Development Finance." Eurodad Report, May 8, Eurodad, Brussels.

———. 2008b. "Addressing Development's Black Hole: Regulating Capital Flight." Eurodad Report, May 8, Eurodad, Brussels.

Franko. P. 2003. *The Puzzle of Latin American Economic Development.* Lanham, MD: Rowman & Littlefield.

Gapper, J. 2009. "How Banks Learnt to Play the System." *Financial Times,* May 6.

Global Witness. 2009. *Undue Diligence: How Banks Do Business with Corrupt Regimes.* Report, March. London: Global Witness. http://www.undue-diligence.org/Pdf/ GW_DueDilligence_FULL_lowres.pdf.

Gordon, D., and R. Levine. 1989. "The Problem of Capital Flight: A Cautionary Note." *World Development* 12 (2): 237–52.

Gordon Nembhard, J. 1996. *Capital Control, Financial Regulation, and Industrial Policy in South Korea and Brazil.* London: Praeger.

Gulati, S. K. 1987. "A Note on Trade Misinvoicing." In *Capital Flight and Third World Debt*, ed. D. R. Lessard and J. Williamson, 68–78. Washington, DC: Peterson Institute for International Economics.

Heggstad, K., and O.-H. Fjeldstad. 2010. "How Banks Assist Capital Flight from Africa: A Literature Review." CMI Report R 2010: 6 (January), Chr. Michelsen Institute, Bergen, Norway.

Hermes, N., and R. Lensink. 1992. "The Magnitude and Determinants of Capital Flight: The Case for Six Sub-Saharan African Countries." *De Economist* 140 (4): 515–30.

Hollingshead, A. 2010. "The Implied Tax Revenue Loss from Trade Mispricing." Global Financial Integrity, Washington, DC. http://www.gfip.org/storage/gfip/ documents/reports/implied%20tax%20revenue%20loss%20report_final.pdf.

Kant, C. 1998. "Capital Inflows and Capital Flight: Individual Country Experiences." *Journal of Economic Integration* 13 (4): 644–61.

———. 2002. "What Is Capital Flight?" *World Economy* 25 (3): 341–58.

Kapoor, S. 2007. "Haemorrhaging Money: A Christian Aid Briefing on the Problem of Illicit Capital Flight." Christian Aid, London.

Kar, D., and D. Cartwright-Smith. 2008. "Illicit Financial Flows from Developing Countries, 2002–2006." Global Financial Integrity, Washington, DC. http://www .gfip.org/storage/gfip/economist%20-%20final%20version%201-2-09.pdf.

Khan, M. H., ed. 2004. *State Formation in Palestine: Viability and Governance during a Social Transformation.* With G. Giacaman and I. Amundsen. Routledge Political Economy of the Middle East and North Africa Series. London: Routledge Curzon.

———. 2005. "Markets, States and Democracy: Patron-Client Networks and the Case for Democracy in Developing Countries." *Democratization* 12 (5): 705–24.

———. 2006. "Determinants of Corruption in Developing Countries: The Limits of Conventional Economic Analysis." In *International Handbook on the Economics of Corruption*, ed. S. Rose-Ackerman, 216–44. Cheltenham, U.K.: Edward Elgar.

———. 2009. "Learning, Technology Acquisition and Governance Challenges in Developing Countries." Report, Research Paper Series on Governance for Growth. School of Oriental and African Studies, University of London, London. http://www.dfid.gov.uk/r4/SearchResearchDatabase.asp?OutPutId=181367.

———. 2010. "Political Settlements and the Governance of Growth-Enhancing Institutions." Report, Research Paper Series on Governance for Growth, School of Oriental and African Studies, University of London, London. http://eprints.soas.ac.uk/9968/.

Khan, M. H., and S. Blankenburg. 2009. "The Political Economy of Industrial Policy in Asia and Latin America." In *Industrial Policy and Development: The Political Economy of Capabilities Accumulation*, ed. M. Cimoli, G. Dosi, and J. E. Stiglitz, 336–77. Initiative for Policy Dialogue Series. Oxford: Oxford University Press.

Khan, M. H., and K. S. Jomo, eds. 2000. *Rents, Rent-Seeking and Economic Development: Theory and Evidence in Asia.* Cambridge, U.K.: Cambridge University Press.

Khan, M. S. and N. Ul Haque. 1985. "Foreign Borrowing and Capital Flight: A Formal Analysis." *IMF Staff Papers* 32 (4): 606–28.

Kindleberger, C. P. 1937. *International Short-Term Capital Movements.* New York: Augustus Kelley.

———. 1990. *Historical Economics.* New York: Harvester Wheatsheaf.

Lessard, D. R., and J. Williamson. 1987. "The Problem and the Policy Responses." In *Capital Flight and Third World Debt*, ed. D. R. Lessard and J. Williamson, 201–54. Washington, DC: Peterson Institute for International Economics.

Myrvin, L. A., and A. J. Hughes Hallett. 1992. "How Successfully Do We Measure Capital Flight? The Empirical Evidence from Five Developing Countries." *Journal of Development Studies* 28 (3): 538–56.

North, D. C., J. J. Wallis, S. B. Webb, and B. R. Weingast. 2007. "Limited Access Orders in the Developing World: A New Approach to the Problem of Development." Policy Research Working Paper 4359, World Bank, Washington, DC.

Palma, G. 2005. "Four Sources of De-Industrialization and a New Concept of the 'Dutch Disease.' " In *Beyond Reform: Structural Dynamics and Macroeconomic Vulnerability*, ed. J. A. Ocampo, 71–116. Washington, DC: World Bank; Berkeley, CA: Stanford University Press.

———. 2009. "The Revenge of the Market on the Rentiers: Why Neo-liberal Reports of the End of History Turned Out to be Premature." Special issue, *Cambridge Journal of Economics* 33 (4): 829–69.

Pollin, R. 2003. *Contours of Descent: U.S. Economic Fractures and the Landscape of Global Austerity.* London: Verso.

Reuter, P., and E. M. Truman. 2004. *Chasing Dirty Money: The Fight against Money Laundering.* Washington, DC: Institute for International Economics.

Rishi, M., and J. K. Boyce. 1990. "The Hidden Balance of Payments: Capital Flight and Trade Misinvoicing in India, 1971–1986." *Economic and Political Weekly* 25 (30): 1645–48.

Schneider, B., ed. 2003a. *The Road to International Financial Stability: Are Key Financial Standards the Answer?* International Political Economy Series. London: Overseas Development Institute; Basingstoke, U.K.: Palgrave Macmillan.

———. 2003b. "Measuring Capital Flight: Estimates and Interpretations." Working Paper 194 (March), Overseas Development Institute, London.

————. 2003c. "Resident Capital Outflows: Capital Flight or Normal Outflows? Statistical Interpretations." Working Paper 195 (March), Overseas Development Institute, London.

————. 2005. "Do Global Standards and Codes Prevent Financial Crises? Some Proposals on Modifying the Standards-Based Approach." UNCTAD Discussion Paper 177 (April), United Nations Conference on Trade and Development, Geneva.

Sharman, J. C. 2008. "Power and Discourse in Policy Diffusion: Anti–money Laundering in Developing States." *International Studies Quarterly* 52 (3): 635–56.

Smithin, J. 1996. *Macroeconomic Policy and the Future of Capitalism: The Revenge of the Rentiers and the Threat to Prosperity.* Cheltenham, U.K.: Edward Elgar.

Tilly, C. 1985. "War Making and State Making as Organized Crime." In *Bringing the State Back In*, ed. P. B. Evans, D. Rueschemeyer, and T. Skocpol, 161–90. Cambridge, U.K.: Cambridge University Press.

————. 1990. *Coercion, Capital and European States.* Oxford: Blackwell.

Tornell, A., and A. Velasco. 1992. "The Tragedy of the Commons and Economic Growth: Why Does Capital Flow from Poor to Rich Countries?" *Journal of Political Economy* 100 (6): 1208–31.

Vos, R. 1992. "Private Foreign Asset Accumulation, Not Just Capital Flight: Evidence from the Philippines." *Journal of Development Studies* 28 (3): 500–37.

Walter, I. 1987. "The Mechanisms of Capital Flight." In *Capital Flight and Third World Debt*, ed. D. R. Lessard and J. Williamson, 103–28. Washington, DC: Peterson Institute for International Economics.

World Bank. 1985. *World Development Report 1985: International Capital and Economic Development.* New York: World Bank; New York: Oxford University Press.

Wray, R. 2009. "The Rise and Fall of Money Manager Capitalism: A Minskian Approach." *Cambridge Journal of Economics* 33 (4): 807–28.

3

The Political Economy of Controlling Tax Evasion and Illicit Flows

Max Everest-Phillips

Abstract

This chapter examines illicit capital flows from developing countries through analysis of one major component of the problem, tax evasion. The political economy definition put forward in the chapter clarifies that the root cause of all illicit capital outflows is ultimately not poor policy or capacity constraints in administration, but the failure of political will. Tax evasion and the other major sources of illegal flows (criminality and corruption) flourish in the absence of the political ambition to build a legitimate, effective state. Such effectiveness, including the effectiveness of tax systems, derives from formal and informal institutional arrangements (political settlements) that establish state legitimacy, promote prosperity, and raise public revenue. The commitment to these arrangements distinguishes illicit from illegal. It requires that political leaders and taxpayers perceive the need for effective tax systems to provide the state with the resources necessary to enforce their own property rights, deliver political stability, and promote economic growth. The extent and form of tax evasion derive from the political consensus to tax effectively and develop the administrative capacity to do so. This, in turn, shapes and reflects the intrinsic willingness to pay taxes (tax morale) of taxpayers. To contain illicit capital flows, including tax evasion, the weak legitimacy of the state in many developing countries must be addressed. If regime leaders and elites are not prepared to tax themselves and prevent free-riding, genuine political ownership of efforts to curb illicit capital flows is problematic.

Introduction: Effective States, Tax Evasion, and Illicit Capital Flows

The G-8 world leaders, meeting in July 2009, recognized "the particularly damaging effects of tax evasion for developing countries."[1] Effective states require effective, efficient, and equitable tax systems. Creating the commitment of citizens not to evade taxation is a political process central to state building; cajoling elites to pay taxes has always been an essential step to any state becoming effective. Bad governance manifests itself through an unjust tax system and rampant tax evasion (the illegal avoidance of paying taxation) (Everest-Phillips 2009a).[2] Throughout history, tax has been a symbol of state authority; tax evasion an indicator of political resistance.[3] Tax evasion is significantly correlated with dissatisfaction with government, political interference in the economy, and weak governance (see, respectively, Lewis 1982; Kim 2008; Hayoz and Hug 2007). In modern times, widespread tax evasion remains a trigger for and indicator of political instability.[4] Political and economic malaise intertwine. For instance, after the Tequila Crisis in Mexico, tax evasion increased from 43 percent of the total take in 1994, to 54 percent in 1995, and to 59 percent in the first half of 1996.[5]

Political economy definition: Flight or flow? Illegal or illicit?

Considerable confusion has arisen in the nascent literature on illicit capital flows from the failure to develop conceptual clarity between capital flight and capital flows and between illicit and illegal. To establish clear definitions requires recognition that effective, legitimate states are crucial for development (DFID 2006). Illicit indicates that the activity is generally perceived as illegitimate, which, in turn, requires the state to be regarded as legitimate. International capital transfers become illicit if they originate from an illegal source (evasion, corruption, or criminality) or are illegal by bypassing capital controls, but also immoral in undermining the state's willingness and capacity to deliver better lives for its citizens. (For simplicity, we treat illicit here to mean immoral *and* illegal, but there also exist potentially immoral, but not illegal capital flows, such as those arising from aggressive tax avoidance.) Flight indicates exit from risk; flow is simply a movement of liquid financial assets. By this definition, illegal capital flight is the rational, but unlawful, shift of assets away from high to low political risk, whereas illicit capital flows take place by choice despite a state's political legitimacy evinced by a credible commitment to development in the national interest (table 3.1). The frequent conflation of illicit and illegal loses the important moral dimension for developing countries and their partners in the international community of the need to tackle poverty and deliver the United Nations' Millennium Development Goals.

The three main drivers of illicit capital flows—tax evasion, corruption, and criminality—are, at once, both causes and effects of the fragility of state institutions and, so, challenge perceived legitimacy. Tax evasion undermines the funding of the state and, thus, the legitimacy associated with the state through the delivery of public services; corruption weakens the moral legitimacy of the state; and criminality challenges the legitimacy of state authority. However, while the rationale for the illicit capital flows driven by these factors is clear, the relative importance of these factors in different contexts and the connections between them remain uncertain and unquantified.[6]

This chapter outlines the political economy of the apparently most common and undoubtedly most politically complex and significant of illicit flows, the flows linked to tax evasion. It argues that, because political

Table 3.1. Proposed Typology: Illegal and Illicit Capital Flows and Capital Flight

Capital movement	Illegal	Illicit
Capital flow (from greed)	Unlawful asset transfer to hide wealth from the state	Asset transfer that immorally undermines a legitimate state's capacity and commitment to development
Capital flight (from risk)	Unlawful asset transfer from a poor to a good governance context to reduce political risk (for example, from arbitrary autocratic rule)	Immoral asset transfer to reduce exposure to political risk (for example, from nascent democracy)

Source: Author compilation.

governance is central to the problem of illicit capital flows, tackling the flows requires more than technocratic solutions. Domestic and international efforts to contain illicit capital flows must include building state legitimacy through a locally credible political vision for sustainable development. It concludes that the key policy concern in attempts to control illicit capital flows must be how to create the political interests and institutional incentive structures so that political leaders and elites will tax themselves, thereby curtailing the potential benefits from those forms of illicit capital flows that may currently be funding their grip on power.

Effective states tackle illicit capital flows

Where poor political governance reflects and exacerbates political insecurity, significant illicit capital flight may occur. Any modern state that is not a tax haven or an oil exporter requires resourcing through an effective tax system capable of constraining tax evasion. The state also requires perceived legitimacy so that taxpayers and citizens in general do not regard illegal capital outflows as licit, that is, as morally legitimate. Yet, many developing states are highly aid dependent and lack legitimacy in the eyes of their citizens; so, they need to strengthen their tax base and the willingness of their citizens to pay taxes (Chabal and Daloz 1999; Everest-Phillips 2011). Overcoming this development conundrum requires recognition that politics shape both the root cause and the potential solution. Tax systems, which comprise legislation, policy, and administration, are part of this, reflecting the national consensus on collective action, through the political process, for resourcing essential public goods such as security, rule of law, and the provision of basic services (Timmons 2005). Taxation reflects the intrinsic legitimacy of the state (based on consent, manifested among taxpayers as tax morale, their inherent willingness to pay taxes) and funds the effectiveness of state institutions (manifested in actual compliance).[7]

The extent of tax evasion thus provides a good indicator of the comparative quality of governance.[8] The state cannot function without revenue; how that revenue is raised (the balance between coercion and consent) mirrors the relationship between society and the state, but also shapes it: tax is state building in developing countries (Bräutigam, Fjeldstad, and Moore 2008; Everest-Phillips 2008a, 2010).[9] While the size and structure of a country's economy significantly influence the types and yield of the taxes that can be collected, the root cause of weaknesses in tax systems in many countries is ultimately not a limited economy, poor tax policy, or capacity constraints in tax administrations (Stotsky and WoldeMariam 1997). Rather, the problem is that taxation reflects political attitudes toward the state and the type of state that taxation should fund.[10]

Tax evasion and the potential illicit capital flows arising from it therefore flourish if there is a lack of political determination to build the legitimacy of the state needed to make taxation effective and deliver development (Therkildsen 2008; Everest-Phillips 2009a).[11] For example, across Africa, the postindependence collapse in governance was reflected in tax evasion: thus, in Malawi, tax evasion increased sevenfold between 1972 and 1990.[12] Corruption also flourished as the state became the vehicle for personal enrichment by the elite, and the state's challenged legitimacy encouraged institutionalized criminality (Bayart, Ellis, and Hibou 1999).

As a result of such dynamics, containing all forms of illicit capital flows requires building state legitimacy and improving political and economic governance. Empirical data consistently confirm the importance of the perceived quality of governance for tax compliance. Public perception of high levels of corruption, for example, is associated with high levels of tax evasion; this is both cause and effect given that higher levels of corruption lower the ratio of taxes to gross domestic product (GDP) (Rose-Ackerman 1999; Ghura 2002). Tax compliance does not depend solely or probably not even largely on a taxpayer's analysis of cost, benefit, and risk of evasion (Alm and Martinez-Vazquez 2003). Instead, taxpayers evade and illicitly move capital abroad not simply because the potential benefit outweighs the perceived risk, but because they believe the state lacks the legitimacy of capable, accountable, and responsive governance (Steinmo 1993).

Indeed, in the face of rampant corruption, criminality, and waste in the public sector, tax evasion is seen as legitimate (Tanzi and Shome 1993). Widespread tax evasion indicates a lack of tax effort: the state lacks the will to engage with its citizens, and citizens do not believe their interests coincide with those of the state. The fiscal social contract—namely, a credible commitment among leaders, elites, and citizens to pay for and deliver sustainable national development—does not exist. The popular Russian attitude toward tax evasion exemplifies the relevant political context found in many developing countries, as follows:[13]

> First, [Russian citizens] rightly did not believe that all "the other" taxpay-
> ers were paying their taxes properly, so it was really no point in being "the
> only one" who acted honestly. The goods (public, semi-public or private)
> that the government was going to use the money to produce would simply
> not be produced because there were too little taxes paid in the first place.
> Secondly, they believed that the tax authorities were corrupted, so that
> even if they paid their taxes, a significant part of the money would never
> reach the hospitals or schools, etc. Instead, the money would fill the pock-
> ets of the tax bureaucrats. (Rothstein 2001, 477)

Thus, tax evasion creates a vicious circle: the perception that others are not paying tax drastically reduces compliance and delegitimizes the state, fueling both capital flight and capital flows. So, for example, the private assets held abroad by Venezuelan citizens more than doubled, from US$23 billion to US$50 billion, between 1998 and 2005 as a result of widespread tax evasion and capital flight arising from the collapse of the political legitimacy of the state as perceived by taxpaying citizens under the divisive populist politics of Chavez's Bolivarian Revolution (Di John 2009). Only if the state formulates an inclusive vision for economic growth and development that is politically credible with a broad base of taxpayers and holders of capital, as well as the wider electorate, does rational capital flight from governance risk become illicit capital flow, that is, an immoral undermining of the state's commitment to poverty reduction, sustainable economic growth, and long-term political stability.

Evasion into illicit outflows: Looting, rent-scraping, and dividend-collecting

Illicit international capital transfers require three drivers: (1) opportunity, particularly facilitated by globalization; (2) pull, that is, attraction to more effective governance contexts with less political risk (flight); and (3) push, that is, the lack of a credible domestic commitment to development (flows). Wedeman (1997) distinguishes three political economies that convert tax evasion into capital flight and outflows: *looting*, or uninhibited plundering or systematic theft of public funds and extraction of bribes by public officials, whereby political insecurity is so endemic that outflows are institutionalized; *rent-scraping*, or political manipulation to produce rents, thereby allowing the scraping off of these rents by public officials so that short-term political gain drives outflows; and *dividend-collecting*, or transfers of a predictable percentage of the profits earned by private enterprises to government officials. Under this last political context, the longer-term consensus on development generates the political security that is essential to constrain outflows.

These different dynamics result in the wide variations in the effectiveness of tax systems. In a looting context such as Zaire under Mobutu, minimal taxation and endemic tax evasion reflected the failure to build the state capacities required to enforce property rights, and the political settlement collapsed. In a rent-scraping environment such as the Philippines under Marcos, the tax system was weak, and tax evasion was widespread and increasing; the ratio of taxes to GDP fell from 12.0 percent in 1975 to 9.6 percent in 1984 as political support for the dictatorship collapsed (Manasan and Querubin 1987). The first finance minister of the post-Marcos Aquino government later noted that "every successful businessman, lawyer, accountant, doctor, and dentist I know has some form of cash or assets which he began to squirrel abroad after Marcos declared martial law in 1972 and, in the process, frightened every Filipino who had anything to lose" (Boyce and Zarsky 1988, 191). A return to formal democracy did little to alleviate the problem, however, and, a decade later, the politics of vested interests in the Philippines continued as rent-scraping, in which "tax avoidance and evasion are evidently largely the province of the rich" (Devarajan and Hossain 1995).

In these rent-seeking contexts, economic opportunities and political order are created and maintained by limiting access to valuable resources (North et al. 2007; North, Wallis, and Weingast 2009). Limited access to the looting of state assets, rent seeking, corruption, criminality, and ease of tax evasion creates the political incentives in any regime to cooperate with the group in power.[14] Access to illicit capital flows and tolerance of tax evasion form part of this rent and are distributed to solve the problem of endemic violence and political disorder. The regime, lacking a broad elite coalition for long-term development, may tacitly or expressly allow the "winning coalition" of its power base to evade tax, while trying to constrain open access to the illicit capital flows and to tax evasion that would undermine the rent seeking on which the stability of the state in these fragile governance contexts depends (North et al. 2007; North, Wallis, and Weingast 2009). Repressive governments may be more inclined to restrain tax evasion by simply avoiding the sources of tax that require a substantial degree of voluntary cooperation (Hettich and Winer 1999).

By contrast, in dividend-collecting contexts, the political importance assigned to building an effective state has meant that evasion has translated less into illicit outflows, and developmental states often emerge (Khan 2000). In a dividend-collecting system, economic growth and political stability are encouraged because political leaders and corrupt officials perceive the payoffs in the long term. This dynamic explains how developing countries often begin to build a national development project despite the initially low tax revenue that undermines their early capacity to deliver services to citizens, potentially reinforcing the lack of legitimacy and the low tax take.

Corruption and tax evasion may be rampant not least so as to fund political stability, but illicit flows are recognized as threatening to sustainable development and are tackled (Khan 2005; North et al. 2007; North, Wallis, and Weingast 2009). This is in contrast to the short-term outlook of the looting model, which destroys economic value. So, while, in all these contexts, grand tax evasion arises from collusion among political and business elites and the top levels of government, the evasion–capital flows process is shaped by different political dynamics. Policies and enforcement may be formulated to permit tax evasion in return for political favors, and they may operate through the overt or tacit complicity of senior tax administrators and fiscal policy officials. Without political support for the high-profile prosecution of tax evaders, grand evasion results in rampant illicit capital flows in looting or rent-scraping contexts, but the politics of dividend-collecting facilitates a pragmatic focus on controlling capital flows for domestic investment and political stability.[15]

Petty low-level tax evasion, by contrast, is probably insignificant for illicit capital flows, but affects the underlying political economy context. The average size of African shadow economies was estimated at 41.3 percent of GDP in 1999/2000, increasing to 43.2 percent in 2002/03), though these figures hide significant grand evasion because the lack of commitment of elites to long-term development morphs into capital flight and flows (Schneider, A. 2007; UNECA 2009). The dynamics of petty evasion also have political implications, however, because of what Tendler (2002) refers to as the "devil's deal," the tacit understanding in patronage politics that petty tax evasion (evasion that does not lead to significant illicit flows) is tolerated as the quid pro quo for political support that allows grand evasion and illicit flows: "if you vote for me . . . , I won't collect taxes from you; I won't make you comply with other tax, environmental or labor regulations; and I will keep the police and inspectors from harassing you" (Tendler 2002, 28). This leaves both vested interests and the informal economy untaxed or undertaxed and deprives the informal sector of the incentive to engage in constructive political bargaining over taxation, the fiscal social contract.[16] At the same time, rulers are left unrestrained to embezzle and misuse public resources to sustain their grip on power, while the public goods and services necessary for poverty reduction and development are underprovided.

This devil's deal underpins the neo-patrimonial politics behind illicit capital flows. Political clients do not act as taxpaying citizens using their votes to improve governance, and political patrons exploit corruption and tax evasion to fund their grip on power, while protecting their long-term prospects outside the country. So, political dynamics shape the capacity of the state to manage evasion and constrain the incentives for political and economic elites to shift the tax burden to middle-size firms and the middle class.[17]

The Political Economy of Tax Evasion

The dynamics outlined above indicate that the political economic determinants of the extent of tax evasion in any specific context reflect a combination of six factors, as follows: (1) the structure of the economy that shapes the potential sources of government revenues; (2) the structure of the political system, that is, the political rules by which politicians gain and hold onto the power that shapes political competition and incentives (constitutions, party structures, electoral processes, legislative and executive rules shaping policy choice, and so on) (Stewart 2007; Schneider, F. 2007); (3) the state's monopoly of violence as the basis for enforcing state tax and other authority (North et al. 2007; North, Wallis, and Weingast 2009); (4) the credibility of the regime's political time horizons that shape the perceptions of tax as an investment in the future prosperity and stability of the state; (5) the potential influence of collective action by taxpayers or other citizen groups to negotiate with political leadership; and (6) the rationale for leaders and elites to build the broad, long-term economic development of their societies, which is influenced by noneconomic interests such as traditional ethnic, kinship, and communal ties and patterns of patronage, as well as other factors such as international pressures.[18]

These six political economy factors, in turn, shape citizen understanding of the legitimacy of taxation.[19] Taxpayer attitudes toward this legitimacy are formed by three more immediate forces, as follows:

- *Tax morale:* taxpayer civic responsibility to support or undermine national goals, that is, the extent to which enforcement is accepted as a legitimate and effective exercise of state power
- *Capacity:* the capacity of tax policy and particularly tax administration, including the effectiveness of political and administrative checks that limit rent seeking and patronage and the political support for the efficiency of the tax administration, measured by tax effort and the tax compliance costs imposed on taxpayers compared across countries at similar levels of development[20]
- *Perceived fairness:* the perceived fairness and effectiveness of taxes and the tax authority (based both on experience and the perception of the extent of the compliance of other taxpayers)[21]

Tax evasion flourishes in poor governance contexts

In light of the above, it is not surprising to find that tax evasion is endemic in contexts of poor governance, for example:

- In the Philippines in the mid-1980s, with the collapsing Marcos regime, income tax evasion grew to account for nearly 50 percent of the potential yield (Manasan 1988). The restoration of democracy under President Aquino was only partly successful in delivering political stability, a weak legitimacy reflected in corporate tax evasion on domestic sales tax at between 53 and 63 percent in the early 1990s
- In Nigeria, persistent political uncertainty was reflected in the federal government estimation in 2004 that, because of tax evasion, corruption, and weak administration, it had collected only around 10 per-

cent of the taxes due and that half the revenue collected was then lost or embezzled (OECD and AfDB 2008).

- In the Central African Republic, ongoing political tensions have facilitated evasion and kept the ratio of taxes to GDP at only 8 percent (World Bank 2009a).[22]

Tax evasion is, however, not static, but fluctuates. A primary variation is the perceived strength of state legitimacy in developing countries, which affects evasion directly through tax morale and indirectly through a lower tax effort (Fjeldstad, Katera, and Ngalewa 2009). This has also been demonstrated in the developed world, in Italy, for example, in the increases in the evasion of the value added tax (VAT) during periods of political uncertainty such as the peak, at 37 percent in the late 1980s, or, in Spain, when shifting political pressures have weakened the administrative effort devoted to tackling tax evasion (Chiarini, Marzano, and Schneider 2009; Esteller-Moré 2005).

Nonetheless, the political roots of the tax evasion driving international capital transfers affect particularly the developing world. In the international development discourse, improving tax systems is too often portrayed as only a technical, apolitical challenge, rather than as a profound litmus test of state legitimacy. Public choice theory's conceptualization of politics as merely self-interest is unfortunately reflected too uncritically in the tax literature.[23] So, it is worth citing the rich evidence showing that tax systems everywhere reflect shifting political legitimacy, as follows:

- In Benin by the late 1990s, during the country's turbulent post–Cold War transition from a Marxist dictatorship, only 10 percent of taxpayers were regularly paying their taxes (van de Walle 2001).
- In The Gambia, in the years immediately before the military coup of 1994, lost revenues rose to 9 percent of GDP, and income tax evasion expanded to 70 percent of the total revenue due (Dia 1993, 1996).
- In Kenya by 2001, the chaotic last year of the Moi presidency, the tax gap had reached at least 35 percent, suggesting significant and increasing evasion (KIPPRA 2004).[24]
- In Madagascar, the political turmoil of the late 1990s saw the tax evasion rate rise to nearly 60 percent, equivalent to 8.8 percent of GDP

(compared with only 8.3 percent of GDP collected in taxes) (Gray 2001).

- In Niger, the political chaos of the 1990s saw rampant tax evasion trigger a major decline in fiscal revenues (Ndulu et al. 2008).
- In Pakistan, as the legitimacy of the state collapsed, the size of the informal economy increased from 20 percent of GDP in 1973 to 51 percent in 1995, while tax evasion more than trebled over the same period and continued thereafter within the climate of continuing political turmoil and military rule; the tax-GDP ratio fell from 13.2 percent in 1998 to 10.6 percent in 2006 (Saeed 1996).
- In Paraguay, the political optimism and improved tax compliance after the end of the Stroessner dictatorship had faded by 2003, when increasing tax evasion and corruption were depriving the state of about two-thirds of potential revenues (Freedom House 2008).[25]
- In West Bank and Gaza during the period 1994 to 2000, the declining perceived legitimacy of the Palestinian Authority reflected an apparently increasing tolerance of tax administrative procedures that facilitated evasion and corruption (Fjeldstad and al-Zagha 2004).

The political foundations of tax systems are apparent in the contrast between states in the Caribbean and states in Latin America given that Caribbean countries inherited parliamentary institutions rather than the presidential regimes of Latin America. This constitutional difference apparently created a broader acceptance of the need for an effective tax system across the Caribbean because parliamentary systems offer the possibility of negotiating a compromise among elites in forming a government. By contrast, Latin American political structures created a vicious circle of political instability and more regressive tax structures (Schneider, Lledo, and Moore 2004).

The collapse of the Soviet Union and the resulting political uncertainties in the transition countries over the progress toward representation through taxation underline the political foundations of tax evasion (Gehlbach 2008).[26] For instance, in Armenia, evasion became endemic as the tax-GDP ratio halved from 29 percent in 1991 to 14.8 percent in 1994. Although it recovered to 17 percent in 1997, the tax-GDP ratio remained well below the level in other transition economies that had a more secure political consensus on national purpose and that had not faced such a dramatic loss of legitimacy (for example, tax-GDP ratios in Estonia of 39 percent or in Poland of 44 percent in 1997) (Mkrtchyan 2001). The World Bank, in 2009, concluded that "fundamental political economy difficulties such as . . . checks to the power of powerful business interests in evading customs and tax payments . . . remain to be seriously addressed" (World Bank 2009c, 4). Armenia, however, highlights the need for further research on the complex international dynamics of illicit capital flight and flows because, despite political and economic fragility, it appears, in recent years, to have had sizable unrecorded capital inflows that may reflect other political economy dynamics in the region (Brada, Kutan, and Vukšic 2009).

Natural experiments in tax evasion and illicit flows

Cross-country comparisons over time illustrate the political dynamics behind state legitimacy and the efficacy of tax systems. In the Central America of the 1950s, Costa Rica and Guatemala shared similar characteristics in geographical location, size, colonial history, position in the world economy, levels of economic development, and reliance on coffee exports, but showed different patterns of illicit capital flows (Fatehi 1994). The Costa Rican political settlement following a brief civil war in 1948 successfully consolidated democracy and delivered economic growth. Taxpayers recognized that making the state effective required an adequate tax base to fund public services. As a result, the political settlement established the political will to tackle tax evasion and minimize illicit capital outflows. The tax compliance and collection rates in Costa Rica are the highest in Central America, and indicate the least evidence of an inclination to capital flight (Torgler 2003).

By contrast, Guatemala has the lowest tax take in Central America and has a long history of widespread tax evasion and capital flight (Erbe 1985). The failure of the political class in Guatemala to develop a wider vision for society resulted in civil war in the 1970s and 1980s. Political bargaining during the drafting of the Constitution of 1985 resulted in three articles being inserted deliberately to weaken the tax authority; as a result, tax evasion in the early 1990s was 58 percent.[27] The peace accord of 1996 has yet to generate any sense of national purpose so that, in the later half of the 1990s, for every quetzal taxed, 65 centavos were evaded, leaving the Guatemalan state without the resources to improve its legitimacy by providing better services for the population (Yashar 1997). The legislature has often appeared to facilitate evasion and avoidance deliberately by making tax laws overly complex.

Without political support to tackle evasion by powerful interests, the revenue authorities have instead directed their anti–tax evasion effort toward small taxpayers. The probability of evaders being caught has been low; in 2003, the Guatemalan revenue administration estimated total tax evasion at more than two-thirds of actual collection, with significant variation across revenue bases, at 29 percent for VAT, but 63 percent for income taxes.[28] If tax evasion is detected, the administrative and legal procedures are complicated and costly for the state. Penalties for tax evasion remain insignificant because of the absence of political determination to impose administrative and judicial sanctions in any effective or timely manner, and tax amnesties are too frequent and generous (Sánchez, O. 2009). The total tax-GDP ratio rose from a low of 6.8 percent when the civil war ended to 10.3 percent of GDP in 2006; citizens still widely regard tax evasion in Guatemala as ethical because the perception remains that "a significant portion of the money collected winds up in the pockets of corrupt politicians or their families and friends" (McGee and Lingle 2005, 489).[29]

Another natural experiment in the links between illicit outflows and the legitimacy of taxation can be seen in the contrast between Argentina and Chile, despite similar cultures, levels of economic development, history, and federal constitutions. Tax evasion in Argentina has consistently been high, the result of political instability and weak institutions (de Melo 2007). Sporadic efforts to crack down on evasion, including by the Menem presidency in the early 1990s, lacked political sustainability.[30]

By contrast, in the early 20th century, Chile achieved a political consensus against tolerating tax evasion and in favor of alleviating poverty and advancing national development through an effective tax system (Bergman 2009). With Chile's return to democracy in 1990, taxpayers were persuaded through the *Concertación* (the Concert of Parties for Democracy) that higher taxation was a small price to pay if democracy was to work by delivering an effective social contract (Boylan 1996; Vihanto 2000; Bergman 2009). Income tax evasion rates in Chile fell from 61.4 percent in 1990 to 42.6 percent in 1995 (Barra and Jarratt 1998). This fiscal social contract covered indirect and direct taxation, so that Chile, with a rate of 18 percent, collected almost 9 percent of GDP in tax revenue. By another contrast, Mexico, with a rate of 15 percent, collected less than 3 percent of GDP (Tanzi 2000). The mix of political will and administrative capacity was then reflected in overall evasion rates that nearly halved in Chile during the early 1990s, from 30 to 18 percent during the euphoria of the return to civilian rule; as the euphoria wore off, evasion had increased again to 25 percent by 1998, but, subsequently, because of rising political concern, matched by administrative effort, declined steadily to under 15 percent in 2004 (World Bank 2006).

As a result, capital flight and illicit capital flows have been consistently lower in Chile than in neighboring Argentina (Schneider, B. 2001; Di John 2006). Politics and institutions, not geography or economic structure, drive rates of capital flight.

Political legitimacy and illicit capital flows

Illicit capital flows arising from tax evasion indicate not only the opportunity for free-riding, but also taxpayer perceptions. If the state does not appear to be aligned with taxpayer interests, this lack of faith in a regime's current legitimacy and its future legitimacy after improving governance shapes the decision to hold assets abroad. However, if taxpaying elites believe in a locally owned political vision for the future, and regimes need their support, evasion may be tolerated by the state, yet not lead to illicit flows. As economic theory suggests, information asymmetries and higher rates of return in capital-scarce developing countries would retain domestic investment rather than encourage capital flow from the developing to the developed world.[31] But, if citizens see no credible long-term future political stability, savers and investors will seek to move their capital abroad to contexts of more effective, more stable governance, even at lower returns on investment and higher tax rates.[32] Where the state lacks political legitimacy, this capital flight, whether legal or not, would, as suggested above, be widely perceived as licit.

Effective tax systems alone are therefore not enough. Bergman (2009, 109) concludes that "moderate efficiency in law-abiding societies generates better results than good administration in a world of cheaters." For the state, the political imperative in curtailing free-riding on taxes is that, while core state functions such as preserving peace and upholding justice are universal expectations, transparent and fair property rights are essential to the dividend-collecting transition to effective, politically open access states and open markets (North et al. 2007; North, Wallis, and Weingast 2009). The creation and enforcement of property rights are, however, not costless (Khan 2005). Historically, the need to raise revenue motivated states to define property rights. In turn, this stimulated economic growth (Tilly 1975). Taxpayers are politically prepared to pay taxes that fund the state capabilities needed to secure their property rights (Khan 2000). In developing polities, the allocation and definition of property rights are continuously evolving, as they did historically in developed countries (Everest-Phillips 2008b; Hoppit 2011). Tackling tax evasion and illicit flows is therefore part of the political bargaining over how and what services, including protection of property rights, the state will provide.

If taxpayers do not accept the legitimacy of the state and are not intrinsically prepared to fund the state's services and the development of their own collective future prosperity, the political incentives for and credibility of the commitment to long-term sustainable development are lacking. Widespread illicit capital flows occur not only because the state is ineffectual, but also because citizens believe that the state has neither the political leadership nor the consensus needed to reform weak or corrupt institutions that threaten peace, justice, and the long-term security of private property rights (Friedman et al. 2001). As van de Walle (2001, 53) notes, the root of the problem is "the political logic of a system in which the authority of the state is diverted to enhance private power rather than the public domain."

Despite the democratization that began in the 1990s in many developing countries, the entrenchment of vested interests has ensured that improvements have been modest.[33] Improvements in the ratio of tax revenue to GDP have also often been short-lived because technical changes dependent on cooperative elites and high tax morale have been overcome by underlying political forces (Orviska and Hudson 2003; Engelschalk and Nerré 2002). So, rampant tax evasion remains widespread in many developing countries despite the seemingly endless tax policy and administration reforms undertaken over the intervening two decades.

Tackling illicit capital flows therefore requires not merely more tightening of tax policy and tax administration, but a shift in citizen attitudes

Figure 3.1. The Political Economy of an Effective State and Tax System

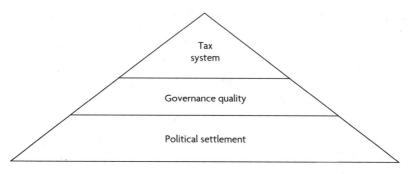

Source: Author compilation.

toward the political institutions shaping the governance context. These operate on three layers, as follows (see figure 3.1):

1. *The political settlement:* the informal and formal rules of the game over political power.[34] This includes both the formal rules for managing politics (peace treaties, constitutional provisions, parliamentary rules, the organization of political parties, and so on) and the informal networks, family ties, and social norms that shape political behaviors.[35] More an iterative process than a critical juncture, the political settlement shapes tax morale as an expression of social order, a collective interest, and a sense of political commitment to improve public institutions, constrain corruption, and deliver public goods (Andreoni, Erard, and Feinstein 1998). The settlement develops from the national political community that delivers the perceived fairness of and trust in a credible state; within this context, the tax system represents a legitimate and effective exercise of state power, while the efficient provision of public goods benefits taxpayers and ordinary citizens (Lieberman 2003). Politics shapes attitudes and behaviors relative to tax evasion, and the differences across groups within a country are potentially as significant as the differences across countries (Gërxhani and Schram 2002).

2. *General quality of governance:* state institutional effectiveness builds on the political settlement. Capital flight (rather than capital flows seeking only higher rates of return) moves from weak to effective governance,

from the generally lower tax contexts of developing countries to the higher tax environment of the developed world. Given overall lower rates of return on such investment, the main rationale would seem to be flight because of a lack of faith in domestic rates of return that derives from a lack of genuine elite commitment to national development, the political risk arising from political instability, and rampant corruption (Fuest and Riedel 2009). This appears to be confirmed by estimates of the capital flight from the African continent of about US$400 billion between 1970 and 2005; around US$13 billion per year left the continent between 1991 and 2004, or a huge 7.6 percent of annual GDP (Eurodad 2008). So, in contexts of poor governance, the wide overlap between capital flight and capital flows is reflected in the frequent conflation of the two terms.

3. *Tax administrative competence*: capacity to contain free-riding and maintain a credible commitment to paying taxes. This is critical to compliance; the state's legitimacy is reflected in the tax authority's powers of enforcement (that is, accountable coercion).[36] In many developing countries, political influence is often pronounced in the selection and promotion of staff at all levels in the revenue administration, thereby facilitating evasion and corruption such as the case of Benin in the late 1990s, when 25 percent of revenues were lost (van de Walle 2001).[37] Tax evasion is also significantly influenced by the interactions between taxpayers and the tax authorities: more respectful behavior on the part of tax authorities is associated with higher rates of tax compliance (Feld and Frey 2002). At the same time, differences in treatment by tax authorities arise from differences in the quality of political participation: "regime type matters in the explanation of the structure of taxation" (Kenny and Winer 2006, 183).

Variations in political governance away from political settlements and the quality of the institutions shaping administrative competence therefore lie at the heart of varying patterns in the tax evasion dimension of illicit capital flows.[38] Citizen perceptions of the legitimacy of taxation and of the effectiveness of the state combine in the calculation citizens make of the tax cost/benefit–burden/contribution equation. Whether taxation is viewed as a value-for-money contribution to society or simply an unproductive burden depends also on how it is raised and used.[39]

Figure 3.2. The Political Economy Model of Tax Evasion Driving Illicit Capital Flows

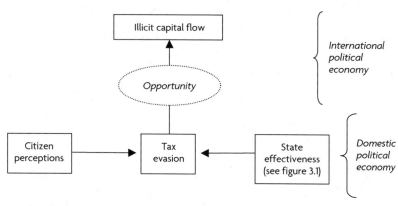

Source: Author compilation.

Alm and Martinez-Vazquez (2003, 158) find that government can decrease evasion "by providing goods that their citizens prefer more, by providing these goods in a more efficient manner, or by more effectively emphasizing that taxes are necessary for receipt of government services." Alm and Martinez-Vazquez (2003, 163) conclude that "compliance is strongly affected by the strength and commitment to the social norm of compliance." This is unlikely, for instance, in Malawi, where, in 2000, the government admitted that a third of public revenues were stolen annually by civil servants.[40] At the other end of the governance spectrum, countries with a strong political settlement and an effective administration, as in Scandinavia, witness the coexistence of large nominal and effective tax rates with low levels of evasion.[41] In effective governance contexts, therefore, taxpayers do perceive taxation as less a *burden* and more of an *investment* in an effective state.[42]

Variation in state effectiveness and, therefore, in the opportunity to turn evasion into illicit capital flows is the meeting point of the domestic and the international political economy (figure 3.2). Efforts to stem capital flight date back to the League of Nations before World War II. The political will to tackle illicit capital flows still requires the combination of effective national commitment to development and international coordination. This has been lacking, because, internationally and domestically, "[tax] is predominantly a matter of political power" (Kaldor 1963, 418).

Controlling illicit capital flows: Governance beyond technical solutions

"Revenue is the chief preoccupation of the state. Nay, more, it is the state."
—Edmund Burke, quoted in O'Brien (2001, 21)

The last decade or so has demonstrated that improving governance in developing countries is not simply a technical task of putting capacities in place, but is a problem of political will shaped by institutions and incentives. As a result, the development challenge has evolved from good governance through good-enough governance to engaging with the specific political drivers of change (Fritz, Kaiser, and Levy 2009). Administrative and policy reforms alone cannot alter the rampant corruption and tax evasion typical of weak states into the strong compliance of citizen-taxpayers in effective liberal democracies. Tax evasion and corruption translate into capital flight and illicit flows not only if the opportunity arises to place assets abroad. Capital flight arises from political risk; illicit flows arise from a perceived lack of political consensus about building an effective state. "A tax regime is conditioned by the power balances and struggles among the major social groups in a country, including the relative strengths of political parties that represent their divergent interests" (Di John 2008, 1). So, as Ndikumana (2004, 290) points out: "Tax evasion is made easier when the taxpayer is also the political client for the decision-maker." Such patrimonial politics, so common in many developing countries, thrives on evasion, corruption, and criminality (Chabal and Daloz 1999).

Illicit capital flows should, as a consequence, be addressed in the context of the political economy of inequality. Nontaxation and wide-scale tax evasion by the rich in high-inequality contexts undermine the capabilities and perceived legitimacy of the state (World Bank 2008a). In many developing countries, extreme inequalities create potential political instability, which, if combined with the lack of a social contract to pay taxes for the common good, fosters illicit capital flows and explains why achieving genuine national ownership of development often proves so problematic.

In such environments, tax system complexity can replace brutal repression as the obfuscation of political choice by elites in a situation in which tax morale is weak. An extreme example is offered by Honduras in

1991. Through legal exemptions alone, a taxpayer there would have required an income 687 times the average per capita income before being liable at the highest marginal tax rate. Given the rampant evasion, the rich in Honduras were, de facto, untaxed. The state consequently lacked broad legitimacy; development stalled; and political instability remained endemic.[43] These dynamics were also evident in Madagascar, for example, where the tax-GDP ratio was only 11.8 percent in the early 1990s. This was the outcome of political interest in permitting the tax system to be too complex for the country's administrative capabilities so as to facilitate widespread evasion for the privileged elites of the regime. This had a disastrous impact on economic growth and job creation; trade taxes discriminated across markets, while profits and wage taxes discouraged investment and employment (IMF 2007).

Elites, in other words, often maintain their power base in highly unequal societies by deliberately making tax systems overly complex, at huge cost to long-term development, not least because this generates illicit capital flows. Successful development, however, such as has occurred in East Asia, is often accompanied by the political imperative to deliver development in the face of internal and external threats, combined with tight capital controls and, thereby, the absence of global opportunities to hold illicit assets abroad. As globalization over the last few decades has created unparalleled opportunity to move capital easily abroad, the political imperative for leaders and elites to deliver national development appears to have weakened. The democratization of the 1990s does not seem to have significantly altered the incentives for corruption and tax evasion. Indeed, the contemporaneous opportunities that opened up with globalization often allowed the political class to accept political reforms, knowing that they could protect their assets by legally, illegally, or illicitly transferring them abroad. This has been manifested in the use of capital flight in response to populist politics such as in Bolivia and República Bolivariana de Venezuela and of illicit flows from many developing countries in the absence of a political commitment to sustainable development.

If controlling illicit flows is inherently a political problem, tax evasion is particularly important because tax structures are among the most measurable manifestations of the political settlement central to state effectiveness. Yet, in many developing countries, particularly the low-income ones, the current political dynamics create little incentive to make the necessary improvements in governance (Bratton and van de Walle 1997; Chabal and Daloz 1999). Tax evasion flourishes if an incomplete political settlement excludes many from the political system. The politically excluded, in turn, exclude themselves from paying taxes, while the lack of political accountability empowers unaccountable elites to exploit their position both to evade and, in the absence of faith in long-term political stability built on legitimacy, to move evaded assets abroad. A weak, corrupt, and illegitimate state drives political flight as citizens disengage from the state, encouraging more illicit flows to escape from the state's grasp.

Such dynamics explain why countries often achieve an uneasy equilibrium in their fiscal systems that reflects the balance of political forces and institutions and remain at this position until shocked into a new equilibrium (Bird, Martinez-Vazquez, and Torgler 2006). Without understanding the underlying political governance determinants of this equilibrium, reforms are unlikely to solve technical problems in the tax system, such as those identified by Le, Moreno-Dodson, and Rojchai-chaninthorn (2008, 16): "tax policies riddled with overly complex structures and multiple—largely ad hoc—incentives that narrow the already limited tax base, create more loopholes for tax avoidance and evasion, intensify the public perception of unfairness of taxes, and generate opportunity for corruption."

As a result, tackling tax evasion is a problem of collective action: funding adequate public goods depends on the discount rates or time horizons of rulers and taxpayers, on the transaction costs involved, and on relative bargaining power (Paul, Miller, and Paul 2006). Intra- and cross-country variation in tax effort and tax-GDP ratios indicates differences not only in the economy or in levels of development or in regime type, but also in the political will to tackle the collective action problem (Bird and Zolt 2007; Cheibub 1998).[44] This applies in developed- and developing-country contexts.[45] So, although low-tax countries tend also to have lower income per capita, there are significant variations in tax effort and tax-GDP ratios. Zambia, for example, had a per capita income of US$785 in 2003 and collected 18.1 percent of GDP in tax, whereas Uganda had a per capita income of US$1,167 but collected only 11.4 percent of GDP. Indonesia, with a gross national product per capita of US$668, collected 16.5 percent, while Lesotho, with a slightly lower per capita gross national product (US$624), collected more than twice as much, at 36.8 percent of GDP (Teera and Hudson 2004).[46] Mozambique's tax revenue, at 13.4 percent of GDP in 2006, represents a remarkable recovery from civil war, but remains well below that of comparable low-income countries in the region, such as Malawi (18 percent) and Zambia (18 percent).[47]

Policy Implication: Strengthen the Political Commitment to Effective States

Effective tax regimes develop when political leaders need effective tax systems. The necessary political commitment to tackle evasion arises when the political costs of the tax effort are outweighed by the political benefits of delivering sustainable development, including by providing the state with the capacity to enforce the property rights of political elites, thereby helping facilitate the emergence of long-term political stability and economic growth. The political incentives around taxes, growth, and property rights are central to this dynamic. An effective tax system offers a general investment in the public goods that the economy and society need. Concepts such as citizenship, fairness, trust, and equality develop practical manifestation through taxation: "the tax system is therefore an effective way of articulating assumptions about the market, consumption and social structures" (Daunton 2001, 21).

Because political ideas, interests, incentives, and identities reflect and are reflected through the tax system, the evolution of tax structures demonstrates a state's political and economic levels of development (Thies 2004; Fjeldstad and Moore 2009). For example, both Finland and Sierra Leone collected 31 percent of total revenue in generally progressive taxation on income and property in 1990; yet, Finland was able to collect more than seven times the revenue take, as a share of GDP, than Sierra Leone (Lieberman 2002). Evasion may express politically passive rather than actively subversive attitudes toward government, particularly where, in the Chinese phrase, "the Mountain is high and the emperor far away." Focused mainly on local taxes and fees, Chinese villagers, in the 1980s, developed a moral politics of evasion (*taoshui*) and tax resistance (*kangshui*) around the perceived extent of reciprocity and mutual obligation with different levels of government. Central to the moral legitimization of evasion was the extent to which the authorities were perceived to be delivering on their responsibilities (*zeren*), from which people then classified taxes as either reasonable (*heli de shui*) or unreasonable (*buheli de shui*) (Ku 2003).

The quality of political institutions therefore has a strong observable effect on tax morale (Torgler et al. 2008; Everest-Phillips 2008a, 2009b). Tax morale, the practical expression of support for national development, as noted above, is particularly significant in developing countries with weak governance quality: citizens across the developing world invariably justify tax evasion through the belief that they do not get an adequate return for the taxes paid.[48] For instance, the U.K. Department for International Development–World Bank survey in the Republic of Yemen of private sector tax morale found that 91 percent of respondents felt that the state had to be seen to be using revenues fairly and efficiently if tax evasion was to be tackled effectively; 97 percent felt they paid a fair amount of tax; and 100 percent felt that tackling corruption was essential (World Bank 2008b; see also Aljaaidi, Manaf, and Karlinsky 2011).

Modern democracies aspire to achieve *voluntary tax compliance*, that is, all citizens willingly comply without the state needing to resort to any compulsion. In reality, all tax systems settle for *quasi-voluntary tax compliance*, recognizing that the free-riding potential always requires some state authority to compel. Levi (1989, 69) categorizes quasi-voluntary compliance as the outcome of "the sanctions, incentives and reciprocity practices that produce social order and conditional cooperation without central state- or ruler-imposed coercion." Yet, the overwhelming focus on tackling tax evasion in developing countries is on fiscal policy and administrative capacity constraints, not on the political governance that makes tax policy and administration effective (Sánchez, O. 2006; Sánchez, J.A. 2008).

Policy Implication: Tackle Illicit Capital Flows by Strengthening the Legitimacy of the State

So, tackling the tax evasion dimension of illicit capital flows requires that one address the underlying political economy constraints to the long-term building of an effective state (Fjeldstad and Moore 2009). Tax is conditional on political performance:

> The quality of political institutions has a strong observable effect on tax morale ... not only the overall index, but also the sub-factors of voice and accountability, rule of law, political stability and absence of violence, regulatory quality and control of corruption exercise a strong influence on tax morale. Moreover, trust in the justice system and the parliament also has a highly significant positive effect on tax morale. (Torgler, Schaffner, and Macintyre 2007, 23)

In other words, every political system constantly struggles to maintain its fiscal legitimacy:

> The achievement of significant quasi-voluntary compliance within a population is always tenuous ... free riding, once begun, is likely to increase. Once quasi-voluntary compliance has declined, it is extremely difficult to reconstitute. Its reestablishment often requires an extraordinary event—such as war, revolution, or depression—that makes people willing to negotiate a new bargain. (Levi 1989, 69–70)

So, tax evasion and the resulting illicit capital flows must be tackled by strengthening the legitimacy of the state in the eyes of current and potential taxpayers. There is evidence in some developing countries, such as Ghana, Indonesia, and Zambia, that, through the messy process of democratic politics, this is happening (Pritchard 2009; Heij 2007; von Soest 2006).

Conclusion

Further research is undoubtedly needed to understand the relative importance and interconnection of tax evasion, corruption, and criminality in driving illicit capital flows in different contexts, but it is clear that tackling the problem will require building effective states responsive to the needs of their societies. Currently, there does not appear to be reliable data on the level of illicit capital that flows South-South or South-North. What we do know is that the governance reforms needed to build effective states and to reduce illicit capital outflows require strong political commitment. Such commitment develops if political institutional incentives and interests are aligned with the goal of building state capacities. This will only occur in developing countries if a broad political consensus in its favor is created. Administrative efforts to tackle illicit capital flows will only be as effective as the constantly evolving political process of state building allows, because "the history of state revenue production is the history of the evolution of the state" (Levi 1989, 1).

Notes

1. "Responsible Leadership for a Sustainable Future," G-8 Leaders Declaration, paragraph 17d, L'Aquila, Italy, July 8, 2009, http://www.g8italia2009.it/static/ G8_Allegato/G8_Declaration_08_07_09_final%2c0.pdf.
2. Recognition of the relationship between tax evasion and effective governance is not new. In the mid-fifth century, the theologian Salvian the Presbyter of Marseilles, seeking to make sense of the decline and fall of the Roman Empire that he witnessed around him, concluded that the empire's collapse lay in the interconnection between poor governance and a weak tax system. Modern research validates Salvian's specific analysis and general thesis: tax evasion was both cause and symptom of Rome's decline: for example, see Wickham (2010).
3. On the fiscal anthropology of power and reciprocal obligations, see Braithwaite (2003). By contrast, tax avoidance, the legal minimization of tax payments, indicates weak policy and ineffectual administration.
4. For example, on the case of Bolivia in the late 1990s, see Mosley (2007); on the long and continuing tradition of Chinese peasant tax evasion as revolt, see Tilly (2003); on Ghana's value added tax (VAT) riots in 1995, see Pritchard (2009).
5. This involved not merely the evasion of direct taxation; for VAT evasion: see Moreno-Dodson and Wodon (2008). For 1998, the estimated level of evasion was 37.5 percent; in May 2000, the Procuradoría Fiscal de la Federación announced that the overall level of evasion and avoidance represented 35 percent of potential collection.
6. Tax evasion, corruption, and criminality are all illegal activities that flourish in domestic and international climates in which personal greed is unrestrained by the political ambition to build legitimate, effective states. Nonetheless, there does not appear to be a single study that has tried to distinguish even conceptually between them, let alone provide clear evidence of their relative importance in different contexts. This chapter is a beginning in addressing the first issue. That much remains to be done is suggested by the findings of Reuter and Truman (2004), according to which tax evasion accounted for over 55 percent of criminal proceeds in the United States in 1990.
7. Tax morale is conceptually distinct from the instrumental willingness based on government performance.

8. Silvani and Baer (1997) offer a typology for the tax gap, ranging from countries with a tax gap at under 10 percent (for example, Denmark or Singapore), which reflects high political will and strong administration, to countries with a tax gap at over 40 percent (for example, Kenya), which reflects limited political will and weak tax administration.

9. The Organisation for Economic Co-operation and Development offers a definition of state building, as follows: "purposeful action to develop the capacity, institutions and legitimacy of the state in relation to an effective political process for negotiating the mutual demands between state and societal groups" (OECD 2008, 14).

10. Musgrave (1996) offers four basic patterns: the service delivery state, the welfare state, the communitarian state, and the government failure state (rather than the market failure state).

11. Legitimacy is a significant component of economic growth in developing-country contexts; see Englebert (2000).

12. As a percentage of actual total tax revenue and of potential tax revenue, tax evasion declined between 1972 and 1974, thereafter rose rapidly, and was about 60 percent of actual tax revenue and 37 percent of potential tax revenue in 1990, representing sevenfold and fourfold increases, respectively. See Chipeta (2002); Therkildsen (2001).

13. In 1999, only 3.4 percent of the Russian population thought they could trust the state (Oleinik 1999).

14. It has been calculated that, in India in the 1980s, up to 45 percent of gross national product was produced by distortionary government policies (for example, artificial price setting, the protection of state-owned enterprises, and government monopolies) (Mohammad and Whalley 1984).

15. In Bangladesh, for example, criminal prosecution for grand evasion is almost unknown; in India, tax evasion, estimated at from Rs 400 billion to Rs 1 trillion, is at the heart of the informal economy, in which politically influential industries operate (Vittal 1999).

16. Schneider and Enste (2000) outline the political determinants of tax evasion and the informal sector.

17. On the missing middle, or the absence of medium-size firms as a result of disproportionate tax burdens, see Kauffmann (2005).

18. Wa Wamwere (2003, 176) describes this as follows: "The cream of government service goes to the ruling ethnic elites, the crumbs to the lesser ethnic elites, and dust to members of the so-called ruling ethnic community." See also Kimenyi (2006).

19. For taxation, four political dimensions of the state then shape the effectiveness of tax systems, as follows: (a) the degree of concentration of state power (for example, a unitary or federal system), (b) the state's reach into society (for example, the capacity to collect information and attain adequate territorial

coverage), (c) the autonomy of the state (the degree of capture, isolation, or embedded autonomy of officials); and (d) the responsiveness of the state to the population (that is, democratic dialogue). See Hobson (1997).

20. Virmani (1987) models corruption that creates higher rates of evasion. The political economy of tackling corruption in the tax administration also involves corrupt tax policy formulation, especially in tax expenditures, through the discretionary powers of politicians and tax administrators. There is an interesting provision in the Lesotho Revenue Authority Act that requires the tax authority to report on the impact of any concessions or waivers granted during the course of the reporting year. Thus, if ministers wish to grant a concession to a specific investor, they may do so, but the nature and the cost of the decision will be reported in the public domain (Charlie Jenkins, former commissioner of the Lesotho Revenue Authority, personal communication, 2009).

21. Thus, the Zambia Revenue Authority has declared that it is committed to the objective of fairness, defined as performing official duties in an impartial manner, free of political, personal, or other bias; this combines with its mission to maximize and sustain revenue collections through integrated, efficient, cost-effective, and transparent systems that are professionally managed to meet the expectations of all stakeholders. See, for example, the Zambia Revenue Authority's "Tax Payer Charter," at http://www.zra.org.zm/charter.php.

22. Decreases in the tax-GDP ratio can also arise from other factors, such as an increase in GDP or in tax avoidance, but the latter reflects weak administration and taxpayer doubt over policy.

23. For instance, "when tax reform enters the political arena, the subtleties of the key issues are usually lost in the midst of self-serving arguments and misleading simplifications" (Slemrod and Bakija 1996, ix).

24. The Kenyan Revenue Authority seems to believe that it is higher, over 40 percent (Waweru 2004).

25. Tax collections increased from 10.3 to 11.9 percent of GDP between 2003 and 2004 and have since stabilized at around 12 percent; see tax system diagnostics in World Bank (2009b).

26. Gehlbach (2008) notes that diversity not only at the national level, but also at the sectoral level was shaped by different political dynamics; the politically powerful were able to secure public goods, while also learning that it was often simpler to evade by running up tax arrears than to hide revenue from the tax authorities.

27. This is based on purchases reported (Guatemala, Ministry of Public Finance, 1990, "Análisis Evaluativo del Sistema Tributario de Guatemala y Apendice Tecnico: Consultoría para Administración Fiscal," July, Policy Economics Group; KPMG; and Policy Research Program, Georgia State University, Washington, DC).

28. In 2006, VAT evasion was 31.6 percent; this compared favorably with the cases of Mexico (45.7 percent), Argentina (40.4 percent), and Bolivia (39.4 percent), but less favorably with the cases of Colombia (28.0 percent) and Chile (19.7 percent), not least because of persisting legal loopholes (World Bank data of 2007).

29. The Guatemalan government has attempted in recent years to address these problems, not least through the Anti-Evasion Law of 2006 (World Bank data of 2007).

30. Thus, under Menem, sanctions against evasion were strengthened, and the temporary closures by the tax authorities of the business premises of enterprises that failed to register for the VAT or to issue invoices rose from 751 in 1990 to 5,021 in the first nine months of 1991. However, this momentum subsequently lapsed; see Morisset and Izquierdo (1993).

31. This, for example, seems to apply to recent Chinese illicit capital flows in round-tripping to benefit from tax incentives that have existed for foreign investment.

32. For this reason, tax havens require good governance, which is often provided or guaranteed by the countries of the Organisation for Economic Co-operation and Development by proxy (for example, Monaco through France) or as colonies or crown dependencies (for example, Isle of Man by the United Kingdom) (Dharmapala and Hines 2006). This centrality of the quality of governance may also help to explain why high-tax countries remain high tax, and low-tax countries remain low tax (Markle and Shackelford 2009).

33. Across Africa, for instance, Keen and Mansour (2008) note that improvements in tax-GDP ratios in recent years have been, overall, almost entirely the result of rising commodity prices.

34. A working paper on state building published by the U.K. Department for International Development (Whaites 2008, 4) defines political settlements as "the forging of a common understanding, usually among elites, that their interests or beliefs are served by a particular way of organizing political power."

35. Bratton and van de Walle (1997) assert that neo-patrimonial regimes in Africa have a cultural system of the quasi-taxation of fiscal-type obligations to the extended circle of family, friends, and tribal chiefs, thereby complicating the idea that evasion arises from governments acting as self-serving Leviathans rather than as maximizers of social welfare.

36. Virmani (1987) points out that higher penalties for evasion could reduce tax revenues by making collusion between taxpayer and tax collector more profitable unless penalties for corruption are strengthened and their implementation is given full political backing.

37. Fjeldstad and Tungodden (2003) argue that discretion and fiscal corruption contribute to undermining the legitimacy of the tax administration and thereby *increase* tax evasion.

38. By contrast, Mahon (2004) finds that tax reform is predicted by the political drive of new administrations, more authoritarian-leaning elected governments, the dominance of the president's party in the legislature, established electoral systems, closed-list proportional representation, less polarized party systems, and more numerous parties.

39. For example, the political settlement requires regional taxpayers to trust the state to redistribute fairly (Ndulu et al. 2007).

40. *The Nation*, Lilongwe, Malawi, April 27, 2000, page 5.
41. Otherwise, high nominal taxes tend to produce considerable tax evasion, including the unrecorded activity of the shadow economy (Schneider and Enste 2000).
42. While some authors have claimed there is causation, Friedman et al. (2001) are not able to find evidence of a negative effect of taxes on the size of the shadow economy. No study has adequately addressed taxpayer perceptions of taxation not as a burden, but as an investment in the political settlement to tackle weak institutions and fund an effective state.
43. By 1997, under the pressure of the International Monetary Fund, the income subject to the highest marginal rate had been substantially reduced, but it was still at the remarkable level of 104 times the average per capita income (Shome 1999).
44. Measurements of tax effort and tax-GDP ratios are notoriously problematic, but, in the absence of other clear indicators, remain the most widely used basis for cross-country comparisons.
45. Thus, Belgium has far greater evasion rates than the Netherlands (Nam, Parsche, and Schaden 2001).
46. By contrast, one of the lowest rates in the world is in Afghanistan, where the government, in 2008, raised only 6.4 percent of national income, or US$750 million, in national revenue across a population of 25 million.
47. International Monetary Fund data for 2007. See Le, Moreno-Dodson, and Rojchaichaninthorn (2008) on tax effort variation.
48. For example, for Pakistan, see World Bank (2004).

References

Abinales, P. N., and D. J. Amoroso. 2005. *State and Society in the Philippines*. State & Society, East Asia Series. Oxford: Rowman & Littlefield.
Aljaaidi, K. S. Y., N. A. A. Manaf, and S. S. Karlinsky. 2011. "Tax Evasion as a Crime: A Survey of Perception in Yemen." *International Journal of Business and Management* 6 (9): 190–201.
Alm, J., and J. Martinez-Vazquez. 2003. "Institutions, Paradigms, and Tax Evasion in Developing and Transition Countries." In *Public Finance in Developing and Transitional Countries: Essays in Honor of Richard Bird*, ed. J. Martinez-Vazquez and J. Alm, 146–78. Studies in Fiscal Federalism and State-Local Finance Series. Cheltenham, U.K.: Edward Elgar.
Andreoni, J., B. Erard, and J. Feinstein. 1998. "Tax Compliance." *Journal of Economic Literature* 36 (2): 818–60.
Barra, P., and M. Jarratt. 1998. "An Analysis of the Chilean Tax System." Report, Division of Studies, Servicio de Impuestos Internos, Santiago, Chile.
Bayart, J.-F., S. Ellis, and B. Hibou. 1999. *The Criminalization of the State in Africa*. African Issues. Oxford: James Currey; Bloomington, IN: Indiana University Press.

Bergman, M. 2009. *Tax Evasion and the Rule of Law in Latin America: The Political Culture of Cheating and Compliance in Argentina and Chile*. University Park, PA: Pennsylvania State University Press.

Bird, R., J. Martinez-Vasquez, and B. Torgler. 2006. "Societal Institutions and Tax Effort in Developing Countries." In *The Challenges of Tax Reform in a Global Economy*, ed. J. Alm, J. Martinez-Vazquez, and M. Rider, 283–338. New York: Springer Science+Business Media.

Bird, R., and E. Zolt. 2007. "Tax Policy in Emerging Countries." International Tax Program Paper 0707, International Tax Program, University of Toronto, Toronto.

Boyce, J. K., and L. Zarsky. 1988. "Capital Flight from the Philippines, 1962–1986." *Philippine Journal of Development* 15 (2): 191–222.

Boylan, D. 1996. "Taxation and Transition: The Politics of the 1990 Chilean Tax Reform." *Latin American Research Review* 31 (1): 7–31.

Brada, J. C., A. M. Kutan, and G. Vukšic. 2009. "The Costs of Moving Money across Borders and the Volume of Capital Flight: The Case of Russia and Other CIS Countries." EMG Working Paper WP-EMG-28–2009, Emerging Markets Group, Cass Business School, City University, London.

Braithwaite, V. A., ed. 2003. *Taxing Democracy: Understanding Tax Avoidance and Evasion*. Aldershot, U.K.: Ashgate.

Bratton, M., and N. van de Walle. 1997. *Democratic Experiments in Africa: Regime Transitions in Comparative Perspective*. Cambridge Studies in Comparative Politics. Cambridge, U.K.: Cambridge University Press.

Bräutigam, D., O.-H. Fjeldstad, and M. Moore, eds. 2008. *Taxation and State-Building in Developing Countries: Capacity and Consent*. Cambridge, U.K.: Cambridge University Press.

Chabal, P., and J.-P. Daloz. 1999. *Africa Works: Disorder as Political Instrument*. African Issues. Oxford: James Currey; Bloomington, IN: Indiana University Press.

Cheibub, J. A. 1998. "Political Regimes and the Extractive Capacity of Governments: Taxation in Democracies and Dictatorships." *World Politics* 50 (3): 349–76.

Chiarini, B., E. Marzano, and F. Schneider. 2009. "Tax Rates and Tax Evasion: An Empirical Analysis and Long-Run Characteristics in Italy." Working Paper 1–2009 (January), Department of the Treasury, Italian Ministry of Economy and Finance, Rome.

Chipeta, C. 2002. "The Second Economy and Tax Yield in Malawi." AERC Research Paper 113 (March), African Economic Research Consortium, Nairobi.

Daunton, M. 2001. *Trusting Leviathan: The Politics of Taxation in Britain, 1799–1914*. Cambridge, U.K.: Cambridge University Press.

de Melo, M. 2007. "Institutional Weakness and the Puzzle of Argentina's Low Taxation." *Latin American Politics and Society* 49 (4): 115–48.

Devarajan, S., and S. I. Hossain. 1995. "The Combined Incidence of Taxes and Public Expenditures in the Philippines." Policy Research Working Paper 1543, World Bank, Washington, DC.

DFID (U.K. Department for International Development). 2006. *Eliminating World Poverty: Making Governance Work for the Poor; A White Paper on International Development.* Secretary of State for International Development. London: Her Majesty's Stationery Office.

Dharmapala, D., and J. R. Hines Jr. 2006. "Which Countries Become Tax Havens?" NBER Working Paper 12802, National Bureau of Economic Research, Cambridge, MA.

Dia, M. 1993. "A Governance Approach to Civil Service Reform in Sub-Saharan Africa." World Bank Technical Paper 225, World Bank, Washington, DC.

———. 1996. *Africa's Management in the 1990s and Beyond: Reconciling Indigenous and Transplanted Institutions.* Directions in Development Series. Washington, DC: World Bank.

Di John, J. 2006. "The Political Economy of Taxation and Tax Reform in Developing Countries." WIDER Research Paper 74, World Institute for Development Economics Research, Helsinki.

———. 2008. "Why Is the Tax System So Ineffective and Regressive in Latin America?" *Development Viewpoint* 5 (June), Centre for Development Policy and Research, School of Oriental and African Studies, University of London, London.

———. 2009. *From Windfall to Curse? Oil and Industrialization in Venezuela, 1920 to the Present.* University Park, PA: Pennsylvania State University Press.

Engelschalk, M., and B. Nerré. 2002. "Gorillas, Gender and Tax Morale: Conservationism, French Catholicism and Female Tax Compliance Rates in Rwanda, 1998–2003." In *Forschungsspektrum aktueller Finanzwissenschaft*, ed. B. Nerré, 142–76. Heidenau, Germany: PD Verlag.

Englebert, P. 2000. *State Legitimacy and Development in Africa.* Boulder, CO: Lynne Rienner.

Erbe, S. 1985. "The Flight of Capital from Developing Countries." *Intereconomics* 20 (6): 268–75.

Esteller-Moré, A. 2005. "Is There a Connection between the Tax Administration and the Political Power?" *International Tax and Public Finance* 12 (5): 639–63.

Eurodad (European Network on Debt and Development). 2008. "Addressing Development's Black Hole: Regulating Capital Flight." Eurodad Report, May 8, Eurodad, Brussels.

Everest-Phillips, M. 2008a. "Business Tax as State-Building in Developing Countries: Applying Governance Principles in Private Sector Development." *International Journal of Regulation and Governance* 8 (2): 123–54.

———. 2008b. "The Myth of 'Secure Property Rights': Good Economics as Bad History and Its Impact on International Development." SPIRU Working Paper 23 (May), Strategic Policy Impact and Research Unit, Overseas Development Institute, London.

———. 2009a. "When Do Elites Pay Taxes? Tax Morale and State-Building in Developing Countries." Paper presented at the World Institute for Development Economics Research Conference, "WIDER Conference on the Role of Elites in Economic Development," Helsinki, June 12–13.

————. 2009b. "Taxation as State-Building: Principles for Reform in Developing Countries." Paper presented at the 65th Annual Congress of the International Institute of Public Finance, Cape Town, August 13–16.

————. 2010. "State-Building Taxation for Developing Countries: Principles for Reform." *Development Policy Review* 28 (1): 75–96.

————. 2011. "Tax, Governance and Development." Discussion Paper 11, Commonwealth Secretariat, London.

Fatehi, K. 1994. "Capital Flight from Latin America as a Barometer of Political Instability." *Journal of Business Research* 30 (2): 187–95.

Feld, L. P., and B. S. Frey. 2002. "Trust Breeds Trust: How Taxpayers Are Treated." *Economics of Governance* 3 (2): 87–99.

Fjeldstad, O.-H., and A. al-Zagha. 2004. "Taxation during State Formation: Lessons from Palestine, 1994–2000." *Forum for Development Studies* 31 (1): 89–113.

Fjeldstad, O.-H., L. Katera, and E. Ngalewa. 2009. "Maybe We Should Pay Tax after All? Citizens' Views on Taxation in Tanzania." REPOA Special Paper 29–2009 (April), Research on Poverty Alleviation, Dar es Salaam, Tanzania.

Fjeldstad, O.-H., and M. Moore. 2009. "Revenue Authorities and Public Authority in Sub-Saharan Africa." *Journal of Modern African Studies* 47 (1): 1–18.

Fjeldstad, O.-H., and B. Tungodden. 2003. "Fiscal Corruption: A Vice or a Virtue?" *World Development* 31 (8): 1459–67.

Freedom House. 2008. "Freedom in the World 2008: Paraguay." Country report (July 2), Freedom House, Washington, DC. http://www.freedomhouse.org/template .cfm?page=22&year=2008&country=7468.

Friedman, E., S. Johnson, D. Kaufmann, and P. Zoido. 2001. "Dodging the Grabbing Hand: The Determinants of Unofficial Activity in 69 Countries." *Journal of Public Economics* 76 (3): 459–93.

Fritz, V., K. Kaiser, and B. Levy. 2009. "Problem-Driven Governance and Political Economy Analysis: Good Practice Framework." World Bank, Washington, DC.

Fuest, C., and N. Riedel. 2009. "Tax Evasion, Tax Avoidance and Tax Expenditures in Developing Countries: A Review of the Literature." Report, Oxford University Centre for Business Taxation, Oxford.

Gehlbach, S. 2008. *Representation through Taxation: Revenue, Politics, and Development in Postcommunist States.* Cambridge Studies in Comparative Politics. Cambridge, U.K.: Cambridge University Press.

Gërxhani, K., and A. Schram. 2002. "Tax Evasion and the Source of Income: An Experimental Study in Albania and the Netherlands." Discussion paper, Tinbergen Institute, Amsterdam.

Ghura, D. 2002. "Tax Revenue in Sub-Saharan Africa: Effects of Economic Policies and Corruption." In *Governance, Corruption, and Economic Performance*, ed. G. T. Abed and S. Gupta, 369–94. Washington, DC: International Monetary Fund.

Gray, C. S. 2001. "Enhancing Transparency in Tax Administration in Madagascar and Tanzania." African Economic Policy Discussion Paper 77 (August), United States Agency for International Development, Washington, DC.

Hayoz, N., and S. Hug, eds. 2007. *Tax Evasion, Trust, and State Capacities*. Interdisciplinary Studies on Central and Eastern Europe 3. Bern: Peter Lang.

Heij, G. 2007. "Who Pulled the Strings? A Comparative Study of Indonesian and Vietnamese Tax Reform. PhD thesis, University of Groningen, Groningen, the Netherlands.

Hettich, W., and S. L. Winer. 1999. *Democratic Choice and Taxation: A Theoretical and Empirical Analysis*. Cambridge, U.K.: Cambridge University Press.

Hobson, J. M. 1997. *The Wealth of States: A Comparative Sociology of International Economic and Political Change*. Cambridge Studies in International Relations. Cambridge, U.K.: Cambridge University Press.

Hoppit, J. 2011. "Compulsion, Compensation and Property Rights in Britain, 1688–1833." *Past & Present* 210 (1): 93–128.

IMF (International Monetary Fund). 2007. "Republic of Madagascar: Selected Issues." IMF Country Report 07/239 (July), IMF, Washington, DC.

Kaldor, N. 1963. "Will Underdeveloped Countries Learn to Tax?" *Foreign Affairs* 41 (2): 410–18.

Kauffmann, C. 2005. "Financing SMEs in Africa." Policy Insights 7 (May), OECD Development Centre, Organisation for Economic Co-operation and Development, Paris.

Keen, M., and M. Mansour. 2008. "Revenue Mobilization in Sub-Saharan Africa: Challenges from Globalization." Draft working paper, August 11, Fiscal Affairs Department, International Monetary Fund, Washington, DC.

Kenny, L., and S. Winer. 2006. "Tax Systems in the World: An Empirical Investigation into the Importance of Tax Bases, Administration Costs, Scale and Political Regime." *International Tax and Public Finance* 13 (2): 181–215.

Khan, M. H. 2000. "Rent-Seeking as a Process: Inputs, Rent-Outcomes and Net Effects." In *Rents, Rent-Seeking and Economic Development: Theory and Evidence in Asia*, ed. M. H. Khan and K. S. Jomo, 70–104. Cambridge, U.K.: Cambridge University Press.

———. 2005. "Markets, States and Democracy: Patron-Client Networks and the Case for Democracy in Developing Countries." *Democratization* 12 (5): 705–24.

Kim, S. 2008. "Does Political Intention Affect Tax Evasion?" *Journal of Policy Modeling* 30 (3): 401–15.

Kimenyi, M. 2006. "Ethnicity, Governance and the Provision of Public Goods." *Journal of African Economies* 15 (1): 62–99.

KIPPRA (Kenya Institute for Public Policy Research and Analysis). 2004. "Tax Compliance Study." Tax Policy Unit, Macroeconomics Division, KIPPRA, Nairobi.

Ku, H. B. 2003. *Moral Politics in a South Chinese Village: Responsibility, Reciprocity, and Resistance*. Asian Voices. Oxford: Rowman & Littlefield.

Le, T. M., B. Moreno-Dodson, and J. Rojchaichaninthorn. 2008. "Expanding Taxable Capacity and Reaching Revenue Potential: Cross-Country Analysis." Policy Research Working Paper 4559, World Bank, Washington, DC.

Levi, M. 1989. *Of Rule and Revenue*. California Series on Social Choice and Political Economy. Berkeley, CA: University of California Press.

Lewis, A. 1982. *The Psychology of Taxation*. Basingstoke: U.K.: Palgrave Macmillan.

Lieberman, E. 2002. "Taxation Data as Indicators of State-Society Relations: Possibilities and Pitfalls in Cross-National Research." *Studies in Comparative International Development* 36 (4): 89–115.

———. 2003. *Race and Regionalism in the Politics of Taxation in Brazil and South Africa*. Cambridge, U.K.: Cambridge University Press.

Mahon, J. E. 2004. "Causes of Tax Reform in Latin America, 1977–95." *Latin American Research Review* 39 (1): 3–30.

Manasan, R. G. 1988. "Tax Evasion in the Philippines, 1981–1985." *Philippine Journal of Development* 15 (2): 167–88.

Manasan, R. G., and R. G. Querubin. 1987. "Revenue Performance of National Government Taxes, 1975–1985." Staff Paper 87–01, Philippine Institute for Development Studies, Manila.

Markle, K., and D. A. Shackelford. 2009. "Do Multinationals or Domestic Firms Face Higher Effective Tax Rates?" NBER Working Paper 15091, National Bureau of Economic Research, Cambridge, MA.

McGee, R. W., and C. Lingle. 2005. "The Ethics of Tax Evasion: A Survey of Guatemalan Opinion." Paper presented at the 60th International Atlantic Economic Conference, New York, October 6–9.

Mkrtchyan, A. V. 2001. "Tax Reform in Armenia." NISPAcee Occasional Paper 2 (3): 44–56, Network of Institutes and Schools of Public Administration in Central and Eastern Europe, Bratislava, Slovak Republic.

Mohammad, S., and J. Whalley. 1984. "Rent Seeking in India: Its Costs and Policy Significance." *Kyklos* 37 (3): 387–413.

Moreno-Dodson, B., and Q. Wodon, eds. 2008. *Public Finance for Poverty Reduction: Concepts and Case Studies from Africa and Latin America*. Directions in Development. Washington, DC: World Bank.

Morisset, J., and A. Izquierdo. 1993. "Effects of Tax Reform on Argentina's Revenues." Policy Research Working Paper 1192, World Bank, Washington, DC.

Mosley, P. 2007. "The 'Political Poverty Trap': Bolivia 1999–2007." WEF Working Paper 0020, World Economy and Finance Research Programme, Birkbeck, University of London, London.

Musgrave, R. 1996. "The Role of the State in Fiscal Theory." *International Tax and Public Finance* 3 (3): 247–58.

Nam, C. W., R. Parsche, and B. Schaden. 2001. "Measurement of Value Added Tax Evasion in Selected EU Countries on the Basis of National Accounts Data." CESifo Working Paper 431, CESifo Group, Munich.

Ndikumana, L. 2004. "Fiscal Policy, Conflict and Reconstruction in Burundi and Rwanda." In *Fiscal Policy for Development: Poverty, Reconstruction and Growth*, ed. T. Addison and A. Roe, chap. 13. Studies in Development Economics and

Policy. Helsinki: World Institute for Development Economics Research; Basing-stoke, U.K.: Palgrave Macmillan.

Ndulu, B. J., S. A. O'Connell, J.-P. Azam, R. H. Bates, A. K. Fosu, J. W. Gunning, and D. Njinkeu, eds. 2008. *Country Case Studies.* Vol. 2 of *The Political Economy of Economic Growth in Africa, 1960–2000.* Oxford: Oxford University Press.

Ndulu, B. J., S. A. O'Connell, R. H. Bates, P. Collier, and C. C. Soludo, eds. 2007. *An Analytic Survey.* Vol. 1 of *The Political Economy of Economic Growth in Africa, 1960–2000.* Oxford: Oxford University Press.

North, D. C., J. J. Wallis, S. B. Webb, and B. R. Weingast. 2007. "Limited Access Orders in the Developing World: A New Approach to the Problem of Development." Policy Research Working Paper 4359, World Bank, Washington, DC.

North, D. C., J. J. Wallis, and B. R. Weingast. 2009. *Violence and Social Orders: A Conceptual Framework for Interpreting Recorded Human History.* Cambridge, U.K.: Cambridge University Press.

O'Brien, P. 2001. "Fiscal Exceptionalism: Great Britain and Its European Rivals; From Civil War to Triumph at Trafalgar and Waterloo." LSE Paper 65/01 (October), Department of Economic History, London School of Economics, London.

OECD (Organisation for Economic Co-operation and Development). 2008. "Concepts and Dilemmas of State-Building in Fragile Situations: From Fragility to Resilience." OECD/DAC Discussion Paper, *Journal on Development* 9 (3), OECD, Paris. http://www.oecd.org/dataoecd/59/51/41100930.pdf.

OECD (Organisation for Economic Co-operation and Development) and AfDB (African Development Bank). 2008. *African Economic Outlook 2008.* Paris: OECD.

Oleinik, A. N. 1999. "A Trustless Society: The Influence of the August 1998 Crisis on the Institutional Organization of the Russians' Everyday Life." Unpublished working paper, Stanford University, Stanford, CA.

Orviska, M., and J. Hudson. 2003. "Tax Evasion, Civic Duty and the Law Abiding Citizen." *European Journal of Political Economy* 19 (1): 83–102.

Paul, E. F., F. D. Miller Jr., and J. Paul, eds. 2006. *Taxation, Economic Prosperity, and Distributive Justice.* Vol. 23, Part 2 of Social Philosophy and Policy. Cambridge, U.K.: Cambridge University Press.

Pritchard, W. 2009. "The Politics of Taxation and Implications for Accountability in Ghana 1981–2008." IDS Working Paper 330, Institute of Development Studies, Brighton, U.K.

Reuter, P., and E. M. Truman. 2004. *Chasing Dirty Money: The Fight against Money Laundering.* Washington, DC: Institute for International Economics.

Rose-Ackerman, S. 1999. *Corruption and Government: Causes, Consequences, and Reform.* Cambridge, U.K.: Cambridge University Press.

Rothstein, B. 2001. "Trust, Social Dilemmas, and Collective Memories: On the Rise and Decline of the Swedish Model." *Journal of Theoretical Politics* 12 (4): 477–503.

Saeed, K. A. 1996. "Principle of Taxation: The Taxation System of Pakistan." *Pakistan Journal of Public Administration,* January–June.

Sánchez, J. A. 2008. "Shaping Taxation: Economic Elites and Fiscal Decision-Making in Argentina, 1920–1945." *Journal of Latin American Studies* 40 (1): 83–108.

Sánchez, O. 2006. "Tax System Reform in Latin America: Domestic and International Causes." *Review of International Political Economy* 13 (5): 772–801.

————. 2009. "Tax Reform Paralysis in Post-Conflict Guatemala." *New Political Economy* 14 (1): 101–31.

Schneider, A. 2007. "Socioeconomic Change, Political Parties, and Tax Capacity: Structure, Agency, and Process in Central America." Paper presented at the American Political Science Association's annual meeting, Chicago, August 30.

Schneider, A., V. Lledo, and M. Moore. 2004. "Social Contracts, Fiscal Pacts and Tax Reform in Latin America." Unpublished working paper, Inter-American Development Bank, Washington, DC.

Schneider, B. 2001. "Measuring Capital Flight: Estimates and Interpretations." Draft working paper, Overseas Development Institute, London.

Schneider, F. 2007. "Shadow Economies and Corruption All Over the World: New Estimates for 145 Countries." *Economics E-Journal* 1 (9): 1–66.

Schneider, F., and D. H. Enste. 2000. "Shadow Economies: Size, Causes and Consequences." *Journal of Economic Literature* 38 (1): 77–114.

Shome, P. 1999. "Taxation in Latin America: Structural Trends and Impact of Administration." IMF Working Paper 99/19, International Monetary Fund, Washington, DC.

Silvani, C., and K. Baer. 1997. "Designing a Tax Administration Reform Strategy: Experiences and Guidelines." IMF Working Paper 97/30, International Monetary Fund, Washington, DC.

Slemrod, J., and J. M. Bakija. 1996. *Taxing Ourselves: A Citizen's Guide to the Great Debate over Tax Reform.* Cambridge, MA: MIT Press.

Steinmo, S. 1993. *Taxation and Democracy: Swedish, British, and American Approaches to Financing the Modern State.* New Haven, CT: Yale University Press.

Stewart, M., ed. 2007. "Tax Law and Political Institutions." Special issue, *Law in Context* 24 (2), Federation Press, Annandale NSW, Australia.

Stotsky, J. G., and A. WoldeMariam. 1997. "Tax Effort in Sub-Saharan Africa." IMF Working Paper 97/107, International Monetary Fund, Washington, DC.

Tanzi, V. 2000. "Taxation in Latin America in the Last Decade." Working Paper 76 (December), Center for Research on Economic Development and Policy Reform, Stanford University, Stanford, CA.

Tanzi, V., and P. Shome. 1993. "A Primer on Tax Evasion." IMF Working Paper 93/21, International Monetary Fund, Washington, DC.

Teera, J. M., and J. Hudson. 2004. "Tax Performance: A Comparative Study." *Journal of International Development* 16 (6): 785–802.

Tendler, J. 2002. "Small Firms, the Informal Sector, and the Devil's Deal." *Bulletin of the Institute of Development Studies* 33 (3): 3–33.

Therkildsen, O. 2001. "Understanding Taxation in Poor African Countries: A Critical Review of Selected Perspectives." *Forum for Development Studies 2001* 28 (1): 99–123.

————. 2008. "Taxation and State Building with a (More) Human Face." DIIS Policy Brief (October), Danish Institute of International Studies, Copenhagen.

Thies, C. 2004. "State Building, Interstate and Intrastate Rivalry: A Study of Post-Colonial Developing Country Extractive Efforts, 1975–2000." *International Studies Quarterly* 48 (1): 53–72.

Tilly, C. 1975. *The Formation of National States in Western Europe.* Princeton, NJ: Princeton University Press.

———. 2003. *The Politics of Collective Violence.* Cambridge Studies in Contentious Politics. Cambridge, U.K.: Cambridge University Press.

Timmons, J. F. 2005. "The Fiscal Contract: States, Taxes, and Public Services." *World Politics* 57 (July): 530–67.

Torgler, B. 2003. "Beyond Punishment: A Tax Compliance Experiment with Taxpayers in Costa Rica." *Revista de Analisis Economico* 18 (1): 27–56.

Torgler, B., I. C. Demir, A. Macintyre, and M. Schaffner. 2008. "Causes and Consequences of Tax Morale: An Empirical Investigation." *Economic Analysis and Policy* 38 (2): 313–39.

Torgler, B., M. Schaffner, and A. Macintyre. 2007. "Tax Compliance, Tax Morale and Governance Quality." CREMA Working Paper 2007–17, Center for Research in Economics, Management and the Arts, Basel, Switzerland.

UNECA (United Nations Economic Commission for Africa). 2009. "Enhancing Domestic Resource Mobilization: Challenges and Opportunities in Southern Africa." Document E/ECA/SA/ICE.XV/2009/3 (May 21), United Nations Economic and Social Council, Geneva.

van de Walle, N. 2001. *African Economies and the Politics of Permanent Crisis, 1979–1999.* Political Economy of Institutions and Decisions. Cambridge, U.K.: Cambridge University Press.

Vihanto, M. 2000. "Tax Evasion in a Transition from Socialism to Capitalism: The Psychology of the Social Contract." BOFIT Discussion Paper 6/2000, Bank of Finland, Helsinki.

Virmani, A. 1987. "Tax Evasion, Corruption, and Administration: Monitoring the People's Agents under Symmetric Dishonesty." DRD Discussion Paper 271, Development Research Department, World Bank, Washington, DC.

Vittal, N. 1999. "Applying Zero Tolerance to Corruption." Unpublished paper, Central Vigilance Commission, New Delhi.

von Soest, C. 2006. "How Does Neopatrimonialism Affect the African State? The Case of Tax Collection in Zambia." GIGA Working Paper 33, German Institute of Global and Area Studies, Hamburg.

Wa Wamwere, K. 2003. *Negative Ethnicity: From Bias to Genocide.* New York: Seven Stories Press.

Waweru, M. G. 2004. "Tax Administration in Kenya: Problems and Prospects." Address presented to the Federation of Kenya Employers, Rift Valley Branch's 16th Annual General Meeting, Nakuru, Kenya, March 10. http://www.revenue.go.ke/speeches/cgspeechtax100304.html.

Wedeman, A. 1997. "Looters, Rent-Scrapers, and Dividend-Collectors: Corruption and Growth in Zaire, South Korea, and the Philippines." *Journal of Developing Areas* 31 (4): 57–78.

Whaites, A. 2008. "States in Development: Understanding State-Building." Working paper, U.K. Department for International Development, London.

Wickham, C. 2010. *The Inheritance of Rome: A History of Europe from 400 to 1000.* London: Penguin.

World Bank. 2004. "Pakistan: Tax Administration Reforms Project." Project Information Document, Report 30640, World Bank, Washington, DC.

———. 2006. "Chile: Development Policy Review." Report 37429 (June), Poverty Reduction and Economic Management Unit, Latin America and the Caribbean Region, World Bank, Washington, DC.

———. 2008a. "The Political Economy of Taxation in Developing Countries: Challenges to Practitioners." In collaboration with U.K. Department for International Development, International Finance Corporation, Washington DC.

———. 2008b. "Tax Perception and Compliance Cost Surveys: A Tool for Tax Reform." In collaboration with U.K. Department for International Development. Investment Climate Advisory Services, World Bank, Washington, DC. https://www.wbginvestmentclimate.org/uploads/TPCCS_Consolidated_Web.pdf.

———. 2009a. "Program Document for a Proposed Economic Management and Governance Reform Grant to the Central African Republic." Report 47559-CF (March 9), World Bank, Washington, DC.

———. 2009b. "Program Document for a Proposed First Public Sector Programmatic Development Policy Loan to the Republic of Paraguay." Report 47712-PY (March 31), World Bank, Washington, DC.

———. 2009c. "Program Document for a Proposed First Development Policy Operation to the Republic of Armenia." Report 48605-AM (June 2), World Bank, Washington, DC.

Yashar, D. J. 1997. *Demanding Democracy: Reform and Reaction in Costa Rica and Guatemala, 1870s–1950s.* Stanford, CA: Stanford University Press.

4

Tax Evasion and Tax Avoidance: The Role of International Profit Shifting

Clemens Fuest and Nadine Riedel

Abstract

In the debate on the impact of illicit capital flows on developing countries, the view is widespread that profit shifting to low-tax jurisdictions undermines the ability of developing countries to raise tax revenue. While the shifting of income out of developed countries is a widely debated issue, empirical evidence on the magnitude of the problem and on the factors driving income shifting is scarce. This chapter reviews the literature on tax avoidance and evasion through border crossing income shifting out of developing countries. We discuss methods and available data sets that can be used to gain new insights into the problem of corporate income shifting. We argue that the results of many existing studies on tax avoidance and evasion in developing countries are difficult to interpret, mainly because the measurement concepts used have a number of drawbacks. We discuss some alternative methods and data sets and present empirical evidence that supports the view that profit shifting out of many developing countries and into tax havens takes place.

Additional tables and figures from this chapter can be found at http://go.worldbank.org /N2HMRB4G20.

Introduction

In the debate on the impact of illicit capital flows on developing countries, the view is widespread that illicit flows undermine the ability of developing countries to raise tax revenue. The reason stated is that illicit capital flows may channel resources to the informal economy or to other jurisdictions, in particular to tax havens, so that the resources escape taxation. A large part of this activity takes place in the shadow economy and largely escapes public attention. Yet, parts of the official economy, particularly multinational firms, are accused of engaging in tax avoidance and tax evasion as well. They are criticized for shifting income out of developing countries and into tax havens to avoid paying corporate income taxes. Since developing countries frequently lack appropriate legislative and administrative resources, they are generally seen to be more vulnerable to income shifting relative to developed countries.

While the shifting of income out of developed countries is a widely debated issue, empirical evidence on the magnitude of the problem and on the factors driving income shifting is scarce. This chapter contributes to the debate as follows. First, we review the literature on tax avoidance and evasion through border crossing income shifting out of developing countries. Second, we discuss methods and available data sets that can be used to gain new insights into the problem of corporate income shifting.

There is a growing number of empirical studies on corporate profit shifting in the countries of the Organisation for Economic Co-operation and Development (OECD). Many of these studies use appropriate data and sophisticated econometric methods, and the results offer valuable insights into corporate profit shifting. Unfortunately, almost none of these studies include developing countries. The main reason is that, for developing countries, significantly fewer data are available. A number of studies, mostly published by nongovernmental organizations (NGOs), try to estimate income shifting and the tax revenue losses suffered by developing countries. These studies have the merit of attracting the attention of a wider public to the issue of income shifting out of developing countries. However, the results of these studies are somewhat difficult to interpret, mainly because the measurement concepts used have a number of drawbacks (Fuest and Riedel 2009).

The setup of the rest of this chapter is as follows. In the next section, we briefly introduce the concept of profit shifting by multinational firms and discuss empirical approaches that have been used to detect profit shifting. In the following section, we review existing studies on profit shifting out of developing countries. The section builds on and extends our earlier work, in Fuest and Riedel (2009). The subsequent section discusses the particular role of tax havens. In the penultimate section, we suggest and discuss the pros and cons of different econometric identification strategies and data sets that can be used to gain new insights into the phenomenon of profit shifting out of developing countries. We also provide some evidence from one of the data sets that supports the view that a significant amount of profit shifting out of developing countries and into tax havens does take place. The last section concludes.

Multinational Firms and the Concept of Profit Shifting

Intrafirm profit shifting

For purposes of taxation, the profits of a multinational firm have to be allocated to the individual jurisdictions where the firm files for income taxation. This is usually accomplished through the method of separate accounting. Each entity (subsidiary or permanent establishment) of the multinational firm individually calculates the income it has generated. Transactions between different entities of a multinational firm (controlled transactions) should, in principle, be treated as transactions with third parties (uncontrolled transactions). However, multinational firms may use controlled transactions to shift income across countries. For instance, they may shift income from high-tax jurisdictions to low-tax jurisdictions using transfer pricing or intrafirm debt.

The concept of income shifting raises the question of whether a true or objective distribution of profits earned by the individual entities of a multinational firm can be identified. Achieving this is complicated for a number of reasons. In particular, the entities of multinational firms typically jointly use resources specific to the firm such as a common brand name or firm-specific expertise. Pricing these resource flows appropriately is difficult because goods traded between unrelated parties are usually different. It is an important characteristic of many multinational firms that the individual entities jointly use resources that could not be used in the same way if they were separate firms. If they could be used in the same way, there would be no reason to create the multinational firm in the first place. For this reason, it is difficult to establish what a profit distribution in the absence of profit shifting would look like.

Most empirical studies on corporate income shifting, however, do not explicitly refer to a hypothetical distribution of profits that would occur in the absence of income shifting. Instead, they focus on particular factors that are likely to drive income shifting, and they try to explore whether these factors affect the distribution of reported income across countries and, if so, how large these effects are. In this chapter, we focus on tax-induced income shifting. Empirical work in this area essentially uses two types of approaches to investigate whether and to what extent firms shift income to exploit tax differences across countries. The first approach looks directly at the use of instruments for profit shifting. For instance, some studies focus on income shifting through debt and ask whether, all else being equal, multinational firms use more debt in high-tax countries relative to low-tax countries (Buettner and Wamser 2007; Huizinga, Laeven, and Nicodeme 2008). Other instruments that have been studied in the context of international profit shifting are transfer pricing and the location of intangible assets (Clausing 2003; Dischinger and Riedel 2008).

The second approach focuses on the result of tax-induced profit shifting: the overall profitability of individual entities of multinational firms in different countries. In the presence of tax-induced income shifting, one would expect to observe a negative correlation between reported profitability and tax levels (Grubert and Mutti 1991; Huizinga and Laeven 2008; Weichenrieder 2009). One drawback of this approach is that a negative correlation between pretax profitability and tax levels may even emerge in the absence of income shifting. The reason is that the location of economic activity itself is influenced by taxes. Firms have incentives to locate highly profitable projects in low-tax jurisdictions.

Both approaches deliver estimates of the (marginal) impact of tax differences on income shifting behavior. Under certain assumptions, these estimates can be used to calculate a hypothetical profit distribution across countries that would occur in the absence of tax differences. For instance, Huizinga and Laeven (2008) analyze a sample of European multinational firms and find that, in 1999, the corporate tax base of Germany, which was the country with the highest corporate tax rate in Europe, would have increased by 14 percent if there had been no tax incentives to shift income to other countries.

Profit shifting and transactions among unrelated parties

Profit shifting as discussed in the previous section takes place through transactions between entities of multinational firms in different countries. If two corporations located in two different countries belong to the same multinational firm or are controlled by the same interest, it is uncontroversial that transactions between these two firms may be used to shift profits across borders. However, some authors have argued that transactions between unrelated firms may also be used to shift profits across borders. This is emphasized, in particular, by Raymond Baker (2005) in his book, *Capitalism's Achilles Heel: Dirty Money and How to Renew the Free-Market System*. There, he quantifies the yearly illicit financial flows out of developing countries through the business sector at US$500 billion to US$800 billion.

Baker's book provides a breakdown of this number according to different activities. The analysis claims that slightly above 60 percent of these financial flows are related to legal commercial activities, whereas the rest is assigned to criminal activity. Baker argues that money earned on legal commercial activities leaves developing countries through three potential channels: the mispricing of goods traded between independent parties, the distortion of transfer prices charged on goods traded within a multinational firm, and fake transactions.

With respect to mispricing between unrelated parties, Baker bases his estimate on 550 interviews he conducted with officials from trading companies in 11 economies in the early 1990s: Brazil; France; Germany; Hong Kong SAR, China; India; Italy; the Republic of Korea; the Netherlands; Taiwan, China; the United Kingdom; and the United States. Because Baker assured anonymity, he does not make the data publicly available, but argues that the data contain appropriate information on trading practices.

He reports that the interviewees confirmed that collusion was common between importers and exporters to draw money out of developing countries. Specifically, he states that "mispricing in order to generate kickbacks into foreign bank accounts was treated as a well-understood and normal part of transactions" by the interviewed managers (Baker 2005, 169). As a result of his study, Baker estimates that 50 percent of foreign trade transactions with Latin American countries are mispriced by, on average, around 10 percent, adding to a worldwide average mispricing of goods traded between third parties of 5 percent. Similar, slightly larger figures are reported for countries in Africa and Asia, suggesting a level of mispricing at 5 to 7 percent.

Studies on International Profit Shifting in Developing Countries

Most existing empirical studies on tax-induced profit shifting focus on OECD countries. Studies on profit shifting in developing countries are scarce. Most studies on tax-induced profit shifting in developing countries (as well as income shifting undertaken for other reasons) have been published by NGOs. Below, we discuss and criticize some of these studies. It should be emphasized, though, that these studies have the merit of attracting the attention of a wider public to this important issue.

The trade mispricing approach

Studies based on the trade mispricing approach start with the idea that firms may manipulate prices of internationally traded goods to shift income across countries. This idea is known from empirical work on income shifting in developed countries (see Clausing 2003 and the literature cited there). The key question is how the manipulation of prices is identified. There are different identification strategies with different implications.

As mentioned in the preceding section, Baker (2005) uses interviews to estimate the extent of mispricing in trade transactions with developing countries. He quantifies the income shifted out of developing countries through mispricing activities by multiplying the low end of his interview-based mispricing estimate (that is, mispricing of 5 percent of import and export value, respectively) with the sum of imports and exports of developing countries, which is equal to approximately US$4 trillion. Given this, he arrives at what he refers to as a lower-bound estimate of US$200 billion for capital outflows due to trade.

The main disadvantage of Baker's approach to the estimation of capital outflows is that it is based on a relatively small number of interviews, and these interviews are confidential. Therefore, the results cannot be replicated.

Another approach to identifying mispricing is used by Pak (2007), who identifies abnormally priced import and export transactions through the price filter matrix method. For example, the method might rely on trade statistics that offer information on the prices of transactions for individual product groups such as U.S. trade statistics that offer information about the prices of refrigerators imported into the country in a given year. One might then classify all transactions as overpriced if they involve prices that exceed the average price for imported refrigerators by a certain amount (for instance, prices in the upper quartile of the price range), while classifying as underpriced all transactions involving prices sufficiently below the average price in that product group. On this basis, one calculates the income shifted into and out of the country. Pak (2007, 120) does so as follows: "the dollar amounts are computed by aggregating the amount deviated from [the] lower quartile price for every abnormally low priced U.S. import and the amount deviated from [the] upper quartile price for every abnormally high priced U.S. export."

The analysis in Pak (2007) leads to the estimate that U.S. imports from all other countries were underpriced by approximately US$202 billion in 2005, or 12.1 percent of total imports. The value of U.S. exports in the same year was overpriced by US$50 billion, or 5.5 percent of overall exports. Zdanowicz, Pak, and Sullivan (1999) investigate the international merchandise statistics between Brazil and the United States and find that the amount of income shifted because of abnormal pricing is between 11.1 percent for underinvoiced exports from Brazil and 15.2 percent for overinvoiced imports to Brazil. Pak, Zanakis, and Zdanowicz (2003) use the same framework to investigate capital outflows from Greece because of the mispricing of internationally traded goods and services. The share of income shifted from Greece to the world varies between 2.0 percent for underinvoiced exports from Greece and 5.9 percent for overinvoiced imports to Greece.

Another study using this approach has been published recently by Christian Aid (2009), which argues that profit shifting out of developing countries through trade mispricing in 2005–07 represented above US$1 trillion, giving rise to a yearly tax revenue loss of US$121.8 billion per year. Using the same approach, Christian Aid (2008) calculates a tax revenue loss of US$160 billion suffered by developing countries in 2008 because of trade mispricing.

The mispricing approach as employed in these studies has the advantage of simplicity and transparency. It uses publicly available data, and it is straightforward to replicate the results of existing studies. Unfortunately, the results of this type of analysis are difficult to interpret, and they effectively reveal little reliable information about income shifting in the context of tax avoidance and evasion. This is so for the following reasons.

First, it is likely that, to some extent, price differences within product groups simply reflect quality differences. If there are price differences within product groups, it would be natural to assume that developing countries tend to export low-end, low-price products, whereas developed countries export high-end products at higher prices. Chinese exports are an example of this pattern, as recently demonstrated by Schott (2008). How this affects the results of income shifting calculations depends on whether or not the trade volumes of different countries in a given product group are considered jointly to identify mispricing. If they are considered jointly and if the quality pattern is as described above, the mispricing approach systematically overestimates income shifting from developing to developed countries. If they are considered separately, this cannot happen, but, in this case, goods that are classified as overpriced in one country may be counted as underpriced in another country. This is inconsistent. As long as it is not possible to disentangle quality differences and income shifting, the interpretation of numbers generated by the mispricing approach is difficult.

Second, identifying the highest and the lowest quartile of observed prices as abnormal prices implies that any price distribution with some variance would be diagnosed to include overpricing and underpricing, even if the observed price differences are small or are driven by factors other than mispricing. Empirical analysis should normally allow for the possibility that a hypothesis—in this case, the hypothesis that income is shifted from developing to developed countries—is not supported by the data. This is excluded by assumption, unless all prices within a commodity group are identical.

Third, the results are difficult to interpret because the counterfactual is not clear. Assume that, in one period, there is only one transaction in the upper quartile price range and only one transaction in the lower quartile price range. All other transactions are priced below the upper quartile price and above the lower quartile price. In this case, the counterfactual, which is a hypothetical situation without mispricing, should be that the two mispriced transactions disappear or their prices are adjusted to within the inner quartile price range. But now assume that, in the next period, the two transactions identified as mispriced in the first period take place at corrected prices, which are between the upper and lower quartile prices identified for the preceding period; everything else remains the same. In this case, the quartile price ranges for the second period would change, and transactions that were not identified as mispriced in the previous period are now identified as mispriced. This inconsistency occurs because there is no well-defined counterfactual.

Fourth, the price filter method, by construction, identifies overpriced and underpriced transactions, so that it always identifies income shifting in two directions: into and out of the country under consideration. Yet, many studies using the approach only report income shifting in one direction and ignore income shifting in the other direction. For instance, Pak (2007) reports underpriced imports into the United States and overpriced U.S. exports, but overpriced imports and underpriced exports (both of which would shift income out of the United States) are neglected. A similar approach is used by Christian Aid (2009) and other studies.

The restriction to one direction in income shifting leads to highly misleading results if the findings are used to estimate the impact of income shifting on corporate income tax revenue collected by a particular country or group of countries such as in Christian Aid (2008, 2009). A meaningful estimate of the tax revenue effects would have to take into account profit shifting in both directions. Consider the following simple example.

Assume that there are three exporters of a good in country A. Firm 1 exports the good at a price of 4; firm 2 exports the good at a price of 8; and firm 3 exports the good at a price of 12. The mispricing approach would identify the transaction at a price of 4 as underpriced and the transaction at a price of 12 as overpriced. Assume, further, that all firms have costs of 4 in country A that are deductible from the profit tax base in country A. The goods are exported to country B, where all three are sold at a price of 14 to consumers in country B.

In this example, the aggregate corporate income tax base in country A is equal to 12. Firm 1 shifts income out of country A, and firm 3 shifts income into country A. In the absence of trade mispricing, the tax base in country A would be the same. The tax revenue loss of country A because of mispricing is equal to 0. A method that only takes into account firm 1 and neglects the implications of mispricing by firm 3 is clearly misleading. The same applies to the impact of income shifting on country B. For illustrative purposes, one might, for instance, consider a developing country with a weak political system and a low corporate tax rate. While some firms may be willing to shift profits into that country to exploit the low corporate tax rate, others may consider it beneficial to transfer profits out of the country to hedge against expropriation risks. This might give rise to the heterogeneous transfer price distortions laid out above. While we do not necessarily want to suggest that income is, in reality, shifted into developing countries, we nonetheless consider that an empirical identification approach should allow for the possibility that this might take place. This hypothesis could then be rejected as a result of the analysis.

What happens if other taxes are considered? For instance, one might be interested in measuring import duty revenue losses that arise because of avoidance or evasion. Assume that there is a proportional import duty in country B. In this case, it is easy to check that tax revenue is the same in the two cases under consideration, and it is of key importance to take into account both under- and overpriced imports to country B. Note also that, in this case, firms would have an incentive systematically to understate the import price. If this happens, income is shifted into the country. This is another reason why neglecting income shifting into developing countries is not appropriate in the context of studies on tax avoidance and evasion. Depending on the question asked, it may be meaningful to consider either net flows or gross flows, but reporting flows in one direction only and ignoring the flows in the other direction are not appropriate and may easily lead to misunderstandings.

Pak (2007) defends his approach by claiming that the price filter method he uses is also applied by the U.S. Internal Revenue Service (IRS regulation 482) to deal with transfer pricing issues. This is not correct.

IRS regulation 482 stipulates that this method can only be applied to uncontrolled transactions (see section 1.482-1e, iii [C]), which means that only transactions between unrelated parties can be taken into account in assessing whether or not a transfer price is acceptable. Transactions within multinational firms must be excluded. The reason is that transactions between unrelated parties are more likely to reflect undistorted prices. Effectively, the IRS approach compares transactions between unrelated firms to transactions between related firms. In contrast, Pak (2007) applies the price filter method to all transactions, including transactions between related parties. This is fundamentally different.

An approach that uses a method consistent with IRS regulation 482 is applied in a study of trade mispricing by Clausing (2003). This study focuses on U.S. external trade, however, not on developing countries in particular. Clausing (2003) compares the prices in trade transactions between related parties with the prices in transactions between unrelated parties and shows that the differences are significantly influenced by tax rate differences. For instance, in transactions between related parties, the prices of exports from low-tax countries to high-tax countries are higher than the prices in transactions between unrelated parties. This suggests that multinational firms try to reduce the taxes they have to pay by manipulating transfer prices.

Of course, one could argue that mispricing is also likely to occur in transactions between unrelated parties. For instance, an exporter located in a low-tax country and an importer in a high-tax country could agree to increase the price of the transaction. This agreement could include a side payment that the exporter makes to the importer. Such a payment would have to be concealed from the tax authorities. If this happens, the approach used in Clausing (2003) systematically understates the impact of tax differences on profit shifting through transfer pricing. However, a mere price manipulation in a transaction between related parties is much easier than a price manipulation, combined with a concealed side payment by which the importer would participate in the tax savings.

Profitability and profit shifting

As mentioned above, a second approach to measuring income shifting directly considers the profitability of firms and asks whether the profitability pattern observed may be explained as a result of income shifting.

As in the case of mispricing, the insights provided by this type of study depend on how profit shifting is identified. Oxfam (2000) estimates that tax revenue losses arising because of corporate profits shifted out of developing countries are equal to US$50 billion per year. This number is calculated as follows. Oxfam multiplies the stock of foreign direct investment (FDI) in developing countries (US$1.2 trillion in 1998, according to UNCTAD 1999) by a World Bank estimate for the return on FDI of 16 to 18 percent in developing countries. Oxfam argues that the true estimate for the return on FDI is even higher since the World Bank figure does not account for profit shifting activities. Thus, they set the rate of return to 20 percent. Next, the paper assumes an average tax rate of 35 percent and thus derives a hypothetical corporate tax payment of around US$85 billion. Since the actual tax payments received are around US$50 billion, this leaves a tax gap of US$35 billion according to Oxfam. Oxfam augments this figure with revenue forgone because of the evasion of income from financial assets held abroad, which is estimated at US$15 billion. This leads to the estimated tax revenue losses of US$50 billion.

This approach raises a number of questions. First, one may question the accuracy of the tax gap estimates. An important weakness of this calculation is the assumption that, with perfect compliance, all income from FDI would effectively be taxed at a rate of 35 percent. The issue is not that the average headline corporate tax rate may have been closer to 30 percent, as Oxfam (2000) recognizes. The key issue is that this approach neglects the existence of tax incentives for corporate investment. In the developing world, these investment incentives play a much larger role than they do in developed countries (Klemm 2009; Keen and Mansour 2008). Many developing countries use tax incentives, for example, tax holidays or free economic zones that offer low or zero corporate taxes, to attract foreign investment. It is controversial whether these incentives are efficient from a national or global welfare point of view (see OECD 2001), but the related revenue impact should be distinguished from the impact of tax avoidance and evasion. Neglecting this implies that the revenue losses caused by evasion and avoidance are overestimated. Moreover, the return on FDI is not identical with the corporate tax base. For instance, if FDI is financed by debt, it cannot be expected that the contribution of the investment to the corporate tax base will be 20 percent of this investment because interest is deductible from the tax base.

Second, one should note that this type of analysis is purely descriptive and does not investigate the factors driving profit shifting. Thus, existing tax gap estimates do not help to explain why multinational firms may have an incentive to transfer profits out of developing economies. Taxation may not be the main factor that causes income shifting out of the developing world. Other factors such as the threat of expropriation or confiscation of private property, economic and political uncertainty, fiscal deficits, financial repression, or devaluation may be the real driving forces, as pointed out by, for example, de Boyrie, Pak, and Zdanowicz (2005). The implementation of effective policy measures against profit shifting from developing countries requires knowledge about the main motivations and incentives behind this type of activity and is thus an important topic for future research.

As mentioned above, there is a growing literature that investigates the role played by taxation as a factor driving income shifting. Unfortunately, most of this work focuses on OECD countries, rather than developing countries.

Grubert and Mutti (1991) analyze profit shifting among U.S. multinational firms and use a data set that includes developed and developing countries. They show that firms systematically report higher taxable profits in countries with lower tax rates. In their analysis, firms in countries with a tax rate of 40 percent would report an average ratio of pretax profit and sales of 9.3 percent, whereas firms in countries with a tax rate of 20 percent would report a profit and sales ratio of almost 15.8 percent. This suggests that some profit shifting that is motivated by taxation does occur.

Azémar (2008) investigates how the effectiveness of law enforcement affects profit shifting. Interacting a summary measure of law enforcement quality and tax profit ratios of firms in her regressions, she finds that a low quality in law enforcement accompanies a high sensitivity in tax payments to corporate tax rates. Her interpretation of this observation is that countries with ineffective law enforcement face greater difficulties in efficiently implementing anti–tax avoidance measures such as thin capitalization rules or transfer pricing corrections. This suggests that developing countries are more vulnerable than developed countries to income shifting.

The Role of Tax Havens

Tax havens are widely viewed as playing a major role in the tax avoidance and tax evasion by multinational firms, as well as by individual taxpayers. Empirical research on income shifting to tax havens encounters the difficulty that data on economic activity are scarce in these places. Nonetheless, there are studies on tax avoidance and evasion in tax havens and on the impact of tax havens on tax revenue collection by other countries. Unfortunately, these studies usually do not focus on developing countries.

First, NGOs have made estimates of the tax revenues forgone because of the existence of tax havens. But these estimates are partly related to the potential impact of tax havens on tax rates set by other countries. For instance, Oxfam (2000) estimates that developing countries may be losing annual tax revenues of at least US$50 billion as a result of tax competition and the use of tax havens. It argues as follows:

> Tax competition, and the implied threat of relocation, has forced developing countries to progressively lower corporate tax rates on foreign investors. Ten years ago these rates were typically in the range of 30–35 percent, broadly equivalent to the prevailing rate in most OECD countries. Today, few developing countries apply corporate tax rates in excess of 20 percent. Efficiency considerations account for only a small part of this shift, suggesting that tax competition has been a central consideration. If developing countries were applying OECD corporate tax rates their revenues would be at least US$50 billion higher. (Oxfam 2000, 6)

The issue here is that the extent is not clear to which the decline in corporate income tax rates that has occurred in both developing and developed countries is caused by tax havens. Tax rate competition would exist even in the absence of tax havens. In addition, some authors argue that, under certain circumstances, tax havens may reduce the intensity of tax competition (Hong and Smart 2010). Of course, the empirical relevance of this analysis remains to be investigated.

However, the main critique of tax havens is not that they force other countries to cut taxes. It is the perception that these tax havens offer opportunities for tax avoidance or tax evasion to multinational firms and individual taxpayers residing in other countries, so that other countries suffer tax revenue losses. One estimate of tax revenue losses because of the existence of tax havens has been published by the Tax Justice Network (TJN 2005). TJN starts with estimates of global wealth in financial assets published by banks and consultancy firms (for example, Capgemini and Merrill Lynch 1998; BCG 2003). This is combined with estimates (for 2004) by the Bank for International Settlements of the share of financial assets held offshore, though this refers to U.S. asset holdings.[1] Based on these numbers, TJN claims that the offshore holdings of financial assets are valued at approximately US$9.5 trillion. This is augmented by US$2 trillion in nonfinancial wealth held offshore in the form of, for example, real estate. TJN thus estimates that, globally, approximately US$11.5 trillion in assets are held offshore. Assuming an average return of 7.5 percent implies that these offshore assets yield US$860 billion. TJN assumes that these assets are taxable at 30 percent and thus calculates a revenue loss of US$255 billion per year (as of 2005).

TJN does not attempt to estimate which part of these revenue losses occur in developing countries. Cobham (2005) uses the TJN (2005) results and estimates the share of developing countries. Assuming that the 20 percent of worldwide gross domestic product that is accounted for by middle- and low-income countries represents a credible share of the offshore wealth holdings of the developing world, he finds that 20 percent of the revenue loss can be assigned to these countries, that is, US$51 billion.

Other estimates of these revenue losses use similar methods. Oxfam (2000) calculates the revenue losses caused by the evasion of taxes on income from financial assets held abroad at around US$15 billion per year. This result is mainly driven by an estimate of the foreign asset holdings of residents in developing countries in 1990 (US$700 billion), which is now outdated. In a more recent study, Oxfam (2009) estimates that US$6.2 trillion of developing-country wealth is held offshore by individuals. This leads to an estimated annual tax loss to developing countries of between US$64 billion and US$124 billion.

It is difficult to interpret these estimates for tax revenue losses because of offshore wealth holdings. They do not unambiguously over- or under-estimate the revenue losses, but they rely on a large number of strong assumptions. These include the assumptions on the distribution of asset holdings across the developed and the developing world, as well as the taxable rates of return and the average tax rates. In addition, there are several open questions that have to be addressed. First, it is unclear whether all income from offshore wealth holdings is taxable on a resi-dence basis. Some developing countries do not tax the foreign source income of residents because it may not be administratively efficient to do so (Howard 2001). Second, even if savings income is taxable on a resi-dence basis, the taxes paid in the source country may be deductible from the taxes owed in the residence country. Third, it is unlikely that all income from financial assets held offshore evades taxation in the coun-try of residence of the owners. There may be other than tax reasons for offshore holdings of financial assets, and it is possible that the owners of these assets declare their incomes in their countries of residence. To the extent that these assets generate passive investment income, they will also be subject to controlled foreign corporations legislation, which means that this income is excluded from the deferral of home country taxation or the exemption granted to active business income.

Additional research is needed to determine, for example, the causal effect that the presence in tax haven countries of multinational affiliates has on the tax revenues paid by these affiliates in the developing world. Such an investigation should follow work by Desai, Foley, and Hines (2006a, 2006b) and Maffini (2009). These papers study the role of tax havens for the European Union and the United States. In the next sec-tion, we discuss methods and data sets that may be used to do similar work on developing countries.

Data Sets and Identification Strategies to Assess Tax Evasion and Avoidance in Developing Countries

Attempts to assess whether and to what extent (multinational) firms in developing countries engage in international tax evasion and tax avoid-ance activities have long been hampered by a lack of appropriate data. Thus, existing evidence on the issue is largely anecdotal with the exception of a small number of studies reviewed in the previous section. As many of these papers face methodological difficulties and their identification strategies partly rely on strong assumptions, more research is needed to identify and quantify corporate tax avoidance and evasion in the developing world. In recent years, a number of data sets have become available that may suit this purpose. In the following, we review a selection of these databases and discuss potential identification strategies. The analysis focuses on microdata sources because we consider these more well suited to the identification of corporate profit shifting activities than macrolevel data given that the former are less prone to endogeneity problems in the estimation strategy.

Identification strategies

The basis for a valid empirical identification strategy is the development and testing of hypotheses that derive effects that are unlikely to capture activities other than corporate profit shifting. In the following, we discuss two identification strategies that, from our point of view, largely fulfill this requirement and that may be applied to microlevel data.

The first identification strategy builds on the notion that companies in developing countries differ with respect to their flexibility and opportunities to shift income out of the host countries. For example, companies that are part of a multinational group can plausibly undertake profit shifting activities more easily than firms without affiliates in foreign countries. This is because they can transfer profits to an affiliated company abroad. Moreover, firms that belong to multinational groups with tax haven affiliates have particularly good opportunities to transfer income out of developing countries. Thus, they can be expected to engage in even larger profit shifting activities. Consequently, the identification strategy is to compare profit shifting measures for the treatment group of multinational firms (with tax haven connections) to a control group of national firms that are expected not to engage in significant profit shifting activities.

To identify profit shifting activities in this context, researchers need detailed information on corporate ownership structures and on company variables that are expected to capture profit shifting activities. According to previous empirical studies on corporate shifting activities in the industrialized world, multinational firms use different channels to transfer taxable resources out of countries, the most important ones being the distortion of intrafirm trade prices and the debt-equity structure, as well as the relocation of profitable assets such as corporate patents (Clausing 2003; Huizinga and Laeven 2008; Buettner and Wamser 2007; Dischinger and Riedel 2008). Testing for this type of profit shifting therefore requires associated information on trade prices, debt levels, and patents. As this is often not available, researchers may also exploit information on corporate pretax profits and corporate tax payments because profit shifting outflows are expected to lower both variables. Thus, following the above identification strategy, we expect that multinational firms in developing countries (especially those with a tax haven connection) should report lower pretax profits per unit of assets, pay lower taxes per unit of assets and per unit of profit, hold higher fractions of (intrafirm) debt, and exhibit stronger distortions of intrafirm trade prices (that is, enlarged import prices and diminished export prices) than the control group of national firms. The obvious challenge of this identification strategy is to account empirically for a potential selection of firms with differing characteristics into the control group (national firms) and the treatment group (multinational firms [with a tax haven connection]). Strategies to solve this problem have been presented in earlier papers for the developed world (for example, see Desai, Foley, and Hines 2006a, 2006b; Maffini 2009; Egger, Eggert, and Winner 2007). If, after accounting for all these issues, no differences between the considered profit shifting variables for national and multinational firms are found, the profit shifting hypothesis is rejected.

A second identification strategy starts with a question: why do companies shift profits out of the developing world? One motive might be that they want to save on tax payments. A second might be that they draw their money out of corrupt and politically unstable countries where they are prone to threats of expropriation. To test for these hypotheses implies to determine whether companies in countries with a high tax rate or a high corruption rate report lower pretax profits per assets, pay lower taxes on their assets and profits, and show higher debt-to-equity ratios and more strongly distorted intrafirm transfer prices. In this case, the challenge is to ensure that the identified effect between taxation-corruption and the profit shifting measures is not driven by an unobserved heterogeneity of firms that are located in high-tax (high-corruption) countries and low-tax (low-corruption) countries. This requires the inclusion of a set of control variables that capture differences between affiliates and host countries. The most convincing approach involves including a set of affiliate fixed effects into a panel data regression, which implies that the researcher accounts for all time-constant affiliate differences, and the identification is achieved via corporate adjustments to changes in taxes or the corruption level. For this identification strategy to be applied, stringent data requirements have to be met. Ideally, accounting data on pretax profits, tax payments, debt levels, or intrafirm transfer prices should be available in panel format for several years; the same should be true of information on corporate taxes and the level of corruption and political stability.

Data sets

A number of data sets may fulfill the requirements associated with the two identification strategies laid out above. In the following, we present a selection of these databases. In a first step, we discuss one of the data sources, Orbis, in some depth. In a second step, we briefly describe alternate databases available for the purpose of testing tax avoidance in the developing world. The tables referenced in this discussion are contained on the website of this volume.[2]

Orbis. The Orbis data provided by Bureau van Dijk contain information on companies worldwide (see table 4A.1 on the website for a description of the data). While the majority of firms in Orbis are located in industrialized economies, the data also include information on countries in the developing world. Orbis is available in different versions, but the largest version of the data set comprises 85 million firms (as of 2011), and new data are added constantly. The data are collected from various (partly private and partly official) sources that may differ across countries. Consequently, it is a well-known problem of the Orbis data that the firm coverage differs across countries, and some economies are poorly represented in relative terms. This problem is especially pronounced in developing countries. While the firm coverage tends to be particularly limited in Africa, information on a sufficiently large number of firms is reported for several economies in Asia and Latin America. Hence, we think that focusing on those developing economies for which good information is available allows the Orbis data to be used for the purpose of identifying corporate profit shifting behavior.

Orbis provides balance sheet information and data on profit and loss account items. Thus, it contains detailed information on pretax and after-tax profit (both operating profits and financial, plus operating profits), as well as tax payments and debt variables. Moreover, information on ownership links is included, especially links to all direct and indirect shareholders of the firm, as well as to subsidiaries within the multinational group. Finally, Orbis provides address information (postal code and city name), which may allow researchers to determine the location of firms (or at least the headquarters) within developing countries and thus to identify, for instance, companies located in free economic zones or to determine the role of taxes levied at the regional level. It is important to stress that, as with other databases provided by private sources, there may be issues regarding the quality of the Orbis data. We believe these problems can be handled by rigorous plausibility checks and data cleaning.

In the following, we present and discuss descriptive statistics on some countries in the Orbis data. Note that the Orbis version available to us contains large firms only. Analyzing the full Orbis version, which also accounts for smaller firms, is likely to enhance the firm coverage compared with our exercise. Moreover, we restrict the analysis to Asia and only employ data for countries with a certain sufficient threshold of firm coverage. The economies included in the sample are China; India; Indonesia; Malaysia; Pakistan; the Philippines; Taiwan, China; and Thailand. Our final data set is a cross section of 87,561 firms for the year 2006 (see table 4A.2 on the website for the country distribution).

Because the Orbis data provide information on ownership connections among firms, they allow us to pursue the first identification strategy described in the previous section. We establish the definition that a firm in a developing country maintains a direct link to a foreign economy if it directly owns a subsidiary in a foreign country through possession of at least 50 percent of the ownership shares or if it is directly owned by a parent firm in a foreign country through a holding of at least 50 percent of the ownership shares. Moreover, we adopt a second, less-restrictive definition of a multinational firm that applies if any affiliate within the multinational group is located in a foreign country (including subsidiaries of the immediate or ultimate global owner that do not have a direct ownership link to the firm under consideration). According to these definitions, 2,202 firms in our data set exhibit a direct ownership link to a foreign affiliate, and 2,807 firms belong to a multinational group in the broader sense that at least one affiliate in the group is located in a foreign country (irrespective of the existence of either a direct or an indirect ownership link).

We face the potential challenge that information on some affiliates within the multinational group is missing in the data. If missing affiliates are located in foreign countries (from the point of view of the firm under consideration), then we might declare that a corporation is a national firm, although it is actually part of a multinational group. Such a mis-classification introduces noise into our analysis and may be expected to bias the results against us. This implies that the results should be interpreted as a lower bound to the true effect.

We undertake a similar exercise to identify firms with ownership links to affiliates in a tax haven country. A tax haven is identified according to the OECD's list of tax havens. We establish the definition that a group of firms has a direct ownership link to a tax haven country if they directly own a tax haven subsidiary through at least 50 percent of the ownership shares or are directly owned through at least 50 percent of the ownership shares by a foreign parent firm in a tax haven. In a second step, we adopt a broader definition of tax haven links that identifies firms in our data that belong to multinational groups with a tax haven affiliate (irrespective of the existence of a direct or indirect ownership link). According to these definitions, 207 firms in our data show a direct ownership link to a tax haven country, while 691 corporations belong to groups that have a tax haven affiliate (directly or indirectly connected to the firm under consideration). Thus, according to the broader definition, 25 percent of the multinational firms in our sample have an ownership link to a tax haven country, while only 9 percent of the firms have a direct ownership link to a foreign tax haven.

We might face the problem that information may not be available for all affiliates belonging to a multinational group. Because a large fraction of multinational firms based in industrialized countries are known to operate subsidiaries in tax haven countries, we run a cross-check on the data and restrict the analysis to firms that are owned by immediate and ultimate global owners (in foreign countries) and on which information on the subsidiary list of the owners is available. Among this subgroup of firms, we find that 63 percent belong to multinational groups with a tax haven affiliate. One should note that missing information on tax haven connections introduces noise into the estimation and biases our results against our working hypothesis, meaning that it would lead us to underestimate the impact of tax haven presence.

Thus, we compare different corporate variables that are expected to capture profit shifting activities among the subgroup of firms as defined above. The Orbis data contain information on a wide range of accounting variables, including unconsolidated corporate pretax profit, tax payments, and debt levels. In table 4A.3 on the website, we provide descriptive statistics that discriminate among, first, all firms in the data; second, firms belonging to groups that own affiliates in a foreign country; third, firms with a direct ownership link via a parent firm or a subsidiary to a foreign country (this is thus a subset of the second group of firms); fourth, firms belonging to a multinational group with an affiliate in a tax haven country; and, fifth, firms having a direct ownership link (via a direct parent firm or subsidiary) in a tax haven country. The rationale behind investigating groups with direct ownership links to foreign countries and tax havens separately is that group affiliates connected through direct ownership are presumed to be more closely tied in an economic sense. This is expected to facilitate profit shifting between the entities.

As table 4A.3 shows, the firms included in the analysis show average total asset investments of US$23.3 million. Multinational firms possess larger asset stocks, with US$98.1 million and US$94.9 million for firms with any link to a foreign affiliate and firms with a direct link, respectively. Moreover, among the multinational firms, corporations with a tax haven link are reported to have higher total asset investments than other multinational firms: at US$140.5 million for firms with any link to a tax haven country and US$172.3 million for firms with a direct link to a tax haven. All the differences are statistically significant as indicated by the 95 percent confidence intervals around the mean.

Table 4A.3 also presents the pretax profit per total assets reported by the companies in our sample. This may be considered a proxy for the corporate tax base of the firms. The average pretax profitability of the firms in our sample is estimated at 0.092. Multinational firms (irrespective of direct or indirect ownership links to foreign countries) show a lower pretax profitability, at 0.071, on average, which is thus significantly lower than the average pretax profitability of the full sample as indicated by the 95 percent confidence interval around the mean. This result may seem counterintuitive at first sight because multinational firms commonly show larger productivity rates than national firms, which suggests that they also report larger pretax profitability values (Helpman, Melitz, and Yeaple 2004). However, as indicated above, they may equally encounter more opportunities to engage in tax avoidance and tax evasion through international channels, and this may lower the reported pretax profits in our sample countries (that do not comprise any tax haven). Or, alternatively, the higher international mobility of their investments may endow them with greater bargaining power with respect to host country governments and allow them to obtain a lower tax base relative to less mobile national firms.

However, firms belonging to multinational groups that include tax haven affiliates do not report significantly lower profitability rates than national firms. Because multinational firms with a link to tax havens are presumed to face more opportunities for tax avoidance and evasion and probably also exhibit more willingness to take up these opportunities, this suggests that the operations of multinationals with a tax haven connection are more profitable than the operations of other multinational firms. This picture prevails if we restrict the profitability variable to rates above 0.

Table 4A.3 also shows the tax payments per total assets reported by the firms in our sample. The broad picture resembles the picture for the profitability rates. While national firms pay the highest taxes per total assets reported, at an average of 0.018, the tax payments per total assets of multinational firms are significantly smaller, at 0.015 and 0.014, respectively, for firms belonging to multinational groups in general and firms with a direct ownership link to a foreign country. The subgroup of multinational firms with a link to tax havens does not make significantly lower tax payments per total assets than national firms. (This outcome is likely driven by the profitability pattern discussed in the paragraphs above.)

Furthermore, we report descriptive statistics on tax payments per pretax profit, which are a proxy for the average tax rate of the observed firms. The results suggest that national firms face the highest average tax rate, at 20.0 percent, which is significantly higher than the average tax rate of multinational firms, at 16.9 and 16.4 percent, respectively, for firms belonging to multinational groups in general and firms with a direct ownership link to a foreign country. Among multinationals, the lowest average tax rate is experienced by firms belonging to multinational groups with a link to tax havens. These firms pay 13.2 and 11.2 percent taxes on their profits, respectively, for firms with any tax haven link and firms with a direct tax haven link, which is significantly lower than the rates faced by multinational firms in general and, thus, also significantly lower than the rates faced by national firms. This suggests that firms with a tax haven connection manage to reduce their corporate tax burden significantly.

To account for the fact that the characteristics of firms belonging to multinational groups with a link to tax havens might differ in ways that may determine the described profit shifting measures, we also run a set of regressions to attempt to control for some of the potential sources of heterogeneity. Table 4A.4 on the website presents the results of a simple ordinary least squares model that regresses the pretax profitability (defined as pretax profits over total assets) of the firms in our sample on two dummy variables, which indicate entities belonging to multinational groups and entities belonging to groups with tax haven affiliates. In specifications (1) to (4), these definitions require the firm to have a direct ownership link to a foreign firm and a tax haven affiliate, respectively, while the multinational and tax haven definitions in specifications (5) to (8) also allow for indirect connections. Specification (1) presents the regression results without any control variables, which derives findings that are analogous to the descriptive statistics in table 4A.3. The results suggest that firms belonging to multinational groups have significantly lower reported pretax profits per total assets than national firms, whereas the pretax profitability of firms belonging to multinational groups with a tax haven affiliation does not statistically differ from the corresponding profitability of national firms.

In specifications (2) to (4), we include additional control variables within the estimation framework to account for heterogeneity in other firm characteristics. Thus, in specification (2), we add a full set of country fixed effects that absorb time-constant heterogeneity in the pretax profitability of firms in various sample countries. This, for example, accounts for time-constant differences in accounting methods across our sample countries. It renders insignificant the coefficient estimate for the dummy variable indicating multinational firms and suggests that the pretax profitability of multinational firms generally and of multinational firms with tax haven connections in particular does not differ from the pretax profitability of national entities. In specification (3), we add a full set of two-digit industry dummies to account for heterogeneity in the profitability ratios of different industries; this does not change the results. Finally, specification (4) additionally controls for the fact that profitability rates may vary according to firm size; it includes the logarithm of the total assets of firms as an additional control variable. The coefficient estimate for the size effect turns out to be negative and statistically significant at the 1 percent level. This indicates decreasing returns to scale, that is, in our sample, large firms tend to report pretax profitability rates that are lower than the corresponding rates among small firms. Accounting for this, in turn, derives positive and statistically significant coefficient estimates for the dummy variables indicating multinational firms (with tax haven connections). Hence, conditional on their size, multinational firms (with tax haven connections) report larger pretax profitability than their national counterparts, which is in line with previous evidence in the literature that suggests the higher productivity—and, in consequence, the higher profitability—of multinational firms. Specifications (5) to (8) reestimate the regression model to account for multinational firm and tax haven definitions that capture direct and indirect ownership links. This derives comparable results.

In table 4A.5 on the website, we repeat the exercise and determine the connection between multinational ownership links (to tax haven affiliates) and the corporate tax payments per assets. Analogously to the previous table, specification (1) regresses the corporate tax payment ratio on dummy variables indicating direct ownership links to foreign firms (in tax haven countries). The results indicate that multinational firms, in general, tend to pay significantly lower taxes on their total asset stock than national firms, while the tax payments of multinational firms with a tax haven connection do not significantly differ. This result prevails if we account for a full set of country fixed effects and industry fixed effects in specifications (2) and (3). In specification (4), we additionally include a size control (the logarithm of total assets). Similar to the results in the previous table, the coefficient estimate for the size variable is negative and significant, suggesting that the tax payments per total assets decrease with firm size. Moreover, conditional on firm size, the specifications indicate that multinational firms in general, but especially those with a tax haven connection report larger tax payments per total assets than national firms. This result may arise because multinational firms tend to show larger underlying productivity and, hence, earn greater profits per total assets, which lead to larger tax payments.

Last, we assess the difference in the average effective tax rate of national and multinational firms (with a tax haven connection) as measured by tax payments over the pretax profits of the firms (see table 4A.6 on the website). To do this, we restrict our sample to firms that show both a positive pretax profit and nonnegative tax payments. Specification (1) regresses the average tax burden on dummy variables indicating multinational firms (with tax haven connections) as determined by direct ownership links. The regression results suggest that multinational firms, in general, are not subject to a lower average tax rate than their national counterparts, while multinational corporations with tax haven links report an average tax rate that is lower by 5 percentage points. Additionally, controlling for a full set of country fixed effects and industry fixed effects equally renders the coefficient estimate for the multinational dummy negative and statistically significant, suggesting that multinational firms in general and multinational firms with a tax haven connection pay lower taxes on their reported pretax profits compared with national firms. This result is, moreover, robust against the inclusion of a size control in the model, as presented in specification (4). Quantitatively, the results suggest that multinational firms pay 1 percentage point lower taxes on pretax profit than national corporations, while multinational firms with a tax haven connection pay 4.4 percentage points lower taxes on their profit. This means that the average effective tax rate of multinational firms with a tax haven connection is around 3.4 percentage points lower than the average effective tax rate of multinational firms without a tax haven connection. In specifications (5) to (8), we rerun the regression to account for indirect ownership links in the definition of the multinational dummy (with tax haven connections) and find comparable results.

Thus, summing up, the results suggest that multinational firms tend to report higher pretax profits and tax payments per assets than comparable national firms, which may mean that they have a higher underlying productivity level. However, we also find that multinational firms, especially those with a tax haven connection, face a significantly lower average tax burden, that is, they make lower average tax payments per pretax profits.

Note that some caution is warranted in interpreting these results. As discussed above, an in-depth analysis requires that we account for the selection of different firms in the groups of national corporations, multinationals, and multinationals with an ownership link to avoid producing results that are driven by unobserved heterogeneity between groups. In interpreting the results, one should also keep in mind that the majority of information exploited is derived from firms in China. Future work should aim to run analyses on a broader basis, including information on other countries in Africa, Asia, Eastern Europe, and South America. One important issue is also to assess to what extent the difference in the average tax rates of national firms and multinationals (with a tax haven connection) is driven by the fact that multinationals tend to benefit from the location in special economic zones or receive special tax breaks from governments through other avenues. This is methodologically feasible as demonstrated by previous studies on the industrialized countries (Desai, Foley, and Hines 2006a, 2006b; Maffini 2009; Egger, Eggert, and Winner 2007). Moreover, it would be necessary to account for any time-varying differences in host country characteristics such as heterogeneity in accounting and tax base legislation. A rigorous analysis that accounts for these issues is beyond the scope of this chapter and is relegated to future research.

The structure of the Orbis data would also allow one to pursue the second identification strategy, that is, determine how changes in the corporate tax rate and corruption parameters affect profit shifting variables. This is possible because Orbis includes rich information on firm and group characteristics that may be used as control variables, and Orbis is available in a panel structure that allows one to control for time-constant differences between affiliates. In the course of this chapter, we determine only the correlation between the corporate statutory tax rate (obtained from various sources) and a corruption index (obtained from

Transparency International) with the profit shifting variables named above, and we find small correlations only. This does not necessarily mean that firms in the sample do not engage in profit shifting behavior, but it does indicate that profit shifting measures are determined by several factors that correlate with the tax rate and corruption indexes. These factors have to be accounted for in a regression framework to make meaningful statements about the effect of taxes and corruption on profit shifting behavior. This is left to future research.

Other data sources. Apart from Orbis, several other data sets may be used to analyze tax evasion and tax avoidance in developing economies. A database that is comparable with Orbis is Compustat Global, which is provided by Standard and Poor's. The data encompass firm-level information on balance sheet items and profit and loss accounts of companies around the world. Thus, information on pretax profits, corporate tax payments, debt levels, interest payments, and research and development expenditure is included, which allows one to identify corporate profit shifting and assess the importance of different profit shifting channels out of the developing world. In total, Compustat covers more than 30,000 companies in 100 countries, including several developing countries. The coverage is especially good in the Asia and Pacific region, where information on almost 16,000 firms is available (see table 4B.1 on the website for a description).

The data have some drawbacks. First, they do not cover ownership information, that is, it is not possible to link subsidiaries and parent firms in the data. Consequently, Compustat does not allow one to apply the first identification strategy because foreign firms and tax haven affiliates cannot be systematically identified. However, because the data are available in panel format for several years, they allow one to pursue the second identification strategy to examine how tax rate changes and changes in the corruption index affect profit shifting measures.

A second drawback of the data is that information is only provided for companies that are listed on a stock exchange. This imposes a sample restriction. Nonetheless, large (listed) firms are likely to be the main profit shifters, and, thus, profit shifting effects should still be identifiable.

Third, as stressed above, the quality of the data sets provided by private institutions has been criticized in the past.

To address this last concern, researchers may consider using data sources provided by official institutions that have become available recently and that allow tax avoidance and evasion to be investigated in the developing world. These data sets encompass information on outward investments by multinational firms. The most widely known data sets of this sort are the Direct Investment and Multinational Companies Database of the U.S. Bureau of Economic Analysis, the Deutsche Bundesbank's Microdatabase on Direct Investment, and the U.K. Annual Inquiry into Direct Investment Abroad (respectively, see tables 4B.2, 4B.3, and 4B.4 on the website). All three data sets contain information on multinational parent firms in the respective countries and their foreign subsidiaries, including subsidiaries in the developing world. The main advantage of these data sources is that the reporting is mandatory by national law, which suggests that the quality of the reported information is high. Moreover, information on directly and indirectly held affiliates is available. Only the U.K. data set is restricted to information on directly held subsidiaries. Despite some limitations, the data sets thus allow for studies based on the first identification strategy.

Moreover, the data include several variables that capture profit shifting behavior such as information on after-tax profits, tax payments, and debt ratios. Nonetheless, the data are somewhat less comprehensive than the data in Orbis or Compustat. Thus, both the German and the U.K. data sets include only information on company profits after taxation, not on pretax profits. This is a disadvantage because information on pretax profits is important for the analysis of profit shifting. Unlike the U.K. and the U.S. data sets, the German data set also does not report any information on the tax bills of the foreign subsidiaries. Still, the data sets possess a major advantage: they include information on intrafirm lending and intrafirm interest flows, which allows one to test for debt shifting activities between affiliates.

Additionally, in the United States, researchers at the U.S. Treasury have access to confidential U.S. firm-level data that are not available to the general public. The data cover information on U.S. tax returns and include variables on the tax payments, profits, and investments of U.S. multinationals in the United States and information on the income and tax payments of foreign-controlled companies, including subsidiaries in developing economies (see table 4B.5 on the website). Finally, table 4B.6

on the website lists other country-specific firm-level data sets that contain information on the foreign activities of domestic companies.

Data on international trade prices may be exploited to investigate profit shifting out of developing countries that takes place through trade mispricing by multinational firms. Previous studies reviewed above use the United States Merchandise Trade Databases, which contain price data according to import-harmonized commodity codes and export-harmonized commodity codes.[3] However, these data hardly allow for a clear identification strategy to ferret out profit shifting behavior. Because the data do not discriminate trade between related and unrelated parties, our first identification strategy is not applicable. This shortcoming can, however, be addressed by using a different data source. Thus, Clausing (2003) exploits data from the International Price Program of the U.S. Bureau of Labor Statistics, which publishes information on 700 aggregate export and import price indexes. The data differentiate trade between related and unrelated parties, which makes the control group approach feasible. Assuming that profit shifting via trade price distortions is negligible between third parties, the trade prices of intrafirm trade between multinational affiliates can be compared with trade pricing between third parties (see Clausing 2003). A different strategy for the development of a valid identification strategy would involve exploiting the panel dimension of the trade price data; this has not been done in existing studies. In this way, one might investigate how trade prices are affected by policy reforms such as tax rate changes or changes in the level of law enforcement or political stability in partner countries, which implies that the countries without tax reforms would serve as a control group.

Conclusion

Tax avoidance and evasion through profit shifting out of developing countries represent an important and widely debated issue. Yet, relatively little is known about the magnitude of and the factors driving profit shifting in the developing world. The main reason is that the available data are limited in terms of both quality and quantity. The results of most existing empirical studies on developing countries are difficult to interpret because the methods used to measure income shifting raise a number of problems. We have suggested and discussed several data sets, some of which have become available recently, and methods to undertake more research on profit shifting in the developing world. While these approaches also have limitations, they do have the potential to improve our understanding of this important issue and to inform policies directed at crowding back tax avoidance and evasion in the developing world.

Notes

1. The website of the Bank for International Settlements is at http://www.bis.org/.
2. See http://go.worldbank.org/N2HMRB4G20.
3. See USA Trade Online (database), U.S. Department of Commerce, Washington, DC, https://www.usatradeonline.gov/.

References

Azémar, C. 2008. "International Corporate Taxation and U.S. Multinationals' Behaviour: An Integrated Approach." Discussion Paper (August), Department of Economics, University of Glasgow, Glasgow.

Baker, R. W. 2005. *Capitalism's Achilles Heel: Dirty Money and How to Renew the Free-Market System.* Hoboken, NJ: John Wiley & Sons.

BCG (Boston Consulting Group). 2003. "Winning in a Challenging Market: Global Wealth 2003." BCG, Boston.

Buettner, T., and G. Wamser. 2007. "Intercompany Loans and Profit Shifting: Evidence from Company-Level Data." CESifo Working Paper 1959, CESifo Group, Munich.

Capgemini and Merrill Lynch. 1998. "World Wealth Report 1998." Capgemini and Merrill Lynch Global Wealth Management, New York.

Christian Aid. 2008. "Death and Taxes: The True Toll of Tax Dodging." Christian Aid Report, May. Christian Aid, London.

———. 2009. "False Profits: Robbing the Poor to Keep the Rich Tax-Free." Christian Aid Report, March, Christian Aid, London.

Clausing, K. A. 2003. "Tax-Motivated Transfer Pricing and US Intrafirm Trade Prices." *Journal of Public Economics* 87 (9–10): 2207–23.

Cobham, A. 2005. "Tax Evasion, Tax Avoidance and Development Finance." QEH Working Paper 129, Queen Elizabeth House, University of Oxford, Oxford. http://www3.qeh.ox.ac.uk/pdf/qehwp/qehwps129.pdf.

de Boyrie, M. E., S. J. Pak, and J. S. Zdanowicz. 2005. "Estimating the Magnitude of Capital Flight Due to Abnormal Pricing in International Trade: The Russia-USA Case." *Accounting Forum* 29 (3): 249–70.

Desai, M. A., C. F. Foley, and J. R. Hines Jr. 2004. "Foreign Direct Investment in a World of Multiple Taxes." *Journal of Public Economics* 88 (12): 2727–44.

———. 2006a. "Do Tax Havens Divert Economic Activity?" *Economics Letters* 90 (2): 219–24.

———. 2006b. "The Demand for Tax Haven Operations." *Journal of Public Economics* 90 (3): 513–31.

Dischinger, M., and N. Riedel. 2008. "Corporate Taxes and the Location of Intangible Assets within Multinational Firms." Discussion Paper in Economics 5294, Department of Economics, University of Munich, Munich.

Egger, P., W. Eggert and H. Winner. 2007. "Saving Taxes through Foreign Plant Ownership." CESifo Working Paper 1887, CESifo Group, Munich.

Fuest, C., and N. Riedel. 2009. "Tax Evasion, Tax Avoidance and Tax Expenditures in Developing Countries: A Review of the Literature." Report, Oxford University Centre for Business Taxation, Oxford.

Grubert, H., and J. Mutti. 1991. "Taxes, Tariffs and Transfer Pricing in Multinational Corporation Decision Making." *Review of Economics and Statistics* 73 (2): 285–93.

———. 2000. "Do Taxes Influence Where U.S. Corporations Invest?" *National Tax Journal* 53 (4): 825–39.

Helpman, E., M. J. Melitz, and S. R. Yeaple. 2004. "Export Versus FDI with Heterogeneous Firms." *American Economic Review* 94 (1): 300–16.

Hong, Q., and M. Smart. 2010. "In Praise of Tax Havens: International Tax Planning and Foreign Direct Investment." *European Economic Review* 54 (1): 82–95.

Howard, M. 2001. *Public Sector Economics for Developing Countries.* Kingston, Jamaica: University Press of the West Indies.

Huizinga, H., and L. Laeven. 2008. "International Profit Shifting within Multinationals: A Multi-country Perspective." *Journal of Public Economics* 92 (5–6), 1164–82.

Huizinga, H., L. Laeven, and G. Nicodeme. 2008. "Capital Structure and International Debt Shifting." *Journal of Financial Economics* 88 (1): 80–118.

Keen, M., and M. Mansour. 2008. "Revenue Mobilization in Sub-Saharan Africa: Challenges from Globalization." Draft working paper, August 11, Fiscal Affairs Department, International Monetary Fund, Washington, DC.

Klemm, A. 2009. "Causes, Benefits, and Risks of Business Tax Incentives." IMF Working Paper 09/21, International Monetary Fund, Washington, DC.

Maffini, G. 2009. "Tax Haven Activities and the Tax Liabilities of Multinational Groups." Working Paper 09/25, Oxford University Centre for Business Taxation, Oxford.

OECD (Organisation for Economic Co-operation and Development). 2001. *Corporate Tax Incentives for Foreign Direct Investment.* OECD Tax Policy Study 4. Paris: OECD.

Oxfam. 2000. "Tax Havens: Releasing the Hidden Billions for Poverty Eradication." Oxfam Briefing Paper. Oxfam International, London.

————. 2009. "Tax Haven Crackdown Could Deliver 120bn a Year to Reduce Poverty: Oxfam." Press release, March 13, Oxfam GB, London. http://www.oxfam.org.uk/applications/blogs/pressoffice/?p=3912.

Pak, S. J. 2007. "Capital Flight and Tax Avoidance through Abnormal Pricing in International Trade: The Issue and the Solution." In *Closing the Floodgates: Collecting Tax to Pay for Development, Tax Justice Network*, 118–22. London: Tax Justice Network. http://www.innovativefinance-oslo.no/pop.cfm?FuseAction=Doc&pAction=View&pDocumentId=11607.

Pak, S. J., S. Zanakis, and J. S. Zdanowicz. 2003. "Detecting Abnormal Pricing in International Trade: The Greece-USA Case." *Interfaces* 33 (2): 54–64.

Schott, P. K. 2008. "The Relative Sophistication of Chinese Exports." *Economic Policy* 23 (53): 5–49.

TJN (Tax Justice Network). 2005. "The Price of Offshore." Tax Justice Network Briefing Paper, March, TJN, London.

————. 2007. *Closing the Floodgates: Collecting Tax to Pay for Development*. London: TJN. http://www.innovativefinance-oslo.no/pop.cfm?FuseAction=Doc&pAction=View&pDocumentId=11607.

UNCTAD (United Nations Conference on Trade and Development). 1999. *World Investment Report 1999: Foreign Direct Investment and the Challenge of Development*. Geneva: UNCTAD.

Weichenrieder, A. 2009. "Profit Shifting in the EU: Evidence from Germany." *International Tax and Public Finance* 16 (3): 281–97.

Zdanowicz, J. S., S. J. Pak, and M. A. Sullivan. 1999. "Brazil–United States Trade: Capital Flight through Abnormal Pricing." *International Trade Journal* 13 (4): 423–43.

Part II
Illegal Markets

5

Illicit Capital Flows and Money Laundering in Colombia

Francisco E. Thoumi and Marcela Anzola

Abstract

In Colombia, the need to send capital abroad to avoid anti–money laundering (AML) controls is not particularly great. During the last few decades, the domestic risk has been low, and so has the incentive for outflows. This phenomenon has been associated with Colombian institutional characteristics: the conflict between the formal (legal) and informal (social) norms that characterizes the country and that serves as a breeding ground for illegal economic activities there. Geography has been a huge obstacle to economic integration and modernization and a main obstacle to effective central state presence in large parts of the country. The country has a large informal economy; financial sector services are expensive and cover only a minority of the population; illegal economic activities are widespread; and violence is frequently used to achieve economic goals. This environment has been fertile for the establishment of the illegal drug industry and provided good support for this industry's resiliency. Law enforcement is a constant struggle. This explains why, although the country's AML legislation is one of the most advanced in the world, the results have been meager. In Colombia, controlling internal and external illegal capital flows presents a daunting policy problem.

Unfortunately, as long as the conflict between the formal (legal) and informal (social) norms persists, illegal economic activities will flourish in Colombia. This is why cultural change should be a main policy goal.

Introduction

Most illegal capital outflows from developing countries are associated with kleptocracy, corruption, and tax evasion and avoidance (Baker 2005). Since criminal gains need to be laundered to disguise their illegal origin, the funds are commonly channeled through scattered accounts at banks situated in offshore financial centers that either facilitate financial transactions without investigating the origin of the funds or do not cooperate in AML investigations. Once the money is laundered abroad, the funds can be used as legal capital anywhere, including in the country of origin.

The need to send illicit funds abroad to be laundered may arise from several situations. Thus, it might arise if the country of origin has the capability to exercise some control over crime and illicit gains. In other cases, as in countries in which presidents or dictators have transferred billions of dollars to hidden accounts in the first world, the fear of losing the illicit money because of political change may explain the need. Countries in which military forces control the territory and support authoritarian regimes have all experienced large illegal kleptocratic capital outflows that have skimmed from the national budget and national resources. Such has been the case in Haiti, Indonesia, Nicaragua, Pakistan, Paraguay, Peru, the Russian Federation, Saudi Arabia, and several African countries (Baker 2005).

The Colombian case differs substantially from the common pattern, however. In Colombia, money laundering has mainly been associated with the illegal drug industry, in which criminal activities cross borders, and payments are commonly made abroad. The main concern for the recipients of these funds is not only to launder the money, but also to bring the money to their countries, including back to Colombia. In the case of kleptocrats, guerrillas, and common organized criminals, even though the illegal funds are, in some cases, sent abroad, they are invested or spent directly in Colombia in most cases. The amounts of funds that these actors wish to send abroad likely pales in comparison with the amounts that traffickers wish to bring back in.

This particular situation is reflected in Colombian AML policy and laws (UIAF 2008). Indeed, in recent decades, the regulatory framework has focused on three dimensions of the effort to combat money laundering in Colombia: the administrative control of financial transactions, the penalization of money laundering and illicit enrichment as separate offenses, and the development of comprehensive asset forfeiture legislation. In this context, financial entities are responsible for adopting adequate and sufficient control measures to avoid being used as instruments for concealing, handling, investing, and, in any other way, using funds or other assets originating from criminal activities or to give an appearance of legitimacy to criminal activities or transactions and funds related to such activities. Colombia has also criminalized the laundering of the proceeds of extortion, illicit enrichment, rebellion, narcotics trafficking, arms trafficking, crimes against the financial system or public administration, and criminal conspiracy (Law 365 of 1997). Additionally, Colombian law provides for both conviction-based and nonconviction-based *in rem* forfeiture.

The academic literature on illicit money flows in Colombia has also focused on illicit inflows, particularly on the macroeconomic effects of these inflows, and has disregarded illicit outflows (Steiner 1997; Rocha 2000, 2005).

This situation raises a question, however: why do Colombian recipients of illicit funds have little or no incentive to send or maintain the funds abroad? The answer is quite simple: in Colombia, despite some of the most advanced AML legislation in the world, there are no real obstacles to invest or spend illegal revenue. Institutional weaknesses have impeded the adequate implementation and enforcement of the AML laws, and the power of the paramilitary, guerrillas, and drug trafficking organizations, particularly at the local level in many regions, and the gap between formal norms and culturally accepted informal norms have shaped an extralegal economy that is immune to traditional mechanisms for combating illegal economic activities.

More precisely, in the case of corruption and illegal drug income, the decision on where to invest the illicit revenues depends on the social and criminal networks in which the lawbreaker participates. For example, a corrupt official who is not part of a criminal network and receives a large sum would be tempted to deposit the sum in an offshore center. However, if this person is part of a group that influences political elections, whose members are friends and relatives of the political elite, and that has a strong private military arm, the corrupt official would be tempted to invest locally. Indeed, doing so, the official will obtain not only an economic return, as he would abroad, but also political influence. So, in this case, there is not much incentive to invest abroad.[1] This explains why most funds generated through corruption are likely to remain in the country. The exceptions are the money paid to local politicians or decision makers by transnational corporations that deposit the funds in foreign accounts or unusually large bribes associated with big government contracts.

Thus, in Colombia, where an important part of the economy is involved in illicit, but socially legitimate economic activities and where corruption is not centralized, but widespread, the need to send capital abroad to avoid seizures and expropriations is not particularly great. As a result, during the last few decades, the domestic risk has been low, and so has the incentive for outflows. Even though this might have changed recently, the incentives to invest illegal capital in Colombia discourage illegal capital outflows. The most recent cases of corruption in Colombia have provided evidence of the existence of bank accounts and investments abroad. However, in many cases, it is possible that the related illicit payments have also been made abroad. The authorities have not yet reported any capital outflows associated with these cases.

This chapter analyzes why Colombian institutions constitute a fertile environment for the laundering and concealment of the proceeds of certain unlawful activities such as the illegal drug industry, kleptocracy, and organized crime, provide good support for their resiliency, and, as a result, encourage illegal capital inflows and reduce the need to launder illegal capital abroad.

Using country-specific characteristics as explanatory variables is discouraged in the social sciences because doing so opens a Pandora box that explains everything through these particularities. However, Colombia has been experiencing almost constant conflict for at least seven decades. As shown below, official data indicate that 9 percent of the country's population has been internally displaced. The International Organization for Migration estimates that, in 2008, there were 4.2 million Colombians living abroad (Ramírez, Zuluaga, and Perilla 2010). This means that about 18 percent of Colombians have been displaced internally or left the country. Colombia is the most important producer of cocaine in the world (despite the many other possible competitors), and, during the last 15 years, it has also been the largest producer of coca. Colombia also has the distinction of being among the foremost countries in the world in number of kidnappings, assassins for hire (*sicarios*), child warriors, landmines and victims of landmines, producers of counterfeit U.S. dollars and other foreign exchange, exporters of Latin American prostitutes, and so on (Rubio 2004; Child Soldiers International 2008; United Nations 2009).[2] It is the country where the term *desechable* (throw away) was coined to refer to indigents and other undesirables who have been socially "cleansed," where "Not for Sale" signs are used widely to prevent fraudulent transactions aimed at stripping property from the legal owners, and where contraband is a socially valid way of life to the point that, in border regions, there have been public demonstrations to demand the right to smuggle.

All these facts have shaped the way in which markets and law enforcement organizations operate. Indeed, Colombians colloquially refer to Colombian capitalism as savage, in contrast with capitalist markets in Europe, the United States, and even developing countries such as Chile. A study of illegal capital flows in Colombia that does not take into account the particular characteristics of Colombian markets and transactions runs the risk of reaching contradictory or erroneous conclusions.

The next section shows how Colombian institutions are an obstacle to law enforcement and help propagate illegal economic activities. The section that follows explains how these institutions represent an obstacle for the enforcement of AML legislation. The penultimate section describes capital flows in and out of Colombia and shows the role of the illicit drug industry. The final section presents a summary and conclusions.

Institutional Obstacles to Law Enforcement and the Upsurge in Illegal Economic Activities

The Spanish Conquest that began in 1492 was never completed in Colombia. Large areas of the country have still not been settled. Local loyalties are strong, and the development of a national identity has been slow and remains unfinished. An important U.S. historian of Colombia refers to the country as "a nation in spite of itself" (Bushnell 1993).

Geography has been a huge obstacle to economic integration and modernization and a main obstacle to effective central state presence in large parts of the country.[3] As a result, Colombia has a large informal economy, significant land concentration, and a wide gap between formal institutions (constitution and laws) and the local culture.

The informal economy

Colombia has a large informal economy that is a principal obstacle to the enforcement of economic laws and facilitates money laundering activities. While there is no agreement on the definition of economic informality, Schneider and Klinglmair (2004), using a combination of statistical procedures, estimate that the informal economy accounted for 39.1 percent of gross domestic product (GDP) in Colombia in 1999/2000. A World Bank study that involved the measurement of informality using employment classifications found that, between 1992 and 2005, independent workers increased their share in total employment in Colombia by 17.3 percent (Perry et al. 2007). It also found that the share of informal independent workers, plus informal wage earners, in total employment in Colombia in 2006 was 66.8 percent. These are workers who do not comply with many legal requirements, contribute little if at all to the social security system, and do not have many social benefits.

A low level of penetration of banking services also creates an environment conducive to economic lawbreaking and money laundering. Data for 1990–99 and 2000–05 show that, in the first period, deposits represented 14 percent of gross national product, which increased to 22 percent in the second period (Rojas-Suárez 2006). These shares are about one-third of the corresponding shares in the developed countries included in the survey and about one-half of the shares in Chile. Similarly, the number of bank offices and automated teller machines (ATMs) per 100,000 inhabitants is low in Colombia: about half the number in Brazil, Chile, and Mexico. These numbers for Colombia are only about 10 percent or less of the numbers found in the developed world. A more detailed study shows that 26.5 percent of the Colombian population resides in municipalities that do not have banking services (Marulanda 2006). These municipalities cover large areas of the country that have a strong guerrilla and paramilitary presence. Data from large urban areas show that only 26.4 percent of the adult population has deposits in or loans from the financial system. Upper-income groups account for a large share of this population segment.

Colombia experienced a financial crisis in 1999 caused by a significant change in the way mortgage balances were estimated. In response to persistent high inflation rates, a constant value unit system was established in the early 1970s. In essence, this set a fixed interest rate on mortgages, although the principal could be adjusted according to inflation. In 1999 in the midst of a financial crisis and high interest rates, the adjustment mechanism was changed, and interest rate levels were used instead of inflation. The values of the principal in mortgages ballooned, and many borrowers found themselves with mortgages that exceeded substantially the value of their properties; the real estate market collapsed. In 1999, Colombia, for the first and only time in the postwar period, showed negative growth in GDP (−4.2 percent). After the financial and real estate crisis, financial institutions had to clean their portfolios, and their total credit exposure declined. Using annual data, Tafur Saiden (2009) shows that, during the 1990s, the ratio of credit to GDP increased, reaching 37.9 percent in 1998. Then it dropped sharply, to the 24–25 percent range in 2002–05.[4]

A tax on financial transactions that was raised from 0.002 to 0.003 percent and then to 0.004 percent was earmarked to support the troubled financial sector. The government, however, found it an expedient source of funds and maintained it after the crisis was over. Today, it gathers in about 1 percent of GDP (Marulanda 2006). Increases in service costs, including many hidden fees, were another response of the financial sector to the crisis. Bank charges now include account management fees, fees to use ATM machines, and even fees to consult balances on ATM machines and the Internet, among many others. Moreover, the interest intermediation gap is probably the largest in Latin America.[5] The penetration of banking services in Colombia faces other obstacles, such as the fear of physical assault following a deposit withdrawal or cashing a check. This type of crime is so common that the police are now offering protection on demand to bank customers who make large withdrawals.

Land concentration and the lack of territorial control

The lack of territorial control by the central state has facilitated the growth of power among local groups. Left-wing guerrillas (Ejército de

Liberación Nacional and Fuerzas Armadas Revolucionarias de Colombia, more well known as ELN and FARC, respectively) and right-wing paramilitary groups have controlled many municipal governments and had sufficient influence on some governments in the country's departments to be able to extract significant amounts from local budgets to fund their activities.

Illegal capital has been a factor in the extreme concentration of land tenancy and the political power of local landlords who, in large parts of the country, have had close ties to the illicit drug industry or have been active in this industry.[6] Illegal drug money could not be easily invested in the modern economy, and drug traffickers purchased large amounts of rural land (Reyes Posada 1997). This concentration has been achieved by purchases, forced purchases under threat, and forced displacements of peasants and has been facilitated by the lack of well-defined, defendable property rights in many regions.

Moreover, in towns controlled by armed groups or local traditional landlords, public land and title registries (*catastros*) are outdated and incomplete, and tax assessments grossly underestimated. Municipal registries that should provide information on ownership are also inadequate, and, frequently, municipal staff refuse to cooperate with the *Fiscalía* (Attorney General's Office) because the staff are controlled by people whose property rights may be challenged for money laundering. Land taxes are woefully low in many regions, and landed interests control municipal councils, where they block any attempts to update the registries and raise rural real estate taxes.

Paramilitary organizations have stripped large amounts of land from peasants. The lack of reliable land records and the fact that many peasants have not had formal property rights to their plots make it impossible to develop accurate estimates on the extent of the plundering. Today, but for Sudan, Colombia has the largest number of displaced citizens in the world. The Internal Displacement Monitoring Centre estimates the number of displaced Colombians, as of June 2010, at 3.3 million to 4.9 million in a total population of 45.7 million.[7]

The gap between formal and informal norms

Geography has also been a main factor in the development of diverse cultures because many regions essentially represent cultural endogamies based on homogeneous values, beliefs, and attitudes (Yunis 2003). This explains why, in Colombia, there is a wide gap and strong contrast between formal institutions (constitution, laws, decrees, and so on) and the informal unwritten norms recognized and followed by many social groups. Scholars have identified this gap as a main problem in establishing the rule of law in Colombia (Thoumi 1987; Herrán 1987; Kalmanovitz 1989; Mockus 1994; Yunis 2003; Puyana-García 2005).[8] One of the principal problems law enforcement efforts face in Colombia is the fact that most decent Colombians break economic laws in some form or another. Some do it without violence. For example, they buy contraband or evade taxes. Others go further and may use social and political influence to get government jobs or contracts; still others may use fraud, violence, or the threat of violence to achieve their goals.

The persistence and diversity of the contrast and conflict in norms, coupled with large internal migrations partially in response to forced displacement, have resulted in a significant number of Colombians developing a deep amoral individualism; they have become anomic: the effects of their actions on others are simply irrelevant.[9] Many Colombians tend to be selective regarding the laws that they comply with and those that they break. Most Colombians simply accept that they should obey "good" laws, but that they may disobey "unjust" laws.[10]

The problem of Colombia is not only the weak state, which could be strengthened, but, rather, that this state is embedded within a lax society in which social controls on behavior have been enfeebled to the point that they are irrelevant for many Colombians. In the Colombian institutional environment, the line dividing legal and illegal economic activities is fuzzy. Indeed, the division of activities between legal and illegal provides only a partial picture of reality. It is more relevant to divide the economy in terms of the law into four sectors: legal and socially legitimate, that is, activities that comply with the law and are accepted and reinforced by unwritten social norms; illegal and legitimate, that is, activities that involve lawbreaking, but that are accepted socially (purchasing contraband, for example); legal and illegitimate, that is, activities that comply with the law, but contradict social norms (abortion, for example, according to the views of conservative religious groups); and illegal and illegitimate, that is, activities that involve breaking the law and contravening the norms of society. Of course, the classification of activities into each of these categories varies across social groups. The issue is how large the numbers of illegal but legitimate activities are and who agrees with the assessment. As these numbers grow, the effectiveness of law enforcement agencies declines, and, if the numbers are large, law enforcement becomes ineffective and the risk associated with lawbreaking is low.

The Failure of Enforcement: The Gap between Formal and Informal Norms

Colombia has one of the most advanced AML legislative frameworks in the world. It is focused on attacking the assets of drug traffickers. However, enforcement has faced huge obstacles, and the results have been meager.

The Financial Information and Analysis Unit has developed a system to manage the risk of asset laundering and the financing of terrorism. The system has been used effectively in the financial sector. However, in Colombia, the financial sector is not the main laundering venue because of its closed and oligopolistic structure and the limited penetration of banking services.[11] The unit acknowledges, for example, that contraband plays a more important role as a means of laundering, and this is why the unit is now turning its attention to the real economy.[12]

The unit has also detected a significant increase in the number of businesses that have been established specifically to provide specialized money laundering services.[13] The Fiscalía finds a similar evolution, noting that, 10 years ago, trafficking organizations were pyramidal. Today, they are fragmented and more collegial. Money laundering firms have increasingly become specialized and offer their services to meet many types of needs. In the past, they were part of the main contraband trafficking structures; today, they are independent. Many of these firms have licit fronts and provide diverse services. In one case, for example, a firm had 1,500 cédulas, the Colombian national identity cards, that it used to make financial transactions (smurfing) for various clients.[14]

Additionally, substantial logistical obstacles impede the adequate implementation and enforcement of AML legislation. The Fiscalía has a large backlog of cases. They have few prosecutors, and the Judicial Police has only 40 officers assigned to fight money laundering. Prosecutorial processes are time-consuming and labor intensive. Because of the prevalence of *testaferros* (front or straw men), prosecutors have to investigate traffickers and all their family members.

In 2004, with the encouragement and support of the United States, Colombia changed its traditional justice system to an accusatory one. The shift to the new system has not been easy, and many lawyers, judges, and prosecutors do not understand the new system. Many young judges are not well qualified, do not understand money laundering issues, and should be trained. High personnel turnover is another problem because it means there must be regular training programs. These have been the main reasons for the large backlog of cases.

Officials of the United Nations Office on Drugs and Crime believe that there is a pressing need to improve the quality of justice system personnel.[15] They think that personnel problems are behind a declining trend in AML convictions. They also think that the quality of the data available on judicial processes are poor. The government agencies involved in fighting money laundering have provided information to the judicial system for prosecutions. However, no information is available about what goes on during the processes.

The National Narcotics Directorate (DNE) is in charge of administering seized assets and forfeitures, but faces great challenges. Its record in administering, managing, and disposing of seized goods has been questionable at best. DNE regularly encounters problems because of the titles of seized properties. Frequently, the relevant records have disappeared. Because of these problems, DNE has opted to accept assets for management only after formal precautionary measures have been completed.

DNE currently manages assets in several special categories: chemical substances; urban real estate; rural real estate; land vehicles; airplanes; boats; cash, art, and other; and businesses. DNE decides how to dispose of the forfeited assets. Both DNE and the Fiscalía have had great difficulty separating front men from good faith asset holders. They know that a large share of the seized assets is in the hands of front men, but this is difficult to prove. Another problem arises because many assets are not productive, but must be stored and maintained and therefore generate substantial cash outflows. Others require special skills to be managed properly.

By the end of November 2008, DNE had received 80,860 assets to manage, while the forfeiture processes were advancing. Of these, 12,397

(15.3 percent) had been returned to their owners, who had obtained favorable court judgments. Only 7,734 (9.6 percent) had been forfeited, and the remaining 60,729 (75.1 percent) were still the subject of judicial processes. The forfeiture process is slow. Indeed, in early May 2008, DNE auctioned property seized from Pablo Escobar, who was killed on December 2, 1993. The fact that the share of the assets that has been returned to asset owners is larger than the share that has been forfeited also indicates the level of problems in the process. DNE officials suggest that the data are misleading because the definition of asset that is used does not refer to an individual piece of property, but to all properties that are seized during each seizure event and that they believe are in the possession of one individual. They claim that some of the forfeited assets include several properties. However, they do not have data to corroborate this.

Table 5.1 summarizes the results of AML efforts involving the seized and forfeited assets of drug traffickers. The official data have been aggregated and do not provide important details. For example, there are no estimates about the value of the assets seized and forfeited. Moreover, the definition of an asset is vague (see above). Despite the data deficiencies, the results are clearly not encouraging.

Table 5.1. The Results of Anti–money Laundering Efforts: Number of Seized and Forfeited Assets
number

Asset type	Returned by judicial decision	In judicial process	Forfeited	Total
Urban real estate	2,571	11,790	2,965	17,326
Rural real estate	1,282	3,659	695	5,636
Businesses	62	2,541	287	2,890
Cash	410	5,420	327	6,157
Controlled substances	525	9,439	653	10,617
Land vehicles	3,823	9,198	585	13,606
Airplanes and helicopters	361	660	44	1,065
Boats	179	571	99	849
Other	3,184	17,451	2,079	22,714
Total	12,397	60,729	7,734	80,860

Source: UIAF 2008.
Note: The data apply to the period up to November 30, 2008.

Several public officials have proposed legal changes to allow the government to sell seized properties and return the proceeds if the owners win their cases. This would eliminate the problem of managing seized property, but raises the issue of how the sale price is to be determined in environments of extremely imperfect markets.

Capital Flows in and out of Colombia: The Role of the Illicit Drug Industry

Colombia began to be a player in the international illegal drug industry some 40 years ago. Since then, asset and money laundering and illegal capital flows have been an important policy issue in the country. Before 1970, policy debates related to illegal capital outflows existed, but the problem did not have a high priority on the policy agenda. The outflows then were generally motivated by the foreign exchange control system and the protectionist policies of the government, the fear of a left-wing political revolution, and the desire to evade Colombian taxes.

Since the illicit drug industry started to grow in Colombia, the debate surrounding illegal capital flows and the related policies have been focused on capital inflows, and the policy concern over capital outflows has been minimal. This has been particularly the case in the last two decades, since the foreign exchange control regime was discarded and the economy was opened up.

Kleptocracy is primarily a local phenomenon in Colombia; it has been limited by the small size of local budgets and the productive activities from which "commissions" may be illegally collected or benefit may be illegally drawn from the associated public contracts.[16] The Colombian military have never controlled the territory; they have relatively low social status, support elected governments, and play only a marginal political role.[17] Colombia has not had a *caudillo* (leader) similar to the ones who, at times, have been typical in other Latin American countries and who have grossly enriched themselves and taken huge amounts of wealth from the country.[18] The most publicized corruption event in Colombia in the 1990s was the funding of the 1994 presidential campaign of Ernesto Samper by the Cali cartel to the tune of some US$8 million. Despite a national scandal and a detailed investigation, Samper was never accused of having personally profited from the money, although some of the funds were deposited in accounts of a close campaign associate in New York who had absconded with some money for his own benefit.

However, this situation may be changing because of the surge in corruption in the past decade. During the eight-year presidency of Alvaro Uribe (2002–10), corruption increased especially in the infrastructure sector, where many large projects were left incomplete or barely begun. While media reports suggest that a large part of the funds remained in the country, a significant, though unknown portion may have been invested abroad. The available information concerning this issue is fragmented and anecdotal, and there are no definitive figures permitting us to describe a pattern of behavior or to reach an acceptable conclusion. Future research might be able to throw light on this issue.

Capital flows and economic policies: From a foreign exchange control regime to an open economy

The literature of the early 1970s describes Colombia as a foreign exchange–constrained economy that has a strict foreign exchange control system (World Bank 1972; Nelson, Schultz, and Slighton 1971). Colombia had the longest running exchange control regime in Latin America. The system was in place from 1931 to 1991. There were several traditional ways for capital to flee the country illegally, including import overinvoicing and export underinvoicing, contraband exports (coffee and emeralds to the developed world and cattle to República Bolivariana de Venezuela were favorites), and, in the case of transnational corporations, transfer prices and payments for patents and royalties.[19] Tax evasion and avoidance were not likely to be an important determinant of capital flight because one could keep one's tax payments low through creative accounting and the frequent tax amnesties that the government periodically enacted.[20]

Colombia did not have large investments by foreign corporations; so, transfer pricing, another illegal capital outflow or inflow modality, was not likely to have been significant, although it was probably used by foreign investors.

The situation had changed drastically by the mid-1970s when illegal drug exports of marijuana and then cocaine grew quickly. From December 1974 until the change in the foreign exchange regime in 1991, the black market exchange rate remained significantly below the official one because drug money was flooding the black market with cash. Also, the net mispricing of international trade changed so that, on average, imports were underinvoiced and exports overinvoiced to bring foreign exchange revenues into the country (Thoumi 1995). The exception to this was 1982–83, when high interest rates in the United States apparently induced Colombian traffickers to purchase U.S. Treasury Bills and other interest-bearing papers abroad. This was a time of high cocaine prices in the United States and a sharp decline of illegal capital inflows in Colombia (Thoumi 1995). Similarly, in 1982 and 1983, worker remittances collapsed, but, "after 1984 Colombian expatriate workers appear to have been a lot more 'generous' with their Colombian brethren" (Thoumi 1995, 191).

After the exchange control regime was eliminated in 1991, the parallel market in foreign exchange remained alongside the official one, although it has declined in Bogotá and other large cities in the last few years, and, today, it is only a couple of percentage points below the official one. Selling foreign exchange in the official market requires that sellers account for the origin of their funds. The gap between the two exchange rates has, at times, been explained by the taxes and fees charged in the official market. The gap has varied not only over time, but also according to geography. In coca-growing regions, for example, peasants are frequently paid in U.S. dollars brought in the same small planes used to export cocaine. In these cases, the peasants sell the dollars at up to a 30 percent discount relative to the official rate. The close current gap between the two exchange rates suggests that there is little if any questioning of suspicious transactions and that the risks associated with money laundering in the country are low.

In the period before 1991, the year the economy was opened and foreign exchange controls were eliminated, capital outflows were associated with the incentives generated by the exchange control regime and political risks. During the 1990s, illegal armed groups gained strength relative to the government, and the illicit drug industry's control shifted from the old Cali and Medellín cartels to armed groups, guerrillas, and paramilitary groups. The increased political uncertainty and the growing risk were clearly reflected in the outflow of legal capital.

Colombian investments abroad are a recent phenomenon. Before 1990, outward foreign direct investment (outward FDI) was rare, and

most of it was the result of the implementation of entrepreneurial strategies under the Andean Pact framework. Starting in the early 1990s,
Colombian enterprises began to invest abroad (see figure 5.1). Such
investments between 1992 and 2002 were directed mainly to Panama,
Peru, the United States, and República Bolivariana de Venezuela. The
most important investments in the first two countries—the largest
investment recipients—were in the financial sector. In 1997, the peak
year, they grew dramatically. The financial sector was a good venue for
people to buy certificates of deposit and other financial instruments
abroad. The investments had a substantial component of capital flight
generated by growing political instability. Indeed, the figures for 1997 are
extraordinarily high, reaching US$687.4 million (see figure 5.1, particu-
larly the data at the bottom).

The growth of outward FDI in the financial sector did not coincide with
large investments by Colombian banks. During these years, the lion's share
of financial investments was in other financial services that included a variety of contracts and activities in which individual investors could partici-

Figure 5.1. Colombia: Outward Foreign Direct Investment, 1994–2010

	1994	1995	1996	1997	1998	1999	2000	2001	2002	2003	2004	2005	2006	2007	2008	2009	2010
OFDI TOTAL	149.0	256.2	327.9	809.4	796.0	115.5	325.3	16.1	856.8	937.7	142.4	4,661.9	1,098.3	912.8	2,254.0	3.088.1	6,528.7
OFDI financial-related services	54.7	141.4	273.5	687.4	292.6	1.5	225.3	–227.4	75.2	32.5	32.1	32.9	184.6	745.9	346.4	204.0	139.1

Source: Central Bank of Colombia.
Note: OFDI = outward foreign direct investment.

pate.[21] After the launch of Plan Colombia and after the guerrilla threat had died down, Colombians began to regain confidence in the economy, and, in 2001, financial sector outward FDI was negative.

After 2002, Colombian outward FDI shifted from the financial sector to industry, mining, and public utilities. Colombian enterprises, like other Latin American enterprises, tend to invest regionally, close to the home country (Ecuador, Panama, Peru, República Bolivariana de Venezuela, and, most recently, Brazil, Chile, and Mexico). While in the 1990s, Colombian outward FDI could be characterized as typical capital flight explained by a loss of confidence in the country, in the last decade by contrast, it has been the result of economic growth and the internalization strategies of Colombian enterprises.

Illegal capital flows associated with the illicit drug industry

Most of the revenues of Colombian drug traffickers has come from foreign markets. A kilogram of cocaine sold per gram in Europe or the United States generates revenues 50 to 100 times the export value in Colombia.

There are no data on the value of all domestic cash seizures, but most have been in U.S. dollars. Fiscalía staff describe a case of the seizure in 2008 of US$3 million in cash. They found that the bills were soiled and smelled of soil, which indicate that they had been stored underground. They interpret this as a sign that the dollars had been brought into the country and stashed away without any intention of sending them abroad. They also claim that, the few times the government has found stashes of Colombian pesos, these have belonged to the guerrillas. These pesos are likely to be the product of kidnappings for ransom and extortions. When the findings have been mixed, both pesos and dollars, the latter account for the vast majority of the find.[22] Remarkably, in Bogotá between August and October 2010, US$80 million and €17 million were found and seized altogether in five locations. These monies supposedly belonged to El Loco Barrera, a well-known trafficker.[23]

A main problem faced by traffickers is how to bring such resources into Colombia.[24] The traditional money laundering system of placing the cash in the financial sector, layering to hide the origin of the funds, and then integrating the resources into the legal economy is not necessarily desired by these people. Drug revenues have been brought into the country in many ways: physical cash, real sector contraband, underinvoicing imports

and overinvoicing exports, and fake labor remittances have been important. Rocha (1997) finds that illegal flows hidden in the current account of
the balance of payments show that the value of underinvoiced imports and
overinvoiced exports, plus Central Bank foreign exchange purchases of
fake labor and other remittances, averaged about US$1 billion a year.[25]
Given that various estimates place the total value of annual illegal drug
revenue brought from abroad in the 1990s at between US$2 billion and
US$5 billion, it is clear that the latter methods were important.[26]

Physical contraband has been another important method for bringing
drug money into the country. As noted above, contraband is socially
acceptable for many Colombians. Every city has a *San Andresito*, a shop-
ping center where contraband is known to be sold openly, mixed with similar legal imports.[27] Computers and other electronic equipment are favorite
illegal imports. These and other bulky items with empty space in the inte-
rior, such as household appliances, are also used to bring U.S. dollars into
the country. Many of these items are imported legally.

In the 1990s, cigarettes were a principal means of laundering drug
money. The international tobacco industry was at least an implicit accom-
plice in this process. Both British Tobacco and Philip Morris exported
huge amounts of cigarettes to Aruba, Curaçao, Margarita Island, Panama,
and other Caribbean locations, from which the cigarettes were smuggled
into Colombia. At almost any traffic light, one could find someone selling
cigarettes. The case of Aruba is remarkable in this respect, as its cigarette
imports were equal to 25 percent of the island's national income (Steiner
1997). For many years, the Philip Morris advertising budget in Colombia
exceeded the value of official Philip Morris cigarette exports to Colombia.
The official Philip Morris response to Colombian officials who questioned these advertising expenditures was simply that they were trying to
increase their market share even though they had over 70 percent of the
market already.[28] When these facts became known, there was a public out-
cry that led to negotiations between the government and the tobacco
companies to suppress this contraband (Thoumi 2003). Several local governments sued the tobacco companies for tax evasion, and, in a June 2009
agreement, Philip Morris agreed to pay US$200 million without acknowl-
edging any wrongdoing or accepting any liability. Cigarette smuggling
was a case in which there was simultaneous capital inflow and outflow.
The tobacco companies were selling their products in Curaçao, a free

port, for consumption in Colombia, thereby evading import and income taxes in Colombia.

During the 1990s, the illegal drug industry evolved substantially. The area under cultivation with illegal crops grew dramatically. The government succeeded in destroying the Medellín cartel. The Cali cartel expanded, but was then also destroyed by the government. Trafficking organizations became smaller, and their armed branches became weaker. The paramilitary organizations that had developed through links with the illegal industry gained ascendancy over the traditional traffickers because they gained control of areas in which cocaine was refined, as well as of trafficking corridors. They also controlled some coca- and poppy-growing regions.

Another change in the industry was caused by the increased involvement of Mexican traffickers in cocaine distribution in the United States. The pressure exerted by the United States on the Caribbean routes beginning in the late 1980s led to the displacement of the traffic to Mexico and the Pacific coast. Colombians started hiring Mexicans to smuggle cocaine into the United States, but Mexicans soon realized that they could have their own distribution networks and the power to gain greater profit by selling directly in the U.S. market. Furthermore, as the large Colombian cartels weakened, the relative power of the Mexican organizations increased. As a result, a significant number of Colombian traffickers now sell their cocaine in Mexico or in Central America to the powerful Mexican cartels. This has lowered the revenues of the Colombian cocaine industry and thus also the amount of money to be laundered in Colombia.

The use of the illegal revenues has also evolved. The early traffickers invested in real estate and some businesses. During the surge in the market for marijuana in the early 1970s, there was a real estate boom in Barranquilla and Santa Marta, the two cities closest to the marijuana-growing region in the Sierra Nevada de Santa Marta. When the Cali and Medellín cartels gained prominence, the cities experienced another real estate boom. Traffickers, mainly from the Medellín cartel, invested heavily in rural land, while traffickers from Cali appeared to prefer urban real estate and investments in various industries and services.[29] The concentration of rural land among armed groups has been substantial. Reyes Posada (1997) estimates that, by 1995, drug traffickers already controlled over 4 million hectares. This process has continued as the territorial control by armed groups strengthened (Reyes Posada 2009).

During the last decade, the control of the industry by warlords has meant that a significant share of the illegal drug revenues has been used to fund the armed conflict: the purchase of weapons, payments to the armed personnel in the counterinsurgency, and the like. This presents a problem in estimating illegal capital inflows because it is difficult to define weapons as capital. A study by the intergovernmental Financial Action Task Force concludes that "a project team investigated the links between narcotics trafficking and terrorist financing, but had to conclude that this subject was less suitable for analysis through publicly accessible information" (FATF 2005, 1). This assertion might be valid in cases of international terrorist organizations that implement suicide attacks or plant bombs, but do not have armies to support. In the case of Colombia, there is no question that drugs have sustained the armed personnel and allowed the guerrillas and paramilitary groups to grow. It is remarkable that, before the expansion of the coca plantings, FARC was able to survive, though it had never become an important problem or a threat to the establishment. Similarly, the paramilitary movement became strong only after coca and cocaine had come to account for important activities.

Conclusion

Over the last 35 years, the main issue in illegal capital flows has been the consequences of the entry of the foreign revenues of the illicit drug industry into the country. In contrast to many other countries, the main policy issue has been the control of illegal capital inflows, not the control of illegal outflows.

From the 1970s onward, these revenues have been invested in the legal economy and have created a particularly grave problem in rural and urban real estate. They have also aggravated rural land concentration, which has been a factor in making Colombia a more violent country, with a displacement of people second only to Sudan in the world. There is no question that, although almost 80 percent of the population is urban, the unresolved land problem remains a key policy issue in Colombia.

The government has been unable to impose the rule of law over the national territory, and various regions have developed their own norms. Other factors, including the persistently high level of violence, have compounded the problem, and civil society has become increasingly indifferent to the rule of law. The decision about whether to respect a law has become similar to an investor's portfolio decision in which the risks of various actions are weighed to determine what to do.

Not surprisingly, law enforcement has become a constant struggle, which reflects the gap between the law and socially acceptable behavior. Many government officials either do not believe in the laws or are unable to enforce them. Thus, although the country's AML legislation is one of the most advanced in the world, the results have been meager, and there is little need to take illegal capital abroad to protect it.

Controlling internal and external illegal capital flows presents a daunting policy problem given that a large proportion of the population considers the law as a grey area that one may or may not respect. As long as the conflict between the formal (legal) and informal (social) norms persists, illegal economic activities will flourish in Colombia. Closing this gap requires significant institutional and cultural change.

Notes

1. For example, Pablo Ardila, former governor of Cundinamarca Department, who was sentenced to jail in 2007 on kleptocracy charges, had transferred substantial assets abroad, but, his lifestyle in Colombia was incongruent with his reported income and caught the attention of the authorities. He regularly brought money from accounts in Panama and other offshore centers back to Colombia to support his high living standard ("Las cuentas del Gobernador," *El Espectador*, November 27, 2007).
2. "Colombia is a major source country for women and girls trafficked to Latin America, the Caribbean, Western Europe, Asia, and North America, including the United States, for purposes of commercial sexual exploitation and involuntary servitude" (U.S. Department of State, *Trafficking in Persons Report, June 2009* [Washington, DC, 2009], 107).
3. "Because of its geography, Colombia was until the early XX century the Latin American country with the lowest per-capita international trade. Palmer (1980, p. 46) shows that as late as 1910 Colombian exports per capita were 77% of the second lowest country (Honduras), 67% of those of Peru, 52% of those of República Bolivariana de Venezuela, 12% of those of Argentina and 9% of those of Uruguay. Only the development of the coffee industry modified this condition" (Thoumi 1995, 18).
4. These data are consistent with a graph in Marulanda (2006, 50) that, unfortunately, does not provide numbers. In the graph, the ratio of deposits to GDP follows a similar path.

5. One of the authors of this chapter, for example, closed a savings account in 2008 that had a balance of about US$7,000 because the interest received was less than the monthly cost of the account.

6. Rural land property has always been a key issue in Colombian society. Land has been a symbol of wealth and power and remains so for many Colombians despite the rapid modernization that the country has experienced (Zamosc 1986; Fajardo 1986). *La Violencia* of the 1940s and 1950s, during which at least 200,000 Colombians (about 1.8 percent of the population) were killed, was, to a great degree, a fight over land, and it generated large displacements of people because armed bands were killing peasants and forcing many others off their land (Guzmán, Fals Borda, and Umaña Luna 1962; Fals Borda 1982).

7. The website of the center is at http://www.internal-displacement.org/countries/colombia.

8. It is remarkable that this gap was the main issue in the campaign for the 2010 presidential election.

9. Over 50 years ago, Banfield's pathbreaking book on southern Italy (1958) referred to the society there as "amoral familism." Today, in Colombia, even this has weakened to the point that we have "amoral individualism."

10. These beliefs are not new. A good example is Augusto Ramírez-Moreno's column in *El Siglo* on March 20, 1936, cited by Acevedo-Carmona (1995, 153): "The Liberal regime has declared civil war on Colombians. . . . There is a need to disobey. Citizens are relieved from obeying the wicked laws and the illegitimate authorities in power." Remarkably, the reference was to the duly elected government and Congress. During *La Violencia*, some Catholic priests, such as Monsignor Builes of Santa Rosa de Osos, incited his flock by preaching that killing Liberals was not sinful.

11. Banks have taken strong measures. Banco de Bogotá, for example, has a team of 50 professionals, each of whom visits 50 clients a month to examine how their businesses operate.

12. The unit is working with Fenalco (the Colombian Retailers Association) and with the Chamber of Commerce of Bogotá. They all support and encourage investigative journalism into issues related to money laundering.

13. Author interviews with staff of the Financial Information and Analysis Unit, March 2009.

14. Author interviews with Fiscalía staff, March 2009.

15. Author interviews with officials of the United Nations Office on Drugs and Crime, March–April 2009.

16. For example, indexes of Transparencia por Colombia show that entities in the municipalities and departments are at substantially greater risk of corruption than the central government agencies that have much larger budgets. See Transparencia por Colombia, http://www.transparenciacolombia.org.co/LACORRUPCION/tabid/62/Default.aspx.

17. Since the new Constitution was enacted in 1991, for example, Congress has always had more members who have formerly been guerrillas than members who have formerly been in the armed forces.

18. For example, see Naím (2005), who covers the main cases of kleptocracy in developing countries; Colombia is not included. Jorge (2008) shows the significant wealth stashed away by Montesinos in Peru during the Fujimori administration.

19. The International Coffee Agreement was signed in 1962 and modified several times. Until 1994, it provided for export quotas for the producing countries, and this induced contraband.

20. Tax amnesties became almost routine as part of the tax reforms enacted by every administration. They were implemented by the López (1974), Turbay (1979), Betancur (1982), and Barco (1986) administrations (Thoumi 1995).

21. Disaggregated data on these investments are not public, but well-informed financial sector professionals agree that this was a period during which people sought ways to take capital out of the country and that it was possible to do so legally through outward FDI in financial services.

22. Author interviews with Fiscalía staff, March 2009.

23. "Más de US$ 200.000 millones hallados en caletas en Bogotá, a manos del Estado," *El Espectador*, March 31, 2011.

24. The physical weight and size of the dollars from sales abroad exceed the volume and weight of the cocaine itself.

25. Since the mid-1970s, the Central Bank has frequently changed its foreign exchange purchasing policies. These changes were particularly important before 1991 when the country had strict foreign exchange controls. Since then, under a system in which there is legal parallel market, a bank policy of easing purchasing requirements has lost importance.

26. Estimates of Colombian GDP in U.S. dollars vary. In the early 1990s, they were around the US$100 billion level. The estimates have increased substantially in recent years.

27. The origin of this term is consistent with the gap in Colombia between legal and social norms. In the mid-1950s, during his presidency, General Rojas-Pinilla wished to develop the Archipelago of San Andrés and Providencia in the Caribbean near Nicaragua, but he decided against a program to attract foreign tourists and promoted tourism by Colombians instead, given that the vast majority could not afford vacations in other Caribbean resorts. To make it attractive for Colombians to visit San Andrés and Providencia, Rojas-Pinilla allowed Colombians who spent a few days there to purchase certain articles tax free while vacationing. This was a time of strict foreign exchange controls, high tariffs, import quotas, and prohibitions. San Andrés became a de facto smuggling-tourism center. Store owners underinvoiced their sales, and tourists brought back expensive and prohibited goods, particularly home appliances: thus, the name San Andresitos.

28. Interview with Miguel Fadul Jr., director of the Colombian Commercial Office in Washington, DC, August 1998.

29. The leaders of the Cali cartel were known for their investments in a large drug store chain, real estate management agencies, several factories, and, at one point, a bank.

References

Acevedo-Carmona, D. 1995. *La mentalidad de las élites sobre la violencia en Colombia (1936–1949)*. Bogotá: IEPRI and El Áncora Editores.

Baker, R. W. 2005. *Capitalism's Achilles Heel: Dirty Money and How to Renew the Free-Market System*. Hoboken, NJ: John Wiley & Sons.

Banfield, E. C. 1958. *The Moral Basis of a Backward Society*. With the assistance of L. F. Banfield. New York: Free Press.

Bushnell, D. 1993. *The Making of Modern Colombia: A Nation in Spite of Itself*. Berkeley, CA: University of California Press.

Child Soldiers International. 2008. *Child Soldiers: Global Report 2008*. London: Child Soldiers International.

Fajardo, D. 1986. *Haciendas, campesinos y políticas agrarias en Colombia, 1920–1980*. Bogotá: Centro de Investigaciones para el Desarrollo.

Fals Borda, O. 1982. *Historia de la cuestión agraria en Colombia, 1982*. Bogotá: Carlos Valencia Editores.

FATF (Financial Action Task Force). 2005. "Money Laundering & Terrorist Financing Typologies, 2004–2005." Report, June 10, FATF, Paris. http://www.fatf-gafi.org/dataoecd/16/8/35003256.pdf.

Guzmán, G., O. Fals Borda, and E. Umaña Luna. 1962. *La violencia en Colombia: estudio de un proceso social*. Bogotá: Tercer Mundo Editores.

Herrán, M. T. 1987. *La sociedad de la mentira*. 2nd ed. Bogotá: Fondo Editorial CEREC–Editorial la Oveja Negra.

Jorge, G. 2008. "La experiencia de Perú: el caso 'Fujimori-Montesinos.'" In *Recuperación de activos de la corrupción*, ed. G. Jorge, 231–51. Buenos Aires: Editores del Puerto.

Kalmanovitz, S. 1989. *La encrucijada de la sinrazón y otros ensayos*. Bogotá: Tercer Mundo Editores.

Marulanda, B. 2006. "Una nueva política para un mayor acceso a los servicios financieros en Colombia." In *La Extensión del crédito y servicios financieros: obstáculos, propuestas y buenas prácticas*, ed. Secretaría General Iberoamericana, 49–60. Madrid: Secretaría General Iberoamericana.

Mockus, A. 1994. "Anfibios culturales y divorcio entre ley, moral y cultura." *Análisis Político* 21.

Naím, M. 2005. *Illicit: How Smugglers, Traffickers, and Copycats Are Hijacking the Global Economy*. New York: Anchor Books.

Nelson, R. R., T. P. Schultz, and R. L. Slighton. 1971. *Structural Change in a Developing Economy: Colombian Problems and Prospects*. Princeton, NJ: Princeton University Press.

Palmer, D. S. 1980. *Peru: the Authoritarian Tradition*. New York: Praeger Publishers.

Perry, G. E., W. F. Maloney, O. S. Arias, P. Fajnzylber, A. D. Mason, and J. Saavedra-Chanduvi. 2007. *Informality: Exit and Exclusion; Building Effective and Legitimate Institutions*. Latin America and Caribbean Studies. Washington, DC: World Bank.

Puyana-García, G. 2005. *¿Cómo somos? Los Colombianos: reflexiones sobre nuestra idiosincrasia y cultura.* Bogotá: Panamericana Editorial.

Ramírez, C., M. Zuluaga, and C. Perilla. 2010. "Perfil Migratorio de Colombia 2010." Report, June, International Organization for Migration, Bogotá. http://publications.iom.int/bookstore/free/PERFIL_27ABRIL_IMPUESTAS.PDF.

Reyes Posada, A. 1997. "La compra de tierras por narcotraficantes en Colombia." In *Drogas ilícitas en Colombia: su impacto económico, político y social,* ed. F. E. Thoumi, 279–96. Bogotá: Editorial Planeta.

———. 2009. *Guerreros y campesinos: el despojo de la tierra en Colombia.* With the assistance of Liliana Duica-Amaya. Bogotá: Friedrich Ebert Stiftung and Grupo Editorial Norma.

Rocha, R. 1997. "Aspectos económicos de las drogas ilegales en Colombia." In *Drogas ilícitas en Colombia: su impacto económico, político y social,* ed. F. E. Thoumi, 141–51. Ariel ciencia politica. Bogotá: Editorial Planeta.

———. 2000. *La economía Colombiana tras 25 años de narcotráfico.* Bogotá: Siglo del Hombre Editores.

———. 2005. "Sobre las magnitudes del narcotráfico." In *Narcotráfico en Colombia: economía y violencia,* ed. A. Rangel, 145–288. Bogotá: Fundación Seguridad & Democracia.

Rojas-Suárez, L. 2006. "El panorama regional." In *La extensión del crédito y servicios financieros: obstáculos, propuestas y buenas prácticas,* ed. Secretaría General Iberoamericana, 17–41. Madrid: Secretaría General Iberoamericana.

Rubio, M. 2004. "Kidnapping and Armed Conflict in Colombia." Paper presented at the Center for the Study of Civil War's workshop, "Techniques of Violence in Civil War," Peace Research Institute Oslo, Oslo, August 20–21.

Schneider, F. G., and R. Klinglmair. 2004. "Shadow Economies around the World: What Do We Know?" IZA Discussion Paper 1043 (March), Institute for the Study of Labor, Bonn. ftp://repec.iza.org/RePEc/Discussionpaper/dp1043.pdf.

Steiner, R. 1997. *Los dólares del narcotráfico.* Cuadernos de Fedesarrollo 2. Bogotá: Fedesarrollo–Tercer Mundo.

Tafur Saiden, C. 2009. "Bancarización: una aproximación al caso colombiano a la luz de América Latina." *Estudios Gerenciales* 25 (110): 13–37, Universidad Icesi, Cali, Colombia.

Thoumi, F. E. 1987. "Some Implications of the Growth of the Underground Economy in Colombia." *Journal of Interamerican Studies and World Affairs* 29 (2): 35–53.

———. 1995. *Political Economy and Illegal Drugs in Colombia.* Boulder, CO: Lynne Rienner.

———. 2003. *Illegal Drugs, Economy and Society in the Andes.* Baltimore: Johns Hopkins University Press.

———. 2005. "Why a Country Produces Drugs and How This Determines Policy Effectiveness: A General Model and Some Applications to Colombia." In *Elusive Peace: International, National and Local Dimensions of Conflict in Colombia,* ed. C. Rojas and J. Meltzer, part 3. New York: Palgrave Macmillan.

UIAF (Financial Information and Analysis Unit). 2008. "Description of Typologies Published by the UIAF, 2004–2008." Report, UIAF, Bogotá.

United Nations. 2009. "Assistance in Mine Action: Report of the Secretary-General." Document A/64/287 (August 12), United Nations General Assembly, New York.

World Bank. 1972. *Economic Growth of Colombia: Problems and Prospects*. World Bank Country Economic Report. Washington, DC: World Bank; Baltimore: Johns Hopkins University Press.

Yunis, E. 2003. *¿Por qué somos así? ¿Qué pasó en Colombia? Análisis del mestizaje*. Bogotá: Editorial Temis.

Zamosc, L. 1986. *The Agrarian Question and the Peasant Movement in Colombia: Struggles of the National Peasant Association, 1967–1981*. Cambridge Latin American Studies. Cambridge, U.K.: Cambridge University Press.

6

Human Trafficking and International Financial Flows

Pierre Kopp

Abstract

Little attention has been paid to the financial flows generated by human trafficking. Nonetheless, adding the many different flows of money linked to human trafficking together into one big number generates a meaningless figure. The socioeconomic consequences of each monetary flow are closely linked to the characteristics of the specific component of trafficking the flow reflects. Following the money flows can provide useful information on the heterogeneity of human trafficking.

The flow of money entering in the source countries and linked to human trafficking is negligible if it is compared, for example, with total remittances. Most of the profits made by petty traffickers stay in the host countries. The only important flow of money internationally results from criminal organizations. It is almost impossible to distinguish the profits of human trafficking from those associated with the core businesses of criminal organizations (prostitution, illegal drugs, counterfeiting, corruption, and so on).

The research described in this chapter, even if preliminary, suggests that money flows entering developing countries and linked to human trafficking are merged into broader flows of criminal money. There is no evidence that the flows have a particular, specific impact on the countries exporting the humans. Whatever the source of the criminal money, the impact is mostly the same.

Introduction

Human trafficking has gained wide attention in recent years. Important debates have focused on the magnitude of the problem, the involvement of criminal organizations, and the share of sexual exploitation in the global phenomenon. However, little attention has been paid to the financial flows generated by this trafficking. This is all the more regrettable because it seems that these flows should be easier to bring to light than the trafficking patterns themselves, which, for obvious reasons, remain shrouded in secrecy. Analysis of the monetary flows is thus likely to provide a precious tool for the representation of a traffic that is difficult to chart directly. Indeed, pursuing the flows of money provides useful information on the design of human trafficking patterns worldwide. Furthermore, it offers an excellent ground for overturning the overly simplistic image of these activities that portrays them as entirely controlled by transnational criminal organizations. Instead, this analysis allows us to construct an image of a world that is deeply fragmented and heterogeneous.

A refined understanding of financial flows can also help build the structure necessary to analyze the impact of the traffic on the developing countries that are home to most of the individuals who are implicated in the traffic. Indeed, if formerly trafficked individuals develop sources of revenue, they often channel part of this revenue back to their countries of origin. On a purely macroeconomic level, the impact of these flows of money is not sensitive to the origin of the victims. Incoming money flows improve the balance of payments; outgoing flows cause a deterioration in the external position of the country. However, tracking the socioeconomic impact of the inflows of money cannot be accomplished with any accuracy if the origin of the victims of trafficking and of the money is not taken into account. The socioeconomic consequences of monetary flows are known to be determined by the characteristics of the activities that generate them. Social relations or a country's reputation can be affected by illegal activities even if these don't account for significant economic transactions and have almost no macroeconomic effect. This might be even truer at the provincial or city levels. For these reasons, the financial repercussions of the trade in human beings must be analyzed with an eye to the specificities of the various activities for which compensation is being received. Only a nuanced account of financial flows can provide the information necessary to distinguish the various types of impacts human trafficking have on source countries.

This chapter aims to structure the elements of a methodological framework for a nuanced analysis of the financial flows of human trafficking. It argues that the methods used to establish global estimates are seriously flawed in that they conflate sources in such a way as to produce nonsensical results. If estimates of the illegal drug trade are added to the turnover associated with heroin and with cannabis, the result fails to take into account the fact that the trafficking networks and the source countries are different. Such problems are compounded if it is a matter of estimating human trafficking: whereas, in the case of drugs, at least the products are clearly identified and the wholesale and retail prices more or less well known (Kilmer and Reuter 2009); in the case of human trafficking, the modes of distribution do not allow for pertinent price observations and make it difficult to identify the various components in the turnover.

The contribution of this chapter will be more analytical than empirical. Our key contention is that more light on how criminal networks are organized and how they run their various activities will allow us to improve our understanding of both the origins and the destinations of the flows of money. This, in turn, will furnish two types of benefits. First, knowing where the money comes from and where it goes to illuminates the various strategies of those people who are active in human trafficking. A clearer understanding of how traffickers conduct their business might provide new suggestions to the authorities who seek to control the trade. Second, identifying the patterns of financial flows can provide a better understanding of their socioeconomic impact on the source countries.

The next section will give some insight into the main theoretical controversies that have surfaced around the definition of human trafficking. The subsequent section describes how the hopes of individuals to find a promised land pushes, more or less voluntarily, millions of people into the hands of criminals. Monetary flows are generated both by the compensation demanded of people for help with illegal border crossings and by the revenue of those criminals who exploit the slaves, prostitutes, and so on that these people become after they have crossed the borders. This is examined in the penultimate section. The last section details the design of the criminal organizations involved in this trafficking and considers their respective needs for money laundering. This section concludes with a taxonomy of the illegal flows generated by human trafficking.

Conceptual Issues

Human trafficking is a part of the shadow economy (Fleming, Roman, and Farrell 2000). The term *traffic* in economics explicitly refers to the idea of transporting merchandise. However, if the merchandise is human, there are specific difficulties in establishing definitions. A major difficulty emerged when United Nations agencies were charged with establishing official definitions of smuggling and trafficking. Nonetheless, we contend that the conceptual problem with which the legal definitions grapple is not necessarily the most relevant angle for studying trafficking from an economic standpoint.

Consider the definitions provided by the United Nations Protocol against the Smuggling of Migrants by Land, Sea, and Air and the United Nations Protocol to Suppress and Punish Trafficking in Persons, Especially Women and Children. The Protocols are supplements to the Palermo convention, the United Nations Convention against Transnational Organized Crime, adopted by the United Nations General Assembly on November 15, 2000 (see UNODC 2004).

The smuggling protocol defines smuggling as "the procurement, in order to obtain, directly or indirectly, a financial or other material benefit, of the illegal entry of a person into a State Party of which the person is not a national or a permanent resident" (article 3), and the trafficking protocol defines trafficking as "the recruitment, transportation, transfer, harbouring or receipt of persons, by means of the threat or use of force or other forms of coercion, of abduction, of fraud, of deception, of the abuse of power or a position of vulnerability or of the giving or receiving of payments or benefits to achieve the consent of a person having control over another person, for the purpose of exploitation" (article 3). The main forms of exploitation are prostitution, forced labor, slavery, and the removal of organs.

Buckland (2008) recalls that those who gathered in Vienna to negotiate the trafficking protocol were united in mandate, but sorely divided when it came to choosing the road ahead. The major cleavage became apparent around the issue of definitions. Is trafficking only about prostitution? Is all prostitution trafficking? Are men trafficked, too? The negotiators' answer (according to Buckland) reflects a certain ambivalence in the fundamental conception of trafficking. While the protocol includes a broad range of activities in the definition, both the title and the statement of purpose cast trafficked people as victims and make clear that the victims of trafficking whom it seeks to protect are, first and foremost, women and children in forced prostitution. The obvious consequence of overemphasizing the victim status is that it allows an artificial and tendentious distinction between smuggled people (painted largely as criminal by international institutions) and trafficked people. As studies have shown, however, smuggled people may be trapped in debt bondage or subject to exploitative working conditions, and it therefore seems problematic to maintain conceptual categories that cast these people simply as criminals rather than victims (Andreas and van der Linden 2005).

Given that intentionality is key to determining the nature of acts in legal terms, it is not surprising that those who drafted the official definitions felt compelled to take a stance on the issue. Our concern, however, is less with ascribing legal responsibility than with reaching an accurate description of this illegal global traffic. For our purposes, it seems that distinguishing between voluntary and involuntary immigration raises more problems than it solves. It seems clear that, if an organ is taken from a dead body and sent to another country to serve as a transplant without consent, this is an involuntary traffic. Likewise, a clandestine migrant whose passport is confiscated and who finds himself enslaved has not chosen this situation. Yet, grouping these two movements together under a label of involuntary (or voluntary) obscures the different sorts of traffic involved in these two cases.

Furthermore, the distinction between voluntary migration in search of opportunity and involuntary trafficking of human laborers may be conceptually satisfying, but applying this distinction in practice is close to impossible. While the conditions of their migration may, indeed, seem shocking, it is far from clear that all migrants who are treated as goods to be exploited are acting involuntarily. What of migrants who turn themselves into transportable commodities because they expect to obtain a better price for their work in a target country? Classic economics theory would hold that such a decision may be deemed rational within a normal economic framework because no one is better placed than the individual to know whether what he is doing is in his self-interest no matter whether or not his decision turns out, in the end, to have been a good calculation. Tens of thousands (perhaps even hundreds of thousands) of clandestine migrants who cross the Mexican–United States border each year purchase the services of smugglers and become part of the flow of smuggled human beings. The persistence of the flow and the fact that the same individuals may recross the border several times, depending upon the state of the employment market (and the riskiness of the crossing), can be taken to indicate that the decision is voluntary.

And, yet, those who might initially be thought merely to be purchasing the services of smuggling networks can, in effect, become subject to trafficking. Massive illegal immigration and the strengthening of controls (for example, with the fence along extensive sectors of the Mexico–United States border) have created situations in which border crossing has become an industry. To improve their chances of successfully crossing the border, candidates for illegal immigration appeal to underground networks for human smuggling. Crossing the border with a network enables one to benefit from the network's investments (trucks, corruption, tunnels, and so on), but such a choice also exposes one to great danger. To avoid endangering their investments, or simply to skimp on costs, smugglers are sometimes prepared to dispose of their human cargo in the sea or in the desert. Furthermore, the condition of absolute dependence into which the individual is placed if he has put his destiny into the hands of people running a network exposes him to all sorts of risks, sometimes dramatic. Clandestine migrants can be robbed of their papers and money; they can be raped and killed. In such circumstances, it becomes disingenuous to maintain that they are not being treated as merchandise.

If one considers, furthermore, that the basis on which the decision to migrate is made may already be determined in part by the smuggling networks, the category of voluntary migration becomes even more problematic. To sustain their activity, smugglers attempt to recruit new candidates for crossings and develop their activities in source countries. While they seem the best source of information, the smugglers, by presenting a false image of the conditions under which illegal emigration can take place, increase the number of their clients and maintain a supply effect. Through this dynamic, the offer of smuggling contributes to an activation of the demand (Jewell and Molina 2009).[1] Insofar as it is created at least in part by false information, even the initial demand for smuggling cannot simply be considered entirely voluntary.

Assessing the voluntary or involuntary character of migration is thus extremely difficult. More importantly, the attempt produces misleading categorizations of activity at least as regards the economic reality. Yet, the principle of this distinction, inherited from legal debates, underlies the conceptual categories used by the international agencies that monitor or assess these activities.

In this chapter, we use the term *trafficking* in a broad sense to cover both smuggling and trafficking as defined by the United Nations. Indeed, we adopt a broad definition of trafficking that includes all means of smuggling, prostitution, organ traffic, slavery, and so on.[2] Some of these activities are clearly coercive; some are not; and some are partially coercive. However, all must be considered if we are to establish a taxonomy of the different flows of money linked to human trafficking.

To underline the stakes in choosing this broad definition, we now briefly consider estimates that have been made of international human trafficking using other definitions so as to emphasize how poor definitions can lead to problematic numbers.

It is exceedingly difficult to estimate the scale of human trafficking. Evaluating illegal markets is always difficult. Their clandestine nature makes them difficult to observe, and the absence of a uniform international standard of illegality renders the comparison and collation of observations a perilous exercise. But the task of evaluating human trafficking is even more difficult than evaluating other illegal markets, such as the market for drugs. In the case of the drug market, the best estimates of quantities and revenues come from national population surveys (for example, Abt Associates 2001). In the case of human trafficking, there is no comparable mass consumer market that can provide demand-side estimates.

In 2001, there were an estimated 175 million people living outside their countries of birth, a number that had doubled since 1975 (United Nations 2002). Most immigrants were living in Europe (56 million), followed by Asia (50 million), and North America (41 million), but most of these came legally. The International Organization for Migration (IOM) is unable to provide figures that accurately reflect the amplitude of the phenomenon of human trafficking as a whole.[3] IOM's global database on human trade contains information on about 13,500 victims who have benefited from IOM assistance. This figure in no way reflects the global reality. Until IOM can collect data through a reliable and systematic method, the following estimates—which must be considered as crude guesses—are being used by IOM to evaluate the amplitude of the global phenomenon of the trade in humans.

According to a handbook for parliamentarians, human trafficking affects 2.5 million individuals every day (UNODC and IPU 2009). This represents a low-end estimate of the number of victims of the trade at any given moment.[4] The estimate is based on analysis of publicly available data published between 1995 and 2004 and presented for the first time in 2005. It has not been updated since.

IOM considers that 800,000 victims of the trade in humans cross international borders every year or are authorized to leave or enter the territory of a country and are thereafter exploited.[5] This is a high-end estimate. It was established by the U.S. government based on data collected in 2006.

Soon, these estimates were no longer being mentioned in the annual report of the U.S. Department of State (2010) on human trafficking in the world. In their place, the report mentioned estimates from the International Labour Organization (ILO) on forced labor, according to which 12.3 million people are victims of forced labor, servitude, forced child labor, or sexual servitude at any given moment in the world (ILO 2009). This is an estimate established by ILO in 2005 and represents stocks of forced labor on a worldwide scale. Among these 12.3 million people, 2.5 million are considered victims of human trafficking. According to ILO, the rest of the people are victims of forced labor who are not considered victims of the trade in humans (that is, their exploitation was unrelated to their entry into the destination country). ILO also indicates that the amount of lost wages from forced labor is US$21 billion.

The United Nations Office on Drugs and Crime has estimated the monetary profits from the worldwide trade in persons at US$7 billion annually (UNODC 2009). About US$3 billion is associated with human trafficking involving around 150,000 victims (which means approximately US$20,000 per victim), and over US$6 billion is associated with the smuggling of migrants, which involves 3 million people (US$2,000 per person). The United Nations Children's Fund estimates the profits at US$10 billion (UNODC 2009; ILO 2009). ILO estimates that the total illicit profits produced by trafficked forced labor in one year at slightly less than US$32 billion (ILO 2009). Others have estimated the profit from commercial sexual exploitation at above US$30 billion a year.

None of these estimates is convincing. The estimates on the numbers of persons involved in human trafficking fluctuate between two extremes. At one extreme, the estimates reflect only the number of people known to have been harmed; in this case, the estimates fail to account for all the victims who are reluctant or incapable of reporting their situation. At the other extreme, the estimates include all illegal migrants, thereby failing to discount for those who have not been trafficked in any sense.

The estimates of the dollar flows generated by human trafficking are often produced for advocacy purposes to underline the magnitude of the problem. However, adding flows together that have nothing in common other than the units in which they are expressed does not produce meaningful values. One of the reasons many of the available data are too flawed to be useful is that they are often produced with an eye to isolating human trafficking from the illegal activities the trafficking facilitates. Human trafficking is, of course, a crime in itself, but its economic raison d'être is to supply a workforce for criminal or illegal activities. In this sense, human trafficking is a means and not an end; it is one step in a complex economic subsystem. If a political agenda drives the desire to separate out this element, it is almost impossible to develop good data.

The dearth of international data is not offset at the national level by good field studies. We know little about national figures on human trafficking. Staring (2006) is an exception; he provides some data on the Netherlands. He makes a distinction between human smuggling and human trafficking. Human smuggling in the Netherlands increased between 1994 and 2002 from 4 cases per year to 201, while human trafficking increased from 63 to 201. Staring notes both that the data are scarce and that, if they are available, the methods used for data collection are unclear.

Slavery and prostitution are other activities that derive from human trafficking. One might be tempted to distinguish between criminal activities that violate universal social norms (*malum in se*) and activities that may be (temporarily) prohibited by law, such as homosexuality or cannabis smoking (*malum in prohibitum*). However, this distinction does not make a great deal of sense from a legal policy standpoint insofar as both sorts of activity trigger law enforcement. It therefore seems reasonable to consider that all legally punishable activity involved in human trafficking is criminal.

These activities do not all cause identical harm to society. Criminal codes reflect these differences by modulating the severity of the punishments associated with various offenses. Obtaining false papers for an illegal migrant or harboring a clandestine person are often only fined, while slavery or prostitution is more severely punished. Other components of human trafficking are even closer to the core activity of classical organized crime. Indeed, human trafficking networks are sometimes intertwined with networks for the transportation of stolen goods or illegal merchandise (stolen cars, drugs). Persons involved in one type of network easily pass to another.

The respective shares of the different components of human trafficking are unknown. In the public imagination, human trafficking is often linked to the sex industry, but labor trafficking is probably more widespread, given the simple fact that the world market for labor is far greater than that for sex (Feingold 1998, 2005).[6] A detailed study by ILO (2005) finds that, of the estimated 9.5 million victims of forced labor in Asia, fewer than 10 percent are trafficked for commercial sexual exploitation. Worldwide, less than half of all trafficking victims are trafficked as part of the sex trade, according to the same report.

Can we describe the market for human trafficking? If we consider that organs or human beings are the merchandise exchanged, several interconnected markets for human merchandise would have to be taken into account: a prostitution market, an organ market, and a market for illegal manpower. As in any market, the suppliers put the merchandise on the market, and the purchasers buy it. The overall market would have the specificity that, occasionally, an individual may, if he has recovered some autonomy, put himself on the market and become both supplier and merchandise.

The market for human beings is not an ordinary market. The usual public policy recipes will not work in the same way they work on a classical market. Criminalization, for instance, directly affects the supply of and the demand for the merchandise (prostitution, organs, slaves, and so on), but it only has a limited and delayed impact on the flow of individuals who cross borders, whether on their own initiative or under the domination of a criminal group. The important point is that the supply of immigrants is not directly affected by the repression of a market segment. Thus, it takes time before repression on the markets of rich countries affects the supply of migration. Numerous buffers slow the transmission of incentives.

The Hope of a Promised Land

The value of accounting is to make goods that are not homogeneous into goods that are homogeneous. A dollar adds to a dollar, but what is there in common between a dollar paid by the clandestine immigrant to his smuggler and the dollar spent by a prostitute's customer? To understand clearly the nature of the various flows of money, we must examine and compare the corresponding components. Figure 6.1 summarizes the functioning of human trafficking.

Figure 6.1 shows that the supply of and demand for services (forced or not) in the markets for sex, illegal X-rated movies, organ transplants, slaves, and so on can be provided by a direct connection between the suppliers and the consumers in exchange (or not) for money. The suppliers of the criminal services can provide the connection. These criminal organizations or public employees corrupted by individual criminals can offer help to the illegal workers and services to consumers. In compensation, they receive money, which will be laundered if the sums are big, the flows are repeated, or the activity is connected to a criminal organization.

Figure 6.1. Human Trafficking: Supply and Demand

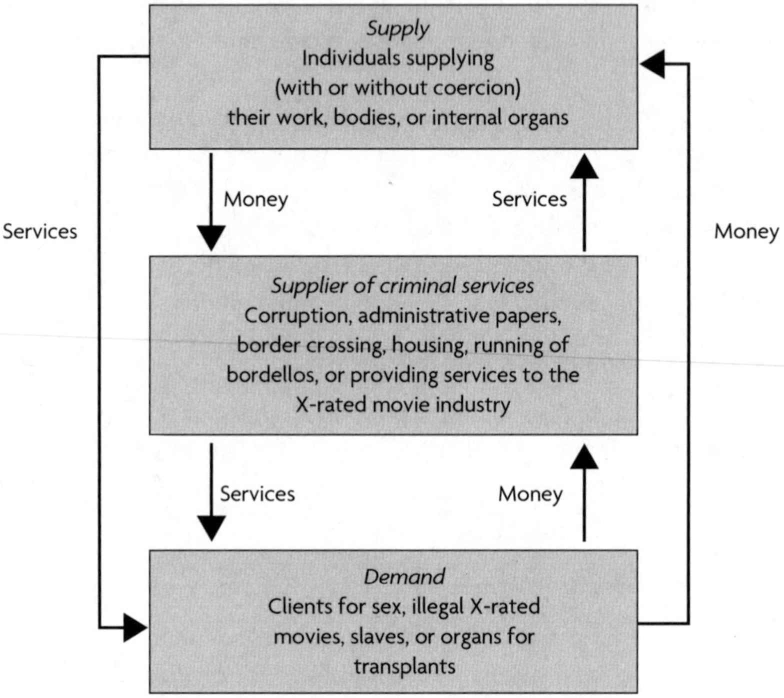

Source: Author compilation.

The motivations of illegal migrants

An act of free will may sometimes determine the decision to seek the help of smugglers to cross a border illegally, the use of *coyotes* (a smuggler of immigrants), for instance, at the Mexico–United States border (Spener 2009). In such cases, illegal immigrants momentarily place their destiny in the hands of the people who run a smuggling network and expect to recover their freedom on the other side of the border. There is a demand on the part of the individual immigrant and a supply of services through a criminal network. The decision of the immigrants may also be forced if the prospective immigrants are recruited or abused by the networks of smugglers and remain dependent on the networks once they have crossed the border. In this case, the individual becomes merchandise; the demand arises from those who want to import human beings, and the supply is provided by the network.

Thus, the supply and demand must be located differently according to whether the decision to cross the border is free or forced. Most often, the smugglers vaunt the benefits they offer. Often exaggerated and romanticized, the descriptions of the benefits are tailored to the expectations or desires of the prospective immigrants.

The economy of illegal immigration is based on the existence of two differentials (Cornelius et al. 2010). The first differential separates the wage levels in the source country and the host country. The second distinguishes the standards of living in the two countries.

First, the illegal immigrant provides manpower at a price that is lower than the price on the market in the host country or fills a gap in manpower of a particular type. This differential persists over time if anti-immigration regulations are sufficiently strict to remain a threat to the illegal immigrant. In the absence of legal barriers to entering the employment market, the wages of the illegal immigrant will tend to become aligned with the wages of the local employee. Recourse to illegal manpower is also a means of exerting pressure on local employees. Historically, illegal manpower is less unionized than the legal workforce, and contractors have often used the supply of illegal immigrants to force down the average union wage rate.

The second differential concerns the living conditions of illegal immigrants and of the local workforce. The fact that the illegal immigrants accept less than average wages normally means that they also live in more straitened circumstances. As long as the illegal immigrants accept or must accept such a differential, the initial characteristics remain intact (the lower wage rate). Over time and in some countries (the United States, but not Saudi Arabia, for example), the illegal immigrants will escape at least some of the initial conditions and will gain professional qualifications and bargaining power that will enable them to gain access to better employment status than they had on arrival.

The more transient the entry barriers, the more illegal immigrants can hope to melt into the legal workforce and make the individual trajectory of their jobs converge with that of the average employee in the country.

Occasionally, an individual may escape the initial conditions relatively quickly. Marriage remains an important possibility. Thus, a demographic gender imbalance can create a greater demand for one gender group (generally women, as in some agricultural areas in Europe). The online dating services that offer to organize dates and marriages between rural French men and women from Asian countries often operate on the borders of legality.

Moreover, some occupations seem always to require more manpower, enabling illegal immigrants to benefit from a certain rent of scarcity. Maids from the Philippines benefit from being Catholic and speaking English, which are valuable characteristics in the eyes of some European employers. These individuals manage to obtain hourly wages that are about 20 percent above the minimum wage. They do not have the social security advantages of the local workforce, but they can sometimes benefit from free health care coverage (in France and some Nordic countries).

Orrenius (2001), in an informative paper, notes that the earliest models of migration emphasize wage differentials as the impetus to mobility. Massey et al. (1987) and Massey (1987) break down the cost of migration into direct monetary costs, information and search costs, opportunity costs, and psychic costs. They demonstr ate that access to migrant networks reduces cost in all four categories. In the case of Mexico, access to a network gives access to more reliable coyotes, lowers the probability of apprehension, facilitates settlement, and shortens the job search.

It thus appears that those who become involved in human trafficking in the wide sense we are using in this chapter are sometimes forced to do so, but may often be considered clients who voluntarily use illegal services to immigrate. The expectation of quick improvement in earnings and the distorted bundle of information available through different channels—media, friends, family, former migrants, and smuggler networks—provide strong incentives for migration. During their journey or once in the host country, immigrants will, perhaps, recover their power to make free decisions. The longer they stay under the influence of a network, a criminal organization, or an employer that forces them to work for almost nothing, the longer they will be part of human trafficking. In the best possible configuration, their connection with trafficking will not last longer than the hours necessary to cross the border.

Monetary compensation

The monetary flows that accompany the flows of people we have described can be divided into three channels.

First are the immediate payments that occur at the border. These payments may be spread among several individuals. For example, a corrupt employee at the consulate of a rich country located in a poor country who delivers a tourist visa will receive a bribe. Most often, visa trafficking is the act of small groups of corrupt embassy employees. The amounts thus collected generally represent fringe benefits for low-level consular employees. Occasionally, the amounts are used to make small investments in the home country of the employees. More often, these amounts are spent locally or enable the satisfaction of vices or double lives. These flows therefore usually remain in the country that is the source of the manpower. Globally, they are insignificant.[7]

Second, clandestine immigrants can benefit from the paid help of a network to ease the border crossing. *Snakeheads* (the term used for smugglers in China) or coyotes (at the Mexican border) are most often members of a network. Sums collected by these networks represent criminal revenue. They are typically used in the country that is the source of the immigration. As a general rule, police control over the monetary flow is weak, and the money is used directly by the criminal organization without having to develop a sophisticated laundering strategy (Amuedo-Dorantes and Pozo 2005).

Third, illegal immigrants may be required to stay in contact with criminal networks after their arrival in host countries. It seems plausible that, particularly in the case of Chinese networks, illegal immigrants are forced to accept the continued collection of payments after their entry and during employment. Our conclusion is highly speculative, but it appears illegal Chinese immigrants may often be forced to pay during longer periods.

One explanation is that organizing the trip from China to the United States is more complicated than organizing the trip from Mexico. Hence, the price demanded for the service is higher, and the number of payments larger. It may also be that Latino workers are more prone to integrate into the general workforce, while Chinese immigrants are more likely to be working for businesses owned by people of Chinese ethnicity. In the first case, the workers are illegal, but are free to choose their employers, while, in the second case, the workers are restricted to a limited set of businesses. The latter workers often have to give a share of their wages to the criminal organization or repay business loans incurred with the criminal organization. Furthermore, the language barriers in the host country are relatively greater for speakers of the many idioms of China than for Spanish-speaking immigrants.

If a new immigrant cannot find a job independently, the connection with a criminal network remains strong. In such situations, the share of the payment made by the immigrant that is transferred to the source country is probably important. Indeed, the criminal organization may have reason to move its income as far as possible from the place where the criminal activity is ongoing. Another, more modest source of regular income for criminal organizations is the assistance provided to illegal immigrants in obtaining new identity papers or in gaining access to medical services.

Flows of money generated by human trafficking partly vanish in the host country if they are one-time payments to acquire a specific, time-limited service. The more personal and specific the illegal service, the more expensive it is. It is also most probably rendered by a criminal organization and not by an individual or small group. Additional payments are scheduled over time. The money ends up in the possession of a more sophisticated criminal organization, and a good part of it is probably channeled out of the host country and sheltered in the country of origin of the criminal organization.

Human Trafficking Is Also a Business

Human trafficking is not only driven by the desire of some inhabitants of poor countries to emigrate to rich countries. The flow must be considered, in part, the creation of a demand in the rich countries. Furthermore, the illegal networks that engineer border crossings and organize the related manpower-intensive criminal activities in rich countries have shown the ability to innovate. Motivated by the desire to increase their profits, they develop new products and services. Indeed, some criminal organizations specialize in the production of criminal goods and services.

Criminal organizations are heterogeneous. Some have originated in the source countries and undertake operations in host countries. An example is the Chinese Triads. The Salvadoran Maras or Mara Salvatrucha, in contrast, originated in the United States and then spread to the home country of many of the members. The methods of these groups, particularly their management of financial flows, vary greatly. This heterogeneity makes it impossible to establish a strict correlation between a given criminal activity and the criminal financial flows.

The criminal portfolio

From a legal perspective, any group of more than two people who are committing crimes together can be deemed a criminal organization. We will, however, use the term only to describe substantially larger groups working together to achieve criminal ends.

Several decades have passed since Schelling (1967) and Buchanan (1973) analyzed the capacity of organized crime to impose its monopoly on criminal activities. Since then, many scholars and law enforcement agencies have conceived of organized crime groups as hierarchical, centralized, and bureaucratic and have come to consider their structure analogous to the structure of a modern corporation; the Mafia remains a paradigm (Abadinsky 1990; Cressey 1969).

Pioneer work has argued against the idea that the monopoly prevails as the natural structure for large-scale criminal activity. Studying the structure of the drug market, Reuter (1983), Reuter, MacCoun, and Murphy (1990), and Kleiman (1989) have underlined the difficulties that criminal organizations face in effectively imposing the barriers to entry necessary to preserve a monopoly. Reuter has challenged the myth of the American Mafia, arguing that, in the 1980s, the Mafia was only able to enjoy high levels of profit because of its prestige, but that it no longer possessed sufficient power to maintain the organization at the level of its reputation. According to Reuter, the Mafia is weakly centralized and has high coordination costs, which are structural consequences of illegality. Insufficient information and a weak definition of property rights of each of its subgroups deprive the Mafia of some of the profits that one might otherwise expect.

The more recent view argues that the concept of organized crime should be abandoned in favor of a criminal enterprise model (Block and Chambliss 1981; van Duyne 2007). Zhang and Chin (2002) note that the latter model suggests that networks are flexible and adaptive and that they can easily expand and contract to deal with the uncertainties of the criminal enterprise. Criminal organizations respond to varying market demands by narrowing or expanding their size; their organizational structures are not so much predesigned as shaped by external social and legal factors. Certain criminal groups, such as those involved in the construction or gambling businesses, may require an elaborate hierarchy and a clear division of labor. These are necessary organizational prerequisites to remaining in the illicit business. In contrast, criminal groups such as those involved in pawnshops and the fencing of stolen goods must respond rapidly to changing demand in the streets and therefore require little or no formal organizational structure. Prostitution, pornographic films, the traffic in organs, and the supply of illegal manpower are often monopolized by criminal organizations. These organizations respond to an existing demand, but they also create new demand. The innovative capabilities of criminal organizations enable them to convert individual preferences into commercial demand.

Some data confirm that, if human trafficking is a big business, it is mostly a disorganized criminal business that depends on individuals or small groups linked on an ad hoc basis. According to Feingold (2005), there is no standard profile of traffickers. They range from truck drivers and "village aunties" to labor brokers and police officers. Traffickers are as varied as the circumstances of their victims. Although some trafficking victims are literally kidnapped, most leave their homes voluntarily and slip into being trafficked on their journey. By the same token, some traffickers are as likely to purchase people as they are to transport them.

Participation in a criminal organization requires specific talents. Not everyone can be a smuggler or a flesh-peddler. Not everyone is prepared to risk prison or violence. The talent is therefore uncommon and attracts a price.

Smugglers. There is a scholarly consensus that most smugglers are not members of a criminal organization. Zhang and Chin (2002) and Zhang, Chin, and Miller (2007) write that Chinese human smuggling is dominated by ordinary citizens whose family networks and fortuitous social contacts have enabled them to pool resources to transport human cargoes around the world. Orrenius (2001) has studied the illegal immigration along the Mexico–United States border and emphasizes the evidence for easy entry into the trafficking industry. In theory, any migrant who has undertaken an illegal border crossing can use the experience to work as a coyote. We disagree with Andreas (2000) for whom the expense involved for the traffickers and smugglers has led to a parallel process of centralization as smaller, poorer, and less sophisticated operators are forced out of the market.

Many specialized roles have emerged in response to the particular tasks required in smuggling operations such as acquiring fraudulent documents, recruiting prospective migrants, serving as border crossing guides, driving smuggling vehicles, and guarding safe houses. These roles correspond to the successive stages of a smuggling operation: the recruiter is active at the beginning, and the debt collector at the end. Most of these activities take place in the host country and do not involve large amounts of money. The income they provide tends to stay in the host country and is probably quickly reinjected into the host economy through consumer spending.

Smuggling activities are normally carried out following negotiations between the smugglers and their clients that leave few opportunities for others to intervene. Smuggling operations consist in secretive and idiosyncratic arrangements known only to those directly involved. Furthermore, the contacts between the organizers of a smuggling operation and their clients are mostly one-on-one. This special business arrangement serves two crucial functions in an illicit economy: (1) it maximizes the smuggler's profit by monopolizing the services critical to specific aspects of the smuggling process, and (2) it minimizes the potential exposure to law enforcement.

Smugglers working along the border are the least skilled people in the trafficking chain. The risk is limited, and the reward is small. There is not a lot of evidence to document the risk. Former border agents consider that one in four illegal migrants is arrested, but many of these migrants make multiple attempts (Slagle 2004). The rates of apprehension by border patrols in Texas show large variations from one period to another (Orrenius 2001).

According to Orrenius (2001), in real terms (1994 U.S. dollars), the median reported coyote price per individual for a single crossing fell from more than US$900 in 1965 to about US$300 in 1994. Higher post-1994 prices (still below US$400) are consistent with the impact of greater enforcement on smuggler fees.[8] Large profits come only with the large numbers of people that can amortize fixed costs (such as regular bribes, safe houses, and so on). Although the value of the time devoted to smuggling should be taken into account, most of the revenue is profit.

Low as the prices of single border crossings are, if they are multiplied by the number of illegal immigrants, they generate revenues on the order of US$700 million annually, which is roughly equivalent to the revenue generated by 30 tons of imported cocaine (300 tons are imported annually).[9] In other words, importing illegal immigrants is a criminal business equivalent in size to 10 percent of the business of importing cocaine. The flow of money generated by this business is, nonetheless, negligible compared with the remittances sent by Mexicans living abroad, mostly in the United States, to their families in Mexico. These remittances are a substantial and growing part of the Mexican economy: in 2005, they reached US$18 billion (World Bank 2006).

A coyote's income does not create wealth in the way drug trafficking does. At a couple of hundred dollars per smuggled person, coyotes make too little to save. This income is mostly a transfer between individual A and individual B. The money is quickly reinvested in the economy without having a specific effect. Whether it is spent by the migrant or by the coyote, the money has the same socioeconomic impact.

Violence and other costs of trafficking. By contrast, other activities of criminal organizations create major costs and expose participants to the risk of arrest and other harms. Revenue from criminal activity should not systematically be interpreted as profit.

We know little about the costs that criminal organizations face, which makes it difficult to differentiate between gross income and profit. We also generally confuse accounting profit and economic profit. This shows up in our omissions of important cost elements accruing to criminal organizations. For example, violence is a specific characteristic of criminal activity. Criminals are exposed to a risk of arrest, but also to being attacked, injured, or killed by their clients or by other criminals. This is a factor in their costs.

Violence directed at migrants is not a necessary part of the illicit market. It is attenuated by the social networks, cultural norms, and contractual relationships in which the market is embedded (Kyle and Scarcelli 2009). Criminal organizations seem much less violent in human trafficking than in the drug market. Perhaps the reason is the absence of territoriality. The final distribution of drugs requires the control of a territory in a way that is not required in human trafficking.[10] Furthermore, the fact that drugs concentrate great value in a small volume creates a singular opportunity because it is possible to steal the stock of drugs from a dealer. It is impossible or, at least, more difficult to steal a stock of organs or clandestine immigrants. Violence is therefore fairly rare among the criminal organizations involved in human trafficking. We may thus legitimately consider that the costs are mainly reduced to the costs associated with logistics and corruption.

The less competitive a market is, the less it will be innovative. Drug markets are conservative, with little product innovation relative to legal market counterparts.[11] However, if a new drug is introduced on the market, waves of violence are observed. We might expect the same for criminal activities based on human trafficking, but what would constitute innovation in this field?

The pornographic film industry provides a good illustration of innovation without (much) violence. Note that it is an extremely competitive market: production costs are low, and entry in the business is easy.[12] Initially, the X-rated industry offered poor-quality films. Little by little, the quality improved. The scenarios became more sophisticated, and the shots improved. Progressively, the industry covered all sexual tastes. Now, the catalogue of X-rated offerings allows the consumer a wide choice of sexual orientation and diverse sexual practices. The supply is thus extremely varied. Having accomplished this range, the X-rated industry has also been able to renew itself by offering home movies and then hidden cameras filming without the knowledge of the participants. There have also been films involving actual violence and murder. The X-rated industry's capacity for innovation is impressive.

The industry requires a lot of labor, which is frequently imported illegally (Mahmoud and Trebesch 2009). Indeed, illegal immigrants often agree readily to perform in the films.

The need for money laundering

Transnational human trafficking is a business without territory. Unlike gambling and prostitution, which tend to serve regular clients and involve activities tied to specific neighborhoods, human trafficking mostly involves one-time transactions. Additionally, although many people want to enter the United States (for example), only a limited number are eligible because smugglers usually select clients based on ability to pay.

Each of the payments that feed the revenue of trafficking organizations is typically small (usually only a couple of hundred dollars), but the revenue can accumulate quickly. The total income is proportional to the number of clients. Some people cross the border many times and spend a lot of money hiring coyotes, but most clients only cross a border once. The relative share of individuals using the service of a coyote only once is certainly higher than the relative share of individuals who use other criminal services, such as prostitution, only once.

The structure of the revenue flows associated with trafficking within a criminal organization depends on the specific activity, whether slavery, the traffic in organs, the sex industry, and so on. In the case of organs, a piece of merchandise can only be sold once. The criminal organization involved carries out most of its activities on the territory of other countries besides the host country. The removal of the organs is usually undertaken in poor countries, and the organs are imported underground into developed countries where they are sold and transplanted. The payments are thus made in the host country, while an important part of the crime is committed abroad. This separation between the location of the crime and the location of the payment makes legal prosecution more difficult. While prosecution for organ trafficking is possible in the host country, it is much more difficult to extend the prosecution to murder even if this is thought to be the source of the organs. We do not address this issue in depth here, but we note that, in this case, the flow of money is collected in the host country. The criminal organization will then either try to launder the money on the territory of the host country or send it back to the source country, which is often also the home country of many of the members of the criminal organization (Kopp 2004).

Prostitution is typically linked to organized crime (Zhang 2009; Zaitch and Staring 2009). The activity takes place in the host country, and the payments are collected there. The money is laundered on the spot or in the country of origin of the traffickers. The logistics of trafficking for prostitution and the sex industry are different from the logistics of organ trafficking. Smuggling dead organs and smuggling living beings present different problems.

The activities linked to living beings imply that the smugglers must maintain contact with the people who are trafficked because these people must be lodged and cared for. Given that they must establish this sort of connection with their clients, criminal organizations take measures to separate manpower and money flows. Police raids and the arrest of prostitutes are almost inevitable; so, the criminal organization must protect its revenue by separating the merchandise (that is, the people) and the money. The money paid by the client is thus usually passed on immediately to a local manager, who then promptly gives it to a collector.

In contrast, organs are discretely removed in a poor country, while the purchasers usually live in rich countries. The transplantation may be carried out in a poor country with good medical infrastructure. We know little about this type of traffic. It is plausible that an organ removed in India, for example, might be transplanted into a Swiss patient who has traveled to Romania for the purpose. In such a scenario, the flow of money is particularly difficult to chart.

Slavery requires different financial circuits. Most often, the individual is offered assistance in entering a host country and then, after the entry, is deprived of his papers. He must then work for a family or, more rarely, a company.[13] The migrant pays the criminal organization. Sometimes, the beneficiary of the labor also pays a fee. The flows are irregular unless the beneficiary wishes to change personnel.

We know little about the laundering techniques used by the criminal organizations involved in human trafficking. It is possible that these organizations have extremely large sums of money and launder them successfully. It is also possible that they possess much more sophisticated laundering systems than anything we have seen in the domain of drugs (Zaitch 1998; Reuter and Truman 2004).

The taxonomy of the flows

We note above that the modes of circulation of the revenue flows created by human trafficking are heterogeneous. It is thus almost impossible to distinguish the sums that correspond to the human trafficking segment of the operations of criminal organizations from the sums that correspond to the pornographic industry, prostitution, or labor. Nonetheless, in table 6.1, we attempt to classify the various flows of money generated by human trafficking according to the most significant characteristics.

Table 6.1. The Financial Flows Generated by Human Trafficking

Provider of the money	Recipient	Service	Frequency	Income	Laundering
Source country					
Illegal migrants	Border patrol	Visas, passports	One time	Profit	No
Criminal organizations	Government officials and bureaucrats	Facilitate the traffic	Repeated	Profit	Depends on the scale
Border					
Illegal migrants	Local police	Passage	One time	Profit	No
Illegal migrants	Coyotes	Passage	One time	Profit	No
Illegal migrants	Criminal organization	Passage	One time	Profit, less cost	Yes
Host country					
Illegal migrants	Employers	Free service (no wages)	Repeated	Value	No
Illegal migrants	Service providers (flesh-peddlers, housing, administrative papers)	Protection services	Repeated	Profit, less cost	Depends on the scale
Illegal migrants	Government officials	Protection	One time	Profit	No
Service providers	Government officials	Protection	Repeated	Profit	Depends on the scale
Criminal organizations	Government officials	Protection	Repeated	Profit	Depends on the scale
Clients and illegal employers	Sex workers, other workers	Services, workforce	Repeated	Profit, less cost	No

Source: Author compilation.

In the table, we first indicate the location of the monetary flow. It can be located in three places: the source country, the border, and the host country. Sometimes, financial flows may transit through one or more third countries. Most of the time, however, this occurs during the laundering process and does not appear in the table. The provider and the recipient indicate who is paying and who is receiving the money. The service gives an indication about what is compensated by the monetary flow. Frequency denotes whether the transaction takes place repeatedly or only once. Income describes whether the flow of money is pure profit or whether the recipient must deduct costs to calculate profit.

The flows of money to the source country, whether originating there or returning from elsewhere, are mainly generated by corruption.

Whether they will or will not be laundered depends on the level of scrutiny of local authorities. Political stability also plays a role. If the government is weak, corrupt government officials and bureaucrats may try to place their assets in other countries where they might plan to go if their security is threatened. These flows are repetitive if they are oriented toward high-level government officials. Most of the time, local bureaucrats can only be corrupted over a short period of time before they are removed from office. There is almost no cost for those who receive the money. The only real cost is the risk of being prosecuted, which is not a monetary cost. This diminishes the economic profit, but not the accounting profit. As long as corrupt officials are not prosecuted, the bribes they collect are both income and profit.

Corruption may occur regularly at border crossings over long periods without this implying that any single individual maintains an income from this corruption for long. Corrupt officials will usually be rotated out of their positions. While their successors may be equally amenable to corruption, and thus the flow of immigrants may be maintained, the window of opportunity for any single officer to take advantage of the demand for illegal border crossings is relatively brief. This implies that individual recipients of bribes do not accumulate sufficiently large sums to be considered to represent a flow requiring laundering. Instead, the sums, which generally amount simply to additional income for local border guards and policemen, are usually spent on consumption or invested with little precaution. Only if a criminal organization establishes an ongoing relationship with a relatively high-level official are the bribes likely to accumulate into sums large enough to warrant a sophisticated laundering scheme.

In the host country, there is a missing monetary flow, which represents the work of those who have, in fact, become slave laborers. It appears in the table as a nonmonetary flow that corresponds to a free service. Another flow represents the services provided by intermediaries who offer protection, housing, and new documents to the illegal workers. These payments are regular. The profit of the intermediaries is the same as the payments they receive as long as they do not have to spend money to provide the service. If they do incur costs, these must be deducted from the income to establish their profit. Generally, the larger the scale of operations, the more likely that intermediaries will incur costs in providing services. Some illegal workers can obtain the services they need directly by paying government officials or bureaucrats. In such cases, the payment is usually made only once, though the corrupt officials and bureaucrats may receive money regularly from many people.

Most of the time, the corrupt officials do not have to pass on part of their profits to other officials above them in a hierarchy, though it may be that numerous corrupt officials have become involved and require payment for the service activity.

Criminal organizations may pay corrupt officials directly for visas or to turn a blind eye toward the border crossings. They include this service in the package they sell to the migrants, and it is simply a cost that must be taken into account in calculating profit. The breakdown of the profit among the various levels of the criminal organization is unclear. The protection bought from corrupt officials may be used in many activities (illegal drugs, human smuggling, prostitution, and so on). We lack information on the level of diversification in the criminal organizations involved in human trafficking. The flows between the criminal organizations and the government officials are repeated. If a contact is caught and prosecuted, the criminal organization identifies a new contact.

The last flow is composed of the direct payments of clients to illegal workers (prostitutes; employers of maids, housekeepers, and gardeners; and so on). These flows are permanent. The flows compensate the services that are provided by the workers.

Conclusion

In this chapter, we provide a methodological contribution to the difficult task of assessing the impact of human trafficking in economic terms. First, we underline the reasons to resist the temptation to add together all the flows of money that are more or less linked to human trafficking. If the results of any analysis are to be meaningful, they must be grounded on a realistic understanding of the complex web of criminal activities that are involved in human trafficking. The money flows associated in human trafficking arise through distinct activities that have different implications. It is important to relate the various money flows to the specific criminal activities that generate them.

Second, we point out that, in certain circumstances, it is plausible that human trafficking may only generate a single flow of money within a single local setting for the benefit of a single criminal organization. However, in other circumstances, for instance, if it is mostly based on geographical competitive advantage (villages close to the border) or if it is associated with a job that involves frequent border crossings (truckers, waterfront workers, and so on), human trafficking is a profitable, but weakly organized activity. In this case, most of the criminal income is spent in consumption, and the remainder is invested without specific precautions. The monetary income from the criminal activity is diffused in the economy without noticeable effects.

Third, large criminal organizations that undertake trafficking in illegal workers, including women, are not necessarily involved in prostitution. The biggest profits, however, are derived from exploiting illegal migrants in sweatshops or houses of prostitution. Trafficking is also necessary to provide a labor force for criminal activities. Trafficking is not a particularly profitable business per se. Most of the profit is made in selling criminal services to end users, not in extorting money to help migrants cross borders.

Fourth, we assume that the flow of money entering the source countries and linked to human trafficking is negligible in comparison with remittances sent back by the illegal immigrants to their home countries. Most of the profits made by petty traffickers stay in the host countries. The only significant flows of money back and forth to source countries and host countries are generated by large criminal organizations. It is reasonable to believe that there are considerable flows of criminal money circulating internationally, but it is almost impossible to distinguish within these flows the profits generated by trafficking and the profits generated by the core businesses of large criminal organizations (prostitution, illegal drugs, counterfeiting, corruption, and so on).

Fifth, developing countries are already aware of the negative socioeconomic impact of criminal money flows. We do not believe that, of this money, the small portion produced by human trafficking generates any unique sort of harm. Good governance and civil society are harmed by the total flows of money generated by criminal activities. Distortion, lack of competiveness, and bad incentives are the well-known consequences of criminal money. Whatever the source of such money, the impact is likely to be similar.

Our research is preliminary, but it already points to a somewhat modest conclusion, as follows. The money flows linked to human trafficking that enter developing countries are merged into bigger flows of criminal money. There is no evidence that these flows have a specific unique impact on these countries.

Notes

1. Orrenius (2001) and Orrenius and Zavodny (2005) have documented the supply effects of networks; see also Mckenzie and Rapoport (2007); Sana and Massey (2005).
2. Organ trafficking is included if it refers to killings that are motivated by the desire to sell the organs internationally. The Palermo convention and the U.S. Department of Justice do not consider organ smuggling a part of human trafficking.
3. See the website of the IOM, http://www.iom.int/jahia/jsp/index.jsp.
4. It is unclear whether this includes only those who are enslaved or also those who use the services of smugglers.
5. Such an estimate uses trafficking in the narrow sense, that is, only those who are exploited.
6. Feingold (2005) reports that statistics on the end use of trafficked people are often unreliable because they tend to overrepresent the sex trade. For example, men are excluded from the trafficking statistics gathered in Thailand because, according to national law, men cannot qualify as victims of trafficking.
7. In Manila, an employee at the consulate of a French-speaking country demanded US$500 to issue a tourist visa to an ineligible person. According to our source, he spent three years at his desk providing not more than 20 visas per month. This last number is an approximation deduced from the waiting time for the visas. The employee's justification for a longer wait (three months) than normal for the visas for the ineligible people was the necessity to merge the visas with a substantial flow of real tourist visas. Imagine that five employees had undertaken the same activity: the flow per year would be US$600,000. In Moscow, a French diplomat was questioned about the origin of the money he used to buy two apartments in the most sought-after location in the city. He resigned from his job at the embassy.
8. The estimate provided by the United Nations Office on Drugs and Crime is higher, close to US$2,000 (UNODC 2010).
9. At US$300 for each of 2 million entrants (allowing for some individuals, say 10 percent, to make two or three entries) yields approximately US$700 million. At

an import price of US$23,000 per kilogram of cocaine, 30 tons of imported cocaine would yield US$700 million.

10. Mexican drug violence is not generated by retail activities, but by the fight for territorial control, which is a broader notion than routes and gross delivery.

11. Alcohol and tobacco are extremely innovative. Products, marketing, and packaging are in permanent evolution.

12. The market is less competitive at the distribution level. (Note that distribution over the Web is not the core of the pornographic film industry.)

13. We concentrate on human trafficking toward rich countries and exclude cases of servitude in low-income developing countries, forced labor in war zones, and so on.

References

Abadinsky, H. 1990. *Organized Crime.* Chicago: Nelson-Hall Publishers.

Abt Associates. 2001. "What America's Users Spend on Illicit Drugs, 1988–2000." Office of National Drug Control Policy, Executive Office of the President, Washington, DC.

Amuedo-Dorantes, C., and S. Pozo. 2005. "On the Use of Differing Money Transmission Methods by Mexican Immigrants." *International Migration Review* 39 (3): 554–76.

Andreas, P. 2000. *Border Games: Policing the U.S.-Mexico Divide.* Cornell Studies in Political Economy. Ithaca, NY: Cornell University Press.

Andreas, P., and M. N. J. van der Linden. 2005. "Designing Trafficking Research from a Labour Market Perspective: The ILO Experience." *International Migration* 43 (1–2): 55–73.

Block, A. A., and W. J. Chambliss. 1981. *Organizing Crime.* New York: Elsevier North-Holland.

Buchanan J. 1973. "A Defense of Organized Crime." In *The Economics of Crime and Punishment,* ed. S. Rottenberg, 119–32. Washington, DC: American Enterprise Institute for Public Policy Research.

Buckland, B. S. 2008. "More Than Just Victims: The Truth about Human Trafficking." *Public Policy Research* 15 (1): 42–47.

Cornelius, W. A., D. FitzGerald, P. Lewin Fischer, and L. MuseOrlinoff, eds. 2010. *Mexican Migration and the US Economic Crisis: A Transnational Perspective.* La Jolla, CA: Center for Comparative Immigration Studies, University of California–San Diego.

Cressey, D. R. 1969. *Theft of the Nation: The Structure and Operations of Organized Crime in America.* With an introduction by J. Finckenauer. New York: Harper-Collins.

Feingold, D. A. 1998. "Sex, Drugs and the IMF: Some Implications of 'Structural Readjustment' for the Trade in Heroin, Girls and Women in the Upper Mekong Region." *Refuge* 17 (5): 4–10.

———. 2005. "Human Trafficking." *Foreign Policy*, 150 (September–October): 26–32.

Fleming, M. H., J. Roman, and G. Farrell. 2000. "The Shadow Economy." *Journal of International Affairs* 53 (2): 387–409.

ILO (International Labour Organization). 2005. "A Global Alliance against Forced Labour." Report of the Director-General. International Labour Conference, 93rd Session, Report I(B), International Labour Office, Geneva.

———. 2009. "The Cost of Coercion." Report of the Director-General. International Labour Conference, 98th Session, Report I(B), International Labour Office, Geneva.

Jewell, R. T., and D. J. Molina. 2009. "Mexican Migrations to the US: A Comparison of Income and Networks Effects." *Eastern Economic Journal* 35 (2): 144–59.

Kilmer, B., and P. Reuter. 2009. "Doped: How Two Plants Wreak Havoc on the Countries That Produce and Consume Them and Everyone in Between." *Foreign Policy* 175 (November/December): 2–6.

Kleiman, M. A. R. 1989. *Marijuana: Costs of Abuse, Costs of Control.* Contributions in Criminology and Penology. Westport, CT: Greenwood Press.

Kopp, P. 2004. *Political Economy of Illegal Drugs.* Routledge Studies in Crime and Economics. London: Routledge.

Kyle, D., and M. Scarcelli. 2009. "Migrant Smuggling and the Violence Question: Evolving Illicit Migration Markets for Cuban and Haitian Refugees." *Criminal Law and Social Change* 52 (3): 297–311.

Mahmoud, O., and C. Trebesch. 2009. "The Economic Drivers of Human Trafficking: Micro-evidence from Five Eastern European Countries." Kiel Working Paper 1480, Kiel Institute for the World Economy, Kiel, Germany.

Massey, D. S. 1987. "Understanding Mexican Migration to the United States." *American Journal of Sociology* 92 (6): 1372–403.

Massey, D. S., R. Alarcón, J. Durand, and H. González. 1987. *Return to Aztlan: The Social Process of International Migration from Western Mexico.* Studies in Demography 1. Berkeley, CA: University of California Press.

Mckenzie, D., and H. Rapoport. 2007. "Network Effects and the Dynamics of Migration and Inequality: Theory and Evidence from Mexico." *Journal of Development Economics* 84 (1): 1–24.

Orrenius, P. M. 2001. "Illegal Immigration and Enforcement along the U.S.–Mexico Border: An Overview." *Economic and Financial Policy Review* 2001 (Q1): 2–11.

Orrenius, P. M., and M. Zavodny. 2005. "Self-Selection among Undocumented Immigrants from Mexico." *Journal of Developments Economics* 78 (1): 215–40.

Reuter, P. 1983. *Disorganized Crime.* Cambridge, MA: MIT Press.

Reuter, P., R. J. MacCoun, and P. Murphy. 1990. *Money from Crime: A Study of the Economics of Drug Dealing in Washington, D.C.* With A. Abrahamse and B. Simon. Santa Monica, CA: Rand Corporation.

Reuter, P., and E. M. Truman. 2004. *Chasing Dirty Money: The Fight against Money Laundering.* Washington, DC: Institute for International Economics.

Sana, M., and D. Massey. 2005. "Household Composition, Family Migration, and Community Context: Migrant Remittances in Four Countries." *Social Science Quarterly* 86 (2): 509–28.

Schelling, T. C. 1967. "Economics and Criminal Enterprise." *Public Interest* 7 (spring): 61–78.

Slagle, J. W. 2004. *Illegal Entries.* Bloomington, IN: AuthorHouse.

Spener, D. 2009. *Clandestine Crossings: Migrants and Coyotes on the Texas-Mexico Border.* Ithaca, NY: Cornell University Press.

Staring, R. 2006. "Controlling Immigration and Organized Crime in the Netherlands: Dutch Developments and Debates on Human Smuggling and Trafficking." In *Immigration and Criminal Law in the European Union: The Legal Measures and Social Consequences of Criminal Law in Member States on Trafficking and Smuggling in Human Beings,* ed. E. Guild and P. Minderhoud, 241–69. Vol. 9 of *Immigration and Asylum Law and Policy in Europe.* Leiden, the Netherlands: Martinus Nijhoff Publishers.

United Nations. 2002. "Secretary-General Stresses 'Clear Need' for International Cooperation on Refugee, Migration Policy." Press Release SG/SM/8522, November 22. http://www.un.org/News/Press/docs/2002/SGSM8522.doc.htm.

UNODC (United Nations Office on Drugs and Crime). 2004. "United Nations Convention against Transnational Organized Crime and the Protocols Thereto." UNODC, Vienna International Center, Vienna.

———. 2009. *Global Report on Trafficking in Persons.* Vienna: UNODC.

———. 2010. *The Globalization of Crime: A Transnational Organized Crime Threat Assessment.* Vienna: UNODC. http://www.unodc.org/unodc/en/data-and-analysis/tocta-2010.html.

UNODC (United Nations Office on Drugs and Crime) and IPU (Inter-Parliamentary Union). 2009. "Combating Trafficking in Persons: A Handbook for Parliamentarians." Handbook 16, UNODC, Vienna.

U.S. Department of State. 2010. *Trafficking in Persons Report, 2010.* Washington, DC: Office To Monitor and Combat Trafficking in Persons, U.S. Department of State. http://www.state.gov/g/tip/rls/tiprpt/2010/.

van Duyne, P. C. 2007. "Virtue and Reality: An Introductory Tale of Two Cities." In *Crime Business and Crime Money in Europe: The Dirty Linen of Illicit Enterprise,* ed. P. C. van Duyne, A. Maljevic, M. van Dijck, K. von Lampe, and J. Harvey, 1–14. Cross-Border Crime Colloquium 7. Nijmegen, the Netherlands: Wolf Legal Publishers.

World Bank. 2006. *Global Economic Prospects 2006: Economic Implications of Remittances and Migration.* Washington, DC: World Bank. http://go.worldbank.org/0ZRERMGA00.

Zaitch, D. 1998. *The Dutch Cocaine Market in European Perspective.* Amsterdam: University of Amsterdam.

Zaitch, D., and R. Staring. 2009. "The Flesh Is Weak, the Spirit Even Weaker: Prostitution Clients and Women Trafficking in the Netherlands." In *Prostitution and Human Trafficking: Focus on Clients*, ed. A. Di Nicola, A. Cauduro, M. Lombardi, and P. Ruspini, 67–121. New York: Springer Science+Business Media.

Zhang, S. X. 2009. "Beyond the Natasha Story: A Review and Critique of Current Research on Sex Trafficking." *Global Crime* 10 (3): 178–95.

Zhang, S. X., and K. L. Chin. 2002. "Enter the Dragon: Inside Chinese Human Smuggling Organizations." *Criminology* 40 (4): 737–68.

Zhang, S. X., K. L. Chin, and J. Miller. 2007. "Women's Participation in Chinese Transnational Human Smuggling: A Gendered Market Perspective." *Criminology* 45 (3): 699–733.

Part III

To What Extent Do Corporations Facilitate Illicit Flows?

7

Transfer Price Manipulation

Lorraine Eden

Abstract

Multinational enterprises (MNEs) are powerful actors in the global economy. Transfer price manipulation (TPM) is one of the benefits of multinationality. By over- and underinvoicing intrafirm transactions, multinationals can arbitrage and take advantage of differences in government regulations across countries. This chapter explains the motivations of firms that engage in TPM, illustrates the ways in which MNEs can arbitrage government regulations, and reviews the empirical estimates on TPM for developed and developing countries. We conclude that the strongest and clearest evidence of TPM comes from transaction-level studies of U.S. intrafirm import and export prices and from firm-level studies using Chinese tax data. No data set is perfect; so, the various estimates are flawed. Still, the balance of the evidence suggests that income shifting does occur through the manipulation of transfer prices. What is needed is greater accessibility to transaction-level data on cross-border export and import transactions and on MNE income statements and balance sheets. This would enable scholars to shine more light in the dark corners of TPM and provide more accurate assessments of TPM impacts on developing countries.

Introduction

World Investment Report 2011 contains the estimate that there are now 103,786 MNE parent firms and 892,114 foreign affiliates (UNCTAD 2011). These numbers have grown enormously since the first United Nations Conference on Trade and Development (UNCTAD) estimate of 35,000 parents and 150,000 foreign affiliates (UNCTAD 1992). Not only are there ever-growing numbers of MNEs, their relative size as a share of the global economy is also growing. Of the world's 100 largest economies, 42 are MNEs, not countries, if one compares firm revenues with country gross domestic product (GDP). The value added by MNEs constitutes about 11 percent of world GDP.

Multinationals likewise bulk large in terms of international trade flows. For example, *World Investment Report 2010* estimates that foreign affiliate exports are now one-third of world exports (UNCTAD 2010). If trade occurs between related parties (that is, between affiliated units of an MNE), the transactions are referred to as *intrafirm trade*. Statistics on intrafirm trade are scarce because most governments do not require MNEs to report their crossborder intrafirm transactions separately from their trade with unrelated parties. The United States is one of the few countries to report intrafirm trade statistics; the U.S. Census Bureau (2010) estimates that 48 percent of U.S. exports and 40 percent of U.S. imports represent trade between related parties. The Organisation for Economic Co-operation and Development (OECD) provides preliminary estimates that related-party trade represents 7–12 percent of world merchandise trade and 8–15 percent of OECD trade (OECD 2010).

The price of an intrafirm transfer is called a *transfer price*, and *transfer pricing* is the process by which the transfer price is determined. Transfer pricing, once an obscure area studied only by a few academics such as Hirshleifer (1956, 1957), Horst (1971), and Rugman and Eden (1985), has now become front-page news because of recent attention to TPM, that is, the over- or underinvoicing of transfer prices by MNEs in response to external pressures such as government regulations (for instance, taxes, tariffs, exchange controls).

For example, Forest Laboratories, a U.S. pharmaceutical company, was profiled in *Bloomberg Businessweek* for using TPM to shift profits on Lexapro, an antidepressant drug, from the United States to Bermuda and Ireland. The headline, "U. S. Companies Dodge US$60 Billion in Taxes with Global Odyssey," compared transfer pricing with the corporate equivalent of the secret offshore accounts of individual tax dodgers (Drucker 2010a). Google was similarly profiled in October 2010 for using transfer pricing and a complex legal structure to lower its worldwide tax rate to 2.4 percent (Drucker 2010b). Politicians have also become involved. The Ways and Means Committee of the U.S. House of Representatives held a public hearing on transfer pricing in July 2010. One report for the hearing, by the Joint Committee on Taxation, explored six detailed case studies of U.S. multinationals using transfer pricing to reduce their U.S. and worldwide tax rates.[1] Sikka and Willmott summarize several recent cases involving transfer pricing and tax avoidance, concluding that "transfer pricing is not just an accounting technique, but also a method of resource allocation and avoidance of taxes that affects distribution of income, wealth, risks and quality of life" (Sikka and Willmott 2010, 352).

Several coinciding forces have raised the visibility of transfer pricing from the academic pages of economics journals to the front pages of major newspapers. All three key actors in the global economy—governments, MNEs, and nongovernmental organizations (NGOs)—now view transfer pricing as critically important.

Government authorities, the first set of key actors, have long recognized that transfer prices can be used by MNEs to avoid or evade national regulations. For example, by setting a transfer price above or below the market price for a product and shifting profits to an affiliate taxed at a lower rate, an MNE can reduce its overall tax payments and achieve a higher after-tax global profit relative to two firms that do not have such an affiliation arrangement.

Most governments of industrialized nations now regulate the transfer prices used in the calculation of corporate income taxes (CITs) and customs duties. The worldwide regulatory standard is the arm's-length standard, which requires that the transfer price be set equal to the price that two unrelated parties have negotiated at arm's length for the same product or a similar product traded under the same or similar circumstances with respect to the related-party transaction (Eden 1998). The arm's-length standard, first developed in the United States, became an international standard when the OECD issued transfer pricing guidelines that were later adopted by OECD member governments (OECD

1979). The purpose behind the guidelines is to prevent undertaxation and overtaxation (double taxation) of MNE profits by national tax authorities (Eden 1998).

Starting in the early 1990s, the legal landscape for transfer pricing changed dramatically. In 1994, the U.S. Internal Revenue Service's major revisions to its transfer pricing regulations became law. In 1995, the OECD published revised transfer pricing guidelines, which have been regularly updated since then (OECD 1995). While only a few governments had detailed transfer pricing regulations attached to their CIT laws before the 1990s, now more than 40 tax jurisdictions around the world—including all the OECD countries and, therefore, the bulk of world trade and foreign direct investment flows—are covered and have highly technical and sophisticated transfer pricing regulations attached to their tax codes (Eden 2009; Ernst & Young 2008).

In 1995, UNCTAD surveyed national governments about current developments in accounting and reporting and asked a few questions about TPM as part of the survey. The results for 47 countries were circulated in an unpublished working paper and analyzed in Borkowski (1997). In the survey, 60 percent of government respondents stated that MNEs in their country engaged in TPM and that it was a significant problem. Almost 80 percent of respondents believed that MNEs were using TPM to shift income, and 85 percent thought this was a serious problem. This belief held regardless of income levels: 11 of 13 low-income, 16 of 18 middle-income, and 13 of 16 high-income country governments believed that TPM was being used to shift income. TPM was seen as a problem because it led to distorted competitiveness between local firms and MNEs, enabled MNEs to withdraw funds from the country, and reduced tax revenues. Governments perceived income shifting by foreign MNEs as more frequent and larger in magnitude relative to home country MNEs.

In the late 1990s, the OECD also launched a major push to deter abusive tax practices, focusing on abusive tax havens (OECD 1998; Eden and Kudrle 2005). While tax havens and TPM are two separate topics and should be treated separately, there are overlaps. Tax havens can encourage abusive transfer pricing practices, for example, by creating CIT differentials between countries that offer pricing arbitrage opportunities to MNEs. Secrecy havens provide opportunities for parking MNE profits away from the eyes of national tax authorities (Kudrle and Eden 2003).

The second key actor in the global economy—MNEs—have long seen transfer pricing as an important international tax issue (Ernst & Young 2010). From an international tax perspective, tax avoidance (tax planning that complies with the law) is viewed by MNE executives and the tax planning industry as both legal and morally acceptable (Friedman 1970).[2] Because the goal of the firm is to maximize shareholder wealth and because transfer pricing can raise the MNE's after-tax profits on a worldwide basis, transfer pricing is a valued activity for the MNE. Transfer pricing has also become an increasingly important issue for MNE executives because government regulations have become more complex and the number of governments that regulate transfer pricing, require documentation, and levy penalties continues to grow (Eden 2009; Ernst & Young 2010). In addition, recent U.S. legislative changes such as Sarbanes-Oxley and FIN 48 have made transfer pricing important for MNE executives from a corporate financial and reporting perspective (Ernst & Young 2008).

Lastly, with the collapse of Enron, WorldCom, and others in the early 2000s and bankruptcies or near bankruptcies among many huge multinationals (for example, General Motors) during the current international financial crisis, NGOs are now paying more attention to corporate fraud, in particular to abusive financial behaviors that may be related to the global financial crisis (for example, see TJN 2007; Christian Aid 2009; Sikka and Willmott 2010). Transfer pricing has been specifically attacked by NGOs. For example, Christian Aid has published reports arguing that transfer pricing is tax dodging, cooking the books, secret deals, or scams that rob the poor to keep the rich tax-free, thereby stripping income from developing countries (Christian Aid 2009). Thus, the third key actor in the global economy—NGOs—is now also paying much more attention to transfer pricing.

The purpose of this chapter is to review the literature on empirical estimates of TPM, focusing, where possible, on developing countries. We also situate this chapter within the context of the work on illicit flows of funds out of developing countries, the theme of this volume. In the next section, we explore the reasons why MNEs engage in TPM. The following section examines expected manipulation patterns in response to particular forms of government regulation. The penultimate section reviews the empirical evidence on TPM. The last section concludes.

Why Engage in Transfer Price Manipulation?

The primary reason why governments have developed the arm's-length standard is that they believe MNEs do not set their transfer prices at arm's length, but rather engage in widespread TPM for the purpose of avoiding or evading government regulations. TPM is the deliberate over- or underinvoicing of the prices of products (goods, services, and intangibles) that are traded among the parent and affiliates of an MNE. Overpricing inbound transfers and underpricing outbound transfers can be used to move profits out of an affiliate located in a high-tax jurisdiction or from a country that does not allow capital remittances. Differences in CIT rates across countries (which are exacerbated by tax havens and tax deferral) create profitable opportunities for MNEs to engage in TPM. Below, we explore the benefit to the MNE of engaging in TPM and the different ways that MNEs respond to these external motivations.

One of the less well known benefits of multinationality is the ability to arbitrage differences in government regulations across countries (Eden 1985). One benefit of internalizing transactions rather than using the open market is that the goals of firms change, and this change makes a big difference. The goals of parties to an intrafirm (intracorporate) transaction are cooperative (the purpose is to maximize joint MNE profit), whereas the goals of arm's-length parties are conflictual (to maximize their individual profits), that is, units of an MNE collude rather than compete in the market. This gives them the ability to reduce overall tax payments and avoid regulatory burdens by under- or overinvoicing the transfer price, the price of the intrafirm transaction.

The fact that two related parties (parent and subsidiary or two sister subsidiaries) can collude in setting the price gives an MNE the ability, which unrelated firms do not legally have, to choose a price that jointly maximizes their profits, the *profit-maximizing transfer price*. The determination of a profit-maximizing transfer price is a complex decision-making process because the MNE must take into account both internal motivations (the costs and revenues of the individual MNE affiliates) and external motivations (the existence of external market prices and government regulations such as taxes and tariffs) that can affect the optimal transfer price (Hirshleifer 1956, 1957; Horst 1971; Eden 1985). Where no external market exists, the MNE should set the transfer price equal to the shadow price on intrafirm transactions; generally, this is the marginal cost of the exporting division. Efficient transfer prices for services and for private intangibles have similar rules; they should be based on the benefit-cost principle, that is, each division should pay a transfer price proportionate to the benefits it receives from the service or intangible (Eden 1998). Where external market prices exist, they should be taken into account in setting the transfer price, that is, divisions should be allowed to buy and sell in the external market. In each case, the purpose is efficient resource allocation within the MNE group.

While economists focus on the TPM benefits in using the profit-maximizing transfer price, managers of MNEs are more likely to focus on practical considerations. First, there may be cases where the MNE has no internal reasons for setting a transfer price; transactions may be small in volume, difficult to value, or occur with extraordinary rapidity. Conventional accounting practice, for example, generally defers valuation of intangible assets until there are arm's-length purchases or sales, creating the balance sheet item "goodwill," which measures the excess purchase price over the fair value of the assets acquired. In such cases, the MNE may ignore the issue altogether and not set transfer prices.

However, in the typical case, the MNE has multiple internal motivations for setting a transfer price. Some of these internal motivations include the performance evaluation of profit centers, motivating and rewarding the managers of foreign subsidiaries, preventing intersubsidiary disputes over intermediate product transfers, more efficient tracking of intrafirm flows, and so on (Borkowski 1992; Cravens 1997; Tang 1993, 1997, 2002). TPM in these situations involves balancing the incentives, reporting, and monitoring activities associated with setting transfer prices for internal efficiency.

MNEs typically also have a variety of external motivations for setting transfer prices. In a world of CIT differentials and tariffs, the MNE has an incentive to manipulate its transfer prices to maximize its global net-of-taxes profits. The benefits from TPM of real flows, as opposed to fiscal transfer pricing, must, however, be traded off against internal distortions. The primary purpose of setting transfer prices now becomes global after-tax profit maximization; such transfer prices, however, may or may not look like the regulatory methods outlined by national government authorities.

Transfer Price Manipulation and Government Regulations

Corporate income taxes and transfer price manipulation

The most well known external motivation for manipulating transfer prices is the differences in CIT rates between countries or between states within countries. For evidence on tax-induced motivations for TPM, see Li and Balachandran (1996); Eden (1998); Swenson (2001); and Bartelsman and Beetsma (2003). There are several ways to engage in TPM in such cases:

- The MNE can overinvoice tax-deductible inbound transfers into high-tax countries and underinvoice them into low-tax countries. This shifts corporate profits from high-tax to low-tax jurisdictions. Examples of inbound transfers include imported parts and components, payments for engineering and consulting services, and royalty payments for intangibles.
- The MNE can underinvoice taxable outbound transfers from high-tax countries and overinvoice them from low-tax countries. This shifts corporate profits from high-tax to low-tax jurisdictions. Examples of outbound transfers include exports of finished goods, charges for the provision of services to other parts of the MNE network, and licensing and royalty payments for outbound intangible transfers.
- If the home government allows deferral of CITs on MNE foreign source income, the MNE can avoid the home country CIT on foreign source income by not repatriating foreign source earnings to the home country. The funds can either be reinvested in the host country or moved to another country in the MNE network.
- If the host country levies a withholding tax on the repatriated profits of foreign affiliates and the withholding tax is not fully creditable against the home country tax, not repatriating foreign source income avoids the tax. In these cases, the MNE can use the rhythm method to time its repatriated earnings only in tax years when the withholding tax is fully credited against the home tax (Brean 1985). In other years, no profits are remitted to the home country.
- If withholding taxes vary according to the form of repatriation (for example, management fees, royalty and licensing payments, and dividends are typically subject to quite different withholding tax rates), the MNE can move the funds out in the form that incurs the lowest

withholding tax. Note that if the MNE receives a full foreign tax credit against the home country tax for the withholding tax, the form by which the MNE moves the funds out becomes irrelevant since the tax is fully credited.

- Tax holidays can also be a motivation for TPM, particularly if the holiday is conditional on the profits earned by the foreign affiliate. In China in the 1980s, the government offered a tax holiday for foreign firms as long as they did not show a profit. Not surprisingly, the foreign affiliates did not show profits until after the law was changed (see below).

- Some forms of intrafirm transfers are more fungible than others and therefore more susceptible to TPM. Management fees are particularly notorious because the MNE parent charges each affiliate for the costs of services provided by the parent to the affiliates, and these charges are difficult to measure. Many host country tax authorities have specific rules limiting the deductibility of the management fees charged by an MNE parent to its foreign subsidiaries because governments see these deductions as a method to eviscerate the host country's national tax base. Governments also levy withholding taxes, in addition to CITs, if foreign affiliates repatriate income to their parent firms. The withholding taxes on management fees are often in the range of 30–35 percent.

- Some forms of intrafirm transfers are easier to misprice simply because there is no open market for the product. (The product is never exchanged between arm's-length parties; an example is highly sophisticated new technologies.) So, arm's-length comparables are impossible to find. Payments for intangible assets are particularly susceptible to TPM because there are often no outside transfers available to determine an arm's-length comparable.

Trade taxes and transfer price manipulation

Trade taxes provide a second external motivation for manipulating transfer prices. For evidence on tariff-induced motivations for TPM, see Eden (1998), Vincent (2004), Goetzl (2005), and Eden and Rodriguez (2004). Some examples of TPM motivated by trade tax include the following:

- If customs duties are levied on an ad valorem (percentage) basis, the MNE can reduce the duties paid if it underinvoices imports. Specific or per-unit customs duties cannot be avoided by over- or underinvoicing.

- If export taxes are levied on an ad valorem basis, the MNE can reduce the export taxes paid if it underinvoices exports. Specific export taxes cannot be avoided through TPM.
- Rules of origin within free trade areas offer another potential arbitrage opportunity. Most rules of origin are on a percent-of-value basis. For example, products qualify for duty-free status if 50 percent or more of the value added is derived from inside one of the countries that is a partner in the free trade area. By overinvoicing the value added, the MNE can more easily meet a rule-of-origin test and qualify for duty-free entry for its products into another country in the free trade area.

Foreign exchange restrictions and transfer price manipulation

A third external motivation for TPM is foreign exchange restrictions. For evidence on foreign exchange rate motivations for TPM, see Chan and Chow (1997a), who find that foreign MNEs were engaged in TPM to shift profits out of China not because of CIT differentials (in fact, Chinese tax rates were lower than elsewhere), but to avoid foreign exchange risks and controls. Examples of TPM in response to exchange rate restrictions include the following:

- If the host country's currency is not convertible so that the MNE cannot move its profits out, the MNE can, in effect, move its profits out despite the nonconvertible currency if it overinvoices inbound transfers and underinvoices outbound transfers.
- If there are foreign exchange restrictions on the amount of foreign currency that can be bought or sold in a particular time period, using overinvoicing of inbound transfers and underinvoicing of outbound transfers enables the MNE to move more funds out than would be permissible with currency controls.

Political risk and transfer price manipulation

Another area susceptible to TPM is political risk. For evidence on the capital flight and political risk motivations for TPM, see Gulati (1987); Wood and Moll (1994); Baker (2005); and de Boyrie, Pak, and Zdanowicz (2005). Examples of TPM in response to various types of political risk include the following:

- If the MNE fears expropriation of its assets in a host country or, more generally, if political risk is great, overinvoicing of inbound transfers and underinvoicing of outbound transfers can be used to shift income out of the high-risk location.
- More generally, policy risk, that is, the risk that the government may change its laws, regulations, or contracts in ways that adversely affect the multinational, also provides an incentive for MNEs to engage in TPM. Policy risks, as discussed in Henisz and Zelner (2010), are opaque and difficult to hedge, and there is typically no insurance. Moreover, the authors estimate that policy risks have risen substantially since 1990. Income shifting through TPM may well be a rational response to policy risk.
- If the host country currency is weak and expected to fall, the MNE can underinvoice inbound transfers and overinvoice outbound transfers to shift profits out of the weak currency.
- Another form of political risk is the requirement that foreign affiliates must take on a forced joint venture partner. Foreign affiliate profits earned in a country with this rule in effect suffer a tax because profits must be split between the MNE and the joint venture partner. In these cases, the MNE may engage in income shifting to move funds out of such a high-tax location.

Empirical Evidence on Transfer Price Manipulation

Let us now turn to empirical work on TPM. The evidence that multinationals engage in TPM to arbitrage or avoid government regulations does exist, but is fragmented and often backward induced, that is, estimated indirectly rather than directly. The extent and significance of TPM, especially for developing countries, is not clear, although, by extrapolating from existing studies, we now have a better understanding of the circumstances under which TPM is likely to occur. Below, we review the empirical evidence on TPM.

Evidence from developed countries

By far, the bulk of empirical research on TPM has been done using U.S. data sets, and almost all studies have been done on U.S. multinationals with controlled foreign corporations overseas.

Income shifting studies. Perhaps the largest number of empirical studies has involved estimates of income shifting from high-tax to low-tax jurisdictions. In these studies, either foreign direct investment or a profit-based measure such as return on assets or return on sales is the dependent variable that is used to test whether MNEs shift income to locations with lower CIT rates (for example, see Bartelsman and Beetsma 2003; Grubert and Mutti 1991; Grubert and Slemrod 1998). Because TPM affects MNE profits at the country level, this approach focuses not on prices, but on profit shifting. These partial and general equilibrium models use national CIT differentials and custom duty rates to predict TPM and to estimate the income moved in this fashion. These studies are more appropriately identified as *fiscal TPM* because they focus on income manipulation and not on the pricing of products per se. Changes in the form of profit remittances from royalties to dividends and the excessive padding of management fees, are examples. A few of the key studies are reviewed below.

In one of the earliest tests, Grubert and Mutti (1991) used a data set of manufacturing affiliates of U.S. MNEs in 33 countries to examine how tax differentials and tariffs generate income transfers because of TPM. The authors aggregated country-level data from the U.S. Bureau of Economic Analysis on foreign affiliates of U.S. multinationals and regressed the profit rates of the affiliates against host country statutory CIT rates. The authors concluded that the empirical evidence was consistent with MNE income shifting from high- to low-tax jurisdictions.

Harris, Morck, and Slemrod (1993), based on a sample of 200 U.S. manufacturing firms over 1984–88, find that U.S. MNEs with subsidiaries in low-tax countries pay less U.S. tax, while those with subsidiaries in high-tax countries pay relatively more U.S. tax per dollar of assets or sales. Income shifting by the largest MNEs is, they argue, primarily responsible for these results. These studies provide, however, only indirect evidence of TPM. For example, the results of the authors can be explained by MNEs shifting income from high- to low-tax locations, but also by cross-country differences in the intrinsic location-specific profitability of MNE subunits. The authors are aware of this possibility, but show evidence that does not support this interpretation.

Grubert (2003) uses firm-level data on U.S. parents and their foreign controlled affiliates to test for evidence of income shifting. He regresses pretax profits against host country statutory tax rates, while controlling for parent and subsidiary characteristics and finds evidence supporting income shifting, particularly among firms with high ratios of research and development to sales.

McDonald (2008) expands on Grubert (2003) by attempting to separate out income shifting arising because of tangibles, research and development, marketing intangibles, and services. In particular, he addresses income shifting through cost-sharing arrangements. He concludes that the empirical results from his tests are "not inconsistent with the existence of possible income shifting" and that there is some evidence that foreign affiliates whose U.S. parents engage in cost-sharing arrangements may also "engage in more aggressive income shifting" (McDonald 2008, 30).

Clausing (2009) uses U.S. Bureau of Economic Analysis data for 1982–2004 to test whether U.S. multinationals engage in income shifting to low-tax locations. She argues that MNEs can engage in both financial and real types of tax avoidance. Financial avoidance is estimated by comparing tax differentials across countries and foreign affiliate profit rates, while real avoidance is estimated by comparing tax differentials and foreign employment. She finds that a host country statutory CIT rate 1 percent below the U.S. rate is associated with a 0.5 percent higher foreign affiliate profit rate; using these estimates, she argues that US$180 billion in CIT had been shifted out of the United States. The losses as measured by real responses to income shifting, however, were about half that: about US$80 billion less in profits and 15 percent less in tax revenues.

The most recent paper on the topic, by Azémar and Corcos (2009), uses a sample of Japanese MNEs and finds greater elasticity of investment to statutory tax rates in emerging economies if foreign affiliates are wholly owned by research and development–intensive parent firms. The authors argue that this is indirect evidence of TPM.

TPM trade mispricing studies. A second approach to estimating TPM has involved examining individual transactions using huge databases of transaction-level import and export data (for example, see Clausing 2003; Swenson 2001; Eden and Rodriguez 2004). The focus of these authors is *trade mispricing,* that is, the under- or overinvoicing of imported and exported goods in response to CIT differences, tariffs, foreign exchange restrictions, and so on. Where the researcher focuses on TPM, we call such studies TPM trade mispricing studies. The idea behind this research is to compare arm's-length comparable prices with the reported intrafirm prices to determine the extent of over- or underinvoicing of related-party transactions.

In the trade mispricing papers, the estimates of trade mispricing are typically done using regression analysis. It may be helpful for the reader if we explain briefly how these models work.

If P_{ijkt} is the transaction price of product i imported by firm j from country k at time t, the researcher regresses the price (the dependent variable) against a vector of independent variables (product and firm characteristics and tax and tariff rates), a dummy variable for related-party trade (1 for transactions between related parties, 0 if the firms are unrelated), and a set of control variables for other possible explanations. The regression equation takes the following form:

$$P_{ijkt} = a + b\,X_{ijkt} + c\,I\,FT + d\,X_{ijkt} \times IFT + Z, \qquad (7.1)$$

where X_{ijkt} is the vector of independent variables, IFT is the intrafirm trade dummy variable, and Z is a vector of control variables. The IFT variable is interacted with the independent variables to see whether there are statistically significant differences between arm's-length and related-party trade if one of the independent variables changes, for example, whether IFT is sensitive to differences in CIT rates or to customs duties. All variables except IFT are normally logged so that the regression coefficients are elasticities, showing the responsiveness (percentage change) in the import price to a percentage change in the independent variables.

It may be helpful to also see this equation as a graph. Figure 7.1 shows a simple regression that relates trade prices to the volume of trade, holding other influential variables constant (for example, product and industry characteristics). By examining and adding up the outliers, one can estimate the extent of mispricing. The key issue is therefore to determine what is an outlier. Under U.S. Code section 6662 on CIT, transfer pricing misevaluation penalties apply if MNEs set their transfer prices significantly outside the arm's-length range of acceptable prices. The arm's-length range, according to the section 482 regulations, is determined by the transfer pricing method that gives the most reliable measure of an

Figure 7.1. Estimating Trade Mispricing from International Trade Data

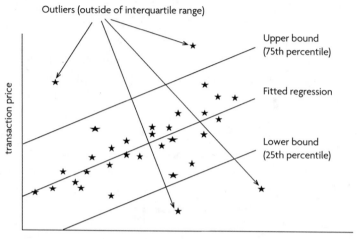

Source: Author.

arm's-length result. In establishing the range, the bottom 25 percent and top 25 percent of observations are normally discarded, leaving the interquartile range (between 25 and 75 percent) as the acceptable arm's-length range. If the MNE's transfer price falls within this range, no section 6662 penalties apply. If it is outside the range, unless the firm has demonstrated a good faith effort to comply with the section 482 regulations (for example, by filing complete, contemporaneous documentation of its transfer pricing policies), penalties do apply (Eden 1998; Eden, Juárez, and Li 2005). We have therefore used the interquartile range to mark outliers in figure 7.1 because these outliers would not normally fall within the arm's-length range.

There are, of course, problems with the TPM trade mispricing approach, not the least of which is, first, that it is critically important to identify which transactions occur within the MNE and which are arm's-length transactions. Too often, the studies attribute all trade mispricing to the MNE, without having the data to determine whether the trade moved within the MNE or not. Second, the key to TPM trade mispricing studies is that the data set must include both arm's-length and intrafirm international transactions, with a clear marker that distinguishes transactions between related parties and transactions between arm's-length firms. The huge advantage of TPM trade mispricing studies over income shifting studies is that the data are transaction-level (not firm-level) data, but the problem is that the marker may be wrong or missing.

Two data sets have been used in the U.S. studies of trade mispricing: U.S. Bureau of the Census data and U.S. Bureau of Labor Statistics (BLS) data. The census data tapes are raw tapes of U.S. export and import transactions. Export figures are reported directly to the Census Bureau; import figures come from the U.S. Customs Service. The data, while extraordinarily rich, suffer from several problems, the most important of which for TPM trade mispricing studies is that the intrafirm trade marker is highly problematic. If the data are taken from shipping documents reported to customs authorities, such markers are widely recognized to be unreliable (Eden and Rodriguez 2004). As a result, empirical studies of trade mispricing using the census data tapes cannot reliably argue that trade mispricing estimates are also estimates of TPM.

For example, Pak and Zdanowicz (1994) use the census data on monthly merchandise export and import prices to look for outliers; they estimate that the U.S. government lost US$33.1 billion in tax revenues because of unreported taxable income. Unfortunately, the authors cannot identify individual transactions as arm's-length or intrafirm transactions; so, they should not (but do) attribute the tax loss to TPM.

Moreover, simply using U.S. Census Bureau data on U.S. merchandise import and export transactions can be quite problematic not only because the intrafirm trade marker may be missing or wrong, but also because prices may be reported for different quantities, leading to spurious estimates of TPM. If the comparability of units cannot be confirmed, it is possible to find huge variations in prices and attribute this to trade mispricing, though the variations are simply caused by differences in units (Eden and Rodriguez 2004; Kar and Cartwright-Smith 2008; Nitsch 2009). For example, comparing the price of a single boxed toothbrush with the price of a freight load of toothbrushes could lead a researcher to conclude that U.S. imports from the United Kingdom were overstated by US$5,655 per unit if the unit in each case were reported as a box (Pak and Zdanowicz 2002). Without the ability to clean the data set to ensure comparability of quantities, such estimates must be regarded as problematic. In addition, the method is only as good as the all-else-being-equal variables, that is, the controls used to ensure comparability between the controlled and uncontrolled transactions. As we stress above, to measure TPM, one must know what the arm's-length price is for comparison purposes, which requires close comparables.

U.S. import data from the U.S. Census Bureau have also been used by Swenson (2001) at the product level by country to test for evidence of TPM over 1981–86. Swenson constructs prices by dividing reported customs values by reported quantities. She finds that a 5 percent fall in foreign CIT rates caused a tiny rise in U.S. import prices. However, she is unable to separate intrafirm from arm's-length trade; so, her study suffers from the same problem as the Pak and Zdanowicz studies.

Recently, Bernard, Jensen, and Schott (2008) used U.S. export transactions between 1993 and 2000 to examine the wedge between arm's-length and related-party transactions and determine how the wedge varies with product and firm characteristics, market structure, and government policy. Their data set is compiled from U.S. export data and U.S. establishment data from the U.S. Census Bureau, as well as U.S. Customs Bureau data. Because they use census data, their results also suffer from unreliable coding for related-party transactions. The price wedge is measured as the difference between the log of the averaged arm's-length prices and the log of the related-party prices at the firm-product-country level. The authors find that export prices for arm's-length transactions are, on average, 43 percent higher, all else being equal, than prices for intrafirm exports. The wedge varies by type of good and is smaller for commodities (8.8 percent, on average) than for differentiated goods (66.7 percent, on average). The wedge is larger for goods shipped by larger firms with higher export shares and in product-country markets served by fewer exporters. The wedge is negatively associated with the foreign country's CIT rate and positively related to that country's import tariff. A 1 percent drop in the foreign tax rate increases the price wedge by about 0.6 percent. Lastly, they find that a 10 percent appreciation of the U.S. dollar against the foreign currency reduces the wedge by 2 percent.

In two situations, however, the quality of the intrafirm trade marker should be quite high, as follows: (1) if government agencies keep data on specific products that are of high salience or (2) if the government is concerned about related-party transactions. In these cases, more than normal attention is paid to data quality and therefore to whether the transactions are intrafirm or arm's length. The most well known example of the first situation (government agencies keeping data on specific products) is the data set on crude petroleum imported into Canada and the United States from the 1970s through the 1980s. The most well known example of the second situation (concern about related-party transactions) is the data set on U.S. export and import transactions collected by BLS, which are used to compute the U.S. export and import price index. We look at each in turn.

Five studies have used confidential data from the Canadian and U.S. governments on crude petroleum imports to test for TPM. Bernard and Weiner (1990, 1992, 1996) find weak evidence of TPM in Canadian and U.S. import prices, which may have been partly related to CIT differentials. Rugman (1985), looking only at the Canadian data, concludes that there was no TPM in Canadian oil import prices in the 1970s. Bernard and Genest-Laplante (1996) examine oil shipments into Canada and the United States over 1974–84 and find that the six largest Canadian affiliates pay the same or lower prices for crude oil imports relative to the prices of third-party transactions; they argue this is evidence of TPM because Canada was a low-tax country relative to the United States over this period.

The second source of high-quality data on intrafirm trade is BLS data on U.S. import and export merchandise transactions. BLS field economists work with approximately 8,000 firms across the United States to identify the most representative export and import transactions, appropriate volumes, and key characteristics, including whether transactions involve related or unrelated parties. Once the transactions have been identified, the firms voluntarily provide transaction-level data on a monthly or quarterly basis to BLS, which cleans the data and uses them to construct U.S. export and import price indexes. As a result, the BLS data are of much better quality for trade mispricing studies in general and for TPM trade mispricing studies in particular. However, there is a sample selection bias problem given that participation in the BLS program is voluntary, and firms can and do refuse to participate.

Clausing has tested the links between CIT differentials and TPM using confidential monthly BLS export and import price data for January 1997–December 1999. She finds a strong relationship indicating tax avoidance: a "tax rate 1% lower in the country of destination/origin is associated with intrafirm export prices that are 1.8% lower and intrafirm import prices that are 2.0% higher, relative to non-intrafirm goods" (Clausing 2003, 16). There are some problems with Clausing's analysis. Her test period most likely underestimates TPM because BLS did not include non–market-based transfer prices until April 1998, and the CIT rate she uses is not the theoretically preferred rate for TPM (the statutory rate adjusted for tax preferences: see Eden 1998; Grubert and Slemrod 1998).

The little evidence we have involving a comparison of the BLS and census data sets can be found in Eden and Rodriguez (2004), who use BLS and U.S. Census Bureau data for January–June 1999 to estimate the responsiveness of U.S. import prices to CIT differentials and tariffs. The authors find that the gap between the BLS- and census-based price indexes widen by 1.3 percent for every 10 percent increase in the share of intrafirm trade and that these results are even stronger where government trade barriers encouraged TPM. Their study suggests that using census data to estimate TPM is problematic; the BLS data set provides superior estimates.

Evidence from developing countries

TPM has long been seen as a way to move funds out of developing countries. The Committee of Eminent Persons at UNCTAD, for example, issued a 1978 report surveying studies of MNEs that use TPM to extract resources from developing countries (UNCTAD 1978). However, the empirical evidence is much more sparse for developing countries than for developed countries (especially in comparison with U.S. studies), which probably is to be expected because careful studies require data sets that often do not exist in developing countries.

The early studies. Most of the research has been in the form of country case studies; for example, Ellis (1981) looked at TPM in Central America; ESCAP and UNCTC (1984) in Thailand; Lecraw (1985) in the countries of the Association of Southeast Asian Nations; Natke (1985) in Brazil; Vaitsos (1974) in Columbia; and Lall (1973) at TPM involving developing countries in general. Some of these studies were highlighted in UNCTAD (1978), Murray (1981), Rugman and Eden (1985), and Plasschaert (1994). UNCTAD (1999) and Eden (1998) provide more recent overviews of this literature.

Some researchers have compared intrafirm prices for selected imports directly with world or domestic prices for the same products. Vaitsos (1974), for example, concluded that foreign MNEs overinvoiced intrafirm imports into Colombia to avoid Colombia's foreign exchange controls. Natke (1985) found that MNEs were overinvoicing imports into Brazil to avoid Brazil's extensive regulations, which included price and credit controls, profit repatriation restrictions, and high CIT rates. Lecraw (1985) concluded that tariffs, relative tax rates, price and foreign exchange controls, and country risk were significant variables explaining transfer pricing behavior in the Association of Southeast Asian Nations. There are also studies of specific industries, such as petroleum and pharmaceuticals, where profit ratios are quite high so that TPM can be an important determinant of income flows among countries. For a recent study on the offshoring of business services, see Eden (2005), which focuses on call centers.

The China studies. China is perhaps the country where TPM has been studied the most frequently, certainly in recent years, primarily because the Chinese government has provided researchers access to firm-level balance sheets, income tax filings, and customs valuation data. Important in the studies is the fact that China has offered tax holidays and other incentives to firms that locate in special economic zones and research parks. A few of the more well known studies are reviewed below.

Chan and Chow (1997a) provide the first evidence on TPM in China. In 1992–93, they collected 81 tax audit cases from city tax bureaus and analyzed the cases for differences across industries, according to firm size, by nationality, and so on. They argue that low tax rates and tax holidays in China should encourage income shifting into China, but the foreign exchange controls and risks would work in the opposite direction. The tax cases, however, involved income shifting out of China (perhaps because that attracted the attention of tax authorities). The six minicases discussed in the article each involved underinvoicing of exports to related parties, creating losses on exports. The authors estimated the extent of underinvoicing by comparing the profits on export sales relative to the profits reported on domestic sales or to industry averages; these are crude measures, but the results are consistent with other case studies of TPM in developing countries.

Chan and Chow (1997b) review the various external motivations that firms in China face and that might lead them to engage in TPM. The authors again argue that, while tax rates are low, which should encourage income shifting into China, foreign exchange controls are an important counterweight encouraging income shifting out of China. Assuming that exchange controls are more important than tax motivations, the authors argue that TPM by foreign firms in China should be visible in their overinvoicing of imports and underinvoicing of exports relative to domestic firms for the same or similar products, that is, foreign firms should be shifting funds out of China through transfer pricing to avoid the foreign exchange controls. To test this hypothesis, the authors subtract the trade transactions of foreign firms from total trade transactions in 1992 to estimate trade by Chinese firms. Comparing foreign with domestic trade patterns, the authors estimate a rate of 11 percent in overinvoicing of imports and 12 percent in overinvoicing of exports among foreign firms relative to Chinese firms. Because the authors find evidence of overinvoicing on both exports and imports, other factors besides foreign exchange controls may be important in this case.

An additional factor affecting transfer pricing in China was the five-year tax holiday for foreign manufacturing affiliates provided by the Chinese government in the 1990s (Chow and Chan 1997a; Chan and Mo 2000). If a foreign affiliate made losses, the firm was exempt from the Chinese CIT. The normal CIT rate was 30 percent, but foreign affiliates in Special Economic Zones were taxed at 15 percent. The tax holiday was structured so that it took effect only after the affiliate declared a profit. For the first two profitable years, the exemption continued, and then the CIT rate was reduced by 50 percent for three more years. After the five-year period, the regular CIT rate would apply. Therefore, while the tax holiday was attractive to foreign MNEs, it was temporary; meanwhile, as long as the foreign affiliate made losses, the firm would be exempt from tax. Foreign MNEs therefore had a strong incentive to underreport profits in China because of the peculiar structure of the tax holiday.

Chan and Mo tested this argument by examining 585 tax audits in 1997; the authors concluded that foreign MNEs "in the pre-holiday position often manipulate taxable income by exaggerating losses before their first profitmaking year, so as to extend their tax holiday" (Chan and Mo 2000, 480). What the authors discovered is that the firms were using TPM (mostly by inflating the cost of sales) to prolong the period of time during which they declared losses. The authors recommended that the Chinese government should limit the preholiday window on tax losses; the government did change the policy and implemented a fixed time period for allowable losses, closing off this particular arbitrage opportunity.

Two other studies of transfer pricing in China report on interviews with financial controllers of 64 foreign affiliates in 2000 (Chan and Chow 2001; Chan and Lo 2004). Both studies find that the perceptions of managers on three environmental variables affect their choice of transfer pricing methods. The more important the interests of local partners and the need to maintain a good working relationship with the Chinese government, the more likely the foreign MNE is to select a market-based transfer pricing method. The more important are foreign exchange controls, the more likely that cost-based prices are used.

The series of Chan and Chow studies are summarized in Chow (2010). She argues that the policy environment in China in the 1990s and 2000s has had a major impact on the transfer pricing policies of foreign MNEs in China. In the 1990s, the combination of tax incentives for foreign MNEs, plus weak regulatory enforcement by inexperienced Chinese tax auditors created a low-tax environment that encouraged TPM. In 2008, China adopted a flat CIT rate of 25 percent that applied to both Chinese and foreign MNEs. The CIT rate remains below the rates of most of China's trading partners except for Hong Kong SAR, China and for Singapore; Chow therefore argues that tax motivations for shifting profits into China still exist. CIT differentials, however, can be offset by other policy environment factors, such as tariffs, foreign exchange controls, political risk, and forced equity joint venture partnerships. Chow discusses each of these factors, concluding that policy liberalization had significantly reduced the impact of the factors by the time of her study, leaving tax incentives as the major factor affecting transfer pricing policies by foreign MNEs in China as of 2010.

Taking a different perspective on TPM, Lo, Wong, and Firth (2010) investigate the impact of corporate governance on earnings management through TPM, using a sample of 266 Chinese firms listed on the Shanghai Stock Exchange in 2004. They measure the manipulation of earnings through TPM by comparing the gross profit margin on related-party transactions with the corresponding margin on arm's-length transactions. The authors find that Chinese MNEs with higher-quality governance structures (for example, a higher percent of independent directors and financial experts on their audit committees) are less likely to engage in TPM. Their results suggest that improving corporate governance of MNEs in emerging markets may lead to less earnings manipulation through transfer pricing.

Looking across these studies of income shifting and trade mispricing, the evidence supports the presumption of TPM in China. Kar and Cartwright-Smith (2008) suggest that China may be the single most important developing country to experience TPM. Perhaps this explains why the Chinese government is now paying so much attention to the development of sophisticated transfer pricing regulations and why Beijing and Shanghai are two of the most rapidly growing transfer pricing locations for the Big Four accounting firms.

Conclusion

In this chapter, we attempt to contribute to the debate on illicit flows and developing countries through the lens of TPM. Based on our literature review, we conclude that empirical evidence for TPM exists, but is not overwhelming. The small number of empirical studies is perhaps not surprising given the fine-grained—individual transactions identified as related-party or arm's-length transactions—and highly confidential nature of the data needed to test for TPM. The best empirical estimates come from transaction-level data collected and processed by statistical agencies that have paid close attention to intrafirm trade, such as the U.S. data set on the prices of crude petroleum imports and the BLS data set used to compute U.S. export and import price indexes. In terms of developing countries, the best and largest number of currently available studies are the Chinese studies. No data set is perfect, and, as a result, all the various estimates are flawed. Still, the balance of the evidence suggests that income shifting does occur through the manipulation of transfer prices.

What would be helpful is greater accessibility to transaction-level data on crossborder export and import transactions and MNE income statements and balance sheets. This would enable scholars to shine more light in the dark corners of TPM, providing scholars and policy makers with the ability to construct more accurate estimates of TPM and its impacts on both developed and developing countries. The Chinese government may be the most well placed to move in this regard, and the rapidly growing number of empirical studies using data on Chinese trade transactions and tax audits suggests we may soon have more reliable estimates of TPM for at least one developing country.

Notes

1. Staff of the Joint Committee on Taxation, 2010, "Present Law and Background Related to Possible Income Shifting and Transfer Pricing," Report JCX-37–10, submitted to the House Committee on Ways and Means, U.S. Congress, Washington, DC, July 20.
2. See the decisions by Judge Learned Hand in *Helvering v. Gregory*, 69 F.2d 809 (CA-2, 1934) and *Commissioner v. Newman*, 159 F.2d 848 (CA-2, 1947).

References

Azémar, C., and G. Corcos. 2009. "Multinational Firms' Heterogeneity in Tax Responsiveness: The Role of Transfer Pricing." *World Economy* 32 (9): 1291–318.

Baker, R. W. 2005. *Capitalism's Achilles Heel: Dirty Money and How to Renew the Free-Market System*. Hoboken, NJ: John Wiley & Sons.

Bartelsman, E. J., and R. M. W. J. Beetsma. 2003. "Why Pay More? Corporate Tax Avoidance through Transfer Pricing in OECD Countries." *Journal of Public Economics* 87 (9–10): 2225–52.

Bernard, A. B., J. B. Jensen, and P. K. Schott. 2008. "Transfer Pricing by U.S.-Based Multinational Firms." Discussion Paper 08–29 (September), Center for Economic Studies, U.S. Bureau of the Census.

Bernard, J.-T., and E. G. Genest-Laplante. 1996. "Transfer Pricing by the Canadian Oil Industry: A Company Analysis." *Applied Economic Letters* 3 (5): 333–40.

Bernard, J.-T., and R. J. Weiner. 1990. "Multinational Corporations, Transfer Prices, and Taxes: Evidence from the U.S. Petroleum Industry." In *Taxation in the Global Economy*, ed. A. Razin and J. Slemrod, 123–60. Chicago: University of Chicago Press.

———. 1992. "Transfer Prices and the Excess Cost of Canadian Oil Imports: New Evidence on Bertrand Versus Rugman." *Canadian Journal of Economics* 25 (1): 101–19.

———. 1996. "Export Pricing in State-Owned and Private MNEs: Evidence from the International Petroleum Market." *International Journal of Industrial Organization* 14 (5): 647–68.

Borkowski, S. C. 1992. "Organizational and International Factors Affecting Multinational Transfer Pricing." *Advances in International Accounting* 5 (1): 173–92.

———. 1997. "The Transfer Pricing Concerns of Developed and Developing Countries." *International Journal of Accounting* 32 (3): 321–36.

Brean, D. 1985. "The Financial Dimensions of Transfer Pricing." In *Multinationals and Transfer Pricing*, ed. A. M. Rugman and L. Eden, 149–64. Croom Helm Series in International Business. London: Croom Helm.

Chan, K. H., and L. Chow. 1997a. "An Empirical Study of Tax Audits in China on International Transfer Pricing." *Journal of Accounting and Economics* 23 (1): 83–112.

———. 1997b. "International Transfer-Pricing for Business Operations in China: Inducements, Regulation and Practice." *Journal of Business Finance and Accounting* 24 (9): 1269–89.

———. 2001. "Corporate Environments and International Transfer-Pricing: An Empirical Study of China in a Developing Economy Framework." *Accounting and Business Research* 31 (2): 103–18.

Chan, K. H., and A. W. Y. Lo. 2004. "The Influence of Management Perception of Environmental Variables on the Choice of International Transfer-Pricing Methods." *International Journal of Accounting* 39 (1): 93–110.

Chan, K. H., and P. L. L. Mo. 2000. "Tax Holidays and Tax Noncompliance: An Empirical Study of Corporate Tax Audits in China's Developing Economy." *Accounting Review* 75 (4): 469–84.

Chow, L. 2010. "Transfer Pricing Environment in Mainland China." *Chinese Management Review* 13 (1): 1–17. http://cmr.ba.ouhk.edu.hk/cmr/webjournal/v13n1/CMR258E09.pdf.

Christian Aid. 2009. "False Profits: Robbing the Poor to Keep the Rich Tax-Free." Christian Aid Report, March, Christian Aid, London.

Clausing, K. A. 2003. "Tax-Motivated Transfer Pricing and US Intrafirm Trade Prices." *Journal of Public Economics* 87 (9–10): 2207–23.

———. 2009. "Multinational Firm Tax Avoidance and Tax Policy." *National Tax Journal* 62 (4): 703–25.

Cravens, K. S. 1997. "Examining the Role of Transfer Pricing as a Strategy for Multinational Firms." *International Business Review* 6 (2): 127–45.

de Boyrie, M. E., S. J. Pak, and J. S. Zdanowicz. 2005. "Estimating the Magnitude of Capital Flight Due to Abnormal Pricing in International Trade: The Russia-USA Case." *Accounting Forum* 29 (3): 249–70.

Drucker, J. 2010a. "Companies Dodge US$60 Billion in Taxes, Even Tea Party Condemns." *Bloomberg Businessweek*, May 14.

———. 2010b. "'Dutch Sandwich' Saves Google Billions in Taxes." *Bloomberg Businessweek*, October 22.

Eden, L. 1985. "The Microeconomics of Transfer Pricing." In *Multinationals and Transfer Pricing*, ed. A. M. Rugman and L. Eden, 13–46. Croom Helm Series in International Business. London: Croom Helm.

———. 1998. *Taxing Multinationals: Transfer Pricing and Corporate Income Taxation in North America.* Toronto: University of Toronto Press.

———. 2005. "Went for Cost, Priced at Cost? An Economic Approach to the Transfer Pricing of Offshored Business Services." *Transnational Corporations*, 14 (2): 1–53.

———. 2009. "Taxes, Transfer Pricing, and the Multinational Enterprise." In *The Oxford Handbook of International Business*, 2nd. ed., ed. A. M. Rugman, 591–622. Oxford: Oxford University Press.

Eden, L., L. F. Juárez, and D. Li. 2005. "Talk Softly But Carry a Big Stick: Transfer Pricing Penalties and the Market Valuation of Japanese Multinationals in the United States." *Journal of International Business Studies* 36 (4): 398–414.

Eden, L., and R. Kudrle. 2005. "Tax Havens: Renegade States in the International Tax Regime." *Law and Policy* 27 (1): 100–27.

Eden, L., and P. Rodriguez. 2004. "How Weak Are the Signals? International Price Indices and Multinational Enterprises." *Journal of International Business Studies.* 35 (1): 61–74.

Ellis, F. 1981. "Export Valuation and Intra-Firm Transfers in the Banana Export Industry in Central America." In *Multinationals beyond the Market*, ed. R. Murray, 61–76. New York: John Wiley and Sons.

Ernst & Young. 2008. "2007–2008 Global Transfer Pricing Survey: Global Transfer Pricing Trends, Practices, and Analyses." Ernst & Young, London.

———. 2010. "2010 Global Transfer Pricing Survey: Addressing the Challenges of Globalization." Ernst & Young, London.

ESCAP (United Nations Economic and Social Commission for Asia and the Pacific) and UNCTC (United Nations Center for Transnational Corporations). 1984. "Transnational Corporations and Transfer Pricing: A Case Study of the Pharmaceutical Industry of Thailand." Working paper, ESCAP/UNCTC Joint Unit on Transnational Corporations, New York.

Friedman, M. 1970. "The Social Responsibility of Business Is to Increase Its Profits." *New York Times Magazine* 33 (September 13): 122–26.

Goetzl, A. 2005. "Why Don't Trade Numbers Add Up?" ITTO Tropical Forest Update 15/1, International Tropical Timber Organization, Yokohama.

Grubert, H. 2003. "Intangible Income, Intercompany Transactions, Income Shifting and the Choice of Location." *National Tax Journal* 56 (1, part 2): 221–42.

Grubert, H., and J. Mutti. 1991. "Taxes, Tariffs and Transfer Pricing in Multinational Corporation Decision Making." *Review of Economics and Statistics* 73 (2): 285–93.

Grubert, H., and J. Slemrod. 1998. "The Effect of Taxes on Investment and Income Shifting to Puerto Rico." *Review of Economics and Statistics* 80 (3): 365–73.

Gulati, S. K. 1987. "A Note on Trade Misinvoicing." In *Capital Flight and Third World Debt*, ed. D. R. Lessard and J. Williamson, 68–78. Washington, DC: Peterson Institute for International Economics.

Harris, D., R. Morck, and J. Slemrod. 1993. "Income Shifting in U.S. Multinational Corporations." In *Studies in International Taxation*, ed. A. Giovannini, R. G. Hubbard, and J. Slemrod, 277–308. Cambridge, MA: National Bureau of Economic Research; Chicago: University of Chicago Press.

Henisz, W. J., and B. A. Zelner. 2010. "The Hidden Risks in Emerging Markets." *Harvard Business Review* 88 (4): 89–95.

Hirshleifer, J. 1956. "On the Economics of Transfer Pricing." *Journal of Business* 29 (3): 172–83.

———. 1957. "Economics of the Divisionalized Firm." *Journal of Business* 30 (2): 96–108.

Horst, T. S. 1971. "The Theory of the Multinational Firm: Optimal Behavior under Different Tariff and Tax Rates." *Journal of Political Economy* 79 (5): 1059–72.

Kar, D., and D. Cartwright-Smith. 2008. "Illicit Financial Flows from Developing Countries, 2002–2006." Global Financial Integrity, Washington, DC. http://www .gfip.org/storage/gfip/economist%20-%20final%20version%201-2-09.pdf.

Kudrle, R. T., and L. Eden. 2003. "The Campaign against Tax Havens: Will It Last? Will It Work?" *Stanford Journal of Law, Business and Finance* 9 (1): 37–68.

Lall, S. 1973. "Transfer-Pricing by Multinational Manufacturing Firms." *Oxford Bulletin of Economics and Statistics* 35 (3): 173–95.

Lecraw, D. 1985. "Some Evidence of Transfer Pricing by Multinational Corporations." In *Multinationals and Transfer Pricing*, ed. A. M. Rugman and L. Eden, 223–40. Croom Helm Series in International Business. London: Croom Helm.

Li, S. H., and K. R. Balachandran. 1996. "Effects of Differential Tax Rates on Transfer Pricing." *Journal of Accounting, Auditing and Finance* 11 (2): 183–96.

Lo, A. W. Y., R. M. K. Wong, and M. Firth. 2010. "Can Corporate Governance Deter Management from Manipulating Earnings? Evidence from Related-Party Sales Transactions in China." *Journal of Corporate Finance* 16 (2): 225–35.

McDonald, M. 2008. "Income Shifting from Transfer Pricing: Further Evidence from Tax Return Data." OTA Technical Working Paper 2 (July), Office of Tax Analysis, U.S. Department of the Treasury, Washington, DC.

Murray, R., ed. 1981. *Multinationals beyond the Market: Intra-firm Trade and the Control of Transfer Pricing.* London: John Wiley and Sons.

Natke, P. 1985. "A Comparison of Import Pricing by Foreign and Domestic Firms in Brazil." In *Multinationals and Transfer Pricing*, ed. A. M. Rugman and L. Eden, 212–22. Croom Helm Series in International Business. London: Croom Helm.

Nitsch, V. 2009. "Trade Mispricing and Illicit Flows." Paper presented at the World Bank's conference, "The Dynamics of Illicit Flows from Developing Countries," Washington, DC, September 14–15.

OECD (Organisation for Economic Co-operation and Development). 1979. "Transfer Pricing and Multinational Enterprises: Report of the OECD Committee on Fiscal Affairs." OECD, Paris.

———. 1995. "Transfer Pricing Guidelines for Multinational Enterprises and Tax Administrations." OECD, Paris.

———. 1998. "Harmful Tax Competition: An Emerging Global Issue." Report, OECD, Paris.

———. 2010. "Intra-firm Trade: A Work in Progress." Document STD/TBS/WPTGS (2010)24 (September 8), Working Party on International Trade in Goods and Trade in Services Statistics, Statistics Directorate, OECD, Paris.

Pak, S. J., and J. S. Zdanowicz. 1994. "A Statistical Analysis of the US Merchandise Trade Data Base and Its Uses in Transfer Pricing Compliance and Enforcement." *Tax Management: Transfer Pricing Report* 3 (1): 50–57.

———. 2002. "U.S. Trade with the World: An Estimate of 2001 Lost U.S. Federal Income Tax Revenues Due to Over-Invoiced Imports and Under-Invoiced Exports." Unpublished working paper, School of Graduate Professional Studies, Penn State University–Great Valley, Malvern, PA.

Plasschaert, S. R. F. 1994. *Transnational Corporations: Transfer Pricing and Taxation.* Vol. 14 of *United Nations Library on Transnational Corporations.* London: Routledge.

Rugman, A. M. 1985. "Transfer Pricing in the Canadian Petroleum Industry." In *Multinationals and Transfer Pricing,* ed. A. M. Rugman and L. Eden, 173–92. Croom Helm Series in International Business. London: Croom Helm.

Rugman, A. M., and L. Eden, eds. 1985. *Multinationals and Transfer Pricing.* Croom Helm Series in International Business. London: Croom Helm.

Sikka, P. N., and H. Willmott. 2010. "The Dark Side of Transfer Pricing: Its Role in Tax Avoidance and Wealth Retentiveness." *Critical Perspectives on Accounting* 21 (4): 342–56.

Swenson, D. 2001. "Tax Reforms and Evidence of Transfer Pricing." *National Tax Journal* 54 (1): 7–26.

Tang, R. Y. W. 1993. *Transfer Pricing in the 1990s: Tax and Management Perspectives.* Westport, CT: Quorum Books.

———. 1997. *Intrafirm Trade and Global Transfer Pricing Regulations.* Westport, CT: Quorum Books.

———. 2002. *Current Trends and Corporate Cases in Transfer Pricing.* Westport, CT: Quorum Books.

TJN (Tax Justice Network). 2007. *Closing the Floodgates: Collecting Tax to Pay for Development.* London: TJN. http://www.innovativefinance-oslo.no/pop.cfm?FuseAction=Doc&pAction=View&pDocumentId=11607.

UNCTAD (United Nations Conference on Trade and Development). 1978. "Dominant Positions of Market Power of Transnational Corporations: Use of the Transfer Pricing Mechanism." Document TD/B/C.2/167, United Nations, New York.

———. 1992. *World Investment Report 1992: Transnational Corporations as Engines of Growth.* Document ST/CTC/130. Geneva: UNCTAD.

———. 1999. "Transfer Pricing." Document UNCTAD/ITE/IIT/11 (vol. I), UNCTAD Series on Issues in International Investment Agreements, UNCTAD, Geneva.

———. 2010. *World Investment Report 2010: Investing in a Low-Carbon Economy.* Geneva: UNCTAD.

———. 2011. *World Investment Report 2011: Non-Equity Modes of International Production and Development.* Geneva: UNCTAD.

U.S. Census Bureau. 2010. "U.S. Goods Trade: Imports & Exports by Related-Parties 2009." U.S. Census Bureau News CB10–57 (May 12), U.S. Department of Commerce, Washington, DC. http://www.census.gov/foreign-trade/Press-Release/2009pr/aip/related_party/rp09.pdf.

Vaitsos, C. V. 1974. *Intercountry Income Distribution and Transnational Enterprises.* Oxford: Clarendon Press.

Vincent, J. R. 2004. "Detecting Illegal Trade Practices by Analyzing Discrepancies in Forest Products Trade Statistics: An Application to Europe, with a Focus on Romania." Policy Research Working Paper 3261, World Bank, Washington, DC.

Wood, E., and T. Moll. 1994. "Capital Flight from South Africa: Is Under-Invoicing Exaggerated?" *South African Journal of Economics* 62 (1): 28–45.

8

The Role of Transfer Pricing in Illicit Financial Flows

Carlos A. Leite

Abstract

As multinationals have become a larger fixture in international trade and the weight of intracompany transactions has increased, the practice of transfer pricing has come under greater and often strident scrutiny. In this chapter, we review the current practice of transfer pricing and its impact on the ability of developing countries to collect tax revenue.

After an overview of the arm's-length principle (ALP), the key concept in modern-day transfer pricing regulations, we discuss the complexities involved in determining prices for transactions between related parties in a context of competing interests and unique transactions. By means of examples drawn from specific real-world cases, we (1) illustrate the difficulties in simultaneously assuring that companies are not double taxed and that competing tax authorities collect their fair share of tax revenue and (2) distinguish between tax avoidance and tax evasion and examine the relationship of each to the illegality of financial flows.

Unfortunately, the existing literature on the impact of transfer pricing abuses on developing countries provides insufficient evidence on the extent of income shifting and the role of transfer price manipulation and few insights into the possible illicit nature of the underlying transactions. We conclude by noting that (1) expanding the use of the ALP is the best option for a theoretically sound and globally consistent approach to transfer pricing, and (2) it is crucial for developing countries to adopt a specific transfer pricing regime and to engage in a higher degree of information sharing among tax authorities.

Introduction

Multinationals are the most successful form of business organization largely because of inherent advantages in the access to crucial knowledge and processes and in the ability to secure economies of scale. Over the past three decades, the number of multinationals has risen 10-fold, from a modest 7,258 in 1970 to nearly 79,000 by 2006 (UNCTAD 2008). Against the background of falling barriers to international commerce, these corporations have played a key role in boosting trade and foreign direct investment (FDI) flows, and, as their far-flung operations have expanded, so has the importance of intrafirm trade.[1] It is estimated that, globally, multinationals account for approximately two-thirds of trade flows, and fully half of these are intrafirm transactions.[2] These developments and trends have distinct consequences for international taxation, and some observers have linked weaknesses in tax collection in developing countries with the propensity of multinationals to use financial artifices, including favorable transfer pricing practices on intrafirm trade, to shift income (illegally) around the world.

As a result, transfer pricing has been raised from the status of an arcane subject solely in the purview of tax administrators and practitioners to a ranking as the most important issue in international taxation in surveys of business people. It has also become a key point of discussion among politicians, economists, and nongovernmental organizations. Technically, transfer pricing refers to the pricing or valuation of intrafirm transactions (a complex task in practice) and the consequent allocation of profits for tax and other internal purposes (a complicated balancing act of competing national interests and public policy choices). On one side of these transactions, multinationals aim, first, at avoiding double taxation (a strong deterrent to international trade) and, second, at minimizing the tax burden (potentially a source of competitive advantage).

Meanwhile, the tax authority of the entity on the selling side of the transaction attempts to raise the price to maximize its own tax collection (on which its performance is judged), and, finally, the tax authority of the entity on the purchasing side of the transaction attempts to lower the price so that its own tax collections can be higher (on which its effectiveness is evaluated). The complexity of the resulting to-and-fro necessitates a specific set of concepts and rules (including transfer pricing regulations and tax treaties) and even a specific interjurisdictional dispute resolution mechanism (the Mutual Agreement Procedure and Competent Authority process).

Following a summary introduction to the building blocks of transfer pricing and a brief discussion of some of the complexities of implementing the ALP, the stage is set for a discussion on the significant differences between tax avoidance and tax evasion and how these concepts intersect with the practice of transfer pricing. Next, we consider the existing literature on the impact of transfer pricing abuses on the tax revenues collected by developing countries; unfortunately, this literature tends to provide, at best, indirect evidence on the extent of income shifting and the role of transfer pricing, but few insights into the motivation or the possible illicit nature of the underlying transactions. We then discuss the importance of developing countries adopting a specific transfer pricing regime; we note, in particular, that a globally consistent tax regime and higher degree of information sharing among tax authorities on the application of transfer pricing policies will help to ensure consistency of application, make the rules clearer for taxpayers, and increase the ability of tax authorities to act in a fair and coordinated manner. We conclude by noting that the ALP and ongoing efforts of the Organisation for Economic Co-operation and Development (OECD) to expand the use of the ALP are the best option for a theoretically sound and globally consistent approach to transfer pricing.

Throughout the chapter, we illustrate some of the implementation and administration complexities faced by multinationals and tax authorities by discussing three cases taken from actual exchanges between taxpayers and tax authorities. In addition to tax-minimizing choices by management, these cases also illustrate the lack of coordination among tax authorities that sometimes risks compromising solid business strategies and valuable commercial relationships.

What Is the Arm's-Length Principle?

A simple theoretical construct

In a world of multijurisdictional taxation and multinational enterprises (MNEs) operating across borders, intercompany transactions have important tax implications, primarily because the associated transfer prices determine the distribution of profits and tax liabilities by jurisdiction.[3] Crucially, however, such transactions are not open-market transactions, which leaves unresolved the issue of the appropriate pricing mechanism (see box 8.1).[4]

For these cases, the pricing mechanism used most often is the ALP initially adopted by the OECD in 1979. The appeal of the ALP resides in its theoretical simplicity: simulate the market mechanism and set the transfer prices as if the transactions had been carried out between unrelated parties, each acting in its own best interest. This simple construct provides a legal framework that easily accommodates the two overriding objectives of an internationally consistent system: governments should collect their fair share of taxes, and enterprises should avoid double taxa-

---

Box 8.1. A Trading Intermediary: A Case of Management Foresight?

Background: A large natural resource company has vertically integrated operations in an industry comprised of a relatively few similarly structured firms and with sales agreements primarily in the form of long-term supply contracts.

Business arrangement: An intermediary subsidiary in a low-tax jurisdiction buys 100 percent of the company's production under a long-term contract and resells the product under a mix of long-term arrangements and spot contracts. The intermediary receives financing from the company, legally holds inventory, and assumes the business risks associated with the negotiating and reselling function.

Market developments: Because of unforeseen circumstances, the market changes (in what amounts analytically to an outward shift of the supply curve), and prices drop. It is during this time that the intermediary is set up. As the reasons for the original supply shift abate and as stronger economic growth boosts demand, the market changes again, and prices rise to historical highs.

Financial results: With long-term purchase contracts in place, the intermediary's financial results benefit significantly from the positive developments in the spot market, and, as some of the long-term sales contracts come up for renewal, its financial results improve additionally.

Bottom line: Should this outcome be attributed to management foresight (or perhaps fortune)? Should it be considered, ex post, as an example of abusive transfer pricing?

tion on their profits. Procedurally, effective application of the ALP in a way that minimizes crossborder disputes requires a system of bilateral tax treaties, together with mutual agreement and competent authority procedures that encourage principled negotiations and timely resolutions between the tax authorities on different sides of each transaction.

The ALP was formally defined in article 9 of the OECD Model Tax Convention on Income and on Capital and, later, in the OECD's transfer pricing guidelines, as follows:

> [When] conditions are made or imposed between . . . two [associated] enterprises in their commercial or financial relations which differ from those which would be made between independent enterprises, then any profits which would, but for those conditions, have accrued to one of the enterprises, but, by reason of those conditions, have not so accrued, may be included in the profits of that enterprise and taxed accordingly. (OECD 1995, I-3)

From this definition, the tax authority retains the right to adjust the transfer prices in a way that restores market prices. In adopting the ALP, a number of countries have gone further in laying out a framework of transfer pricing rules, including the following:

- Specific provisions for recharacterization and adjustments of transactions (that is, repricing carried out by the tax authority)
- Documentation requirements (typically, on a contemporaneous and transactional basis)
- Penalty provisions for noncompliance (typically focused on penalizing egregious failures of compliance rather than good faith errors)
- Advance pricing arrangements (which allow an ex ante agreement between taxpayers and tax authorities on the treatment of specific transactions)

Less than an exact science at the implementation level

Notwithstanding the broadbased agreement on the underlying theoretical principle and an extensive framework for settling disputes, the application of the ALP tends to be fact intensive and judgment-based, which poses challenges and opportunities for tax authorities and taxpayers alike (box 8.2). In other words, while the more popular discourse centers on potential transfer pricing abuses by MNEs, there is also no guarantee of a fair application of the ALP by tax authorities. During competent authority negotiations, for example, officers and representatives of separate tax authorities may be more concerned about protecting their respective tax bases than about a straightforward application of the ALP.[5] Additionally, the formal dispute resolution mechanisms do not mandate an outcome that necessarily avoids double taxation or even a timely conclusion, despite the emphasis on principled negotiations.

Consider, for example, the recent case of a company with well-known brands that were initially developed in the United States and that are legally owned by the U.S. parent, but that are marketed globally. How much of a royalty for the use of the brand should the U.S. parent charge its Canadian subsidiary, or, equivalently, how much of the operating profit of the Canadian subsidiary should be attributed to the value of these brands? The U.S. parent continues to expend substantial amounts

---

Box 8.2. A Trading Intermediary: Redux

Accounting treatment: The trading intermediary records all the revenue from its contracts, the cost of purchasing the goods from the parent company, and the cost of subcontracting the parent company for administrative and other business functions (at the equivalent cost, plus a market-related markup). The remaining profit is booked by the intermediary.

Possible taxpayer's position: The trading intermediary should be compensated for the business and market risks it has assumed. It trades on its own account, signs purchasing and sales contracts, takes legal possession of inventory, and has sufficient working capital to finance its own operations. Management had the foresight to set up the business structure at an opportune time (and, if market developments had gone in the other direction, the intermediary would have incurred losses).

Possible tax authority's position: The trading company is recording larger than market-related profits because it is overpricing the risks assumed, or, equivalently, it is underpricing the unique contribution of the strategic guidance provided by the parent company, particularly on the negotiation of contracts.

Current debate: The ability of taxpayers to modify their business structures in conformity with the ALP is currently a topic of much debate. In this case, the question could be framed around the sufficiency of the economic substance in the trading company effectively to take on all the risks that the parent company ascribes to its subsidiary, where, in the opinion of some tax authorities, the risks necessarily follow the assets and functions. In this case, the taxpayer could argue that the negotiating functions are more routine (based quite simply on the widely available spot price and market trends), and some observers would argue that the tax authority is simply adapting its own conceptual framework to ensure short-term revenue maximization (which is generally not good public policy).

on research and development, and it both develops and guides marketing campaigns around the world. Its transfer pricing policy specifies a
royalty of 4 percent of sales. The U.S. tax authority looked at the value of
the brand and indicated that, based on analysis of comparable transactions, a more appropriate charge would be in the range of 7–11 percent
(thus increasing the U.S. reported income). In looking at the same transaction, the Canadian tax authority analyzed company functions in Canada and indicated that it would disallow any crossborder royalty; it indicated that the marketing campaign in Canada, together with other
activities and investments of the Canadian entity, created local brand
awareness and equity.

In this dispute, the MNE is essentially neutral: the Canadian subsidiary is 100 percent owned, and internal transfers are a zero-sum game,
plus the tax rates in the two jurisdictions are broadly similar, and the
business environment is sufficiently comparable. Still, it now faces a
conundrum on how to set its transfer prices as it is pulled by one tax
authority and pushed by the other; failure to comply immediately with
both demands could mean large penalties and late-interest payments.[6]
Ultimately, the company could simply let the dispute go to competent
authority, let the tax authorities decide how to benchmark the royalty
charge, and focus on avoiding double taxation. However, there is no certainty of a settlement that fully eliminates double taxation, and the process of appeals and arbitration is a costly and time-consuming exercise.[7]
In other words, despite the focus in the public discourse on the potential
for transfer pricing abuses, there is a flip side that places MNEs at risk of
being caught between competing tax authorities and ending up with
double taxation (a significant cost if corporate tax rates are in the range
of 30–35 percent in Canada and the United States) and large interest
payments, as well as heavy penalties (which could amount to 10 percent
of any adjustments proposed by a tax authority).

This case highlights the fact that the theoretical simplicity of the ALP
is matched by judgment and complexity in implementation, but it also
illustrates some of the tough choices faced by MNEs in navigating the
sometimes choppy waters of a multijurisdictional taxation system. In this
case, the underlying transaction involves a unique intangible asset and
wide-open questions on the existence, ownership, and localization of the
asset. In practice, the absence of exactly comparable market transactions

from which to extract a market price necessitates approximations from either a range of similar transactions (adjusted for key comparability differences) or the use of valuation techniques that fundamentally rely on subjective assessments of economic contributions and company-specific financial forecasts. In such cases, the transfer pricing analysis tends to generate a range of prices, and any point within that range may be considered an arm's-length price.

Transfer pricing is not an exact science, and the OECD guidelines explicitly state as follows:

> There will be many occasions when the application of the most appropriate method or methods produces a range of figures all of which are relatively equally reliable. In these cases, differences in the figures that make up the range may stem from the fact that in general the application of the arm's-length principle only produces an approximation of conditions that would have been established between independent enterprises. (OECD 1995, I-19)

Furthermore, the OECD guidelines specify the following:

> A range of figures may also result when more than one method is applied to evaluate a controlled transaction. For example, two methods that attain similar degrees of comparability may be used to evaluate the arm's-length character of a controlled transaction. Each method may produce an outcome or a range of outcomes that differs from the other because of differences in the nature of the methods and the data, relevant to the application of a particular method, used. Nevertheless, each separate range potentially could be used to define an acceptable range of arm's-length figures. (OECD 1995, I-19)

To guide the process of selecting appropriate comparable transactions, transfer pricing reports include extensive functional analyses of a company's assets employed, functions undertaken, and risks borne.[8] Even if the product transacted is a commodity for which market prices are widely available, differences in circumstances and timing issues likely necessitate comparability adjustments. Consider, for example, a hypothetical multinational oil company selling a cargo of oil from Cabinda, Angola. Starting with the published price of Brent crude, you need to adjust (at least) for differences in chemical characteristics between the two types of crude and for transportation costs.[9] As the type of product or service becomes less of a traded commodity and more of the intermediate good that is often the subject of intrafirm transactions or even a more unique service or intangible, transfer pricing comes to rely even more on (1) comparability adjustments and ranges of prices obtained from a group of similarly comparable transactions and (2) profit-based methods, rather than product-based prices.[10]

In practice, derived ranges for arm's-length pricing can be quite broad. In a cost-markup situation, for example, it is not uncommon for a range with a central point (or average) at 10 percent to have a minimum of less than 5 percent and a maximum of around 15 percent. The range arises from differences in results across comparable companies and may also be affected by adjustments for differences in comparability between the tested party (the company for which the range is being calculated) and the comparable companies (which provide the market evidence).

In addition, to account for possible differences in the business and economic cycles, a three- or five-year average of results is typically used as the market benchmark (OECD 1995). The OECD guidelines recognize that, particularly in applying profit-based transfer pricing methods, it is necessary to take account of business cycles and special circumstances, such as the startup of a business, that cannot be fully addressed through comparability adjustments. Absent this option, a profit-based method might indicate that a transfer pricing adjustment is called for (simply) because the tested party is at the bottom of its business cycle when the uncontrolled comparables are at the peak of theirs.

Finally, differences in approach across tax authorities (for example, Canada with its general reliance on form and the United States with its general reliance on economic substance) create interstate frictions. Moreover, inconsistencies in domestic tax codes also create domestic frictions and additional opportunities for tax planning; for example, Canada actually blends an application of legal form for general anti-avoidance purposes with a reliance on economic substance for transfer pricing regulations.[11] These frictions can become either a source of concern for multinationals aiming to comply with differing provisions or an opportunity for tax arbitrage in the presence of creative tax planning and a favorable fact pattern. At the least, these frictions make MNEs base their decisions on transfer pricing issues not only on the underlying facts and the legal requirements, but also on the degree of aggressiveness (and capacity of monitoring) of each of the tax authorities. In other words, the decision framework becomes a risk-based compliance exercise driven by a fact-intensive and judgment-based analysis.

In summary, application of the ALP is more complex in practice than suggested by the relatively elegant theoretical construct. In recent years, the higher propensity for intrafirm trade to involve services, as well as intangible and financial assets, has raised particularly complex issues.

Tax Avoidance and Tax Evasion

Tax avoidance and tax evasion are fundamentally different

The courts first established the difference between tax avoidance and tax evasion in *IRC v. Duke of Westminster* ([1936] 19 TC 490). In this case, payments were made by the taxpayer to domestic employees in the form of deeds of covenant, but which, in substance, were payments of remuneration. The House of Lords refused to disregard the legal character (form) of the deeds merely because the same result (substance) could be brought about in another manner. Lord Tomlin commented, as follows: "Every man is entitled, if he can, to order his affairs so that the tax attaching under the appropriate Acts is less than it otherwise would be." In other words, taxpayers are entitled to arrange their tax affairs in the most tax efficient way, and this is the principle behind tax planning and tax avoidance.

Tax evasion, in contrast, involves an element of illegality and clearly gives rise to illicit financial flows.[12] Those participating in tax evasion may underreport taxable income or claim expenses that are nondeductible or overstated.[13] Tax evaders generally face criminal prosecution, and criminals are sometimes charged with tax evasion (given their usual reluctance to report income from criminal activities) if there is insufficient evidence to try them on the underlying criminal action. In the context of a transfer pricing system based on the ALP, income shifting could be characterized as illicit to the extent that it is not commensurate with a shift in assets, functions, and risks.

In recent years, the public debate has focused on activities that may be said to fall in a grey area, or situations open to an interpretation of the law. In this context, some commentators have described selected avoidance tactics as unacceptable because they may take unfair advantage of tax rules or run counter to the intentions of the legislators. The behavior of corporations in pursuing these more aggressive forms of tax avoidance has sometimes been labeled contradictory to the notion of corporate social responsibility. Others argue that the evenhanded administration of taxation is a matter of statutory interpretation of the tax statutes and should not be open to appeals to the intentions of legislators or vague notions of corporate social responsibility.

Business restructuring as a form of tax avoidance: An old concept

In a world of mobile factors of production, significant differences in tax rates across countries will inevitably lead to tax-based locational advantages, and profit-maximizing global companies will be at the forefront of securing the benefits of structuring their supply chain in a manner consistent with business objectives and tax minimization. However, the idea of structuring business operations in a way that minimizes tax liabilities is not, by any stretch of the imagination, a new construct. In ancient Greece, sea traders avoided the 2 percent tax imposed by the city-state of Athens on imported goods by using specific locations at which to deposit their foreign goods; in the Middle Ages, Hanseatic traders who set up business in London were exempt from tax; and, in the 1700s, the American colonies traded from Latin America to avoid British taxes.

Securing tax-based advantages will sometimes mean relocating production, development, and even administration centers to minimize the tax burden in a legally consistent manner. The resulting shift in assets, functions, and risks will inevitably also shift profits to those countries that offer an environment more consistent with profit maximization. Such a shift in profits, as long as it is accompanied by a commensurate shift in assets, functions, and risks, is a legally acceptable strategy; this is the essence of tax planning and tax avoidance. The related financial flows could not be considered illicit.

However, shifting profits without a business justification (that is, in a manner not commensurate with the assets employed, the risks borne, or the functions provided) is clearly illegal and should be considered illicit. For corporations engaging in such manipulative practices (which effectively means that the transfer prices employed are outside of the relevant arm's-length interval), the penalties can be costly. For example, Glaxo SmithKline announced, in September 2006, that they had settled a long-running transfer pricing dispute with the U.S. tax authorities, agreeing to pay US$3.1 billion in taxes related to an assessed income adjustment because of improper transfer pricing and also agreeing not to seek relief from double taxation (which is available through the bilateral tax treaty between the United Kingdom and the United States).

A case of windfall profits

Consider the case of a large petroleum company doing business in a high-risk country. During a typically turbulent period (in a recess from open conflict and in the run-up to a contentious election), the government solicits the assistance of the company's local subsidiary in building an electricity generating station (not normally an activity that the company would choose) and agrees to pay in barrels of oil (from government stocks) valued at the spot-market price (fixed over the term of the contract).[14] In the circumstances, the level of conflict escalates; the current government is removed from power; and the world price of oil rises considerably. For the company, the contract terms yield a windfall: it is able to sell the in-kind payment for roughly three or four times the fixed value set in the contract. In the normal course of business, the local subsidiary sells its local oil production to a foreign-related party (the group's trading subsidiary), which onsells to oil traders or refineries.

In a country with ALP transfer pricing regulations, the difference between the price set by the contract and the arm's-length price for local crude would likely be attributed to the local subsidiary as income. In turn, the trading subsidiary would be accorded a normal trading profit. In other words, given that the key value-driver in generating this income was the local contract and the related business risks assumed by the local subsidiary, an ALP-consistent allocation of profits would call for the bulk of the total profit to be declared in the source country, and the trading operation would earn a return consistent with comparable companies (that provide similar services to third parties).

Additional considerations are as follows:

- During this time period, the source country had no specific transfer pricing legislation, a marginal corporate tax rate of 60 percent, and a generally weak tax administration.
- By contrast, the OECD country where the trading subsidiary resides had a highly competent tax administration (which would certainly

have pressured the MNE into an ALP-consistent treatment if the country roles were reversed), a substantially lower marginal corporate tax rate of 35 percent, and a (legal) scheme that allowed a recharacterization of non–ALP-consistent inbound transactions (through a practice known as informal capital rulings).

- The local subsidiary was generally worried about the high-risk environment (including the possibility of expropriation) and a binding limit on its ability to repatriate profits.

In the end, the MNE managed to assign the (bulk of the) windfall profits to the trading subsidiary, which used an informal capital ruling to achieve a highly favorable tax treatment in the OECD country (likely at a tax rate of 1 percent for what was considered a capital contribution instead of taxable income).

Should this be considered a case of tax avoidance or tax evasion? In the absence of a legal requirement for related-party transactions to be carried out at arm's length, the local subsidiary honored its contract with the government, assumed the risk of a fixed price compensation scheme, benefited from the subsequent rise in oil prices, and onsold the oil to its related party at the same price it negotiated with the government. In the tax system of the source country, there was nothing that would label this transaction as illegal.[15]

Suppose, for instance, that the local subsidiary (which only has expertise in exploration and not in trading) had presold the oil receivable under the contract to its trading subsidiary at the time that it initially entered into the contract in an attempt to hedge its position. The impact on the assignment of profits would have been similar to a later transfer at the contract price. Should this transaction be labeled as a cautious business approach, or should it be characterized, ex post, as income shifting and, possibly, tax evasion?

Global tax planning and transfer pricing practices in developing countries

The case of the large petroleum company and its allocation of trading profits from the country of exploration to a low-tax OECD jurisdiction raises important questions about the tax system in developing countries and global tax cooperation. This discussion is particularly significant for resource-dependent economies that tend to have a large proportion of national production under the control of MNEs.

Currently, the centerpiece of international tax coordination is the bilateral tax treaty, which provides for specific tax treatment for taxpayers having sources of income in both countries and, possibly, crossborder transactions and generally includes certain obligations in terms of information sharing. Some of the key objectives for entering into such a treaty are the reduction of barriers to trade and investment, the reduction of double taxation (under the principle that the same source of income should only be taxed once), and elimination of tax evasion (including through information sharing). By specifying the tax treatment of certain transactions and instituting mechanisms for dispute resolution, tax treaties generally improve certainty for taxpayers and tax authorities. Under these treaties, specific mutual agreement procedures are used to resolve international tax grievances, including double taxation issues arising out of a transfer pricing transaction. The government agency responsible for implementing these dispute resolution procedures (and negotiating with other national tax authorities) is the competent authority of the country, which has the power to bind its government in specific cases.

While the network of tax treaties is fairly extensive among OECD countries, most developing countries have relatively few tax treaties in place. This severely restricts the ability of their tax authorities to share information and coordinate enforcement across borders. In addition, while internationally consistent transfer pricing regulations have been almost universally adopted throughout the OECD, relatively few developing countries have specific transfer pricing regulations. This helps to explain the recourse in some developing countries to specific arrangements for individual projects and individual MNEs (through, for example, individually negotiated production-sharing contracts, which effectively lay out a complete legal, tax, and customs regime specific to individual projects), although, given the general lack of negotiating capacity and sector-specific expertise, it would seem more appropriate to lay out one general regime by which all related projects would abide.

However, the practice of bilateral company-by-company negotiations raises the level of influence of specific bureaucrats and politicians. This situation often leads to practices that are judged as corrupt in OECD countries, and companies operating in such corrupt environments face thorny issues on the legality and licit nature of certain transactions. In countries with highly corrupt regimes or stringent exchange controls (the two often go hand in hand), companies may consider the manipulation of transfer prices—which is particularly easy in the absence of specific transfer pricing regulations—as an acceptable method of profit repatriation. In the case above of the large petroleum company, this consideration was likely important given the state of the business environment and the existence of severe restrictions on profit repatriation at the time. It is questionable whether such a technically illegal attempt to shift income out of a corrupt regime should be considered an illicit flow of funds.

More recently, with the substantial reduction in exchange controls across the world, the concern of tax authorities, particularly in OECD countries, has shifted to how easy it has become for taxpayers to conceal foreign-based income on which residents should pay national tax. By accessing foreign jurisdictions offering low or zero tax rates and failing to report the proceeds to their home authorities and then not reporting the foreign-based income, these taxpayers evade their tax obligations with respect to their country of residence. Required reporting under exchange controls has provided information that is helpful in tracking the flows of funds and, therefore, in assessing tax obligations. Without transfer pricing regulations or exchange controls in the country in which the income is earned, taxpayers may find it particularly easy to evade tax obligations through a combination of transfer price manipulation and access to a tax haven.[16]

Empirical Evidence on Illicit Financial Flows from Developing Countries

The wide variations in tax rates across the globe certainly lead MNEs to respond to the incentives created by these differences. We have good evidence that recorded profits of MNEs shift among countries after a change in tax rates.[17] Of course, MNEs are likely to respond in a similar fashion to comparable arbitrage opportunities created by the different mix of skills and costs among different locations within countries and across countries. After all, their performance is judged by shareholders on their ability to maximize after-tax profits, and economic efficiency is generally raised by the search for lower costs. What is less clear is how much of this profit shifting is associated with tax evasion, and, within that category, how much is due to transfer pricing. In other words, given that transfer pricing analyses typically provide a range of prices or profit levels consistent with the ALP, is it the case that MNEs simply select a point within the range that legally minimizes their tax liability, or is it, instead, the case that MNEs effectively choose a point outside the ALP range?

The role of transfer pricing

To date, there is no direct evidence on the role that transfer pricing plays in tax evasion (box 8.3). It is likely true, however, that MNEs routinely choose prices within the ALP range in a tax efficient manner, but this would be classified, at most, as tax avoidance. Two recent studies, Bartelsman and Beetsma (2003) and Clausing (2003), provide direct evidence on the related issue of profit shifting associated with transfer pricing. Their findings are broadly consistent with tax minimization strategies, but neither of these studies distinguishes between tax avoidance and tax evasion. Both studies find that a 1 percentage point increase in a country's tax rate leads to a decline in reported taxable income of roughly 2.0–2.5 percent. These findings are consistent with the interpretation that a lower corporate tax rate tends to encourage firms to anchor their

---

Box 8.3. A Measure of Tax Evasion in the United States

In what is likely the most rigorous exercise of its kind, the U.S. tax authority estimated that the gross tax gap for the U.S. taxation year 2001 was close to US$350 billion, of which US$30 billion was due to the corporate sector (on account of nonfiling, underreporting, and underpayment).[a] It is not clear how much of this was associated with transfer pricing issues. In any case, this estimate is also likely to be an overestimate given that the U.S. tax authority would not have taken account of the reverse situation in which a United States–resident corporation overreports income in the United States (because the other jurisdiction is the high-tax country).

a. The gross tax gap is defined as "the difference between what taxpayers should have paid and what they actually paid on a timely basis"; it excludes the impact of penalties and late interest collected by the tax authority. In the U.S. study, the bulk of the tax gap arose from underreporting on individual tax returns (close to US$200 billion) and on employment returns (close to US$55 billion).

transfer pricing policy at different points within the ALP range or else to restructure their businesses in a way that increases reported profits in the taxing country.

For developing countries, Kar and Cartwright-Smith (2008) and Christian Aid (2009) provide estimates of trade misinvoicing practices by which profits are shifted out of developing countries. The former study suggests that, between 2002 and 2006, approximately US$370 billion in profits were shifted out of the developing world every year, and the latter study suggests that the figure for the period between 2005 and 2007 is more than US$1 trillion. The headline number in these reports is the estimated tax revenue loss, which is calculated at close to US$120 billion per year. (This compares with global flows of official development assistance of roughly the same magnitude in 2008.)

These figures are not widely accepted, and the academic literature has raised important questions with respect to the methodology and the strength of the conclusions.[18] For our purposes, these studies do not allow any conclusions on the role of transfer pricing because they do not use company-level data; given that transfer pricing is intrinsically fact-dependent, the extent of non-ALP transfer pricing can only be determined by analyzing transaction-level data to ensure that apparent income shifting in the aggregate data is not caused by (1) reasonable comparability differences, (2) variations in product quality, or (3) a reflection of shifts in assets, functions, and risks.[19] In fact, these studies do not even distinguish between transactions involving unrelated and related parties.

Impact on local economies and tax collections

What is also less clear is the impact on the economies and on tax collections of developing countries. In fact, during the recent globalization drive that included a substantial increase in the number of MNEs and in the share of intrafirm transactions in trade flows, corporate tax revenues remained stable across the world. So, why are there differences in the perceived widespread effects of transfer pricing practices and the available empirical analyses? First, the existing estimates are derived from studies with substantial methodological shortcomings, and, second, the evidence of these studies runs counter to the observed response of FDI to tax rates and the recent buoyancy in corporate tax revenues.

As recently reviewed by Fuest and Riedel (2009), the existing studies are purely descriptive, employ the marginal tax rate to calculate the tax gap, and do not account for the reverse effects of profits shifted into developing countries, some of which do have significantly lower corporate tax rates.[20] In addition, recent work on the demand for tax haven operations suggests that tax havens may not have purely negative consequences (Desai, Foley, and Hines 2006). This work indicates the following:

- Multinational parent companies in industries that typically face low foreign tax rates, those that are technology intensive, and those in industries characterized by extensive intrafirm trade are more likely than others to operate in tax havens.
- Firms with growing activity in high-tax countries are most likely to initiate tax haven operations, and the reduced costs of using tax havens are likely to stimulate investment in nearby high-tax countries.

The same studies that provide estimates of large tax gaps created in developing countries by illicit flows from tax-induced manipulations also need to provide answers to puzzles related to (1) the sensitivity of FDI to tax rates, (2) the broadly similar levels of tax rates across countries, and (3) the buoyancy of tax collections in the 1990s.

Consistent with economic theory, we have good empirical evidence that FDI responds to statutory tax rates and other features of the tax system.[21] Meanwhile, it is popularly thought that MNEs are finding more and more ways to shift income (including by optimizing financing structures, choosing advantageous accounting treatments, and using offshore financial centers and tax havens).[22] Taken together, these facts suggest that the sensitivity of FDI to tax factors should be decreasing over time given that the increasing availability of income shifting practices suggests that the burdens of high host country rates can be more easily avoided (without the need for costly reallocations of real investment). However, the sensitivity of FDI to tax factors appears, if anything, to be increasing over time.[23] This is consistent with tax avoidance rather than tax evasion.

Stöwhase (2006) finds that, in addition, the elasticity of FDI to tax incentives in the European Union differs strongly according to economic sector. While taxes are insignificant as a determinant of FDI in the primary sector, tax elasticity is substantial in manufacturing, and it is even greater in service industries.[24] The increasing differentiation of products and the growing reliance on service transactions and intangibles as one moves from the primary to the secondary and tertiary sectors would make it easier to shift profits simply by manipulating transfer prices, without the need for costly reallocations. While this finding, as indicated by Stöwhase, amounts to (indirect) evidence of income shifting, the responsiveness of FDI is evidence that profits are moving in a way commensurate with FDI flows (that is, with shifts in assets, risks, and functions). In other words, this evidence is more consistent with legal tax planning and tax avoidance strategies rather than with tax evasion.

We also know that corporate tax rates are broadly similar in developing countries and developed countries, notwithstanding differences in tax rates and tax structures across countries (World Bank 2004).[25] For transfer pricing, this implies that manipulations that are purely tax motivated should involve a tax-evading higher import price into a developing country and a tax-inducing higher export price from a developed country as much as a tax-evading higher import price into a developed country and a tax-inducing higher export price from a developing country. In this context, it is not clear why MNEs would consistently engage in tax-driven practices geared strictly to stripping out profits from developing countries. Yet, many studies consider only one direction in mispricing transactions, which results in a significant overestimation of the net tax revenue losses; this includes estimates prepared by tax departments of OECD countries.

Finally, some commentators point out that the revenue collected tends to be lower in developing countries than in developed countries, notwithstanding broadly similar tax rates. Data of the World Bank's World Development Indicators suggest that the average ratio of tax revenue to gross domestic product in the developed world is approximately 35 percent compared with 15 percent in developing countries and only 12 percent in low-income countries.[26] This gap, it is further argued, is a sign of a nexus of phenomena, such as encroaching globalization and corporate profit shifting, that work against the ability of developing countries to collect needed tax revenue (generally dubbed the harmful tax competition argument).

Developments during the 1990s do not appear to support the argument of a race to the bottom, however. As the pace of globalization picked up in the 1990s, there was a substantial increase in the number of MNEs and a significant extension of the set of options available for the manipulation of tax liabilities. Concurrently, there were significant increases in the share of intrafirm transactions in trade flows, but either slight increases or, at worst, stability in corporate tax revenues across the world (despite falls in marginal tax rates).[27]

Thus, clear evidence on the tax motives of transfer pricing abuses requires a disaggregated empirical analysis using evidence on how companies actually set their transfer pricing policies and a comparison with arm's-length price ranges by transaction. In addition, to assess whether any related tax gap could be remedied by a tax-system response would also require evidence on the extent to which tax considerations influence transfer pricing decisions. Limited by the availability of data, the resulting analyses now tend to be conducted at too high a level of aggregation and without a sufficient theoretical foundation to provide any direct evidence on the extent of the problem or any insight into the motivation of the participants.[28] Most careful analysts now explicitly recognize that care must be taken in interpreting the results of the typical regression analysis of subsidiary profitability on tax rates.[29] On the ground, the buoyancy of corporate tax revenues across the world during a period characterized by a substantial increase in the share of intrafirm transactions suggests that transfer pricing did not play a significant role in the manipulation of tax liabilities.

A Plan of Action for Developing Countries

Developing countries need primarily to become more effectively integrated into the international taxation regime.[30] In particular, these countries should do the following:

- Strengthen tax administration and enforcement (institutions matter)
- Improve the exchange of tax information between governments (reflecting the globalized state of business transactions and MNE operations and the consequent need for international coordination among tax authorities)[31]

In the area of transfer pricing, they should adopt the following:

- Globally consistent regulations for transfer pricing (implement best practice)

- Contemporaneous documentation requirements (to facilitate enforcement)
- The use of advance pricing agreements, which hold the promise of simplifying the negotiation and monitoring of transfer pricing practices, including by generating relatively quickly a much-needed body of locally relevant precedents[32]

The call to strengthen enforcement is a common refrain, but it is nonetheless of primary importance. Low tax collection rates occur more often in countries where fundamental issues of tax administration and institutional weaknesses tend to complicate (severely) the enforcement of the existing tax regime, regardless of choices on tax policy. The operational challenges include not only questions of organizational design (encompassing accountability mechanisms, the relationship between policy and administration, and risk management practices), but also capability in basic tools such as auditing and a sound knowledge of legal principles.

The fact that these economies tend to be economically less diversified actually enhances the ability to make quick progress toward effective implementation of the ALP. MNEs operate in relatively few sectors in these economies, and tax auditors require a clear understanding of only a few types of business models, that is, by strengthening their degree of familiarity with the assets, functions, and risks deployed in only a few sectors, tax auditors can typically cover a significant proportion of the tax clientele that uses transfer prices in determining tax liabilities (for example, see the case of Zambia in box 8.4).

The other recommendations (exchange of information and a globally consistent transfer pricing regime) are crucial because taxpayers tend to view transfer pricing (primarily) from a risk-management point of view. As a result, there is a natural tendency for companies to undertake more efforts to comply with the requirements of those countries that have more effective regulations (including documentation requirements) and enforcement capacities (so as to minimize the possibility of compliance penalties and negative publicity). By the adoption of clear and globally consistent transfer pricing regulations, developing countries should be able to nudge MNEs into a more balanced risk assessment, which would permit the revenue authorities to direct their limited resources to

Box 8.4. Zambia: Tax Collection in the Copper Sector

A recent boom in the copper sector in Zambia resulted in a substantial increase in copper exports, but only minimal increases in tax revenue: mining royalties received by the Zambian government in 2006 represented only 0.6 percent of sales. As identified by advocacy group Southern Africa Resource Watch, the culprits were the fiscal terms in agreements signed by the government during the slump experienced in the copper sector in the late 1990s. Faced with falling levels of investment, a collapsing state-owned mining conglomerate, and low global prices, the government agreed to renegotiate the original contracts and include sector-specific incentives designed to make mining investments more attractive (Horman 2010).

As a result, the new mining tax regime proposes to raise tax rates, reduce incentives, and require that transfer prices be based on the price of copper quoted at the London Metal Exchange or the Shanghai Stock Exchange.

For purposes of transfer pricing, the commodity nature of unprocessed copper (as exported by Zambia) makes the use of market-quoted prices the undisputed choice for a transfer pricing methodology (possibly with an adjustment for differential transportation costs). In other words, the simple adoption of the ALP would bring about the desired result with relatively little need for upfront capacity building (market quotes are widely available) and would also avoid an ad hoc sector-specific approach to the problem.

enforcement areas where they are most needed.[33] At the same time, the enhanced opportunities for international cooperation and access to a wider set of knowledge resources will tend to strengthen efforts at capacity building.

Consistent with these priorities, OECD has focused its tax evasion work on the widespread adoption of the OECD transparency and exchange of information standard. In the circumstances, the number of tax information exchange agreements, a key platform of this approach, doubled to over 80 during the first six months of 2009. This should make it easier for tax authorities to share information and cooperate on cases of tax evasion, and it may even lead to the increased use of simultaneous examinations (by different tax authorities of the same taxpayers).[34]

Conclusion

In discussing the role of transfer pricing in illicit financial flows in developing countries, we start with a review of the current OECD-supported system based on the ALP, and we examine the differences between tax avoidance and tax evasion. Although an elegant and simple concept as a theoretical construct, the ALP becomes a fact-intensive and judgment-based system at the implementation level. Often, the benchmarking of comparable transactions and companies provides a range of acceptable prices and the conclusion that any point inside this range is consistent with arm's-length pricing. In this context, selecting a lower (or higher) price within the arm's-length range of prices, whether in response to tax objectives or otherwise, cannot be construed as anything other than a legal practice or, at most, as tax avoidance. Similarly, shifting income from one country to another in a manner that is commensurate with a shift in assets, functions, and risks cannot be construed as anything other than a legal way of business restructuring.

Alternative proposals for a transfer pricing system, including grandiose schemes involving a global tax authority and global apportionment formulas, have been proposed and debated. Overall, these alternatives not only lack theoretical rigor, but are also less likely to win international agreement (which is crucial to ensuring that rules are consistently and fairly applied). Therefore, we argue that the current framework provides a construct that should help corporations avoid double taxation and should also help tax administrations receive a fair share of the tax base of multinational enterprises. While any set of rules can be potentially manipulated, the OECD-led initiative to develop and extend the reach of transfer pricing guidelines based on the ALP represents the best alternative for a system that is theoretically sound and amenable to being implemented in an internationally coordinated and consistent manner.

We also review the empirical evidence on the impact of transfer pricing in illicit flows from developing countries. Essentially, there is no direct evidence of such an impact. The majority of available studies are conducted at an aggregate level, and even the studies that provide direct evidence on the extent of income shifting arising from transfer prices do not distinguish between ALP-consistent price changes (tax avoidance) and non–ALP-consistent changes (tax evasion). There is also a dearth of analytically rigorous evidence on the impact of income shifting on developing countries and their ability to collect taxes.

Finally, we discuss the importance of introducing a specific transfer pricing regime in developing countries (rather than relying on ad hoc measures and general antiavoidance provisions). This would ensure that tax structures and policies are more well integrated with international best practice, and, for the private sector, it would make the rules of the game more globally consistent and transparent. However, it is clear that, at the implementation level, developing countries face significant challenges in adopting the OECD-style transfer pricing regime, owing not only to the malleability of the ALP concept, but also the lack of access to appropriate benchmarks by which to assess transfer prices. The impact of these difficulties is likely to be more acute for those countries that are highly dependent on revenues from natural resources, a sector that tends to be dominated by multinationals and intrafirm trade.

Notes

1. Intrafirm trade is defined here as crossborder trade among affiliates of the same multinational corporation.
2. The coverage of data on intrafirm trade is not comprehensive. For the United States, the best estimates now suggest that intrafirm trade accounts for approximately 50 percent of all imports, and transactions involving other countries of the Organisation for Economic Co-operation and Development (OECD) are significantly more likely to involve related parties.
3. For a complementary discussion, see chapter 7 by Lorraine Eden in this volume.
4. The ability to collect tax revenues from the corporate sector is particularly important for developing countries, which tend to rely relatively more on corporate taxes as a source of revenue. Developing countries tend to collect about half the tax revenue, as a share of gross domestic product, relative to developed countries and to rely much more heavily on indirect and trade taxes (Tanzi and Zee 2001).
5. Competent authority refers to a national body entrusted with interpreting and implementing tax conventions. The competent authority deals with situations in which taxpayers are subject to taxation not in accordance with the provisions of the relevant tax convention, including situations of double taxation.
6. In Canada, transfer pricing penalties effectively amount to 10 percent of the resulting adjustment to the transfer prices. This is a non–tax-deductible expense.
7. The start of this process involves a tax audit that may occur up to five or six years after the relevant fiscal year and that may take years to complete. Thereafter, settlements from the competent authority process typically take years to conclude, and the negotiation process requires multiple stages of written submissions. The complexity of this process means that, in most cases, the taxpayer employs highly specialized tax advisers over the course of the tax audit and the deliberations by the competent authority.
8. The types of risks that must be taken into account include market risks; risks of loss associated with the investment in and use of property, plant, and equipment; risks associated with the outcome of research and development activities;

risks of collection of accounts receivable; risks associated with product liability; and financial risks such as those caused by currency exchange rate and interest rate variability.

9. Adjustments routinely undertaken in transfer pricing analyses account for differences in accounting practices for inventories, intangible assets, or depreciation; level of working capital; cost of capital; level of market; treatment of foreign exchange gains; and impact of extraordinary items. The total of these adjustments can sometimes produce a substantial cumulative adjustment to the underlying market price, in which case the OECD guidelines question whether the degree of comparability between the selected companies and the tested party is sufficiently high, but, in practice, there are no specific criteria by which to make this determination. Of course, in the absence of a more adequate method or more comparable data, the analysis in question may remain the most feasible, and, in any case, it may still produce a relatively tight range of arm's-length prices.

10. The OECD views profit-based methods (such as the transaction net margin method or, in the United States, the comparable profit method) as generally less reliable than the traditional transaction methods such as the comparable uncontrolled price, which is a product comparable method. The latter, however, requires the identification of transactions involving the same product and third parties (to be used as the comparable uncontrolled transaction by which to price the related-party transaction), and, in practice, companies tend not to transact with a third party on the same terms as a related party. Differences in transactions with related and unrelated parties include (a) volume or other size or scale factors, (b) level of the market, (c) temporary versus permanent relationship, (d) primary sourcing versus secondary sourcing, and (e) after-sales service, warranty services, and payment terms. Thus, either comparability adjustments are necessary (if a potential comparable uncontrolled transaction can even be identified) or profit-based methods must be used.

11. In this context, form means that the legal setup or structure of the transactions takes precedence in terms of its characterization (and treatment) for tax purposes, whereas economic substance implies that the underlying business or economic rationale is paramount (regardless of the legal form). Where the economic substance concept applies, for example, tax authorities may look through intermediate transactions and merely consider the aggregate effect for purposes of tax treatment. In the specific case of Canada and the United States, this has promoted the use of hybrid transactions that are characterized differently in each country (so that the same transaction, for example, may be viewed as a dividend receipt by one jurisdiction and an interest payment by the other jurisdiction).

12. As defined in Wikipedia (http://en.wikipedia.org/wiki/Tax_avoidance_and_tax_ evasion [accessed August 31, 2009]), "tax avoidance is the legal utilization of the tax regime to one's own advantage, in order to reduce the amount of tax that is

payable by means that are within the law. By contrast tax evasion is a felony and the general term for efforts to not pay taxes by illegal means." Consistent with these definitions, the OECD has been focusing on combating tax evasion (OECD 2009).

13. Concerns with egregious cases of tax evasion have recently come to the fore with the widespread publicity accorded to the 2008 case involving LGT Bank of Liechtenstein. After the initial case became public in Germany, a U.S. Senate investigations committee extended the inquiry to possible abuses by American taxpayers; other countries followed suit; and the issue of tax evasion and tax havens has since become a key agenda item at various international policy forums. The report by the U.S. committee estimated that offshore tax havens supported tax evasion schemes that reduced tax collections in the United States by about US$100 billion per year (compared with annual gross domestic product of around US$14.2 trillion, annual federal tax revenue of close to US$2.5 trillion, and annual federal spending on Medicare and Medicaid of some US$675.0 billion) (see Permanent Subcommittee on Investigations, 2008, "Tax Haven Banks and U.S. Tax Compliance: Staff Report," Report, U.S. Senate, Washington, DC, July 17).

14. In this region of the world, government routinely collects royalty and tax payments in kind. At the time the contract was signed, the price of the commodity was near historical lows.

15. In the absence of a specific transfer pricing regulation, there was no specific authority to enforce compliance with the ALP even though the tax laws included general antiavoidance provisions (which are typically vaguely worded, difficult to interpret without legal precedents, and cumbersome to implement).

16. Tax authorities in some OECD countries are combating the lack of disclosure that is part of these tax evasion schemes by accessing a wider set of information. In the United States, for example, the Internal Revenue Service has started relying on records from American Express, MasterCard, and Visa to track the spending of U.S. citizens using credit cards issued in Antigua and Barbuda, The Bahamas, and Cayman Islands. As a direct result of such information, the accounting firm KPMG admitted that its employees had criminally generated at least US$11 billion in phony tax losses, often routed through Cayman Islands, which cost the United States US$2.5 billion in tax revenue, and, in 2007, the drug maker Merck agreed to pay US$2.3 billion to the government to settle a claim that it had hidden profits in a Bermudan partnership.

17. For example, Maffini and Mokkas (2008, 1) find that "a 10 percentage points cut in the statutory corporate tax rate would increase multinationals' measured [total factor productivity] by about 10 percent relative to domestic firms, consistent with profit-shifting by multinationals."

18. For a review, see Fuest and Riedel (2009). Even for the United States, where more disaggregated and higher-quality data are available, the U.S. Government Accountability Office recognizes that the usefulness of the available estimates

and our ability to interpret the results crucially "[depend] on how many of the important nontax characteristics have been included in the analysis" (GAO 2008, 5). This is because the statistical relationships exploited by most studies are liable to be considerably affected by the researchers' ability to control for significant industry- and corporate-specific effects. The importance of these controls is highlighted by the U.S. Government Accountability Office (GAO 2008), which indicates that, for the United States, foreign-controlled domestic corporations tended to report lower tax liabilities than United States–controlled domestic corporations between 1998 and 2005 (by most measures), but also that the percentage reporting no tax liability was not statistically different after 2001. Most importantly, these two types of corporations differ significantly in age, size, and industry, and companies in different sectors are likely to have different financial characteristics (including levels of assets) and therefore different levels of receipts and profitability. The U.S. Government Accountability Office does not attempt to explain the extent to which such factors affect differences in reported tax liabilities (GAO 2008).

19. There is, for example, empirical support for the notion that price differences within product groups are mostly related to quality differences, where "developing countries tend to export low-end/low-price products whereas developed countries export high-end products with higher prices" (Fuest and Riedel 2009, 33).

20. For more detailed considerations, see Fuest and Riedel (2009) and our discussion elsewhere in the text on the incentives for mispricing on both the import side and the export side.

21. The empirical evidence also confirms that FDI is responsive to other locational advantages such as country risk, public inputs, and skill availability.

22. For a more scholarly summary, see Altshuler and Grubert (2006). For a more populist treatment, see recent publications by the Tax Justice Network, Christian Aid, and Oxfam, among others.

23. See, for example, Mutti and Grubert (2004) and, for a brief summary, Zodrow (2008).

24. The results of this research are summarized in Haufler and Stöwhase (2003), as follows:

   • FDI in the primary sector (consisting of agriculture, fishing, mining and quarrying) has a tax elasticity of around zero, implying that FDI is not driven by tax incentives.
   • Investment in the secondary sector (manufacturing) is negatively and significantly affected by an increase in effective taxation. The tax elasticity is around −2, implying that a 1 percent increase in the tax rate of the host country decreases FDI by roughly 2 percent, all else being equal.
   • Compared with the secondary sector, FDI in the tertiary sector (consisting of investment in service industries such as transport, communication, and

financial intermediation) is even more strongly affected by an increase in tax rates, and the tax elasticity for this sector is around −3.
- By weighing sector-specific elasticities with the sector's share of total FDI, we obtain an average tax elasticity of −2.5. This average tax elasticity is comparable to the results derived in more aggregated studies.

25. In fact, the statutory tax rates in the most economically significant developing countries tend to be lower than the average in OECD countries (Gordon and Li 2009).

26. See World Development Indicators (database), World Bank, Washington, DC, http://data.worldbank.org/data-catalog/world-development-indicators/. Economists contend that these differences in revenue collection can be explained by both (a) the fact that demand for public services increases more than proportionally as income rises and (b) weaknesses in the ability of developing countries to raise the revenue required for the provision of adequate public services. On the latter, the World Bank (2004) emphasizes the narrowness of the tax base and problems in tax administration.

27. World Bank (2004) reports that the only exception to this outcome was the region of Central and Eastern Europe and Central Asia, where revenues fell because of privatization and a general contraction in the size of the state.

28. Fuest and Riedel formulate the issue as follows:

> Attempts to estimate the amount of tax avoidance and tax evasion therefore have to build on concepts which exploit correlations between observable and statistically documented variables and evasion. These data problems may explain why there is very little reliable empirical evidence on tax avoidance and evasion in developing countries. The existing studies mostly rely on highly restrictive assumptions and have to make use of data of mixed quality. (Fuest and Riedel 2009, 6)

29. For example, see Fuest and Riedel (2009); GAO (2008); McDonald (2008).

30. We adopt the view that, in the presence of an international tax regime, countries are effectively constrained to operating in the context of that regime and not free to adopt any international tax rules they please. This view is espoused in Avi-Yonah (2007). The basic norms that underlie this international tax regime are the single tax principle (that is, that income should be taxed once, no more nor less) and the benefits principle (that is, that active business income should be taxed primarily at the source and that passive investment income should be taxed primarily at residence).

31. For a discussion on the role of information sharing in international taxation, see Keen and Ligthart (2004), who consider that this form of administrative cooperation may be a feasible substitute for the difficult-to-achieve target of the coordination of tax systems.

32. For a strong argument on the role of advance pricing agreements and tax treaties in improving the current international tax regime, see Baistrocchi (2005).

33. This behavior by taxpayers and the suggested policy response are broadly consistent with economic models of tax evasion (following the work on the economics of crime by Nobel laureate economist Gary Becker and the tax evasion
model of Allingham and Sandmo), which contend that the level of evasion of
income tax depends on the level of punishment provided by law. The suggestion
herein extends this notion to the practice of tax avoidance.

34. For some developing countries, a key obstacle to effective implementation of
information sharing is the lack of the capacity required to determine what information should be requested from other countries and also to make proper and
timely use of the information received.

References

Altshuler, R., and H. Grubert. 2006. "Governments and Multinational Corporations
in the Race to the Bottom." *Tax Notes* 110 (8): 459–74.

Avi-Yonah, R. S. 2007. "Tax Competition, Tax Arbitrage and the International Tax
Regime." Working Paper 07/09, Oxford University Centre for Business Taxation, Oxford.

Baistrocchi, E. 2005. "The Transfer Pricing Problem: A Global Proposal for Simplification." *Tax Lawyer* 59 (4): 941–79.

Bartelsman, E. J., and R. M. W. J. Beetsma. 2003. "Why Pay More? Corporate Tax
Avoidance through Transfer Pricing in OECD Countries." *Journal of Public Economics* 87 (9–10): 2225–52.

Christian Aid. 2009. "False Profits: Robbing the Poor to Keep the Rich Tax-Free."
Christian Aid Report, March, Christian Aid, London.

Clausing, K. A. 2003. "Tax-Motivated Transfer Pricing and US Intrafirm Trade
Prices." *Journal of Public Economics* 87 (9–10): 2207–23.

Desai, M. A., C. F. Foley, and J. R. Hines Jr. 2006. "The Demand for Tax Haven Operations." *Journal of Public Economics* 90 (3): 513–31.

Fuest, C., and N. Riedel. 2009. "Tax Evasion, Tax Avoidance and Tax Expenditures in
Developing Countries: A Review of the Literature." Report, Oxford University
Centre for Business Taxation, Oxford.

GAO (U.S. Government Accountability Office). 2008. "Tax Administration: Comparison of the Reported Tax Liabilities of Foreign- and U.S.-Controlled Corporations, 1998–2005." Report GAO-08-957 (July 24), GAO, Washington, DC.
http://www.gao.gov/products/GAO-08-957.

Gordon, R., and W. Li. 2009. "Tax Structures in Developing Countries: Many Puzzles
and a Possible Explanation." *Journal of Public Economics* 93 (7–8): 855–66.

Haufler, A., and S. Stöwhase. 2003. "Taxes as a Determinant for Foreign Direct Investment in Europe." CESifo DICE Report 4 (2): 45–51, CESifo Group, Munich.

Horman, Chitonge. 2010. "Zambia's Development Agreements and the Soaring Copper Prices." *Resource Insight* 11 (September 29), Southern Africa Resource Watch,
Johannesburg.

Kar, D., and D. Cartwright-Smith. 2008. "Illicit Financial Flows from Developing Countries, 2002–2006." Global Financial Integrity, Washington, DC. http://www.gfip.org/storage/gfip/economist%20-%20final%20version%201-2-09.pdf.

Keen, M., and J. E. Ligthart. 2004. "Incentives and Information Exchange in International Taxation." CentER Discussion Paper 2004–54, Center for Economic Research, Tilburg University, Tilburg, the Netherlands.

Maffini, G., and S. Mokkas. 2008. "Transfer-Pricing and Measured Productivity of Multinational Firms." Unpublished working paper, Oxford University Centre for Business Taxation, Oxford.

McDonald, M. 2008. "Income Shifting from Transfer Pricing: Further Evidence from Tax Return Data." Technical Working Paper 2, Office of Technical Analysis, U.S. Department of the Treasury, Washington, DC.

Mutti, J., and H. Grubert. 2004. "Empirical Asymmetries in Foreign Direct Investment and Taxation." *Journal of International Economics* 62 (2): 337–58.

OECD (Organisation for Economic Co-operation and Development). 1995. "Transfer Pricing Guidelines for Multinational Enterprises and Tax Administrations." OECD, Paris.

————. 2009. "An Overview of the OECD's Work on Countering International Tax Evasion." Background Information Brief, August 28, Centre for Tax Policy and Administration, OECD, Paris.

Stöwhase, S. 2006. "Tax-Rate Differentials and Sector Specific Foreign Direct Investment: Empirical Evidence from the EU." *FinanzArchiv: Public Finance Analysis* 61 (4): 535–58.

Tanzi, V., and H. Zee. 2001. "Tax Policy for Developing Countries." *Economic Issues* 27 (March), International Monetary Fund, Washington, DC.

UNCTAD (United Nations Conference on Trade and Development). 2008. *World Investment Report 2008: Transnational Corporations, and the Infrastructure Challenge.* Geneva: UNCTAD.

World Bank. 2004. *World Development Report 2005: A Better Investment Climate For Everyone.* New York: World Bank; New York: Oxford University Press.

Zodrow, G. 2008. "Corporation Income Taxation in Canada." *Canadian Tax Journal* 56 (2): 392–468.

9

Accounting for the Missing Billions

Richard Murphy

Abstract

This chapter considers, first, whether substantial transfer mispricing by major corporations that contributes to a loss of at least US$160 billion a year to developing countries is plausible in the context of total likely corporate profits earned worldwide in a year.[1]

Second, it tests whether corporate activities in developing countries and in the extractive industries in particular might be especially prone to this abuse.

Third, it considers whether this sum could be hidden from view within the accounts or financial statements of the multinational corporations (MNCs) that might be perpetrating the mispricing.

Fourth, it explores the possibility that the MNCs might use secrecy jurisdictions to assist in hiding these transactions from view.

Some of the data used in this chapter have been researched for the Mapping the Faultlines Project of the Tax Justice Network (TJN), financed by the Ford Foundation, the results of which are being published at http://www.secrecyjurisdictions.com/. The author is research director of that project.

Additional tables and figures from this chapter can be found at http://go.worldbank.org /N2HMRB4G20.

In each case, it is suggested that the behavior described is plausible and that, as a consequence, losses of the estimated amount are also plausible, although not proven to exist as a result of this work.

Introduction

Since 2000, a body of literature, mainly emanating from nongovernmental organizations (NGOs), has developed suggesting that systematic transfer mispricing is taking place within the world's MNCs. This literature asserts, in the first instance, that the flows in question abuse international standards on transfer pricing implicit in the arm's-length pricing rules of the Organisation for Economic Co-operation and Development (OECD) and that the abuse results in significant loss in revenues to developing countries.[2]

Estimates of the loss vary. Christian Aid's estimate (2008) finds that transfer mispricing and related abuses result in the loss of corporate tax revenues to the developing world of at least US$160 billion a year, a figure that, it notes, is more than 1.5 times the combined aid budgets of the rich world, which totaled US$103.7 billion in 2007.

Raymond Baker (2005) proposes that total annual illicit financial flows (IFFs) might amount to US$1 trillion, asserting, in the process, that these flows pass illegally across borders aided by an elaborate dirty money structure comprising tax havens, financial secrecy jurisdictions, dummy corporations, anonymous trusts and foundations, money laundering techniques, and loopholes intentionally left in the laws of western countries.[3] Of this amount, Baker estimates that some US$500 billion a year flows from developing and transitional economies. He suggests that at least 65 percent of these flows may be accounted for by transfer mispricing.

Baker's findings have been endorsed by Kar and Cartwright-Smith (2008), who estimate that, in 2006, developing countries lost US$858.6 billion to US$1.1 trillion in illicit financial outflows. Note that the term *illicit* is appropriately used in this chapter. The *Oxford English Dictionary* defines illegal as contrary to or forbidden by law, but illicit as forbidden by law, rules, or custom. The distinction is important. Transfer mispricing is illicit; it is contrary to known rules or customs, but, in many of the transactions of concern, it is not illegal because, as noted later in this chapter, double tax agreements (DTAs) that would make it so are not in place, nor are relevant local laws.

NGOs and civil society organizations are not the only source of literature proposing that transfer mispricing might be used to reallocate profits across jurisdictions. There is a substantial body of academic literature asserting that this practice is commonplace, although this literature does not focus on developing and transitional economies in coming to its conclusion. For example, Dischinger and Riedel (2008) state that intangible assets such as patents and trademarks are increasingly seen as the key to competitive success and as the drivers of corporate profit, but also constitute a major source of the opportunity for profit shifting in MNCs because of the highly nontransparent transfer pricing process. They argue that this provides MNCs with an incentive to locate intangible property in jurisdictions with relatively low corporate tax rates. They find evidence to support this activity, showing that the lower a subsidiary's tax rate relative to other members of a multinational group, the higher the subsidiary's level of intangible asset investment.

Harry Huizinga (2009), in a wide-ranging review, indicates that MNCs can relocate profits in a number of ways. First, they could change real activity, that is, where they locate; second, they could manipulate transfer prices; third, they could choose the location of intangible assets and associated income such as royalties (as Dischinger and Riedel 2008 emphasize); or, fourth, they could choose the location of their headquarters to create possible favorable international double taxation consequences. Having reviewed the current literature within Europe on this issue, Huizinga concludes that international profit shifting erodes the corporate tax base in Europe, that the best approach to tackling the problem is to eliminate incentives for firms to shift profits, and that international policy cooperation is necessary to achieve this.

Notably, the academic studies, in contrast to those by NGOs, find that the scale of income shifted is relatively small, only a few percentage points, at most, of the tax base. For example, in chapter 4 in this volume, Fuest and Riedel posit that Baker (2005), Kar and Cartwright-Smith (2008), Christian Aid (2008), and others all overstate the extent of transfer mispricing, although all these authors reject the assertion because Fuest and Riedel make a fundamental error by assuming that overpriced inflows and underpriced outflows may be netted off for the purposes of assessing resulting tax losses, when, in fact, these sums should be aggregated for this purpose. In chapter 10 in this volume, Nitsch also questions the same group of estimates, suggesting that the forging of documentation relating to IFFs may not be motivated by taxes. It is a curious argument if the consequence is tax loss whatever the motive.

There are, however, reasonable methodological grounds that explain why this low level of transfer mispricing is reported by academic studies, all these grounds deriving from significant methodological weaknesses in the studies.

First, most academic studies on this issue use database information supplied by agencies that summarize accounting data; as a result, they do not use the accounts themselves as their data source, losing considerable vital information on tax as a consequence (see below).

Second, these data sets tend to result in the use of pretax profit as a proxy for taxable income—which is rarely appropriate—and in the use of profit and loss account tax charges as a proxy for taxes paid. This use of the profit and loss account tax charge as an indicator of taxes paid is almost always inappropriate. This is because these charges are invariably made up of two parts. The first is the current tax charge. This is the tax that a company actually believes will be paid within 12 months of a period end as a result of the profit arising during the accounting period. It is, therefore, a reasonable measure of the tax liability accruing during the period. The second component of the tax charge in a profit and loss account is described as the deferred tax charge. Deferred tax is not tax at all. Rather, it represents an accounting entry relating to taxes that may potentially (but will not definitely) be paid in future periods as a consequence of transactions that have occurred in the current period. So, for example, if the tax relief on the acquisition of fixed assets in the period exceeds the charge for depreciation on these assets in the profit and loss account, there is a potential deferred tax charge in future periods if the situation were to reverse. The liability is provided in the accounts, even though it may never arise simply because the situation may not reverse. Similarly, if transfer mispricing can defer the recognition of profit in a high-tax parent-company location by the current relocation of the profits in question to a secrecy jurisdiction where tax is not currently due on the profits, then a deferred tax provision can be made for the potential liability arising on the eventual remittance of the profits to the parent company, but there is no guarantee that this sum will ever be due. As a consequence, many consider deferred tax charges as accounting fiction and as unreliable, and they are, curiously, the only liability included in the set of accounts whether or not there is any prospect of their settlement. In this case, to include them in the tax charge in considering the real taxation paid by corporations is seriously misleading and undermines many existing studies of effective taxation rates among MNCs. Thus, the methodology used in these studies is inappropriate for appraising the transfer mispricing that these studies survey.

Using accounting data from the companies, Murphy (2008) shows that the largest 50 companies in the FTSE 100 increased their net deferred tax provisions (that is, the cumulative provisions that are made by a company for deferred taxation arising over the period of trading to date and that are shown as a long-term liability on balance sheets) from £8 billion to £46 billion between 2000 and 2006. This hints at the existence of significant tax avoidance that database information on the taxation charges in company accounts is unlikely to reveal.

The room for disagreement is thus substantial on whether there is, or not, a major transfer mispricing issue that might have particular relevance to developing nations and in which secrecy jurisdictions may play a significant part in a way that policy change may need to address.[4]

It is not the purpose of this chapter to resolve whether the mispricing takes place or not. The chapter has another purpose, which is approached from an accounting and auditing perspective. An audit tests the credibility of reported data. This is not a test of whether the variable is right or wrong: financial audits do not offer an opinion on this to their users. Instead, the audit seeks to test whether the variable may be true and fair. In seeking to prove or disprove the credibility of data, auditors have, for some time, realized that a microapproach, that is, verification based on transactional data alone, is unlikely to provide all (and, in some cases, any) of the data needed to determine the likely credibility of the overall stated position. The alternative approach involves verifying data by testing the credibility of sums in total.

This testing can take a number of forms. For example, do the data fall within the known range of plausible outcomes based on the third-party data that are available? Alternatively, are the data within the likely pattern of outcomes that may be observed within the entity that is being tested? And are the total data plausible in that they are consistent with other known totals?

Importantly and, in the current case, crucially, all such tests must take into consideration the broader commercial, regulatory, legal, and risk environments in which the transactions or balances being considered occur. An auditor is not allowed to consider numerical data in isolation; the use of such data must be contextualized.

This chapter seeks, first, to test the hypothesis according to which transfer mispricing by major corporations that gives rise to tax losses amounting to at least US$160 billion a year among developing countries is plausible in the context of the total likely worldwide corporate profits in a year during the same period of reference (that is, pre-2008).

Second, it tests whether corporate activities in developing countries and, particularly, in the extractive industries may be especially prone to this abuse.

Third, it considers whether this sum may be hidden from view within the accounts and financial statements of the MNCs that might be perpetrating the mispricing.

Fourth, it explores the possibility that MNCs may use secrecy jurisdictions to assist in hiding these transactions from view.

The rest of the chapter is divided into five sections. The next section explores the tax rates that MNCs have and are likely to face; it shows that much of the existing literature on this subject offers misleading indications of likely effective tax rates.

In the subsequent section, the state of transfer pricing regulation and practice within the extractive industries is explored on the basis of a range of sources on which the author has worked over a number of years.

The following section looks at the way in which MNCs are structured and how this structure interacts with the corporate and tax law of the locations that host some of these MNCs; it also contrasts these relationships with the requirements of International Financial Reporting Standards (IFRSs), which are the standards that govern the financial reporting of most such entities now that U.S. Generally Accepted Accounting Principles are converging with the standards issued by the International Accounting Standards Board.

The penultimate section considers the nature of secrecy jurisdictions. Data on the use of such locations by MNCs are presented. The role of the Big Four accounting firms is touched upon.

The evidence is drawn together in the concluding section.

Multinational Corporations and Their Tax Rates

Data sources

This part of the chapter seeks to compare the corporate tax rates offered by a wide range of jurisdictions over time. The basic data source for the time series data on tax rates used in this report is the annual corporate tax rate reviews published by KPMG, a Big Four firm of accountants and business advisers. KPMG has been publishing the reviews since 1996, and, although the jurisdictions reviewed have varied slightly over the period, the data have always covered between 60 and 70 jurisdictions in each annual report up to and through 2008, all of which have been included in the current survey. The KPMG data consistently cover 30 OECD countries and the 15 preenlargement members of the European Union (EU). The other jurisdictions surveyed vary widely. A consistent feature is that few of the places are recognized secrecy jurisdictions. The data on populations and gross domestic product (GDP) used in this part of the chapter were extracted from the CIA World Factbook in July 2009.[5]

As a result of the omission of tax rate data for secrecy jurisdictions, an alternative data source for these locations has been used. Given that the KPMG data were, without doubt, produced for marketing purposes, another, similar source has been sought. The source the author of the chapter has settled on is a data set downloaded from OCRA Worldwide.[6] These data, which were extracted in November 2008, relate to the corporate tax rates of secrecy jurisdictions as applied to foreign source income. This is relevant for the purpose of this review because one is concerned with transfer pricing, and the income that will pass through these locations in connection with intragroup trades is likely to be considered foreign source income in these jurisdictions; the tax rates provided by OCRA will therefore be the appropriate tax rates to consider.

Methodology

The KPMG data are summarized in table 9A.1.[7] The data are categorized according to the following characteristics for the purposes of the analysis:

1. Whether or not the jurisdiction was a member of the OECD
2. Whether or not the jurisdiction was one of the 15 EU preenlargement states (the EU15)

3. Whether the jurisdiction was large or small (for these purposes, a large jurisdiction has a population over 15 million, which splits the data into two broadly equal parts)

4. Whether the jurisdiction had a high or low GDP per head (for these purposes, a high GDP is above US$25,000 in 2009, which splits the data into two roughly equivalent parts)

5. Whether or not the jurisdiction had a high proportion of government spending in relation to GDP (in this case, 30 percent government spending as a proportion of GDP indicates high spending)

The categories have been chosen broadly to reflect developed and less-developed nations (the developed nations are the OECD members) and large and small jurisdictions. Categorizing according to a high or low tax spend also broadly reflects the effectiveness of the tax system in the jurisdiction because it is likely that those jurisdictions with low spending had ineffective tax collection systems given that this is commonplace in developing countries.

The average data for each year have then been calculated for each of these groups. The resulting data set is reproduced in table 9A.2.[8]

Initial results

The initial results are best presented graphically. An overall summary of the data is shown in figure 9.1.

There is a strong and, in almost all cases, persistent downward trend in nominal corporate tax rates over the period under review. This, however, does not reveal much of the subtlety inherent in what is happening, which greater exploration of the data reveals.

First, with regard to the OECD countries (of which the EU15 are an effective subset), there has been a significant decline in notional rates that has seen them converge with the rates offered by the other, non-OECD countries. Rather surprisingly, in 2008, OECD country rates fell, on average (weighted by the number of countries), below the average rate of non-OECD countries. Given the substantial differential of more than 6 percentage points in 1997, this is a remarkable change. The playing field, much talked about in OECD circles over many years, appears to have been leveled.

Figure 9.1. Corporate Tax Rates, Initial Results, 1997–2008

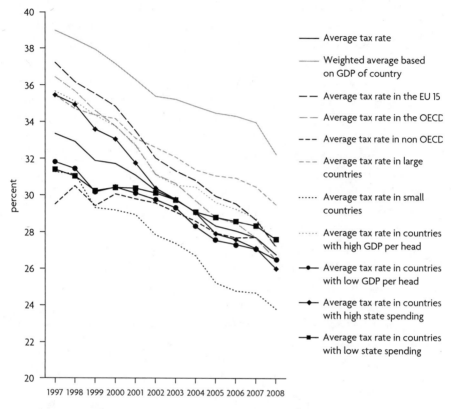

Legend:
- Average tax rate
- Weighted average based on GDP of country
- Average tax rate in the EU 15
- Average tax rate in the OECD
- Average tax rate in non OECD
- Average tax rate in large countries
- Average tax rate in small countries
- Average tax rate in countries with high GDP per head
- Average tax rate in countries with low GDP per head
- Average tax rate in countries with high state spending
- Average tax rate in countries with low state spending

Source: Author compilation, based on data of Tax Tools and Resources (database), KPMG, Zug, Switzerland, http://www.kpmg.com/Global/en/WhatWeDo/Tax/tax-tools-and-resources/Pages/default.aspx.

This story is not repeated elsewhere. The data for large and small jurisdictions do, for example, show a persistent gap in tax rates between these two groups, the extent of which marginally increases during the period. The trend in rates seems clear: smaller jurisdictions (those with populations of less than 15 million people) would appear to wish to create competitive advantage by having lower corporate tax rates.

This trend is also found by comparing jurisdictions with high GDP per head and jurisdictions with low GDP per head. In this case, it is, however, clear that the margin is closing: a level playing field is being created between these sets of jurisdictions. This is not surprising: there is significant overlap between the high-GDP jurisdictions and the OECD countries.

A comparison of jurisdictions with high and low state spending in proportion to GDP shows an even more marked contrast. Quite surprisingly, by 2008, the jurisdictions with high state spending (in excess of 30 percent in proportion to GDP) were offering lower notional corporate tax rates than jurisdictions with a lower (under 30 percent) proportion of GDP going to state spending. The implications of the change would appear clear: this is the consequence of a shift in the tax burden in high-spending jurisdictions from corporations to individuals that was rapid and marked.

These findings are significant. They confirm what other literature (of which there is a considerable body) has also shown, that is, that corporate tax rates are steadily falling. However, unlike most surveys of such rates, which are concentrated most often solely on EU or OECD countries, these data show that the issue of changing corporate tax rates is more complex than one may suspect at first sight.[9] There are strong differences in the trends that a simple analysis does not reveal.

Even so, the analysis noted here does not show the whole picture with regard to notional tax rates because a simple averaging methodology has been used to present the data. This means that the tax rates surveyed have been totaled over the set of jurisdictions and divided by the number of jurisdictions within the set. This standard methodology is flawed. To assume that all jurisdictions stand equal in the assessment of changes in average tax rates is inappropriate: it would seem that weighting should be an essential part of any analysis.

There are a number of ways to weight these data. The usual method is simply to attribute an equal weight to each jurisdiction. This would be misleading. The method gives an undue emphasis to the tax rates of small economies with limited populations. Because such economies are frequently associated with secrecy jurisdiction activity, there is an obvious risk of inherent bias. It is precisely for this reason that an alternative weighting has been used in the current exercise, resulting in a perspective that is different from the one usually provided by analyses of this sort, which are undertaken, in most cases, by members of the accounting profession, who have an inherent bias (as noted elsewhere below) toward secrecy jurisdiction activity. As a necessary alternative, a different weighting has been used here. We have weighted by the GDP of the jurisdiction offering the tax rate. There is a good reason for this choice: GDP is a reasonable indication of the size of national markets, and this is a good proxy for the capacity to generate profits. Because this exercise is focused on the taxation of profits in particular locations, this weighting is likely to indicate the effective tax rates that companies are seeking to avoid by transfer pricing activity given that the taxation of profits is the motive for using transfer pricing. The only other viable method that might indicate the impact of profit shifting through transfer mispricing is to weight tax rates by the population of the jurisdictions: such an exercise would indicate a shift from locations with high populations, requiring taxation revenue to service local need, to locations with low population, requiring little taxation to service the needs of the population (this is also, of course, a characteristic of secrecy jurisdictions). This second weighting method is also considered in the analysis offered below.

Weighting by GDP supplies a different picture of average tax rates, as shown in figure 9.2. The weighting in figure 9.2 has been carried out using notional 2009 GDPs expressed in U.S. dollars as a consistent ranking mechanism that is unlikely to have introduced distortion because relative positions are unlikely to have changed materially for this purpose over time.

Average tax rates fall within the ranges noted within the standard economic literature mentioned above. This literature gives, however, a misleading view. Because of the presence of the biggest economy in the

Figure 9.2. Corporate Tax Rates, Weighted by GDP, 1997–2008

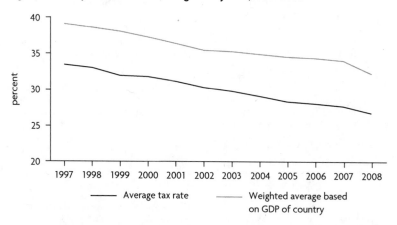

Source: Author compilation using 2009 GDP data taken from World Factbook (database), Central Intelligence Agency, Washington, DC, https://www.cia.gov/library/publications/the-world-factbook/.

world (the United States), which has one of the highest effective tax rates on corporate profits in the world (notionally stated, as are all rates used here) if federal and state taxes are combined, and many other major countries that combine high absolute GDPs and high tax rates, the average corporate tax rate weighted by GDP is much higher than the apparent simple average; in 2008, the difference was about 5 percent.

This is significant. Murphy (2008) finds that the effective current rates of corporation tax paid by the largest 50 companies in the FTSE 100 fell steadily, from 26 percent in 2000 to about 22 percent in 2006, both compared with a headline rate of 30 percent. This closing rate differential of 8 percent looks substantially more significant, however, if it is compared with the worldwide weighted average tax rating of about 34 percent in 2007 calculated on the basis noted above. A 12 percent differential, assuming (as is likely) that many of these companies have significant sales in the United States, seems high indeed.

Including data from the OCRA data set on some secrecy jurisdictions—only those secrecy jurisdictions on which OCRA provides data have been used in the survey discussed hereafter, and only those on which OCRA provides specific rate data have been included in the exercise—changes the perspective on these data once again.[10] Data are only available for 2008; so, trend analysis cannot be offered, but, even so, the position is quite different. The data are summarized in table 9A.3.[11] The summary in table 9.1 is based on the 90 jurisdictions used for computational purposes. The equivalent data, excluding secrecy jurisdiction locations, are shown in table 9.2.

Table 9.1. Summary Data: Corporate Tax Rate, Including Secrecy Jurisdiction Locations, 2008

percent

Description	Rate
Notional simple average of corporate tax rates	20.30
Corporate tax rate weighted by GDP	32.10
Corporate tax rate weighted by population	29.90

Source: Author compilation based on data of Jurisdiction Centre (database), OCRA Worldwide, Isle of Man, United Kingdom, http://www.ocra.com/jurisdictions/index.asp; Tax Tools and Resources (database), KPMG, Zug, Switzerland, http://www.kpmg.com/Global /en/WhatWeDo/Tax/tax-tools-and-resources/Pages/default.aspx; World Development Indicators (database), World Bank, Washington, DC, http://data.worldbank.org /data-catalog/world-development-indicators/ (for GDP).

Table 9.2. Summary Data: Corporate Tax Rate, Excluding Secrecy Jurisdiction Locations, 2008

percent

Description	Rate
Notional simple average of corporate tax rates	26.77
Corporate tax rate weighted by GDP	32.10
Corporate tax rate weighted by population	29.90

Source: Author compilation based on data of Jurisdiction Centre (database), OCRA World-wide, Isle of Man, United Kingdom, http://www.ocra.com/jurisdictions/index.asp; Tax Tools and Resources (database), KPMG, Zug, Switzerland, http://www.kpmg.com/Global /en/WhatWeDo/Tax/tax-tools-and-resources/Pages/default.aspx; World Development Indicators (database), World Bank, Washington, DC, http://data.worldbank.org /data-catalog/world-development-indicators/ (for GDP).

The secrecy jurisdictions all have 0 percent tax rates. They therefore do not change the weighted data, but they do significantly reduce the simple average data. It is obvious that excluding secrecy jurisdiction data from a sampling of average corporate tax rates, as has been conventional in most academic reviews to date, makes a substantial difference in the presentation of information. If the simple averaging method is used and secrecy jurisdictions are excluded from review, a quite misleading perspective on current likely effective tax rates is presented.

There is one computation to note. For several of the jurisdictions in the KPMG data set, OCRA notes that a differential tax rate is available for foreign source income. For these jurisdictions alone and only if OCRA could indicate the alternative rate that was available, we have undertaken further analysis using this rate for foreign source income. The jurisdictions for which this has been done are Hong Kong SAR, China; Hungary; Iceland; Israel; Luxembourg; the United Kingdom, where limited liability partnerships are tax transparent; and the United States, where limited liability companies offer the same fiscal transparency. Singapore and Switzerland offer differential rates, but we do not restate them here because OCRA does not indicate the alternative rate, which varies according to the circumstances. Our results are shown in table 9.3.

The resulting tax rate data weighted by GDP look much closer to the tax rate actually found if one examines effective corporate tax rates declared by companies, as noted by Murphy (2008), than to any tax rate data one may present by undertaking calculations weighted simply by

Table 9.3. Summary Data: Tax Rate on Foreign Source Income, Selected Secrecy Jurisdiction Locations, 2008
percent

Description	Rate
Notional simple average of corporate tax rates	18.48
Corporate tax rate weighted by GDP	20.70
Corporate tax rate weighted by population	27.20

Source: Author compilation based on data of Jurisdiction Centre (database), OCRA World-wide, Isle of Man, United Kingdom, http://www.ocra.com/jurisdictions/index.asp; Tax Tools and Resources (database), KPMG, Zug, Switzerland, http://www.kpmg.com/Global /en/WhatWeDo/Tax/tax-tools-and-resources/Pages/default.aspx; World Development Indicators (database), World Bank, Washington, DC, http://data.worldbank.org /data-catalog/world-development-indicators/ (for GDP).

the number of jurisdictions based on the notional tax rates of all jurisdictions that are not secrecy jurisdictions. Ring-fences increase the number of jurisdictions offering low tax rates. In combination with the weighted and secrecy jurisdiction data, this understanding adds a new approach to analyzing these data.

The developing-country perspective
A final dimension to this issue needs to be noted. The KPMG data include some transition countries, but few developing countries, and Africa is, for example, seriously underrepresented. Keen and Mansour (2009) provide some data to correct this omission, although only in graphical form, as shown in figure 9.3.

The statutory corporate income tax rate plot relating to tax rates is relevant here. Simple averaging of the tax rates in Africa (with all the inherent faults in this process, which is used here, as elsewhere in most economic literature on this issue) shows that corporate income tax rates in Africa fell from 44.0 percent, on average, in 1990 to 33.2 percent in 2005. The rate of 33.2 percent might compare favorably (only barely) with the weighted average rate noted above, but it does not compare well with any other. The reality is that, on the basis of simple weighted averages, Africa has high corporate tax rates on profits, at least 5 percent above the KPMG simple weighted average for the same year and much higher than the weighted average, including secrecy jurisdictions, in 2008.

Figure 9.3. Corporate Income Tax, Africa, 1980–2005

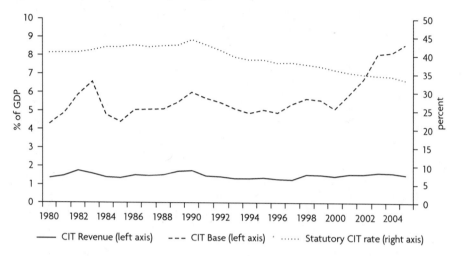

Source: Author compilation based on Keen and Mansour (2009) and data of International Bureau for Fiscal Documentation and International Monetary Fund.
Note: CIT = corporate income tax. Revenue excludes oil, gas, and mining companies.

These findings are important. It is likely that the incentive to avoid taxes through transfer pricing is based on two considerations. The first is the differential between the tax rates of the countries through which ownership of the goods might pass as part of the transfer pricing supply chain. The greater the differential in tax rates across jurisdictions in the intragroup supply chain, it may be suggested, the greater the prospect that a group of companies will profit from transfer mispricing. The second consideration likely to feature significantly in the decision process on mispricing is the chance that the activity may take place without discovery within the intragroup supply chain. The first issue is considered here; the second, in later parts of this chapter.

The literature that finds evidence for substantial IFFs relating to transfer mispricing also finds evidence that this process is facilitated by the existence of secrecy jurisdictions, most or all of which offer no taxation on foreign source income (Baker 2005; Christian Aid 2008; and so on). As the data noted above show, this 0 rate tax offering has, over time, had a slightly diminishing impact as simple weighted average tax rates have fallen, but, with the rates still hovering at around 27 percent in many of the measures noted, the differential remains large.

The differential is even more significant if comparison is made with the simple weighted average tax rates in Africa. The incentive to tax avoid through transfer mispricing from that continent would appear to be strong, a theme to which we return below.

What does need to be assessed is whether the incentive based on tax rate differentials is sufficient to justify the claimed US$160 billion or more of transfer mispricing that is said to take place each year. Analytical review techniques such as are found in auditing are used here with the objective of testing whether the claimed audit outcome (in this case, that transfer mispricing results in losses to developing countries of US$160 billion a year) is within the plausible range of data outcomes that population information implies may be likely.

It is proposed that, in analytical review terms, the estimates of transfer mispricing would be considered plausible if the total estimated amount of tax lost to transfer mispricing were materially less than the amount of tax lost as measured by the differential between weighted average headline tax rates (which would indicate tax due if corporations were tax compliant) and the tax likely actually to be paid calculated using likely cash paid tax rates, as noted above. In this context, tax compliance is defined as an effort to pay the right amount of tax (but no more) in the right place at the right time, where right means that the economic substance of the transactions undertaken coincides with the place and form in which they are reported for taxation purposes.

Data on tax rates have already been developed above. The other data needed are as follows:

- A measure of world GDP, because the trade that is transfer mispriced is a proportion of world GDP, and that proportion must be credible
- An indication of corporate profits as a proportion of world GDP, because, ultimately, it is profits that are shifted as a result of transfer mispricing

These data, if combined, will generate the following:

- A measure of worldwide corporate taxable profits
- If weighted by the tax rate data noted above, the measure of worldwide corporate taxable profits will give measures of both the likely tax paid and the tax lost because tax rates weighted by GDP are not paid by major corporations, as noted above

Worldwide GDP was approximately US$61 trillion in 2008.[12] The IFFs that give rise to the estimated tax loss calculated by Christian Aid (2008) amount to between US$850 billion and US$1 trillion a year, representing, in some cases, sums as high as 10 percent of GDP (Kar and Cartwright-Smith 2008). These calculations are based on actual trade data. Illicit flows of this scale are considered plausible for the purposes of this chapter.

As Murphy (2010a) notes, the U.K. tax authorities estimate that 15 percent of total value added tax due on U.K. gross sales and imports in 2008–09 was not collected (HMRC 2010). The part not collected was associated with what might reasonably be described as IFFs using the definitions offered by Kar and Cartwright-Smith (2008). By extrapolation, the total tax loss over the entire U.K. economy was at least 5 percent of GDP in that case. The United Kingdom is considered a well-regulated economy with low levels of tax evasion, although the domestic tax authority acknowledges that one-sixth of total gross commercial financial flows are outside the tax system. It is widely accepted that a significant amount of lost value added tax arises as a result of international unrecorded trading flows and illicitly recorded transactions, a matter that has been of considerable concern in the United Kingdom and the rest of the EU for many years. In this circumstance, the estimates of IFFs in developing countries that Kar and Cartwright-Smith (2008) provide appear to be well within the plausible data range based on comparison with alternative reliable information.

Total corporate added value in the U.K. economy represented by the gross operating surplus of corporations is in excess of 20 percent of GDP.[13] In 2008, this gross operating surplus of corporations amounted to £339 billion. Yet, this sum is stated before charges such as interest are offset against profit. Total corporation tax revenues in the same year were £46 billion.[14] On gross value added, this implies an effective tax rate of 13.6 percent. However, Murphy (2008) states that an effective average tax rate of about 22 percent should be anticipated. If this latter rate were applied to tax paid, the gross added value after the interest offset is reduced to £210 billion, a sum that was 14.5 percent of U.K. GDP in 2008.

Data on the same ratio in the United States for 2006, 2007, and 2008 imply that corporate profits were lower, less than 11 percent of GDP and on a downward trend (12.0 percent in 2006, 10.9 percent in 2007, and

9.4 percent in 2008).[15] Nonetheless, this excludes the profits of private companies (which are included in the U.K. data). In this case, one may presume that the two ratios are largely consistent, and a total profit rate of approximately 10 percent of GDP might be considered to be associated with large entities likely to undertake multinational trade. This is probably a reasonable estimate of global corporate profits given that the United Kingdom and the United States are the two largest centers for the location of MNCs in the world. Assuming that this rate may be indicative of worldwide rates, this leads one to suspect that, based on worldwide GDP of US$61 trillion, corporate profits may be conservatively estimated at a total of approximately US$6 trillion in 2008.

We have used secondary sources to check this conclusion. Global data on profits are remarkably difficult to source. However, McKinsey has published a review of the after-tax profits of the top 2,000 companies in the world in 2006 and established that the after-tax earnings of this group in that year were US$3.2 trillion (Dietz, Reibestein, and Walter 2008). Murphy (2008) finds that declared tax rates for companies registered in the United Kingdom and quoted on the stock exchange for that year averaged 25.8 percent (this rate reflecting their worldwide rates and not merely the rate applicable in the United Kingdom), which suggests that the worldwide pretax profits of the McKinsey sample may be US$4.3 trillion. This figure is, of course, somewhat lower than US$6 trillion, but a sample of 2,000 companies is also somewhat lower than the total population of MNCs. There are, for example, more than 2,200 companies quoted in the United Kingdom alone (London Stock Exchange 2010). That 2,000 companies might represent 72 percent of total global profits likely to be of concern does seem plausible, however, and this is considered strong supporting evidence that the estimates of global profits are reasonable.

On this global profit estimate of US$6 trillion, the tax due at weighted average tax rates based on GDP noted above (32.1 percent) might be about US$1.9 trillion. If secrecy jurisdictions and ring-fences are considered, this might fall to a tax figure as low as US$1.2 trillion at a rate of 20.1 percent, as noted above. The rates are selected from among those noted above because, first, it is suggested that the average tax rate weighted by GDP indicates the taxes that would be due if companies were tax compliant, that is, if they paid the right amount of tax (but no more) in the right place at the right time, where right means that the economic substance of the transactions undertaken coincides with the place and form in which they are reported for taxation purposes and that profits arise where third-party sales (for which GDP is a proxy) occur. Second, the rate, including secrecy jurisdictions and ring-fences, reflects the reality of the tax system that, this chapter notes, MNCs can actually exploit, that is, the rate is used in recognition of the fact that secrecy does allow the relocation of profits and that ring-fences for foreign earnings might be used to apply low tax rates to profits reallocated by transfer mispricing techniques behind the veil of secrecy.

It is plausible that the differential in taxes paid, based on the varying assumptions, of some US$700 billion might include transfer mispricing effects of US$160 billion that have been claimed (Christian Aid 2008). Transfer mispricing abuse would represent 22.8 percent of the tax deferral on this basis, and one may note that, because some of this deferral may be represented as deferred tax provisions in the accounts of MNCs, the actual impact on the tax charge in the accounts of MNCs may be lower than this implies without diminishing the cash loss to developing countries.

A ratio of this proportion allows ample margin for numerous other factors that may reduce declared tax rates, including advanced capital allowances (by far the biggest claimed factor in tax deferral noted in Murphy 2008), nonremittance of profits (perhaps transfer mispricing induced), tax holidays, and so on. If private company profits were to be included in the profit base on which the calculation has been undertaken, the margin for these other factors would obviously be higher still.

What is clear is that these data suggest that US$160 billion in transfer pricing abuse affecting developing counties is plausible within the framework of the world economy given what we know of corporate profits, corporate tax rates, and the opportunities for corporate tax planning.

The risk of being caught

If it is plausible that transfer mispricing of the suggested order may have taken place, we must then ask if the transfer mispricing could have taken place without detection or sanction.

First, this would not happen if all corporations sought to be tax compliant (see above). While some corporations are risk averse, by no means all are.[16] In this case, it is unlikely that all corporations are tax compliant.

The likelihood of noncompliance is increased because of the limited application of the OECD arm's-length pricing rules, which are meant to govern transfer pricing in international trade (see above). For the purposes of this chapter, transfer mispricing is considered a breach of these rules. Because these rules usually only apply if legislation requires or if a DTA is in existence requiring the trade between two jurisdictions to be priced in accordance with these principles, it is likely that transfer mispricing is commonplace.

In EU and OECD countries, which have been used as the basis for much of the published research on transfer mispricing, such DTAs usually exist, as do the resources to monitor the application of these agreements. As a result, it is now often said at tax conferences that mispricing in the trade in goods is rare or almost unknown, although the same is not said of intangibles. Such comments, however, ignore the fact that this is a select sample base that gives little indication of the opportunity for abuse in much of the world.

For example, even a brief review shows clearly that DTAs are notable by their absence in Africa. While South Africa has an impressive range of DTAs, other countries are in a different position.[17] Botswana has 10.[18] Zambia has 17, but most are old, and none has been signed since 1989.[19] The Democratic Republic of Congo has only two DTAs.[20] Angola is far from alone in having no DTAs. The lack of progress in developing new agreements implies that the resources devoted to monitoring the issue are limited in Africa.

Especially since the G-20 summit in April 2009, DTAs have been supplemented by new tax information exchange agreements. These, however, are limited to information exchange issues, as their name implies, and not the regulation of transfer prices (in other words, they exclude standard article 9 of the OECD Model Tax Convention; see OECD 2003). Moreover, as research by Tax Research LLP and the Tax Justice Network (TJN) has shown, as of November 2009, Brazil, China, India, Japan, most of Africa, and almost all developing countries were notable absentees from the list of states that had signed tax information exchange agreements with secrecy jurisdictions (Murphy 2009b). The implication is obvious: the places most likely to be subject to transfer mispricing abuse are also the places least likely to enjoy protection from such abuse.

It is accepted that other regulation, such as controlled foreign company rules, might limit the opportunity for such abuse, but, as secondary protection, they do not do so efficiently. First, they do not restore correct pricing between the parties that initiated the trade; so, tax remains inappropriately allocated to jurisdictions given that the application of these rules to transfer mispricing only gives rise to an additional tax payment in the jurisdiction in which the ultimate parent company is located, not in the jurisdiction that lost out initially. Second, the abuse has to be discovered in the parent company jurisdiction. For the reasons noted below, this can be difficult. Consequently, the chance that transfer mispricing will take place without being detected is high.

The Particular Problem in Developing Countries

The issue of enforcing transfer pricing rules in developing countries is particularly acute, as many published reports have shown.[21]

Global Witness has published a report on the operations of Mittal Steel (now Arcelor Mittal) in Liberia. The report provides commentary on the tax provisions of Mittal's mineral development agreement, noting that "probably the single biggest problem with this agreement is that it gives the company [Mittal] complete freedom to set the price of the iron ore, and therefore the basis of the royalty rate" (Global Witness 2006, 7).

There were no restrictions at all in the original agreement between Mittal Steel and Liberia on the transfer prices the company could use. As a result, while there is no suggestion of impropriety, the possibility that transfer mispricing occurred was increased by the absence of any regulation intended to prevent it. In this case and as a direct result of the work of Global Witness, the contract was revised. The changes were noted in a new commentary issued by Global Witness, which reported that "under the amended agreement the [transfer] price is set under the arms length rule, which means that it will be based on the international market price of the ore" (Global Witness 2007, 1).

It would be pleasing to report that all such risks of transfer mispricing have been eliminated so speedily, but the evidence is clear that this is not the case. Problems with transfer mispricing have been found after similar

NGO studies of the extractive industries in many countries. For example, in Zambia, Christian Aid has stated that "in his budget speech in February 2006, the minister of finance estimated that the government was likely to receive less than US$11 million from royalty payments in 2006: that's 0.1 per cent of the value of production in 2005" (Christian Aid 2007, 24). Christian Aid believes that this is in no small part caused by transfer mispricing, which has an impact, in this case, on both royalty payments and declared taxable profits. This is unsurprising. The Investment Act 1993 of Zambia, like its predecessor, the 1991 Investment Act, does not address the issue of transfer pricing (Mwenda 1999). Nor, it seems, do many of the mineral development agreements that have been negotiated in Zambia. This is a situation that may have been addressed by amendments in the Zambian Income Tax Act, passed by parliament in April 2008, which stipulated that royalties are to be calculated based on the average monthly cash price on the London Metal Exchange, *Metal Bulletin*, or any other metals exchange as agreed with the government (Open Society Institute et al. 2009). The impact may be limited, however: most Zambian mineral development agreements have stability clauses exempting them from the effects of any changes in tax law for up to 20 years (Christian Aid 2007).

In the logging sector in the Democratic Republic of Congo, Greenpeace notes as follows:

> Internal Danzer Group documents show in great detail the price fixing arrangements between the Group's Swiss-based trading arm Interholco AG and the parent firm's logging subsidiaries in the DRC and the Republic of the Congo. The DRC-based Siforco sells its wood to Interholco at an official price below the true market value of the wood. The shortfall is made up through unofficial payments into offshore bank accounts in Europe. (Greenpeace 2008, 3)

A review undertaken for this report found no evidence that issues related to transfer pricing were addressed in five mineral development agreements signed from 1994 to 2007 between the government of Tanzania and companies mining gold in Tanzania. Royalty rates were fundamental to anticipated government revenues from royalties and, ultimately, from profits in each case, but on no occasion was the basis specified for setting the price of exports. The tax base on which royalties were to be charged was thus capable of discretionary determination by the company liable to make the payment of the taxes due. In addition, all the agreements include fiscal stability clauses, and most specify that the basis of the pricing of gold (even though unspecified) should not be unilaterally changed, presumably by the government of Tanzania. For this reason, recent changes to Tanzanian law introducing transfer pricing regulation are likely to have little or no impact in this critical Tanzanian export sector.

The problem has also been found within the Extractive Industries Transparency Initiative. In a review of the first audit of the initiative in Ghana, Murphy (2007, 10) notes that the audit objective to "ascertain the appropriateness of payments made with regards to mineral royalties; ground rent; dividends; taxation on profits and for mineral rights" had not, in the opinion of the reviewer, been fulfilled, largely because of the use of indeterminate prices unrelated to verifiable benchmarks and the use of apparently uncorroborated exchange rates for valuing gold exports, both clear indications that proper transfer pricing controls were not in operation.

The evidence appears to be telling: there is a pattern of transfer pricing abuse or at least the risk of such abuse in developing countries. The evidence from mineral development agreements implies there is no change in the prospects in this area even if legislation to introduce arm's-length pricing rules is enacted because companies in the extractive industries are almost entirely immune to legislative changes affecting the way in which their tax liabilities are computed for periods of up to 30 years after signing mineral development agreements.

It is also important to note another key feature emphasized by this work: the transfer pricing abuse in these cases is highly unlikely to be motivated by taxes on corporate profits alone. The abuse is likely to extend to royalties, sales and purchase taxes, dividends, abuse of profit-sharing agreements, and more. The incentives to abuse are high, indeed; the consequences of not tackling the issue are considerable; and the prospects for tackling the abuse within current legislative and contractual constraints are not good.

Even if arm's-length transfer pricing rules do exist in developing countries, there appear to be almost insurmountable problems in enforcing them. As one of the rare cases of suggested transfer pricing abuse ever brought to court in Africa has shown (*Unilever Kenya Ltd v. Commissioners of Income Tax*, Kenya Income Tax Appeal 753, 2003), the absence of the accounts of the related party with whom trade was being undertaken in the destination jurisdiction is a significant cause of the failure to prove that profit was being shifted through the transfer mispricing of goods; this is what the Kenyan authorities were seeking to prove had occurred using the OECD arm's-length principle. Although the accounts in question were necessarily available to the group of companies the Kenyan subsidiary of which made the appeal in this case, they were not made available to the court. It is likely that the withholding of this accounting data, albeit entirely legal, had a material impact on the resulting decision of the court in Kenya.

Secrecy prevented the proper determination of a transfer pricing issue in this case, whether rightly or wrongly. This is a recurring theme of work in this area, as is the persistence of the assertion that developing countries are particularly vulnerable to the effects of secrecy. If this is the case, it is important that the mechanisms for creating this secrecy that permits transfer mispricing to take place undetected, unchallenged, or uncorrected be considered. Unless it can be shown that corporations can make use of secrecy to achieve this outcome, then it remains implausible that transfer mispricing of the alleged scale takes place. If, in contrast, significant secrecy is available to corporations, then corporations have the opportunity to transfer misprice, as some believe is taking place.

How Multinational Corporations Exploit Secrecy

The modern MNC is a complex entity. This is not the place to explore all aspects of the nature of the MNC or the motivations for creating some of the structures MNCs use, but, without consideration of the interaction of the corporation, jurisdictions, corporate law, and tax law, testing the proposition that transfer mispricing can take place within MNCs and be hidden from view within the accounts and financial statements of MNCs is not possible.

The MNC is almost invariably headed by a single company, the parent entity, which is almost always a limited liability corporation. The parent entity comprises a number of other, usually similar limited liability corporations spread over one or more other jurisdictions. For example, in the course of researching this report, we noted that United Kingdom–based BP plc has more than 3,000 subsidiaries in over 150 jurisdictions.

Subsidiaries need not be limited liability corporations. As noted in International Accounting Standard 27 (IAS 27, 2009), a subsidiary is an entity, including an unincorporated entity such as a partnership, that is controlled by another entity (known as the parent).[22] Subsidiaries can therefore also be limited liability partnerships in any form, whether trusts, charities, or other arrangements, but limited liability corporations are the most common by far. The key is that the parent company controls the subsidiary. Control is widely defined by IAS 27, but most commonly means that the parent has direct or indirect control of a majority of the equity shares.

However control is established, if a parent entity governed by the IFRSs (which, in this respect, operate almost identically to the U.S. Generally Accepted Accounting Principles) has subsidiary entities, then IAS 27 requires that consolidated accounts and financial statements be prepared. These are the financial statements of a group of entities presented as if they were those of a single economic entity.

It is immediately apparent that, within this requirement, there is an obvious conflict of interest. The parent entity of such a group may be required to present the group's accounts as if the group were a single entity, and, yet, in practice, the group may be made up of thousands of entities that are under the control, but not necessarily the sole ownership, of the parent entity. Thus, in substance, each entity within the MNC may remain legally distinct, and each may be subject to the rules of accounting, taxation, and disclosure of the jurisdiction in which it operates. In a real sense, each subsidiary is therefore without obligation to the other members of the group, barring the duty the directors and managers of the entity may owe to the owners to whom they report under the law of the jurisdiction in which the entity is incorporated, and this duty varies widely from place to place.

Curiously, according to the one nearly constant assumption in company law, the shareholders and the owner do not have the right to manage the entity: that right belongs to the directors. Of course, the shareholders may have the right to appoint the directors, but, it is important to note, the assumption underpinning group accounts pierces the veil of incorporation that, in turn, underpins the notion of the limited liability entity. The dichotomy is that the assumption accomplishes this in the effort to reinforce the division inherent in the act of incorporation through the presentation of the group as one undertaking distinct from the owners, who obtain only the limited information the directors may wish to supply, subject to legal constraints.

The inherent conflict in reporting results is exacerbated by a number of other factors. First, the definition of control used for accounting may be different from the definition used by some jurisdictions for tax. So, some entities that are within the group for tax purposes in some locations may not be within the group in other locations. For example, tax may require 75 percent control, while accounting requires 50.01 percent in most cases. Therefore, entities that, for accounting purposes, may be related parties requiring inclusion in a common set of consolidated accounts and financial statements may not be so treated for transfer pricing purposes.

Second, note that some entities are deliberately structured to exploit the rules on consolidated financial reporting. In particular, the financial services industry has become expert at creating orphan entities. These are companies that are created by a parent organization and that are deliberately structured by the parent entity so that they are off the balance sheet; thus, the assets or liabilities that the orphans own are excluded from consolidation in the parent entity's accounts and financial statements, as are the results of the trading of the orphans.

A common way to engineer this outcome is to create a company to which are transferred the off–balance sheet assets and liabilities the parent entity wishes to hide from view. The new entity is owned by a charitable trust, for example. As such, it is not considered to be under the ownership or control of the parent entity. This is why it is described as an orphan; it has become parentless, although it is utterly dependent on the parent entity.

These entities are hard to spot, but commonplace. While the entities are used to exclude liabilities from accounts, the rules that permit this will, in most cases, also allow them to be used for transfer mispricing, which may pass undetected, subject to the caveat that the proceeds must then be used for purposes that the group may wish to keep at quasi-arm's length. This purpose may be fraudulent.

Third, it is widely assumed that consolidated accounts and financial statements are created by adding together all the accounts of the individual entities that make up the group and then eliminating all the intragroup transactions and balances. This is a simplistic, but not wholly inappropriate view of what should happen. The reality is that MNCs can deliberately obscure the relationship between the underlying accounts and financial statements of the subsidiary companies and the group accounts in ways that make it almost impossible to detect what is really happening within the group.

The first method to achieve this is the use of different accounting year-end dates for group companies. IAS 27 (section 26) says this should not occur and that any differences should be explained, but the reality is (as the author has frequently witnessed) that noncoterminous year-ends are commonplace and almost never disclosed or commented upon. If noncoterminous year-ends are used, transfer mispricing may then be relied on to shift profits (and losses) around the group almost at liberty and almost entirely undetected.

Next, nonstandard accounting policies may be used in different places to recognize transactions even though, according to IAS 27, this should not occur. This is now commonplace. The parent company might account using IFRSs, but local entities may well account using local Generally Accepted Accounting Principles, and there is nothing to prevent this. Some significant transactions have different tax treatments depending on the accounting standards used. There are, for example, conflicts between the United Kingdom and the International Accounting Standards on financial derivatives for tax purposes. These differences and conflicts have been exploited by international banks.

In addition, entries can be made in the consolidated accounts alone, without ever appearing anywhere in any of the accounts of the underlying entities. In principle, this should not occur because the accounts can then be said not to reflect the underlying books and records of the MNC that is publishing them, but, in practice, if the entries are considered a nonmaterial adjustment in the assessment from the point of view of the user of the financial statements, which both the International Accounting Standards Board and the U.S. Federal Accounting Standards Board define as "a provider of capital to the company," then no auditor is likely to object. This can, however, disguise radically different presentations of profit on trades between related undertakings in group consolidated accounts and financial statements and individual entity accounts and financial statements, especially if the tax implications are considered, so that the benefit may be hidden from view in the accounts of the group as a whole. Interview-based evidence indicates that this practice may be commonplace. It will never be discovered by tax authorities because it is the accounts and financial statements of the individual subsidiary entities that are used to determine tax liabilities in each jurisdiction in which these entities trade. The consolidated accounts and financial statements are deemed to have no tax interest to tax authorities (although it is not clear that this is true), and, as such, in jurisdictions such as the United Kingdom, the tax authorities are not entitled to ask questions about the entries that make up these published accounts.

This last point is, perhaps, of the greatest significance because the exact entries that are eliminated from view when the consolidated accounts and financial statements are prepared are those same transactions that will always have the potential to give rise to transfer pricing disputes. For this reason, the most useful evidence that consolidated accounts and financial statements could provide to tax authorities—the data relating to transfer pricing issues, which are the data on the "most contentious issue in tax," according to a poll of U.S. tax directors in 2007—is denied to the tax authorities who need it.[23]

This omission is exacerbated by a number of other practices, all endorsed by the IFRSs and all of which make it easier to hide transfer pricing abuse. First, in the individual accounts and financial statements of the subsidiaries that make up an MNC, it would seem obvious that the transactions with other group companies should be highlighted if only to indicate that they will disappear upon consolidation. This is theoretically required by another International Accounting Standard, IAS 24, on related-party transactions. Broadly speaking, IAS 24 (section 9) defines a party as related to an entity if one party directly or indirectly controls the other, but associates, joint venturers, and some other arrangements are also included in the definition. IAS 24 defines a related-party transaction as a transfer of resources, services, or obligations between the related parties regardless of whether a price is charged (section 9). As a result, it would seem that all transactions among group companies must be disclosed in a group's financial statements because a long list of disclosable transactions of this sort is included in the standard.

Unfortunately, the prospect of disclosure that this requirement creates is then dashed. IAS 24 proceeds to state that, while the disclosure must be made separately for the parent company, subsidiaries, and other identified categories of related parties, the information within each such category "may be disclosed in aggregate except when separate disclosure is necessary for an understanding of the effects of the related party transactions on the financial statements of the company." As a result, all trading by a subsidiary with all other subsidiaries can be aggregated into one number in most cases, and no indication need be given of the other party in a trade, what has been traded, or on what terms and where the other side of the transaction might be recorded.

The result is obvious: the accounts and financial statements end up providing no meaningful information at all on transfer pricing issues. The information is excluded from consolidated accounts and financial statements because related-party trades between parents and their subsidiaries and between fellow subsidiaries are always excluded from these accounts, while the disclosure requirement on individual group members is so limited that forming a view on transfer pricing is almost impossible in most cases: it is rare for the other party to any transaction to be disclosed, especially within a large and complex group.

This might be thought an accident. Regrettably it is not, as IAS 24 makes clear. In the latest version of the standard, introductory note IN7 states that "discussions [in the standard] on the pricing of transactions and related disclosures between related parties have been removed because the Standard does not apply to the measurement of related party transactions."

This is an extraordinary statement. Accounts prepared under IFRSs and their U.S. equivalents are the basis of corporate taxation in a great many countries in the world, but the International Accounting Standard that is responsible for their promulgation says that it is not the purpose of the standard to assist in the measurement of matters related to transfer pricing. Moreover, it offers no suggestion on how such matters should be considered or measured.

What is clear is that it is not the intent in the standards that the only other part of the IFRS environment that might provide information on the issue—IFRS 8, on segment—do so. IFRS 8, by default, usually only applies to companies quoted on a stock exchange in a jurisdiction that has adopted IFRSs (as all countries in the EU have done, for example). It defines an operating segment as a component of an entity:

- that engages in business activities from which it may earn revenues and incur expenses;
- the operating results of which are reviewed regularly by the entity's chief operating decision maker so as to make decisions about the resources to be allocated to the segment and assess its performance; and
- for which discrete financial information is available.

IFRS 8 requires an entity to report financial and descriptive information about the entity's reportable segments. These are operating segments or aggregations of operating segments that account for more than 10 percent of the revenues, profits, or assets of the entity. Smaller segments are combined until ones of this size are created, supposedly to reduce information overload. In practice, this might, of course, hide necessary detail.

Required disclosure by reportable segments targets trading data, including profit and loss, assets and liabilities, and limited geographical analysis. Such a summary does not, however, show the true level of problems inherent within IFRS 8, which also allows segment data to be published using accounting rules that are not the same as those used in the rest of the accounts and financial statements, meaning, as a result, that segment data may be formulated in a way harmful to the appraisal of transfer mispricing. In addition, IFRS 8 does not require that segments cover all of the MNC's activities, meaning some information may be omitted, providing more opportunity for transfer mispricing to be hidden from view.

As a consequence, considerable support has developed for an alternative form of segment accounting called country-by-country reporting, created by the author of this report (Murphy 2009a). Country-by-country reporting would require an MNC to disclose the name of each country in which it operates and the names of all its companies trading in each country in which it operates. Currently, these data are usually unavailable. Country-by-country reporting would then require publication of a full profit and loss account for each country in which the MNC operates, plus limited cash flow and balance sheet information. Radically, the profit and loss account would break down turnover between turnover involving third parties and turnover involving group entities. Costs of sale, overhead, and finance costs would have to be broken down in the same way, while a full tax note would be required for each country, as is presently necessary for IFRSs.

In addition, if the company operates within the extractive industries, one would also expect to see all those benefits paid to the government of each country in which the MNC operates broken down across the categories of reporting required in the Extractive Industries Transparency Initiative.

As Murphy (2009a, 18) notes, "country-by-country reporting does not [stop transfer mispricing]. What it does do is provide data that . . . tax departments . . . can use to assess the likely risk that exists within the accounts of a multinational corporation. They can do this by

- "Assessing the likelihood of risk within the group structure;
- "Reviewing the overall allocation of profits to countries within the group to see if there is indication of systematic bias towards low-tax jurisdictions;
- "Assessing whether the volume and flows of intragroup trading disclosed by country-by-country reporting suggests that this outcome is achieved as a result of mispricing of that trade;
- "Using that information to assess where that abuse is most likely to occur so that an appropriate challenge can be raised."

So far, the International Accounting Standards Board has only indicated willingness to consider this issue with regard to the extractive industries, and current indications are that, despite the considerable lobbying, there is little prospect of an advance on this issue. The conclusion is inescapable: as one board member said when the issue of country-by-country reporting was being discussed by the International Accounting Standards Board, "this looks like it deals with the issue of transfer pricing, and we do not want to go there."[24] The comment is succinct and neatly summarizes the design of current accounting standards, which seem purpose-made to hide the subject of transfer pricing from view.

The Role of Secrecy Jurisdictions

The literature that alleges substantial transfer mispricing abuse by MNCs also finds that tax havens play a significant role in the process. The term *tax haven* is, however, so widely misunderstood that this chapter does not use it, preferring instead to use the term *secrecy jurisdiction*. For a more detailed consideration of the term, the nature of a secrecy jurisdiction, and the economic significance in the matters under consideration here, see chapter 11 in this volume. A list of the places currently considered significant secrecy jurisdictions is available in table 9A.4.[25]

The term secrecy jurisdiction is considered more appropriate for the purposes of the current analysis because, although the process of transfer mispricing to which this chapter refers seeks to secure a tax advantage (by way of reduced tax payment) for those who pursue the activity, this advantage is not normally available unless the abuse giving rise to the advantage—the artificial relocation of activities to one or more secrecy jurisdictions—can be hidden from view behind a veil of secrecy. Secrecy jurisdiction opacity is often, of course, linked to low tax rates (see above).

The combination of low tax rates and secrecy has obvious attractions for those seeking to transfer misprice. However, to demonstrate whether or not MNCs actually use secrecy jurisdictions and which ones they might use if they do, TJN has coordinated, under the direction of the author of this chapter, a survey of the locations of MNC subsidiaries, paying particular attention to the secrecy jurisdictions TJN has identified. The results of the study by the U.S. Government Accountability Office of December 2008 (GAO 2008), "Large U.S. Corporations and Federal Contractors with Subsidiaries in Jurisdictions Listed as Tax Havens or Financial Privacy Jurisdictions," have been used as part of the survey. Because the U.S. survey excludes data on the Netherlands, the United Kingdom, and the United States, these locations have also been excluded from the TJN survey. Austria (for practical rather than methodological reasons), Belgium, and Madeira (because of difficulties in isolating data independently from Portugal) have also been excluded.

The total sample of MNCs surveyed is shown in table 9.4.

It should, however, be noted that the data selection has been pragmatic: the U.K. data should have been the entire FTSE 100, that is, the 100 largest companies in the United Kingdom, designed to match the U.S.

Table 9.4. Multinational Corporations Surveyed by the Tax Justice Network

number

Country	MNCs sampled
France	39
Germany	28
Netherlands	23
Switzerland	20
United Kingdom	33
United States	100
Total	243

Source: Mapping Financial Secrecy (database), Tax Justice Network, London, http://www.secrecyjurisdictions.com/index.php (accessed December 12, 2009).

sample. In practice, although all United Kingdom–quoted companies are legally required to publish the names, places of incorporation, and percentage of the holdings for all their subsidiary companies annually either in their audited accounts and financial statements or as an appendix to their annual declaration made to the U.K. Registrar of Companies, only 33 of the FTSE 100 companies did so. Enquiries found that no company had ever been prosecuted for failing to file this information. It is a curious example of the United Kingdom's opacity (see table 9A.5).[26]

It should also be noted that substantial problems were encountered with all other samples. The French data undoubtedly underreport the number of subsidiaries because they only relate to principal subsidiaries, not all subsidiaries. German companies do not always make the distinction between subsidiaries and associates clear. The Dutch and Swiss data have been taken from databases, not original documentation, which implies that there are inconsistencies in approach, particularly about whether dormant subsidiaries are counted or not, and so on. All such issues do, however, reveal one consistent theme: it is immensely difficult to determine the composition of an MNC.

Detailed analysis of the regulatory requirements of the 60 secrecy jurisdictions surveyed by TJN highlights the issues. Of the 60 jurisdictions surveyed, accounts of companies were available on easily accessible public record in only six.[27]

Table 9.5. Secrecy Jurisdiction Locations of Multinational Corporation Subsidiaries

number

Rank	Secrecy jurisdiction	MNC subsidiaries
1	Cayman Islands	1,130
2	Ireland	920
3	Luxembourg	824
4	Switzerland	771
5	Hong Kong SAR, China	737
6	Singapore	661
7	Bermuda	483
8	Jersey	414
9	Hungary	252
10	British Virgin Islands	244
11	Malaysia (Labuan)	177
12	Mauritius	169
13	Bahamas, The	156
14	Guernsey	151
15	Philippines	126
16	Panama	125
17	Isle of Man	99
18	Costa Rica	85
19	Cyprus	69
20	Netherlands Antilles	68
21	Uruguay	67
22	Malta	60
23	United Arab Emirates (Dubai)	58
24	Israel	56
25	Gibraltar	54
26	Barbados	51
27	Latvia	40
28	U.S. Virgin Islands	37
29	Monaco	35
30	Liechtenstein	32

Source: Mapping Financial Secrecy (database), Tax Justice Network, London, http://www.secrecy jurisdictions.com/index.php (accessed December 12, 2009).

The situation was worse for the beneficial (as opposed to nominal) ownership information on public record. Only Monaco requires that these data be available. In all other cases, nominee ownership may be recorded, or there is simply no requirement to record data on public record at all.[28]

It is readily apparent, as a consequence, that, unless data are required from MNCs on the companies making up or not making up their group and the operations of each, as shown by the audited accounts, then the current legal requirements for data registration within secrecy jurisdictions ensure that the information required to assist in the appraisal of MNC activities, including those relating to transfer mispricing, will simply be unavailable to most people and, quite possibly, to many tax authorities if that is the MNC's wish, as it will be if the MNC is seeking to hide transfer mispricing activity.

This would not be an issue if MNCs did not use secrecy jurisdictions. The reality is that they do use secrecy jurisdictions extensively. Of the European and U.S. samples, 97.2 and 84.0 percent, respectively, had secrecy jurisdiction subsidiaries as defined by the TJN. Table 9.5 indicates the number of subsidiaries by location according to the TJN survey. (Data on the 24 additional, smaller jurisdictions have been ignored; these jurisdictions are immaterial for the purposes of this chapter.)

It is readily apparent that some locations stand out, but the data make a lot more sense if they are plotted against two control variables: population and GDP (figure 9.4).

The data in figure 9.4 are ranked by the number of subsidiaries by GDP in billions of U.S. dollars. In most cases, the correlation with a ranking by the number of subsidiaries per head of population is clear. These weighted data give a much better view of the relative importance of these secrecy locations. It is apparent that some show extraordinary amounts of activity relative to their size. There is only one explanation for this: the secrecy jurisdictions are not creating entities for use by the local population, but, as the definition of these jurisdictions in this chapter suggests is likely, for the use of people resident elsewhere. The companies that are registered in these jurisdictions do little or nothing in these locations.

Figure 9.4. Top 20 Subsidiaries by Secrecy Jurisdiction, Population, and GDP

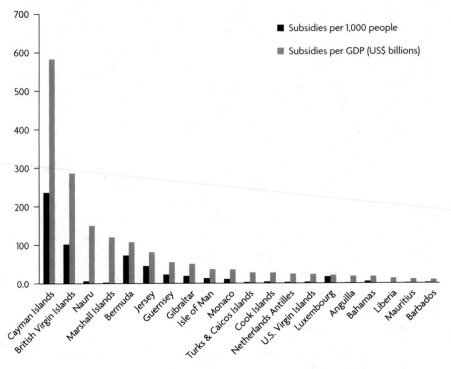

Source: Mapping Financial Secrecy (database), Tax Justice Network, London, http://www.secrecyjurisdictions.com/index. php (accessed December 12, 2009).

That this must be true is indicated by the number of subsidiaries active in financial services as a proportion of the total working population in the secrecy jurisdictions. As TJN has noted, this exceeds 20 percent in Cayman Islands, Guernsey, Isle of Man, and Jersey and 10 percent in Bermuda, Liechtenstein, and Luxembourg.[29] Financial service sectors of this size crowd out the possibility of any other significant economic activity taking place. The overlap between this list (figure 9.4) and the locations with the most MNC subsidiaries (table 9.5) is obvious, and the implication is clear: these locations do not create value. Their sole raison d'être is the provision of corporate and financial service structures that may record value, but do not generate it. Of course, one way in which this value may be relocated into these places is through transfer mispricing.

The existence of the Big Four firms of accountants—Pricewater-houseCoopers, Deloitte Touche Tohmatsu, Ernst & Young, and KPMG—in many secrecy jurisdictions in which their location cannot possibly be justified solely by the needs of the local populations reinforces this view. As Murphy (2010b) shows, the Big Four firms are significantly overrepresented in small secrecy jurisdictions (those with less than 1 million population) compared with other locations of this size (see table 9A.6).[30] As he also shows, these locations of the Big Four have an average GDP per head that is approximately four times greater than the average GDP in similar locations in which the Big Four are not present. Of course, cause and effect cannot be proven based on this circumstantial evidence, but the possibility exists, especially in the smallest of such locations, that the income in question is not earned in these places, but is transferred in through transfer mispricing, and, in that case, the Big Four firms, as Murphy suggests, facilitate the structures that allow the transfer mispricing to occur.

Conclusion

This chapter has sought, first, to test the credibility of the claim that at least US$160 billion a year may be lost by developing countries as a result of transfer mispricing by MNCs.

Second, it has sought to demonstrate that developing countries and, particularly, the extractive industries may be especially prone to this abuse.

Third, it has considered whether this sum may be hidden from view within the accounts or financial statements of the MNCs that may be perpetrating the mispricing.

Fourth, it has explored the possibility that these MNCs may use secrecy jurisdictions to assist in hiding these transactions from view.

As the chapter indicates, the incentive to transfer misprice is great. This is because, first, the differential in effective tax rates between the jurisdictions in potential supply chains is higher than the existing literature on tax rates suggests would normally be the case. Second, it is because the structure of international tax regulation at present suggests that the chance of detection of transfer mispricing is low.

The chapter then shows that the risk that transfer mispricing may go undetected within the extractive industries that supply much of the external earning capacity of many developing countries is great. As the chapter also notes, transfer mispricing in this sector is unlikely to be motivated by a desire to avoid taxes on corporate profits alone. The abuse is likely to extend to royalties, sales and purchase taxes, dividends, abuse of profit-sharing agreements, and more. The incentives to abuse for all these reasons are substantial, and the consequence of not tackling the issue considerable, but, as the chapter shows, the prospects of tackling the issue are limited given the current legislative and contractual constraints.

The chapter also reviews a number of IFRSs, in particular the standards addressing consolidated accounts and financial statements, related-party transactions, and segment reporting: the three standards most likely to relate to disclosure of intragroup trade within the accounts of MNCs. The analysis shows that these standards are not designed to, and are not capable of, leading to the disclosure of these transactions and the associated transfer pricing. It proposes that this failure may be intentional.

The chapter defines secrecy jurisdiction and argues that secrecy jurisdictions are deliberate constructs. Secrecy jurisdictions are used disproportionately by MNCs as measured relative to local populations and GDP. In the secrecy jurisdictions most popular with the MNCs, there is little prospect of any real added value arising because, as the chapter shows, the economies of these secrecy jurisdictions are largely dedicated to the supply of financial services, part of which activity is administered by the MNC subsidiaries. This pattern of use does, however, accord with the proposed definition of a secrecy jurisdiction, suggesting that the purpose of these jurisdictions is to disguise the true nature of activity undertaken elsewhere so that compliance with the regulations of other states can be avoided or evaded. Transfer mispricing may be only one abusive activity that may be occurring.

What overall conclusions may one draw from this evidence? The following conclusions are proposed.

First, it is apparent that there is a stronger incentive to transfer misprice than the existing literature has suggested. Second, developing countries are particularly susceptible to this activity. Third, this activity can be hidden from view in accounts. Fourth, secrecy jurisdictions provide an additional layer of opacity to disguise this activity. Fifth, the combination of the secrecy inherent in accounting rules and secrecy jurisdiction legislation provides a deep opacity that limits the possibility of discovering transfer mispricing activity. As a result, the chapter finds that transfer mispricing may be taking place undetected.

In this case, is it also plausible that the quantum of the loss to developing countries may be as much as US$160 billion per annum? As noted in the chapter, this seems to be quite plausible on the basis of data verified from a variety of sources and therefore considered a credible basis for the analytical review techniques common in auditing methodology.

Thus, on the basis of the methodologies noted, the chapter concludes that substantial transfer mispricing by major corporations contributing to a loss of at least US$160 billion a year to developing countries is plausible in the context of the total likely corporate profits earned worldwide in a year.

Notes

1. Transfer mispricing occurs if two or more entities under common control that are trading across international borders price transactions between them at rates designed to secure a tax advantage that would not be available to third parties trading in the same goods or services across the same borders.
2. The arm's-length principle is the international standard that OECD member countries have agreed should be used to determine transfer prices for tax purposes. It is set forth in article 9 of the OECD Model Tax Convention, as follows: where "conditions are made or imposed between the two enterprises in their commercial or financial relations which differ from those which would be made between independent enterprises, then any profits which would, but for those conditions, have accrued to one of the enterprises, but, by reason of those conditions, have not so accrued, may be included in the profits of that enterprise and taxed accordingly" (Centre for Tax Policy and Administration, "Annex 3: Glossary," OECD, Paris, http://www.oecd.org/document/41/0,3343,en_2649_33753 _37685737_1_1_1_1,00.html, accessed October 13, 2011). See also chapter 7 in this volume.
3. IFFs are defined by Kar and Cartwright-Smith (2008) as "the proceeds from both illicit activities such as corruption (the bribery and embezzlement of national wealth), criminal activity, and the proceeds of licit business that become illicit when transported across borders in contravention of applicable laws and regulatory frameworks (most commonly in order to evade payment of taxes)."
4. Secrecy jurisdictions intentionally create regulation for the primary benefit and use of nonresidents in the geographical domain. The jurisdiction regulation is

designed to undermine the legislation or regulations of another jurisdiction. The jurisdictions create a deliberate, legally backed veil of secrecy that ensures that those from outside who use the jurisdiction regulations cannot be identified by others.

5. See World Factbook (database), Central Intelligence Agency, Washington, DC, https://www.cia.gov/library/publications/the-world-factbook/.

6. Jurisdiction Centre (database), OCRA Worldwide, Isle of Man, United Kingdom, http://www.ocra.com/jurisdictions/index.asp.

7. The table may be found on the website of this volume, http://go.worldbank.org /N2HMRB4G20.

8. The table may be found on the website of this volume, http://go.worldbank.org /N2HMRB4G20.

9. Devereux, Lockwood, and Redoano (2002) are typical of the other surveys in that they also entirely ignore the tax haven–secrecy jurisdiction issue.

10. Jurisdiction Centre (database), OCRA Worldwide, Isle of Man, United Kingdom, http://www.ocra.com/jurisdictions/index.asp.

11. The table may be found on the website of this volume, http://go.worldbank.org /N2HMRB4G20.

12. Based on International Monetary Fund–World Bank data summarized at http:// en.wikipedia.org/wiki/List_of_countries_by_GDP_(nominal) (accessed March 3, 2010). In each case, the data are in the range of US$60 trillion to US$61 trillion. Original sources are linked through the website noted.

13. Data of the U.K. Office for National Statistics.

14. HMRC (HM Revenue & Customs), 2009, "HM Revenue and Customs Annual Receipts," data sheet, December, London, http://www.hmrc.gov.uk/stats/tax _receipts/table1-2.pdf.

15. Data of the Bureau of Economic Analysis, U.S. Department of Commerce.

16. Anecdotal evidence based on conversations with high-ranking officials of HM Revenue & Customs leads us to believe that approximately 35 percent of all large companies in the United Kingdom are considered to have little appetite for taxation risk, while at least 40 percent are considered to have exposed themselves to high risk in the management of their taxation affairs.

17. See South African Revenue Service, http://www.sars.gov.za/home.asp?pid=3906 (accessed August 17, 2009).

18. Lowtax, Global Tax and Business Portal, "Botswana: Double Tax Treaties." http:// www.lowtax.net/lowtax/html/botswana/jbo2tax.html (accessed August 17, 2009).

19. Zambia Revenue Authority, "Tax Treaties." http://www.zra.org.zm/Tax_Treaties _Agreemnet.php (accessed August 17, 2009).

20. See United Nations Conference on Trade and Development, http://www.unctad .org/sections/dite_pcbb/docs/dtt_Congo_DR.PDF.

21. It is appropriate to note that the author of this chapter has acted as adviser on transfer pricing or contractual issues to the authors of most of the reports referred to in this section.

22. See Standards (IFRSs) (database), International Accounting Standards Board, London, http://www.ifrs.org/IFRSs/IFRS.htm.
23. For the citation, see "US Tax Directors' Poll: TP Is Most Contentious Issue," *TP Week*, December 12, 2007, http://www.tpweek.com/Article.aspx?ArticleID= 1786798.
24. Reported by Richard Murphy, September 2006.
25. The table may be found on the website of this volume, http://go.worldbank.org /N2HMRB4G20.
26. The table may be found on the website of this volume, http://go.worldbank.org /N2HMRB4G20.
27. See Mapping Financial Secrecy (database), Tax Justice Network, London, http:// www.secrecyjurisdictions.com/index.php (accessed December 12, 2009).
28. See Mapping Financial Secrecy (database), Tax Justice Network, London, http:// www.secrecyjurisdictions.com/index.php (accessed December 12, 2009).
29. See Mapping Financial Secrecy (database), Tax Justice Network, London, http:// www.secrecyjurisdictions.com/index.php (accessed December 16, 2009).
30. The table may be found on the website of this volume, http://go.worldbank.org /N2HMRB4G20.

References

Baker, R. W. 2005. *Capitalism's Achilles Heel: Dirty Money and How to Renew the Free-Market System.* Hoboken, NJ: John Wiley & Sons.

Christian Aid. 2007. "A Rich Seam: Who Benefits from Rising Commodity Prices?" Christian Aid Report, January. Christian Aid, London.

———. 2008. "Death and Taxes: The True Toll of Tax Dodging." Christian Aid Report, May. Christian Aid, London.

Devereux, M. P., B. Lockwood, and M. Redoano. 2002. "Do Countries Compete over Corporate Tax Rates?" CEPR Discussion Paper 3400, Centre for Economic Policy Research, London.

Dietz, M., R. Reibestein, and C. Walter. 2008. "What's in Store for Global Banking?" *McKinsey Quarterly*, January.

Dischinger, M., and N. Riedel. 2008. "Corporate Taxes and the Location of Intangible Assets within Multinational Firms." Discussion Paper in Economics 5294, Department of Economics, University of Munich, Munich.

GAO (U.S. Government Accountability Office). 2008. "Large U.S. Corporations and Federal Contractors with Subsidiaries in Jurisdictions Listed as Tax Havens or Financial Privacy Jurisdictions." Report GAO-09–157 (December), U.S. Government Accountability Office, Washington, DC.

Global Witness. 2006. "Heavy Mittal? A State within a State: The Inequitable Mineral Development Agreement between the Government of Liberia and Mittal Steel Holdings NV." Report, October, Global Witness, Washington, DC.

————. 2007. "Update on the Renegotiation of the Mineral Development Agreement between Mittal Steel and the Government of Liberia." Update, August, Global Witness, London.

Greenpeace. 2008. "Logging Sector Review: Conning the Congo." Report, July. http://www.greenpeace.org/raw/content/international/press/reports/conning-the-congo.pdf.

HMRC (HM Revenue & Customs). 2010. "Measuring Tax Gaps 2009." Report, March (revised), HMRC, London. http://www.hmrc.gov.uk/stats/measuring-tax-gaps.pdf.

Huizinga, H. 2009. "Profit Shifting Activities in Europe." Paper presented at the Taxation and Customs Union's Brussels Tax Forum 2009, "Tax Systems in a Changing World," European Commission, Brussels, March 30–31. http://ec.europa.eu/taxation_customs/resources/documents/taxation/gen_info/conferences/taxforum2009/pres_Huizinga.pdf.

Kar, D., and D. Cartwright-Smith. 2008. "Illicit Financial Flows from Developing Countries, 2002–2006." Global Financial Integrity, Washington, DC. http://www.gfip.org/storage/gfip/economist%20-%20final%20version%201-2-09.pdf.

Keen, M., and M. Mansour. 2009. "Revenue Mobilization in Sub-Saharan Africa: Challenges from Globalization." IMF Working Paper 09/157, International Monetary Fund, Washington, DC.

London Stock Exchange. 2010. "Market Statistics." Main Market Fact Sheet, February, London Stock Exchange, London. http://www.londonstockexchange.com/statistics/historic/main-market/february-10.pdf.

Murphy, R. 2007. "Ghana's EITI: Delivering on the Promise? A Review of the First Report on the Aggregation/Reconciliation of Mining Benefits in Ghana." Report, March, Tax Research LLP, Downham Market, U.K.

————. 2008. "The Missing Billions: The UK Tax Gap." Touchstone Pamphlet 1, Trades Union Congress, London.

————. 2009a. "Country-by-Country Reporting: Holding Multinational Corporations to Account Wherever They Are." Report, June 17, Task Force on Financial Integrity and Economic Development, Washington, DC.

————. 2009b. "The TIEA Programme Is Failing." Richard Murphy on Tax and Economics, November 27, Tax Research UK, London. http://www.taxresearch.org.uk/Blog/2009/11/27/the-tiea-programme-is-failing/.

————. 2010a. "Tax Justice and Jobs: The Business Case for Investing in Staff at HM Revenue & Customs." Report, March, Tax Research LLP, Downham Market, United Kingdom. http://www.taxresearch.org.uk/Documents/PCSTaxGap.pdf.

————. 2010b. "Where 4 Art Thou? A Geographic Study of the Big 4 Firms of Accountants and the Implications of Their Location for Illicit Financial Flows." Report, Tax Research LLP, Downham Market, U.K. http://www.taxresearch.org.uk/Documents/Where4ArtThou.pdf.

Mwenda, K. 1999. "Legal Aspects of Foreign Direct Investment in Zambia." *Murdoch University Electronic Journal of Law* 6 (4), Murdoch University, Perth, Australia. http://www.murdoch.edu.au/elaw/issues/v6n4/mwenda64.html.

OECD (Organisation for Economic Co-operation and Development). 2003. "Articles of the Model Convention with Respect to Taxes on Income and on Capital." January 28, OECD, Paris. http://www.oecd.org/dataoecd/52/34/1914467.pdf.

Open Society Institute, Third World Network Africa, Tax Justice Network Africa, Nairobi Action Aid International, and Christian Aid. 2009. "Breaking the Curse: How Transparent Taxation and Fair Taxes Can Turn Africa's Mineral Wealth into Development." Report, March, Open Society Institute of Southern Africa, Johannesburg.

10

Trade Mispricing and Illicit Flows

Volker Nitsch

Abstract

A potential vehicle to move capital unrecorded out of a country is the mis-invoicing of international trade transactions. Exporters may understate the export revenue on their invoices, and importers may overstate import expenditures, while their trading partners are instructed to deposit the balance for their benefit in foreign accounts. Aiming to quantify the extent of trade mispricing, studies have analyzed asymmetries in matched partner trade statistics or examined price anomalies in transaction-level price data. This chapter critically reviews these empirical approaches and briefly describes an alternative methodology. Overall, the accuracy and reliability of estimates of illicit financial flows (IFFs) based on trade mispricing are questioned. In particular, it is argued that estimates of trade mispricing are critically dependent on assumptions on how to interpret observed asymmetries in trade statistics. For instance, various reasons for discrepancies in bilateral trade statistics are discussed, and incentives for faking trade invoices other than capital flight are highlighted. Also, aggregate trade data may mask considerable variation in trade discrepancies at the transaction level. Most notably, the importance of trade mispricing as a method for the unrecorded crossborder transfer of capital is generally unclear.

Introduction

The (in)accuracy of international trade statistics has recently (once more) become an issue of much debate. Trade data are often critically reviewed (more than other economic statistics) for at least three reasons. First, data on international trade are of considerable economic relevance. Crossborder shipments of goods and services often have sizable effects on a country's economic activity. Also, for some countries, taxes on international trade constitute a significant share of government revenue. Second, a country's trade data allow, in principle, for full cross-checks with data from other countries. Individual trade transactions are recorded separately by both trading partners so that it should be quite easy to compare these records. As Naya and Morgan (1974, 124) note, "comparable double accounts are not usually available for domestic economic transactions." Finally, recent research has reemphasized that trade activities are subject to criminal behavior. Fisman and Wei (2009) show that the level of smuggling of cultural property is related to the level of corruption in the country of origin. Baldwin (2006) discusses the effect of value added tax (VAT) fraud on intra-European trade figures.

A feature of international trade statistics that has frequently attracted considerable attention is the potential asymmetry in partner country trade statistics arising from mispricing. More specifically, it has been argued that the faking of trade invoices is a commonly used method to move money out of developing countries. If trade declarations are manipulated such that the stated value of imports exceeds the actual value (overinvoicing) or the stated value of exports is below the actual value (underinvoicing), financial resources are implicitly transferred abroad without any official record of this having taken place. Conversely, it is assumed that, to proxy for such IFFs (often labeled capital flight), trade statistics may provide some useful empirical indication. For instance, Kar and Cartwright-Smith (2008) explore gaps in mirror trade statistics; also see Bhagwati, Krueger, and Wibulswasdi (1974) for an early contribution. De Boyrie, Pak, and Zdanowicz (2004) examine the variation of trade prices at the transaction level.

This chapter provides a detailed discussion of issues associated with trade mispricing. It reviews various incentives for faking trade invoices, critically examines empirical approaches to quantify the extent of mispricing (thereby also highlighting other potential reasons for discrepancies in bilateral trade statistics), and analyzes differences in mirror trade statistics at the product level (which may be associated with mispricing behavior). It also assesses how trade mispricing may be reflected in capital flight and illicit flow estimates.

The plan of the chapter is as follows. The first section reviews evidence on asymmetries in international trade statistics. IFFs are typically generated by underinvoicing exports and overinvoicing imports. However, dozens of other reasons for the over- and underinvoicing of trade activities have been identified in the literature; these reasons include overinvoicing of exports to benefit from export subsidies and underinvoicing of imports to avoid payment of import tariffs. As a result, some of these misinvoicing activities may offset each other. In addition, there are other reasons for incorrect trade invoices and, thus, discrepancies in official trade figures. These manipulations may be the result of intended (criminal) behavior such as smuggling or carousel fraud (explained below). Similarly, however, they could simply reflect inaccuracies in compiling trade figures (for example, because of the Rotterdam effect) and thus result from unintended behavior.

Based on the discussion of incentives for misreporting trade flows, the chapter next analyzes empirical approaches to quantifying the extent of mispricing. The trade-based approach in Kar and Cartwright-Smith (2008) and the price-based work by Pak and Zdanowicz (with various coauthors) are critically reviewed.

The chapter then examines how trade mispricing fits into the illicit flow estimates. Kar and Cartwright-Smith (2008) use the gap in trade statistics (along with other approaches) to provide detailed estimates of IFFs by country. This section examines the robustness of their findings. For instance, results are compared with estimates derived from the product-level approach of Fisman and Wei (2009). Similarly, it may be useful to relate Kar and Cartwright-Smith's estimates of illicit flows to other country characteristics that have been found to be associated with trade mispricing, such as corruption.

The final section concludes.

Discrepancies in Trade Statistics

Conceptually, country i's exports to country j are equivalent to j's imports from i. In practice, however, recorded trade figures differ in official matched partner country trade statistics. The reasons for asymmetries in trade statistics are manifold, but they can be broadly grouped into two categories: legitimate statistical reasons and intended misdeclarations. For illustration, this section briefly summarizes some of the main explanations for the discrepancy in officially reported export and import figures. Morgenstern (1950), in a classical paper, provides a more detailed account.

Statistical reasons

The most notable source of discrepancy between the exports of one country and the imports of the other is the conceptual difference in valuation. Exporting countries report the value of goods at the initial point of departure (free on board [f.o.b.]), while import values refer to the value at the point of final destination, thereby including cost, insurance, and freight (c.i.f.).[1] As a result, the c.i.f.–f.o.b. ratio has been frequently used in the literature as a measure of transportation costs. Limão and Venables (2001) provide a recent application of this approach; see Hummels and Lugovskyy (2006) for a detailed critique.

Apart from the different treatment of shipping costs, there are other methodological difficulties in matched partner trade statistics. For instance, the correct identification of the source or destination country may be a problem. If the country of final destination is not known at the time of exportation, the exporter declares the country of last shipment; the country of final destination, in contrast, classifies its imports by country of origin. Herrigan, Kochen, and Williams (2005) provide an illustration of this "Rotterdam effect" in trade statistics whereby import and export statistics are distorted because of the transit through intervening countries. They note as follows:

> Crude oil is imported from the UK via Portland, Maine in the USA, and then sent by pipeline to Canada. This is recorded in Canada as [an] import from the UK, whereas the UK records an export to the USA. The USA do not record either flow, as it is simple transit. Thus the UK records more oil exports to the USA [than] they record importing, and [records] less oil

exports to Canada [than] they record importing. (Herrigan, Kochen, and Williams 2005, 9)

Another potential issue of importance is timing. Because there are often notable time lags between the departure and arrival of a shipment (for example, arising from long-distance sea cargo, a delay in customs declaration, or temporary storage in a warehouse), trade may be recorded in different calendar years. More importantly, statistical offices in the source and destination countries may value goods at different prices or exchange rates. Finally, recorded trade at the commodity level may differ because of the omission of individual transactions in one of the partner countries (for example, because of varying thresholds for the low value of trade across countries), the exclusion of certain product groups in a country's trade statistics (such as military material or repair trade), or differences in commodity classifications (for example, a regrouping of a transaction into chapter 99, which covers "items not elsewhere classified," for reasons of confidentiality).

Fraudulent trade activities

Discrepancies in trade statistics may also result from intended misdeclaration of trade activities. Transactions may be hidden completely (so that official statistics underreport trade), purely imaginary (so that trade is overstated in the data), or mispriced in trade invoices (with, a priori, unknown effects on trade statistics).

Unreported trade. For unreported trade activities (that is, smuggling) to affect asymmetries in partner country trade statistics, the transactions have to be recorded by one of the partners. This is the setup that Fisman and Wei (2009) have in mind. For antiques and cultural property, there are often strong export restrictions such that there is an incentive to smuggle the goods unrecorded out of a country. Imports, however, are properly declared since there are generally no constraints for the entry of such goods, and there is even the risk of seizure if there is a false declaration.

Fictitious trade. An example of imaginary trade transactions (where official trade figures are artificially inflated) is missing trader VAT fraud in intra–European Union (EU) trade. For intra-EU trade, for which no barriers to trade exist, and, thus, there are no customs declarations, trade statistics rely on the VAT system; that is, firms declare to fiscal authorities, as part of the VAT return, trade activities with customers and suppliers in EU member countries. Trade statistics are then affected by two types of VAT fraud. In acquisition fraud, goods are regularly imported VAT free and then sold on the home market (for example, to the next trader) at a price that includes VAT. Instead of paying over the VAT to tax authorities, however, the importer disappears. As a result, because of the missing VAT declaration, imports also remain unrecorded. A more elaborate version of this form of criminal attack on the VAT system is carousel fraud whereby, after a series of sales through home companies, the imported goods are reexported to the country of origin (or any other EU member country) and, thus, move in a circular pattern. The exports are properly declared, while the imports are not captured in trade data, which may lead to substantial asymmetries in partner country trade statistics. When, in 2003, the United Kingdom's Office for National Statistics made corrections to trade figures for VAT fraud, real growth in gross domestic product for previous years was lowered by up to 0.2 percentage points.[2]

Misreported trade. Finally, trade may be recorded, but invoices are faked such that the declared value of a trade transaction deviates from the true value. A plausible explanation for trade mispricing is capital flight. If there are exchange restrictions, overinvoicing of imports and underinvoicing of exports are popular methods for the unrecorded movement of capital out of the country. However, there are other reasonable explanations for mispricing. Some of these explanations work in a similar direction. For instance, underreporting of exports allows firms to acquire foreign exchange that is not disclosed to national authorities; the foreign currency can then be freely used by exporters without complying with controls and regulations (for example, a potential option may be the sale of foreign currency in the parallel exchange rate market). Furthermore, authorities may use information on the export activities of firms to infer the production of these firms. As a result, firms that seek to hide output (for example, to evade domestic taxes) will automatically also seek to hide exports. Dabla-Norris, Gradstein, and Inchauste (2008) provide a description of informal activities by firms.

Others work in the opposite direction. For instance, if there are import restrictions, there is an incentive to underinvoice imports; the misdeclaration of cargo is an obvious solution to circumvent these trade restrictions. Bhagwati (1964) provides an early empirical assessment of such activities. Similarly, to benefit from export subsidies, exports can be overinvoiced. Celâsun and Rodrik (1989) argue that a sizable share of the increase in Turkish exports after 1980 is caused by a change in invoicing practices among domestic entrepreneurs (to take advantage of generous export subsidies).

Summary

The finding that official trade statistics may suffer from misreporting and faked declarations is a fact well known not only to statisticians of international trade. Bhagwati (1964, 1967) provides an early economic discussion of incentives for misinvoicing in trade; Bhagwati and Hansen (1973) develop a trade model to examine the welfare effects of smuggling.

Using trade statistics to quantify the extent of misreporting, however, appears to be difficult. Misreporting can work in either direction, so that some activities may offset each other in aggregate trade statistics. Also, the extent to which transactions are reported at all (and thus show up in the trade statistics of at least one of the trade partners) may vary. Increased surveillance of trade transactions have apparently little measurable effect.[3] Finally, discrepancies in trade statistics may simply arise from statistical factors. A quantitative assessment of such factors in a bilateral context has been provided for trade flows between Australia and the EU; reported trade figures differ, on average, by about 10 percent between the two trade partners. Table 10.1 summarizes the results. As shown, the largest source of discrepancy between recorded exports and imports is the difference in (c.i.f.–f.o.b.) valuation, which inflates European import data by, on average, about 9 percent. In contrast, goods that are imported by Australia and are subsequently reexported to the EU may have initially artificially lowered the discrepancy (since they are recorded in Australia's exports, but not in the EU's imports). In view of all these difficulties, the EU, though aiming to reduce the declaration burden on businesses, still refrains from using mirror (single-flow) trade statistics.[4]

Table 10.1. Asymmetries in Australia–European Union Trade: A Statistical Practitioner's Assessment

Indicator	1992	1993	1994	1995	1996	1997
a. Australian exports (f.o.b.) ($A, millions)	7,711	7,476	7,247	8,007	8,381	8,678
Adjustments						
Country classification						
Australian reexports	-400	-417	-327	-451	-394	-333
EU indirect imports	101	133	120	137	242	185
EU reimports	215	195	240	245	275	315
Exchange rate	-25	-4	7	-1	1	-28
Ships	80	—	—	—	—	—
Adjusted Australian exports	7,682	7,383	7,286	7,937	8,504	8,815
b. EU imports (c.i.f.) ($A, millions)	8,721	7,159	7,979	8,813	8,526	9,570
Adjustments						
Valuation	-728	-605	-658	-737	-708	-795
Timing	-93	25	81	54	62	23
Exchange rate	-41	13	-7	—	-6	-15
Ships	—	—	—	—	236	—
Nonmonetary gold	63	484	126	-4	119	—
Adjusted EU imports	7,922	7,077	7,520	8,124	8,228	8,782
c. Discrepancy						
Unadjusted	1,010	-316	732	806	145	892
percent	13	-4	10	10	2	10
Adjusted	240	-306	235	187	-276	-34
percent	3	-4	3	2	-3	—

Source: ABS 1998.
Note: — = not available.

Trade Mispricing and Illicit Financial Flows

IFFs are, by definition, unobservable in official statistics. However, based on the assumption that trade mispricing is an important method for the unrecorded movement of capital out of a country, a number of papers have examined trade statistics to provide a rough empirical indication of the magnitude of IFFs. In the following, two of these approaches are discussed in detail: the analysis of asymmetries in trade statistics and the analysis of price anomalies in transaction-level trade data.

Conceptual issues

It may be useful to address briefly some conceptual issues on the definition of IFFs. In describing capital flows, one often applies different concepts to classify capital transactions. For instance, as noted by the International Monetary Fund (IMF), there is an occasional tendency to
identify any capital outflow from a country as capital flight (IMF 1992).
Kar and Cartwright-Smith appear to follow this (broadest possible)
approach for capital outflows from developing countries; they argue that
"the term flight capital is most commonly applied in reference to money
that shifts out of developing countries, usually into western economies"
(Kar and Cartwright-Smith 2008, iii).

While this approach may be applicable, a possible shortcoming of this
general definition is that it also covers all standard (or normal) crossborder capital transactions. Therefore, a number of authors prefer to take a
more restrictive approach that includes only a subset of capital movements and also justifies the negative connotation (capital flight). Walter
(1987), for instance, emphasizes the importance of motivations for flight
(such as macroeconomic mismanagement or fear of confiscation) by
arguing that flight capital is capital that flees. Cumby and Levich (1987)
focus on the type of transaction by excluding all freely organized legal
transactions from their definition of capital flight. It might thus seem
reasonable to distinguish capital transactions along various dimensions,
such as the source of capital, the method of transfer, and the motivation
for the transaction.

A similar reasoning may also apply to the definition of IFFs. Kar and
Cartwright-Smith (2008, iv) provide a comprehensive approach, treating all unrecorded capital transfers as illegal and note, more generally,
that "illicit money is money that is illegally earned, transferred, or utilized."[5] Another plausible definition, by contrast, also takes into account
the motivation for such behavior. IFFs may then be defined as any capital
transaction that intentionally moves capital out of a country in a manner that is not recorded; trade mispricing is therefore one of (potentially
many) possible conduits for such conduct.[6]

Examining asymmetries in trade data

A prominent approach to quantifying the extent of misinvoicing is the
analysis of matched partner country trade statistics. Based on the principle

of double counting in trade statistics, a country's exports to a partner are compared to what the partner reports as its imports (mirror statistics). The difference may then provide a reasonable indication of illicit flows that occur through mispricing. A recent application of this approach is Kar and Cartwright-Smith (2008); an early contribution is Bhagwati, Krueger, and Wibulswasdi (1974).

Trade asymmetries ≠ mispricing. Any estimate of IFFs derived from asymmetries in trade statistics has to deal explicitly with three types of problems. The most notable issue is related to the accuracy of trade statistics in general. As noted above, partner country trade data typically differ for various reasons. As a result, trade figures have to be adjusted before any possible remaining statistical asymmetry can be reasonably interpreted as deriving from mispricing. At a minimum, trade data have to be corrected for differences in valuation, which is most likely to be the main reason for a discrepancy in mirror statistics. However, the information on transportation costs that is needed for the conversion from f.o.b. to c.i.f. values is rare; for precisely this reason, some trade economists have used the c.i.f.–f.o.b. ratio as a proxy for transportation costs.[7]

Two approaches have frequently been applied in the literature to deal with this issue. First, the analysis may focus particularly on episodes in which f.o.b. export values exceed the corresponding c.i.f. import values. Because the latter include additional price components (transportation costs) and, therefore, should, by definition, be larger than the former, such perverse statistical findings may indicate that mispricing has occurred; this argument was first made by Bhagwati (1964) in an empirical analysis of the underinvoicing of imports. Capital outflows through trade mispricing, however, work exactly in the opposite direction; these activities are associated with overinvoicing of imports and underinvoicing of exports, which tend to inflate the observed difference between c.i.f. and f.o.b. values so that this approach is of little help.

Second, a number of papers apply a flat c.i.f.–f.o.b. conversion factor. Typically, with reference to conventions by international organizations, a 10 percent difference between c.i.f. and f.o.b. values is assumed. For instance, in using partner data to supplement their trade database, the IMF generally applies a c.i.f.–f.o.b. factor of 1.1. Any discrepancy in mirror statistics that exceeds this correction might then be attributed to mispricing; for instance, see Bhagwati, Krueger, and Wibulswasdi (1974). However, this approach provides, at best, only a crude empirical indication of the potential presence of misinvoicing because the assumption of a fixed conversion factor that varies neither over time nor among trading partners is clearly challenging.

Mispricing $\neq$ illicit flows. To the extent that discrepancies in trade statistics indeed reflect mispricing, over- and underinvoicing of trade transactions may be completely unrelated to IFFs (narrowly defined). An obvious reason to underinvoice trade is to avoid the payment of trade taxes; similarly, overinvoicing allows a trader to benefit from trade subsidies. More specifically, if export duties are ad valorem, the motive to reduce the effective tax rate by underinvoicing exports is indistinguishable from a flight-motivated capital outflow in the analysis of mirror statistics in international trade. In similar fashion, the overinvoicing of imports (for other reasons than capital flight) may occur if a firm seeks to reduce its before-tax profits (and, hence, the effective tax on profits) by overstating the cost of imported inputs. As a result, an assumption has to be made about the extent to which trade mispricing is, indeed, a channel for illicit flows.

Illicit flows $\neq$ trade asymmetries. Conversely, it is questionable whether the extent of illicit flows is detectable from asymmetries in aggregate trade data. Various incentives to fake trade invoices that work exactly in the opposite direction relative to the capital flight motives can be identified. The effects of these explanations on trade (that is, underinvoicing of imports and overinvoicing of exports) have been widely documented. For instance, Celâsun and Rodrik (1989, 723) note that the introduction of export subsidies in Turkey in the early 1980s led to substantial overinvoicing: "Turkish entrepreneurs, never too shy in exploiting arbitrage opportunities, used the wedge [between the profitability of manufactures exports and the profitability of other means of earning foreign exchange] to their advantage." Celâsun and Rodrik conclude (1989, 729–30) that, "once fictitious exports are eliminated, the average growth rate of Turkish exports . . . is not nearly as spectacular as [that] . . . calculated from official statistics." The existence of obvious incentives for underinvoicing imports has been recently documented empirically by Yang

Table 10.2. Motives for Mispricing in International Trade

Trade	Overinvoicing	Underinvoicing
Exports	Capturing export subsidies	Capital flight, avoiding export taxes
Imports	Capital flight, lowering domestic profits	Evading import duties

Source: Adapted from Dornbusch and Kuenzler (1993).

(2008), who examines an increase in enforcement in Philippine customs that targets a specific method of avoiding import duties. He nicely illustrates that increased enforcement (by lowering the minimum value threshold for preshipment customs inspection for shipments from a subset of origin countries) reduced the targeted duty-avoidance method, but caused substantial displacement in an alternative method (shipping via duty-exempt export processing zones).

In sum, there are various motives for mispricing in trade invoices. Table 10.2 lists some of these motives. As these effects partly work in opposite directions, they may easily cancel each other out at the aggregate trade level. For instance, if a shipment is underinvoiced in the exporting country to move capital unrecorded out of the country, and the shipment carries the same mispriced invoice in the importing country to evade import tariffs, no discrepancy in mirror trade statistics will occur.[8] Reviewing the various motives, Bhagwati, Krueger, and Wibulswasdi (1974) argue that underinvoicing of exports, rather than overinvoicing of imports, is more often used as a vehicle of capital flight, also because export controls are less restrictive. Gulati (1987) even finds that, if trade invoices are faked, the underinvoicing of imports more than outweighs the underinvoicing of exports so that, for a number of countries, (illicit) capital inflows are observed.

Kar and Cartwright-Smith (2008). In view of these difficulties, it is interesting to review recent estimates by Kar and Cartwright-Smith (2008) of capital flight arising because of trade mispricing.[9] These authors analyze international trade statistics, address the above-mentioned relevant issues in a consistent and transparent way, and estimate, based on this analysis, the volume and pattern of IFFs. While their efforts have provoked useful debate, it should also be clear that the reliability of the estimates crucially hinges on the assumptions made and the conventions chosen.

A first set of methodological issues in Kar and Cartwright-Smith (2008) relates to the interpretation of observed asymmetries in matched partner trade statistics. As noted above, trade asymmetries may arise for a variety of reasons and, therefore, do not necessarily reflect trade mispricing. Kar and Cartwright-Smith (2008) acknowledge the difficulty in properly identifying mispricing from trade data by providing a definition for trade asymmetries of interest. Specifically, after a careful discussion of the limitations of various models in estimating illicit flows, they provide two sets of estimates of trade mispricing by country. In their baseline model, they apply a gross excluding reversals method. This method is based on the assumption that episodes of bilateral export underinvoicing and import overinvoicing reflect capital outflows, while they argue that episodes of pair-wise trade gaps in the opposite direction (possibly representing capital inflows) are spurious because of data issues (and therefore simply set to zero). As a result, if a country reports low export figures relative to recorded imports in the corresponding partner country, this discrepancy is defined, according to Kar and Cartwright-Smith, as mispricing. In contrast, a statistical discrepancy similar in magnitude that results from the same country's relatively large exports relative to another partner's imports is, by definition, ignored. This selective interpretation of trade asymmetries appears to inflate estimates of IFFs artificially. Indeed, if offsetting capital flows are additionally taken into account, a country's net position is obtained, which is often sizably lower than the estimated gross excluding reversals result. With this extension, many aggregate country estimates even change signs. However, Kar and Cartwright-Smith argue that results derived from such an approach are distorted and unrealistic and focus instead on their method.

Kar and Cartwright-Smith's (2008) interpretation becomes particularly troublesome if one also takes the treatment of transportation costs in their analysis into consideration. A major source of discrepancy between exports and the corresponding imports is the difference in valuation concepts, so that c.i.f. imports must be converted to f.o.b. values. Kar and Cartwright-Smith apply a c.i.f.–f.o.b. conversion factor that is fixed (at 1.1) across all bilateral country pairs (irrespective of trade distance and the commodity composition of trade) and over time. In practice, however, c.i.f.–f.o.b. ratios in international trade statistics often lie outside a reasonable range of variation. According to Hummels and

Lugovskyy (2006), roughly half of all observations in the IMF's Direction of Trade Statistics database lie outside a (1, 2) range (which would be consistent with ad valorem transportation costs between 0 and 100 percent); the remaining observations contain substantial errors in levels.[10] Still, Kar and Cartwright-Smith classify, after a flat 1.1 correction, any c.i.f.–f.o.b. ratio larger than 1 as evidence of trade mispricing, while ratios below this threshold (often covering substantial fractions of trade) are treated as noise.[11]

Another set of issues refers to the difficulty of identifying mispricing and estimating IFFs from aggregate trade data. Mispricing occurs at the level of the individual trade transaction, whereas Kar and Cartwright-Smith (2008) examine trade asymmetries at the country level. Their focus on aggregate trade, however, is likely to produce inconsistent results. Assume, for instance, that trade gaps at the commodity level cancel each other out at the aggregate level; these trade gaps remain uncaptured by Kar and Cartwright-Smith, potentially leading to aggregation bias. More realistically, if trade gaps are concentrated in a few product categories with serious difficulties in properly reporting trade flows (for example, crude oil), the resulting trade asymmetries at the country level are taken as evidence of trade mispricing (and, thus, IFFs).

Moreover, any pooled estimate of asymmetries in aggregate trade data may mask considerable variation in export and import behavior. Therefore, if one computes trade gaps for a large set of countries, it appears particularly helpful to distinguish between and report results separately for the underinvoicing of exports and the overinvoicing of imports. In principle, there should be no difference between the two methods: both activities involve faking of trade declarations, and both activities may be instruments to facilitate illicit capital flows. In practice, however, there are typically large differences in the observed degrees of export underinvoicing and import overinvoicing; see, for instance, Gulati (1987). Bhagwati, Krueger, and Wibulswasdi (1974) argue that, especially, the incentive to overinvoice imports as a vehicle of capital flight is often overcome by other motives to fake trade invoices. As a result, there is an asymmetry of conduit behavior for IFFs that should be documented in empirical findings to aid the proper interpretation of the results.

Examining transaction-level price data

In a series of papers, Simon Pak and John Zdanowicz analyze price data in transaction-level trade statistics. In a typical analysis, such as de Boyrie, Pak, and Zdanowicz (2005), the authors examine information from individual export declarations and entry forms in U.S. external trade. The data set is huge; it contains about two million records per year.[12] Specifically, Pak and Zdanowicz are interested in the product code, the partner country involved in the trade, and the price quoted in the trade document. With this information, it is possible to analyze, for each product-country pair, the range of prices recorded in trade transactions. More notably, based on this price range, transactions with abnormal prices can be identified; Pak and Zdanowicz define prices that fall outside the interquartile range as abnormal. These improperly priced transactions are then assumed to constitute illegal capital flows, and the capital outflow is determined by the dollar value of the over- or underinvoicing of a transaction based on its deviation from interquartile prices.

What is a product? Although Pak and Zdanowicz's idea of using micro-level trade data is generally intuitive, their approach is not without difficulties. An obvious issue is the definition of a product. Pak and Zdanowicz rely on the harmonized classification of products in international trade statistics. At the most detailed level (for U.S. external trade), this commodity code system contains about 20,000 product categories. It is unknown, however, whether these products are, indeed, homogeneous; there may be considerable differences in product characteristics (such as quality) and, thus, in product prices within categories. As a result, the price range within a category may be wide so that mispriced transactions remain undetected. Alternatively, a transaction may be mistakenly identified as improperly priced if most transactions within a category are in low-value products, while a single transaction is in an expensive high-quality product.

The relevance of product definitions has been recently highlighted by Javorcik and Narciso (2008), who argue that there is broader scope for faking invoices in differentiated products because it is difficult to assess the quality and thus the price of such products. Examining trade gaps in mirror trade statistics for German exports to 10 Eastern European countries, they find that the responsiveness of the trade gap to the level of tariffs is greater for differentiated products than for homogeneous goods.

In addition, it should be mentioned that the product categories are defined for customs purposes. This implies, for instance, that some products are properly and tightly defined, while there are plenty of product codes that simply collect all other types of products. For illustration, consider the description of the 2009 harmonized tariff schedule.[13] The tariff schedule lists 28,985 product categories (including subheadings), of which about half (12,581 categories) contain the catchall "other" in the description. Examples are shown in table 10.3. As indicated, the first category of heading 4901 covers printed material in single sheets. This material is categorized into "reproduction proofs" and all "other" single-sheet material; the other single-sheet material may range from plain black-and-white leaflets to expensive art prints on special paper, and there is no further qualification in the customs statistics. The category "art books" is divided into subcategories by price alone: less than US$5 or more than US$5 for each book. However, it is obvious that art books that cost more than US$5 may still vary considerably in style, format, and quality (and therefore also price). Finally, the unit of quantity for "tankers" is the number of ships; differences in the size and equipment of such ships may imply considerable price differences per unit.

Abnormal prices. Another challenge facing the Pak and Zdanowicz approach is the arbitrary definition of abnormal prices.[14] The focus on the interquartile price range appears to be taken from U.S. legal regulations aimed at detecting transfer price manipulation in trade between related parties. However, there is no economic reason to describe prices above or below a certain threshold level as abnormal a priori. In fact, even for products with minor variations in prices, the method may, under specific circumstances, identify improper pricing.

More importantly, any analysis that is based on the distribution of prices appears to be sensitive to the number of observations. For example, transactions involving products for which a similar range of traded prices is observed may be classified as normal or abnormal depending on the number of trade transactions. Alternatively, the occurrence of an additional data point may lead to a reclassification of a transaction from normal to abnormal or vice versa. In general, the distribution of prices

Table 10.3. Examples of Product Categories in the U.S. Tariff Schedule, 2009

Heading/subheading, statistical suffix	Description
4901	Printed books, brochures, leaflets and similar printed matter, whether or not in single sheets
4901.10.00	In single sheets, whether or not folded
20	Reproduction proofs
40	Other
	Other
4901.91.00	Dictionaries and encyclopedias, and serial installments thereof
20	Dictionaries (including thesauruses)
40	Encyclopedias
4901.99.00	Other
10	Textbooks
20	Bound newspapers, journals and periodicals provided for in Legal Note 3 to this chapter
30	Directories
	Other
40	Bibles, testaments, prayer books, and other religious books
50	Technical, scientific, and professional books
	Art and pictorial books
60	Valued under US$5 each
65	Valued US$5 or more each
	Other
70	Hardbound books
75	Rack size paperbound books
	Other
91	Containing not more than 4 pages each (excluding covers)
92	Containing 5 or more pages each, but not more than 48 pages each (excluding covers)
93	Containing 49 or more pages each (excluding covers)
8901	Cruise ships, excursion boats, ferry boats, cargo ships, barges and similar vessels for the transport of persons or goods
8901.10.00 00	Cruise ships, excursion boats and similar vessels principally designed for the transport of persons; ferry boats of all kinds
8901.20.00 00	Tankers
8901.30.00 00	Refrigerated vessels, other than those of subheading 8901.20
8901.90.00 00	Other vessels for the transport of goods and other vessels for the transport of both persons and goods

Source: Author compilation based on data of United States International Trade Commission, "Official Harmonized Tariff Schedule," http://www.usitc.gov/tata/hts/index.htm.

should become more representative, the greater the number of price observations available. For many products, however, there are typically few bilateral trade transactions.

Price variations over time. Prices above or below a certain threshold are mechanically classified as faked, but the results are potentially difficult to interpret. Differences in prices at the transaction level may arise for various reasons. These reasons may be trivial, such as mistakes in filling the form. However, there may also be differences in prices across markets (within the United States or internationally). Also, if variations in prices are analyzed over a longer time horizon, transaction dates may matter. For instance, seasonality may lead to considerable price fluctuations.[15]

Quantity faking. An issue that remains untouched by the Pak and Zdanowicz approach is misinvoicing of quantities. Instead of faking prices or unit values, a trader may fake the invoice by misstating the quantity shipped, that is, the container holds a quantity that is different from the invoiced quantity. Although the method is perhaps more detectable than unit value faking, Bhagwati (1981, 417) notes that this is a "rather common form of illegality." In addition, there are other ways of misinvoicing, including, for instance, the omission of invoiced spare parts.

Trade pairs. Since Pak and Zdanowicz's results are exclusively based on data from U.S. customs, it is unclear to what extent they can be generalized. Anecdotal evidence suggests that the faking of trade invoices occurs especially in trade with a main trading partner that is not necessarily the United States. For instance, Celâsun and Rodrik (1989) find strong evidence of misreporting only in Turkey's trade with Germany. For African countries, trade with South Africa, the regional economic and financial center, may be the preferred target for misdeclaration.

Trade Asymmetries: An Empirical Analysis

For illustration, this section briefly examines trade asymmetries at the commodity level.[16] This empirical exercise relies on the United Nations Comtrade database for export and import data at the 4-digit (harmonized system [HS]) product level.[17] The database contains detailed (annual) trade statistics reported by statistical authorities of close to 200 countries or territories and standardized by the United Nations Statistics Division. Among the records of shipments to the five largest importing nations in the world (China, Germany, Japan, the United Kingdom, and the United States), there are more than 1,200 product categories at the 4-digit level. We use the most recent commodity classification (HS 2002); the data are available for five years, covering the period from 2002 to 2006.

We begin by exploring the full sample of annual country pair-specific trade gaps at the 4-digit product level, that is, we compute, for each country pair and product, the percentage difference between reported imports and corresponding exports. Table 10.4 lists the five largest discrepancies in bilateral trade by importer, along with the exporter and the 4-digit product code. A few empirical regularities emerge from this rough tabulation. For instance, most experiences where recorded import values greatly exceed corresponding exports appear to be concentrated in a single product category, "petroleum oils, crude" (HS code 2709). As Yeats (1978) notes, this discrepancy is often associated with problems in valuing petroleum and the frequent diversion of petroleum exports from their original destination during transit. For other product categories, in contrast, the export values (even though transportation costs are disregarded) are considerably larger than the imports in mirror statistics. These categories include "other aircraft (for example, helicopters, aeroplanes), spacecraft" (8802), "cruise ships, excursion boats, ferry-boats, cargo ships, barges and similar vessels for the transport of persons or goods" (8901); and "gold (including gold plated with platinum)" (7108). A possible explanation is that, especially for bulky items characterized by low-frequency trading, the time lag between exportation and importation may be particularly important. Also, to the extent that there is any geographical pattern in misreporting, the overinvoicing of exports appears to be a more frequent problem in trade with neighboring countries.

To analyze the geographical pattern in misreporting, we examine differences in trade gaps across countries in more detail. In particular, we aim to identify countries that consistently understate their exports (and, thus, appear to be particularly prone to trade mispricing or smuggling).

Table 10.4. Largest Trade Gaps, 2004

a. Underreporting of exports
percent

	Importer														
	United States			Germany			China			United Kingdom			Japan		
Exp.	Prod.	Gap	Exp.	Prod.	Gap	Exp.	Prod.	Gap	Exp.	Prod.	Gap	Exp.	Prod.	Gap
SAU	2709	23.8	PHL	2709	22.0	PHL	8542	22.4	BWA	7102	21.5	SAU	2709	23.4
VEN	2709	23.7	GBR	8803	21.2	AGO	2709	22.3	SAU	2710	20.6	QAT	2709	22.4
NGA	2709	23.5	DNK	9999	21.2	SAU	2709	22.3	KWT	2710	20.4	IDN	2711	22.3
IRQ	2709	22.9	SAU	2709	20.7	OMN	2709	22.2	PHL	8542	20.3	KWT	2709	22.1
AGO	2709	22.2	SYR	2709	20.7	IRN	2709	22.0	EGY	2709	19.7	ARE	2711	21.6

b. Overreporting of exports
percent

	Importer														
	United States			Germany			China			United Kingdom			Japan		
Exp.	Prod.	Gap	Exp.	Prod.	Gap	Exp.	Prod.	Gap	Exp.	Prod.	Gap	Exp.	Prod.	Gap
DEU	8901	-19.9	CHN	8901	-20.3	HKG	8703	-20.8	USA	8803	-21.2	SWE	8802	-18.9
FIN	8901	-19.9	BEL	0803	-19.8	HKG	4101	-19.3	DEU	8802	-21.0	SGP	2204	-18.5
PRT	8802	-19.2	AUT	8901	-19.7	HKG	7108	-19.2	HKG	7108	-20.8	SGP	2208	-18.0
MEX	8602	-19.1	DNK	2716	-19.1	JPN	7108	-18.6	CAN	7108	-20.7	NZL	2709	-17.9
KOR	8901	-18.7	BLR	2709	-18.7	ARE	9999	-18.5	USA	8802	-20.7	BHR	7604	-17.6

Source: Author computation based on data of UN Comtrade (United Nations Commodity Trade Statistics Database), Statistics Division, Department of Economic and Social Affairs, United Nations, New York, http://comtrade.un.org/db/.

Note: Exp. = exporter. Prod. = 4-digit HS product code. Gap = percentage difference between reported imports by the country listed in the top row and the corresponding exports reported by the country listed in the columns.

In a first exercise, we compute, for each exporter, the average trade gap across all products. Because there may be sizable product-specific differences in reported trade values between the exporting and the importing country, taking the arithmetic mean of these reporting gaps over often hundreds of products is a simple way to identify (hopefully) country-specific differences in trade reporting. Table 10.5 lists the five countries with the largest average percentage share of missing exports by importer. As shown, we find, indeed, a strong and consistent mismatch in international trade statistics, with continuous underreporting, for instance, by Equatorial Guinea, Indonesia, and the Philippines. More importantly, reviewing the full distribution of exporting countries, we find that the extent to which countries tend to misreport exports is broadly similar across trade destinations. The correlation of exporter-specific average trade gaps across importing countries is astonishingly high, on the order of about 0.9. Table 10.6 reports a set of simple bivariate correlation coefficients; Spearman rank correlations (unreported) provide similar results. These consistent patterns of misreporting in trade appear to provide a useful basis for further research.

In Berger and Nitsch (2012), for instance, we use regression analysis to examine the association between observed trade gaps and country-specific corruption levels. Holding constant a variety of other determinants of discrepancies in trade statistics, we find that the reporting gap in bilateral trade is, indeed, strongly associated with the level of corruption, especially in the source country. In countries with corrupt bureaucracies, it seems easier (and perhaps even common practice) to ignore legal rules and procedures. To the extent that this misbehavior also affects international trade transactions, our findings suggest that reporting gaps in official trade statistics partly reflect illegal activities for which the illicit movement of capital may be one motivation.

Conclusion

A potential vehicle to move capital unrecorded out of a country is the misinvoicing of international trade transactions. Exporters may understate the export revenue on their invoices, and importers may overstate import expenditures, while their trading partners are instructed to deposit the balance for their benefit in a foreign account.

Table 10.5. Underreporting of Exports by Country, 2002–06
percent

	United States		Germany		China		United Kingdom		Japan		All five	
Importer	Exporter	Gap	Exporter	Gap	Exporter	Gap	Exporter	Gap	Exporter	Gap	Exporter	Gap
	Libya	14.5	Equatorial Guinea	12.1	Equatorial Guinea	14.9	Indonesia	12.1	Iraq	16.3	Equatorial Guinea	12.6
	Lesotho	13.5	Indonesia	11.9	Congo, Rep.	13.5	Lao PDR	11.5	Equatorial Guinea	14.0	Indonesia	12.4
	Indonesia	13.3	Ukraine	11.4	Congo, Dem. Rep.	12.7	Myanmar	11.5	Western Sahara	13.7	Philippines	11.6
	Philippines	12.7	Philippines	11.2	Chad	11.8	Falkland Islands	11.2	Indonesia	13.2	Iraq	11.4
	Iraq	12.5	Serbia and Montenegro	11.0	Rwanda	11.8	Philippines	11.5	Botswana	12.8	Western Sahara	11.3

Source: Author computation based on data of UN Comtrade (United Nations Commodity Trade Statistics Database), Statistics Division, Department of Economic and Social Affairs, United Nations, New York, http://comtrade.un.org/db/.

Table 10.6. Correlation of Exporter-Specific Average Trade Gaps

Country	United States	Germany	China	United Kingdom	Japan	All
United States	1.0000					
Germany	0.9245	1.0000				
China	0.8357	0.7824	1.0000			
United Kingdom	0.9368	0.9571	0.7986	1.0000		
Japan	0.9015	0.8572	0.8963	0.8582	1.0000	
All five importers	0.9700	0.9494	0.9120	0.9564	0.9548	1.0000

Source: Author computation based on data of UN Comtrade (United Nations Commodity Trade Statistics Database), Statistics Division, Department of Economic and Social Affairs, United Nations, New York, http://comtrade.un.org/db/.
Note: The table is based on 202 observations.

This chapter critically reviews empirical approaches to quantify the extent of trade mispricing. There are at least two sorts of problems. First, mispricing behavior is hard to identify. The analysis of discrepancies in bilateral trade statistics appears to be of generally limited value because gaps in trade statistics also typically arise for reasons unrelated to mispricing. The second set of issues refers to the motivations for fraudulent trade behavior. Even if mispricing is properly identified, there are incentives for faking trade invoices other than the desire to transfer capital.

Overall, the accuracy and reliability of estimates of IFFs based on trade mispricing are questioned. This finding is in line with Bhagwati (1967, 63), who argues that, "whereas it is easy to establish the conditions under which the faking of trade values . . . will occur, it is in practice extremely difficult to set about determining whether such faking is actually occurring. It is further impossible to find out how much faking is going on."

Notes

1. This difference is based on agreed guidelines for international trade statistics as published by the United Nations (1998). Some countries, however, also report imports on an f.o.b. basis (for example, Australia).
2. Ruffles et al. (2003) provide a more detailed description.
3. Winston (1974, 64) argues that, "regardless of the sincerity of efforts, it is virtually impossible to control overinvoicing considering the myriad ways it can, in fact, be done."
4. For an early attempt, see the European Commission's initiative Simpler Legislation for the Internal Market, which is documented at http://ec.europa.eu/internal_market/simplification/index_en.htm.

5. Kar and Cartwright-Smith (2008, iii) argue that "by far the greater part of unrecorded flows are indeed illicit, violating the national criminal and civil codes, tax laws, customs regulations, VAT assessments, exchange control requirements and banking regulations of the countries out of which unrecorded/illicit flows occur."

6. For instance, for some transactions, the avoidance of trade taxes rather than capital transfer may be the primary motivation.

7. For an early critical assessment of this approach, see Moneta (1959).

8. A more fundamental issue revolves around the fact that illicit flows through trade mispricing may not necessarily show up in trade invoices (for example, if there are unofficial agreements).

9. Kar and Cartwright-Smith (2008) also apply other methods (such as the World Bank residual model) to derive estimates of IFFs. Since one term in the computation of the World Bank residual is the current account balance, which may be distorted downward by trade mispricing, both results are added to obtain an aggregate estimate.

10. Direction of Trade Statistics (database), International Monetary Fund, Washington, DC, http://elibrary-data.imf.org/FindDataReports.aspx?d=33061&e=170921.

11. Hummels and Lugovskyy (2006) note that, for New Zealand and the United States, episodes in which f.o.b. exports exceed corresponding c.i.f. imports constitute about one-third of the IMF data.

12. The data are obtained from the U.S. Merchandise Trade Databases; see USA Trade Online (database), U.S. Department of Commerce, Washington, DC, https://www.usatradeonline.gov/.

13. See the archive section at United States International Trade Commission, "Official Harmonized Tariff Schedule," http://www.usitc.gov/tata/hts/index.htm.

14. See also the discussion in Fuest and Riedel's contribution to this volume (chapter 4).

15. Gopinath and Rigobon (2008) examine monthly price data for approximately 20,000 imported goods and find that the (trade-weighted) median price duration in the currency of pricing is 10.6 months.

16. This section draws on Berger and Nitsch (2012).

17. UN Comtrade (United Nations Commodity Trade Statistics Database), Statistics Division, Department of Economic and Social Affairs, United Nations, New York, http://comtrade.un.org/db/.

References

ABS (Australian Bureau of Statistics). 1998. "Bilateral Merchandise Trade Statistics Reconciliation: Australia and the European Union, 1992 to 1997." International Merchandise Trade, Australia 5422.0 (September): 10–21, ABS, Canberra.

Baldwin, R. E. 2006. "The Euro's Trade Effects." ECB Working Paper 594 (March), European Central Bank, Frankfurt.

Berger, H., and V. Nitsch. 2012. "Gotcha! A Profile of Smuggling in International Trade." In *Illicit Trade and the Global Economy*, ed. C. Costa Storti and P. De Grauwe. CESifo Seminar Series. Cambridge, MA: MIT Press.

Bhagwati, J. N. 1964. "On the Underinvoicing of Imports." *Oxford Bulletin of Economics and Statistics* 27 (4): 389–97.

———. 1967. "Fiscal Policies, the Faking of Foreign Trade Declarations, and the Balance of Payments." *Oxford Bulletin of Economics and Statistics* 29 (1): 61–77.

———. 1981. "Alternative Theories of Illegal Trade: Economic Consequences and Statistical Detection." *Weltwirtschaftliches Archiv* 117 (3): 409–27.

Bhagwati, J. N., and B. Hansen. 1973. "A Theoretical Analysis of Smuggling." *Quarterly Journal of Economics* 87 (2): 172–87.

Bhagwati, J. N., A. Krueger, and C. Wibulswasdi. 1974. "Capital Flight from LDCs: A Statistical Analysis." In *Illegal Transactions in International Trade: Theory and Measurement*, ed. J. N. Bhagwati, 148–54. Studies in International Economics. Amsterdam: North-Holland.

Celâsun, M., and D. Rodrik. 1989. "Debt, Adjustment, and Growth: Turkey." In *Country Studies: Indonesia, Korea, Philippines, Turkey*, ed. J. D. Sachs and S. M. Collins, 615–808. Vol. 3 of *Developing Country Debt and Economic Performance*. National Bureau of Economic Research Project Report. Chicago: University of Chicago Press.

Cumby, R. E., and R. M. Levich. 1987. "On the Definition and Magnitude of Recent Capital Flight." In *Capital Flight and Third World Debt*, ed. D. R. Lessard and J. Williamson, 26–67. Washington, DC: Peterson Institute for International Economics.

Dabla-Norris, E., M. Gradstein, and G. Inchauste. 2008. "What Causes Firms to Hide Output? The Determinants of Informality." *Journal of Development Economics* 85 (1–2): 1–27.

de Boyrie, M. E., S. J. Pak, and J. S. Zdanowicz. 2004. "Money Laundering and Income Tax Evasion: The Determination of Optimal Audits and Inspections to Detect Abnormal Prices in International Trade." *Journal of Financial Crime* 12 (2): 123–30.

———. 2005. "The Impact of Switzerland's Money Laundering Law on Capital Flows through Abnormal Pricing in International Trade." *Applied Financial Economics* 15 (4): 217–30.

Dornbusch, R., and L. T. Kuenzler. 1993. "Exchange Rate Policy: Issues and Options." In *Policymaking in the Open Economy: Concepts and Case Studies in Economic Performance*, ed. R. Dornbusch, 91–126. EDI Series in Economic Development. Washington, DC: World Bank; New York: Oxford University Press.

Fisman, R., and S.-J. Wei. 2009. "The Smuggling of Art, and the Art of Smuggling: Uncovering the Illicit Trade in Cultural Property and Antiques." *American Economic Journal: Applied Economics* 1 (3): 82–96.

Gopinath, G., and R. Rigobon. 2008. "Sticky Borders." *Quarterly Journal of Economics* 123 (2): 531–75.

Gulati, S. K. 1987. "A Note on Trade Misinvoicing." In *Capital Flight and Third World Debt*, ed. D. R. Lessard and J. Williamson, 68–78. Washington, DC: Peterson Institute for International Economics.

Herrigan, M., A. Kochen, and T. Williams. 2005. "Edicom Report: Analysis of Asymmetries in Intra-Community Trade Statistics with Particular Regard to the Impact of the Rotterdam and Antwerp Effects." Statistics and Analysis of Trade Unit, HM Revenue & Customs, Southend-on-Sea, U.K.

Hummels, D., and V. Lugovskyy. 2006. "Are Matched Partner Trade Statistics a Usable Measure of Transportation Costs?" *Review of International Economics* 14 (1): 69–86.

IMF (International Monetary Fund). 1992. *Report on the Measurement of International Capital Flows.* Washington, DC: Research Department, IMF.

Javorcik, B. S., and G. Narciso. 2008. "Differentiated Products and Evasion of Import Tariffs." *Journal of International Economics* 76 (2): 208–22.

Kar, D., and D. Cartwright-Smith. 2008. "Illicit Financial Flows from Developing Countries, 2002–2006." Global Financial Integrity, Washington, DC. http://www.gfip.org/storage/gfip/economist%20-%20final%20version%201-2-09.pdf.

Limão, N., and A. J. Venables. 2001 "Infrastructure, Geographical Disadvantage, Transport Costs, and Trade." *World Bank Economic Review* 15 (3): 451–79.

Moneta, C. 1959. "The Estimation of Transportation Costs in International Trade." *Journal of Political Economy* 67 (1): 41–58.

Morgenstern, O. 1950. *The Accuracy of Economic Observations.* Princeton, NJ: Princeton University Press.

Naya, S., and T. Morgan. 1974. "The Accuracy of International Trade Data: The Case of Southeast Asian Countries." In *Illegal Transactions in International Trade: Theory and Measurement,* ed. J. N. Bhagwati, 123–37. Studies in International Economics. Amsterdam: North-Holland.

Ruffles, D., G. Tily, D. Caplan, and S. Tudor. 2003. "VAT Missing Trader Intra-Community Fraud: The Effect on Balance of Payments Statistics and UK National Accounts." *Economic Trends* 597 (August): 58–70.

United Nations. 1998. "International Merchandise Trade Statistics: Concepts and Definitions." Document ST/ESA/STAT/SER.M/52/Rev.2, Studies in Methods, Statistics Division, Department of Economic and Social Affairs, United Nations, New York.

Walter, I. 1987. "The Mechanisms of Capital Flight." In *Capital Flight and Third World Debt,* ed. D. R. Lessard and J. Williamson, 103–28. Washington, DC: Peterson Institute for International Economics.

Winston, G. C. 1974. "Overinvoicing, Underutilization, and Distorted Industrial Growth." In *Illegal Transactions in International Trade: Theory and Measurement,* ed. J. N. Bhagwati, 49–65. Studies in International Economics. Amsterdam: North-Holland.

Yang, D. 2008. "Can Enforcement Backfire? Crime Displacement in the Context of Customs Reform in the Philippines." *Review of Economics and Statistics* 90 (1): 1–14.

Yeats, A. J. 1978. "On the Accuracy of Partner Country Trade Statistics." *Oxford Bulletin of Economics and Statistics* 40 (4): 341–61.

Part IV

Policy Interventions

11

Tax Havens and Illicit Flows

Alex Cobham

Many citizens of developing (and developed) countries now have easy
access to tax havens and the result is that these countries are losing to tax
havens almost three times what they get from developed countries in aid.
If taxes on this income were collected billions of dollars would become
available to finance development.
—Jeffrey Owens, Director, Centre for Tax Policy Administration,
Organisation for Economic Co-operation and Development,
January 2009

We will set down new measures to crack down on those tax havens that
siphon money from developing countries, money that could otherwise
be spent on bed nets, vaccinations, economic development and jobs.
—Gordon Brown, Prime Minister, United Kingdom, March 2009

We stand ready to take agreed action against those jurisdictions
which do not meet international standards in relation to tax
transparency. . . . We are committed to developing proposals, by end
2009, to make it easier for developing countries to secure the benefits of
a new cooperative tax environment.
—G-20 Declaration, April 2009[1]

Additional tables and figures from this chapter can be found at http://go.worldbank.org
/N2HMRB4G20.

Abstract

Only limited research has been carried out on the links between tax havens and developing countries. This chapter provides a brief, critical survey of the state of knowledge on the impact of tax havens on development and then uses existing data to extend that knowledge by examining bilateral trade and financial flows between havens and developing countries to identify the exposure of developing countries of different types.

Three key results emerge. First, the chapter shows that the exposure of developing countries to tax havens is on a par with, if not more severe than, that of high-income countries of the Organisation for Economic Co-operation and Development (OECD). This supports efforts to ensure that developing countries benefit from initiatives to require greater transparency, particularly in terms of international tax cooperation. Second, the differences in developing-country exposure across different income groups of countries and regions are substantial, and recognition of this must lead to more detailed and careful study and, over time, appropriate policy responses. Finally, the research has been repeatedly blocked by a lack of high-quality, internationally comparable data. An agenda for research and for data collation and dissemination is proposed that would allow greater certainty of the scale of the impact of tax havens on development.

Introduction

In the wake of the financial crisis, a consensus emerged that international measures were required to limit the damage caused by tax haven secrecy and that developing countries must be included to ensure that these countries also benefit.

Research demonstrating the damage caused by havens, especially to developing countries, remains limited, however. If international policy efforts are to be well directed and, ultimately, to be effective in removing obstacles to development, then further work is needed. It is regrettable that policy research at multilateral institutions has almost completely neglected these issues until now. The research that has been carried out, at least until recently, when these issues began moving rapidly up the policy agenda, has largely been conducted by academics and civil society researchers.

This chapter sets out the key questions on this important research agenda that has now become an urgent one also for policy. There are three main areas requiring further analysis: the definition of tax havens, the broad development impact of tax havens, and the specific impact on particular developing countries in different regions and at various income levels. An additional issue that should be addressed urgently is the lack of data to examine these questions.

The chapter addresses these questions in turn. We begin by considering three related, but distinct concepts—tax havens, offshore financial centers, and secrecy jurisdictions—and the various definitions that have been offered for each. The lack of clarity in definitions has been a significant barrier to greater understanding, and it emerges from our discussion that the fundamental feature of these concepts relates not to the provision of low(er) tax rates, nor to the provision of financial services to nonresidents, but to the secrecy associated with each provision. The financial secrecy index (FSI) is therefore identified as a potentially valuable tool for further research.

We then briefly survey the literature on the development impact of secrecy jurisdictions. This serves to highlight two main points. First, the key damage appears to stem from the functions attributed to secrecy jurisdictions, rather than to the functions of the alternatively defined entities discussed. Second, the literature identifies a range of powerful arguments about the impacts, but does little to differentiate among developing countries and tends to treat the experience of these countries as homogenous. Greater evidence of direct causality is also required.

The next section takes the first steps toward providing a more differentiated analysis of development links. By considering a range of bilateral flows and stocks in trade and finance, we identify the key areas in which different types of developing countries are most exposed to the damage that relationships with secrecy jurisdictions can engender. The claim sometimes made that developing countries are less at risk than richer economies finds no support in terms of the recorded scale of developing-country exposure. In addition, important differences in exposure emerge among developing countries in different regions and at different income levels.

This chapter does not set out to prove causal links between the exposure to secrecy jurisdictions and damage to development. It does, however, close by setting out a clear agenda for future research that would address the need for more information on these links. Without such research by academics and policy researchers not only at nongovernmental organizations, but also at international financial institutions, there can be no guarantee that the well-meaning efforts of the G-20 or other international policy coordination groups will generate the potentially substantial benefits for development. The requirement for more research must be addressed without delay.

Tax Havens: Offshore Financial Centers or Secrecy Jurisdictions?

To undertake serious analysis of the impact of tax havens, the analyst must assert a specific definition that is objectively quantifiable and directly related to the harm believed to occur. This is necessary if the impact of those jurisdictions designated as tax havens is to be evaluated statistically. On this issue, there is a broad literature focusing on academic interests, advocacy, and official policy positions and encompassing a range of views.

Definitions

The most common term—tax haven—is probably also the most problematic. As long ago as 1981, the Gordon Report to the U.S. Treasury found that there was no single, clear objective test that permits the identification of a country as a tax haven (Gordon 1981). While originally intended, presumably, to indicate a jurisdiction with lower tax rates than elsewhere, the term came to be used to cover jurisdictions with a great range of functions, many largely unrelated to taxation.

Eden and Kudrle (2005), for example, draw on the literature to identify two categories of havens: one based on type of taxation, and one based on activity. The first category, following Palan (2002), separates havens into "countries with no income tax where firms pay only license fees (e.g., Anguilla, Bermuda), countries with low taxation (e.g., Switzerland, the Channel Islands), countries that practice so-called 'ring-fencing' by taxing domestic but not foreign income (e.g., Liberia, Hong Kong), and countries that grant special tax privileges to certain types of firms or operations (e.g., Luxembourg, Monaco)" (Eden and Kudrle 2005, 101).

The second category, following Avi-Yonah (2000) and Kudrle and Eden (2003), distinguishes among production havens, which relocate real value added (for example, Ireland in the 1990s); headquarters havens, which provide incorporation benefits (for example, Belgium and Singapore); sham havens, which provide little more than addresses for financial companies in particular (for example, Cayman Islands); and secrecy havens, the main advantage of which is opacity (and which include most sham havens).

Analysis under the heading tax haven tends to focus, understandably, on tax aspects. This view is most commonly associated with the OECD. While an earlier report (OECD 1987) focused on reputation ("a good indicator that a country is playing the role of a tax haven is where the country or territory offers itself or is generally recognised as a tax haven" [cited in OECD 1998, 21]), there is somewhat more precision in the 1998 report. Specifically, the 1998 report emphasizes no or only nominal taxes as the starting point for the identification of a tax haven, but allows, in addition, lack of an effective exchange of information, lack of transparency, and no substantial activities as further key factors.

The overarching rationale for the existence of tax havens that emerges from this approach is the provision of relief to businesses or individuals from the rates of tax that apply elsewhere. If real economic activity (in substance) is not moved to a new location from the original jurisdiction, then taxing rights have to be transferred by other means (manipulation of the form). This may involve taking advantage of genuine legal differences (for example, the distinction between the tax liabilities of corporate headquarters and the tax liabilities associated with locations where real economic activity takes place), of the absence of coordinated international tax policy (for example, exploiting differences between the calculation of domestic and foreign tax liabilities in two or more jurisdictions), or of asymmetric information across jurisdictions (for example, hiding information about the true ownership of assets or income streams and, therefore, responsibility for the associated tax liabilities).

The second frequently used term is offshore financial center (OFC). This term is preferred, for example, by the International Monetary Fund (IMF), the mandate of which is more closely aligned to issues of international financial regulatory oversight and stability than to issues of tax.

Palan explores some of the difficulties of consistent definition in this case, as follows:

> In financial literature, . . . offshore is used . . . to describe unregulated international finance. . . . Rather confusingly, however, the International Monetary Fund and the Bank for International Settlements consider only tax havens as Offshore Financial Centres, though the City of London, which does not qualify as a tax haven, is considered the hub of global offshore finance. (Palan 1998, 64)

Palan goes on to distinguish between spontaneous OFCs, which have grown up as entrepôts over time, such as the City of London and Hong Kong SAR, China, and international banking facilities that have been more recently created as part of a deliberate strategy, such as New York and Singapore.

An important IMF Working Paper by Ahmed Zoromé (2007) discusses the definitional issues in some detail and proposes new criteria (discussed in the following subsection). After surveying most of the key references, Zoromé concludes that "three distinctive and recurrent characteristics of OFCs have emerged from these definitions: (i) the primary orientation of business toward nonresidents; (ii) the favorable regulatory environment (low supervisory requirements and minimal information disclosure); and (iii) the low- or zero-taxation schemes" (Zoromé 2007, 4).

This shifts the focus onto specific actions taken by jurisdictions, whereas other definitions tend to emphasize specific results. Zoromé's subsequent application of these criteria offers one solution to Palan's point about the City of London: Zoromé classifies the United Kingdom as an OFC.

The third main term used—increasingly so since it was promoted by Murphy (2008)—is secrecy jurisdiction. The focus remains on specific actions taken, but is more explicit in emphasizing the legal steps. In this, it follows the logic of Palan (2002), who discusses the commercialization of sovereignty: the decision by certain jurisdictions to obtain economic advantage by allowing selected political decisions (over, for example, the taxation of nonresidents) to be dictated by likely users (for example, financial, legal, and accounting practitioners). The term jurisdiction is therefore used, rather than, for example, center or some other less specific term, because it is precisely the legal system that is the locus of the specific actions.

The emphasis on secrecy is necessary, Murphy argues, so that nonresidents can take advantage of favorable changes in the jurisdiction's legal framework with the confidence that they will not fall foul of the legal system in the place where they reside. There are thus two key characteristics that define a secrecy jurisdiction:

- "The secrecy jurisdiction creates regulation that they know is primarily of benefit and use to those not resident in their geographical domain"
- "The creation of a deliberate, and legally backed, veil of secrecy that ensures that those from outside the jurisdiction making use of its regulation cannot be identified to be doing so." (Murphy 2008, 6)[2]

By focusing on what makes them attractive, the secrecy jurisdiction concept therefore relies, above all, on an assessment of the comparative advantage of the jurisdictions in question. The route the secrecy jurisdictions have chosen to attract (the declaration of) foreign economic or financial activity is the provision of relatively favorable terms to users. In effect, this indicates a reliance on regulatory arbitrage (potentially, but not necessarily including tax regulation).[3] Because some arbitrage is inevitable in the absence of comprehensive global standards, this also runs the risk of excessive breadth; the damaging element relates to arbitrage that is effective because it frustrates the intentions behind regulatory standards in other jurisdictions in regard to activities that remain substantially in those other jurisdictions.

Criteria and approaches

The success of attempts to identify the jurisdictions of concern has been mixed. Table 11A.1 reproduces a set of lists compiled by Murphy in chapter 9.[4] The table outlines most of the main efforts by academics and institutions over the last 30 years. For the most part, these have drawn on definitions that, while generally made explicit, lack a basis in objective, measurable criteria.

To consider how such criteria might be created and applied, it is useful to start with Zoromé (2007). Having established key characteristics of OFCs, Zoromé proposes a definition, as follows: "an OFC is a country or jurisdiction that provides financial services to nonresidents on a scale that is incommensurate with the size and the financing of its domestic economy" (Zoromé 2007, 7).

He proposes to identify such OFCs by examining the ratio of net financial service exports to gross domestic product (GDP) from IMF balance of payments data and by looking at jurisdictions with especially high values.[5] In practice, the limited data availability on these flows means that the data search must be supplemented with data interpolated from stock variables using proxy indicators created from data on variables reflecting crossborder holdings of portfolio investment assets (the IMF Coordinated Portfolio Investment Survey) and international investment positions (using data from International Financial Statistics).[6]

The key difference between the IMF's existing list and Zoromé's findings can be seen by comparing the columns denoted "IMF (2000)" and "Zoromé (2007)," respectively, in table 11A.1. Most of the definitions coincide (for those jurisdictions for which Zoromé had data), but an important addition to the latter's list is the United Kingdom. While there are some issues with the proxy indicators and the interpolation from stock to flow data, the approach illustrates clearly the value of using objective criteria: a level playing field (including politically uncomfortable findings) may be more likely to emerge.

In keeping with the emphasis on the OFC discourse, Zoromé (2007) relies on the relative intensity of the provision of financial service to nonresidents by scaling for jurisdictional GDP. Alternative criteria include the following:

- Openness to international trade in financial services (that is, taking the sum of exports and imports as a ratio to GDP, which might capture more about the role of jurisdictions as conduits)
- Net exports of financial services (exports, minus imports as a ratio to GDP), as an indicator of specialization
- Netted trade in financial services (the lower of exports and imports, as an indicator only of the extent to which the jurisdiction acts as a conduit)
- The absolute contribution to the global provision of financial services to nonresidents (that is, each jurisdiction's provision of financial services to nonresidents as a ratio to the total global provision of services to nonresidents across all jurisdictions, rather than as a ratio to the jurisdiction's own GDP)

If we are looking for a measure to capture the relative importance of jurisdictions so as to consider the appropriate policy response at a global level, this last criterion may be appropriate. Table 11A.2 compares the results of the use of the relative approach of Zoromé and the use of the absolute approach, showing the top five jurisdictions identified by each approach.[7] Taking global contribution rather than relative intensity in the provision of financial services to nonresidents leads to quite a different picture: per 2007 data, the former criterion points to Cayman Islands, Luxembourg, Switzerland, the United Kingdom, and the United States, while the latter points, instead, to Bermuda, Cayman Islands, Guernsey, Jersey, and Luxembourg.

Finally, however, we may consider the implications of the secrecy jurisdiction approach. While the relative or absolute approach to offshore specialization may capture something about the success of jurisdictions in following this path, it has nothing directly to say about the secrecy or otherwise with which this has been achieved.

The ideal objective criteria for the identification of secrecy jurisdictions might therefore contain two separate components: one reflecting each jurisdiction's importance in the global provision of financial services to nonresidents (the absolute contribution approach) and one reflecting each jurisdiction's (objectively measurable) performance against one or more key indicators of secrecy.

A final advantage of such a composite approach is that it would allow users to step away from reliance on lists, which, by necessity, dictates that a given jurisdiction either does or does not meet certain criteria. More powerful both for policy making and for research might be a measure that falls on a sliding scale. A method of measuring progress that is more nuanced than a blacklist may eventually produce more positive responses; see, for example, Kudrle (2008, 16), who, on the limitations of blacklisting, writes that "the evidence does not suggest that blacklisting made an important systematic difference."

The FSI jointly produced by Christian Aid and the Tax Justice Network reflects this analysis.[8] The FSI combines a secrecy score based on objectively measurable criteria that reflect the secrecy or otherwise of the jurisdiction in key areas (for example, banking secrecy, the exchange of tax information) with a quantitative measure of the absolute contribution as discussed above, here labeled the global scale weight (table 11A.3).[9]

By combining measures of secrecy and measures of the importance to global offshore finance, the index presents a picture that is different from the one commonly envisaged. First, many of the usual suspects do not feature as significantly as they do in policy discussions. For example, Guernsey does not make the top 20, while Monaco ranks only 67th. Among developing countries, many oft-named Caribbean jurisdictions also rank low; thus, for example, Antigua and Barbuda ranks 58th, and Grenada 61st.

At the same time, many other usual suspects do feature at the top of the index; for example, Switzerland, Cayman Islands, and Luxembourg occupy the top three places, in that order. However, the top five also include the United States, despite powerful statements in recent years about the damage done by financial opacity. The United Kingdom and the United States each account for around a fifth of the global total of financial service provision to nonresidents, but the United Kingdom ranks only 13th because of a substantially better secrecy score.

It seems uncontroversial that a measure of the global damage caused by financial secrecy would include measures equivalent to both the secrecy score and the global scale weight. Less likely, however, is agreement on the relative importance of the two in establishing a final ranking. The value of the FSI resides less in providing a categorical final ranking than in focusing the attention of policy makers on the two elements, instead of on the opacity measures alone, which has historically supported a perhaps unjustified concentration on smaller, less economically and politically powerful jurisdictions. From the global perspective, strong opacity in a major player may do more damage than complete secrecy in a tiny one.

A particular concern is that the FSI may exclude the possibility that no jurisdictions legitimately offer high-quality banking, accounting, and legal services, but also rely on a transparent regulatory framework. The United Kingdom is often cited by those who have such concerns because it is said to have a genuine comparative advantage that does not depend on lax regulation. This chapter does not offer the space to explore this issue in detail, but the role of the United Kingdom's network of tax havens in the development of London as a key financial center is certainly worth considering (Shaxson 2011).[10] Establishing appropriate counterfactuals about the development of financial centers, absent opacity, especially in the presence of significant agglomeration benefits in financial services, is inevitably challenging.

In the penultimate section of this chapter, we use the existing list approach to identify links between developing countries and secrecy jurisdictions. However, we believe the FSI has the potential to provide valuable new insights on the issue of links, and the relevant research is under way. Econometric analysis of the differential impact of commercial and financial links with more or less extreme secrecy jurisdictions may offer much more powerful and illuminating results, and we explore some suggestions here. Additionally, an anonymous referee has suggested the value of creating sub-FSI indexes that reflect the relative importance of jurisdictions in specific types of financial services, which would allow analysis of the benefits or damage attributable at this more granular level. Data constraints are a major obstacle, but such an analysis, if possible, would be revealing.

The terms *tax haven* and *secrecy jurisdiction* are used interchangeably hereafter.

Development Impact

Before assessing the extent of the links between development and secrecy jurisdictions, we survey the literature on the potential development impact. Our intention is to establish the key relationships that require empirical testing.

The literature is unfortunately somewhat limited; it has two general characteristics: a focus on developed-country impact, accompanied by the study of havens, and a general neglect of tax as a development policy issue (see Cobham 2005a on the latter). A recent assessment by an expert commission reporting to the Norwegian government represents a useful step forward in outlining the key claims and much of the existing evidence.[11] Seven major claims are considered, the first three of which (at least) will affect all countries, while the other four may be especially relevant to developing countries:

1. Tax havens increase the risk premium in international financial markets.
2. Tax havens undermine the functioning of the tax system and public finances.

3. Tax havens increase the inequitable distribution of tax revenues.
4. Tax havens reduce the efficiency of resource allocation in developing countries.
5. Tax havens make economic crime more profitable.
6. Tax havens can encourage rent seeking and reduce private incomes in developing countries.
7. Tax havens damage institutional quality and growth in developing countries.

Of these, 1 relates to systematic global financial risk, 2–4 relate primarily to the damage done to effective tax systems, 5 relates to the damage done through crime, and 6 and 7 relate to distortions to economic activity, including corruption. We treat these in turn and also the major positive claim that tax havens can encourage investment in developing countries.

Aside from the systemic stability issue, the Norwegian commission's breakdown is in line with the most widely quoted analysis of illicit global financial flows, which suggests that the volume of outflows from developing countries reaches US$500 billion–US$800 billion a year (Baker 2005; subsequently revised upward by Kar and Cartwright-Smith 2008). Of this amount, 60–65 percent is estimated to be associated with commercial tax evasion (overwhelmingly in the form of mispricing and misinvoicing in trade both between unrelated parties and within multinational groups), 30–35 percent to the laundering of criminal proceeds (for example, drug and human trafficking), and around 3 percent to the corruption of public officials.

The Norwegian commission summarizes these important estimates and a good deal of additional literature that deals with the general scale of illicit capital flows. We do not treat this broader literature in more detail here, but concentrate only on those contributions that specifically address the role of tax havens. The subsections below survey the literature on the main areas of development impact, considering efforts at quantification and broader arguments about the channels of impact.

Systemic financial risk

Christian Aid (2008) advances the argument that the financial crisis was, effectively, a capital account liberalization bust, following a classic boom (see Williamson and Mahar 1998). Over a quarter of a century or more, the richer economies engaged in competitive deregulation of financial markets. Secrecy jurisdictions took this to an extreme, exploiting the gaps left by the national regulation of global finance.

The key regulatory arbitrage occurred around the regulation of banks and other financial institutions, particularly regulation that, to protect depositors from undue risk, limits the amount of assets banks may acquire as a proportion of their own capital base. The Basel II capital accord allows assets of US$1,250 for each US$100 of capital. In merely one example of an excess, Stewart (2008) has discovered that the Irish holding company of the now-collapsed U.S. bank Bear Stearns held US$11,900 in assets for each US$100 of capital. The late-2011 collapse of broker-dealer MF Global revealed a ratio in excess of 80:1 (Christian Aid 2011).

The crisis was driven by two key factors that allowed an unsustainable expansion in credit. One was the complexity of the new financial instruments, which confused investors and regulators about the true ownership of assets and liabilities. The other was the opacity of the shadow banking system, that is, financial activities outside the traditional banking system, from hedge funds and private equity to the structured investment vehicles and other conduits of investment banks and others, all taking advantage of regulatory arbitrage to operate through secrecy jurisdictions.

U.S. Treasury Secretary Timothy Geithner (then president of the New York Federal Reserve Bank) has estimated that only a portion of these activities exceeded the total assets of the entire U.S. banking system: "Financial innovation made it easier for this money to flow around the constraints of regulation and to take advantage of more favorable tax and accounting treatment" (Geithner 2008, 1).

The genesis of the crisis was undoubtedly complex, and attempts to strictly apportion blame are likely ultimately to be futile. It does seem clear, however, that the role of secrecy jurisdictions was nonnegligible at the least. An important policy response to the specific problems posed by regulatory arbitrage was the decision by G-20 finance ministers in September 2009 to call for "the setting of an overall leverage ratio, which will take into account off-balance-sheet activities, in order to limit the amount of borrowing conducted by institutions *outside the formal banking regime*."[12]

While researchers will continue for many years to reexamine the genesis of the crisis and the long period of deregulation and liberalization that underpinned the crisis, a successful and sensible attempt to quantify the role of tax havens is difficult to imagine. Yet, without such a quantification, a credible estimate of the cost of tax havens to developing countries through increased systemic financial risk is also unlikely. It does not follow, however, that this channel of impact should be ignored.

Tax systems

The most high-profile and clearly quantified claims made about the damage done by tax havens to developing countries relate to the undermining of tax systems, both in the ability of these systems to deliver the revenues needed for the provision of public services and for growth-enhancing investment in, for example, infrastructure and high-quality administration and in their ability to meet social preferences for redistribution.

The importance of tax systems for development is becoming more widely recognized in policy-making circles, although much remains to be done. Ultimately, tax can make a great contribution to the four Rs: most obviously, revenues and redistribution, but also the repricing of economic and social "bads" and political representation (Cobham 2005b; on the important links between taxation and governance, see Bräutigam, Fjeldstad, and Moore 2008).

There are multiple reasons why tax systems in developing countries fail to deliver these contributions, as follows:

- A damaging tax consensus pushed by donors and the IMF, in particular (Heady 2004; Cobham 2007)
- Lack of capacity in domestic tax administrations
- Lack of engagement by civil society to hold governments to account for tax policies and practices
- The opacity of corporate accounting (on the scale of profit shifting within Europe, see Huizinga and Laeven 2008; on the scale of trade mispricing and revenue losses in the developing world, see Christian Aid 2009; on a key policy option, see Richard Murphy's contribution,
- The opacity of this scheme) jurisdictions in facilitating profit shifting, but also in facilitating the underdeclaration of income or assets by individuals[13]

Note that these issues are largely independent of the additional problem of the smaller per capita tax base in developing countries because of lower per capita GDP, while the problems associated with large informal sectors are primarily a result, rather than a cause, of these other issues (see the discussion on compliance below).

There have, as yet, been no serious attempts to estimate the cost of secrecy jurisdictions in terms of forgone redistribution, repricing, or representation. Useful attempts have, however, been made to address the revenue effects.

The systemic impact of tax havens on development was first addressed not by researchers at international financial institutions, but by a nongovernmental organization, which relied on academics and haven insiders to build its analysis. The report, by Oxfam (2000), included an estimate that developing countries were losing around US$50 billion a year to tax havens. This estimate draws on global figures for foreign direct investment and the stock of capital flight, combining these with estimated returns to investment and interest income, along with estimated tax rates: the sum is around US$35 billion in untaxed foreign direct investment and US$15 billion in untaxed personal income.

Subsequent work by the Tax Justice Network (TJN 2005) suggests that the global revenue loss to the untaxed savings incomes of individuals may be as much as US$255 billion annually, and Cobham (2005b) notes that proportions equivalent to the shares of world GDP would imply a loss to developing countries of around US$50 billion a year. As Fuest and Riedel (2009) clarify, this would imply a potential tax haven total of US$85 billion a year, which is close to the total of aid received for the period in question. A subsequent Oxfam study puts the estimated loss on individual income alone at US$64 billion–US$124 billion (Oxfam 2009). More recently, Ann Hollingshead (2010) has estimated that US$98 billion to US$106 billion is the developing-country tax loss on some form of the trade mispricing that Christian Aid assesses and notes that her Global Financial Integrity study therefore well supports the work of Christian Aid.

This is the extent, currently, of attempts to quantify the revenue damage done by havens to developing countries. Two main criticisms can be made. First, the assumptions involved are necessarily nontrivial. Global estimates of asset return, for example, are open to criticism because opacity shields both the likely motivations and the actual portfolio choices of those holding assets in secrecy jurisdictions. Criticisms of this nature have not, however, been made, in general, by scholars offering superior alternative approaches.

The second major criticism of these approaches is that no reasonable counterfactual is put forward. Imagine, for example, that there are two main channels for illicitly reducing tax liabilities in developing countries. If the second is, say, 95 percent as effective as the first, then shutting down the first is likely to yield only a small revenue benefit. In a world with multiple channels of illicitly reducing tax liabilities, it is unrealistic to expect a definition of an appropriate counterfactual to estimate the benefit of closing down any particular channel. In effect, however, this criticism applies not to the quantification approaches, but to a popular interpretation that the resulting estimates represent readily available revenues.

In addition, such assessments of the impact of secrecy jurisdictions do not do justice to the impact on tax compliance more broadly. The experimental economics literature strongly suggests that compliance is heavily influenced by the perceptions of the compliance of others, so that high-profile noncompliance—fueling, for example, the perception that all rich citizens or multinational companies are hiding their incomes and profits in havens—is likely to have substantial multiplier effects on compliance and revenue throughout a whole economy and over the long term, given how slowly compliance is observed to shift in practice (Bosco and Mittone 1997; Mittone 2006).

While refinements in these approaches can be envisaged, the key contribution of the literature on revenue losses has been to establish that there exists an obstacle to the development of sufficient scale in estimates to warrant serious attention from civil society and from policy makers. It is not immediately clear at this stage what additional value could be offered to the policy debate by alternative estimates of global scale; more nuanced work, as suggested in the sections below, may be more valuable now.

Few would argue that the United Nations Development Programme's human development index is a truly appropriate measure of human development in all its complexity. The index has, however, undeniable benefits in shifting the emphasis in media reporting and policy discussions on poverty away from unhelpfully narrow GDP per capita measures and toward a broader and more human-level analysis. A similar argument may apply to Oxfam's seminal 2000 report. The value of the report in drawing attention to the issue is certain, not least by catalyzing the emergence of the Tax Justice Network, which has played a central role in raising awareness among policy makers, civil society, and the public.

A number of potential approaches to quantifying the scale of revenue losses on a country-specific basis are worth consideration, although they suffer from certain weaknesses also. One approach would involve pursuing the Huizinga and Laeven method (2008) using data from multinational companies on the performance of their subsidiaries to estimate the extent of profit shifting on a global basis, rather than only in Europe. The data have been questioned by those more familiar with corporate accounting (see, for example, Richard Murphy's contribution in this volume, in chapter 9), but are standard in the corporate finance literature; so, they may at least provide some benchmark estimate of the revenue losses occurring specifically because of the behavior of multinational companies.

The other avenue available is to use data on the financial positions of secrecy jurisdictions with regard to specific developing countries and, given the relative secrecy and administrative capacity of each, to make estimates about the likely extent of returns and income declarations. Current political processes through the G-20 and bilaterally mean that more data will become publicly available about the secrecy jurisdiction location of hidden assets and income streams (of richer economies at least) and, importantly, about the actual forgone tax yields. These data will provide a practical backstop to ensure that estimates for developing-country revenue losses are demonstrably anchored in reality.

Neither approach seems entirely satisfactory from an academic standpoint. However, as long as secrecy is the issue under study, any impact assessment will be subject to considerable margins of error.

In the longer term, a more promising avenue may be to work toward a better understanding of the nature of the problem, rather than specific quantifications of the scale in revenue terms alone. In particular, if a consistent indicator is available to capture the secrecy of jurisdictions, then it will be possible to use panel data regression analysis to estimate the various impacts of economic and financial links between secrecy jurisdictions and developing countries. (This is explored in greater detail in the following sections.) Potentially, this would allow the assessment not only of revenue effects, but, for example, also of the impact on the extent of redistribution, channels of political representation, standards of governance, and so on.

An additional reason to consider broader impacts, even if the focus is revenue, is a point stressed by the Norwegian commission: tax treaties between havens and developing countries are typically negotiated with the former in a position of strength, and, as a result, the havens receive a transfer of taxing rights from the developing countries, which hope that greater investment (and subsequent economic benefits) will follow.

The three hypotheses that make up this argument should be the subject of empirical scrutiny. First, do revenue patterns reflect such effects as a result of newly signed treaties? Second, do investment patterns respond as predicted? Third, does such investment deliver economic benefits? (If so, it would be interesting to consider whether the benefits are sufficient to offset any revenue losses discovered in the shorter term.)

Governance

We will not revisit the range of arguments on the importance of effective taxation for improvements in governance and channels of political representation (see Christian Aid 2008 and chapter 3, by Everest-Phillips, in this volume for more details, including considerable empirical evidence). Nor do we consider the generic arguments about the contribution of illicit flows to making crime pay (see chapters 6 and 12, by Kopp and Levi, respectively, on aspects of money laundering and crime). The specific role of tax havens with regard to the laundering of the proceeds of crime is relatively well explored, not least because it has been the focus of some of the more effective international coordination efforts; for example, see Hampton and Christensen (2002) for a discussion of the establishment, in 1989, of the intergovernmental Financial Action Task Force and its subsequent impact in terms of promoting anti–money laundering legislation at least in havens.[14]

There is, however, little academic analysis of the links between the opportunities provided by havens and the damage done to developing countries. Perhaps the main innovation offered by the Norwegian commission is in this area. Torvik (2009) goes beyond the generic arguments about tax and governance to make a specific case against havens by drawing parallels with the well-established literature on the paradox of plenty (the poor economic performance often associated with a country's natural resource wealth). Torvik argues that havens distort developing countries, above all, by changing incentives. First, the balance between productive activity and rent-seeking behavior is pushed toward the latter because of the availability of secrecy, which allows the capture of higher returns to rent seeking. This process can occur in any context, but may be particularly potent in the presence of natural resources.

The secondary effects may be even more powerful because they relate to the institutional and political context. Most narrowly, the availability of haven services can support the undermining or disestablishment of institutions by politicians so as to conceal corruption and financial malfeasance generally. Furthermore, the incentives of politicians to achieve a shift toward political systems that make elite capture easier (that is, presidential rather than parliamentary systems) will also be strengthened by haven opportunities. Finally, if havens support the returns to narrow self-interest over more broadly based progress, Torvik argues that they may increase the chances of conflict and contribute to the weakening of democratic processes.

Torvik summarizes his conclusions thus:

> The negative effects of tax havens are greater for developing countries than for other countries. There are many reasons for this. Reduced government income will have a greater social cost for developing countries than for industrialized countries. In addition, other mechanisms make themselves felt in countries with weak institutions and political systems. (Torvik 2009, 188)

While the theoretical arguments set out are compelling, what remains unavailable at this point is empirical verification of the haven links in the series of hypotheses that connect natural resource wealth, political systems, and institutional quality with particular outcomes. Research should build on the valuable insights of Torvik (2009) and test a range of hypotheses in two directions: to assess the impact of natural resource wealth, political systems, and institutional quality on the extent of economic links with tax havens and to assess the impact of economic links with tax havens on the growth-reducing effects of natural resource wealth on the development of political systems and on institutional quality.

Haven benefits

A common argument made by defenders of offshore finance is that the key service provided by secrecy jurisdictions is not secrecy, but a tax-neutral platform from which investors based in a range of jurisdictions, with potentially quite different tax treatments, can join to make an investment in another, particular jurisdiction. The tax neutrality is generally claimed to represent a safeguard against double taxation, rather than a tool for avoiding or evading taxation altogether.

Internet searches for "tax-neutral platform" identify those jurisdictions that most commonly make this claim, but a somewhat more analytical approach is offered by the Big Four accounting firm Pricewaterhouse Coopers, which proposes a set of criteria for an investment platform (in a briefing recommending Ireland as such), including that it have an "attractive tax regime for holding and financing activities" and "an attractive treaty network and low or zero statutory withholding tax rates on interest and dividend flows" (Arora, Leonard, and Teunissen 2009, 1).[15]

Leaving aside the question of whether such a platform is likely to facilitate or encourage the avoidance or evasion of single taxation, the hypothesis that follows from such claims is that the existence of havens makes investment in other jurisdictions more profitable. The Orbis database on the accounts of the subsidiaries of multinational companies would allow a partial testing of this hypothesis using the Huizinga and Laeven approach (2008), but this would miss the phenomenon of financial vehicles relying on multiple investors in different jurisdictions.[16]

Because the opacity of such jurisdictions and financial vehicles militates against direct testing in this case, a less direct hypothesis may be needed. If profitability is, indeed, raised by the use of haven platforms, then the level of investment should respond accordingly and be higher where havens are involved.

One paper claims to have tested this hypothesis: Desai, Foley, and Hines (2006a). Using results from their longer paper (2006b), the authors offer a different interpretation, which, they claim, shows that "careful use of tax haven affiliates permits foreign investors to avoid some of the tax burdens imposed by domestic and foreign authorities, thereby maintaining foreign investment at levels exceeding those that would persist if tax havens were more costly" (Desai, Foley, and Hines 2006a, 223).

The model is dismissed by the Norwegian commission. The model is based on "the assumption that an investor can make real investments with a real level of activity in a tax haven," the commission states on page 72 of its report.[17] "In fact, foreigners who use the preferential tax regime are not permitted to invest locally, have local employees or use the country's currency. The Commission accordingly takes the view that the assumption underlying the analysis is based on ignorance of investor regulations in tax havens."

The empirical results can be criticized because they are based on a limited sample of U.S. multinationals and therefore, as indicated above, may not capture the main benefits claimed. Certainly, the results are insufficient to support the claims made for the benefits of tax havens. As with the claims about damage discussed above, they require closer scrutiny.

Further research should assess more carefully whether any causal relationship can be established between haven origin investment and (1) the total level of inward investment and (2) the total level of investment from any source (because round-tripping may lead to artificially inflated declarations of inward investment with no necessary associated increase in actual investment levels). Additional research should also examine whether investment received through havens has different economic and political impacts relative to other investment flows.

Economic and Financial Links

There are three main issues in the emerging research agenda on the links between havens and development: first, that assessments of the extent of these links are lacking; second, that empirical verification is needed of the key claims surveyed above about the impact of these links; and, third, that little work has been done to analyze whether different developing countries are affected differently, which seems to be a key issue, not least for policy makers, in prioritizing responses. This section lays out some evidence relating to the first issue, the extent of the links, and highlights additional sources that can be tapped for future research. The data presented will also form the basis for econometric analysis to address the second issue, the extent of the development impact of the links.

The third issue is perhaps the most interesting. One aspect of dealing with it would involve assessing whether the links vary quantifiably across developing countries and whether there are systematic differences according to income group or region. Some attention is given to this question here. Another aspect, which will remain for future research, is whether the strength of the impact of the links differs from country to country, whether, for example, the impact of haven access in undermining governance is strongest in low-income countries, natural resource countries, countries with presidential systems, South Asian countries, and so on.

Two broad sets of competing hypotheses could usefully be examined: first, whether lower-income countries are generally less closely linked to *and* less affected by havens because their institutions, including their tax systems, are sufficiently weak that haven structures are not required to facilitate rent seeking, for example, by reducing tax payments (or avoiding other regulation), and, second, whether lower-income countries are more closely linked to and affected by havens because they are less able to respond to the associated challenges.

According to a more nuanced and interesting hypothesis, there are certain groups of (probably developing) countries in the middle of the income distribution that are the most closely linked to and affected by havens, while the poorest countries and the developed economies may be relatively less affected for different reasons (respectively, the simplicity of financial abuse in the former and the capacity of tax authorities and the relative political power of the latter).

The following subsection discusses data issues in examining bilateral links between developing countries and secrecy jurisdictions, while the subsequent subsection presents initial findings.

Data

Ideally, to capture the full range of economic links, data would be available on a bilateral basis on each relevant (trade) flow and (financial) stock, as follows:

- *Trade in goods.* UN Comtrade provides bilateral data, on the basis of a detailed commodity breakdown if necessary, for most countries and for up to around 30 years.[18] Here, we take data for the period 1995–2008, by Standard International Trade Classification (SITC), revision

3.[19] Limitations include the absence of certain reporting jurisdictions of interest, for example, Channel Islands, which are counted with the United Kingdom for overseas trade purposes. This data set consists of some 580,000 observations dealing with total trade only (that is, no commodity breakdown below the SITC 3 total). Future work could expand this data set by combining totals reported on different SITCs and other bases and, eventually, by exploring patterns in particular commodity codes (for example, natural resource codes).

By coding each reporter and partner country individually and according to groups (for example, regions, income groups, or various secrecy jurisdiction lists), one may obtain values for the share of trade carried by each country with members of other groups. To present the data, we have partially aggregated the jurisdictions into groups by income level and region, according to World Bank classifications. The key information is the share of trade carried out with secrecy jurisdictions.

- *Trade in services.* The United Nations also provides bilateral data on services trade, but this database is relatively recent and currently has much weaker coverage. We do not use it here, in part because of the especially weak coverage of bilateral reporting by developing countries. Future work should investigate in more detail the availability and value of these data, possibly with a view to encouraging reporting.
- *Portfolio investment.* The IMF Coordinated Portfolio Investment Survey reports stocks of the following categories of portfolio investments on an annual basis: equity securities (for example, shares, stocks, participations, and similar documents such as American depositary receipts, where these denote the ownership of equity), long-term debt securities (for example, bonds, debentures, and notes, where these generally give unconditional rights to a fixed future income on a given date and have an original maturity greater than a year), and short-term debt securities (for example, treasury bills, commercial paper, and banker acceptances, with an original maturity of less than a year).[20]

For 2007, 74 jurisdictions reported; these were the most recent data available when this chapter was presented, and we use them here. Data are provided on the assets and liabilities of jurisdictions, but based only on reporting from the creditor side. Because each reporter therefore provides data for all other jurisdictions in which they have investment positions, investment is reported in a total of 237 jurisdictions. There are relatively few developing countries among the reporting jurisdictions, but a good many smaller secrecy jurisdictions do report. In contrast to the goods trade data, there is better direct coverage of links originating in secrecy jurisdictions, but less direct coverage of links originating in developing countries. No data set examined offers comprehensive coverage from both angles. As with the goods trade data, the 2007 IMF Coordinated Portfolio Investment Survey was coded to allow summary of the links by group.

- *Foreign direct investment.* The United Nations Conference on Trade and Development provides bilateral data on foreign direct investment positions, but at greater expense than was possible for this research.[21] Future work should seek to obtain these data and assess their coverage and quality.

- *Claims on foreign banks.* The Bank for International Settlements provides data on the extent of foreign claims on banks of reporting jurisdictions. These data are available on a quarterly basis with a short lag. We use the December 2008 data, the most recent confirmed data available when this chapter was presented (BIS 2008). Sadly, these data are available only on a bilateral basis for consolidated, rather than locational, statistics. This means that apparent links between a developing country and a particular secrecy jurisdiction must be interpreted with caution, because, for example, Argentine deposits in a Bermudan bank operating out of Buenos Aires would be recorded as a Bermudan liability. Until locational statistics are made available by the Bank for International Settlements, which would be a valuable contribution to transparency, this is the only possibility; so, this strong caveat should be borne in mind.

Main findings

As noted elsewhere above, it would be preferable if we could judge jurisdictions using an indicator of secrecy on a sliding scale, thereby allowing us to measure gradual change where appropriate. For the moment, however, we make do with the range of existing lists. To present the results simply, we report trade shares for two groups: the larger group of secrecy jurisdictions identified by the Tax Justice Network (see table 11A.1 and the note to table 9A.4) and a narrower group closer in composition to the usual suspects. The latter are defined as those jurisdictions that feature on a majority of the 11 lists shown in table 11A.1 (that is, on six or more).[22]

Table 11A.4 and figures 11.1 and 11.2 present the main results.[23] If the results for narrow and broad secrecy jurisdiction lists are examined and different stocks and flows are compared, a number of interesting patterns emerge. There is considerable variation among developing country groups both by income and by region. Analyses that fail to take this into account will be incomplete. We highlight a few other key points below.

First, the trade flows of developing countries are generally more exposed (as a share of total economic links) to the effects of secrecy jurisdictions than are the trade flows of high-income OECD countries, which we take as a benchmark throughout. This is particularly pronounced in developing-country exports and in East and South Asia most of all. The differences in exposure between narrow and broad secrecy

Figure 11.1. Intensity of Economic Exposure: Implied Ratios of Secrecy Jurisdiction Shares to GDP, by Income Group

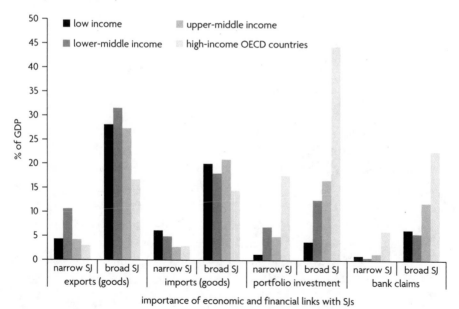

importance of economic and financial links with SJs

Sources: Trade data: UN Comtrade (United Nations Commodity Trade Statistics Database), Statistics Division, Department of Economic and Social Affairs, United Nations, New York, http://comtrade.un.org/db/. Portfolio investment data: IMF, "Coordinated Portfolio Investment Survey," Washington, DC, http://www.imf.org/external/np/sta/pi/cpis.htm. Data on bank claims: BIS 2008.

Note: SJ = secrecy jurisdiction. "Narrow" and "broad" refer to shorter or longer lists of secrecy jurisdictions (see the text).

Figure 11.2. Intensity of Economic Exposure: Implied Ratios of Secrecy Jurisdiction Shares to GDP, by Region

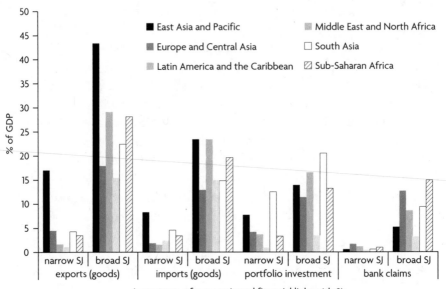

Sources: See figure 11.1.

Note: SJ = secrecy jurisdiction. "Narrow" and "broad" refer to shorter or longer lists of secrecy jurisdictions (see the text).

jurisdiction lists are often driven, as in the case of Latin American trade, by the inclusion of the United States in the latter list.

Striking examples emerge from the underlying country-level data. One example is highlighted in figure 11.3, which shows the total value of Zambian trade from 1995 to 2008, as well as the shares attributable to only one secrecy jurisdiction, Switzerland.

Note that the share of declared Zambian exports to Switzerland in the total declared exports of Zambia (that is, exports declared at and subsequently reported by Zambian customs) rise from a fraction of 1 percent in 1995–98 to more than 50 percent in 2008. The growth in exports over the period reflects Zambia's emergence as a major copper producer. However, copper is not a product for which particular demand or processing capacity is noted in Switzerland, although relatively opaque metal trading does take place there. This highlights a major concern about the data and emphasizes the need for transparency. If one were to assume

Figure 11.3. Zambian Trade: Swiss Role, 1995–2008

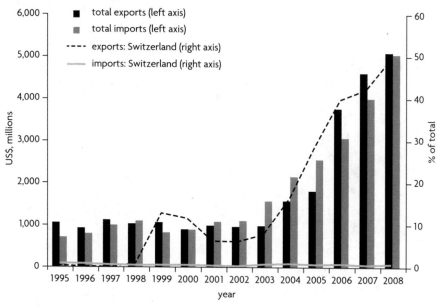

Source: UN Comtrade (United Nations Commodity Trade Statistics Database), Statistics Division, Department of Economic and Social Affairs, United Nations, New York, http://comtrade.un.org/db/.

that Zambian copper is of the same quality as any copper in the Switzerland trade data in the same detailed commodity categories (for example, coils of copper at thicknesses of less than 0.35 millimeters), so that Zambian copper exports to Switzerland should be priced at the same level as the declared Swiss trade in the same items, then the implied illicit capital flow out of Zambia is in the region of 30 times the declared export value. Clearly the impact on Zambian GDP would also be dramatic.

However, the declared Swiss imports from Zambia and the declared total exports from Zambia are a tiny proportion of the Zambian-declared exports to Switzerland; so, such an estimate of the illicit flow cannot be supported on this basis. The use of Switzerland for transit in commodities in this way is well known, but remains highly opaque (for example, see Berne Declaration 2011). What is absolutely clear is that declared Zambian copper exports, on which the country depends economically, effectively disappear once they leave the country. The potential for this opacity to undermine the country's development is equally apparent.

The second broad result is that developing countries in general are more exposed to (more reliant on) secrecy jurisdictions in portfolio investment stocks. East and South Asia are especially exposed, reflecting the regional location of particular secrecy jurisdictions (for example, Hong Kong SAR, China; Singapore). To take an arbitrary example, the U.K. Crown Dependency of Jersey was responsible, in 2007, for more than 30 percent of the declared portfolio investment in six countries: Algeria, Guinea, and the Syrian Arab Republic (between one-third and one-half of declared investment), and Djibouti, Libya, and Turkmenistan (99.5 percent or more).

Third, the picture is somewhat more mixed if bank claims are considered. With respect to the narrow secrecy jurisdiction list, this is the one set of results in which high-income OECD countries are notably more exposed than each developing country group. On the broad secrecy jurisdiction list, however, developing countries are a little more exposed, particularly countries in South Asia and Sub-Saharan Africa. An arbitrary example: more than 20 percent of the revealed foreign claims of Eritrea and neighboring Ethiopia at the end of 2008 were against banks in one country, Switzerland. However, this may be the result of a Swiss bank operating out of, for example, Addis Ababa and taking deposits. The available data do not allow us any certainty about the locational aspects.

Table 11A.5 presents the results on a different basis: the implied percentage of GDP.[24] We use additional data on economic aggregates and then extrapolate on the assumption that the shares of bilaterally reported trade (or other flows and stocks) that are associated with secrecy jurisdictions are equal to the shares of these jurisdictions in total trade (or other measures). This may be somewhat heroic, and it would clearly be preferable to have full data available. Nonetheless, for this exercise, which involves making broad comparisons across different country groups, there seems no particular reason to expect that our method would introduce a systematic distortion.

The main results are twofold. First, the trade exposure of developing countries to secrecy jurisdictions relative to the total size of the economies of these countries is notably greater than that of the high-income OECD countries. Second, the reverse pattern holds with regard to portfolio investment and foreign bank claims. It is important to understand the difference that allowing for GDP makes: developing countries generally have a much lower ratio of portfolio investment to GDP; so, while secrecy jurisdictions are responsible for a much higher proportion of the investment received (table 11A.4), the secrecy jurisdiction investment as a proportion of GDP (table 11A.5) is much lower in developing countries than in high-income countries. As might be expected, the international financial integration of developing countries is broadly correlated with the per capita income levels of these countries. The results in table 11A.4 show that the intensity is not significantly different (that is, the share of secrecy jurisdictions in the existing level of financial integration), but the lower levels of integration mean that the total secrecy jurisdiction exposure through these channels is less.

Next steps

Subsequent work should extend these findings in three ways. First, researchers (and research funders) should prioritize the construction of a consistent data set containing as much information as possible on bilateral trade and financial flows and stocks. Major actors such as the IMF, the Bank for International Settlements, the OECD, and perhaps even the World Bank should aim to emulate, for various financial flows, the trade transparency that the United Nations has achieved. The absence of detailed results in this field can largely be blamed on the lack of transparency not of individual jurisdictions, but of the major players in the economic system. An effort to achieve a greater understanding of the global economy, as well as of the major elements that form illicit flows, calls for an economic transparency initiative of the type being pursued by the Task Force for Financial Integrity and Economic Development.[25]

This would facilitate more detailed comparisons of this sort, but it would also help fulfill the second requirement: rigorous econometric work to establish whether there are, indeed, systematic impacts on developing countries because of their exposure to secrecy jurisdictions, such as impacts, in particular, on tax revenues, on economic growth, on inequality, and on governance outcomes. Finally, this work should be extended along the lines argued in this chapter, that is, to include the FSI or equivalently nuanced tools for capturing the relative opacity of jurisdictions.

Conclusion

This chapter has drawn together the literature on the impact of tax havens on development and considered the need for further research in this neglected area.

It is clear that the data on bilateral trade and financial flows, while frustratingly limited in some areas, do provide a sufficient basis on which to draw quite clear conclusions about the relative exposure of developing countries to tax havens or secrecy jurisdictions, specifically: *in general, developing countries do not appear to be any less exposed than high-income OECD countries to secrecy jurisdictions, and, in some cases, they are much more highly exposed.* Therefore, the G-20 and others are correct in demanding that developing countries be included in any mechanism to require increased transparency from secrecy jurisdictions.

In addition, there are clearly important differences in the exposure of developing countries across different income groups and regions. This warrants further investigation and analysis, which is likely, ultimately, to lead to the identification of distinct policy recommendations.

Although this brief summary of the state of research makes clear that there are more questions than answers, there can be no doubt that secrecy jurisdictions are an important issue for developing countries and that the damage done by them to development is also potentially large. For researchers, research funders, and policy makers, this is an area of work that must be given an increasingly greater priority.

Notes

1. See, respectively, Owens (2009, 2); Gordon Brown, quoted in Christian Aid (2010, 22); and Declaration on Strengthening the Financial System, G-20 London Summit, April 2, 2009, 4–5, http://www.g20.org/Documents/Fin_Deps _Fin_Reg_Annex_020409_-_1615_final.pdf.
2. The second criteria is related to the characteristic that the OECD's Towards a Level Playing Field Initiative seeks to measure through the consistent assessment of jurisdictions on a range of legal and regulatory features (OECD 2006).
3. See Christian Aid (2008) for a discussion of how this process of regulatory arbitrage caused secrecy jurisdictions to play an important role in the unfolding of the financial crisis.
4. The table may be found on the website of this volume, http://go.worldbank.org /N2HMRB4G20.

5. For the IMF data, see http://www.imf.org/external/np/sta/bop/bop.htm.

6. For the Coordinated Portfolio Investment Survey, see http://www.imf.org /external/np/sta/pi/cpis.htm. For International Financial Statistics, see International Financial Statistics (database), IMF, Washington, DC, http://elibrary-data .imf.org/FindDataReports.aspx?d=33061&e=169393.

7. The table may be found on the website of this volume, http://go.worldbank.org /N2HMRB4G20.

8. See Financial Secrecy Index, Tax Justice Network, London, http://www.financial secrecyindex.com/index.html.

9. The table may be found on the website of this volume, http://go.worldbank.org /N2HMRB4G20.

10. See also "The British connection" and "Chart 2: The British Empire by Secrecy Scores," Financial Secrecy Index, Tax Justice Network, London, http://www .financialsecrecyindex.com/significance.html#british.

11. Norway, Minister of the Environment and International Development, 2009, *Tax Havens and Development: Status, Analyses and Measures*, Oslo: Government Commission on Capital Flight from Poor Countries, http://www.regjeringen .no/upload/UD/Vedlegg/Utvikling/tax_report.pdf.

12. *Financial Times*, "Hurdles Remain for G20 Pact," September 7, 2009; emphasis added.

13. This opacity is also used to hide the origin or beneficial ownership of the proceeds of crimes unrelated to tax, including other forms of corruption, but also, for example, the trafficking of drugs and people, the financing of terrorism, and so on. Some implications of these activities for developing countries are treated elsewhere in this chapter; see also the chapters by Kopp and Levi in this volume (chapters 6 and 12, respectively).

14. See Financial Action Task Force, http://www.fatf-gafi.org/.

15. A casual investigation shows that The Bahamas, British Virgin Islands, Cayman Islands, and Isle of Man feature prominently in the Internet searches on claims about a tax-neutral platform.

16. For the Orbis data, see Bureau van Dijk, http://www.bvdinfo.com/Products /Company-Information/International/Orbis.

17. Norway, Minister of the Environment and International Development, 2009, *Tax Havens and Development: Status, Analyses and Measures*, Oslo: Government Commission on Capital Flight from Poor Countries, http://www.regjeringen. no/upload/UD/Vedlegg/Utvikling/tax_report.pdf.

18. See UN Comtrade (United Nations Commodity Trade Statistics Database), Statistics Division, Department of Economic and Social Affairs, United Nations, New York, http://comtrade.un.org/db/.

19. See United Nations, "Detailed Structure and Explanatory Notes, SITC Rev.3 (Standard International Trade Classification, Rev.3)," United Nations Statistics Division, http://unstats.un.org/unsd/cr/registry/regcst.asp?Cl=14.

20. See IMF, "Coordinated Portfolio Investment Survey," Washington, DC, http://www.imf.org/external/np/sta/pi/cpis.htm.

21. See Data Extract Service, Division on Investment and Enterprise, United Nations Conference on Trade and Development, Geneva, http://www.unctad.org/Templates/Page.asp?intItemID=3205&lang=1.

22. Tables 9A.4 and 11A.1 may be found on the website of this volume, http://go.worldbank.org/N2HMRB4G20.

23. Table 11A.4 may be found on the website of this volume, http://go.worldbank.org/N2HMRB4G20.

24. Table 11A.5 may be found on the website of this volume, http://go.worldbank.org/N2HMRB4G20.

25. See the Task Force on Financial Integrity and Economic Development, Washington, DC, http://www.financialtaskforce.org/.

References

Arora, P., B. Leonard, and O. Teunissen. 2009. "Ireland Emerging as an Onshore Investment Platform." PwC Alternatives 4 (1), PricewaterhouseCoopers, New York. http://download.pwc.com/ie/pubs/IrelandEmergingAsAnOnshoreInvestmentPlatform.pdf.

Avi-Yonah, R. S. 2000. "Globalization, Tax Competition, and the Fiscal Crisis of the Welfare State." *Harvard Law Review* 113 (7): 1573–676.

Baker, R. W. 2005. *Capitalism's Achilles Heel: Dirty Money and How to Renew the Free-Market System.* Hoboken, NJ: John Wiley & Sons.

Berne Declaration. 2011. "Commodities: Switzerland's Most Dangerous Business." Berne Declaration, Zurich. http://www.evb.ch/cm_data/2011_09_19_Berne_Declaration_-_Commodities_-_English_Sample.pdf.

BIS (Bank for International Settlements). 2008. *BIS Quarterly Review*, December 8, BIS, Basel, Switzerland. http://www.bis.org/publ/qtrpdf/r_qt0812.htm.

Bosco, L., and L. Mittone. 1997. "Tax Evasion and Moral Constraints: Some Experimental Evidence." *Kyklos* 50 (3): 297–324.

Bräutigam, D., O.-H. Fjeldstad, and M. Moore, eds. 2008. *Taxation and State-Building in Developing Countries: Capacity and Consent.* Cambridge, U.K.: Cambridge University Press.

Christian Aid. 2008. "The Morning After the Night Before: The Impact of the Financial Crisis on the Developing World." Christian Aid Report, November, Christian Aid, London. http://www.christianaid.org.uk/Images/The-morning-after-the-night-before.pdf.

———. 2009. "False Profits: Robbing the Poor to Keep the Rich Tax-Free." Christian Aid Report, March, Christian Aid, London. http://www.christianaid.org.uk/Images/false-profits.pdf.

———. 2010. "Blowing the Whistle: Time's Up for Financial Secrecy." Christian Aid Report, May, Christian Aid, London. http://www.christianaid.org.uk/images /blowing-the-whistle-caweek-report.pdf.

———. 2011. " 'My Word Is My Bond': Responsible Finance and Economic Justice." Accounting for Change 3 (November), Christian Aid, London. http://www .christianaid.org.uk/images/accounting-for-change.pdf.

Cobham, A. 2005a. "Taxation Policy and Development." OCGG Economy Analysis 2, Oxford Council on Good Governance, Oxford.

———. 2005b. "Tax Evasion, Tax Avoidance and Development Finance." QEH Working Paper 129, Queen Elizabeth House, University of Oxford, Oxford. http://www3.qeh.ox.ac.uk/pdf/qehwp/qehwps129.pdf.

———. 2007. "The Tax Consensus Has Failed! Recommendation to Policymakers and Donors, Researchers and Civil Society." OCGG Economy Recommendation 8, Oxford Council on Good Governance, Oxford.

Desai, M. A., C. F. Foley, and J. R. Hines Jr. 2006a. "Do Tax Havens Divert Economic Activity?" Economics Letters 90 (2): 219–24.

———. 2006b. "The Demand for Tax Haven Operations." Journal of Public Economics 90 (3): 513–31.

Eden, L., and R. Kudrle. 2005. "Tax Havens: Renegade States in the International Tax Regime." Law and Policy 27 (1): 100–27.

Fuest, C., and N. Riedel. 2009. "Tax Evasion, Tax Avoidance and Tax Expenditures in Developing Countries: A Review of the Literature." Report, Oxford University Centre for Business Taxation, Oxford. http://ec.europa.eu/development /services/events/tax_development/docs/td_evasion_riedel_fuest.pdf.

Geithner, T. F. 2008. "Reducing Systemic Risk in a Dynamic Financial System." Speech to the Economic Club of New York, New York, June 9. http://www .newyorkfed.org/newsevents/speeches/2008/tfg080609.html.

Gordon, R. A. 1981. Tax Havens and Their Use by United States Taxpayers: An Overview; A Report to the Commissioner of Internal Revenue, the Assistant Attorney General (Tax Division) and the Assistant Secretary of the Treasury (Tax Policy). Publication 1150 (4–81) (January 12). Washington, DC: U.S. Department of the Treasury.

Hampton, M., and J. Christensen. 2002. "Offshore Pariahs? Small Island Economies, Tax Havens, and the Reconfiguration of Global Finance." World Development 30 (9): 1657–73.

Heady, C. 2004. "Taxation Policy in Low-Income Countries." In Fiscal Policy for Development: Poverty, Reconstruction and Growth, ed. T. Addison and A. Roe, 130–48. Studies in Development Economics and Policy. Helsinki: World Institute for Development Economics Research; Basingstoke, U.K.: Palgrave Macmillan.

Hollingshead, A. 2010. "The Implied Tax Revenue Loss from Trade Mispricing." Global Financial Integrity, Washington, DC. http://www.gfip.org/storage/gfip /documents/reports/implied%20tax%20revenue%20loss%20report_final.pdf.

Huizinga, H., and L. Laeven. 2008. "International Profit Shifting within Multinationals: A Multi-country Perspective." *Journal of Public Economics* 92 (5–6): 1164–82.

Kar, D., and D. Cartwright-Smith. 2008. "Illicit Financial Flows from Developing Countries, 2002–2006." Global Financial Integrity, Washington, DC. http://www.gfip.org/storage/gfip/economist%20-%20final%20version%201-2-09.pdf.

Kudrle, R. T. 2008. "Did Blacklisting Hurt the Havens?" Paolo Baffi Centre Research Paper 2008–23, Paolo Baffi Centre on Central Banking and Financial Regulation, Bocconi University, Milan.

Kudrle, R. T., and L. Eden. 2003. "The Campaign against Tax Havens: Will It Last? Will It Work?" *Stanford Journal of Law, Business and Finance* 9 (1): 37–68.

Mittone, L. 2006. "Dynamic Behaviour in Tax Evasion: An Experimental Approach." *Journal of Socio-Economics* 35 (5): 813–35.

Murphy, R. 2008. "Finding the Secrecy World: Rethinking the Language of 'Offshore'." Report, Tax Research LLP, Downham Market, U.K. http://www.taxresearch.org.uk/Documents/Finding.pdf.

OECD (Organisation for Economic Co-operation and Development). 1987. "International Tax Avoidance and Evasion: Four Related Studies." Issues in International Taxation 1, Committee on Fiscal Affairs, OECD, Paris.

———. 1998. "Harmful Tax Competition: An Emerging Global Issue." OECD, Paris.

———. 2006. *Tax Co-operation 2006: Towards a Level Playing Field; 2006 Assessment by the Global Forum on Taxation.* Paris: OECD.

Owens, J. 2009. "Tax and Development: Why Tax Is Important for Development." *Tax Justice Focus* 4 (4): 1–3. http://www.oecd.org/dataoecd/10/22/43061404.pdf.

Oxfam. 2000. "Tax Havens: Releasing the Hidden Billions for Poverty Eradication." Oxfam Briefing Paper, Oxfam International, London. http://www.taxjustice.net/cms/upload/pdf/oxfam_paper_-_final_version__06_00.pdf.

———. 2009. "Tax Haven Crackdown Could Deliver 120bn a Year to Reduce Poverty: Oxfam." Press release, March 13, Oxfam GB, London. http://www.oxfam.org.uk/applications/blogs/pressoffice/?p=3912.

Palan, R. 1998. "The Emergence of an Offshore Economy." *Futures* 30 (1): 63–73.

———. 2002. "Tax Havens and the Commercialization of State Sovereignty." *International Organization* 56 (1): 151–76.

Shaxson, N. 2011. *Treasure Islands: Tax Havens and the Men Who Stole the World.* London: Bodley Head.

Stewart, J. 2008. "Shadow Regulation and the Shadow Banking System." *Tax Justice Focus* 4 (2): 1–3. http://www.taxjustice.net/cms/upload/pdf/TJF_4-2_AABA_-_Research.pdf.

TJN (Tax Justice Network). 2005. "The Price of Offshore." Tax Justice Network Briefing Paper, March, TJN, London.

———. 2008. "Creating Turmoil," pp. 9–217 in *Written Evidence to the UK House of Commons Treasury Select Committee on Offshore Financial Centres*, London: HMSO, http://www.parliament.uk/documents/upload/OFCWrittenEvidence.pdf.

Torvik, R. 2009. "Appendix 1: Why Are Tax Havens More Harmful to Developing Countries Than to Other Countries?" In *Tax Havens and Development: Status, Analyses and Measures*, ed. Norway, Minister of the Environment and International Development, 155–94. Oslo: Government Commission on Capital Flight from Poor Countries. http://www.regjeringen.no/upload/UD/Vedlegg/Utvikling/tax_report.pdfpp.

Williamson, J., and M. Mahar. 1998. "A Survey of Financial Liberalization." Princeton Essays in International Economics 211 (November), International Economics Section, Princeton University, Princeton, NJ.

Zoromé, A. 2007. "Concept of Offshore Financial Centers: In Search of an Operational Definition." IMF Working Paper WP/07/87, International Monetary Fund, Washington, DC. http://www.imf.org/external/pubs/ft/wp/2007/wp0787.pdf.

12

How Well Do Anti–Money Laundering Controls Work in Developing Countries?

Michael Levi

Abstract

Much of the attention to the link between corruption and money laundering understandably has focused on the developed world, given that it is the businesses of the developed world that mostly pay the bribes and that it is the banks and other institutions of the developed world that receive and recycle the bribes. However, this is not the whole picture. Substantial sums arising from corruption are often retained or even imported into developing countries to pay off political rivals, satisfy obligations to families, friends, and clans, and invest in local businesses and property. Kleptocrats usually wish to retain power and therefore require such funds.

Historically, the principal benefit of anti–money laundering (AML) regimes in developing countries has been the international political and economic acceptance and the avoidance of sanctions that they bring. This has to be set against the substantial costs of introducing such regimes in human resource–poor countries. If nations are to be required to have AML measures, one component of optimizing the benefits involves using these measures to combat corruption, especially corruption at a high level. Namibia and Nigeria excepted, there do not appear to be any cases in which internal AML reporting within developing countries has led to major cases against in-favor politically exposed persons (PEPs). However, suspicious activity reports (SARs) can be useful against out-of-favor PEPs and in helping to accumulate information about assets held in the actual or beneficial ownership of in-favor and out-of-favor PEPs. If no recording systems are in place, financial investigators in the aftermath of criminal cases would face greater difficulty in identifying assets.

Unless the national financial intelligence unit (FIU) is believed to be both discreet and independent of the government, potential whistle-blowers might be afraid of exposure as sources of information. If suspicions are communicated to the FIU, what could the FIU plausibly do with the report? This highlights the importance of the relationship between FIUs and effectively independent investigation and prosecutorial bodies, which may be needed if AML regimes in developing countries are to have a significant impact on domestic grand corruption. Local and foreign investigations running in parallel might produce benefits; so, too, might better domestic coordination with anticorruption bodies. Achieving this level of competence and independence is a major task.

Introduction

AML is a major element in the standard list of interventions with apparent potential to reduce the flow of illicit funds both into and out of developing countries and into developed ones, usually for the purpose of storing wealth or for expenditure on conspicuous consumption. It is the first such intervention that has been put into place on an almost universal basis. This chapter represents an assessment of what is known about the effects of AML regimes within developing countries in dealing with internal money laundering and kleptocratic wealth.

The international AML system is over 20 years old, but, prior to 2001, it was primarily focused on the countries of the Organisation for Economic Co-operation and Development (OECD) and on financial havens (OECD or not) in which funds from drugs and fraud were laundered. Since 2001, it has been implemented in most countries, partly with the aim of protecting the West from the export of terrorism, but also to deal with grand corruption and organized crime, often arising from crimes committed outside a jurisdiction, but also from crimes within it. In many developing countries, the system is new. For example, most African countries have only passed AML laws since 2005, usually under pressure from the developed world, and some jurisdictions have adopted such laws irrespective of the insignificance of their financial service systems domestically or internationally. Examples of the latter include Malawi, Namibia (the Financial Intelligence Act 2007), and the formerly blacklisted (by the Financial Action Task Force [FATF]) South Pacific island of Nauru, where, in the last few years, more than a third of the laws passed have related to AML, even though Nauru is no longer any sort of financial services center, and there is nothing left there to regulate that could plausibly cause serious harm.[1] The fact that a country is not a financial center does not, of course, mean that there is no money laundering there. All countries have domestic crime and the possibility of both transnational and domestic bribery in contract negotiations and may be conduits for terrorism and the financing of terrorism. Given the broad definitions of laundering generally in place, this creates scope for AML. The question is: How much impact can we expect in such countries to justify the expenditure of scarce resources that AML requires?

Given the recency of these laws in many parts of the developing world, it would be unreasonable to expect much evidence of effectiveness yet. Moreover, the empirical links between reductions in serious crime for gain and any measures against serious crime (including AML) are difficult to demonstrate (Levi and Maguire 2004; Levi and Reuter 2006). The arguments about the effective implementation of AML can be tautological in both the developed and the developing worlds. The waters are further muddied by the fact that most of the grand kleptocracy cases that are known occurred before the significant implementation of AML in developing countries in Africa, Asia, or Central and South America, so it would be improper to deduce that AML failed in these regions.

This chapter, then, has an important speculative element with respect to effectiveness. For example, it examines the plausibility of a kleptocratic regime allowing a local FIU to be effective and fulfilling any other requirement to enable this effectiveness to be translated into broader preventive or criminal justice action. It briefly describes the historical evidence that anticorruption agencies that have had significant success (such as in Kenya, Nigeria, and Zambia) have generally been dismantled either by the governments they have attacked or by successor governments (Ribadu 2010). This reflects the political economy reality of AML: it requires the support of the powerful who, in a corrupt country, have the most to fear from its effectiveness.

The chapter also examines the role of domestic AML in dealing with (1) the proceeds of corruption and (2) those proceeds of crime and licit activities that are used to finance corruption within developing countries. It suggests that dictators and elected kleptocrats usually plan on staying in power and expect to do so. For these purposes, they require funds, as well as career positions to distribute to those who are useful in maintaining their power and gaining rent-seeking opportunities. They may also purchase vehicles and properties in their domestic jurisdictions in excess of their official incomes. So, opportunities exist for AML interventions locally, as well as in the rich world.

The Goals of AML Policies in Developing Countries

Looked at historically, the growth of AML measures has been motivated largely by the desire of rich countries to reduce the impact of crimes upon their own citizens, residents, and businesses.[2] The theory is that AML will demotivate offenders, shorten criminal careers, and disrupt or prevent the loose construct known as organized crime. It does this by incapacitating organizational growth and stripping those assets under the control of criminals that offenders cannot demonstrate they have acquired by legitimate means.[3] Another aim of AML is to increase public satisfaction with criminal justice and administrative regulation and to reduce the attractiveness of criminals as role models by showing that crime does not pay.[4] Note, however, that past lifestyle expenditure cannot, in practice, be recovered. The applicability of this model to grand corruption is taken for granted in the literature, and, in particular, it is assumed that, if PEPs and their close families cannot deposit large sums in rich countries, they will not commit corruption.

The mechanism for achieving these goals is to develop an international chain with no weak link, making it impossible for people to retain the proceeds of multifarious crimes both outside and inside their own jurisdictions. Though most mutual legal assistance is requested by rich countries from other rich or from poor countries, this also tends to be true, paradoxically, in most grand corruption cases, though rich countries do not always help as much as they could. AML is also available for purely domestic cases, in which offenders try to conceal their criminal income within the local financial sector.

Whether from corruption or not, some alleged proceeds of crime can make a significant difference to welfare within developing countries, though it may be countered that—as with some Russian oligarch émigrés in the West—people are seeking to buy their immunity from extradition by courting popular support. Kobi Alexander, an Israeli technologist whose extradition from Namibia has been sought by the United States since 2006 on charges of stock options securities fraud related to his firm Comverse Technology (and who agreed to a U.S. Securities and Exchange Commission civil settlement in 2010 for US$54 million), brought substantial, if disputed funds with him to Namibia and has invested or given away millions to finance low-cost high-technology housing projects and endow educational funds for Namibians.

> Alexander transferred 120m. Namibian dollars (N$16.9m.) from Israel to Namibia and was granted a two-year work permit on a pledge to spend N$300m. in the country. . . . He had invested N$11m. in the country, including N$3.4m. in low-cost housing in the western town of Swakopmund, because of demand created by the opening of the Langer Heinrich uranium mine. . . . Alexander invested another N$5.9m. in an auto-body shop business in Windhoek and bought a N$3.5m. house on a golf estate. He also enrolled his children in the 275-pupil Windhoek International School, where fees last year ranged between N$18,000 and N$118,000 a year. . . .
>
> "I have invested responsibly and with a view to engaging previously disadvantaged Namibians," Alexander said.[5]

There is no extradition treaty between Namibia and the United States, and, as of November 2011, Alexander is out on bail of N$10 million pending a High Court challenge to the United States.

In addition to governmental pressures, AML has, in recent times, been regularly supported by large international banks. These have the capacity to implement the required sophisticated control systems. They have successfully called for an extension of such controls to their smaller commercial competitors (including money transmission businesses), driving up the latter's costs of doing business and the cost of remittances by expatriates to poor countries. However, cooperation over tax issues by some banks (and some governments) remains an item of serious contention (Chaikin 2009; Sharman 2011; Shaxson 2011).

In regard to the methods of laundering, the conventional wisdom since the 1980s is that they entail a three-stage process of (1) the placement of funds into the financial or other sector, (2) layering steps to make the money trail harder to follow, and (3) integration of the cleansed capital into the legitimate economy after the illegitimate origins have been obscured. This process does not necessarily involve international money flows, especially not in cases of self-laundering (see below). Nonetheless, the existence of international flows of funds, criminal precursors (such as chemicals), and international illicit markets (such as drugs, people smuggling, and human trafficking) provides leverage for peer pressure between states in the form of mutual evaluations (Levi and Gilmore 2002). Such evaluations have long been extended to corruption through the Council of Europe's Group of States against Corruption and, more tentatively, to those nations that have ratified the United Nations Convention against Corruption (UNCAC). A different form of expert evaluation occurs within the framework of the OECD Convention on Combating Bribery of Foreign Public Officials in International Business Transactions (more well-known as the OECD Anti-Bribery Convention).

To implement AML controls, a broad network of FATF-Style Regional Bodies has been developed; AML legislation has been adopted; and an ever-widening range of private sector businesses and professions has become involved. These last include car dealers, jewelers, money exchanges and transmitters, real estate vendors, and, in Europe, but in few places elsewhere, lawyers who are required to make reports to their national FIUs on their subjective suspicions about their clients. Much less commonly, they also include objective cash receipts that exceed a modest level.[6]

The privacy of high net worth individuals with regard to their own governments, foreign governments, and the risk of criminal extortion is a matter of great political sensitivity. Thus, the person who runs an FIU (for example, typically, the central bank, the attorney general, or the police) makes a great difference in the extent to which the FIU is trusted by those it regulates and with whom it has to cooperate.[7] This also makes a difference in how efficient an FIU is in follow-up action. As of July 2010, there were 127 members of the Egmont FIU Group, including the richest jurisdictions and poorer countries. FIUs are absent altogether only in the poorest countries, and some of these countries are not admitted to Egmont or have been suspended from the group because, it is felt, they have not reached a sufficient standard of competence and independence. Hitherto, most of the attention has been paid to laundering and the financing of terrorism because these affect developed countries (and their associated commercial and security interests worldwide). The interest of developed countries in developing countries has mainly taken the form of reviewing the ways in which the tolerance or alleged tolerance of the latter is inhibiting the success of efforts to control drugs, organized crime, human trafficking, and terrorism.

There are signs of increased systematic action against grand corruption and laundering. The G-20 Seoul Summit Action Plan of November 2010 requires an annual follow-up.[8] These corruption-related reputational issues and collateral harms and benefits arguably have become part of the goals of AML. Swiss regulators and investigative judges might have expected even greater credit for their ingenious use of their powers and creative applications of the law from Marcos onward (for a more skeptical view, see Chaikin and Sharman 2009). The Swiss use this as political capital to compare themselves favorably with the United Kingdom, the United States, and the latters' "satellite states," while continuing to advertise Swiss banking secrecy unless criminal investigations yield sufficient evidence to generate mutual legal assistance.

Measurement and Patterns of Laundering Relative to Corruption

One of the difficulties faced by any study in this area is that the definition of corruption may be narrowly interpreted to include only bribery (as the criminal law and criminal statistics do) or—as is now more common in analytical discourse—may be more broadly interpreted to include the misuse of office to steal funds or to acquire assets for private gain at significantly below true market value. If a PEP has a substantial measure of control over a country's treasury, there is no need to bribe treasury staff: in addition to the custom of obedience, threats—including the threat of unemployment or homicide or any form of harm to relatives—can be sufficient to induce compliance. The PEP may bypass domestic controls anyway, for example, when Marcos instructed the Philippine Central Bank to generate large disbursements from its account at the New York Federal Reserve, rather than using the bank's Manila office (Briones 2007). Analytically satisfactory estimates are affected by the definitional problems that bedevil white-collar crime studies generally: acquitting former President Chiluba in August 2009, the Zambian court appeared to accept the defense that Zambian law did not lay down any upper limit on the gifts the president could accept.[9] The Zambian authorities did not proceed with an appeal against this ruling, but this would mean that what to some might look like kleptocracy does not constitute criminal corruption. Unless one is imposing an objective standard of corruption that disregards the legal requirements of the mental element to prove crime, one presumably should drop such sums from the total in estimates. Such considerations do not appear to be incorporated in the corruption estimates embodied in the governance indicators developed by Kaufmann (2005) or others. To focus only on criminal corruption or laundering cases that have passed through the final stages of appeal would be too strict a test. On the other hand, to allow anyone to impose their own judgment of whether any given conduct was corrupt would likely generate many different estimates without any clear way of adjudicating among them. This is not an appropriate place to rehearse corruption definitions, but depending on whether or not the private sphere is included in the victim category, corruption might be *the use of illegal means for private gain at public expense* or *the misuse of public trust or authority in private enterprises or nonprofit organizations.*

Sums transferred might be referred to as funds rather than bribes to express the possibility that large tranches of profit might arise (1) from transfers for fictitious or partly fictitious goods and services (that is, false accounting) or (2) from undervalue privatizations (including land sales) to nominees of the officials or to apparently independent third parties as part of patron-client relationships. Noncash payments could take many forms, including (1) electronic funds, which are less anonymous than cash because, excepting some prepaid cards for which there is no serious know-your-customer effort, they leave audit trails; (2) jewels, real estate, vehicles, and so on regulated under the European Union's third anti–

money laundering directive and other legislation; or (3) education or health payments to family and friends, which can be substantial and can be paid from corporate or third-party funds, usually overseas. An important question is what proportion of bribes is retained internally (from domestic sources) or imported (from external sources); conversely, what proportion is exported (from domestic sources) and retained overseas without being imported (from external sources)? Unfortunately, data are unavailable to examine this, and it is unclear what proxies could defensibly be used instead.

It is conventional to start with a discussion of the extent to which the proceeds of corruption are laundered, but, because the issue is dealt with elsewhere in this volume, I make only cursory reference here. Thus, Goredema and Madzima (2009), Chaikin and Sharman (2009), and Shaxson (2011) reiterate the estimated global figure of US$1 trillion in bribes, which itself derives from Baker (2005) and Kaufmann (2005).[10] This figure is at risk of becoming a "fact" by repetition, but, irrespective of arguments about its validity, the numbers are big enough to matter to developing countries. Most of it may well go to routine low-level bribes, incidental to the hazards of everyday interactions with officials in many poor countries; these rarely lead to a demand for money laundering services, but simply help to finance the modest daily lives of low-level officials. It is the high-level corruption that is salient to AML measures.

It is often asserted that large sums have been exported by kleptocratic public officials, but much smaller sums are usually detected in overseas accounts, and even smaller sums are recovered. This is true even if no deals are done, as they were with the Abacha family, thereby allowing family members to keep many millions, while they agreed to return larger sums to the national treasuries (see Maton and Daniel's chapter 13, in this volume). Some of the attrition may result from sophistication in the layering of beneficially owned corporate secrecy vehicles, as well as from inadequacies or corruption in the pursuit of the money trail. In addition to secrecy over the value of exports in the extractive industries, cases in different parts of the world indicate that the nontransparency of contracts in the security and intelligence areas offers great scope for corruption and the nondetection of corruption in the awarding of contracts both for goods and for protection services, overriding whatever normal internal audit controls may exist (Daniel and Maton 2008; Salonga 2000;

Wrong 2000, 2009). The same is true of the privatization of public assets at below value.[11] The 18 contracts that were awarded by the Kenyan government to Anglo-Leasing totaled US$751 million (Wrong 2009). Many of the contracts were for illusory supplies, but the literature does not discuss what proportion of the bribes (or the marginal difference between the purchase price and the proper market price) reached the domestic parties locally.[12]

Some definitional discussion may be helpful in illuminating the dimensions of the phenomenon. There are at least two significantly different ways in which people use the term *money laundering*. The first way refers to the act of hiding the illicit origins of funds so as to make tainted wealth look sufficiently legitimate to withstand significant scrutiny (which it may never receive). This plausibly is what most people who encounter the term would expect money laundering to mean. The second way refers to the act of acquiring, possessing, using, or disposing of the proceeds of crime and covers all acts that fall within the criminal laws and regulations against money laundering. These laws and regulations are intentionally framed broadly to stimulate business, finance, and the professions to develop and report their suspicions, thereby making it more difficult for criminals to legitimize their wealth in the first sense above. It also penalizes broadly defined self-laundering by those who commit the primary money-generating crimes (in this case, giving, receiving, or extorting bribes, locally and transnationally) to such an extent that almost anything the offenders do with the proceeds constitutes laundering. This can generate some legal complexities if, as is common in developing and many developed countries, successful mutual legal assistance and prosecution depend on an act being criminal in both countries in which the money laundering process occurs.[13]

A figure one might consider using is the total assets available for asset recovery, which would be a combination of the saved proceeds of corruption, the total value of the contract (under English law, for example), and the criminal and regulatory fines imposed on the financial intermediaries (though such fines are not usually available as compensation for the developing country). Here, to avoid confusion, we examine only the total proceeds of corruption. We divide these into *PC (E)*, representing the total paid and stored or spent outside the developing country, and *PC (I)*, representing the total internally stored or spent, though *PC (I)* may originally have been paid externally. *PC (I)* might be anticipated to vary positively with the desire and the expectation of kleptocrats to remain in power and need the funds so stored to sustain political and military support.

One component of the AML regime involves steps to prevent people from integrating the proceeds of crime into the legitimate economy; though this may act as a deterrent to the involvement of people in crime or shorten the length of criminal careers, it may also prevent people from "going legit" (becoming actually respectable rather than only apparently respectable). It is a tenable explicit policy aim to show criminals that, however much they may reform, they can never enjoy the fruits of their crimes, including the fruits derived from legitimate investments made possible through crime (the doctrine of the fruit of the poisoned tree). This would nullify the personal ambition to become socially integrated of persons such as the bankruptcy fraudster who was interviewed by Levi (2008) and observed that he only wanted to make enough money to be able to afford to be honest.[14] The netting out of harms lies outside the scope of this chapter, but the interviews conducted for this report with a convenience sample of public officials in some developing countries (including countries in the former Soviet ambit) since 1988 suggest that some of the officials are privately ambivalent about whether it is a bad thing to accept tainted funds into their economies. Such thoughts might invite negative reactions if expressed in official meetings and are normally suppressed for that reason.[15] Irrespective of personal greed and benefits, politicians may obtain political and social credit from inward investment, whatever the source of the funds, if it creates employment and a multiplier effect from expenditure. In major financial centers in the developed world, it is difficult to acknowledge inflows of criminal funds as an acceptable economic benefit, and the OECD Anti-Bribery Convention expressly excludes economic interests as justifications for not prosecuting transnational bribery.

Informal value transfer systems, including *hawala*-type money movements, have received some significant interest, especially post-9/11 (Passas 2005; Rees 2010).[16] Most of this interest has focused on the transmission of terrorist finance to operational sites from Muslims in developing and developed countries and on terrorist finance and the proceeds of organized crime remittances from developed countries to developing countries. However, the significance of informal value transfer systems for the proceeds of corruption has received scant attention. Perhaps this is because grand corruption payments from multinationals seem unlikely to be sent in this way—though there is no reason, in principle, why they cannot be so sent—and partly because they seem an implausible conduit for payment into the large international banks in the West on which the substantial legal actions and popular protests have focused. There is no evidence from published investigations such as the case of the French Elf-Aquitaine frigates purchased by Taiwan, China, and similar cases in which informal transfer channels have been used (beyond the cash smuggled in diplomatic bags and containers or on private planes). Large corporations would have to unlaunder the money, turning it from white to black money, prior to sending it over informal channels (as they might also have to do with cash bribes). To the extent that informal value transfer is unattractive for grand corruption, its significance for money laundering generally is reduced.

One reason this area is important is the fact that, to maintain power, corrupt leaders may have to engage in patron-client deals to purchase support locally or regionally (Wrong 2000). There is no motive, in principle, why such formal or informal political funding should have to come from the money laundering circuit in the developed or the financial haven world. What can we learn from cases such as Abacha, Marcos, Mobutu, Montesinos, and Suharto about this local distribution and about the extent to which the existence of local FIU regimes and legislation targeting the proceeds of crime might be drivers for international outflows of corrupt finance now or in the future? Logically, for the internal proceeds of corruption regimes to drive funds to leave countries because these countries reject accounts or actively share information, the regimes would have to be more draconian than the regimes existing in money centers elsewhere.[17]

This chapter focuses on the flows of corrupt funds into and circulating around developing countries, rather than the more usual issue of estimates of the amount of money stored overseas in major financial centers. One component is the question of how funds obtained through corruption are spent. This has not received much systematic attention in research; the inference in high-profile cases is that corrupt funds are spent on affluent lifestyles in the West, including homes and so on, and are stored in American, British, and Swiss banks as a part of a strategy, presumably, to avoid confiscation should there be an unfriendly regime change at home. However, because many regimes involve political clientelism, it seems likely that some of the funds, even if they originate in Western financial institutions, are recycled domestically in developing countries (Warutere 2006; Wrong 2000, 2009; ongoing allegations in Nigeria). Although Mobutu (like other high-living suspect African, Asian, Caribbean, and Latin American leaders) undoubtedly required a great deal of money to purchase and maintain properties overseas, Wrong (2000) makes a convincing case that he was more interested in power than in money. Mobutu needed large amounts of cash in what is now the Democratic Republic of Congo, as well as the ability to confer well-remunerated government posts on the *grands légumes* (big vegetables: the elite) who sought to feed at his table without actually doing anything other than not opposing him. The redistributed bribes gave Mobutu the ability to defuse threats and monitor and act effectively against internal abuses by potentially rival rent seekers.

It may be hypothesized that some institutional variables may affect the relationship between financial institutions and the vulnerability to corruption, though a report of the Eastern and Southern Africa Anti–Money Laundering Group discusses the variables as a static preordained classification rather than as a dynamic process that can change over time and place.[18] It seems plausible that an additional cultural-personality variable is whether the bribe recipients are—in the typology of the Knapp Commission investigation into police corruption in New York in 1973—meat-eaters (actively in search of rent-seeking opportunities) or merely grass-eaters (passively accepting the bribes offered to them).

Another important dimension of the visibility of the corruption-laundering link is the origin of the corrupt funds. Large blocks of funds from bribes in the awarding of large contracts to transnational corporations might be more visible than smaller, more frequent insider contracts to non–arm's-length companies. Import monopolies or privileges among family members or party members might be one important route for rent seeking. There might, however, be nothing wrong, on the surface at least, with the awarding of national or transnational contracts to the relatives of senior public officials directly or through companies that may be known to be associated with such officials or more obscurely held.[19] Whereas, in other cases, bribes, shares, or charitable donations may be given in return for permission to engage unmolested in illegal enterprises such as drug trafficking, and these bribes may sometimes, ultimately, help finance terrorism, as in Afghanistan (U.S. Senate 2009), the privileges assigned to family members as in the cases described above may, at the other ideological extreme, merely finance conspicuous consumption, private education (schools and universities), and health care overseas. How and in what countries and currencies are the latter paid for? A typology is proposed by the Eastern and Southern Africa Anti–Money Laundering Group (see table 12.1).

This typology leaves out the fact that financial institutions may simply be afraid of or feel loyal to the national leadership—who may belong to the same ethnic group—and may benefit from the trickle down symbolized by the first part of the title of Wrong's book (2009) *It's Our Turn to Eat: The Story of a Kenyan Whistle-Blower*. Therefore, the bank may continue to launder money for its friends or may avoid doing so out of a fear of capricious closure or other economic detriment caused by those in power.

This typology also assumes that the financial institution has detected the laundering (or is in a position to do so with modest effort). If the

Table 12.1. Vulnerabilities in Financial Intermediation

Category	Characteristics of a financial intermediation institution	Comment
A	The institution involved is corrupt from inception.	The institution is primed to be a vehicle for money laundering; its use to launder the proceeds of crime is thus inevitable.
B	The institution is corrupted by subsequent changes in ownership or management or in the operating environment.	Although not at first intended to be a vehicle for money laundering, it eventually drifts in that direction.
C	The institution has corrupt employees who provide money laundering on an ad hoc and noninstitutionalized basis.	The institution could be separated from the corrupt employees.
D	The institution unwittingly facilitates money laundering because it has no mechanisms to detect money laundering.	Although the institution may not benefit from money laundering, it sabotages the AML system.

Source: Goredema and Madzima 2009.

funds are prelaundered by placement in a real business venture (rather than a shell company, the beneficial ownership of which may not be transparent), then how they may be identified as proceeds of corruption or any other form of crime is not obvious. This is yet another note of caution: it would be unwise to assume that the within-country identification of the proceeds of corruption is easy whether the country is a poor one or a rich one. It may be that the families of corrupt politicians in developing countries find it easier than corresponding families in rich countries to integrate the proceeds of corruption (including political and economic extortion) into their businesses. This issue will require more analysis.

Alternatively, one might adapt Levi's typology (2008) of bankruptcy (and other) frauds to the involvement of individuals and businesses in money laundering. The typology is as follows:

- Preplanned frauds, in which the business scheme is set up from the start as a way of defrauding victims (businesses, the public sector, individuals)
- Intermediate frauds, in which people start out obeying the law, but consciously turn to fraud later
- Slippery-slope frauds, in which deceptions spiral out of control, often in the context of trying—however absurdly and overoptimistically— to rescue an essentially insolvent business or set of businesses, thereby escalating the losses of creditors

By analogy, some schemes are set up principally for the placement, layering, or integration of the proceeds of crime; some existing businesses knowingly hire themselves out or are pressured into selling out to would-be launderers; and others drift into occasional part-time laundering by assisting large corporations or full-time criminal enterprises if they need the business to keep going, but never intending to become full-time launderers. Given the absence of systematic data collection and the low probability that laundering schemes will be detected and acted against, it is plausible that intermediate and slippery-slope laundering will occur more often during economic downturns. In short, the motivation to defraud and the motivation to launder are heterogeneous rather than a single phenomenon.

Situational opportunity models of corruption

It is illuminating to examine the different conditions under which situational opportunities for corruption are created and exploited. Public corruption cases typically involve either (1) a legal or natural person outside the government (the corruptor) who pays a person inside the government (a corrupt PEP) in exchange for a government benefit, or (2) a PEP who (with or without active collusion) embezzles public funds. In the second type, corruptors outside the government are not usually involved in the scam, though they may set up corporate or other non-transparent vehicles and act as bankers or other types of value transferors. The price extracted for the corrupt benefit may be modest in the view of the corruptor, but significant in the view of the recipient, or it may be significant for both. The potential funds transfers are a function of this and other expenditures. The development of land for tourism—the alleged source of corruption that, not for the first time, led to the suspension of local government in the Turks and Caicos Islands and has been the subject of a major criminal investigation by the U.K. government (Auld 2009)—may generate substantial rewards for all parties, though only if the infrastructure actually is developed.[20]

Gordon (2009) argues that, in almost all grand corruption cases, the corrupt proceeds are already within the financial system at the time of their generation (that is, no cash is involved), while, in two cases, much of the proceeds may not have been in cash. This is not surprising given that the sources of corrupt proceeds are primarily kickbacks on government contracts and bribes to receive a government benefit. The corruptor might therefore normally be a businessperson who receives the government benefit in the form of checks or wire transfers directly from the state. If—before or after the award of the contract, depending on the level of trust and other factors—the corrupt government contractor withdraws cash and transfers it to a corrupt PEP, this would break the chain of bank records connecting the two. However, a new problem is generated because the corrupt PEP may be required to deposit cash back into the financial system. If the problems associated with this redeposit of cash by the corrupt PEP are considered to outweigh the benefits of breaking the chain of financial records, the PEP and the "donors" often attempt to mask their association with the funds by hiding the identity of the beneficiary.[21] The donor—who may be at risk of being discovered by prosecutors because of offenses connected with the OECD Anti-Bribery Convention—and the corrupt PEP need to (1) hide the ownership and control of the assets, (2) disguise the fact that the assets are illegitimate, or (3) do both. One of the most effective ways of accomplishing this is to interpose accounts under different names or separate legal persons or other secrecy vehicles or between the origin of the illegal funds and the ultimate control by the corrupt PEP. Alternatively expressed, the successful corruptor simply utilizes the benefit granted to him (for example, contract, franchise, license, permit, and so on) in a legal way, including tax payments that lawful tax planning requires, while the corrupted official (or bribe-demander) may receive benefits the legitimacy of which will appear dubious if a serious, high-quality investigation occurs and must therefore launder the benefits or have them prelaundered. Of course, if the corrupted (or extorting) official is bypassed because the briber pays the official's associates or political supporters on the official's behalf, then the connection with the corrupt benefit may be difficult to prove.

We now consider case studies of grand corruption, irrespective of whether or not the AML framework might have made a significant contribution to the prevention, investigation, prosecution, or recovery of the proceeds. To the extent that the AML framework lacks utility, our understanding of the conditions under which the framework is or is not effective may need to be nuanced.

Case studies

The Montesinos case offers an unusual amount of insight because of the video recordings systematically made by Montesinos and recaptured (and retransmitted on television to a fascinated public). A valuable study on Peru by Dumas (2007, 3) notes as follows:

> It was estimated that during Fujimori's administration more than US$2 billion were stolen from the state, a figure equal to nearly 9 percent of Peru's current stock of external public debt. A total of US$1 billion is believed to have been sent overseas, while Montesinos alone is suspected to have amassed a fortune worth US$800 million.

Dumas focuses on the US$1 billion believed to have been sent overseas, of which US$184 million had been repatriated at that time (mostly from Cayman Islands, Switzerland, and the United States), while a further US$56 million had been frozen. The fate of the missing US$1 billion estimated to have been looted, but not sent abroad, is not discussed explicitly, nor can it be deduced readily from the data. Dumas (2007, 7) clarifies as follows:

> Through bribery and extortion, Montesinos was able to capture the Judiciary, the Media and the Legislature. . . . the average bribe given to a Supreme Court and Superior Court judge was between US$5,000 and US$10,000 a month. Members of the print media received initial payments as high as US$1.5 million, and also requested additional sums for manipulating headlines ($3,000–4,000), and stories on the inside pages ($5,000). The television media received bribes that ranged between US$2 [million] and US$9 million. Fujimori undermined all checks and balances and was able to concentrate executive, legislative and judiciary powers in himself. The manipulation of the press and the capture of other watchdog groups within civil society further reduced Fujimori's public accountability.

If bribes were collected within Peru, the cash was transformed into bearer certificates (now almost unavailable anywhere because of ex post FATF pressure), which were then given to Montesinos. As the custodian of the certificates, Montesinos would use a local bank to wire the certificates to a foreign bank that would remit monies to a financial haven or acquire assets abroad (see figure 12.1). If this were to happen today, it would arouse concerns or SARs from compliance officers because the funds so exceeded Montesinos's known income and wealth. Given his control over the state apparatus, however, reporting might have proved hazardous for the bankers (and might have been considered dangerous by them), and successful action against Montesinos would have been extremely unlikely at that time.

Inbound laundering operations greatly benefited from a domestic law, the Repatriation of Foreign Currency Act, that came into force in 1988 in the context of balance of payments difficulties. This law allowed the repatriation of foreign currency without tax and information requirements. Using different legislative measures, Fujimori kept this practice legal and, so, facilitated the repatriation of illegal funds for the purpose of election campaign financing and the bribing of judges, members of Congress, and the mainstream media.

Figure 12.1. The Case of Montesinos: Laundering Maneuvers if Monies Were Collected in Peru

Cash ⟹ Local banks

Bank transformed cash into certificates issued to the bearer.

Assets were acquired for money laundering purposes.

Vladimiro Montesinos ⟹ Foreign banks

Montesinos kept custody of the certificates.

Montesinos transferred certificates to foreign bank through a local bank.[a]

Monies were remitted to financial havens.

Financial haven

Source: Dumas 2007.

a. In Peru, Banco de Comercio handled over US$220 million in transfers for Montesinos.

The Philippine literature tends to focus more on the international than on the internal aspects, but Briones (2007, 10) summarizes it well when she observes that "a part of the Marcos ill-wealth stayed in the Philippines and included corporations which were acquired on his behalf by his cronies, land, machinery, etc." One might add that trust enables beneficial ownership to be disguised more easily, especially if this is achieved by noncompetitive tendering. The Marcoses might have had to rely on their network's informal sanctions and friendships to secure benefits in the event of their fall from power. One anonymous source has observed to this author that Imelda Marcos has experienced significant difficulty in resuming control of assets placed in the hands of some nominees: one of the problems of using clandestine laundering methods. In the event, Briones states, the assets taken domestically from the Marcos network—mainly by sequestering 69 beneficially owned corporations—totaled US$11.8 billion, though this figure may relate only to assets frozen rather than sequestered.[22]

An indicator of the size of the assets taken by Marcos is the fact that the Agrarian Reform Program of the Philippines is funded in part from the illicit gains of the Marcos regime. According to an unpublished 2010 report of the Philippine Institute of Development Studies, approximately ₱74.5 billion was recovered over the period 1987–2008 by the Presidential Commission on Good Government, that is, US$1.6 billion has been recovered in total. Given that this figure includes at least US$600 million recovered from Swiss accounts, this would mean that less than US$1 billion has been recovered from domestic sources.

Gordon (2009) has generated some 21 case studies on corruption. Of these, we have excluded from our examination all developed-country cases and, with the partial exception of the Salinas case (discussed below), those cases in which payments were primarily made to offshore accounts and in which there is no evidence (in Gordon or elsewhere) that significant funds were reimported. Thus, if a bribe-payer sets up a foreign credit card that is used to pay the expenditures of a kleptocrat overseas (as was alleged in relation to Swiss accounts of former Russian President Yeltsin), we exclude the case as irrelevant, though some of the purchases may be physically imported into developing countries. Our aim is not merely to demonstrate corruption laundering mechanisms, but also to analyze bribes and laundering that may or may not have been detected and acted against.

It is important to think of AML as a dynamic process over time. If an AML system is having any effect, then bribe-payers and bribe-takers or bribe-demanders will adapt their modes of laundering to changes in the methods of control. As in the areas discussed elsewhere above, one may wonder what has changed other than risk aversion, which is generating a growing preference for corporate vehicles as intermediaries. The number of PEPs reported on to FIUs is not disclosed in public reports, so we do not know if this subcategory is an exception to Takats's (2007) economic model of a rising trend in defensive SAR disclosures. We return to this topic below.

The cases below are adapted from Gordon (2009). In some of the cases (for example, the funds given by Japanese donors to Apenkai, a charitable foundation, for the rebuilding of Peru), the moneys appear to have simply been stolen by Fujimori factions after they had been handed over to the Embassy of Peru in Japan and passed on to Apenkai.

Case 1. When he was president of Nicaragua, Arnoldo Aleman misappropriated millions in public funds for his personal benefit, as well as for the benefit of his family and associates. Many of the officers in his cabinet were his close personal friends and assisted in the theft and laundering of state funds. Most of the funds that Aleman misappropriated were funneled through the Nicaraguan Democratic Foundation (FDN), a nonprofit organization incorporated in Panama by Aleman and his wife.

The Nicaraguan Directorate of Income was headed by Byron Jerez, a close friend of Aleman. He set up a system whereby ENITEL, the main public telecommunications company, would pay for the operation of the directorate. A number of shell and real companies set up by friends of Aleman provided the necessary goods and services. As compensation for this expenditure, ENITEL received a tax benefit equal to the amount expended. ENITEL transferred funds to the shell companies, which had opened bank accounts for their accounts receivable. From there, these companies transferred the funds to a consultancy firm, and eventually the funds were transferred to the FDN.

ENITEL also guaranteed a loan to a state-owned insurance company. These funds were later transferred to an account of the Ministry of the Presidency; under Nicaraguan law, the funds could be spent at the complete discretion of the president. The president invested the money in a company controlled by Jerez and his wife. This entity also received funds from a secret account of the Nicaraguan Treasury set up by the director of the Treasury; these funds were then donated to a nonprofit organization controlled by Aleman and his wife and subsequently donated to the FDN.

The state agency in charge of privatization also funneled funds from winning bids into the FDN, as did the state-owned Channel 6 station. At a low price, the government sold a telecommunications frequency to a company controlled by Aleman associates. The sale was financed using funds from Channel 6, which gave a fake commercial rationale for the origins of the money. Aleman used the FDN to pay for the personal credit cards of himself and his family. The FDN also purchased a building and then transferred the title to a company controlled by Arnold Aleman. Finally, the FDN gave a loan to a company owned by Aleman and his associates that held many of Aleman's real estate purchases, and the loan was never called in.

These are all examples of the embezzlement of public assets, but they also represent methods of laundering the proceeds from the thefts via commercial entities in the reasonable expectation that no one would be attempting seriously to oppose the conduct. It seems unlikely that these actions would have been picked up by an AML process, though a competent tracking investigation did eventually detect them.

Case 2. Upon the election of his brother as president of Mexico, Raul Salinas was appointed to several positions, one of which was to manage Conasupo, a store set up to sell basic goods to the underprivileged at subsidized prices. Raul Salinas used this position to create disguised profits that he diverted to himself, often by reporting prices for Conasupo's purchases that were higher than the sums actually paid or by selling subsidized products at market rates. In one case, at an extremely low price, Conasupo imported 39,000 tons of powdered milk contaminated at Chernobyl and then sold the milk to the poor at a profit. In another case, corn provided by the United States for distribution to the poor was sold by Conasupo at market rates; the corn was made into tortillas and sold back to the United States. The hidden profits were then transferred to personal accounts in Mexican banks.

Raul may also have profited by financing winning bids during privatization. An example of this was the government sale of Azteca Television to Ricardo Salinas Pliego through Salinas Associates. Profits from Azteca were used to make payments to Raul, which Pliego claimed were repayments on a loan Raul had made to him to finance the acquisition. The loan was provided at a suspiciously low interest rate.

To show that there had been a loan and that the payments were not kickbacks, Raul made payments from his account to finance the loan, in effect showing he was only an intermediary. Raul would deposit the funds into Mexican banks. Then his wife, Paulina, acting under the alias of Patricia Rios, would withdraw the funds and transport them to a Mexican branch of Citibank. This money would be transferred into a mass concentration account used by Citibank to transmit internal funds. A vice-president at the Mexican Division of Citibank would then extract these funds from the concentration account and transfer them to London and Switzerland to Citibank accounts of Trocca, a shell corporation formed by Cititrust in Cayman Islands and controlled by Raul through nominees.

Raul Salinas may have used his influence over two banking groups, Grupo Financiero Probursa and Grupo Finaciero Serfin, both purchased from the Salinas government during privatization, to convince them not to apply extended (or indeed any) due diligence to accounts controlled by him and his confederates. In any event, under current rules that require identification only of foreign and not domestic PEPs, he would not have been classified as a PEP by a domestic bank, and it is implausible that domestic regulators or prosecutors would, in that era, have taken action against bankers for failing to conduct AML actions in relation to Raul's businesses.

Case 3. Joseph Ejercito Estrada served as vice president to Fidel Ramos and then as president of the Philippines. He began his term on June 30, 1998, but was ousted in less than three years, having been accused of amassing over US$11 million in kickbacks from illegal gambling and tobacco excise taxes. Proceeds from these kickbacks were allegedly used to finance companies formed to purchase real estate for Estrada.

One of these companies was allegedly St. Peter's Holdings, which was 99.8 percent owned by Jose Luis Yulo, the former president of the Philippine Stock Exchange and a close associate of Estrada. On October 6, 1999, a ₱142 million check was allegedly drawn from an account of Velarde, a friend of Estrada at Equitable PCI Bank, and deposited into Yulo's personal account at the Bank of Philippine Islands branch. Yulo then withdrew ₱50,000 from his account to open a corporate account for St. Peter's Holdings, where he later deposited the ₱142 million. St. Peter's Holdings purchased the Boracay Mansion in New Manila, Quezon City, for ₱86 million. The home was then used by Laarni Enriquez, allegedly one of Estrada's mistresses. Yulo also executed three cashier's checks made payable, one, for ₱86,766,960.00, to Vicente AS Madrigal (a former senator and power industrialist whose daughter currently serves in the Senate) and two others. The St. Peter's Holdings bank account only had ₱2,000–₱5,000 after the ₱142 million transaction. It is not clear if or how illicit funds were acquired by Velarde to make payments to Yulo's account.

Estrada allegedly acquired over 18,500 square meters of real estate in luxury subdivisions, as well as other valuable property using similar transactions through other corporate vehicles. On the other hand, he did not appear to engage in the massive development contract corruption schemes that were a noted feature of the Marcos regime.

Case 4. Following the election of the Workers Party candidate Luiz Inácio Lula da Silva as president of Brazil, the government attempted to solidify its power in the legislature, where it did not have a working majority. To accomplish this, it allegedly began paying certain legislators an amount that eventually reached around US$12,000 per month. To finance some of these payments, senior Workers Party leaders allegedly contacted Marcos Valerio, a wealthy Brazilian businessman, to assist in making the payments. In exchange for a sham contract from the Brazilian government for his advertising firm, SMP&B, Valerio was asked to guarantee a loan made to the Workers Party by Bank BMG. The Workers Party defaulted on this loan, and Valerio paid the loan with funds from SMP&B, creating a kickback payment from Valerio to the Workers Party. Cash payments were then made from the party directly to legislators.

Comments on the cases. These cases illustrate the variety of ways that regimes generate corrupt moneys and use them internally, including—in Estrada's case and in other cases about which the risk of suit for defamation induces caution—local property, suggesting that the perceived danger of subsequent sequestration was low. Leaders and extended family or clan members may also enjoy and want to be seen to enjoy a higher standard of living within their own countries (though this does not emerge in the case studies above). Also, though infrequently, the cases show the drip-feed of funds for local patronage. Wrong's account (2000) of the Mobutu regime and the ever-increasing number of grands légumes whom Mobutu found expedient to buy off and neutralize expresses this particularly vividly. Given the investigations and prosecutions in France relating to deal making in recent decades, it would be a mistake to view patron-client relationships and their corrupt manifestations as a feature restricted to developing countries; nor is a developing country necessarily prone to heavy corruption and such relationships. It is important to analyze carefully what an AML regime would require in developing and developed countries (including parallel cross-country investigations) to identify such activities and engage in appropriate preventive or criminal enforcement actions. It must be emphasized that the integrity and confidentiality of national FIUs, though important, is not sufficient for a system to work. There must also be confidence among potential SAR-writers that information will not leak to those on whom they are reporting or to their allies. The risk of the use of personal violence by kleptocratic regimes is real both against those who submit SARs and any investigators and prosecutors who are not corrupt.

Accounting for the Lack of Impact

It is not only in the rich world that strategic approaches have been applied to address serious crimes. Governance issues have been significant among development activists for some time. Corruption and the related financing and financial consequences have ascended the ladder of political attention in the 21st century, exemplified by the more active profile of the OECD Working Group on Bribery in International Business Transactions and by development of the UNCAC, now in force. Nonetheless, until recent G-20 pronouncements and the Seoul Action Plan 2010 and the follow-up in 2011, there has been comparatively little talk, at least in the developed world, about the need for a war on corruption and only a modest, though increasing focus among official mainstream AML bodies on the role that AML can play in combating corruption (FATF 2010). Stimulated by nongovernmental organizations such as Transparency International and Global Witness, as well as a succession of major scandals, greater attention has been focused on the role of major offshore financial centers in laundering the proceeds of grand corruption, as intermediary transit points in concealing bribes, or as the site of accounts held by or on behalf of kleptocrats.[23] Prior to the development of a variety of scandal-driven regulations introducing PEP regimes, offshore financial centers offered two advantages to corrupt public servants and to their (official and unofficial) families with respect to the deposit and long-term storage of large sums of money: (1) trustworthiness toward their clients and (2) a studied lack of interest in the origins of the capital. The new AML regime should have removed the latter advantage by making it difficult for people to store and transform the proceeds of corruption (and other crimes) without risky, active criminal conspiracy by financiers, which might be detected by regulators or criminal investigators (police or anticorruption officials) in their own countries or elsewhere. Other chapters in this volume deal with the extent to which this may still be the case.

However, the discussions among nongovernmental organizations on grand corruption and AML have understandably focused exclusively on the role of financial institutions in the developed world in holding the accounts of PEPs and failing adequately to scrutinize outgoing bribe payments and the incoming proceeds of bribery. Partly because of this political pressure and partly because of the way that corruption has been conceptualized as a poor-to-rich country process of capital flight, the public and professional debate has focused exclusively on the laundering links between rich and poor countries, the bribes paid by companies based in the former to leaders in the latter, and the return of the bribe money to financial institutions or as investments in rich countries. In this process, laundering that is largely internal to the poor world has been neglected. Indeed, this is implicit in the way that most poor (and rich) countries define PEPs: most include only foreign, not domestic, public officials, and few include subnational politicians, the military, the police, and so on, though the rent-seeking capacities of these may be great (see Chaikin and Sharman 2009, for a critical review of such legal differences). According to the current FATF definition, PEPs are individuals who are or have been entrusted with prominent public functions in a foreign country, for example, heads of state or of government, senior politicians, senior government, judicial, or military officials, senior executives of state-owned corporations, or important political party officials. Business relationships with family members or close associates of PEPs involve reputational risks similar to those with PEPs. The definition is not intended to cover middle-ranking or more junior individuals in the foregoing categories. Thus, although poor countries are expected, almost required, to have AML legislation and FIUs, their financial institutions and other regulated bodies are not expected to pay extra due diligence to their own de facto and de jure political leadership, who are precisely the people most likely to be corrupt.[24]

Whatever the legal requirements may be, international financial institutions generally use commercially compiled global lists such as World-Check or LexisNexis, and these include relatives and associates of PEPs.[25] Many FIUs, at least in jurisdictions that can afford the commercial fees, also use these. However, such lists do not include companies of which PEPs are undisclosed beneficial owners, nor do many countries assist by publishing lists of all government officeholders on the Internet or even in print. This has not been an internal priority for countries, nor—at least until the FATF began to focus recently upon beneficial ownership—has it been the subject of significant pressure from the FATF or the International Monetary Fund–World Bank monitoring process. Neither developed nor developing countries currently collate lists of PEP holdings in their countries (and major international banks claim that this is impracticable), though there is pressure upon them to do so. It would take a major transformation in the current frailties of the global AML system to trap corrupt funds paid in developing countries or to link most bribes paid elsewhere to corrupt public officials through the nominees of these officials.

Analysts of the corruption-laundering nexus typically explain the persistence of the nexus in terms of the following:

- The relative lack of FATF interest in the subject, though this has changed recently
- The lack of passage or implementation of AML legislation on corruption
- Political influence on offices of prosecutors and the judiciary either to prosecute regime opponents and financial institutions or not
- The disconnect between anticorruption and AML bodies that may not even be aware of each other, let alone working cooperatively (ADB and OECD 2007; Chaikin and Sharman 2009; Goredema and Madzima 2009; Sharman and Mistry 2008)

The general theme is missed opportunities for control and what might be needed to generate tougher controls. Thus, Goredema and Madzima point to five countries in the region that have included unexplained wealth provisions in their legislation, but none of which has established a record of enforcement, principally, it is claimed, because the privately held financial data are "not normally within the purview of an anti-corruption agency" (Goredema and Madzima 2009, 26). This leads to recommendations to combine or coordinate FIUs, anticorruption agencies, and similar bodies and to ensure their autonomy from government, though the method by which these aims are to be achieved (and the way in which the unmentioned necessary confidence of financial and other regulated institutions to make reports is to be attained) remains vague. It would be surprising if there were not an inverse relationship between transparency and the exploitation of corrupt opportunities.[26] Under such circumstances, the prospects for the local impact of AML on grand or even mesolevel corruption are poor: the degree of political control (and the democratization of proceeds in terms of the bribery of judicial authorities) might protect corrupt PEPs against serious action.[27] Goredema and Madzima state as follows:

Member countries have generally not adopted the identification and application of enhanced scrutiny of financial transactions linked to Politically Exposed Persons as required by the narrow approach [foreign PEPs only] in the FATF prescriptions or the broad [national, as well as foreign PEPs] prescriptions of the UNCAC. Only [Tanzania] requires reporting institutions to conduct enhanced due diligence of transactions conducted with PEPs. It also requires that such institutions consider the fact that a PEP is based in a country with no AML measures as a red flag. Unfortunately there are no explicit penalties for non-compliance. (Goredema and Madzima 2009, 60)

One might counter that so few countries have no AML measures that this is too generous a baseline. Indirect indicators might be the number of SARs aimed at suspected public officials and activities connected with them and submitted by financial and other regulated institutions within developing countries and the number of developing-country FIUs investigating these SARs or requesting assistance from financial centers overseas. The legal secrecy that (appropriately) surrounds SARs in most jurisdictions makes it difficult for the authorities to demonstrate their impact to skeptical outsiders or, alternatively, for skeptical outsiders to demonstrate that nothing significant is happening. After all, the FIUs cannot, in most circumstances, prosecute PEPs or even regulated persons for failing to implement AML; so, they can argue that it is unfair to blame them or the AML system (narrowly construed) for failures. This raises the question of how one might evaluate the efficiency or effectiveness of AML. In politically sensitive cases, anonymization would be impossible without neutering the value of case studies, but, in principle, there could be some global quantification of flows of requests without risking the identification of the people or institutions submitting SARs.

The Development and Processing of Anti–Money Laundering Suspicions

Under the money laundering recommendations of the FATF, financial Institutions and other regulated bodies must do the following:

- Identify customers (and beneficial owners, if these are different).
- Establish and maintain up-to-date customer profiles.[28]

- Monitor transactions to determine if they match customer profiles.
- If they do not match, examine the transactions to determine if these might represent the proceeds of crimes, including by examining the sources of funds.
- If they do appear to represent the proceeds of crimes, report the transactions to the FIU.

These institutions must apply enhanced due diligence in the case of higher-risk customers (of which PEPs are a required category) and reduced due diligence in the case of lower-risk customers. However, this is not self-implementing; there is much discretion, for example, on how far compliance officers must go to ascertain the identity of beneficial owners.[29] The FATF preventive measures do not describe with any precision at what point in the risk continuum financial institutions should identify transactions as suspicious (a term that, analytically, should be redefined as suspected) and report them; nor is it clear whether financial institutions should report to the FIU those people they decline to accept as customers so as to alert the FIUs. Discussions with compliance officers indicate that they do sometimes turn away PEPs altogether or, if the PEPs have accounts, bar them from particular activities that are viewed as inconsistent with their official roles and incomes. However, many PEPs have access to numerous banks, and barring them from making particular transactions may not be effective overall.[30] PEPs also have local accounts in developing countries, though a developing country may not require institutions to apply enhanced due diligence to national PEPs, at least formally. Little is publicly known about the perceptions of risk among compliance officers and regulators in developing countries.

One of the few clear-cut cases where a SAR has been used by a developing-country FIU to prosecute grand corruption locally occurred in Namibia, which took action against local elites for massive alleged corruption involving the airport security technology firm run by a son of Chinese leader Hu Jintao (see box 12.1).[31]

Although he was not a PEP, another example of success by an AML system in a developing country is the case of Kobi Alexander, wanted by U.S. authorities since 1996 for alleged securities fraud. A Namibian bank report arising from a large transfer into Alexander's recent Namibian account may have triggered his arrest.

Box 12.1 A Suspicious Activity Report Leads to a Transnational Corruption Investigation

According to press reports, the Chinese government gave a loan to Namibia of US$100 million through the Export-Import Bank of China (Exim) for the purchase of scanners for airports in Namibia after a visit by Chinese President Hu Jintao in 2007. The loan was given at a low rate on the condition that the Namibian government subsequently buy the scanner technology from Nuctech under a US$55.3 million contract (although less-expensive options were available from competitors).

It was arranged that the Namibian government would make a down payment of US$12.8 million, and the rest of the contract was financed by Exim. After the down payment had been paid from government coffers, a payment was made by Nuctech to Teko Trading for facilitating the contract. It was alleged that Nuctech had negotiated with Teko Trading to receive 10 percent of the contract if the average price of one scanner was US$2.5 million. If the selling price was over this amount, the company would receive 50 percent of the difference, and a subsequent negotiation fixed the payment for this agreement at the equivalent of the Namibian government's down payment.

According to a report in the New York Times, the scam was discovered "because of a new money laundering law that requires Namibian banks to routinely report large money transfers to investigators."[a] An official from the Windhoek bank implemented the procedure and alerted the Finance Ministry when a large amount was received into the account of Yang Fan, the Chinese Nuctech representative for Africa.

Yang allegedly deposited US$5.3 million into the account of Teko Trading on March 11, 2009. Teko then sent invoices to Nuctech for US$12.8 million, which was the amount of the down payment paid by the Namibian Ministry of Finance. Yang and the Namibian owners of Teko Trading—Teckla Lameck (a public service commissioner) and Jerobeam Mokaxwa—were arrested and charged with corruptly accepting gratification for giving assistance in the procuring of a contract with a public body.[b]

Yang also transferred US$2.1 million into an investment fund, while the other two accused spent large amounts of funds purchasing vehicles and houses. The Namibian court subsequently froze the assets of the accused and US$12.8 million of Nuctech's assets under Namibia's Organized Crime Prevention Act.

a. Wines, M., "Graft Inquiry in Namibia Finds Clues in China," New York Times, July 21, 2009.
b. As of July 2010, the case was still ongoing, but Chinese authorities were reportedly cooperating with the local investigation in Namibia.

A clerk at the Namibian supervisor of banks' office noticed an unusual influx of capital into the country—in fact, tens of millions of dollars—into accounts that Alexander had opened. The clerk thought that suspicious, especially since Alexander was not a resident and had no business contacts in Namibia, and he had only arrived a few days earlier. The clerk lodged a query with Interpol, which contacted the FBI, and the rest is history.[32]

Developing-country reporting bodies and FIUs might theoretically have an effect in any area except external sources and external account deposits. Yet, developed countries almost never receive requests from developing countries on their own domestic PEPs unless PEPs have fallen from political favor.[33] There are few economies similar to Botswana and Hong Kong SAR, China, where the anticorruption regimes are widely claimed to have been a success and where international jurisdictional reputation is high. However, the political conditions of autonomy are rarely appropriate for pursuing elites while they are in power; not even in Hong Kong SAR, China, before (or after) its absorption into China as a special administrative region, where police and administrative corruption were undoubtedly endemic at the time of the formation of the Independent Commission against Corruption, were business and political elites the targets of the enforcement and prevention efforts. Financial investigation powers were probably used against the commission's targets, but the proactive volunteering of suspicions by regulated bodies characteristic of the ideal-typical AML regime was rare at that early period. Rather than being triggered by suspicious activity reports, investigations relied on classic intelligence-led policing operations and the application of financial investigation tools.

There are plausible fears that government knowledge about the wealth and bank holdings of prominent individuals will increase the risk of kidnapping and the levels of extortion in some countries. Banks have made reports to FIUs on leading national politicians, and the information has leaked back to the politicians. Part of the political capital of leaders such as Fujimori of Peru, Mobutu of Zaire, and Suharto of Indonesia was that their intelligence apparatus was omnipresent, and, whatever the formal constitutional status of FIUs, beliefs about the penetration of official bodies are bound to have a chilling effect on AML reporting (and on the audit of institutions within the country), as, indeed, it is intended to have. The need to finance this internal intelligence apparatus and to buy subservience, if not loyalty, demonstrates why not all the proceeds and financing of corruption flow from poor to rich countries: substantial sums may be needed internally to retain power. One expert source has observed that, whereas President Estrada gave contracts and other benefits to a modest number of his media circle, President Marcos, lacking this level of popular support and legitimacy, lavished huge cash sums, as well as contracts on a wider range of potential threats and needed supporters. In environments where economic power is more concentrated and where investigative and criminal justice institutions may be seen to be and may actually be less independent of government than in most (but not all) developed countries, how can police, anticorruption commissions, prosecutors, and judges be expected to deal properly with reports on elites? How can local FIUs in developing countries deal effectively with SARs that are reported to FIUs in developed countries and passed on to authorities in the developing countries for intelligence development? Such action may not be necessary in the developing countries if money laundering charges can be made in developed countries against the foreign PEPs, but prosecutions are not always successful; those undertaken in English courts have been subject to serious delays and difficulties exacerbated at the intersection between the human rights of the defendants and transnational investigative powers.

Conclusion

This chapter represents a difficult venture into an underdeveloped literature on a policy area that has been caught up in a process of permanent expansion over the past two decades. It is clear that the substantial financial proceeds arising from corruption are often retained or even imported into developing countries to pay off political rivals, satisfy obligations to families, friends, and clans, and invest in local businesses and property. The steps necessary so that local AML measures can be used to identify and act against such activities remain somewhat uncertain. If suspicions are communicated to national FIUs or, conceivably, by international banks to foreign FIUs, what could these FIUs plausibly do with the reports if investigators and prosecutors are not truly independent? (In the latter case, it seems unlikely that the kleptocracy would have developed in the first place.) However, the combination of local and foreign investigations running in parallel might yield more than the sum of the two. The inward movement of cash or the corporate and charity vehicles can be a way of bringing funds into, as well as out of, developing countries. Estimating the size of these internal-internal and external-internal flows has not been attempted here.

Key questions remain about the implementation and impact of AML controls in developing countries in relation to corruption and other crimes that depend on corruption. For example, how do AML controls function in environments in which financial institutions and professionals—those expected to submit SARs and cash deposit and transfer reports—may be afraid of leaks reaching powerful private sector and state actors, gain profit from dealings with them, or have relatively few alternative sources of profit?

The Western powers have, arguably, considered AML and its associated legislative infrastructure mainly as a device to ensure mutual legal assistance. Perhaps AML also helps prevent criminal activities from harming developed countries, though the crimes have been thrust on the developing world. (However, within the developing world, there are huge variations in implementation levels and difficulties, as well as in the support for the idea of AML.)[34] The amount of evidence collected systematically is modest, but not only the FATF, but also the FATF-Style Regional Bodies have been encouraged to develop their own money laundering typologies and assess trends in laundering and the impact of controls.[35] Both of these present serious analytical challenges, not least in disentangling the extent to which the visible tip of the crimeberg reflects real changes or merely or mostly investigatory foci. The decision to have a typology on a particular subject (such as the use of the timber trade or e-gambling) can generate a sharper analytical focus among member states that can bring to light issues not formerly addressed. This can create the illusion that there is a trend, but may merely have revealed more of the dark side of this sort of activity. Typologies also present communicative challenges because anonymization can easily render cases unmemorable, defeating the object of the typology. Without a greater understanding of these elements of implementation and impact, it is difficult to gauge the extent to which the continuance of corruption (and other serious crimes for gain, including tax fraud, at least in principle) may be due to theory failure or to implementation failure in the AML regime.

It is arguable that the principal benefit (and perceived benefit) of AML regimes in developing countries is the political and economic acceptance that AML brings, allowing membership in the international economic community, rather than anything more specific. This has to be set against the substantial costs of introducing such regimes in countries poor in human resources. The travel and associated costs of participating in Egmont, FATF-Style Regional Bodies, and so on—often paid for out of aid or budgets for law enforcement assistance—are substantial.

Under certain circumstances, such as the plethora of reforms that followed Montesinos and, to a lesser extent, Marcos, a plausible case can be made that economic benefits outweigh economic costs, but this is rarely the trend in the evidence. Their case studies of Barbados, Mauritius, and Vanuatu led Sharman and Mistry (2008) to express the judgment that the international AML regime has imposed undue costs on small commonwealth (and, by inference, other) jurisdictions. One expert interviewed for this project noted that at least one-fifth of the qualified accountants in Niger were employed in the FIU there, but had little to do. This (and the Malawi and Nauru examples cited elsewhere above) looks like an egregious waste of resources to avoid even more damaging external economic sanctions. Perhaps the Sharman and Mistry analysis took insufficient account of the damage done not only to their case study jurisdictions, but to other jurisdictions as a result of regulatory deficiencies, for example, through the use of corporate secrecy vehicles to commit fraud or grand or meso corruption embezzlement elsewhere. AML, after all, is about reducing global sociopathy in sanitizing the proceeds of crime elsewhere. What does seem clear is that some regimes receive a small proportion of their gross domestic product from fees from the corporate and financial service sector and that maintaining serious AML capability makes this of little net value to a country.

If regimes are to be required to have AML measures in general, the case is undeniable that they should optimize the benefits by using them to combat corruption, especially corruption at a high level. This would require not only better liaison with anticorruption bodies within their own jurisdictions, but also with financial crime investigators and intelligence units abroad, perhaps in parallel or in tandem. Namibia and Nigeria excepted, there do not appear to be any cases in which internal AML reporting in developing countries has led to major cases against in-favor PEPs, but this does not rule out the utility of SARs against out-of-favor PEPs or in accumulating evidence of assets directly or beneficially owned by national or international PEPs. In one middle-income non-OECD country, corruption and fraud-related SARs triggered the prosecution of senior in-favor politicians even though, as national figures, they were not formally classified as PEPs.[36] However, this is a jurisdiction in which confidence in the independence of the FIU and the prosecutorial process is high.

More generally, what is required is to work out the details of how the identification, reporting, investigation, and intervention processes might produce fewer false positives and false negatives and of how the laundering indicators of corruption differ from or resemble those for other offenses. In short, as the example of the Nigerian Economic and Financial Crimes Commission demonstrated (before changes were implemented among key personnel), a vigorous developing-country FIU, combined with an independent investigative and prosecutorial body, can receive SARs from and transmit SARs to foreign countries and use these to investigate corrupt senior figures at home and abroad (Ribadu 2010). However, such examples are rare, especially in the long term, and the impact of AML within developing countries in controlling grand corruption remains limited. The policy implications of this merit further reflection, and, although there are welcome signs that the international community appreciates the need for risk-based resource allocation in poor countries, the transformation of this into AML evaluations requires more subtlety than has been evident to date (de Koker 2009).

Notes

1. "Malawi is not and does not aspire to be an international financial center, nor has it been associated with money laundering or the financing of terrorism. Speaking at an international financial summit in September 2006, the Minister of Economics and Planning recounted how his country had come to adopt the standard package of AML regulations. The Minister was told that Malawi needed an AML policy. The Minister replied that Malawi did not have a problem with money laundering, but was informed that this did not matter. When the Minister asked if the package could be adapted for local conditions he was told no, because then Malawi would not meet international standards in this area. The Minister was further informed that a failure to meet international AML standards would make it harder for individuals and firms in Malawi to transact with the outside world relative to its neighbors, and thus less likely to attract foreign investment. The Minister concluded: 'We did as we were told'; the country adopted the standard package of AML policies." (Sharman 2008, 651)

2. A parallel argument could be made about mutual legal assistance treaties, including extradition.

3. The national proceeds of crime confiscation schemes vary. The most common are postconviction schemes that either (a) require offenders who wish to retain assets to show that the assets have been acquired legitimately for value or (b) require the prosecution to prove that the specific assets have been illicitly acquired by the convicted persons. The latter was the conventional approach until the 1990s. However, there are, additionally, civil forfeiture–asset recovery schemes that require proof that assets have been illicitly acquired only on a balance of probabilities test. These include some, primarily, common law jurisdictions in the developed world such as Australia, Ireland, the United Kingdom, and the United States, but also legislation of the newly established AML regimes of developing countries, such as Lesotho, Namibia, and South Africa.

4. The lifestyle of the grand corrupt (and other offenders) may excite admiration and emulation (as well as fear and hatred) even if their savings are confiscated or frozen.

5. Kaira, C., and V. Wessels, "Namibian Firm Formed by Ex-Comverse Chief Alexander," *Jerusalem Post*, February 26, 2007, http://www.jpost.com/Home/Article.aspx?id=52744.

6. It should be borne in mind that threshold reporting sums such as US$10,000 or €15,000, which are modest in rich countries, may represent large sums in poor ones.

7. This is not merely a question of the perception of corruption within the FIU (the police are often mistrusted in developing countries); it is also a question of whether the FIU can be trusted to be discreet if reports are submitted on PEPs or local business elites.

8. A White House press release (2010, 1) nicely expresses the issues, as follows:

> Under the Action Plan, G-20 Leaders agreed to lead by example in key areas, including: to accede or ratify and effectively implement the UNCAC and promote a transparent and inclusive review process; adopt and enforce laws against the bribery of foreign public officials; prevent access of corrupt officials to the global financial system; consider a cooperative framework for the denial of entry to corrupt officials, extradition, and asset recovery; protect whistleblowers; and safeguard anticorruption bodies.

9. The acquittal of Chiluba was appealed by the prosecutor, but the Zambian government of the time (defeated in the 2011 elections) dismissed the prosecutor and withdrew the appeal for undisclosed reasons. It also declined to enforce an order against Chiluba and others in the London High Court for the return of US$46 million in stolen funds. (See *Attorney General of Zambia for and on behalf of the Republic of Zambia (Claimant)* and *Meer Care & Desai (a firm) & Ors [2007] EWHC 952.*) In 2011, Chiluba died, and the future of these funds remains uncertain despite the change in government.

10. Kaufmann notes that the range is US$600 billion–US$1.5 trillion; so, US$1 billion is (almost) at midpoint. The methodology is set out in his appendix.

11. One of the common mistakes is to equate the losses arising from corrupt contracts with the bribes (and the sums laundered therefrom). Logically, the bribe-payer's income and the bribe recipient's income both count as proceeds of corruption. So, in the context of this chapter, it is what happens to the profits and where the funds are disbursed and distributed that count.

12. Technically, under some legislative systems, such as in England and Wales, the entire purchase price constitutes the proceeds of corruption and is liable to postconviction confiscation. However, analytically, such sums are not available in bribes and certainly not for redistribution or savings, unless the goods or services supplied are wholly fictitious. See also the discussion of the meaning of laundering in the text.

13. This can be a particular problem for offenses such as illicit enrichment, which is a criminal offense in many former British colonies and mandated in the Convention of the Organization of American States, but not implemented by Canada or the United States because of an assessed incompatibility with the constitutions of these two countries. The OECD Anti-Bribery Convention aims to make transnational bribery criminal whether or not the act is criminal in the receiving country.

14. Whether such claims are true, even if believed by their authors, remains an open question. It is difficult to generalize from ex post statements about motivations and future intents.

15. It is important to bear in mind, though, that we may misjudge or be misinformed about the likely consequences of accepting criminal money.

16. Hawalas are informal systems for transferring money that are traditional in Arab countries and South Asia.

17. The longer-term impact of the UBS settlement with the U.S. authorities over money flows from Switzerland, of the information leaks from Bank Julius Baer in Zurich and from LGT Bank in Liechtenstein, of the subsequent tax settlements with Germany, and of the market anticipation of the more general effects of such cases remains to be determined.

18. The report (Goredema and Madzima 2009, 29) notes as follows:

   If endemic, corruption can render the AML system dysfunctional by clogging it with a large volume of cases to deal with:

   • Because of its connection to money laundering, corruption will try to prevent the adoption of effective measures against money laundering, and may succeed in doing so if not detected and confronted;
   • The implementation of AML measures that have been adopted can be impeded by corruption, such as by interfering with the capacity of mandated institutions to perform their duties, or influencing the relevant officials;

- By corrupting institutions in the private sector on whose co-operation prevailing AML systems increasingly rely, to secure their collusion in sabotaging the effective implementation of AML measures;
- Corruption will take advantage of differences in levels of implementation of AML measures in different countries to frustrate trans-national co-operation to investigate money laundering or track proceeds of crime.

19. No wrong has been done, that is, except through the process by which the concessions are granted.
20. Wrong (2000) identifies the nonperformance of the extraction industry in the postcolonial period as a key problem in Mobutu's Zaire.
21. In cases of extortion by PEPs, the normal normative model of a bad corporation and a less bad bribe-taker is, arguably, reversed. However, in both cases, public welfare is diminished. The relative impact of models such as "publish what you pay" is not clear if government personnel are the extortionists rather than the more passive recipients of bribes.
22. This might appear like a good recovery rate, though, in common with data on the seizure or confiscation of the proceeds of crime generally, it is often difficult to disentangle what is seized or frozen from the assets that are merely ordered to be confiscated and the assets actually recovered. Chaikin (personal communication) notes that, according to the Report of the Presidential Commission on Good Government's Accomplishments for the year 2001, there were 24 civil cases (involving over 100 companies) pending before the Anti-Corruption Court in the Philippines to determine ownership of alleged illicit assets connected with the Marcos regime. These cases concern equities and domestic real properties worth a total of ₱208 billion. (At current prices, this amounts to about US$4.5 billion.) The 2001 figures are not current, but other sources state that there have been few if any new domestic cases, and the Philippine government is likely to have lost some cases in court. The data problems are indicative of the difficulties in externally tracking evidence in even well-attested cases.
23. *Offshore financial center, financial haven,* and *secrecy haven* have been replacing the more limited, older term *tax haven.*
24. The European Union third anti–money laundering directive refers to "natural persons who are or have been entrusted with prominent political functions and immediate family members or persons known to be close associates of such persons." (Article 3 [8]). Article 2(a) of the UNCAC states that "public official" shall mean: (a) any person holding a legislative, executive, administrative, or judicial office of a State Party, whether appointed or elected, whether permanent or temporary, whether paid or unpaid, irrespective of that person's seniority; (b) any other person who performs a public function, including for a public agency or public enterprise, or provides a public service, as defined in the domestic law of the State Party and as applied in the pertinent area of law of that State Party; (c) any other person defined as a "public official" in the domestic law of a State Party.
25. See "Wolfsberg FAQ's on Politically Exposed Persons," Wolfsberg Group, http://www.wolfsberg-principles.com/faq-persons.html.

26. Though the declaration of interests can simply demonstrate a sense of impunity by elites.
27. There is a useful typology of levels of corrupt penetration and possible responses (see table 12.1).
28. Presumably, if a customer profile suggests the proceeds of crime are involved, the financial institution should skip directly to the penultimate step.
29. After the event, regulators may apply hindsight standards, but the collateral consequences of bringing down large multinational or national financial institutions may deter heavy corporate sanctions beyond fines and restrictions on the access of particular individuals to fill banking posts that need to be approved.
30. The fact that PEPs may have accounts with several institutions means that counting PEP accounts within a jurisdiction is a poor guide to the number of PEPs because there will be double counting unless the names and other personal and corporate account identifiers are available. Meanwhile, undisclosed beneficial ownership may generate an undercount.
31. In 2011, a similar deal was concluded between Chinese firms and Namibia, but without the involvement of Teko Trading. See Smit, N., "Namibia: Tender Exemption for Chinese Firms," AllAfrica.com, November 18, 2011, http://allafrica.com/stories/201111180336.html.
32. Yom-Tov, S., "Kobi Alexander Will Be Facing Charges of Money-Laundering," *Haaretz*, September 29, 2006.
33. Confidential interviews by the author among FIU staff, 2009.
34. The levels of support for AML are hard to determine. One of the interesting aspects of the phenomenon, notable more strongly in discussions about terrorist finance, is the way—even in Islamic countries—the perception that money laundering is harmful and that AML is needed have become the conventional wisdom. One consequence is that it is difficult to find officials who express skepticism about keeping the proceeds of crimes out of their economies, though critical discussion is commonplace about the impracticality of mechanisms to develop and report suspicions and act upon them.
35. "Money laundering typologies" is rather an elastic construct lacking in the rigor normally associated with the noun *typology* in scientific usage. In the AML world, a typology normally refers simply to a method of laundering. See Goredema and Madzima (2009) for a review of money laundering and measures against corruption in that region (for example, table 12.1): these connections are found in other FATF-Style Regional Bodies.
36. Personal communication to the author.

References

ADB (Asian Development Bank) and OECD (Organisation for Economic Co-operation and Development). 2007. *Mutual Legal Assistance, Extradition and Recovery of Proceeds of Corruption in Asia and the Pacific.* ADB/OECD Anti-Corruption Initiative for Asia and the Pacific. Paris: OECD.

Auld, R. 2009. *Turks and Caicos Islands Commission of Inquiry 2008–2009: Into Possible Corruption or Other Serious Dishonesty in Recent Years of Past and Present Elected Members of the Legislature.* London: Foreign and Commonwealth Office. http://www.tci-inquiry.org/index.html.

Baker, R. W. 2005. *Capitalism's Achilles Heel: Dirty Money and How to Renew the Free-Market System.* Hoboken, NJ: John Wiley & Sons.

Briones, L. M. 2007. "The Philippine Experience." Unpublished paper, World Bank, Washington, DC.

Chaikin, D. 2009. *Money Laundering, Tax Evasion and Tax Havens.* Sydney: University of Sydney.

Chaikin, D., and J. C. Sharman. 2009. *Corruption and Money Laundering: A Symbiotic Relationship.* London: Palgrave Macmillan.

Daniel, T., and J. Maton. 2008. "Recovering the Proceeds of Corruption: General Sani Abacha; A Nation's Thief." In *Recovering Stolen Assets,* ed. M. Pieth, 63–78. Bern: Peter Lang.

De Koker, L. 2009. "Identifying and Managing Low Money Laundering Risk: Perspectives on FATF's Risk-Based Guidance." *Journal of Financial Crime* 16 (4): 334–52.

Dumas, V. 2007. "The Peruvian Experience." Unpublished case study, World Bank, Washington, DC.

FATF (Financial Action Task Force). 2010. "Corruption: A Reference Guide and Information Note on the Use of the FATF Recommendations to Support the Fight against Corruption." FATF, Paris. http://www.fatf-gafi.org/dataoecd/59/44/46252454.pdf.

Gordon, R. 2009. "Laundering the Proceeds of Public Sector Corruption: A Preliminary Report." Unpublished report, World Bank, Washington, DC.

Goredema, C., and J. Madzima. 2009. "An Assessment of the Links between Corruption and the Implementation of Anti–money Laundering Strategies and Measures in the ESAAMLG Region." Report, May 18, Eastern and Southern Africa Anti–Money Laundering Group, Dar es Salaam, Tanzania.

Kaufmann, D. 2005. "Myths and Realities of Governance and Corruption." In *Global Competitiveness Report 2005–06: Policies Underpinning Rising Prosperity,* ed. A. Lopez-Claros, M. E. Porter, and K. Schwab, 81–98. Basingstoke, U.K.: Palgrave Macmillan.

Levi, M. 2008. *The Phantom Capitalists: The Organisation and Control of Long-Firm Fraud.* 2nd ed. Aldershot, U.K.: Ashgate.

Levi, M., and W. Gilmore. 2002. "Terrorist Finance, Money Laundering and the Rise and Rise of Mutual Evaluation: A New Paradigm for Crime Control?" *European Journal of Law Reform* 4 (2): 337–64.

Levi, M., and M. Maguire. 2004. "Reducing and Preventing Organised Crime: An Evidence-Based Critique." *Crime, Law and Social Change* 41 (5): 397–469.

Levi, M., and P. Reuter. 2006. "Money Laundering." In *Crime and Justice: A Review of Research,* vol. 34, ed. M. Tonry, 289–375. Chicago: University of Chicago Press.

Passas, N. 2005. "Informal Value Transfer Systems, Terrorism and Money Launder-ing: A Report to the National Institute of Justice." Document 208301, National Institute of Justice, Washington, DC. http://www.ncjrs.gov/pdffiles1/nij/grants /208301.pdf.

Rees, D. 2010. "Money Laundering and Terrorist Financing Risks Posed by Alterna-tive Remittance in Australia." AIC Report, Research and Public Policy Series 106, Australian Institute of Criminology, Canberra.

Reuter, P., and E. M. Truman. 2004. *Chasing Dirty Money: The Fight against Money Laundering.* Washington, DC: Institute for International Economics.

Ribadu, N. 2010. "Show Me the Money: Leveraging Anti–Money Laundering Tools to Fight Corruption in Nigeria; an Insider's Story." Report, Center for Glo-bal Development, Washington, DC. http://www.cgdev.org/files/1424712_file _Ribadu_web_FINAL.pdf.

Salonga, J. 2000. *Presidential Plunder: The Quest for the Marcos Ill-Gotten Wealth.* Manila: Regina Publishing.

Sharman, J. C. 2008. "Power and Discourse in Policy Diffusion: Anti–money Laun-dering in Developing States." *International Studies Quarterly* 52 (3): 635–56.

———. 2011. *The Money Laundry: Regulating Criminal Finance in the Global Econ-omy.* Ithaca, NY: Cornell University Press.

Sharman, J. C., and P. S. Mistry. 2008. *Considering the Consequences.* London: Com-monwealth Secretariat.

Shaxson, N. 2011. *Treasure Islands: Tax Havens and the Men Who Stole the World.* London: Bodley Head.

Takats, E. 2007. "A Theory of 'Crying Wolf': The Economics of Money Laundering Enforcement." IMF Working Paper WP/07/81, International Monetary Fund, Washington, DC.

U.S. Senate. 2009. "Afghanistan's Narco War: Breaking the Link between Drug Traf-fickers and Insurgents." Report (August 10), Committee on Foreign Relations, United States Senate, Washington, DC.

Warutere, P. 2006. "Detecting and Investigating Money Laundering in Kenya." In *Money Laundering Experiences,* ed. C. Goredema, 55–72. ISS Monograph Series 124 (June). Cape Town: Institute for Security Studies.

White House. 2010. "G-20: Fact Sheet on a Shared Commitment to Fighting Corrup-tion." Press Release (November 12), Office of the Press Secretary, White House, Washington, DC.

Wrong, M. 2000. *In the Footsteps of Mr. Kurtz: Living on the Brink of Disaster in Mobutu's Congo.* London: Fourth Estate.

———. 2009. *It's Our Turn to Eat: The Story of a Kenyan Whistle-Blower.* London: Fourth Estate.

13

The Kleptocrat's Portfolio Decisions

James Maton and Tim Daniel

Abstract

This chapter contains five corruption case studies relating to politically exposed persons (PEPs) from Indonesia, Kenya, Nigeria (two cases), and Zambia; two of these PEPs were heads of state. It details the methodology of amassing corrupt fortunes and the ways in which the politicians and officials involved have sought to put those fortunes beyond the reach of the law using a variety of jurisdictions perceived as havens for illicitly acquired funds. It tracks the efforts made to recover these funds and the obstacles encountered, resulting in success in some cases and failure in others. It emphasizes the importance of utilizing civil asset recovery powers, in conjunction with the compulsion powers of criminal law enforcement agencies. International mutual assistance is vital to successful recoveries in this area, but is by no means a given in cases that are, by their nature, politically high profile. Shortcomings in the law in this area are regularly exposed by lawyers acting for defendants who are frequently more well funded than the people pursuing them. International conventions recognize the need for concerted action, but, ultimately, the leaders in individual states have to summon the political will to tackle those who have gone before them and resist the temptation of simply following them, or nothing will ever change for the disadvantaged of this world. This chapter shows that the effective use of the law has the power to bring about change: it aims to share experiences that may help those dedicated to the pursuit of assets stolen from the people of too many nations by their corrupt leaders.

Introduction

The U.K. lord chancellor and minister for justice introduced the United Kingdom's new foreign bribery strategy at Chatham House in January 2010 with these words:

> By definition, it is hard to assess the costs of bribery. But the estimates we do have are staggering. The World Bank estimated that around US$1 trillion is paid each year in bribes. Transparency International estimates that 15% of companies in industrialised countries have to pay bribes to win or keep business. In Asia it is estimated that 30% do so. . . .
>
> Politicians and officials in developing and transition states alone are estimated to receive between US$20 [billion] and US$40 billion in bribes; the equivalent of 20 to 40% of development assistance. And this is bribery alone. It does not include wider forms of corruption; embezzlement of public funds; theft or misuse of public assets; distortions in public procurement. And it takes no account of fraud in the private sector.
>
> These are dreadful figures. And beyond these figures lie innumerable individual tragedies. . . .[1]

Great steps forward to combat bribery and corruption have been taken, particularly in the last 10 years, by a variety of international actors, including the United Nations, the Organisation for Economic Co-operation and Development (OECD), and the World Bank.[2] Guidelines have been established; individual states have been urged to bring their own legislation into order; and peer review mechanisms have been set up. These measures have had as their objective not only successful prosecution of bribery offenses, but also, and at least as importantly, the prevention of bribery and corruption. Chapter V of the United Nations Convention against Corruption (UNCAC) and the Stolen Asset Recovery Initiative have as their focus, however, the recovery of assets paid in bribes or embezzled by officials, generally high-ranking ones, politicians, and, most egregiously, heads of state.

The chapter considers four cases from Africa, and one from Southeast Asia. It addresses the acts generating the corrupt funds and the mechanisms and techniques by which corrupt funds were transferred and then held and managed. It identifies where the corrupt funds ended up in the developed world and examines the assistance provided by financial institutions and professional advisers in the transfer and maintenance of the funds and assets. The chapter then details mechanisms by which some of the corrupt funds have been recovered and looks at some of the hurdles faced and why recovery efforts sometimes end in failure.

The importance of understanding the issues involved was recently underlined in the United States by the work of the Levin Committee, which, in February 2010, released a 330-page report on four other case histories (U.S. Senate 2010), all relating to African PEPs who "used gaps in U.S. law and the assistance of U.S. professionals to funnel millions of dollars in illicit money into the United States." The report makes a series of recommendations, for, as Senator Levin says, "Stopping the flow of illegal money is critical, because foreign corruption damages civil society, undermines the rule of law, and threatens our security."[3]

The case studies considered in this chapter now follow.

Sani Abacha, Head of State of Nigeria, 1993–98

Overview

It is estimated that Abacha stole between US$3 billion and US$5 billion during his four and a half years in office. To date, approximately US$2.3 billion has been or is in the course of being recovered. Of this sum, approximately US$750 million was handed over voluntarily by the Abacha family following Sani Abacha's death in June 1998. Contrary to their assertion that everything that had been stolen had been handed back, it was discovered that there were substantial additional funds in bank accounts situated mainly in Europe. Thus, protracted litigation in Switzerland ultimately resulted in a judgment in favor of Nigeria, and over US$500 million worth of assets were repatriated to Nigeria. Proceedings in the United Kingdom, in England, resulted in a payment of US$150 million.[4] Funds held in Jersey by Abubakar Bagudu, who was the right-hand man of Mohammed Abacha, the eldest son and mastermind of the entire enterprise, amounted to about US$160 million.

Bagudu was allowed to keep US$40 million in return for unconditional surrender of the balance.[5] Sums of the order of US$400 million were held by banks in The Bahamas and Luxembourg, and US$200 million was held in Liechtenstein.[6] In November 2010, the court in Geneva ordered confiscation of the US$400 million held in the banks in The Bahamas and Luxembourg in accounts controlled by Mohammed's younger brother, Abba, and imposed a two-year suspended jail sentence, but, in March 2011, the sentence was quashed and a retrial ordered on the grounds that Abba had been unable to attend court because his visa had not come through in time.[7] It is anticipated that these funds, as well as those held in Liechtenstein, will be repatriated to Nigeria in due course.

Acts generating corrupt funds

On July 23, 1998, following Abacha's death in June, the interim government of Abdulsalami Abubakar set up a special investigation panel under the direction of Peter Gana, a deputy police commissioner and a member of the National Security Council. The panel was instructed to ascertain whether Abacha and his entourage had embezzled public funds and, if so, to seek to recover them. In November 1998, the panel published a report, according to which Abacha and his accomplices (namely, among others, Ismailia Gwarzo, the national security adviser; Anthony Ani, the former minister of finance; Bagudu; and Mohammed Abacha) had arranged payments to themselves between January 1994 and June 1998 of sums in excess of US$1.5 billion and £415 million (equivalent in all to US$2.3 billion) from the Central Bank of Nigeria (CBN).[8] These sums were made up of cash, traveler's checks, and interbank transfers. The report states that the panel was able to recover a total of US$625 million and £75 million. This was the "voluntary" return of monies by the Abacha family.

The panel report stated that records from the CBN revealed that a total of US$2.25 billion had been withdrawn from the CBN on the approval of General Abacha and Ismailia Gwarzo and largely diverted into foreign bank accounts and the acquisition of real estate and other assets. The *modus operandi* was for Gwarzo to use security needs as a fake reason for applying to the CBN for funds. These monies are thus generally referred to as the security vote monies.

The methodology was almost comically simple. Between March 1994 and April 1998, Gwarzo wrote some 45 letters to Abacha. The first, dated March 25, 1994, was, as the letter itself stated, "very modest"; it read:

Request for Special Allocation
I am constrained to request very modestly US$2m (Two million dollars) for very urgent operation (sic) overseas.
I will appreciate your kind approval for this amount to enable this imperative operation to commence immediately.[9]

The entire sum was approved by Abacha, who countersigned the letter, which was then taken to the CBN, and the CBN paid out to Gwarzo six tranches of traveler's checks totaling US$2 million on the same day. Thomas Cook traveler's checks issued by the CBN under license were a favorite instrument used extensively by government ministers to make overseas payments during the time of the Abacha regime.

The scheme with the traveler's checks worked so well that Abacha and Gwarzo moved on to obtain direct cash withdrawals from the CBN. Between February 1995 and May 1996, 33 cash withdrawals or telegraphic transfers were made. The cash withdrawals were made mainly in large denomination dollar bills delivered personally to Gwarzo. The telegraphic transfers were made mainly to accounts held at European banks by offshore entities beneficially owned by the Abachas.

By April 1998, Gwarzo's letters were much more ambitious: the last of these letters referred to Abacha's "charismatic leadership and a vote of confidence from all five political parties." However, it said there were "insincere voices" that felt "others should be given a chance to run the race with you. These sorts of characters," the letter said, "are being aided and abetted by some foreigners who do not wish this nation any good." Therefore, the letter went on, "we should put on an aggressive public enlightenment and mount strategies of countering these miserable miscreants with a view to furthering the solidity of your teaming (sic) admirers both at home and abroad."

The letter finished by stating: "A lot of resources will be needed for use both at home and abroad. I recommend as follows one hundred million US Dollars ($100m), fifty million-pound sterling (£50m) and five hundred million Naira (N500m). Kindly consider and approve."

Before that single-candidate election could be held, Abacha was dead; this was in June 1998. It was claimed subsequently that one of the reasons Abacha amassed all that he did was to build up his war chest to fight the elections.

The total security vote withdrawals comprised US$1.13 billion and £413 million in banknotes, US$43.3 million and £3.5 million in traveler's checks, and US$328.5 million in telex or telegraphic transfers abroad. A small fraction (US$15 million) of the cash was given in aid to some neighboring African states, and around US$100 million may have been lost in currency exchanges. The balance of unrecovered funds was put at US$748 million and £341 million.

Mechanisms and techniques used to transfer funds. The Abachas had to find ways to manage the colossal sums they had stolen. Mohammed Abacha admitted in evidence in other proceedings that, sometimes, there was as much as US$50 million–US$100 million in banknotes at his house in Abuja. These monies were then either retained by the Abacha family and used for their personal purposes or passed on to associates to be laundered and concealed.

Cash shipments out of Nigeria were sometimes intercepted. In August 1995, US$7.5 million and £250,000 in cash and US$1.5 million in traveler's checks were intercepted by the Nigerian customs service in transit from Union Bank of Nigeria to the bank's London branch. As a result, a directive was issued that, in future, currencies "evacuated" from the country should be transferred through the CBN. Bagudu said, in evidence, that, despite this directive, individuals could still buy currency and take it out of the country in cash and that this means of removal from Nigeria was still practiced on a widespread scale.

In February 1998, a Mr. Daura of Sunshine Bureau de Change was caught with US$3 million in cash after he had landed at Heathrow in a private jet. HM Customs & Excise then made an application for the money to be forfeited, assuming it to represent the proceeds of drug trafficking.[10] Daura and his Bureau de Change were big recipients of security vote monies. He deposited the monies with the local branch of First Bank and other Nigerian banks. He then exchanged the amounts held in the accounts that were in his name in Lagos and had them transferred to branches of the same banks abroad. These were then transferred from

Daura's overseas accounts to accounts held in the names of the Abachas and their associates. As much as US$100 million was thus exported by Daura.

Another method used was for cash and traveler's checks to be deposited in accounts held with local commercial banks in Nigeria, including, in particular, accounts held in the name of Bagudu with Inland Bank of Nigeria and Union Bank of Nigeria. The funds were then transferred on to accounts maintained at banks outside Nigeria in the names of entities owned or controlled by the Abachas.

Following the CBN directive, the Nigerian banks were used to undertake what Bagudu referred to as "cash swaps." Bagudu made deposits of foreign currency and traveler's checks at local Nigerian banks. These were then deposited by the local bank with the CBN, which made a corresponding transfer from one of its overseas foreign currency accounts to the overseas domiciliary account (held by banks such as Commerzbank and Citibank) of the relevant local bank. The sums held in the relevant bank domiciliary accounts would be held for their clients, the Abachas or their associates, who would then give transfer instructions to the relevant banks to effect transfers from the domiciliary accounts to recipient accounts. Huge sums were transferred this way.

Structures through which corrupt funds were transferred, held, and managed. The Abachas and their accomplices used traditional methods to launder the monies stolen from the CBN, such as multiple accounts. Estimates vary, but it is thought that probably around 1,000 different accounts were opened in different jurisdictions. These accounts were all owned or controlled by members of the Abacha family and their accomplices or by persons who were not readily identifiable. The use of multiple accounts is a recognized device used by money launderers because it impedes the monitoring and tracing of client activity and assets by banks, allows the quick and confidential movement of funds, disguises the true extent of an individual's assets, and hides and facilitates illicit activities.

Shell companies incorporated in offshore locations such as The Bahamas, British Virgin Islands, Isle of Man, and others where there is little publicly available information in relation to ownership, control, or financial position were used liberally. None of these companies had any commercial business of their own; they were simply incorporated or acquired to receive and transmit monies through recognized banks.

Many of the companies utilized by the Abacha family and their accomplices were also bearer share companies. All of these were incorporated in British Virgin Islands, and the shares were generally held by Bagudu or Mohammed Abacha. Bearer share companies are used by money launderers because, unless a bank maintains physical possession of the shares, it is impossible to know with certainty who, at any given moment, is the company's true owner.

Many of the accounts owned or controlled by the Abachas were special name accounts, that is, accounts held under a special name or pseudonym, thus disguising the identity of the real account holder from those who make transfers to or receive transfers from the accounts. These accounts were generally set up in London or New York by Citibank Private Bank. Numbered accounts were used extensively in Switzerland, at about a dozen different (well-known) banks. A number of trusts were also set up in Guernsey (with bank accounts in London), British Virgin Islands, and Nassau, in The Bahamas, with bank accounts in Switzerland. Apartments purchased by the Abachas in Kensington (London) were owned by companies incorporated in Isle of Man.

Finally, security vote monies were used to purchase Nigerian par bonds. These par bonds were issued by Nigeria in exchange for rescheduled bank loans. The government paid interest by way of coupon payments on the bonds, and the government would purchase the bonds at face value on expiry. In the meantime, there was a limited market in the par bonds.

Destinations, assistance, and the recovery process

On September 30, 1999, four months after democratically elected President Obasanjo took office, Nigeria informed the Federal Police Office in Switzerland of its intention to request mutual assistance from Switzerland for an ongoing investigation against the friends and family of the late Sani Abacha. The original Nigerian request was accompanied by a request for interim freezing orders made by Enrico Monfrini, a Swiss lawyer in Geneva instructed by the Nigerian government. The freezing orders were made two weeks later.

However, as the investigation showed later, many of the bank accounts identified in the original request for assistance had been closed, and the assets transferred to other jurisdictions such as Jersey, Liechtenstein, Luxembourg, and the United Kingdom. Had Nigeria waited for the transmittal of evidence by Switzerland through the formal mutual legal assistance route, it would only have received the documents necessary to send additional requests to those jurisdictions in about August 2003. Such delays would have repeated themselves in those jurisdictions, and Nigeria would probably never have been able to freeze any meaningful assets.

To avoid these delays, Monfrini lodged, in late November 1999, a criminal complaint alleging fraud, money laundering, and participation in a criminal organization, with the attorney general of Geneva. A list of the suspects and their companies was provided, and Nigeria also made a formal request to be admitted in the criminal proceedings as a civil party suing for damages. The attorney general opened a criminal investigation, and, within a matter of days, Nigeria was also admitted as a civil party.[11] A blanket freezing order was sent by the Swiss authorities to all Swiss banks and financial institutions (at that time, there were about 11,000), listing the names of the suspects, their aliases, and their companies.

Following the lodging of the criminal complaint, dozens of accounts with assets totaling more than US$700 million were frozen in Switzerland in the context of the domestic criminal proceedings. This was the consequence of banks reporting all suspicious accounts following the blanket freezing order and the media coverage of the investigation.

Accounts and insurance policies were found to be held at a number of leading banks, including Warburgs, Union Bancaire Privée, Crédit Suisse, Baring Brothers, Crédit Agricole Indosuez, UBS, and Goldman Sachs. These accounts were held in the names of Abacha family members and the companies set up by them. In the court proceedings that followed in Switzerland, it was clear that all these banks had been all too willing to assist the Abachas.

After several years of litigation in Swiss courts, the matter reached the Swiss Federal Supreme Court. The accounts in question had the characteristics of what the court called "transitional accounts," which do not relate to any identifiable activity and have a high frequency (at intervals of only a few days) of payments of significant sums, apparently unrelated to any consideration. These accounts were used to transfer on (launder) the sums sent in checks and cash either by Bagudu himself or his accomplices, all of whom were Swiss nationals.

The court was in little doubt that the sums in question were derived from withdrawals from the CBN. The main perpetrators undoubtedly remained the Abachas themselves, particularly Mohammed and Bagudu. To a large extent, they duped the banks. How they did this emerges in the Swiss Federal Supreme Court judgment.[12]

The court noted that certain accounts were held by unidentified Nigerian nationals calling themselves such names as Sani Mohammed, Abba Muhamad Sani, Ibrahim Muhammad Sani, Abba Sani, Sani Abdu Mohammed, Sani Ibrahim, Ibrahim Muhammad, Sani Abba Muhammad, and Sani Abdu Muhammad. Abacha's three sons were named Ibrahim, Mohammed, and Abba.

The defendants stated that, in accordance with the traditions of Muslim families of northern Nigeria, from which they originated, their real surname is Sani. They claimed, further, that it is usual to reverse the surname and forename or to use nicknames to distinguish persons bearing the same forename (sometimes as between brothers in the same family). The evidential value of the legal opinion to which they referred on these points was queried because it came from a person who had close links with the defendants. The court stated that, interesting though the considerations expressed by the expert on customs relating to personal names in Nigeria might be, they were not of such a nature as to explain the fact that three individuals opened the accounts in question under different identities and presented different passports on each occasion. It was clear to the court that the persons who opened the accounts in question not only used false names, but deliberately sought to mislead the banking institutions they approached by causing confusion over their real identities. The defendants did not attempt to indicate to which of them the various surnames and forenames used in combination every time they opened an account specifically belonged; they also did not contest that they were all known under their usual name of Abacha in the criminal proceedings against them in Nigeria.

The repatriation of funds. The investigations conducted by the Geneva authorities, with the cooperation of Nigeria, enabled the Swiss Federal Office to have a clear view of the origin of the frozen funds and determine that it was manifestly criminal. Consequently, in August 2004, the Federal Office, utilizing a provision in the Federal Law on Mutual Assistance in Criminal Matters, decided to transmit to Nigeria all the assets in Switzerland beneficially owned by the Abacha family, about US$500 million, waiving the need for a prior judicial forfeiture decision in Nigeria.

That decision was upheld by the Swiss Supreme Court, which also confirmed that Abacha, his sons, and accomplices formed a criminal organization within the meaning of the Swiss Penal Code and that any asset controlled by such member should be forfeited unless it could be shown to have been legally acquired, that is, there was a reversal of the burden of proof relating to these funds. All funds in Switzerland have now been repatriated.

In the event, Switzerland was reluctant to exercise its jurisdiction to hold the main criminal trial of the members of the Abacha criminal organization, deeming that it was more appropriate that such a trial should take place in Nigeria. However, the criminal trial of the Abacha sons, who were charged in September 2000 before the High Court of Abuja, has yet to begin because of the innumerable appeals lodged in the Nigerian courts by the Abachas' massive team of attorneys and their apparent ability to delay or halt any legal process in Nigeria.

Mutual legal assistance. Based on the information and documents discovered through the Geneva criminal proceedings, requests for mutual legal assistance were lodged by Nigeria in Jersey, Liechtenstein, Luxembourg, and the United Kingdom.[13] In the following months, an additional US$1.3 billion was frozen in those jurisdictions at the request of Nigeria.

The results then obtained in those jurisdictions depended much on whether their respective authorities initiated their own criminal investigation into money laundering or not. Thus, in Jersey and Liechtenstein, the local law enforcement authorities, with the active participation of Nigeria, identified and froze more accounts than simply those designated in the requests for mutual legal assistance.

In Luxembourg, no such investigations took place, and only the accounts in the banks designated in the Nigerian request of February 2000 were frozen. The assets in these accounts have been forfeited by the Luxembourg authorities, and recognition of that decision is being sought in the Luxembourg courts. Nigeria, as victim, should be entitled to receive the proceeds of the forfeiture. This outcome is, however, once again, being contested by the Abacha family.

In October 2006, a criminal trial of Mohammed Abacha began in Vaduz, Liechtenstein. Because in absentia criminal proceedings do not exist in Liechtenstein, and Mohammed Abacha did not appear at the first hearing, the proceedings have been converted into autonomous forfeiture proceedings, targeting the US$200 million frozen in Liechtenstein. At the end of the proceedings, Nigeria, as victim of the crimes, should again be entitled to the forfeiture proceeds. There have been legal obstacles to the process both in Liechtenstein and Nigeria, but it is hoped they will be resolved soon.

The United Kingdom. Virtually no action was taken by the U.K. authorities following Nigeria's request for mutual legal assistance that was lodged in June 2000. The Financial Services Authority, which was involved in the early part of the enquiry in the United Kingdom, only reprimanded the banks involved in laundering US$1.2 billion through the City of London; it took no steps to initiate a domestic criminal investigation into money laundering, nor would it disclose the names of the banks involved.[14] When the Home Secretary finally announced that an investigation would be undertaken, the Abachas challenged the decision by way of judicial review. They failed, but another three years were to pass before the U.K. authorities announced they were ready to transmit to Nigeria the evidence they had gathered; at which point, the Abachas requested a judicial review of the decision to transmit. They failed again, but the evidence regarding the targeted accounts, which had, for the most part, been closed in the meanwhile, was ultimately only transmitted by the U.K. authorities in December 2004 and was insufficiently complete to allow outgoing transfers to be traced.

In September 2001, frustrated by the lack of progress on the official front, Nigeria's counsel acted. Separate civil proceedings, making proprietary claims on behalf of Nigeria to the monies, were commenced in London against more than 100 defendants. The embezzlement was claimed of US$2 billion from the CBN under the false pretense that the monies were needed for security purposes. The monies were said by Nigeria to be held on constructive trust for the state. The civil proceedings sought and obtained freezing and disclosure orders against the first 20-odd respondents (all banks) of their books and records, in particular bank statements, relating to the accounts held in the names of the remaining 90 respondents. These respondents were incorporated in jurisdictions such as British Virgin Islands, Ireland, Isle of Man, and Liechtenstein (there were also quite a few Nigerian corporations). No satisfactory explanation was ever given by Mohammed Abacha as to the provenance of the monies: he relied on the privilege against self-incrimination.

Full disclosure was made by the banks named as defendants in the U.K. proceedings, and, within six weeks, all the information that it had taken the U.K. authorities four years to transmit had been obtained. However, only about £50 million remained in the U.K. bank accounts. This money was frozen, but, over the ensuing years, the court allowed much of it to be disbursed to pay the Abachas's legal fees, which had been substantial.

This being the case, little effort went into pursuing the named companies in offshore jurisdictions. The value of such an exercise would, in any event, have been highly dubious. There was sufficient evidence from Switzerland to show that these offshore entities were connected with the Abacha enterprise. Expending time, effort, and money on trying to establish the beneficial ownership of these offshore entities would therefore have been a largely futile exercise. The assumption that these were Abacha-related companies was never challenged by the Abachas in such evidence as they saw fit to file in the various proceedings.

The U.K. action never proceeded beyond freezing all the Abacha assets held by the named banks and disclosing all the account information. The freezing order was a worldwide one and remains in force. Although such orders made by the U.K. courts can be difficult to implement overseas, they do have the effect of putting major international banks on notice all around the world, and, in practice, banks avoid breaching such orders in case it opens them up to liability before the U.K. courts. Continuing the action might have yielded further information, and it might ultimately have led to a judgment. This could have been useful for enforcement purposes in other jurisdictions, but, in practice, other ways have been found to secure compliance.

Conclusion

Abacha is probably still the single most successful case in terms of assets recovered by a state. Some of the hurdles faced have been referred to above. Recovery efforts continue.[15] Perhaps as much as US$3 billion may one day be repatriated to Nigeria. Success has been the result of the rapid establishment of an investigative process in Nigeria, followed by the cooperation of the (offshore) Swiss authorities who instituted criminal proceedings, demanded the disclosure of information by all Swiss financial institutions, and then joined Nigeria as a civil party to the proceedings, thus allowing Nigeria's own lawyer access to all the criminal evidence, enabling him to assist the investigating magistrates in a direct fashion and to obtain rapid cooperation in other havens, notably Jersey, Liechtenstein, and Luxembourg. This shows the value of identifying a proactive lead jurisdiction to demand action in such cases.

It has taken the U.K. common law system a while to learn the lessons the Abacha case has taught, but the next case study in this chapter, on Alamieyeseigha, is testimony to some of the lessons learned.

Governor Alamieyeseigha of Bayelsa State, Nigeria

Introduction

Diepreye Peter Solomon Alamieyeseigha was elected governor of Nigeria's Bayelsa State in May 1999 and reelected in 2003. His term of office was supposed to run until May 2007, but was cut short by impeachment for corruption in December 2005.

Between the start of his period of office in May 1999 to late 2005, Alamieyeseigha accumulated (outside Nigeria) known properties, bank accounts, investments, and cash exceeding £10 million in value.

His portfolio of foreign assets included accounts with five banks in the United Kingdom and additional accounts with banks in Cyprus, Denmark, and the United States; four London properties acquired for a total of £4.8 million; a Cape Town harbor penthouse acquired for almost £1 million; possible assets in the United States; and almost £1 million in cash stored at one of his London properties.

Some of the foreign assets were held in his name and the name of his wife, but the bulk were held by companies and trusts incorporated in the following jurisdictions:

- The Bahamas: Falcon Flights Incorporated, the company that maintained the bank account with UBS AG in London

- British Virgin Islands: Solomon and Peters Limited, the company that acquired the four London properties
- South Africa: Royal Albatross Properties 67 (Pty) Limited, the company that acquired the South African property
- Seychelles: Santolina Investment Corporation, the company that held the bank accounts in Cyprus, with Barclays Bank plc; in Denmark, with Jyske Bank A/S; and in London, with the Royal Bank of Scotland plc

The companies used to hold the assets were established and managed by third parties. Solomon and Peters Limited was incorporated for Alamieyeseigha by a Nigerian associate resident in London. Santolina Investment Corporation was incorporated for Alamieyeseigha by a London trust and companies service provider, which also opened and managed at least some of the accounts. Falcon Flights Incorporated was established and managed by the private banking department of UBS Bank plc.

The source of the funds
Alamieyeseigha's wealth derived from a combination of the theft of public funds, principally from the Bayelsa State Development Fund, and bribes paid by contractors for the award of public contracts by Bayelsa State. Evidence of the illicit activities was obtained during criminal investigations by the Economic and Financial Crimes Commission in Nigeria and the Metropolitan Police in London in the form of documents and witness statements from contractors and financial institutions. Foreign banks and advisers were variously told that Alamieyeseigha's wealth derived from inheritances, property sales, and businesses said to have been operated prior to his election as governor. No evidence of this was ever produced.

The U.K. criminal proceedings
In September 2005, Alamieyeseigha was arrested in London by officers of the Proceeds of Corruption Unit of the Metropolitan Police, questioned, and subsequently charged with three counts of money laundering contrary to the Criminal Justice Act 1988 and the Proceeds of Crime Act 2002.

On the day of his arrest, police officers searching one of his London properties discovered almost £1 million in cash. A worldwide criminal restraint order over his assets was obtained under the Criminal Justice Act 1988 from the English High Court by the U.K. Crown Prosecution Service and was enforced in Cyprus and Denmark through requests for mutual legal assistance.[16] A criminal restraint was also obtained in the United States.

Alamieyeseigha was initially remanded in custody after failing to persuade the court that he should be permitted to return to Nigeria for four weeks to attend to the affairs of Bayelsa State. After three weeks in custody, he was released on bail on conditions, including the surrender of his passport, the payment of £1.3 million into court by sureties, and daily reporting to the police.

He then sought to challenge his arrest and prosecution in the United Kingdom on the basis that, as a Nigerian state governor, he enjoyed sovereign immunity under English law. That argument was robustly rejected both by the English Crown Court and on appeal by the High Court.

In November 2005, despite his bail restrictions, Alamieyeseigha managed to flee the jurisdiction and return to Nigeria. He was subsequently impeached and charged with various corruption offences.

His flight led to the confiscation of the bail monies put up by his associates. (Subsequent scrutiny of the financial affairs of one of these associates led to the associate's prosecution and conviction in the United Kingdom for mortgage fraud and the confiscation of his London property.)

Proceedings to recover the assets

A variety of criminal and civil mechanisms were used to recover Alamieyeseigha's assets.

After he had absconded, criminal confiscation of U.K. assets on conviction was no longer possible. Alternative mechanisms were necessary.

The assets that had been frozen comprised cash, properties, and bank balances. The cash was straightforward. The United Kingdom has an uncomplicated procedure for the forfeiture of cash representing the proceeds of unlawful conduct, under the Proceeds of Crime Act 2002. An application can be made to a magistrates court by the police, among others, and, in cases of theft or fraud, the true owner of the cash can intervene under the Proceeds of Crime Act to seek its return. This procedure was successfully used. The Metropolitan Police applied for the confiscation of the cash seized from Alamieyeseigha, and Nigeria intervened to seek an order as victim for its return. The police did not oppose Nigeria's application for the return of the funds. The court ordered the cash to be forfeited and returned to Nigeria.

That left the properties and bank balances in London (and Cyprus and Denmark), to which the simple cash forfeiture mechanism could not apply.

Nigeria brought civil proceedings in the English High Court against Alamieyeseigha and others for the recovery of bank balances and properties in Cyprus, Denmark, and London.

The civil proceedings faced an initial difficulty. The Metropolitan Police had obtained a mass of evidence of Alamieyeseigha's corrupt activities in Nigeria and the laundering of the proceeds of those activities internationally. Nigeria needed that evidence to advance its proceedings. However, the evidence had primarily been obtained under compulsion from banks, solicitors, and other advisers using investigatory powers granted to the police by statute. The police owed duties of confidence to the owners of the documents, which prevented them voluntarily from handing over that evidence for use by Nigeria in private civil proceedings.

The English rules of civil procedure permit the court to compel third parties to disclose documents if they are likely to support the case of the applicant and if disclosure is necessary to permit a claim to be determined fairly or to save costs. Those powers can even be exercised against the police, provided it is in the public interest to do so.

The civil proceedings therefore commenced with an application by Nigeria for a court order requiring disclosure by the police of the evidence that the police had collated. That application was made without the knowledge of Alamieyeseigha or any other defendants on the basis that to allow them knowledge could cause Alamieyeseigha to conceal assets that had not yet been identified. Nigeria argued that it was in the public interest to order disclosure because it intended to use the documents to secure and recover the proceeds of corruption and because successful proceedings would assist in efforts to reduce corrupt activities, would demonstrate that the United Kingdom was not a safe haven for corruptly acquired assets, and would permit their recovery, whereas Alamieyeseigha's flight from the country could otherwise thwart the criminal confiscation process. The police confirmed that disclosure would not jeopardize further criminal investigations and did not oppose the application. The judge agreed that disclosure should be ordered.

The documents enabled Nigeria fully to articulate its case and to apply for its own civil freezing injunction over Alamieyeseigha's assets. A civil freezing injunction was granted to Nigeria by the English High Court in December 2005, expressed to take effect worldwide with the exception of Nigeria, together with a disclosure order requiring additional banks and Alamieyeseigha's London financial adviser to disclose more information about his assets and activities.

Alamieyeseigha sought to defend the proceedings, claiming that there were innocent explanations for the assets that were claimed. The bank balances, it was said, largely represented unused donations to his election campaign funds. He also denied any knowledge of the cash found in his bedroom in one of his London properties, saying that it was planted by political adversaries to "create the sensation that has coloured this case from the beginning." The explanations contradicted those given contemporaneously to banks and solicitors and sometimes contradicted assertions made by Alamieyeseigha when he was interviewed by the police in London and Nigeria. Alamieyeseigha was unable, save in relation to one property, to produce any documents supporting his explanations. The provenance of those documents was disputed.

Nigeria applied for summary judgment, a process intended to bring a swift end to proceedings without the need for a full trial on the basis that there is no genuine defense to a claim. It was supported by substantial affidavit and documentary evidence. Alamieyeseigha achieved significant delay in the determination of this application on the grounds of his alleged illness. He relented only after an independent medical examination in Nigeria ordered by the English court at Nigeria's request concluded that he was capable of giving instructions to his lawyers.

The subsequent summary judgment hearing was heard in the High Court in February 2007, but failed. The judge decided that Nigeria had a strong case and that Alamieyeseigha "had a lot of explaining to do," but he also decided that allegations of corruption against an elected public official were so serious that Alamieyeseigha should be given the opportunity to "confront his accusers" at a trial, following the exchange of all material evidence.

However, in July 2007, Alamieyeseigha put an end to delays in the Nigerian criminal proceedings. He pleaded guilty to six charges of making false declarations of assets and caused two of his offshore companies to plead guilty to 23 charges of money laundering. He was sentenced to two years in prison for each personal charge, to run concurrently. A confiscation order was made over some (but, for technical reasons, not all) of his domestic and international assets, which was enforced domestically and could have been enforced overseas. However, by that stage, it appeared that the assets would be recovered more quickly using the existing civil proceedings rather than starting a new process by seeking to enforce the Nigerian confiscation order through a request to the United Kingdom for mutual legal assistance.

Nigeria reapplied for summary judgment in the civil proceedings in relation to those assets deriving from the criminal conduct that had been admitted by Alamieyeseigha and his companies, arguing that the guilty pleas meant that Alamieyeseigha's defense had no reasonable prospect of success in relation to those assets. That application succeeded in December 2007. The court agreed that the guilty pleas destroyed the already weak defense and that Alamieyeseigha had been given the opportunity to "confront his accusers," but had, instead, accepted the charges made against him.

The civil proceedings continued in relation to the remaining assets. Nigeria made applications for orders requiring Alamieyeseigha to disclose information and documents. He failed to do so. In February 2008, Nigeria obtained an order requiring Alamieyeseigha to comply with the orders, with the sanction that his defense would be struck out and judgment granted to Nigeria if he failed to do so. The required information and documents were not provided, and, on July 2, 2008, Nigeria obtained judgment over the remaining assets in Cyprus, Denmark, and London.

Foreign proceedings

The English judgment over the Cypriot and Danish bank accounts was enforced under European Community legislation for the mutual recognition and enforcement of civil judgments.

The Cape Town penthouse was secured by a freezing injunction obtained by the South African authorities in support of requests for mutual legal assistance in criminal matters from Nigeria and the United

Kingdom. The property and rental income from the property were forfeited in July 2006 by the High Court of South Africa in civil forfeiture proceedings on the application of the national director of public prosecutions acting through the Asset Forfeiture Unit. Nigeria successfully intervened in the proceedings seeking an order for the return of the proceeds of sale.

Conclusion

Alamieyeseigha is a good example of coordinated international asset recovery. The case involved the full set of criminal and civil asset recovery mechanisms: criminal proceedings in Nigeria and the United Kingdom, including criminal restraining orders over assets; requests for mutual legal assistance between these jurisdictions and others; criminal confiscation of assets in Nigeria, civil forfeiture of cash in the United Kingdom; private civil proceedings in the United Kingdom, including a worldwide freezing injunction; enforcement of the civil judgment in Cyprus and Denmark; and civil forfeiture proceedings in South Africa.

There were a number of factors leading to success in the Alamieyeseigha proceedings, as follows:

- Thorough investigations into the corrupt activities of Alamieyeseigha in Nigeria by the Economic and Financial Crimes Commission and by the Metropolitan Police in the United Kingdom
- Effective and quick execution of requests for mutual legal assistance, including the use of a criminal restraint order to secure assets
- Close cooperation between the Nigerian and U.K. authorities and, as far as was permissible, between the U.K. authorities and civil lawyers in Nigeria
- The availability of the documents gathered by law enforcement agencies for civil proceedings
- A package of civil and criminal efforts to recover assets
- Relentless pressure in the civil proceedings to force Alamieyeseigha properly to explain his defense, in particular, the alleged legitimate source of his wealth, coupled with the court's willingness to enter judgment following repeated failures to comply with orders for disclosure of information and documents

Tommy Suharto, Son of President Suharto of Indonesia

Introduction

Tommy Suharto's father was president of Indonesia for 30 years, from 1968 to 1998; he died in 2008. It was alleged by *Time Magazine*, in an article published a few months after Suharto was deposed, that, during his 30 years in office, his family had acquired cash and assets in excess of US$70 billion.[17] By the time he was deposed, *Time Magazine* reckoned that the family controlled assets worth US$15 billion. Of these assets, it was estimated that the president's favorite son, Tommy, controlled nearly US$1 billion.

Transfer of funds

In July 1998, scarcely a month after his father's resignation as president, Tommy Suharto opened an account with the Guernsey office of BNP Paribas (Suisse) SA in the name of Garnet Investments Limited, a company incorporated in British Virgin Islands. Between August 1998 and June 1999, some £8 million and US$59 million were paid into Garnet accounts at BNP in Guernsey.

In July 2002, Tommy Suharto was convicted in Indonesia of the following:

- Unlawfully possessing fire arms and ammunition
- Arranging the murder, on July 26, 2001, of Supreme Court Judge Syafiuddin Kartasasmita, who had convicted him of corruption on September 22, 2000
- Preventing a public servant from performing his duty (by failing to surrender to serve his sentence after his conviction for corruption and the rejection of his petition for clemency)

In October 2002, while Tommy was in prison following his conviction for the above offenses, Garnet instructed BNP to make payments from its accounts totaling €36 million. BNP had previously notified Guernsey's financial intelligence unit, the Financial Intelligence Service (FIS), of its suspicion that Tommy Suharto was involved in corruption. BNP accordingly sought consent from the FIS to make the payments requested by Garnet. In November 2002, the FIS refused consent and has done so ever since. Therefore, BNP declined to make the payments.

Proceedings in Guernsey

Nearly three and a half years after BNP's first refusal to make the payments, in March 2006, Garnet, which Tommy admitted, early on, was his company, began proceedings against BNP in Guernsey seeking declarations that BNP was obliged to comply with its payment instructions.[18] In September 2006, the Royal Court of Guernsey ordered that the Indonesian Embassy in London should be notified of the proceedings and asked whether it wished to make any claim to the money in Garnet's account with BNP. As a result of this notification, Indonesia took steps to intervene in the proceedings and was joined as a third party in January 2007.

Indonesia immediately applied for a freezing order on Garnet's account with BNP, which was granted by the Guernsey court. The freezing order was continued in subsequent applications. However, the court in Guernsey made it clear from an early date that it did not want to be the sole focus of Indonesia's endeavors to recover what were alleged to be the proceeds of corruption among members of the Suharto family. Tommy maintained that the monies in the account represented the sale of his shares in Lamborghini, the luxury car maker. That may have been so, but begs the question where the money came from to purchase those shares.

The Guernsey court said that Indonesia needed to demonstrate that action was being taken by the authorities in Indonesia against Tommy for corruption. Ideally, the court in Guernsey would have liked to have seen a conviction obtained in Indonesia. However, all attempts by the Indonesian government to bring civil claims and obtain a judgment against Tommy failed.

Difficulties in Indonesia

In 2008, the Indonesian courts dismissed the last of the government's claims. Indonesia appealed and won, but, in the meantime, the freezing injunction in Guernsey had been released. This was the result of a decision of the Court of Appeal in Guernsey in January 2009. The Court of Appeal's decision was appealed to the Privy Council in London, which is the highest Court of Appeal for Guernsey. The Privy Council refused leave to continue with the appeal, but the Guernsey Financial Intelligence Service, which had originally frozen the funds, has withheld its consent to removal of the monies. The matter is before the courts in Guernsey again at the time of writing.

If the monies are ultimately released, it will obviously be an extremely unfortunate result for Indonesia, but the question has to be asked: Why has it not been possible for the authorities in Indonesia to bring a successful prosecution against Tommy? This is particularly so in light of the substantial allegations of corruption that have been made against the Suharto family in general and Tommy in particular. It may have to be recognized that the Indonesian authorities face insurmountable difficulties in bringing successful proceedings against members of a family that has been protected by years of political immunity in Indonesia, amounting to near total impunity under Indonesian law.

Following the failure of the proceedings in Guernsey, various events took place in Indonesia that may shed light on the difficulties the government has faced in succeeding against Tommy. A number of revelations came out in the wake of a botched attempt to discredit two of the commissioners at Indonesia's anticorruption agency, the KPK. One revelation was that anyone with sufficient monies could hire *markuse*, who, in the words of the *New York Times*, are "middlemen who can persuade corrupt police officers, prosecutors and judges to drop a case against a client for the right amount of money."[19]

This case does not represent a failing by the offshore haven involved, Guernsey, which has tried to assist Indonesia by continuing to freeze these assets for as long as possible within the limits of Guernsey law, but it does demonstrate the huge difficulties a government faces bringing proceedings in a foreign jurisdiction if it is, for whatever reason, unable to bring a successful case in its own jurisdiction.

Kenya: The Anglo Leasing Affair

Introduction

This is a rather different type of case. It does not involve a single kleptocrat, but rather a conspiracy among high-ranking members of the government and dishonest businessmen to defraud Kenya of huge sums of money. The methods used and the failings in the Kenyan system are revealing.

Anglo Leasing is the generic description given to some 18 contracts, two of which involved a shell company called Anglo Leasing and most of which were entered into by the Kenyan government over a period of two or three years. This period straddled the end of the rule of President Daniel arap Moi and the election of President Mwai Kibaki in 2003. Twelve of the contracts were placed during Moi's term of office, and six after Kibaki came to power.

The contracts were for a wide range of equipment and services spread across a number of government departments. These ranged from the Prison Service, the Police, the Police Air Wing, the Administration Police (responsible for country districts), the Passport Office, the Post Office, the Kenyan navy, and the Meteorological Department. The equipment in question for each of these departments included digital communications networks for the prisons, the Post Office, and the Administrative Police; weapons, security equipment, vehicles, and a forensic science laboratory for the police Criminal Investigations Department; helicopters for the Police Air Wing; an oceanographic survey vessel for the navy; and a weather surveillance radar system for the Meteorological Office. The total value of these contracts was close to US$1 billion. An evaluation of the contracts by a leading international firm of accountants concluded that the majority were vastly overpriced given that the equipment was often either outdated and useless or far too sophisticated to be supported adequately.[20] The actual need for the majority of the equipment was, in any event, highly questionable.

All of the contracts had many or all of the same suspicious features, some of which may be summarized as follows:

- The projects were not subject to the normal public procurement processes as laid down by government circulars prior to 2001 and by regulations since 2001.
- The procurement processes were normally avoided on the basis that the projects were a matter of national security, or that there was effectively only one available supplier, or that there was the utmost urgency to undertake the project. None of these assertions was ever effectively challenged or investigated.

- As a result, each of the cotractors was presented as a single-source supplier on the basis of either no tender process whatsoever or, at best, a deeply flawed tender process.
- No due diligence was carried out on any of the contractors.
- There was little or no negotiation of the contractual terms, which were dictated by the supplier and not adequately scrutinized by the commissioning department or the Finance Ministry.
- Contractors frequently represented that they were based in major commercial jurisdictions, such as the Netherlands, Switzerland, or the United Kingdom, whereas they were registered in offshore jurisdictions.

Links among the contracts

Investigations have clearly established that, apart from the numerous shared features summarized above, there are also numerous links of personnel, addresses, banking arrangements, and other matters in respect of the companies involved in the contracts. Broadly, the contracts can be shown to fall into two groups: 13 can be shown to be associated with the Kamani family, and 5 were associated with Anura Leslie Perera.

The Kamani family includes prominent Kenyan businessmen who are also involved in businesses overseas, most notably in India and the United Kingdom. In the mid-1990s, the family, which had been heavily linked to contracts with the Kenyan government, was involved in two major scandals, one concerning defective boilers sold to the Kenya Prisons Department and the other concerning Mahindra jeeps that were sold to the Kenya Police Department and were wholly unsuitable for the requirements. As a result, in 1997, the family was blacklisted from government business. The structure of these newer contracts, with a series of apparently unconnected companies used as fronts, appears to have evolved as a way of avoiding this prohibition.

Anura Leslie Perera has lived in Kenya and done business with the Kenya government for many years, but is said currently to reside in northern Cyprus. He is of Sri Lankan origin and has an Irish passport.

Kenya is not alone in having suffered from such dubious contracting practices. A combination of corrupt officials and unscrupulous businessmen is a pattern that appears all too often in emerging markets, to the huge detriment of the countries concerned.

Attempts to bring the perpetrators to justice

When the Kenya Anti-Corruption Commission (KACC) investigated these matters, it was clear that all the contracts had been masterminded by the two groups.[21]

The full extent of the scam only became gradually apparent to John Githongo, Kibaki's newly appointed secretary for governance and ethics, who called on the government to cancel the contracts when it became clear to him what had been happening. Githongo's attempts to expose the affair led directly to harassment, which included death threats and various attempts at blackmail; as a result, he fled the country and sought asylum in the United Kingdom.[22] Already, large sums of money had been paid out, but this did not stop at least three of the contractors from initiating proceedings in Europe to claim the unpaid balances on their contracts.

One of these sets of proceedings was undertaken in Switzerland.[23] In an endeavor to gather evidence from Switzerland, the KACC issued letters of request for mutual legal assistance. Acting on one of these requests, the Swiss authorities raided the premises of a shell company used by the plaintiffs. Papers and records were removed. Within 48 hours, proceedings were issued by that company in Nairobi seeking orders of certiorari and prohibition in respect of Kenya's 2003 Anti-Corruption and Economic Crimes Act.[24]

It was claimed that the KACC had no power to issue letters of request to a foreign government. The case came up for trial, and the judge at first instance upheld the claims that KACC had, in effect, acted unconstitutionally, despite the fact that express power was given to the KACC to request from and to give mutual legal assistance to foreign governments in the statute under which it was incorporated.[25]

The effect of this decision was interpreted by Kenya's attorney general to mean that the KACC could not either give or receive mutual legal assistance until the court decision had been appealed and overturned or until new legislation, which was before Parliament, had been passed.

As a direct result, the Serious Fraud Office in England issued a press release at the beginning of February 2009 in which it stated that it was suspending investigations being carried out on behalf of the Kenyan government because they could not foresee receiving adequate cooperation from Kenya.[26]

In 2010, the Kenyan court decision was successfully appealed, and cooperation has resumed, but two valuable years were lost.

The Swiss press has, however, been following the proceedings in Geneva closely, and a number of articles have been published that have had the effect of widening the scope of the investigation.[27]

The Swiss authorities have also made great efforts to cooperate with the Kenyans, but little progress has been made to date in prosecuting the wrongdoers. The fault has almost certainly lain more with Kenya than with Switzerland. Various attempts have been made by the Kenyan Parliament to obstruct investigations into this and other, older corruption investigations, and the head of the KACC and his deputies were not reappointed when their contracts came to an end. It remains to be seen whether the political will exists now to pursue these investigations to a conclusion.

Zambia: President Frederick Chiluba

Introduction

This matter was litigated in the English courts over the course of five years.[28] It involved a claim brought by the attorney general of Zambia to recover monies belonging to Zambia that had allegedly been fraudulently misappropriated by means of money transfers made by the Ministry of Finance (MOF) between 1995 and 2001, during the presidency of the late Frederick Chiluba.

The money in question was transferred on the grounds that it was required to pay debts owed by the government. Some of the money was used in this way, but most of it was diverted for private purposes in favor of various of the defendants. The case fell into three distinct parts, as follows:

- A claim relating to the transfer of about US$52 million from Zambia to a bank account operated outside ordinary government processes, the Zamtrop account, at the Zambian National Commercial Bank Limited (Zanaco) in London (the Zamtrop conspiracy)

- A claim relating to a property company registered in the United Kingdom and owned by the Zambian government in respect of which it was alleged that one of the defendants had breached his fiduciary duty by improperly obtaining a consultancy agreement in relation to the letting of a property owned by the company
- A claim relating to payments of about US$20 million made by the Zambian government pursuant to an alleged arms deal with a Bulgarian company (the BK conspiracy)

In respect of the first claim, the court found that the Zambian defendants in the case had conspired to misappropriate US$25 million through the Zamtrop conspiracy. In respect of the second claim, the court found that the defendant in question had not breached his fiduciary duty in obtaining the consultancy agreement. In respect of the third claim, the court found that there had, indeed, been a conspiracy to misappropriate US$20 million through the BK conspiracy, and the defendants were found fully liable for that amount.

The Zamtrop conspiracy

The Zamtrop conspiracy arose following the collapse, in early 1995, of the Meridien Bank of Zambia, of which Meridien International Bank Limited, registered in The Bahamas, was the parent; the ultimate parent was ITM International S.A., a company registered in Luxembourg. On May 19, 1995, the then minister of finance in Zambia, Ronald Penza, announced that the Bank of Zambia would seize the Zambian subsidiary of Meridien under powers in the Banks and Financial Services Act. Receivers were appointed on June 5, 1995, and compulsory liquidation was subsequently ordered.

There was an investigation into the collapse by the accounting firm KPMG, which reported in November 1995, but no proceedings were brought. It was the attorney general's case that the conspiracy was hatched in April 1995. Xavier Chungu, the fourth defendant, was the permanent secretary at the Office of the President, Special Division, also known as the Zambian Security Intelligence Services, of which Chungu was the director-general. Chungu wrote to Penza seeking financial assistance for the Security Intelligence Services for unspecified projects.

Funding was sought on the grounds that debts left behind by the former regime had to be met. In the letter, Chungu wrote as follows:

> I wish to recommend that these debts be treated as part of the national debt. The amounts involved are quite modest and can, therefore, be accommodated within the external debt service budget without drawing the attention of the IMF [International Monetary Fund] and the donor community. I stand ready, Hon. Minister, to work with your Permanent Secretary and the Director of Budget and Loans Investments . . . in order to come up [with] a repayment program.[29]

This letter was written shortly before the Meridien collapse.

A series of letters was then written by Chungu stating that the Security Intelligence Services would provide a company, Access Financial Services Limited, with funds to be utilized for selected projects. This company was licensed hard on the heels of Meridien's collapse. Penza authorized a financial services license to be granted with immediate effect in October 1995 without any previous evaluation by the Bank of Zambia. The company was licensed as a nonbank financial institution and authorized to conduct financial, but not banking services. Penza was murdered in 1998, although no evidence was adduced at the trial as to why or by whom he was murdered.

Chungu would then, from time to time, give the company instructions on disbursements to be made from the account. The company was assured that it would not be asked to disburse funds for unlawful activities. As the letter stated, "you are relieved from making an enquiry about, and will often be unable to know, the use of application of funds after you have disbursed them." Chungu thus purported to give immunity from claims by others or any successor government officials.

At the same time, a woman, Stella Chibanda, the sixth defendant and one of the conspirators, was, first, assistant director (loans and investments) at the MOF; then director of external resource management, an internal MOF department, in December 1997; and, finally, permanent secretary, MOF, in December 1999. She was a powerful figure whom nobody dared to cross. Until September 1998, monies were transferred from the MOF account at the Bank of Zambia on the authority of MOF letters carrying two signatures. After that date, a new system of payment authorization forms was introduced. Thereafter, transfers were made under payment authorizations bearing only Stella Chibanda's signature.

Over US$1.2 million of the money paid out of the account went to the president's tailor in Switzerland for expensive suits. The president was well known for his smart clothing.[30] Other payments were simply cash payments for the president or to Chungu to pay off Chungu's credit card debts and school fees or to purchase jewelry. A "charitable donation" of US$180,000 was made to "churches in America" at the direction of the president.

The Zambian conspirators were aided and abetted in all their activities by two London-based firms of solicitors, Meer Case & Desai and Case Malik & Co., respectively, the first and second defendants.[31] Both firms acted for Access Financial Services Limited and Access Leasing Ltd. The judge found partners in both firms to be coconspirators in the Zamtrop conspiracy.

In the judgment, Chiluba, Chungu, Chibanda, and two other coconspirators were found liable to repay US$25.75 million, and Chungu was to pay an additional US$600,000 in damages for conspiracy. The partners in the two firms of solicitors were found liable for sums of US$7 million and US$2 million, respectively, for conspiracy and dishonest assistance. Sums were awarded against various other individuals, including US$1.2 million against Basile, Chiluba's Geneva tailor, for dishonest assistance and conspiracy.

The BK conspiracy

A letter of intent dated April 1999 was initially signed by Chungu on behalf of Zambia and appointing a Mr. Soriano, also known as Emmanuel Katto, a close associate of Chiluba and Chungu, as a consultant to act for Zambia in negotiating and purchasing arms, ammunition, and equipment. In August 1999, an agreement was supposedly entered into between a company called Teraton of Sofia, Bulgaria, and Zambia for the procurement of four helicopters, two fighter aircraft, arms, and equipment, at a price of US$81 million.

A facility agreement dated September 1999 was purportedly made under which Soriano, as lender, agreed to make available to Zambia, as borrower, a 10-year facility of US$100 million to provide financing for specific select projects and institutions for the purposes of provision of equipment and the need to replace obsolete facilities. Delivery was specified to be within 30 days after the contract came into force. Payment was to be made by means of a 20 percent down payment, 20 percent after inspection by letter of credit, and 60 percent after delivery by letter of credit.

An account was opened at ABN-AMRO in Basel, Switzerland, and a second account was opened at KBC Bank Brugge in Bruges, Belgium. The latter was called BK (Betti Katumbi was the wife of Moses Katumbi, Soriano's brother). The attorney general's claim was for US$20 million paid into the ABN-AMRO account and the KBC account. This amount was allegedly stolen from Zambia by virtue of the conspiracy.

Despite the fact that Zambia was supposed to be the borrower under the September agreement, the first down payment of US$10 million, also paid in September 1999, was paid by Zambia, not received by Zambia as the borrower. It was credited to the ABN-AMRO account as advised by Soriano. Subsequent payments were made between December 1999 and November 2001. A total of US$2.8 million was transferred to the ABN-AMRO account, and US$17.5 million to the KBC account.

Soriano had suggested that the purchase of the arms was related to a need to defend Zambia from threats from Angola and the Democratic Republic of Congo. In these circumstances, the official concerned said he felt compelled to sign the documents even though the facility agreement was not beneficial to the government and the manner in which the agreement had been brought to him was not in accordance with proper procedures: a familiar story. In the event, no arms were purchased, and the court was satisfied that the monies paid into the two accounts simply dissipated.

All payments into the bank accounts originated from the MOF and were authorized by Stella Chibanda. Soriano authorized onward payments from the accounts. In the judgment, Soriano was found liable for US$20 million, plus US$1 million personally received by him. Chiluba, Chungu, Chibanda, and one other coconspirator were also found liable for the US$20 million. The firms of solicitors were found liable for sums actually received: US$1.3 million by Meer Case, and US$450,000 by Case Malik.[32]

There have been press reports indicating that enforcement of the judgments has run into serious difficulties, particularly in Zambia. On

August 17, 2009, a magistrate in Zambia acquitted Chiluba of any wrong-doing: a finding that speaks volumes on many levels about the problems of bringing proceedings against African leaders in their own countries. So far as is known, no monies have ever been repatriated to Zambia, and, in June 2011, Chiluba died.

Conclusion

There are a number of common, not unexpected features in all these cases, such as the use of traditional havens to incorporate offshore entities to hold accounts in well-established banking centers and the use of intermediaries such as lawyers, accountants, and businessmen operating in Europe. One notes also the complicity of the banks involved, not one of which has, to date, been prosecuted or sued for the part they played.[33]

While the use of well-known banks in major banking centers may facilitate the recovery of funds as regulatory supervision tightens, particularly in the areas of know your customer and increased awareness of the dangers posed by assisting PEPs, there remain vast lacunae. In the United States, these have most recently been vividly demonstrated by the work of the Levin Committee to which we refer in the introduction.

It is also apparent that, while the jurisdictions in which the banks operate have become increasingly cooperative (this is particularly true of Switzerland and the United Kingdom and its dependent territories, Jersey, Guernsey, and Isle of Man), serious deficiencies may still exist in the jurisprudence of these states in returning stolen assets to the peoples from whom they have been taken.

This has most recently been vividly demonstrated by an extraordinary juxtaposition of events. On January 12, 2010, the Swiss Supreme Court ruled that over US$5.5 million in Swiss bank accounts beneficially owned by Jean-Claude "Baby Doc" Duvalier, the former dictator of Haiti, should be returned to his family. This decision overturned a lower court decision that had awarded the monies to charities working for the good of the people of Haiti. The new decision was based on a statute of limitations that had the effect of preventing the prosecution of any crimes committed by the Duvalier clan before 2001. Within hours of the court's decision, the devastating earthquake struck Haiti that killed over 200,000 people. The Swiss government was appalled. "This is a public

The Swiss government

relations disaster for Switzerland," said Mark Pieth, the well-known Swiss professor and anticorruption campaigner.[34] The money would have fed over one million Haitians for at least two weeks. The Swiss government was hugely embarrassed and immediately stepped in and stated the money would not be returned to the Duvaliers. It then rushed through new, retroactive, legislation, the Duvalier Law, which will be used by Switzerland if there is a perception that there is no longer a functioning judicial system in a victim country: prosecutors will have 10 years from the date on which monies are frozen in which to bring confiscation proceedings.[35] This legislation is potentially groundbreaking because it appears to remove the necessity for the victim state to request assistance, one of the great weaknesses of the UNCAC regime.

However, the uncomfortable fact is that Switzerland has been caught up in this sort of scandal before. In 2009, the heirs of Mobutu Seise Seko, the notorious dictator of the former Zaire, now the Democratic Republic of the Congo, who is reckoned to have misappropriated about US$12 billion in aid money, provided largely by the World Bank, recovered about US$7.4 million, despite assurances given by the Swiss foreign minister in 2007 that the money would be returned to the Congolese people (Wrong 2000). The reason, apparently, why this money was not returned to the people was that the Congolese government did not request the return.

These are but two examples of failures in asset recovery that are high profile. The reality is that the efforts to recover stolen assets are all too often thwarted. International asset recovery depends on cooperation among states. If this cooperation is not given by the state that has been the victim of the grand corruption involved, there is often little that can be done by other states to assist. It is hoped that other states will consider following the lead of Switzerland in this regard.

The case studies in this chapter demonstrate that there are a number of unique features in high-level state corruption that are the more striking for their repetition across cases. An example is the use of national security as the pretext for the urgent and secret disbursement of funds of the central government. One sees this with Abacha and Chiluba, and in Kenya. In the case of the Suhartos, the methodology was different, although the president was a former general and ran a quasi-military dictatorship. More surprising, perhaps, is the seeming ease of extracting the money—for example, simply by writing phony letters—that arises, directly or indirectly, from being associated with the highest office in the land. There is also the ever-present threat of violence against those who resist these people: the loss of a job and even death.

The tracking down and recovery of looted assets also yield common features. In the first instance, there is no real substitute for an initial investigation by law enforcement agencies, ideally in the country of origin. A lack of political will to carry out or continue with such an investigation can be disastrous. This can manifest itself in a variety of ways, from failure to pass enabling legislation to failure to mobilize resources to pursue malefactors and failure to pay lawyers to pursue them. Often, after initial enthusiasm for a recovery exercise within a state, political reality intervenes, interest wanes, people disperse, and instructions are increasingly difficult to obtain. Attempted emasculation of anticorruption agencies is an increasingly common phenomenon: Indonesia, Kenya, Nigeria, and Zambia have all shown the experience. Donor nations are starting to take action. The United States withheld aid to Kenya and placed travel bans on a number of Kenyan PEPs. A great deal more could be done. Kleptocrats and, especially, their wives and children, intensely dislike being denied the opportunity to flaunt their wealth in developed countries. Nongovernmental organizations in France have, however, brought civil proceedings in Paris against three African rulers in an attempt to have their assets in France confiscated, and the proceeds of sale repatriated to the peoples of the countries concerned.[36] The use of civil proceedings to recover assets is steadily being recognized as a powerful adjunct to criminal confiscation; the standard of proof is easier to meet, and, often, civil recovery is more attractive than high-profile criminal prosecutions for victim states. The World Bank recently launched a guide to nonconviction-based asset forfeiture to assist states in formulating policies and legislation in this regard (Greenberg et al. 2009).

In all the cases, there can be no doubt that the immediate self-interest of those who support the kleptocrats overrides any conception of the long-term damage corruption does to their nations. This underlines once again the huge importance of raising awareness of the fight against corruption, particularly in the developing world. The UNCAC and its proposed peer review system is, in large measure, directed toward this end.[37] Bringing kleptocrats to justice is only one small part of the fight, but an important one not only in effecting recoveries, but also in testing the political will of the states involved. International sanctions for failure to act should become an increasingly recognized option.[38] A number of those engaged in this area have opined on a need for a supranational jurisdiction. In this regard, thoughts turn to the jurisdiction of the International Criminal Court. There is surely a strong argument to be made that the enduring effects of corruption at the highest levels is at least as devastating, in terms of loss of life through lack of clean water and disease, as any genocidal conflict. A court that is internationally objective, addressed by independently funded lawyers, and able to deliver internationally recognized judgments that can be registered and that are enforceable in domestic jurisdictions is, as Hamlet said, "a consummation devoutly to be wished."[39]

Notes

1. Ministry of Justice, 2010, "Launch of UK Foreign Anti-bribery Strategy," Speech by Jack Straw, Justice Secretary, London, January 19, http://www.justice.gov.uk/news/speech190110a.htm.
2. The United Nations Convention against Corruption (UNCAC), which came into effect on December 14, 2005; the OECD Convention on Combating Bribery of Foreign Public Officials in International Business Transactions, 1977; and the Stolen Asset Recovery Initiative, launched jointly by the United Nations Office on Drugs and Crime and the World Bank in 2007.
3. The quotations are taken from "Investigations Subcommittee Holds Hearing on Keeping Foreign Corruption out of the United States: Four Case Histories," Permanent Subcommittee on Investigations, Committee on Homeland Security and Government Affairs, U.S. Senate, February 4, 2010, http://hsgac.senate.gov/public/index.cfm?FuseAction=Press.MajorityNews&ContentRecord_id=9a9a2e09-5056-8059-76f6-1b9eb33b29b2&Region_id=&Issue_id=.
4. These proceedings were separate from the recovery proceedings, involving the Abachas selling a US$150 million debt that they had purchased through offshore entities back to the Nigerian government for US$300 million. The debt was originally incurred in the construction of a steel plant at Ajaokuta. As a result of the judgment, Nigeria recovered the US$150 million profit the Abachas had hoped to make from the deal.
5. This took place in August 2003 after Bagudu was extradited from Houston by the authorities in Jersey, where he would have stood trial had a settlement not been reached.

6. These sums would undoubtedly have been greater. The amount banked in Luxembourg was US$600 million originally. The banks holding the funds seemingly used their discretionary powers imprudently, making high-risk investments and incurring substantial losses.

7. "Nigerian Dictator's Son Wins Retrial: The Verdict Passed by a Geneva Court against a Son of Former Nigerian Dictator Sani Abacha Last Summer Has Been Quashed and a Retrial Ordered," swissinfo.ch (March 10, 2011), http://www.swissinfo.ch/eng/swiss_news/Nigerian_dictator_s_son_wins_retrial.html?cid=29692974.

8. The panel report has not been published and only redacted versions have been presented to foreign courts.

9. The content of this and other correspondence was disclosed in affidavits sworn to in the proceedings.

10. This led, ultimately, to a confrontation between President Obasanjo and Tony Blair as to which country had the better claim to this money. Nigeria won.

11. The notion of *partie civile* in the context of criminal proceedings does not exist as such in common law systems, but it is an extremely useful tool in civil law jurisdictions. The condition for being admitted as a civil party is to be able to show, as the victim of the crime, direct loss or ownership of the assets that are the subject of the crime. A foreign state, local entity, or public company may, acting in a private capacity, as a matter of right, be admitted as a party suing for damages in cases of corruption or embezzlement of public funds. In most civil law systems, the civil party, once joined, is granted the same rights as the criminal suspect, namely, access to the examining magistrate's file during the investigation, participation in the interrogation of suspects and witnesses, and the right to request measures to be taken by the investigating magistrate, most notably the freezing of assets and seizure of documents at home or abroad. Although, sometimes, access to the file may have to await a certain event, such as the indictment of a suspect, the civil party can interact on a daily basis with the investigating magistrate through local counsel and can thus feed the local investigators with additional information or evidence and can request that new measures be adopted, such as the interviewing of certain witnesses.

12. Swiss Federal Court Decision (1A.215/2004/col), February 7, 2005.

13. The mutual legal assistance request to Jersey resulted in the extradition of Bagudu referred to in the text.

14. The Financial Services Authority issued a press release in March 2001 to the effect that 19 City of London banks had been involved in this laundering process, of which 15 had inadequate money laundering compliance regulations in place. These banks were "spoken to" by the Financial Services Authority, but no further action was taken.

15. In 2010, a leading Indian businessman was convicted in Jersey of money laundering in connection with the monies he had received from Nigeria during the Abacha regime by exporting Tata trucks and tractors at five times their actual

price to the Nigerian army. US$184 million held in an account at the Bank of India in Jersey was confiscated by the Jersey authorities, and Mr. Bhojwani, the Indian businessman, was sentenced to six years in jail. See Pidd, H., "Jersey Court Jails Former Nigerian Dictator's Business Associate," *Guardian*, June 27, 2010, http://www.guardian.co.uk/uk/2010/jun/27/nigeria-dictator-businessman -jailed-jersey.

16. The court system of the United Kingdom is divided among the courts of England and Wales, the courts of Northern Ireland, and the courts of Scotland.

17. Colmey, J., and D. Liebhold, "The Family Firm," *Time Magazine*, May 24, 1999, http://www.time.com/time/world/article/0,8599,2056697,00.html.

18. In a second set of proceedings, Tommy is suing BNP for losses incurred by BNP in investing Garnet funds.

19. Onishi, N., "In Indonesia, Middlemen Mold Outcome of Justice," *New York Times*, December 19, 2009, http://www.nytimes.com/2009/12/20/world/asia /20indo.html.

20. The police helicopters were secondhand East European models that required lengthy pilot training and heavy maintenance schedules to be kept in the air. Within four months of being supplied, the pilot trainers departed, leaving no skilled pilots, and the helicopters were grounded. The Post Office computers were to be supplied to all 800 rural post offices to provide interactive access to accounts all over Kenya. This would have required expensive satellite access and, more basically, a regular supply of electricity, which simply does not exist in remote rural areas, where the demand for such services was, in any case, nonexistent.

21. KACC was superseded by the Ethics and Anti-Corruption Commission in August 2011.

22. A full account of the Anglo-Leasing affair and Githongo's role is found in Wrong (2009), who highlights the wider political implications.

23. Many of the contracts required payment directly to banks in Switzerland.

24. In the High Court of Kenya at Nairobi misc Civil Application 695 of 2007.

25. Reading this decision, it is impossible not to recall the slogan paraded by members of the Law Society of Kenya a few years ago: "Why hire a lawyer, when you can buy a judge?"

26. The suspension is now in the process of being lifted in relation to some of the contracts.

27. In particular and quite startlingly, the Swiss press has made a connection with Bradley Birkenfeld, a U.S. citizen sentenced in the United States in August 2009 for having masterminded transfers of billions of dollars in U.S. taxpayer monies to UBS in Switzerland to evade payment of U.S. taxes. Birkenfeld's cooperation with the Swiss federal authorities has been the key to the recovery of these monies from UBS. A court order has, however, been obtained since his sentencing in an effort to prevent him from cooperating with the Swiss and Kenyans on the same grounds as the KACC cooperation with the Serious Fraud Office in the U.K. was halted.

28. The writers' firm was not involved in this matter, but it has made an important contribution to the jurisprudence in this field. The fullest account of the facts is contained in the judgment reported at [2007] EWHC 952 (Ch).

29. The content of this and other correspondence was disclosed in affidavits sworn to in the proceedings.

30. The BBC reported that few could remember ever seeing Chiluba in the same shirt or suit twice; this in a country where millions barely scrape a living (court judgment, 19).

31. Ultimately, they were not found liable.

32. The solicitors were found liable for dishonest assistance at first instance. However, the finding was overturned on appeal on the grounds that they were not dishonest, merely foolish and incompetent *Attorney General of Zambia v. Meer Case & Desai (A Firm)* [2008] EWCA Civ 1007.

33. See the report published by Global Witness (2010) that details, among other issues, the failure to learn lessons from U.K. bank deposits in the Abacha case, as demonstrated by the deposits made in the Alamieyeseigha case and the continued failure of the authorities to prosecute the banks involved.

34. Professor Pieth set up the International Centre for Asset Recovery at the Basel Institute on Governance, heads the OECD Working Group on Bribery in International Business Transactions, and was a member of the panel that investigated the Iraq oil-for-food scandal.

35. " 'Duvalier Law' Enters into Force: The New Swiss Law on Returning Illicit Dictator Funds Has Come into Force, Providing a New Framework for the Restitution of Assets to Failed States," swissinfo.ch (February 1, 2011), http://www.swissinfo.ch/eng/politics/Duvalier_Law_enters_into_force.html?cid=29395684.

36. Transparency International and a fellow nongovernmental organization, Sherpa, brought proceedings in Paris. The case called for the French authorities to investigate how a large amount of expensive real estate and other assets was acquired in France by three African presidents: Denis Sassou N'Guesso (the Republic of the Congo), Omar Bongo-Ondimba (Gabon), and Teodoro Obiang Mbasogo (Equatorial Guinea), their families, and close associates. It was dismissed at first instance for lack of jurisdiction, but, in November 2010, the Cour de Cassation overturned that decision and ordered that files be opened by investigating judges. For background, see Transparency International–France, "Corruption Case Filed by Transparency International France and a Gabonese Citizen Ruled Partially Admissible: First Step towards the Recognition of the Rights of Victims of Corruption," May 5, 2009, Transparency International, Paris, http://www.transparency.org/news_room/latest_news/press_releases_nc/2009/2009_05_06_france_case.

37. The effectiveness of the review process is itself kept under review by various nongovernmental organizations, including Global Witness and Transparency International. The relevant statements and reports of these organizations on the review process as applied to individual states were included in the documenta-

tion provided at the Fourth Session of the Conference of the States Parties to the UNCAC, Marrakech, Morocco, October 24–28, 2011 (see CAC/COSP/2011/ NGO/1–17, http://www.unodc.org/unodc/en/treaties/CAC/CAC-COSP-session4 .html).

38. The imposition of financial sanctions is, however, a notoriously difficult area because of the tendency of sanctions to harm the most those they are designed to help.

39. The case for the jurisdiction of the International Criminal Court to be engaged in certain international corruption cases is made by Bantekas (2006), but an amendment to the Rome Treaty was not on the agenda at the Review Conference on the Rome Statute of the International Criminal Court, in Kampala, Uganda, May 31–June 11, 2010.

References

Bantekas, I. 2006. "Corruption as An International Crime and Crime against Humanity: An Outline of Supplementary Criminal Justice Policies." *Journal of International Criminal Justice* 4 (3): 466–84.

Global Witness. 2010. *International Thief: How British Banks Are Complicit in Nigerian Corruption.* London: Global Witness. http://www.globalwitness.org/library /british-banks-complicit-nigerian-corruption-court-documents-reveal.

Greenberg, T. S., L. M. Samuel, W. Grant, and L. Gray. 2009. *Stolen Asset Recovery: A Good Practices Guide for Non-Conviction Based Asset Forfeiture.* Stolen Asset Recovery Initiative. Washington, DC: World Bank. http://siteresources .worldbank.org/FINANCIALSECTOR/Resources/Stolen_Assest_Recovery.pdf.

U.S. Senate. 2010. "Keeping Foreign Corruption out of the United States: Four Case Histories." Report (February 4), Permanent Subcommittee on Investigations, Committee on Homeland Security and Government Affairs, U.S. Senate, Washington, DC.

Wrong, M. 2000. *In the Footsteps of Mr. Kurtz: Living on the Brink of Disaster in Mobutu's Congo.* London: Fourth Estate.

———. 2009. *It's Our Turn to Eat: The Story of a Kenyan Whistle-Blower.* London: Fourth Estate.

Part V

Conclusions and the Path Forward

14

The Practical Political Economy of Illicit Flows

Mick Moore

Abstract

Aspects of late 20th-century globalization—growing international income inequality, the financialization of the economy, the rise of tax havens, increasing rents from exports of energy and mineral resources, and the large international drug economy—have interacted to reshape the political economies of many of the poorest countries and left them particularly vulnerable to the adverse economic and political effects of illicit capital flows. The increasing scope for the illicit expatriation of capital exacerbates problems of corruption, low investment, the unequal sharing of tax burdens across different parts of the private sector, the lack of legitimacy of private enterprise, and relatively authoritarian and exclusionary governance. The international community is already developing a range of interlocking tools to deal with the nexus of problems around illicit capital flows, capital flight, corruption, money laundering, tax avoidance, tax havens, and transfer mispricing. Improvements in the design of these tools and greater vigor in their implementation should have especially beneficial effects within many of the poorest countries, notably, in increasing private investment and economic growth, reducing the popular mistrust of private enterprise, and providing more space for more democratic governance. More effective international action against illicit capital flows would be complementary rather than competitive with attempts to improve from within the quality of public institutions in the poorest countries.

Introduction

Illicit capital flows is a difficult topic. As we see from the other chapters in this volume, there are differing definitions of the concept itself and contrasting views both on how it might be operationally defined for the purpose of producing estimates of magnitudes and on the analytic procedures that should be used to produce these estimates. The wise researcher might park the big questions about the dimensions and effects of illicit flows and focus on developing a better understanding of the components and correlates of the flows: capital flight, corruption, money laundering, tax avoidance, tax havens, and transfer mispricing. These topics, too, are challenging. I make a case here for continuing to work with the broader concept. Illicit flows have serious, systematic adverse effects on the economic and political development of many of the poorest countries. While it is impossible to block all illicit flows, there are significant, feasible opportunities to reduce them and mitigate their consequences through coordinated international action. The better we understand the adverse effects of these flows, the greater the likelihood of mobilizing more effective international action. These propositions cannot be proven beyond doubt. My case is based on deduction from interlocking bits of evidence. It is strong enough to merit more serious inquiry.

This is an exercise in political economy. For some purposes, it is useful to separate the economic causes or consequences of illicit flows from the political counterparts. Illicit flows certainly damage the quality of governance. They undermine democracy. The opportunities they create for personal or institutional enrichment create or exacerbate incentives for powerful people and interest groups both to be corrupt and to weaken public institutions so that they can continue to be corrupt (Reed and Fontana 2011). I focus more on a less familiar thread of argument: the ways in which the system that permits illicit flows discourages domestic investment in poor countries and therefore reduces rates of economic growth. The economic and political aspects of this system are deeply intertwined. In the poorest countries, illicit capital flows contribute to a vicious circle of weak and illegitimate domestic capitalism. (Potential) domestic capitalists expatriate much of their capital and invest only limited amounts in the domestic economy. They have inadequate incentives to nurture the domestic institutions that would protect and encourage private investment. They therefore continue to face an array of incentives to keep much of their capital overseas, and capitalist enterprise remains suspect and politically vulnerable, in part because it typically has a high foreign component. The more large-scale private investment is seen to be an indigenous activity, the more quickly it will become legitimate and the more likely property rights will be respected. All else being equal, a reduction in illicit flows is likely to lead to higher domestic investment.

The phenomenon of illicit capital flows is systemic in two senses. First, political and economic variables interact closely. Second, they do so on a global canvas (see the section on globalization). The apparently internal issues of weak institutions in poor countries both contribute to the prevalence and adverse effects of illicit flows and are partly caused by these flows. The appropriate policy response is not to focus only on these putatively domestic political and institutional problems, setting aside for later the problem of controlling and reducing illicit international flows. This is because the causation also works the other way: illicit flows exacerbate domestic political and institutional problems. Better global regulation of illicit flows should benefit both the polities and the economies of the poorest, weakest states.

Perspective

Mainstream economics tells us that international capital mobility can bring many benefits and that we need to scrutinize carefully any argument for restricting it, even where it is in some sense illicit. Equally, it is now widely accepted that, in the highly financialized contemporary global economy, excessive international financial mobility can do damage. It has become conventional wisdom that capital accounts should be liberalized slowly and that it may make sense to tax and discourage short-term capital inflows. One basis for these arguments is that the economies of smaller, poorer countries with relatively weak economic and political institutions may need protection from the destabilizing effects of large flows of highly mobile capital. Arguments about capital flows—or, indeed, any other form of international economic transaction—may mislead if they assume a population comprising only similarly placed high-income countries with relatively robust economic institutions and financial systems. What is good for those countries may not be good for the more disadvantaged parts of the world. This emphasis on the ways in which international economic inequality might challenge conventional economic wisdom has underpinned development studies since it emerged as a distinct field in the 1950s. The argument I make here is fully within that tradition and reflects the tradition's characteristic emphasis on the interactions of polity and economy. The world about which I write is characterized by a relatively systemic pattern of politico-economic inequality and advantage-disadvantage among countries. Until recently, economic inequality between the richest and poorest countries had been steadily increasing over several centuries. The quality of political and economic institutions largely mirrors average income levels. Poorer countries generally have less legitimate, stable, and effective governance systems. Property rights are less secure.

I depart from traditional development studies in that I do not posit a fundamental distinction in the global economy between a poor Third World and a rich (capitalist, industrialized, Organisation for Economic Co-operation and Development [OECD]) core. Neither am I entirely comfortable with the convention of equating political jurisdictions with countries. In particular, contemporary tax havens are highly consequential jurisdictions in terms of their impacts on the global political economy, but often are not countries. As I explore further elsewhere below, we need a minimum of four categories of political jurisdictions to understand the adverse effects of illicit capital flows on the poorest countries: the poorest parts of the world (labeled weak states), the OECD jurisdictions, tax havens, and a residual category that includes, in particular, those big, rapidly growing emergent economies that do not enjoy the questionable benefits of large reserves of point natural resources in the form of minerals, oil, and gas, most notably Brazil, China, India, and Turkey. To understand the emergence and significance of these categories of political jurisdictions, we need to look more broadly at the consequences of late 20th-century globalization.

Late 20th Century Globalization and Weak States

I use the term *globalization* in its most general sense to refer to the increasing frequency and intensity of interactions across different parts of the globe (Scholte 2000). There is broad agreement among scholars that a period of globalization in the late 19th and early 20th centuries was followed by an era of retraction and nation-centricity that lasted from World War I until approximately the 1960s. This was succeeded by late 20th-century globalization. Some of this globalization's most visible, generic manifestations are the rapid expansion of international trade, fueled in part by the containerization revolution; the even more rapid growth of transnational capital movements; and the enormous improvements in long-range communications consequent on the marriage of telephony and digital technologies. The following, more specific aspects of the globalization process are especially relevant to later sections of the chapter.

Growing income inequality

The recent rapid growth of the Chinese and other Asian economies may herald the reversal of a long-term process of growing divergence in per capita incomes between the poorest and the richest countries in the world. However, it has been divergence rather than convergence that has characterized most of the period since 1970. The OECD economies have grown at similar rates, and their citizens have become steadily wealthier than the populations of most of Africa and of other poor parts of the world (Pritchett 1997).[1] Late 20th-century globalization thus took place when average income disparities between the richest and the poorest countries were at the highest levels ever recorded. This inequality interacts with other factors listed below. For example, the existence of high-income markets in one part of the world generates large markets for commodities that, because they are either scarce (oil, gas, many minerals, diamonds) or illegal (drugs), generate high rents for those who control the sourcing in poor countries.

Financialization

Understood broadly, financialization refers to the increasing influence of financial markets, financial actors, and financial institutions in the operation of domestic and international economies. More specifically, it includes the increasing dominance of the finance industry in the sum total of economic activity, of financial controllers in the management of corporations, of financial assets among total assets, of marketized securities and, particularly, equities among financial assets, of the stock market as a market for corporate control in determining corporate strategies, and of fluctuations in the stock market as a determinant of business cycles (Dore 2000). Braudel's concept of disembedded capitalism points in the same direction: capitalism is "a series of layers built on top of the everyday market economy of onions and wood, plumbing and cooking. These layers, local, regional, national and global, are characterized by ever greater abstraction, until at the top sits disembodied finance, seeking returns anywhere, uncommitted to any particular place or industry, and commodifying anything and everything" (Mulgan 2009, 10–11). There is a wide consensus that financialization has been a dominant feature of late 20th-century globalization. The volume of transnational capital movements has expanded exponentially since the 1970s, having long ago ceased to reflect trade financing requirements, despite the fast growth of international trade (Cohen 1996). As the forest of legitimate transnational capital movements has blossomed and thickened, the opportunities to hide illegal or illicit capital assets within it have multiplied.[2]

Tax havens

Some tax havens have their historical roots in the 19th century, but their explosive growth dates from the early 1970s (Palan, Murphy, and Chavagneux 2010). Conceptually, tax havens are easy to define. They are "jurisdictions that deliberately create legislation to ease transactions undertaken by people who are not resident in their domains, with a view to avoiding taxation and/or regulations, which they facilitate by providing a legally backed veil of secrecy to make it hard to determine beneficiaries" (Palan, Murphy, and Chavagneux 2010, 236). They are characterized by high levels of secrecy and the ease with which companies and other legal entities, including trusts, can be established and registered. There are enormous disputes over which jurisdictions should formally be labeled as tax havens. For our present purposes, it is useful to distinguish two broad categories. The first are basic tax havens, as exemplified by Cayman Islands. These are secrecy jurisdictions that "remain mere 'paper centers,' providing a home for shell companies and trusts, proxy banking institutions, and captive insurance companies" (Palan, Murphy, and Chavagneux 2010, 27). They add little economic value and employ few people relative to the number of companies and other legal entities to which they are formally home. They exist purely to facilitate the hiding of assets, money laundering, and the evasion of tax. These basic tax havens are an outcome of high levels of international economic inequality. Most were originally small island colonial dependencies, especially of the United Kingdom, that moved into the tax haven business in response to decolonization, the disappearance of imperial subsidies, and serious difficulties of identifying alternative new sources of national income and government revenue (Palan, Murphy, and Chavagneux 2010). The second type of tax havens are offshore financial centers, which provide some of the basic tax haven services of secrecy, money laundering, and tax avoidance, but employ more people, undertake a wider range of financial services, and, to some extent, do add economic value. While basic tax havens tend to be small island jurisdictions, often in the Caribbean, offshore financial centers are more likely to be located within the financial service sectors of larger and more prosperous economies, including Singapore, Switzerland, the United Kingdom, and the United States (Palan, Murphy, and Chavagneux 2010). Both kinds play a central role in illicit financial flows. Their existence increases the opportunities to transfer money clandestinely and then store it secretly and securely. It rewards and thus motivates illicit movements of money across international borders and the illicit activities such as grand corruption or transfer mispricing that often underlie these movements.

Natural resource rents

In quantitative term, rents from point natural resources—that is, minerals and energy—have grown considerably in recent decades.[3] Although the international energy and minerals economies tend to be unstable, demand and prices have tended upward in recent decades, and extraction activities have spread into poorer regions hitherto considered too difficult politically or technically. Relative to the 1960s and 1970s, resource rents are now less concentrated in the Middle East and North Africa and have become more important around the Caspian Basin (the Caucasus, Central Asia, and the Russian Federation) and in Sub-Saharan

Africa.[4] Because the rents from mineral and energy extraction are so large and because the extraction processes are so distinctive, concentrated, and rooted in particular locations for long periods of time, we now know quite a lot about their impacts on politics and governance in the source countries.[5] First, the extraction of point natural resources, in almost all cases, greatly enriches the political elites that control the locations where the extraction takes place. It provides revenues to both political elites and states. Even in more bureaucratically organized states with some elements of formal electoral democracy, state energy corporations, often described as a state within a state, are bastions of privilege and extraconstitutional power (de Oliveira 2007; Winters 1996). Second, the extraction of point natural resources tends to generate relatively exclusionary, monopolistic, and militarized rule. Third, governments funded principally through point natural resource extraction tend to treat their citizens badly in terms of civil and political rights, health and education services, and public infrastructure provision because they have so little need of their citizens. Natural resource wealth frees governments from their normal motivations to nurture at least some prosperous taxpayers, affluent mass consumers, healthy and educated workers, appreciative voters, or fit and skilled military recruits (Bräutigam, Fjeldstad, and Moore 2008; Moore 2007). Cash from oil and minerals obviates the need for a booming economy and tax revenues and pays for the recruitment of mercenaries and (politically docile) immigrant workers to provide essential skills.

The international drug economy

Since the 1960s, there has been a big increase in opportunities for illegal rent-taking through the production of drugs in poorer countries and drug trafficking into rich countries. One cause has been increasing wealth and growing consumer demand in rich countries. Another has been the growth in air travel. The third is symbolized by the 1961 United Nations Single Convention on Narcotic Drugs, which represented the creation, under U.S. leadership, of an activist, punitive global antidrug regime that increased the monetary rewards for producers, traffickers, and the people in authority who were bribed to cooperate with them.[6]

In part because of these dimensions of late 20th-century globalization, a new concept and a new problem have, over the past two decades, come to occupy a prominent place on international policy agendas: the notion of fragile, failing, or weak states.[7] Let us term this the *weak state phenomenon*. While the terms and definitions remain diverse and to some degree contested, it is widely accepted that we are dealing with a new, generic phenomenon, which is found, in particular, in Central America, parts of Central Asia and Pakistan, significant parts of the Andean region of South America, and much of Sub-Saharan Africa.[8]

Governance failures are not new. They are, rather, the historical norm. Most attempts to establish legitimate and effective public authority fail somewhere along the way and end in disorder (Keefer, Loayza, and Soares 2008; Reuter 2008). The novelty of the current situation lies in the combination of several related factors. The weak state phenomenon became widespread across the globe within a short time. It arises in part because political elites in the poorest countries can enrich themselves by acting as gatekeepers between their own political jurisdictions and the global political economy. They can profit from the large rents attached to natural resource exports, drug trafficking, and various other kinds of illicit activities such as illegal diamond exports. Armed conflict may help them extract resources in this fashion or provide other opportunities to profit, for example, from arms trading or from the provision of transport and other logistical services to international humanitarian operations.

Historically, the political uncertainty and instability that typically follow war or internal conflict elicited a drive toward political resolution. Different interests and parties competed actively for state power. Either one party emerged as dominant, or public authority was reestablished through compromise among the leading contenders. A distinctive feature of the situation in some parts of the contemporary world is that these processes of political resolution and the reestablishment of relatively effective public authority are weak and slow. Failing governments have not been ousted militarily or supplanted by expanding neighboring states. Weak governance and continuous internal conflict have become routine. For every case of apparently successful resolution, such as Sierra Leone, there are several in which success is not yet in sight (Maconachie and Hilson 2011). A major reason is that, if they can continue to act as rent-taking gatekeepers, elites often lack strong incentives to put an end to weak governance or disorder and may actively profit from them (Munkler 2005). Control of rent-taking nodes becomes more rewarding than ruling territory and population through the contemporary state institutions with which we are most familiar. Political elites have limited incentives to nurture or build the institutions that might ensure peace and the rule of law (reliable and effective militaries, police, judiciaries, and prison services), mobilize large numbers of people into politics (political parties), encourage political bargaining among different inter-est groups (legislatures), collect revenue for public purposes (tax agen-cies), make informed policy decisions and implement them consistently (civil services), encourage private investment (property rights systems and predictable policy-making processes), or provide the technical sup-port needed to hold government to account for the use of public money (public audit offices). Effective institutions of these kinds become barri-ers to the pursuit of particularistic strategies aiming at the enrichment of family members and small associated groups.[9]

What does this all look like in practice? In chapter 13 of this volume, James Maton and Tim Daniel detail five rather spectacular cases relating to individual kleptocrats from Indonesia, Kenya, Nigeria, and Zambia. There may be no better case than Nigeria, a country that suffered pre-cipitous declines in institutional quality around 1970 when it suddenly became a major oil exporter.

> The problem is not simply one of embezzlement and bribery. The entire state machinery exists to siphon off cash. Many functions of government have been adapted for personal gain. It starts at the frontier. Access to the fast-track channel at Lagos airport can be bought from touts for $10. Bor-der guards in cahoots with them work extra slowly to make this option more attractive.
>
> A universe of red tape engulfs the economy. In a survey by the Interna-tional Finance Corporation, Nigeria ranks 178th out of 183 countries when it comes to transferring property. In some Nigerian states, gover-nors must personally sign off on every property sale; many demand a fee.
>
> Senseless restrictions and arcane procedures abound. Procter & Gam-ble had to shelve a $120m investment in a factory to make bathroom products because it could not import certain types of specialist paper. An American airline waited a year for officials to sign off on an already agreed route from Atlanta to Lagos.
>
> Massive economic failure is the result. Employment in industry has shrunk by 90% in the past decade, "almost as if by witchcraft", says one

sheepish boss. The few jobs that exist are mostly offered by cartels. These control imports, too. The need for new infrastructure is vast, but the price of a 50kg bag of cement is three times higher than in neighbouring countries. Fighting cartels is hard. Customs officers are bent, hindering foreign competitors. Judges are easily bought. The police are, at best, ill-equipped. One in four cops exist only on paper: chiefs collect the extra pay.

Nigeria is the leading oil producer in Africa, with a revenue stream of about $40 billion a year. The effect of this wealth is mostly corrosive. . . . Three-quarters of the government budget goes toward recurrent expenditure, including salaries. Parliamentarians are paid up to US$2m a year, legally. Very little is invested in infrastructure. State governors all receive big slices of the oil pie. This has attracted some very shady characters into politics.[10]

Categorizing Contemporary Political Jurisdictions

At the end of the section titled "Perspective," I suggested that it is useful to think of the contemporary world divided into four categories of political (more or less national) jurisdictions.[11] Informed by the analysis in the subsequent section of the impact of late 20th-century globalization, I explain in this section, in a little more detail, the differences among these categories that are most relevant to understanding the effects in poor countries of illicit capital flows.

OECD jurisdictions

These are wealthy countries that have shared similar rates of economic growth for many decades and similar economic and political institutions. All are liberal democracies in which the historic compromise between capital and labor has held for decades and become almost naturalized. The compromise faces little fundamental political critique. Property rights are strong. Workers and consumers exercise considerable power through electoral democracy, while controllers of capital continue to nudge and discipline governments through less visible channels: their autonomy either to refrain from reinvestment and, increasingly, to relocate in other jurisdictions (Winters 1994). Governments raise increasing proportions of gross domestic product (GDP)—now averaging 40 percent (IMF 2011)—to meet the needs of voters for services and welfare and the needs of capitalists for infrastructure and other kinds of support. The high proportion of the world's private companies that are rooted, historically and in terms of activities and beneficial ownership, in OECD countries face significant tax bills and pressures to relocate their profits formally to low-tax jurisdictions.

Weak states

These tend to be small countries, although Nigeria is also included, characterized by relatively weak public institutions and by political elites that face unusually strong temptations to enrich themselves through the ways in which they intermediate between domestic and international actors, institutions and resources (see the section on globalization). Commercial and banking confidentiality is not guaranteed. Legal and penal systems often function slowly and badly. Property rights tend to be weak. A relatively small proportion of the population are employees in the formal private sector. Private enterprise is often associated with immigrant foreigners or ethnic minorities and is still widely considered illegitimate or immoral (Chaudhry 1994; Moore 1997; Riggs 1964). Almost paradoxically, this limited political and cultural legitimacy of capitalism coexists with a relatively high dependence of governments for their revenue on what they can collect directly from private companies.

In general, the capacity of governments to raise revenue is substantially dependent on the structure of national economies. Above all, the proportion of GDP that accrues to governments increases predictably as average incomes rise.[12] Historically, the governments of poorer countries have depended heavily for revenue on easy-to-collect import and export taxes. This remains broadly true of the contemporary world, but is, however, much less true than 20 years ago. In the intervening period, governments of poorer countries have reduced tariff rates substantially and introduced a value added tax (VAT) to substitute, not always completely, for the revenue forgone (Baunsgaard and Keen 2005; Keen and Lockwood 2010). To that extent, their formal tax structures have come to resemble those of the OECD countries. However, they lack the capacity of the OECD's richer countries to raise large revenues through personal income taxes collected by employers on a withholding basis (see table 14.1).

The net effect of these factors is that governments of poorer countries—the best proxy we have for weak states—are relatively highly depen-

Table 14.1. Summary Statistics on Sources of Government Revenue, by Country Category

Country category	Low income	Lower-middle income	Upper-middle income	High-income non-OECD	High-income OECD
a. Government revenue, % of GDP	18.4	26.4	28.5	33.8	41.5
b. Corporate income taxes, % of GDP	2.2	2.9	3.4	2.4	3.1
c. VAT, % of GDP	4.9	5.0	5.2	6.2	6.8
d. Trade taxes, % of GDP	3.7	4.9	4.6	2.7	0.6
e. Corporate income taxes, % of government revenue	12.0	11.0	12.0	7.1	7.2
f. Corporate income taxes, plus VAT, % of government revenue	38.6	29.9	30.2	27.2	23.9
g. Corporate income tax rate %	39.0	33.5	33.3	28.9	33.8

Source: IMF 2011.
Note: The table covers 174 countries. The numbers show the means within each category and relate to recent years.

dent for revenue on taxes paid directly to them by private companies. This phenomenon is measured in two ways in table 14.1. First, in row (e), we can see that corporate income taxes account for a higher proportion of government revenue in poorer countries. But this is not the full story. The VATs now nominally in place in virtually every poor country are often, in practice, different from the formal model and the OECD practice. They often cover only some parts of the economy, notably the larger firms in the more organized sector, and, in practice, resemble additional sales, excise, or import taxes.[13] To a significant degree, VAT collections have a corporate tax element. Therefore, in table 14.1, row (f) presents the figures on the joint contribution of both corporate income tax and VAT to government revenue.

Both sets of figures illustrate the significant dependence of governments on taxes paid directly by private companies. Yet, we know that formal or informal tax exemptions for companies are widespread in poorer countries, especially in Sub-Saharan Africa (Cleeve 2008; Keen and Mansour 2010).[14] We can also assume that most illicit capital flows from weak states pay no tax at home, for the major mechanisms used by companies, in particular transfer mispricing and possibly also the manipulation of intragroup debt, seem explicitly designed to evade taxes through reassigning profits to other jurisdictions. This information is consistent with the fact that companies paying taxes in poor countries complain they are required to pay at high rates. While some companies are exempt, others face the full brunt of the appetites of governments for revenue. In Sub-Saharan Africa between 1980 and 2005, the total take from corporate income taxes in all sectors, except oil, gas, and mining, held up as a proportion of GDP despite the spread of tax holidays (Keen and Mansour 2010). It seems unlikely that the ratio of corporate profits to GDP could have expanded sufficiently to account for this stability. Some, at least, must have come from high levels of extraction from those companies in the tax net. Other evidence points in the same direction: globally, corporate income tax rates are higher in poorer countries than in richer countries, while corporate income taxes comprise a lower proportion of GDP (table 14.1).[15] The tax efforts made by revenue collection agencies in poorer countries are not inferior to those of their counterparts in high-income countries (IMF 2011).[16] Someone is paying taxes in poor countries. All too often, the taxpayers are the legitimate, formal sector companies that do not engage in large-scale transfer mispricing or lack the political clout to get tax exemptions. This highly uneven playing field does not make for a good investment climate. Illicit capital flows alone are not responsible, but they exacerbate the existing distortions.

Tax havens

Tax havens, in particular, tend to be jurisdictions rather than countries. Sometimes, most classically in the case of Switzerland, the distinction is unnecessary. However, many tax havens comprise territories within larger political structures that enjoy a special status and make their own laws, including Channel Islands and other dependencies of the United Kingdom and the state of New Jersey within the United States (Palan, Murphy, and Chavagneux 2010). As explained in the section on categories of jurisdictions, the category includes both basic tax havens that employ few people and exist simply to facilitate secrecy, tax evasion, and money laundering and offshore financial centers that provide a wider range of financial services, while still performing the basic tax haven functions. Both offer relative security for financial assets. Basic tax havens typically offer greater opportunities for secrecy, while offshore financial centers are better points from which to integrate illicit assets in more visible, recorded activities.

Other jurisdictions

This residual category includes most of the world's most rapidly growing large economies, including Brazil, China, India, Indonesia, and Turkey, and a number of rapidly growing medium-sized economies such as Argentina; Chile; the Republic of Korea; Malaysia; and Taiwan, China. They are relatively peripheral to the concerns of this chapter because they do not yet provide environments in which illicit capital can be kept, invested, or laundered easily, securely, and anonymously, especially not by foreigners without good local political connections. Some are major sources of illicit international flows, sometimes as a part of relatively distinct localized flow patterns. We know that large quantities of illicit flows out of India are routed through Mauritius before they return to India to take advantage of the privileges granted to foreign investment. Similarly, an even larger proportion of total global illicit flows take the form of business profits or the proceeds of corruption generated in China that are illicitly expatriated, partly to avoid the risk and burdens of foreign exchange controls, and often reappear in China to benefit from tax exemptions for foreign investment.[17]

The Location of Capital and Profits

As the global economy has become more liberal and financialized in recent decades, the people who own and control large amounts of capital face wider choices about where they locate it, where they book their profits for accounting and tax purposes, and how they transfer capital between jurisdictions. Many factors affect these choices, not least the real profitability of investment. All else being equal, investment will flow to the places where it can generate higher returns. But there is, in addition, a range of other political, institutional, and policy factors that affect these decisions. Six such factors seem particularly consequential for the pattern of illicit capital flows, as follows:

1. The degree of property security. This, in turn, reflects the interaction of four main considerations: the degree of political stability; the extent to which political power-holders are likely, because of combinations of incentive and opportunity, to prey on the property of others; the extent to which there is effective protection against private

predation or theft; and the extent to which capitalism and profit making are normatively suspect at the level of public opinion and political rhetoric.

2. The extent of the opportunities for grand corruption. This results, in particular, from the interaction of (a) the existence of opportunities for large rent-taking through the exercise of political power, which is especially likely in countries with large amounts of point natural resources such as oil, gas, and minerals, or where drug trafficking and smuggling are widespread; and (b) weak political and institutional checks on corruption.

3. The scope for secrecy in asset ownership.

4. The capacity of government institutions, especially tax authorities and central banks, to monitor, regulate, and tax capital.

5. Effective rates of tax on capital.

6. The degree of socioeconomic and political inequality.

Table 14.2 compares these six political, institutional, and policy (extraeconomic) factors across the four categories of contemporary political jurisdictions.[18] The table sketches on the canvas with a broad brush, and I am aware that the boundaries between my categories of jurisdictions are fuzzy and that there are wide variations within them. The comparisons suggest some conclusions about where people who own or control large amounts of capital prefer to locate it.

Table 14.2. Major Political, Institutional, and Policy Characteristics Affecting Decisions on the Location of Large-Scale Private Capital

Characteristic	OECD	Weak states	Tax havens	Other jurisdictions
Degree of property security	high	low	high	mixed
Extent of opportunities for grand corruption	low	high	low, or — (few residents)	mixed
Scope for secrecy in asset ownership	low	mixed	high	mixed
Capacity of government to monitor, regulate, and tax capital	high	low	mixed	mixed
Effective tax rates on capital	high	mixed or low	low	mixed
Degree of socioeconomic and political inequality	low	high	—	mixed

Source: Author compilation.
Note: — = not available.

The first inference that we can make is that, even if the rates of return on capital investment were the same across all four types of jurisdictions, people who own or control large amounts of capital from within weak states would prefer to expatriate (some of) it to other jurisdictions. There are three interacting reasons, as follows:

1. In weak states, property rights are, anyway, relatively insecure. These are, on average, not good places for companies or wealthy individuals to keep abundant assets, especially liquid assets.

2. Especially in contemporary weak states, large capital accumulations in private hands are often the result of corruption, the abuse of political power, and theft of public assets. Such accumulations are always vulnerable to changes of political fortune. New power-holders will tend to try to expose the sins and corruption or take a share in the assets of the people they replace. Placing illicitly acquired money elsewhere in the world, above all in a tax haven, is the best protection against political opponents or political successors at home, domestic tax authorities, global investigatory authorities, and campaigning international nongovernmental organizations.

3. Companies operating in weak states frequently face a trade-off between (a) paying the relatively high headline rates of tax on their operations or (b) making political contributions to purchase formal or informal exemptions, tax holidays, or other favorable treatment from tax authorities. We can assume—hard evidence on this point is particularly elusive—that the people concerned would prefer to understate profits and expatriate capital clandestinely to reduce their vulnerability to this kind of political squeeze. Transfer mispricing is likely the dominant means.

Owners and managers of capital have significant extraeconomic incentives to expatriate capital secretly from weak states. They also have opportunities to do so at relatively low cost. First, central banking and tax authorities tend to be weak and, thus, do not constitute much of a barrier to transfer mispricing or other mechanisms of illicit outflow. Second, other attractive locations for capital have become increasingly available. The OECD countries have some allure, but the disadvantage that their governments mostly require significant tax payments. Tax havens more closely meet the three major needs: security of ownership, the secrecy needed to hide the recent origins of the capital, and low tax rates. Much of the capital passing through tax havens might be laundered and then appear as direct foreign investment in other jurisdictions.

The first-round consequence of the institutional configuration I have sketched out is that the people who own or control capital in weak states have powerful incentives to convert the capital into illicit outflows and significant opportunities to do so.[19] Even if we remain agnostic about the various estimates of the aggregate size of these outflows from weak states, we could reasonably conclude that the combination of the extra-economic incentives to expatriate capital and the opportunities to do so will tend to reduce the rates of investment and economic growth in weak states. However, only when we examine the second and third order effects of this institutional configuration can we appreciate the extent to which it may be doing consistent economic and political damage to weak states, as follows:

- The potential to hide illicit capital securely in tax havens is a direct stimulus to corruption and other illicit activities such as transfer mispricing. It decreases the chances of detection and therefore increases the likely returns.
- Especially in polities characterized by high degrees of socioeconomic inequality and little or no effective institutionalized popular control of the actions of political elites, those fractions of the political elites that are able and willing to participate in this nexus of corrupt internal accumulation and illicit capital outflows are also motivated and able to create or change the rules of the game to ensure that they can continue playing it in a rewarding way. In practice, this is likely to mean tax agencies that collect enough money to run basic government services, but have low overall capacity, especially in dealing with complex international issues such as transfer pricing; police services that lack investigatory powers; court systems vulnerable to corruption; weak public audit offices that lack independent authority; legislatures that lack collective cohesion and authority; fragile, unstable political parties motivated by money and patronage; and public services that lack a collective, professional ethos. Indirectly, these processes may further weaken the protection of property rights through their incentive effects on political elites. Powerful groups that control considerable (illicit) capi-

tal, but locate much of it overseas, do not have strong incentives to strengthen property rights at home (for everyone).[20]

• Not only do people who control capital domestically have extraeconomic incentives to expatriate it (illicitly), but also the domestic investment climate suffers collateral damage. First, a certain fraction of legitimate, formal business tends to face unfairly and inefficiently high tax burdens because much capital evades the tax net, especially through transfer mispricing and extensive tax holidays (see elsewhere above). Second, the knowledge that businesses are engaged in illicit capital transfers reinforces public and political suspicion of capitalism and profit making and increases the political vulnerability of the private sector. A not unfamiliar figure in weak state parts of the globe is the head of state who routinely lambastes the private sector for greed and failure to invest adequately in productive activities, yet regularly grants large tax holidays to investors on grounds that are less than formal or transparent.

Conclusion

Let us imagine that the international community extends and more actively uses the range of interlocking tools that it has been developing to deal with the nexus of problems implied by the term *illicit capital flows*, including capital flight, corruption, money laundering, tax avoidance, tax havens, and transfer mispricing. This action would take the form of greater international cooperation to identify and sanction transfer mispricing, further limiting the scope for the abuse of tax havens, easing and introducing more automaticity into the exchange of information among national tax authorities, requiring banks to be more vigilant against illicit funds and money laundering, expanding the scope of the Extractive Industries Transparency Initiative, more vigorously extending and implementing legislation that criminalizes acts of corruption overseas by citizens of and companies registered in the more economically influential countries, reforming international accounting standards, strengthening mechanisms and laws to facilitate the recovery of stolen assets located overseas, increasing watchfulness in relation to the financial affairs of politically exposed persons, reinforcing the regulation or self-regulation of corporate service providers, and requiring larger transnational corporations to give more information in their accounts about the location of their sales or profits.[21]

What would be the political and economic consequences for the typical weak state? The analysis in this chapter and elsewhere in this book suggests that they would be complex, because many variables interact. I suggest there would be a definable causal chain, sequenced approximately as follows:[22]

1. The net volume of illicit outflows would decline for two proximate reasons. First, transfer mispricing would diminish because it would be easier to detect, and the penalties would increase. Second, the overall level of corruption would decline because the opportunities to transfer and hide the proceeds overseas would decrease, and the chances of detection nationally or internationally would increase.

2. More capital would stay within the country.

3. The level of legitimate investment in productive activities would increase for several reasons. More capital would be available. The burden of taxes on the corporate sector would be spread more evenly, improving the investment environment for companies and sectors that currently bear high tax burdens. Political elites would be more motivated to improve the domestic investment environment. They would have two reasons to do so. One arises from group self-interest: because the incentives and opportunities to expatriate their own licit and illicit capital assets would be reduced, they would be more concerned about domestic investment opportunities. The other stems from their political dominance and interest in public revenue. The more domestic capital that is potentially available for investment, the more likely it is that improvements in the investment environment would bring returns to those who run the state through increased investment leading to higher public revenues. Through these incentive mechanisms, one could expect various kinds of public organizations and institutions to be strengthened, including the overall security of property rights.

4. The greater visible engagement of elites in productive domestic investment would help increase the overall legitimacy of capitalism.

5. Democratic institutions and practices should be strengthened because political elites would have less interest in controlling political

institutions and processes to facilitate and hide their own illicit activities in the form of corruption and the illicit expatriation of capital.

Does this all sound too rosy? If the list of intensified actions set out above were interpreted as a new policy program, then skepticism would be appropriate. We do not know the magnitudes of any of the causal processes outlined above. The arguments might be valid, but the causal relations and the impacts are weak. But this is not a new policy program. The scenario I have sketched out here involves simply the further development of a set of tools for the regulation of perverse and damaging transnational transactions that the international community has been crafting for many years. These are the right tools to use not only in the broad interest of much of the world, but from the specific perspective of the problems of institutional, economic, and political weaknesses in weak states. These weaknesses have strong internal roots, but they also reflect the ways in which the economies and political elites of weak states interact with global forces of various kinds, and illicit capital outflows play a significant role. Anything that makes illicit flows significantly more costly or risky for the beneficiaries and their agents is likely to have positive effects on the economies and the institutions of those states that have emerged from late 20th-century globalization with predatory elites, weak institutions, and flawed investment climates. Reducing illicit flows is not a substitute for internal reforms. Neither is it competitive with them. Rather, there is every reason to believe it is strongly complementary.[23]

Notes

1. See also Maddison, A., "Historical Statistics of the World Economy, 1–2008 AD," Datasheet, Groningen Growth and Development Centre, University of Groningen, Groningen, the Netherlands, http://www.ggdc.net/maddison/Historical _Statistics/horizontal-file_02-2010.xls; World Economy (database), OECD Development Centre, Paris, http://www.theworldeconomy.org/index.htm.
2. Correspondingly, diamonds seem to have lost some of their previous value as a mechanism for illicit capital flows.
3. Point natural resources are concentrated and extracted—normally mined— through large-scale, capital-intensive operations. The political consequences are different from the exploitation of agricultural and forestry resources, which, almost by definition, are widely dispersed, far less likely to generate high rents, and far less prone to monopoly capture.

4. For a relatively sophisticated database on the size of these rents, by country, see Adjusted Net Saving (database), World Bank, Washington, DC, http://go.world bank.org/3AWKN2ZOY0. Until World War II, the developed countries collectively were largely self-sufficient in energy resources, mainly coal, but also significant domestic oil production in the United States. Their dependence on oil from the Middle East (and República Bolivariana de Venezuela) increased considerably in the 1950s and 1960s, but in a context whereby the governments of the main oil-producing states (the Islamic Republic of Iran, Iraq, Kuwait, Libya, Saudi Arabia, and República Bolivariana de Venezuela) were generally dependent on and subservient to the United Kingdom and the United States, in particular. However, the balance of power gradually shifted from Western governments and companies to local politicians. The Organization of the Petroleum Exporting Countries, founded in 1960, was able to take advantage of oil shortages in 1973 to engineer production limits, rapidly push up the price to what were considered crisis levels, and, at a stroke, transfer something like 2 percent of the world's gross national product from oil purchasers into its own coffers. This set in motion two processes that, amid all the volatility of the oil industry (and, increasingly, the allied natural gas industry), have continued up to the present. First, the average rents from oil and gas production have been high, and governments have generally succeeded in capturing a large proportion for themselves, to the extent that they have become wealthy and potentially powerful. Second, the large relative decline in the North American contribution to global oil and gas production has been substituted by new sources, nearly all in areas with few nonenergy income streams: the Russian Federaton, the Caucasus, Central Asia, and parts of Sub-Saharan Africa (Harris, Moore, and Schmitz 2009).
5. There is a large literature examining the diverse effects of large resource rents on politics and governance. Among the many sources, see Bornhorst, Gupta, and Thornton (2008); Bulte, Damania, and Deacon (2005); Collier (2006); Daniele (2011); and Torvik (2009).
6. For good, brief general accounts of the international drug economy and its developmental consequences, see Keefer, Loayza, and Soares (2008) and Reuter (2008).
7. As other chapters in this volume demonstrate, issues such as human trafficking and the production and smuggling of counterfeit goods are a peripheral part of the story. They are neither large in volume terms nor themselves major drivers of the system. They matter to the extent that that they add more noise to cross-border capital flows and make it more difficult to determine what is going on.
8. The differences between overlapping concepts—such as collapsed, failed, failing, fragile, kleptocratic, neo-patrimonial, predatory, shadow, shell, rhizomic, and weak states (Blundo 2006)—are not relevant to this chapter. Some useful distinctions can be made. For example, Stewart and Brown (2009) distinguish among states that can be considered fragile because they lack authority, because they lack legitimacy, or because they fail to provide services. However, there is a

high degree of overlap between the various lists of weak or failed states. Lang-bein and Knack (2010) show that, despite the effort that goes into the construc-tion of the World Bank's flagship Worldwide Governance Indicators, the indica-tors are highly correlated. For the present purposes, the concepts of state weakness or fragility can be considered to refer to a common syndrome. See Worldwide Governance Indicators (database), World Bank, Washington, DC, http://info.worldbank.org/governance/wgi/index.asp.

9. For literature on the incentives for elites to weaken state institutions deliberately, see Ganev (2007) and Mathew and Moore (2011).

10. Abuja, Kano, and Onitsha, "Nigeria's Prospects: A Man and a Morass; Can the New Government of Goodluck Jonathan Clean Up Corruption and Set Enter-prise Free in Africa's Most Populous Country?" *Economist*, May 28–June 3, 2011, 28–29.

11. My classification differs from that employed by Stephanie Blankenburg and Mushtaq Khan in their chapter in this volume mainly in that I treat tax havens as a distinct category.

12. The other features of economic structure that consistently correlate with a higher tax take are (a) the size of the nonagricultural economy and (b) the ratio of foreign trade to GDP (Gupta 2007; Pessino and Fenochietto 2010; Piancastelli 2001). For explanations of the higher taxability of high income economies, see Gordon and Li (2009) and Moore (2008).

13. There is little or no effort to implement the core process of a true VAT: the rec-onciliation of mandatory invoices relating to interbusiness transactions.

14. We also know that tax exemptions for companies have become more common in Sub-Saharan Africa since 1980, especially in the more damaging form of tax holidays, as opposed to investment allowances that can be offset against tax lia-bilities (Keen and Mansour 2010).

15. Ideally, we would measure the corporate income tax take as a proportion of corporate profits. However, the latter figures are not available.

16. Tax effort is defined as actual tax collection as a percentage of the collections one could expect given the structure of national economies.

17. See chapter 7 by Lorraine Eden in this volume. A report released by China's Central Bank in June 2011 and quickly recalled suggested that, from the mid-1990s up until 2008, between 16,000 and 18,000 officials and employees of state-owned companies had fled China, mainly to the United States, having used off-shore bank accounts to transfer more than US$120 billion overseas. See "Chinese Officials Stole $120 Billion, Fled Mainly to US," BBC News Asia-Pacific, June 17, 2011, http://www.bbc.co.uk/news/world-asia-pacific-13813688.

18. I have not provided detailed statistical evidence to support table 14.2. This sup-port is generally to be found in major data series such as the World Bank's Worldwide Governance Indicators, where the best national level proxy scores for the concepts I have used in table 14.2 generally correlate significantly with aver-age per capita income levels. There are important questions about the extent to

which these correlations are valid or reflect biases in the construction of the indicators and how far broad concepts such as rule of law reflect the kind of property rights systems that are actually required to stimulate private investment (Andrews 2008; Haggard, MacIntyre, and Tiede 2008; Haggard and Tiede 2011). For our present purposes, we can reasonably assume that relative national scores in the Worldwide Governance Indicators are substantively meaningful. See Worldwide Governance Indicators (database), World Bank, Washington, DC, http://info.worldbank.org/governance/wgi/index.asp.

19. It is likely that some jurisdictions experience significant illicit inflows also because they offer the advantage of such factors as tax holidays for foreign investment or temporarily high interest rates.

20. To the extent that they wish to protect some of their own assets at home and protect their families against the future loss of political influence, they might create institutions such as capital markets as a way of laundering illicit wealth. However, capitalism has a powerful institutional logic. Institutions protecting property rights as private or club goods may expand to provide collective goods (McVey 1992).

21. Reed and Fontana (2011) provide a basic introduction to this field of regulating international transactions.

22. Specialists in this field might like to compare this argument with Brigitte Unger's work (2007) on money laundering. She detects 25 effects of money laundering, most of them adverse, but also explains well the difficulties of making strong claims and of finding suitable evidence.

23. Most anticorruption mechanisms operate only within individual jurisdictions. They are notoriously ineffective (Reed and Fontana 2011). It is as if the United States or some other large federal country decided to dispense entirely with any national-level crime fighting agency, even for the purposes of coordinating state police forces.

References

Andrews, M. 2008. "The Good Governance Agenda: Beyond Indicators without Theory." *Oxford Development Studies* 36 (4): 379–407.

Baunsgaard, T., and M. Keen. 2005. "Tax Revenue and (or?) Trade Liberalization." IMF Working Paper 05/112, International Monetary Fund, Washington, DC.

Blundo, G. 2006. "Dealing with the Local State: The Informal Privatization of Street-Level Bureaucracies in Senegal." *Development and Change* 37 (4): 799–819.

Bornhorst, F., S. Gupta, and J. Thornton. 2008. "Natural Resource Endowments, Governance, and the Domestic Revenue Effort: Evidence from a Panel of Countries." IMF Working Paper 08/170, International Monetary Fund, Washington, DC.

Bräutigam, D., O.-H. Fjeldstad, and M. Moore, eds. 2008. *Taxation and State-Building in Developing Countries: Capacity and Consent.* Cambridge, U.K.: Cambridge University Press.

Bulte, E. H., R. Damania, and R. T. Deacon. 2005. "Resource Intensity, Institutions and Development." *World Development* 33 (7): 1029–44.

Chaudhry, K. A. 1994. "Economic Liberalization and the Lineages of the Rentier State." *Comparative Politics* 27 (1): 1–25.

Cleeve, E. 2008. "How Effective Are Fiscal Incentives to Attract FDI to Sub-Saharan Africa?" *Journal of Developing Areas* 42 (1): 135–53.

Cohen, B. 1996. "Phoenix Risen: The Resurrection of Global Finance." *World Politics* 48 (2): 268–96.

Collier, P. 2006. "Is Aid Oil? An Analysis of Whether Africa Can Absorb More Aid." *World Development* 34 (9): 1482–97.

Daniele, V. 2011. "Natural Resources and the 'Quality' of Economic Development." *Journal of Development Studies* 47 (4): 545–73.

de Oliveira, R. S. 2007. "Business Success, Angola-Style: Postcolonial Politics and the Rise and Rise of Sonangol." *Journal of Modern African Studies* 45 (04): 595–619.

Dore, R. P. 2000. *Stock Market Capitalism: Welfare Capitalism; Japan and Germany versus the Anglo-Saxons.* Oxford: Oxford University Press.

Ganev, V. I. 2007. *Preying on the State: The Transformation of Bulgaria after 1989.* Ithaca, NY: Cornell University Press.

Gordon, R., and W. Li. 2009. "Tax Structures in Developing Countries: Many Puzzles and a Possible Explanation." *Journal of Public Economics* 93 (7–8): 855–66.

Gupta, A. S. 2007. "Determinants of Tax Revenue Efforts in Developing Countries." IMF Working Paper 07/184, International Monetary Fund, Washington, DC.

Haggard, S. M., A. MacIntyre, and L. Tiede. 2008. "The Rule of Law and Economic Development." *Annual Review of Political Science* 11 (1): 205–34.

Haggard, S. M., and L. Tiede. 2011. "The Rule of Law and Economic Growth: Where Are We?" *World Development* 39 (5): 673–85.

Harris, D., M. Moore, and H. Schmitz. 2009. "Country Classifications for a Changing World." IDS Working Paper 326 (May), Institute of Development Studies, Brighton, United Kingdom.

IMF (International Monetary Fund). 2011. "Revenue Mobilization in Developing Countries." Policy Paper, Fiscal Affairs Department, IMF, Washington, DC.

Keefer, P., N. V. Loayza, and R. R. Soares. 2008. "The Development Impact of the Illegality of Drug Trade." Policy Research Working Paper 4543, World Bank, Washington, DC.

Keen, M., and B. Lockwood. 2010. "The Value Added Tax: Its Causes and Consequences." *Journal of Development Economics* 92 (2): 138–51.

Keen, M., and M. Mansour. 2010. "Revenue Mobilisation in Sub-Saharan Africa: Challenges from Globalisation II; Corporate Taxation." *Development Policy Review* 28 (5): 573–96.

Langbein, L., and S. Knack. 2010. "The Worldwide Governance Indicators: Six, One, or None?" *Journal of Development Studies* 46 (2): 350–70.

Maconachie, R., and G. Hilson. 2011. "Artisanal Gold Mining: A New Frontier in Post-Conflict Sierra Leone?" *Journal of Development Studies* 47 (4): 595–61.

Mathew, S., and M. Moore. 2011. "State Incapacity by Design: Understanding the Bihar Story." IDS Working Paper 366, Institute of Development Studies, Brighton, U.K.

McVey, R. 1992. "The Materialization of the Southeast Asian Entrepreneur." In *Southeast Asian Capitalists*, ed. R. McVey, 7–34. Ithaca, NY: Cornell University Southeast Asia Program Publications.

Moore, M. 1997. "Societies, Polities and Capitalism in Developing Countries: A Literature Survey." *Journal of Development Studies* 33 (3): 287–363.

———. 2007. "How Does Taxation Affect the Quality of Governance?" *Tax Notes International* 47 (1): 79–98.

———. 2008. "Between Coercion and Contract: Competing Narratives on Taxation and Governance." In *Taxation and State-Building in Developing Countries: Capacity and Consent*, ed. D. Bräutigam, O.-H. Fjeldstad, and M. Moore, 34–63. Cambridge, U.K.: Cambridge University Press.

Mulgan, G. 2009. "After Capitalism." *Prospect* 157 (April 16). http://www.prospect magazine.co.uk/2009/04/aftercapitalism/.

Munkler, H. 2005. *The New Wars*. Cambridge, U.K.: Polity Press.

Palan, R., R. Murphy, and C. Chavagneux. 2010. *Tax Havens: How Globalization Really Works*. Cornell Studies in Money. Ithaca, NY: Cornell University Press.

Pessino, C., and R. Fenochietto. 2010. "Determining Countries' Tax Effort." *Hacienda Pública Española/Revista de Economía Pública* 194 (4): 65–87.

Piancastelli, M. 2001. "Measuring the Tax Effort of Developed and Developing Countries: Cross-Country Panel Data Analysis, 1985/95." IPEA Discussion Paper 818, Institute of Applied Economic Research, Brasília, Brazil.

Pritchett, L. 1997. "Divergence, Big Time." *Journal of Economic Perspectives* 11 (3): 3–17.

Reed, Q., and A. Fontana. 2011. "Corruption and Illicit Financial Flows. The Limits and Possibilities of Current Approaches." U4 Issue 2, U4 Anti-Corruption Resource Centre, Chr. Michelsen Institute, Bergen, Norway.

Reuter, P. 2008. "Can Production and Trafficking of Illicit Drugs Be Reduced or Merely Shifted?" Policy Research Working Paper 4564, World Bank, Washington, DC.

Riggs, F. W. 1964. *Administration in Developing Countries: The Theory of Prismatic Society*. Boston: Houghton Mifflin.

Scholte, J. A. 2000. *Globalization: A Critical Introduction*. London: Macmillan.

Stewart, F., and G. Brown. 2009. "Fragile States." CRISE Working Paper 51 (January), Centre for Research on Inequality, Human Security, and Ethnicity, University of Oxford, Oxford.

Torvik, R. 2009. "Why Do Some Resource-Abundant Countries Succeed While Others Do Not?" *Oxford Review of Economic Policy* 25 (2): 241–56.

Unger, B. 2007. *The Scale and Impacts of Money Laundering*. London: Edward Elgar.

Winters, J. A. 1994. "Power and the Control of Capital." *World Politics* 46 (3): 419–52.

———. 1996. *Power in Motion: Capital Mobility and the Indonesian State*. Ithaca, NY: Cornell University Press.

15

Policy and Research Implications of Illicit Flows

Peter Reuter

Domestic resource mobilization lies at the heart of development. Illicit financial outflows drain development resources.
— Task Force on the Development Impact of Illicit Financial Flows[1]

Introduction

The preceding chapters cover a wide range of topics (criminal markets, trade flows, the foundations of state legitimacy, internal firm pricing, and tax collection) and a moderately broad range of methods (accounting, criminology, economics, political theory, and law). This reflects the reality that illicit flows, like most interesting policy phenomena, touch many domains and require a variety of approaches to aid understanding.

In the face of such diversity, this concluding essay makes no claim to comprehensiveness. It offers observations on four matters. First, is it useful to focus policy attention on illicit flows, given that they represent a consequence of more fundamental and troubling problems (corruption, tax evasion, criminal markets, and so on)? Second, are illegal markets likely to be an important source of such flows? Third, what can be concluded from the existing estimates, given the lack of any systematic technical assessment of the most frequently cited figures? The final section of the chapter reviews potential research paths.

Illicit Flows and Policy

There is no doubt that illicit financial flows (IFFs) from developing countries are substantial. Even if the correct figure is only a 10th of the often-cited Global Financial Integrity estimates (about US$1 trillion annually according to Kar and Cartwright-Smith 2008), that is, around US$100 billion, it is large relative to either official development assistance (about US$70 billion) or total foreign direct investment in the developing world (around US$250 billion in 2004 according to UNCTAD 2009). Eliminating this outflow, all else being equal, would be an enormous gain to developing countries.

This alone does not imply, however, that IFFs constitute a good focus for policy. IFFs are a specific consequence of more fundamental problems that have long been of great concern. Most notably, corruption and the payment of bribes to major government officials have become a central issue for the World Bank and for the development community generally, at least since World Bank President James Wolfensohn put it on the Bank's agenda in the mid-1990s. Similarly, the failure of developing countries to collect taxes has also come more into focus in the last decade; the reliance on official development assistance is seen as, importantly, a consequence of the inability of these countries to tax their own resources (Bräutigam, Fjeldstad, and Moore 2008). The root cause argument, then, is that one should focus on ways of reducing the underlying problems: corruption, tax evasion, and so forth. The international flows are only a manifestation of these problems. Cut down on corruption, tax evasion, and the rest, and the IFFs will take care of themselves.

The argument for focusing on causes rather than symptoms is a common one in many domains of policy. For example, many analysts argue that crime is a manifestation less of individual failings or moral turpitude than of social failure (Sykes, Cullen, and Merton 1992). Thus, they say, the most effective way of responding to crime is not detection and punishment of offenders, which treat only the symptom, but elimination of social inequality, improving the conditions in which the poor live, and better schools and social programs, which treat the true causes of crime. In fact, there is evidence that society can usefully do both. Police and prison do reduce crime, at least through incapacitation, and social programs such as early childhood interventions also reduce the propensity to crime (Spelman 2000; Greenwood et al. 1998).

There are other domains in which policy focuses on root causes, but with little attention to amelioration of harms. For example, the current debate about financial regulation, in the wake of the global fiscal crisis, emphasizes rules to correct fundamentals rather than postfailure remedies.

There is thus no general approach. For some problems, ameliorative programs have a minimal role; focusing on the root causes is, indeed, the only path to reduction of the problem. For others, treating the symptom is also useful. What may be said about illicit flows in this respect?

A distinctive feature of the IFF issue is that the illicit flows may themselves exacerbate the underlying harms, that is, even if the tax evasion, corruption, and criminal markets continued unabated and all that one accomplished was to prevent the resulting funds leaving the home country, the result would appear to be welfare enhancing. Assuming that the owners of the illicit funds want to do more than hide their assets under mattresses, there would be more money for domestic investment and, perhaps, also a stronger tax base. Mick Moore takes this up in chapter 14.

It is also possible that trapping funds in the source countries reduces the attractiveness of corruption, tax evasion, and so on. A focus on the consequences might then reduce the underlying activities. This reduction could occur through at least two mechanisms. First, the returns associated with having to spend the money at home, with only the goods and services available, for example, in Congolese markets, may make the marginal dollar less valuable and, thus, lower the incentive to steal from the state. With increasing globalization, however, the consumption possibilities in developing countries are approaching those available elsewhere, at least in terms of perishables. Substitutes for homes in the south of France may remain difficult to find in poorer countries (indeed, in almost any country). Second, the funds are less secure at home than abroad. This will also lower the marginal return of another dollar stolen in an ex ante calculation because a change in regime may lead to the seizure of some of these assets. The calculation of the probabilities of seizure is no doubt complicated, but the fear of such a loss surely weighs heavily in small countries with kleptocratic traditions. The fear may increase the current kleptocrats' incentives for retaining power given that flight will separate them from their wealth.[2] However, this seems a modest effect; few kleptocrats quit power easily, even with vast amounts of wealth overseas, as evidenced by Muammar Ghaddafi's refusal to leave Libya under extreme pressure, despite the availability of billions of dollars in overseas accounts.

It is unclear how one should assess the plausibility of the above arguments: one is at a loss to identify instances in which it has, in fact, been difficult to transfer money from a developing country. The arguments do not seem persuasive. One suspects that trapping the funds at home will not much reduce the temptations for corruption and tax evasion, but that is pure conjecture.

There are, however, potential negative effects of preventing international transfers as well; those forced to keep their funds at home will have incentives to pay more bribes to protect their assets, now more vulnerable to the kleptocratic regime. Whereas a one-time payment may have sufficed to get the funds out of the country illegally, protecting them at home year after year might require frequent payments. The share of total gross domestic product (GDP) devoted to corruption may actually rise. Assessing how important this effect might be is also difficult, but it is probably not large under most circumstances.

Stephanie Blankenburg and Mushtaq Khan, in chapter 2, offer an argument why IFFs might be the wrong focus for policy efforts. They see the flows as the consequence of more fundamental failures of governance, which generate grand corruption and a reduced willingness to pay taxes, a theme also of chapter 3 by Max Everest-Phillips. The argument is almost one of feasibility rather than relative effectiveness. It is only possible to reduce the outflows from developing countries by improving governance, and, anyway, good governance produces many other gains. For example, a significant share of illicit flows in some countries arise in response to policies that lower the domestic returns available to investors outside of a favored elite who have access to the best opportunities. The sources of the income that is seeking higher returns overseas may be legitimate, but, if the government has imposed strict limits on currency conversion to stimulate domestic investment, money will flow overseas illegally. Eliminating the restrictive policies may be a precondition to cutting illicit flows, flows that some see as having a moral legitimacy lacked by the regime, which, among other excesses, is unfairly rewarding its supporters. In effect, the argument is that IFFs can only be reduced domestically by actions that will also reduce the underlying distortions that fuel the flows in the first place.

There is also the question of whether the political resources freed up for reform are best spent addressing the IFFs as opposed to the root causes. At the international level, there is only a limited amount of energy available for these kinds of efforts, which require commitments of time by heads of state and other senior policy makers. At this level, IFFs score well. They represent a target that can be dealt with through well-established entities such as the Financial Action Task Force (FATF), which has managed to obtain at least formal compliance in many nations through the establishment of specialized governmental agencies or through forums such as the G-8 and G-20.[3]

Nonetheless, the fundamental problems are essentially domestic. There is not much that outsiders, even major international financial institutions such as the International Monetary Fund or the World Bank, can do to address corruption, tax evasion, or criminal markets. The failure of the coalition supporting the government of Afghanistan is an extreme illustration of the limits of interventions on these matters: even 150,000 troops do not make much difference with respect to heroin production and broadbased corruption in that country (Caulkins, Kleiman, and Kulick 2010).

One of the benefits of focusing on the flows is that the developed world can play a direct role. These funds do not mysteriously disappear from developing countries. In large part, they flow into legitimate and, often, even highly respected financial institutions in the developed world. Thus, governments of the rich countries that serve as the domicile for many of the recipient banks can, through legislation, more forcefully push the institutions to ensure they are not taking in illicit flows.

Controlling the Flows

Numerous proposals aim at reducing the flows rather than targeting the fundamentals. Many of these are associated with nongovernmental organizations such as the Tax Justice Network, Global Financial Integrity, and

Christian Aid. Some proposals, such as country-by-country reporting of revenues and taxes by corporations that has been advocated by Richard Murphy and referred to by him in chapter 9, seek to reduce the extent of transfer mispricing (Murphy 2009). Others, such as tightening the regulation of tax havens and secrecy jurisdictions, broadly target all methods behind IFFs (TJN 2007). Still others, such as strengthening anti–money laundering (AML) efforts, build on existing initiatives.

One rhetorical merit of the term *flows* is it makes clear that there is both a destination and a source. Should both ends receive the same focus? Michael Levi, in chapter 12, points to the difficulty of enhancing AML controls in developing countries, illustrating the political economy point made by Blankenburg and Khan in chapter 2. Inasmuch as AML aims to curb the fruits of corruption, it often requires those who benefit most from the theft to build stronger controls that either prevent the crime or increase the probability of detection. It is fanciful to imagine that Marcos, Mobutu, or Suharto would have allowed the operation of an effective domestic AML, whatever laws they might have permitted to be placed on the books. It may be that the AML controls that matter more for developing countries are those that operate in destination countries. Tim Daniel and James Maton, in their review of recent cases (chapter 13), show that courts and police in Switzerland and the United Kingdom have helped return stolen assets to Nigeria, whereas the systems in African countries such as Kenya have singularly failed in dealing with their own grand corruption (Wrong 2009). In his talk at the conference at the World Bank in September 2009 at which the papers forming the basis of this volume were presented, Nuhu Ribadu, the former anti-corruption chief of Nigeria, stressed that a major aim of his early efforts in Nigeria was to induce cooperation from investigative bodies in the United Kingdom and the United States because, relative to his agency, they had more expertise and greater legal powers. He sought to demonstrate to these bodies that he was serious about recovering the stolen assets, and he accomplished that goal. As a consequence, after successful prosecutions in British and Swiss courts generated by his Nigerian initiatives and cooperation from the British and Swiss governments, there was a sharp reversal in flows of illicitly generated funds; large sums flowed from the United Kingdom and Switzerland, where they now seemed exposed to confiscation, back to Nigeria.

Surely, AML systems can be made more effective globally so that those who transfer illegally obtained funds are at greater risk of losing the assets or of being prosecuted.[4] The risk, at present, is generally thought to be negligible; it certainly is far less than 1 percent (in the share recovered) if the estimates of hundreds of billions of dollars in IFFs are correct.[5] More information exchange agreements among nations, more well-drafted laws, more dedicated investigative units will all raise the effectiveness of AML in many countries. Nonetheless, it is worth noting that the United States, which has a strong set of laws and a reasonably committed and honest enforcement system, has had little success in seizing laundered moneys or catching launderers or their clients. Reuter and Truman (2004), admittedly using data that do not reflect the increased effort since 9/11, estimate that only about US$700 million in laundered money is seized annually and offer a speculative calculation that the probability a launderer will be arrested during the course of a year is no more than 1 in 15. Perhaps radical changes in the status of tax havens would make a large difference, but the record suggests that AML initiatives have had little effect on illegal flows through the financial system. Databases containing suspicious activity reports have given investigators and prosecutors in a few countries a valuable additional source of information, but this has hardly transformed the effort to identify and punish those seeking to conceal criminal earnings. In countries without a tradition of independent and vigorous prosecution, it is even more difficult to be optimistic about the creation of an effective system, especially if (unlike the United States) senior political elites are also the probable targets of such prosecutions.

The fundamental problem for AML and, perhaps, for IFFs is the plethora of channels by which money can be laundered. AML controls initially were targeted only at banks, which had a public utility element in their role of providing liquidity. As reflected in the FATF guidelines, the controls soon expanded to financial enterprises more generally; insurance companies and stockbrokers also had to develop AML specialists to monitor transactions. In some countries, the systems have expanded still more broadly to cover all businesses that might be able to provide useful money laundering services. In the United Kingdom, all businesses must report cash purchases involving more than US$10,000. The FATF 40+9 regulations, published in 2004, impose obligations on a great array of businesses. No country has been found to be in compliance with the entire set of regulations. Even if a nation were in compliance, there are other channels, such as *hawalas* (informal systems for transferring money that are traditional in Arab countries and South Asia), for which the regulations are barely meaningful. AML regulations have certainly complicated the lives of felons with large incomes and helped remove some of the barriers to imprisoning sophisticated offenders. It is much less clear that they have reduced the criminal activities they have targeted.

Can the set of proposals for controlling IFFs accomplish more? Country-by-country reporting, transparency rules for traditional secrecy jurisdictions, and better tracking of politically exposed persons are all major reforms that would importantly change the ways in which business is conducted. The need of major corporations, both financial and other, to maintain working relationships with the international financial system provides a strong incentive for compliance with these rules, as may be indicated by the apparent success of recent efforts to isolate the Iranian economy. Such sanctions have the advantage of a well-defined target, whereas those aimed at IFFs are, by definition, not so narrowly targeted. It would be premature to make a judgment whether these reforms would do more than change the modalities by which illicit money moves internationally. Perhaps kleptocrats sleep less comfortably because of these changes.

Alex Cobham, in chapter 11, points to the significant exposure of developing countries to secrecy jurisdictions (which are usually called tax havens) in terms of the share of capital flight that passes through financial institutions domiciled in these places. These jurisdictions are now seen as a threat to the effectiveness of financial regulation and macroeconomic policy globally. A number of international bodies, such as the European Union and the Organisation for Economic Co-operation and Development, have taken steps to make them more transparent; see the survey and critique of such efforts in the report of the Norwegian Government Commission on Capital Flight from Poor Countries.[6]

Despite the high level of rhetoric on this issue from world leaders, it is fair to say that little progress has been made in the fundamentals (Eurodad 2009). The barriers to change with respect to tax havens are the standard ones for international economic policy reform, well described in recent tracts by distinguished academics such as Joseph Stiglitz. The suggested barriers extend from protectionism by leaders of countries and an inherent difference in pace between financial globalization and the international financial regulatory system to the procyclicality of financial systems.[7] The reform mill may grind slowly, but, if even the massive crisis of 2008–09 does not generate meaningful reform, one has to be concerned whether such reform is possible.

In summary, it is not clear how much effort should go toward halting illicit flows, as opposed to dealing with the underlying phenomena. There are political arguments that favor the effort, but also serious questions about how effective the targeted controls can be. It is likely that some effort should go specifically toward IFF control, but also that such control should be seen mostly as a component of the agenda for helping deal with corruption and tax evasion in developing countries.

Transfer Price Manipulation

Transfer price manipulation (TPM), the explicit subject of chapter 7, by Lorraine Eden, and chapter 8, by Carlos Leite, and part of the scope of chapter 9, by Richard Murphy, and chapter 4, by Clemens Fuest and Nadine Riedel, falls in another category. TPM is both a means by which illicit funds are generated and a method for transferring illegal funds generated by other economic activities.[8] There is a shallow consensus that TPM is reasonably well controlled in the developed world; there are intricate and heavily monitored agreements among countries that can occasionally even lead to a twinge of sympathy for a multinational firm caught between two aggressive national tax authorities.[9] This suggests that the TPM problem for developing countries can be solved through negotiation of agreements comparable with those found among members of the Organisation for Economic Co-operation and Development and through training of the relevant officials.

However, this takes us back to the conundrum raised in chapter 2 by Blankenburg and Khan, who treat all these regulatory issues as an exercise in political economy. TPM can occur for two quite distinct reasons. In one case, the multinational firm has more technical competence than the government with which it is engaged, and the TPM is simply undetected. This problem of government is, in principle, easily addressed through technical assistance. The other reason is that TPM is the result of corrupt dealings, whereby, for example, the original contract governing the transaction has involved bribes to government officials. The TPM is easily detected, but is allowed by the contract. There are many detected instances of this sort of problem (Global Witness 2006; Greenpeace 2008). We are therefore taken back again to the conundrum; can effective domestic restrictions on IFF be developed without tackling the underlying corruption?

Perhaps the actions initiated by rich nations can provide the missing element because transfer pricing involves two nations (or, at least, two jurisdictions given that so many of the secrecy jurisdictions are dependencies).[10] Even more than the other controls of IFFs, transfer pricing involves highly technical accounting issues that are difficult for non-experts to assess.

Illegal Markets

Chapter 5 on Colombia by Francisco E. Thoumi and Marcela Anzola points to a fundamental problem in the current view of how illicit markets contribute to illicit flows. Consider illegal drugs, the most well studied and probably largest of the global criminal markets.[11] The main flow is of drugs (particularly opiates and cocaine) from producer and transit countries, which are mostly in the developing world, to rich consuming countries that account for most of the expenditures, though not necessarily most of the quantities consumed.[12] The reverse flow is of funds from consumers in rich countries to the traffickers, who are predominantly in the source countries. Indeed, it is an oddity of the drug market that, in contrast to legal markets, the dominant earners in the international trade have come from poorer countries. Pablo Escobar (Colombia), Arellano Félix (Mexico), and Khun Sa (Myanmar) were all prominent figures who made massive fortunes from the international drug trade; if there are comparably rich European and U.S. traffickers in recent decades, they have managed to keep their identities concealed.

At first impression, this suggests that illegal drugs would generate illicit *inflows* to developing nations. It is often claimed that opium and heroin add one-third or more to the measured GDP of Afghanistan (UNODC 2009). Most of this comes not from the production of opium, but from the smuggling to Afghanistan's neighbors and possible involvement in other transactions entirely outside Afghanistan (Paoli, Greenfield, and Reuter 2009). There may be some financial outflows as richer drug traffickers seek to find more liquid and secure locations for wealth generated by wholly domestic transactions. However, it is more likely that some of the foreign earnings are brought back to Afghanistan. Those earnings have not been generated in the country and never enter the national income accounts even theoretically. The net flow may well be inward.

Thus, it is not surprising that Thoumi and Anzola, in chapter 5, find that the fiscal problem for Colombia related to drug earnings has been precisely the effects of the inflow of dollars on its financial system and exchange rate. The demand for pesos has been so great that the peso, rather than the dollar, has commanded premiums in the illicit exchange market that arose in response to currency controls. Drug trafficking and production have many adverse consequences on Colombia, but outflows of domestic earnings is not one of them.

A few developing nations have substantial international monetary flows related to drug markets; Afghanistan, Bolivia, Colombia, Mexico, Myanmar, Peru, Tajikistan, and (in percentage terms) a number of microstates in the Caribbean may exhaust the list of jurisdictions with 5 percent or more of GDP originating in drug production or trafficking. The newer human trafficking markets, analyzed by Pierre Kopp in chapter 6, are much more widely spread across the developing world; the Kyrgyz Republic, Moldova, Paraguay, and Thailand are a few of the countries mentioned. The flows have a different dynamic relative to the flows associated with drugs. They are often highly dispersed. Instead of a 100 kilogram shipment of cocaine, which may have a value for the smuggler of US$1.5 million, there are many coyotes at the Mexican border that earn US$1,000–US$10,000 for each crossing with a few illegal immigrants.[13] There may also be large payments for more complex human trafficking ventures such as the smuggling of a large number of Central Asian women to brothels in Western Europe (Shelley 2010). The extent to which this traffic is in the hands of residents of the sending countries has not been determined. Whether there are equivalents in human trafficking to Pablo Escobar and Khun Sa in drug trafficking is also unknown.

Keefe (2009) describes in detail the workings of Chinese human traffickers in the United States. The central figure in his account is a Chinese citizen who received most of her revenues in the United States from other Chinese immigrants (families of her customers), who had earned the money in the United States. She spent some of the money in her home village in China; many of her agents spent their money exclusively in the United States.

However, even for these markets, it is not clear that there is any substantial outflow from the source countries of funds from activities that are properly included in domestic GDP. The Netherland income from the prostitution of a coerced Moldovan woman, if it is included in any GDP, is counted in the country in which it becomes income, the Netherlands.[14] The money may be repatriated to the source country by the prostitute or by the smuggler.[15] There is a loss of human capital and associated earnings as a result of human trafficking, but the people who are smuggled are generally in the lower quantiles of earnings in their own nations; the loss may be minor relative to the loss of human capital associated with, for example, the admission under various U.S. immigration programs of medical physicians and skilled technology workers trained abroad.

Raymond Baker (2005) identifies other illegal markets that make substantial contributions to the illicit flows from developing and transitional economies: counterfeit goods, smuggling, and racketeering. The only method of determining the actual outflows of these markets would be to examine the dynamics of each market separately. It is easy to argue that there are substantial illicit inflows associated with, at least, counterfeit goods. These are often exports from developing countries that undercut products bearing the same name that are made in a variety of countries. The net effects on any individual country depend on various elasticities of substitution about which prior speculation is essentially impossible. Smuggling, while it certainly deprives governments of legitimate revenues, may involve net inflows to developing countries if the smuggling occurs from poorer countries to richer countries.

Existing Estimates

The debate about IFFs has been dominated by reference to estimates of the large scale of the phenomenon that are associated with Global Financial Integrity (Baker 2005; Kar and Cartwright-Smith 2008). These estimates, which are apparently the only ones to date, have been extremely valuable. They have focused attention on an issue that had previously been quite marginal. In this respect, they fit well into the modern pattern by which policy issues acquire a public identity; it is numbers as much as stories that attract scrutiny (Andreas and Greenhill 2010).

Thus, the numbers have been taken up by the advocacy community and used extensively to press for various policy proposals. For example, they are used to support the case for paying more attention to AML regimes in developing countries and for curbing tax havens and secrecy jurisdictions (DIIS 2009; Christensen 2009; FitzGerald 2010; Helleiner 2009; Purje, Ylönen, and Nokelainen 2010). As discussed in chapter 1, these estimates also have the troubling possibility of undercutting the case for providing official development assistance simply because they imply that there is a solution to the development problem that is both more constructive and less expensive for the wealthy nations that currently provide official development assistance, namely, preventing illicit financial outflows. Thus, it matters a great deal if they are substantial overestimates, a problem that is exacerbated by reference to missing items that might make them conservative estimates.

We address two related issues here: how well the measures match with the concept of illicit as formulated for policy purposes and the unexpected and troubling pattern of the distribution across countries in the estimates. The interested reader can find other concerns scattered in the chapters by Fuest and Riedel, by Eden, and by Nitsch (chapters 4, 7, and 10, respectively).

Concepts and Measures

Kar and Cartwright-Smith apply an unusually sweeping definition of their target measure, as follows:

> Illicit financial flows involve the transfer of money earned through activities such as corruption, transactions involving contraband goods, criminal activities, and efforts to shelter wealth from a country's tax authorities. Such flows may also involve funds that were earned through legitimate means. It is in transferring legitimately earned funds in direct contravention of applicable capital controls that the transfer becomes an illicit flow, regardless of the fact that the funds were earned in a legitimate activity. (Kar and Cartwright-Smith 2008, 1)[16]

In terms of the Blankenburg and Khan taxonomy of definitions of capital flight in chapter 2, this definition is legalistic, with its emphasis on the formal law, regardless of whether the regime enacting the law has social legitimacy. It ignores the distinction between the terms *illegal* and *illicit*, whereby the latter term covers concepts of morality.

Illicit includes some actions that are not covered by illegal, and vice versa.[17] For example, if Zambia has no transfer pricing regulations, then a contract with abusive transfer pricing terms may be illicit, but not illegal. Meanwhile, moving private funds out of Myanmar almost certainly will be illegal, but may not be illicit if it represents the assets of an individual escaping the inhumane rule of that nation.

Whether the distinction turns out to be important cannot be determined a priori; it involves sensitive judgments. If governments lacking moral legitimacy account for a small share of IFFs, then this becomes a minor issue. However, the estimates do not allow such a simple solution. The government of China, which accounts for such a large share of IFF estimates, has delivered extraordinary economic prosperity to its people over the last 30 years. It may not be democratic, but its achievement gives the government an important element of legitimacy. Does this imply that all violations of the government's many unreasonable restrictions on economic activities and individual mobility should be considered illicit?

The Russian Federation, also among the top 10 nations in terms of estimated IFFs, presents another difficult case. The government has been democratically elected, but has used capital control violations for political ends. This was one of the weapons it used to close down Yukos Oil Company and target the Yukos chief executive officer, Mikhail Khodorkovsky, for allegedly political reasons (Sakwa 2009). Are all violations of the Russian government's controls illicit?

One argument for using a legally oriented definition is that it simplifies the task. However, it does so at the expense of conceptual clarity. Moreover, it grants a legitimacy to regimes with foundations that are anything but licit. Major developing countries such as Iraq, Libya, Nigeria, and Pakistan have, at times in the last 20 years, been ruled by regimes that violated any notion of democracy and created legal systems that benefited only a small, privileged subset of the population. To assert that each of these nations would have been benefited if legitimately earned moneys had not been smuggled away from brutal and corrupt regimes is to take an unusually strong stand for the inherent legitimacy of the government. Such issues also raise difficult problems for the legitimacy and socioeconomic impact of suspicious activity reporting schemes if these are used in such countries for tax recovery or other purposes. When does extortion become the "recovery of stolen money"?

Which countries have large IFFs?

A striking feature of the final estimates is the dominance of China. The estimated annual normalized IFF from China is US$238.5 billion (Kar and Cartwright-Smith 2008). This is almost exactly equal to the total of the next nine countries with the largest flows. Indeed, China accounts for about 25 percent of the global total. Note that there is evidence, referred to by Lorraine Eden in her chapter, that TPM is a particularly important phenomenon for China. Only considering the 57 developing countries in the study by Kar and Cartwright-Smith, the China estimates range from 58 percent of the gross unadjusted mispricing estimates to 83 percent of the net unadjusted trade mispricing estimates for these countries, a major element of the illicit flows.

The focal policy concern about IFFs at the national level has been lack of domestic investment; this is clearly not an issue in China. Over the last 30 years, since its economy was released from command and control, China has experienced sustained domestic growth rates higher than the rates achieved by any other nation over such a long period. Moreover, the well-being of China has not been adversely affected by a lack of capital for investment. Some of that investment has been subject to lower taxation because it falsely appears as foreign direct investment, the result of illicit transactions that allow domestic capital to move overseas rather than appear as domestic investment; Hong Kong SAR, China, seems to be a particularly important location for faked capital movement. The comment here is not that the outflows have no consequence, but that the most dire one—the lack of investment—is absent.

It is also striking that five of the next seven countries ranked by the size of IFFs are countries of which the exports are dominated by oil (Saudi Arabia, Russia, Mexico, Kuwait, and República Bolivariana de Venezuela). Two of these nations (Saudi Arabia and Kuwait) are not developing countries at all; they have high per capita GDP.[18] The other three are middle-income countries, with high levels of corruption and low levels of tax collection. However, the dominance of oil is highly relevant because there are specific factors that can explain outflows related to oil. Indeed, it is well known that oil trade statistics are particularly error-ridden because of the fluid (pun intended) nature of the trade (Statistics Norway 2006; Laherrere 2007; Sinton and Fridley 2001). For example, a tanker may leave Saudi Arabia bound for the Netherlands (and be so recorded in Saudi Arabia's trade statistics), but then be diverted to Mumbai because a better price has been negotiated for delivery there. It will show up as an Indian rather than a Netherland import. Moreover, the supposed price when it leaves Saudi Arabia will be lower than the price when it arrives in India.

None of these concerns invalidates the estimates. They do raise questions about exactly what the numbers mean, a matter we take up below in the research agenda portion of this chapter.

Do illicit inflows matter?

Critics of the large Global Financial Integrity estimates of IFFs, such as Fuest and Riedel (chapter 4) and Nitsch (chapter 10), have pointed out that net illicit flows may be substantially smaller than gross outflows because there are reasons to bring funds in illicitly. Capital flight, from which the estimates are derived, has always been considered potentially a two-way flow. While temporary events might lead to rapid exits (flight having a time dimension), these might then reverse after the events. Political unrest is an example; money that has exited during a period of instability might return after a new regime has been established. Even in the period 2002–06, which is covered by Kar and Cartwright-Smith (2008), a large share of the developing world had restrictions on currency conversion and international funds flows that gave individuals and firms incentives to carry out such transactions illegally.

Kar and others have correctly pointed out that illicit inflows generate their own problems for governments.[19] The ability of the government to conduct effective economic policy, whether fiscal or monetary, is undermined by these flows. Illegal organizations can gain power by access to these unregistered funds. The illicit funds are likely to avoid taxation.

Governments, indeed, make great efforts to force such flows above ground. The government of Bangladesh, faced with a flow of unrecorded remittances from overseas workers, developed methods to make the use of the formal banking system more attractive to the senders and recipients of remittances: user costs were lowered; time to delivery was decreased; and the density of branches in Bangladesh was increased, so as to facilitate access for recipients. As a result, a large share of remittances moved into official financial accounts, and the share of GDP originating in remittances rose from 4 to 8 percent between 2001 and 2006 (Hasan 2006; Barua, Majumder, and Akhtaruzzaman 2007).

The problems associated with the two sets of flows are quite different. However, if the focus is on development potential, then netting them out can serve a useful purpose. Even if the Bangladesh remittances enter illegally, as a portion of them still do through the Bangladesh equivalent of hawalas (*hundis*), they provide resources for development. Indeed, remittances hardly represent tax-evading flows because such a large share of the funds go to poor households with minimal tax obligations even if they declare all relevant income. One needs at least to pay some attention to whether efforts to stop illegal outflows have negative consequences for illegal, but beneficial, inflows.

A Research Agenda

The research agenda should be diverse both methodologically and in terms of the unit of analysis. Beyond the disciplines represented in this volume, ethnographic and forensic accounting approaches should be added. Instead of focusing only on broad aggregates, there should be studies of the phenomenon in the small as well.

The overall goal of the research agenda is to increase understanding of the determinants of the phenomenon and to inform policy discussion of proposals to reduce IFFs. This section will provide a sketch of what is needed.

The existing estimates can serve an important function for future research. If they hold up to further scrutiny, then the national estimates become data. It may be possible to estimate a set of equations that examine both causes and consequences of IFFs. While the estimates are certainly noisy, they may not be much different in this respect from measures such as Transparency International's corruption index and the World Bank's various governance indicators that are now the staple of economists' modeling.

Generally, however, the focus on aggregate figures obscures the dynamics of the phenomenon; it has a black box quality to it. The aggregates do not allow the analyst to determine composition. Kar and Cartwright-Smith note (2008, 1) that their "paper makes no attempt to link illicit financial flows with the nature of underlying activities whether legal or illegal." It could be argued that, if IFFs constitute a useful target for policy purposes, then the tools are generic. It does not matter whether the flow is generated by bribery, tax evasion, or circumventing exchange controls. These all involve similar mechanisms for moving money to another country, probably a rich one, and can be dealt with through the various reform proposals: tightened AML controls, country-by-country reporting, a requirement that transfer pricing regulations be instituted in all countries, and so on. All that is needed is evidence that the problem is large, and the proposals should then be adopted.

In fact, we know far too little about the causes and consequences to take such a reductionist approach at this stage. It is likely that the outflows have varied sources, channels, and destinations across countries. Nigeria's IFFs have historically come primarily from high-level corruption in the oil industry; in Mexico, tax evasion has probably been substantially more important. The high estimates for China show that trade mispricing is a particularly serious problem in that nation, whereas it has been a relatively minor channel in many other developing countries. As Alexander Cobham shows in chapter 11, Switzerland plays a central role in Zambian flows, while the Isle of Jersey is important in the case of Algeria. Some channels will be more difficult to shut down; some destinations, more recalcitrant; and some sources, more innovative in circumventing particular controls. The discussion above also suggests that the adverse consequences differ among the various components of illicit outflows.

Moreover, IFFs are almost certainly driven by different factors across countries and over time. As with capital flight generally, political events may be important. Population dynamics matter as well; countries with large diasporas may see high inflows, as well as outflows given that émigrés provide facilitating networks for placing funds overseas.

The existing estimates provide a useful basis for selecting case study countries. The dominance of China in the Global Financial Integrity calculations suggests that it should be a prime target for research. As Lorraine Eden notes, Chinese government agencies have been cooperative in prior studies of trade mispricing. While this does not mean they will cooperate in all aspects of illicit flows research, it does suggest the possibility of obtaining the kind of information, for example, on the extent of informal moneylending, that can help identify the methods other than trade mispricing that are important in the transfer of illicit funds overseas. The recent release of a study by the Bank of China, "Investigation on the Asset Transfer Routes Used by Corrupt Officials and the Corresponding Surveillance Methods," is further indication of the Chinese government's interest in the phenomenon of IFFs.[20]

At the microlevel, it may be possible to learn from case studies of specific channels that have been hypothesized as important channels in particular countries. Ethnographic techniques involving participant observation or, at least, close and lengthy immersion may help increase our understanding of how, for instance, hawalas in East Africa serve to facilitate such flows, who are the customers, which are the destinations, perhaps even, what are the sources of the money being transferred.

As the number of successful asset recovery actions increases, a database could be developed on the portfolio decisions of kleptocrats. This may be fertile ground for forensic accountants, particularly if the case records allow the creation of a historical record of the movements of the associated assets. The recent studies by the World Bank of the portfolios of Abacha, Marcos, and Montesinos are indicative of the potential of this kind of research (Dumas 2007).

Policy shifts may also provide important research opportunities. The loosening of exchange controls, for example, should reduce the incentives for at least certain kinds of illicit outflows. Building models that allow for the separate identification of these effects, first, on the outflows themselves and, then, on the real economy, would be a worthwhile challenge.

IFFs have complex origins and varied consequences and present difficult policy options. Research will require a mix of opportunism and imagination.

Notes

1. See "Final Report from the Task Force on the Development Impact of Illicit Financial Flows" (2008, 4), at http://www.leadinggroup.org/IMG/pdf_Final_report_Task_Force_EN.pdf.
2. Thanks goes to Michael Levi for this point.
3. See FATF, Paris, http://www.fatf-gafi.org/. Though FATF has only 36 members, it covers a majority of countries through counterparts, associates, and affiliates such as the FATF-Style Regional Bodies. For example, the Egmont Group of Financial Investigative Units lists approximately 120 member units throughout the world; see http://www.egmontgroup.org/about/list-of-members.
4. AML laws require that the funds be generated by specified predicate offenses, that is, underlying crimes. Money laundering itself is not a predicate offense.
5. Though most of the attention is placed on the collective uncertainty about the size of the outflows, it is also worth noting that there are no global and few national estimates of the total assets recovered.
6. Norway, Minister of the Environment and International Development, 2009, *Tax Havens and Development: Status, Analyses and Measures*, Oslo: Government Commission on Capital Flight from Poor Countries, http://www.regjeringen.no/upload/UD/Vedlegg/Utvikling/tax_report.pdf.
7. For example, see Gordy and Howells (2004); Saccomanni (2008); "All's Fair: The Crisis and Fair-Value Accounting," *Economist*, September 18, 2008, http://www.economist.com/node/12274096.
8. The focus of the Eden and Leite chapters is the use of TPM to transfer excess firm profits. However, TPM can also be used to assist other parties who wish to move illicit money out of a country; in that case, side payments may be made in the destination country.
9. Leite provides an example in chapter 8.
10. TPM involving only two developing nations is rare.
11. This is a conjecture; systematic estimates of the size of other illegal markets have not been made.
12. Rich countries can serve as transit and producing countries. The Netherlands was, at one time, perhaps the major producer of Ecstasy. The Netherlands and Spain are the entry points for much of the cocaine coming to Europe, as indicated by seizures (EMCDDA 2010). Paoli, Greenfield, and Reuter (2009) present data on the world heroin market that support these statements about that drug. Cocaine use is concentrated in North America and Western Europe as measured by volume and expenditures.
13. The price at which a kilogram of cocaine is exported from Colombia is about US$2,000. At its first sale in the United States, it might attract US$15,000–US$20,000 (Kilmer and Reuter 2009). On the prices of coyote services at the border, see Massey and Durand (2003).
14. The United Nations System of National Accounts includes earnings from illegal markets in national income accounts (see OECD 2002). However, little effort is

made to create the relevant estimates, and they are not, to our knowledge, included in the routine official GDP estimates of any nation.

15. There is a conceptual complexity mentioned in Kopp's chapter, namely, how to deal with the location of the earnings of smugglers. Assume that the prostitute is smuggled by a Moldovan trafficker who is paid in the Netherlands: Putting aside issues of legality, in which country should the value added (so to speak) be recorded?

16. They also offer an even broader definition, as follows: "money that is illegally earned, transferred or utilized" (Kar and Cartwright-Smith 2008, 1). They do not subsequently develop the concept of "illegally utilized."

17. It is useful to repeat here the distinction between illegal and illicit provided in chapter 1. A typical definition of illicit, presented at dictionary.com, shows two meanings: "1. not legally permitted or authorized; unlicensed; unlawful," and "2. disapproved of or not permitted for moral or ethical reasons." See http://dictionary.reference.com/browse/illicit.

18. The World Bank lists Kuwait number 7 in terms of per capita income (adjusted for purchasing power parity); Saudi Arabia is number 37.

19. The issue is dealt with directly in Kar and Cartwright-Smith (2010).

20. The translated report can be found on the website of this volume, http://go .worldbank.org/N2HMRB4G20.

References

Andreas, P., and K. Greenhill. 2010. *Sex, Drugs, and Body Counts: The Politics of Numbers in Global Crime and Conflict.* Ithaca, NY: Cornell University Press.

Baker, R. W. 2005. *Capitalism's Achilles Heel: Dirty Money and How to Renew the Free-Market System.* Hoboken, NJ: John Wiley & Sons.

Barua, S., A. Majumder, and M. Akhtaruzzaman. 2007. "Determinants of Workers' Remittances in Bangladesh: An Empirical Study." Bangladesh Bank Working Paper 0713, Policy Analysis Unit, Research Department, Bangladesh Bank, Dhaka, Bangladesh.

Bräutigam, D., O.-H. Fjeldstad, and M. Moore, eds. 2008. *Taxation and State-Building in Developing Countries: Capacity and Consent.* Cambridge, U.K.: Cambridge University Press.

Caulkins, J. P., M. A. R. Kleiman, and J. D. Kulick. 2010. "Drug Production and Trafficking, Counterdrug Policies, and Security and Governance in Afghanistan." June, Center on International Cooperation, New York University, New York.

Christensen, J. 2009. "Giving with One Hand, Taking with the Other: The Danger of Tax Havens Use for Development." Media presentation, Counter Balance, Brussels.

DIIS (Danish Institute for International Studies.) 2009. "Combating Illicit Financial Flows from Poor Countries: Estimating the Possible Gains." DIIS Policy Brief:

Governance in the Global Economy, November, DIIS, Copenhagen. http://www.diis.dk/sw86518.asp.

Dumas, V. 2007. "The Peruvian Experience." Unpublished case study, World Bank, Washington, DC.

EMCDDA (European Monitoring Center for Drugs and Drug Addiction). 2010. "2010 Annual Report on the State of the Drugs Problem in Europe." November, EMCDDA, Lisbon.

Eurodad (European Network on Debt and Development). 2009. "From London to Pittsburgh: Assessing G20 Action for Developing Countries." Eurodad Briefing, September 16, Eurodad, Brussels. http://www.eurodad.org/uploadedFiles/Whats_New/News/Assessing_G20_Development_Pledges_Eurodad_Sept09.pdf?n=7274.

FitzGerald, V. 2010. "International Tax Cooperation and International Development Finance." Paper prepared for the 2010 World Economic and Social Survey, United Nations Department of Economic and Social Affairs, New York. http://www.un.org/esa/analysis/wess/wess2010workshop/wess2010_fitzgerald.pdf.

Global Witness. 2006. "Heavy Mittal? A State within a State: The Inequitable Mineral Development Agreement between the Government of Liberia and Mittal Steel Holdings NV." Report, October, Global Witness, Washington, DC.

Gordy, M. B., and B. Howells. 2004. "Procyclicality in Basel II: Can We Treat the Disease without Killing the Patient?" Unpublished working paper (May 12), Board of Governors, Federal Reserve System. http://www.bis.org/bcbs/events/rtf04gordy_howells.pdf.

Greenpeace. 2008. "Logging Sector Review: Conning the Congo." Report, July. http://www.greenpeace.org/raw/content/international/press/reports/conning-the-congo.pdf.

Greenwood, P. W., K. Model, C. P. Rydell, and J. Chiesa. 1998. "Diverting Children from a Life of Crime: Measuring Costs and Benefits." Monograph Report MR-699–1, Rand Corporation, Santa Monica, CA. http://www.rand.org/pubs/monograph_reports/MR699-1.html.

Hasan, R. Al. 2006. "Harnessing Remittances for Economic Development of Bangladesh." INAFI Bangladesh Working Paper 1 (April 30), International Network of Alternative Financial Institutions, Dhaka, Bangladesh.

Helleiner, E. 2009. "The Contemporary Reform of Global Financial Governance: Implications of and Lessons from the Past." G-24 Discussion Paper 55 (April), Intergovernmental Group of 24, United Nations Conference on Trade and Development, Geneva. http://www.unctad.org/en/docs/gdsmdpg2420092_en.pdf.

Hollingshead, A. 2010. "The Implied Tax Revenue Loss from Trade Mispricing." Global Financial Integrity, Washington, DC. http://www.gfip.org/storage/gfip/documents/reports/implied%20tax%20revenue%20loss%20report_final.pdf.

Kar, D., and D. Cartwright-Smith. 2008. "Illicit Financial Flows from Developing Countries, 2002–2006." Global Financial Integrity, Washington, DC. http://www.gfip.org/storage/gfip/economist%20-%20final%20version%201-2-09.pdf.

————. 2010. "Illicit Financial Flows from Africa: Hidden Resource for Development." Global Financial Integrity, Washington, DC. http://www.gfip.org/storage / gfip/documents/reports/gfi_africareport_web.pdf.

Keefe, P. R. 2009. *The Snakehead: An Epic Tale of the Chinatown Underworld and the American Dream.* New York: Doubleday.

Kilmer, B., and P. Reuter. 2009. "Doped: How Two Plants Wreak Havoc on the Countries That Produce and Consume Them and Everyone in Between." *Foreign Policy* 175 (November/December): 2–6.

Laherrere, J. 2007. "Uncertainty of Data and Forecasts for Fossil Fuels." Paper presented at the University of Castilla–La Mancha, Spain, April 24. http://www .oilcrisis.com/laherrere/Castilla200704.pdf.

Massey, D. S., and J. Durand. 2003. "The Costs of Contradiction: US Immigration Policy 1986–1996." *Latino Studies* 1: 233–52.

Murphy, R. 2009. "Country-by-Country Reporting: Holding Multinational Corporations to Account Wherever They Are." Report, June 17, Task Force on Financial Integrity and Economic Development, Washington, DC.

OECD (Organisation for Economic Co-operation and Development). 2002. *Measuring the Non-Observed Economy: A Handbook.* Paris: OECD.

Paoli, L., V. A. Greenfield, and P. Reuter. 2009. *The World Heroin Market: Can Supply Be Cut?* New York: Oxford University Press.

Purje, H., M. Ylönen, and P. Nokelainen, ed. 2010. "Illegal Capital Flight from Developing Countries: 'Development Assistance' from the Poor to the Rich." Service Center for Development Cooperation, Helsinki. http://www.kepa.fi/tiedostot /julkaisut/illegal-capital-flight.pdf.

Reuter, P., and E. M. Truman. 2004. *Chasing Dirty Money: The Fight against Money Laundering.* Washington, DC: Institute for International Economics.

Saccomanni, F. 2008. "Managing International Financial Stability." Edited text of remarks at the Peterson Institute for International Economics, Washington, DC, December 11. http://www.bis.org/review/r081217c.pdf?noframes=1.

Sakwa, R. 2009. *The Quality of Freedom: Khodorkovsky, Putin and the Yukos Affair.* Oxford: Oxford University Press.

Shelley, L. 2009. *Human Trafficking: A Global Perspective.* New York: Cambridge University Press.

Sinton, J. E., and D. G. Fridley. 2001. "A Guide to China's Energy Statistics." Working paper, April 29, Energy Analysis Department, Lawrence Berkeley National Laboratory, Berkeley, CA. http://minotaur.lbl.gov/china.lbl.gov/sites/china.lbl.gov /files/LBNL_49024._A_Guide_to_Chinas_Energy_Statistics._Apr2001.pdf.

Spelman, W. 2000. "The Limited Importance of Prison Expansion." In *The Crime Drop in America*, ed. A. Blumstein and J. Wallman, 97–128. Cambridge Studies in Criminology. New York: Cambridge University Press.

Statistics Norway. 2006. "Oil Industry in Official Statistics: A Norwegian Statistical Quality Project." Report summary, Statistics Norway, Oslo. http://www.ssb.no /ocg/oil_industry_in_official_statistics.pdf.

Sykes, G. M., F. T. Cullen, and R. K. Merton. 1992. *Criminology*. 2nd ed. Fort Worth: Harcourt College Publishing.

TJN (Tax Justice Network). 2007. *Closing the Floodgates: Collecting Tax to Pay for Development*. London: TJN. http://www.innovativefinance-oslo.no/pop.cfm? FuseAction=Doc&pAction=View&pDocumentId=11607.

UNCTAD (United Nations Conference on Trade and Development). 2009. *World Investment Report 2009: Transnational Corporations, Agricultural Production and Development*. Geneva: UNCTAD.

UNODC (United Nations Office on Drugs and Crime). 2009. *Addiction, Crime and Insurgency: The Transnational Threat of Afghan Opium*. Vienna: UNODC.

Wrong, M. 2009. *It's Our Turn to Eat: The Story of a Kenyan Whistle-Blower*. New York: HarperCollins.

Index

Boxes, figures, notes, and tables are indicated by italic b, f, n, and t following page numbers.